KELTIC FOLK &
FAERIE TALES

ABOUT THE AUTHOR

'From earliest childhood I had pronounced psychic abilities which developed into especial (through un-disciplined talents) by the age of 16–18. From this age I embarked upon a deep, extensive and disciplined study of many ancient Religions. Mythologies and Wisdom-Traditions. From 1974–1982 I was Group Leader of a Qabalah Group in Edinburgh. From 1979–1984 President of the Keltic Research Society. In 1982 I founded and became Director of Studies for The College of Druidism, which since its inception has developed into the most important Keltic-based Initiatory Organisation in Great Britain & Abroad. Since 1982 I have amalgamated the Quabalah Group I was leading with the C. of D. Edin Mother Group. In 1984 I was appointed General Secretary of the European Pan-Keltic League. Over the last ten years I have given many dozens of Workshops and Lectures to small Groups and large Conferences throughout Great Britain'.

Kaledon Naddair

BY THE SAME AUTHOR

Keltic Shamanistic Calendar (2 vols.)
Keltic Tree Lore (2 vols.)
Keltic Bird Lore
Keltic Animal Lore (2 vols.)
Pictish and Keltic Art Symbolism
Cup and Ring Marks and Sacred Rock Art
The Shaman and Ritual Drumming
(other titles listed in bibliography)

Kaledon Naddair is Editor and main Article Contributor to the following three Keltic Journals/Magazines:

Inner Keltia (The Leading Journal of the Keltic Renaissance)

The Pictish Shaman (This new magazine focusses on the Initiatory Wisdom of the Primal Kelts – the Kruithni/Ffichti/Picts)

Awen (Religious, Mythological, Nature-Worship, Erotic and Romantic Poetry from the leading Keltic-Pagan Poets)

Further details and copies available from:

Keltia Publications
PO Box 307
Edinburgh
EH9 1XA

Keltic Folk & Faerie Tales

Their Hidden Meaning Explored

Kaledon Naddair

CENTURY
LONDON MELBOURNE AUCKLAND JOHANNESBURG

Front cover illustration by Gordon Wain

A Rider Book published in the Century Paperback series by
Century Hutchinson Ltd, Brookmount House, 62–65 Chandos Place, Covent Garden, London WC2N 4NW

Century Hutchinson Australia (Pty) Ltd
PO Box 496, 16–22 Church Street, Hawthorn, Melbourne, Victoria 3122

Century Hutchinson New Zealand Ltd
32–34 View Road, PO Box 40–086, Glenfield, Auckland 10

Century Hutchinson South Africa (Pty) Ltd
PO Box 337, Bergvlei 2012, South Africa

Set by Avocet Marketing Services, Bicester, Oxon.
Printed and bound in Great Britain by
Anchor Brendon Ltd, Tiptree, Essex

British Library Cataloguing in Publication Data

Naddair, Kaledon
Keltic folk and faerie tales: their hidden meaning explained.
1. Tales Celtic — History and criticism
Rn: J.A. Johnston 1. Title
398.2′1′094 GR137

ISBN 0–7126–1679–9

CONTENTS

Dedication & Credits

I should like to dedicate this book to the Wildman and my other 'Allies' from the magical Otherworlds; for without the secret keys that they entrusted to me I would have been just one more diligent researcher among so many others – understanding from without, but not from within (the heartland of the mysteries).

Having agreed to write this book at short notice, and to a tight deadline, I am absolutely certain that it could not have been achieved without the unstinting help of my lovely lady Lorraine Jordan. For Lorraine not only typed the whole of this intricately worded endurance test, but she also raked out hundreds of notes, unearthed Lore and Tales, produced diagrams, and did 101 fiddly little jobs that the public never see. All this she managed whilst coping with my wolf-toothed impatience and my latest record blasting out (be that Bruce Sringsteen the Boss's *Live 1975–85* or Matt Johnson's *Infected* or *Stairway to Heaven*, etc.) – for such fortitude my deep gratitude and love.

Next, my Pictish colleague Alan Miller deserves major mention, for a great deal of the traditional Lore that has been woven into this book was painstakingly gathered by Alan from many long-buried sources. In a consumerist push-button world few people have the patience to wade their way through old dictionaries or dusty volumes in the search for pieces of our neglected tradition, but also few people draw close to the Gods through the old knowledge. For all Alan's research contributions I (and the common Duchas/Treftdaeth) are deeply indebted.

Greater awareness brings unpleasant realizations in this crazy world, thus Brothers and Sisters of the Inner Way are valued to ease the pain. I therefore thank Linda Lees for the healing, and keeping me sane (not to mention the inspiring Keltic Mandalas).

Thanks to my other group members: Kirsty (my half wolf-sister), Robert II for visibly changing (thus showing that men can), Edward O'Donnelly for getting there (and for the great calligraphy to add the polish), to Stuart for the special-angle insights he shared and for permission to include his mighty poem in this book, to Ruth (when the energy is up), to Chris (for being forthright), and to Vivien for the Pictish roots.

Other people of merit, like Rhode (Irene), Bel Bucca and Mike Brydon, deserve a nod for their friendship.

Thanks to Gordon Wain for the superb front-cover illustration (and other artwork). Thanks also to Dr Derek Bryce for his translations of Breton material. To Stuart Akers for illustrations on p. 203; to Gerald Dodd for W11, p. 141 foot and for quote; to Val Biro for Fig. 75; to Wendy Woods for the illustration of the Magical City of Emrys on p. 169; Edward O'Donnelly for the Otherworld castles and sea islands illustrations Fig. E; to Paul Screeton and Thorsons for the quotation from *Quicksilver Heritage*. My thanks to that great man J. R. R. Tolkien for the quotes from *Tree and Leaf*, and George Allen and Unwin, his publishers; likewise to Anthony Roberts and Zodiac House, Martin Buber and Fontana, and Daniel Corkery and Mercier Paperbacks. (Also to Sandy and staff at Dupli-Quick for the preparatory work.)

Plus a great debt of thanks to the hundreds of good Initiates, storytellers, collectors and researchers who have kept the tradition alive and healthy.

Finally, I am indebted to Carlos Castaneda for having the courage and phenomenal skill to write his astonishing series of books, crucial to 'the Path'.

Introduction

Y Gwir yn Erbyn y Byd
To the man who has no magic in his blood, the
cavern of Keltic profundity is for ever sealed.

May I offer you a hearty welcome to what I guarantee is a quite revolutionary book on Keltic Folk and Faerie Tales. It may not be found an easy read, but mayhap it shall be found a spiritually rewarding one.

Before I attempt to describe what this book aims to achieve, it would perhaps be wise to explain what it is *not*.

First of all, its prime intention is not to be a 'collection' of Tales – for most of the best collections were done in the nineteenth century or in the first quarter of the twentieth century – any recent such books are usually no more than a reshuffling of earlier material. Although not primarily a 'collection' then, the book nevertheless owes a massive debt of gratitude to such commendable collectors and translators as Jeremiah Curtin (and Pádraic O'Siochfhradha), Lord Archibald Campbell, P. W. Joyce, J. F. Campbell, Whitley Stokes, Kuno Meyer, Standish Hayes O'Grady, Eugine O'Curry, Lady Gregory, Edward Davies and the like.

Whilst this book is very learned, complex and well thought-out, it is not remotely what I would call an academic study of Folk or Faerie Tales. For I could not, nor would I deem it desirable to, adopt a detached analytical stance of implied intellectual superiority to the ancient storytellers. Nor would I dream (even in my worst nightmares) of contaminating these Tales with the intellectual cancer of post-industrial materialistic philosophy. Thus I shall not dissect these numinous Tales upon the operating table of fundamental orthodox dogma, nor shall I scrutinize them with the cold logic of patronizing disbelief. I am not interested in reductive investigation to establish their lowest common denominator, for the items that constitute these Tales should always be seen in relation to the whole organic systems that initially gave them life and function within the Tale. Thus I am happy to state that I write from within the Keltic Folk tradition; I am passionately interested in the message and mode of communication (language) employed in these Tales; as much as I can, I seek contact with and experience within the realm of Faerie, and this has led to certain beings becoming indubitable experiential realities for me. Therefore most of my comments, observations and ideas related in the following chapters have been made from *within* the living ethos of the Keltic Folk and Faerie tradition: if that renders this book an academic failure – whooopee! – for at the very same time it might vouchsafe its psychic and spiritual potency.

Nor shall I be spending too much time tracing motifs from Keltic Tales into European or Oriental 'equivalents'. For I would have thought it obvious that Indo-European peoples, whose language and religious mythology has been proven to have arisen from common origins, should also have elements of their Folk and Faerie Tales in common. I would also hope that it would later become obvious that seers from many traditions have experienced identical, or very similar, Otherworld realities; thus it should not come as too much of a surprise that they have sometimes described things in very similar ways, employing similar images. Indeed, it seems that academic Folklorists often have an uncanny knack of doing exactly what is not required in any given situation. Imagine oneself walking through a sunny meadow and a white butterfly suddenly brushing against one's forehead. Now, some people will chase after this butterfly; but, if they see an even whiter butterfly flitting over a neighbouring field, they will climb over the fence and start chasing that; but then, if they see a red admiral in an orchard, over the wall they go; and thus the chase for the butterfly 'motif' goes on through various fields, gardens and woodlands. But wait: if the omen (sign-communication from nature/the Otherworlds) were fully to take stock of the particular white butterfly that brushed against the brow-centre, then in pursuing others one would have failed to grasp the essential significance of the 'message'. Other people might have simply stood on the spot and let their eyes follow the white butterfly, then another butterfly, then another, over the surrounding countryside; but, if it had been important to keep our attention devoted to that particular white butterfly then, in relinquishing sight of it, we would also have failed. Other character types would of course have fished out their portable net, caught the butterfly and then rushed back to the study to pin it to the entymologist's board to examine whether there was anything special in its thorax or wing muscles to account for the prodigious jolt it had given the captor's forehead. With regard to the *living* omen-carrier, in its *living* environment, this approach is a miserable failure; not least because it fails to realize that the soul-essence of a being cannot be explained by studying the anatomical workings of its physical parts. On another tack, if the white butterfly had brushed against our brow to tell us that we had just stood upon a powerful geomantic spot in that meadow, then if we went off chasing that, or any other butterfly, we would have failed, for the omen-sign in this case was to take stock of the context and exact surrounding of the spot on which the omen happened. Perhaps what the butterfly was asking/telling us to do was to meditate on that very spot, or do some other suitable magical act.

In relation to such Shamanistic lines of reasoning, it should be noted that a wise man or woman is one who is conversant with a range of suitable approaches, and, come the omen-event, they are open enough to a higher intelligence (their own or otherwise) to be guided into the most suitable course of action and interpretation.

That modern people, especially mere rational analysts, have become divorced from signs, omens, hidden messages and all the ingredients of a truly magical life is the result of adverse conditioning upon the individual, population and society. Martin Buber describes the situation perfectly in *Between Man and Man*:

> Each of us is encased in an armour whose task is to ward off signs. Signs happen to us without respite, living means being addressed, we would need only to present ourselves and to perceive. But the risk is too dangerous for us, the soundless thunderings seem to threaten us with annihilation, and from generation to generation we perfect the defence apparatus.

Now, in erecting such an armour, some humans mistakenly think they are free of superstition, but as such people still live in the world to a certain extent and interact with it, it would be worth considering how 'free' they are from things, as Carlo Suarés so astutely observes:

> As long as a man does not understand his surroundings he is controlled by his reactions to them, and therefore controlled by the surroundings. The accumulated reactions are the sum of the species' mechanical past, it is therefore the past of the 'functionally maimed individual'.

In attempting fully to understand ourselves and our surroundings, it boils down to whether we are prepared to encounter or deal with non-physical beings or situations. As Keltic Folk and Faerie Tales are replete with such Otherworld beings and dimensions, this is obviously a key question. It is thus also of great significance whether those who are writing about Folk and Faerie Tales are aware of psychic and spiritual realities or are closed off to such phenomena due to a materialistic philosophy that they have applied to their daily life. Too many establishment writers on Folk and Faerie Tales are of the latter disposition; thus they will always remain half sceptical, half noncomprehending outsiders to the subject they are spouting forth upon.

In speaking thus, I am not neglecting the faculty of healthy criticism, for genuine Druidical

Shamanism involves as high (or higher) discernment than is normally applied in everyday life. (Remember the discernment needed to make the 'right' choice with regard to the butterfly omen.) By the end of this book you will become aware that a healthy amount of *Gevurah* (perceptive discernment) has indeed been employed.

Discernment is also required in deciding what you should or should not do to Folk and Faerie Tales when 'interpreting' them. Whilst writing this book I came across Bruno Bettleheim's *The Uses of Enchantment: The Meaning and Importance of Fairy Tales*, and was staggered by the cretinous level of discernment displayed within. For example, when relating 'motifs' to 'Freudian concepts' he assures us that in Tales, birds = the superego, animals = the ordinary ego, and toads/reptiles/amphibians = the id (sexual drive); this is of course total rubbish. It does not even bear thinking about as a hopelessly inadequate generalization, for in the Shamanistic traditions there are many animals that are magically more important and powerful than certain birds, as there are certain reptiles (e.g., snakes and lizards) and amphibians (e.g., toads and newts) that are more significant than certain birds. Such modern inanities also do not do justice to the complex richness of Shamanistic Lore and the principles upon which it operates. (For example, a wild goose is more of a power-bird in November/December than a skylark; similarly, a seal out of water is a cumbersome character, but swimming in the icy sea it is another magical story.) As there is no conception by such academics of the time or place that the 'motif' is found within, they will never be able to understand why the mighty Faerie Queen might appear through a 'noble' white hind at one point in the year's cycle, and yet through a 'lowly' frog (as was recorded in Arran) in another part of the Shamanistic cycle.

The general rule would seem to be to employ discernment and continually shape or expand your conceptions accurately to fit what the ancient sages actually related; do not squash and mutilate the ingredients of our best Folk and Faerie Tales into the pathetically inadequate thought-moulds of Freudian, Jungian or other such analysts.

The other ingredients needed to improve our perceptive awareness as it is applied to Folk and Faerie Tales I will explore in chapter 6.

But before that I should like to sketch for you the environment in which the ancient sages (who formulated the earliest versions of these Tales) lived. If you enter (at least conceptually) into their world as much as you can, this will set you in good stead for the Tales.

pob hwyl, Kaledon Naddair
Kaer Eidyn, upon the Winter Solstice (Alban Arthuran), 1986

CHAPTER 1

The Environment In Which The Tales Were Set, And In Which The Original StoryTellers and Initiates Lived

I am the land of their fathers.
In me the virtue stays.
I will bring back my children,
After certain days.

R.K.

For any of us moderns to envisage the environment of our ancient Keltic ancestors is very difficult – I tend to feel impossible – but, if we are to stand any chance of properly understanding ancient Tales, then we must make a wholehearted and sincere attempt.

From 4000 to 100 BC most of the Keltic lands were covered in vast primeval forests, the richness and depth of which are hard to describe. Many villages started in clearings made near the edges of the vast woods and, with dispensations from the priests, further ground was allowed to be cleared of trees for cultivation purposes. The Colleges of Druidical Training were originally far into the depths of these forests (smaller Initiatory spots would be in mountain/sea-coast caves). The Druids knew full well the priceless value of these giant woods, for not only do such numbers of trees exude an etheric healing, but they are also the haunt of mighty beings whom these Shaman Initiates worked with intimately. Thus, in early times the Druids imposed fines and punishments upon anyone found cutting down any members of the noble tree tribes. The amount of severity of the fines depended upon how important or sacred the tree species was adjudged (e.g., for felling one of the 'chieftain' trees – oak, hazel, holly, apple, ash, yew, pine, also a sacred thorn – one could have oxen confiscated, be fined several pigs/sheep/goats, have a hand chopped off; or, if it had been a 'prayer' tree, one might have been put to death).

Such an order of priorities may seem strange to some of us moderns, but this simply shows how much our value-system has been turned on its head. You see, apart from building materials, tools and weapons, occasional boats, and land for farming (which were all allowed), there were not many other major needs for the felling of lots of trees. With such a massive number of standing trees (of various ages), there were always enough wind-fallen branches and top-heavy keeled-over trees to provide firewood. As the Druids and Druidesses were practical as well as religious people, they would have, where appropriate, allowed certain areas of trees to be felled for utilitarian purposes. The system of fines was an ever-present reminder that there were spiritual values to be borne in mind, such that it was not wise to offend the nature spirits (by heedless destruction), nor to disappoint the Gods by needlessly removing their channels of communication.

During this forest-dwelling period, the woods, which were teeming with game, provided ample food for those who had a fair skill in hunting. This diet was supplemented with seasonal fruits, berries, nuts and fungi; and domesticated herds of swine were turned into the autumn woods to fatten off the acorns and beechmast. The rivers, helped by good tree cover, were at this time very healthy and immensely fertile, having hundreds of salmon, trout, eels, etc., all there for the catching. With the small hamlets of clustered huts often being surrounded on at least three sides by woodland, some degree of shelter was afforded from the worst of the winter gales.

(I am reminded here of the occasion a few years back when I was exploring some chambered cairns and hut circles in the North-east of Alban and happened to read a guidebook written by a female archaeologist who was puzzled why these early folk chose to live in such bleak windswept places; I in turn marvelled at the thoughtless stupidity of this academic who had not realized that these hut circles would have originally stood in sheltered woodland clearings, for the ancient forests of this part of Pictland had only been cut down in the sixteenth to nineteenth centuries. In saying this I do not wish to undermine the great hardiness of our ancestors, for they did indeed live upon bleak mountainsides or on windswept Western/far-Northern islands, but simply to give one example of 'the experts' failing accurately to envisage the environs of a particular group of hut circles and chambered cairns.)

Of course in early times there were elements of very real danger that lurked in forests; for example, wild boars could attack and disembowel a man with their nine-inch-long tusks shaped like a curved knife; Kaledonian brown bears would occasionally set upon and dismember a human who had strayed into their territory; *aurochs* (fierce wild oxen) were best avoided unless one wanted to be gored by their five-foot-long sharp horns; mountain lions were not too much of a problem unless one strayed into their cave, but packs of wolves down from the mountains in winter were very dangerous and best kept well away from, unless you were a certain type of Initiate. Although these were only very occasional dangers, when they were coupled together with other risks, such as that of drowning whilst trying to cross a river in spate or of being ambushed by a hostile tribe's war-party, they helped people to retain a sharpened awareness in the face of their own possible bloody death or maiming. These were some of the aspects of everyday life that kept it very 'real' and very much in the now.

Another element of everyday life that helped to keep people earthed and real was food. Most was grown or reared or gathered by the people who ate it. If you hadn't attended to it with your own bare hands, then the person who had would usually live nearby (and, as most goods at this time were exchanged for barter, you would had to have given him/her something of worth that probably you yourself had produced). In those times all food was natural, nothing artificial, coloured or chemicalized; thus there was nothing in what people ate that could render their bodies even in the slightest unnatural ('off' eggs or rancid butter would have only temporarily upset the natural balance of the bodies). The obtaining of food involved nearly all men and women exerting themselves physically (coordinating eyesight, deft hands and the work of arms and legs). Men did all the hunting and most of the heavy ploughing and land maintenance; women sowed and planted crops, gathered the fruits and mashed the meal and flour to bake with. The slaughtering, disembowelling and dressing of animals and fowl would usually be done by a member of the family who was about to eat it – thus blood, death and the sacrifice of an animal's life so that a human could thrive were very much closer experiences to most people than they are today. (Although the chieftains and Keltic aristocracy deputized servants to do the more menial food preparation, they kept in touch with the life and death process by riding out with their horses and hounds on a hunt, sometimes to face a wild boar with only their spears to hand, or quivers full of arrows to bring down prey.) Although modern vegetarians may deplore so much animal suffering and slaughter, we should recognize that our ancestors were at least much more personally in touch with the moral significance of their food-making actions. Too many present-day meat-eaters fob off the moral responsibility onto some unknown, unthoughtabout, unspecified third party in our nice, clean, neat, supermarket foodchain.

Similarly, the clothing and footwear made and worn in ancient times was very intimately involved with animals that had just been slaughtered. Whether it was skinned furs, tanned hides, thick cowhide leather or spun and woven sheep's wool, most items to keep folk warm and dry had been obtained, with much intensive physical labour, from our animal brethren. Indeed, flax and *cannah* (bog cotton) were some of the few plant substances extensively employed for clothing.

Travel was also a very different proposition for our ancient Keltic forebears. For most, this would have meant quite simply walking the many miles to their destination (often getting foot-sore and leg-

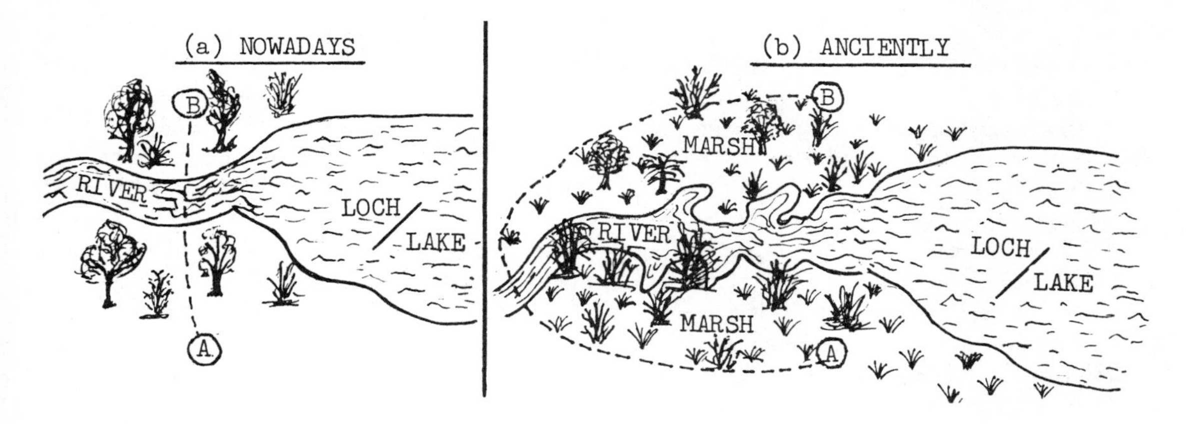

weary before arriving there). Some merchants, and only during certain times of the year, could employ wagons (even this would often require physical exertion, e.g. to assist the horses in getting over a river or up a steep slippy brae). The most fortunate could enjoy the exhilarating, but still somewhat taxing, method of horse-travel (however, owing to their weight, horses could not cross very extensive stretches of bogs and moorland). Even getting from A to B was not quite as simple as it is nowadays; let me depict for you a personal experience which I know was much more common in the undrained environment of the ancient Europeans – see figure above.

Anciently, where a river or a confluence of streams flowed into a loch or mere-pool, there would be extensive marshes. In such a muddly quagmire one has to progress by carefully jumping from tussock to tussock, and from half-submerged log to log, else one sinks into grey-black slime up to the knee or thigh. If one wishes to traverse more solid ground then one has to be prepared to make a detour of several miles to skirt along the edges of the marshes. (Of course, hunters, with special-tipped arrows and dogs, would deliberately venture into such expanses of water, mud, reeds, willows and alders to hunt the waterfowl that inhabited such conditions.)

As there was next to no artificial lighting, any travelling done at night (even if the person had good 'night-eyes') was likely to involve rough physical contact with the terrain.

In olden times, if you wanted a house or farmsteading, then you built one yourself from cut and trimmed logs and local stones (no 'builders' were employed). If you were fortunate, some friends and neighbours would come along to assist with the heavier labour. But it would have been a matter of personal pride for each houseowner (man or woman) to possess the required skills. The vast amount of hard graft needed in the creation obviously made the resultant house/rath/farm-outhouse much more valuable to its owner, and hence worth defending.

Certain forms of dwelling in particular required enormous labour; these were the *krannogs* or lake-dwellings. Some were supported by hundreds of alder or oak piles driven down through the water and into the peat bed; others were built upon mounds constructed from retaining piles holding criss-crossed logs, layers of compacted brushwood and rubble, plus tons (up to 150 tons per dwelling) of heavy, water-resistant clay. All such construction materials had to be carried to the site and, in the case of some of the stonework, this could be from several miles away. *Krannog* builders in the Lake of Menteith even went to such lengths as to build an artificial island out in the loch. (It is perhaps worth noting here that in lake villages such as that at ancient Glastonbury (Innis Wytrin), there could be encountered flocks of pelicans, cormorants, herons and bitterns, as well as the more common ducks, swans, grebes and coots; also, beavers and wild cats were fairly common amongst the wild animals (boars, deer, foxes, otters, hedgehogs, etc.), whilst domesticated sheep were kept and eaten by the hundred, along with many Keltic oxen, pigs, horses and goats.

As moving overland could be somewhat arduous and toilsome (even along the ancient drove trails and 'green roads'), all possible navigable stretches of river were travelled along; long before the times of the Romans, the Gaulish and Pictish Kelts maintained fleets of stout-bodied high-hulled *birlinns* and war galleys; when conveying goods down a long coastline, sea transportation could sometimes reduce the carriage time to one sixth of the up-hill and down-dale equivalent.

With so many aspects of daily life requiring such great physical labour, one might have expected that folk would have done as little as possible over and above this; but, the strength of the human spirit being what it is, many people lavished hundreds of caring hours upon producing jewellery, decorative artwork or religious objects.

As the better hand-crafted items required hundreds, sometimes thousands, of hours of work, they were obviously contemplated much in the making, and treasured for long afterwards. This being so, the fact that spiritual and esoteric concepts were employed regularly, not only in symbols and meaningful ornamentation, but also in the geometrics of shape and form, is a fact that needs to be fully evaluated by modern-day investigators. (For years I have been indicating such matters, and I am glad to see that Keith Critchlow has been pointing out some other angles in his excellent book *Time Stands Still*; and Schwaller De'Lubitz is good on Egyptian equivalents.) Even in the stage of production before esoteric embellishment was applied, certain technical skills of our ancestors should be properly appreciated. Think, for example, of the skill required in drilling three holes several inches long, but only a few millimetres in diameter, through a piece of jet, to meet at a point inside it, and to appear at the other end as one straight hole – all this flawlessly achieved without the use of high-powered electric drills or tungsten-tipped drill-bits; or the skill required to make a perfectly smooth sphere out of a lump of solid granite, without the use of any mechanized tools. Some such masterpieces of the Pictish craftsmen appear unpraised in museum display cases; others gather dust in storage; whilst praise is lavished upon the artefacts of virtually any other culture, more than it is upon our own native Keltic genius.

Probably very few modern-day folk would like to re-adopt the physically more demanding life-styles of our ancestors, especially as we seem to be designing ever more appliances to deal with the most elementary tasks. As many of the major inventions (washing machines, electric drills, gas-cookers, etc.) can indeed be hailed as wonderful time-savers, perhaps the aim should be some sort of balance between saving ourselves unnecessary manual chores and keeping ourselves physically fit. Western society seems to have become noticeably out of balance, for perhaps one tenth to one quarter of the population still do physical hard work for their wage packets; whilst over three quarters engage in purely cerebral, paper-shuffling, button-pushing jobs. Another whole industry comes into being whereby pear-shaped podgy businessmen go on crash-courses at health farms or jog around the block a few times before heading off into the rush-hour traffic; other beer-gutted young men decide to get themselves back into condition, and so go into the gym to work out and 'pump iron'; the ladies in the meantime pay out lots of money for packs of vitamin tablets, flab-shaking machines and aerobics classes.

Whatever other advantages we can claim, as far as personal fitness goes, our ancestors were ten times leaner, more supple and physically robust than most of us are. So, although fetching water in buckets from the nearest well or stream may have been a tiresome task, it did at least provide regular walks in the fresh air, across dew-covered meadows to draw truly refreshing drinking water (unlike the strange, dead, chemicalized liquid that we drink as 'water' nowadays). In the long-gone days when there was enough space to bathe in a river or pool undisturbed, such a process, although cold, was immensely stimulating to the circulation and general tone of the body. In such activities it is often the individual's personal attitude that affects the result. Thus, if you go into the river timidly, as a weak chittering human, then you are likely to catch a cold. On the other hand, one can swim in an icy mid winter river (as I have done several times) in an attitude of powerful at-one-ment, and one can emerge healthily invigorated with the water-serpent energy.

I would recount the commendable attitudes of the French painter Mistral, who, even when famous and wealthy (from well-priced paintings), chose most days to go out and chop his own firewood, and along with his staff go down into the fields and plant and tend his own vegetables and fruits. He believed that any human being, but especially every artist or creative person, should strive not to lose touch with reality; should remain aware of the changing seasons, the quality of light, the beauty of flowers and blossoms, the pulsation of the earth, and the lusty joy that all life has to re-create. Without retaining such an 'awareness', Mistral thought, no painter's work (or that of a poet or religious writer) could be truly real, because it was not in touch with reality.

Therefore we see that each of us has a choice. We need not employ all the technological gadgetry that the advertisers tell us we need; we need not eat junk food or drink artificial drinks; we need not become unhealthy consumerist puppets; and, most importantly of all, we need not become aliens to our own natural environment.

For, mark my words, a degree of personal health and harmony within this physical world of reality can supply one with enough 'ooomph' to make the leap into the very real magical Otherworlds.

It is my opinion that there is all too much in this debilitated world that hinders individuals who are trying to gather enough personal power (psychic and spiritual) to cross the thresholds over into the Faerie Otherworlds; whereas in ancient times it was there for the gathering. Can I describe it like this: the role of the Druids, Shamans and priestesses was to teach trainee Initiates how to *generate* and *gather* Magical power; this was somewhat easier in ancient times, as I will relate. The standing stones and circles radiated power, being part of a geometric distribution network; all the millions of unregimented trees exuded etheric power; the lush meadows oozed out a gentle power; all the wild animals (and even the more characterful farm animals) had a lot more spirit and exuberant energy, thus their flesh and skins were charged with power; all the corn, fruit, vegetables, nuts, seeds and berries were brimming over with the rich fertile power of the soil; the cockles and mussels and other seafood still spoke to stomachs of the ocean's mighty power; the trout, salmon and river water in those days was alive with the black-serpent power; certain of the mountain-tops shot great plumes of ozone power up into the atmosphere, which the winds then distributed far and wide; all in all the living Earth continually breathed out a great exaltation of power in days of yore. (This the Initiates garnered directly into themselves and their pupils and those who came requesting healing; occasionally the Shaman would acquire special batches of power from their Wildfolk allies, who were and are the hidden guardians of nature.)

Then came the Romans 'who created a wasteland and called it peace'; next came the Church of Rome and Orthodox Church suppression; next the English Empire; and recently the American, German and Japanese multi-nationals. All the native Keltic wise men and bards could do against this massive destruction was to 'make their moan' and lament the unfeeling despoilation that they witnessed:

> *Is dith kreach bhur gkoillte ar feochadh.*
> Woe, your woods are withering away.
>
> AODHAGAN O'RATHAILLE
>
> What shall we henceforth do without trees,
> The last of the great woods is fallen.

As Daniel Corkery so incisively described it in his brilliant book on the Munster poets, *Hidden Ireland*:

> Everywhere the giant woods were being cut down – the woods that like a magic cloak had sheltered the Gael in every century. The undertakers, the land-pirates, not ever quite sure of their standing in so strange a country, were selling the timber on the estates at sixpence a tree – they were rifling the ship they had boarded. Trees to the value of £20,000 (at 6d/tree) were cut down, soon after the Revolution, upon a single estate of Sir Valentine Brown in Kerry.

And ever since then the ecological carnage has continued, at an ever-increasing pace – a 'civilization' gone crazy with greed, heedless of the long-term cost, peopled and run by an alien breed of humans, bereft of wild nobility or spiritual power, leaving only a grossly polluted environment and a dying planet behind them.

CHAPTER 2

The Purpose Of The Original Tales and Their Esoteric Dependability

Culture isn't a passive element. There is no culture where no culture is in operation. So long as it doesn't act, it doesn't exist.

IAN HAMILTON FINLAY

The purpose of such Tales as are featured in this book was to preserve the Keltic cultural tradition, for in this ancient period up to 95 per cent of knowledge was transmitted by oral means. That is, from mouth to ear, and mouth to ear, down through the scores of generations. The subject matter of these Tales varied from topographical lore (*Din Seanchaes*), to accounts of the deeds of great chiefs, warriors or Initiates; from encounters with Faerie beings to descriptions of the magical Otherworlds; from satirical diatribes against stingy patrons to beautiful, romantic and passionate love stories.

Overall the Tales were designed to elevate and inspire the inner faculties of the listeners; those that did this most effectively tended to survive the passage of time (barring outside disruption, of course). Such ideas are preserved in the Kymraeg (Welsh) word for 'story' and 'storyteller', as follows:*

> The Old Welsh word for 'story', *kyfarwyddyd*, means 'guidance', 'direction', 'instruction', 'knowledge', 'skill' and 'prescription'. Its stem, *arwydd*, means 'sign', 'symbol', 'manifestation', 'omen', 'miracle', and derives from a root meaning 'to see'.

The storyteller (*kyfarwydd*) was originally a seer and a teacher who guided the souls of his hearers through a world of 'mystery'.

The *kyfarwydd*, ('guide to the mysteries through sacred stories') was just one of a range of associated wise teachers in the Keltic tradition; which I have grouped approximately as follows:

	English	*Old Ghaidhlig (and Middle Irish)*	*Old Kymraeg (and Middle Welsh)*	*Gaulish*
1	Druid and Shaman	*Druidh*, *Draoi*	*Dryw* (pl. *Drywyddon*)	*Druid* (*Druwis*)
2	Prophet and Omen-reader	*Faidh*, *Faith*	*Gwawdydd*, *Gwydd* or *Awenydd* (Inspired Seer)	*Vate* (*Vatis*)
3	Wise Seer and Initiated Poet	*Fili*, *File*, *Filidh*	*Gweledydd*, *Awenydd* (Inspired Poet)	*Veleda* (*Veledus*)
4	Master of Learning	*Ollamh*, *Olaf*	*Athraw* (Master Teacher)	–
5	Storyteller, Historian, Genealogist	*Seanachaidhe*, *Seanchai*, *Seanchais*, *Shanachi*, *Rann-ter* (*Recitor*)	*Kyfarwydd* (Story-guide) *Pen-kerdd* (Chief Poet/Musician) *Hanesydd* (Praise-poet of Patron)	–
6	Wise Judge	*Breithamhain* (*Brehon*) *Breathamh*	*Brawdydd*	–
7	Poet and Singer	*Bard*	*Bardd*	–

* From Alwyn Rees and Brinley Rees, *Celtic Heritage*.

The functions of these various sages would occasionally overlap, and down through the centuries certain titles came more into vogue, whilst others dropped out of verbal currency or became altered in meaning. (For example, a 'ranter' was originally an inspired recitor of bardic verse, the stanzas of which were called *ranns* in Gaelic.)

Accounts of the Irish system of Bardic training at least are fairly complete.

Young students came to the masters to learn the intricacies of Keltic Bardism. Originally the colleges of learning would have been situated deep in the forests; latterly they were large houses in the countryside, around which soon sprang up various ancillary buildings. During the Dark Half of the Year (Samhain to Beltaine) the students would dwell exclusively within the Bardic colleges, supported by grants from their parents; then during the Light Half of the Year (from Beltaine to Samhain) they would accompany a more experienced poet to one of the chieftains' residences (there to earn a good living from composing suitable verse, for marriages, births, battles, elopements, strange happenings and deaths. The Dark Period in the Bardic colleges was used for some very intensive training in versecraft, over twelve hours per day, seven days per week, for those six months in the year). This study would include all the Bardic devices: alliteration, assonance, cross-consonance, *kennings* (poetic paraphrases), verbal symbolism and Ogham lore; to this would be added religious lore (of the Gods and mythological characters), plus lore on the ancient sites and the individuals who had contributed to the history of Irish culture. Late each afternoon the students would be allocated a topic or theme upon which they had to compose a poem; then, come dusk and darkness, all the students would retire to their small rooms, where they would compose, and memorize their newly composed verses, and at about midnight they would be summoned to the main hall, where they would recite what versecraft they had made, and have its strengths and weaknesses commented upon by the Master Poet of the college. As Dermot O'Byrne describes it in his book *Children of the Hills*:

> In accordance with the regulations of the bardic schools the sons of learning were at this time lying upon their beds in their windowless cells, composing the exercises in prosody which later in the evening were to be written down and submitted to the Ard-File for his judgement.

The intensity and strictness of this training method is hard for us, standing at a distance, to grasp; yet, as it was leavened with humour and comradeship, it was by many counted as some of the happiest periods in their lives. And, after eight years of such indepth training, they could qualify as a Bard, and enter one of the regions of Eirinn to ply this noble craft. The overall aim and effect of such a training system was to pass on the wisdom and techniques of the elders to the students, and to maintain a phenomenal standard of accuracy within the transmission of the ancient tradition. As these Bardic colleges were perhaps at their intellectual and spiritual peak in pre-Roman and pre-Christian times, it can be noted that in the centuries of persecutions that followed, some of the ancient wisdom gradually became lost, confused or mistranslated; repeatedly the most learned of the Fili would attempt to cleanse and faithfully reinterpret the hidden secrets (as I have done). Once again Dermot O'Byrne gives us an excellent imaginative picture of one such attempt:

> This glorious harvest of the ripe and golden past, known to learned ones as the Great Skin-book of Bere, is written in a style so divinely and nobly obscure that its contents have been the feeble gleam of jewels in clouded water to many of the learned and more of the unlearned in old years. And of this I judge from the glosses in the margins of the first ten leaves. I myself have spent ten years of my life in the elucidation of the great mysteries contained therein, and have at least accomplished the task, as I believe, of dispelling the clouds raised by the incompetency and ill-judgement of other commentators.

The device of writing such texts being 'in a style so divinely and nobly obscure' was deliberately employed by the Fili and Druids to bamboozle those that had lazy or undeveloped minds. It was in a way a celebration of their own skill, for like a good chess game with a worthy opponent, if someone could solve the Bardic *kennings* (poetic hieroglyphs) then it would bring him/her immense joy and satisfaction, and confirm in the process that they had a well-cultivated mind. Thus, unlike the modern-day gutter press, trashy novels, soapbox stories and bland American hype, and all the other similar dregs of 'literature', the ancient Keltic word-craftsmen attempted rather to set their standards very high, and then inspire the population to ascend to the heights of contemplation.

When the young man (usually in his early twenties) had become qualified as a Bard, he then had to make a choice: he could either go and work for some chieftain (who would provide a house, land and provisions for the Bard and perhaps future wife and prospect of a family), or he could undergo a further four years' hard training in the more esoteric sciences, thereby to become an Initiated Fili. To those that then wished to undertake it (and to those that were adjudged suitable) a further eight years' training was available to become a genuine Shaman Druid (unlike the pathetic parodies that pose as such nowadays). For those interested in reading a description of the full range of secret skills and magical knowledge that was involved within this highest grade of seership, embodied by the Druids, Druidesses and Arch Druids, I would refer you to my booklet *Modern Keltic Druidism: An Assessment*.

This great hierarchical system of seership was originally based solely upon individual merit, and not upon unfair advantage. That it possessed a vertical structure is nothing to complain about, although those that are scared of healthy discipline often do. Such pseudo-anarchistic types fail to realize that the overseeing discernment inherent in such a profound system ensured that any errors introduced by a less perceptive individual would be compensated for and rectified by the presiding Awareness permeating the Druidical colleges (flashes of individual genius were, of course, welcomed and assimilated to enrich the tradition). This obviously resulted in a *dependability* of teachings and symbolism in the Keltic tradition of esoteric knowledge. Thus, as regards the more dependable early Tales, our main task should be to discern this underlying system of symbolism – and that is exactly what I have undertaken in this and other books.

The commonest feature of these Tales is that of an Otherworld journey, whether that be overland, underground, over seas or under them – likewise with lochs, lakes and mere-pools – or through the sky. We are hence charting the various planes of existence in the Keltic kosmos. Occasionally the Tale is used as an allegory for the development of the inner faculties of human consciousness, hence delineating the various physical, astral and spiritual bodies of a man or woman. Clever Tales do both at once.

To say that the composers of these Tales used a great deal of flexibility towards spatial directions – e.g. North, South, East and West – is to fail to appreciate the metaphysics employed in their system of symbolism. For in many cases what is meant is ***not*** the normal physical spatial direction, but rather the *Shamanistic direction*. For example, if an Initiate instructed me to go tomorrow and attune myself with a *Shamanistic Western* place, then I would get on a train and travel some miles in a northerly direction to a certain loch that I know to possess very *Shamanistic West* qualities, and that is what is important; similarly, if I was instructed to go and check out a *Shamanistic Northern* spot, I could travel due South to a certain part of a wooded valley which I know to be very strongly *Shamanistic North* in character. Academics writing upon Keltic mythology and Folktales have, as yet, failed to grasp these essential principles, although they are common ones throughout many different Shamanistic traditions, and within the Chinese geomant's system of *Feng-shui*. Also it must be firmly grasped that when one encounters the King of Greece/Spain/Lochlann/Alba in a Tale, then that being most probably does not rule over the geographical regions we normally associate with those names. Rather what the *Seanchaithe* intended us to understand was that they were indicating an area in the Keltic magical Otherworlds. Thus, as far as my understanding goes, in most of the authentic Irish Initiatory Tales *Alba* refers to the Shamanistic Northern and North-eastern region nearby ordinary Eirinn; *Lochlann* is the distant Shamanistic North and North-east region away from normal Erinn; *Greece* is Shamanistic East and North-east; *Spain* is Shamanistic South-east and Shamanistic South; and also the Mythical *Hy-Brasil* may well be Shamanistic West and South-west. As John Rhys so accurately surmised, Lochlann has in fact little to do with Scandinavia, for the Men of Lochlann are simply latter day replacements of the *Fomori* (*Fomors*) = *fo* (under, below) and *muir* (sea), hence meaning 'the Men from Under the sea'; they are linked to the Scottish *Fomhair* (*Fahms*, 'giants') and the Irish *Fir Domnann* ('People of the Goddess of the Deep'). Thus one can truly sail due West from the West coast of Eire and reach 'Lochlann', it being the region below the Otherworld Astral Sea (which one can reach by embarking in any geographical direction, so long as at one point one goes *in/under/down into* or *up into* the Watery Astral Plane.

Great care must be applied when we are analysing Otherworld Tales, for intellectual simplicity has no place in Keltia: e.g., Domhnail Donn (the Lord of the Underworld) has as his main 'Station' Shamanistic North, but one can enter into his domains by the 'crack in the worlds' where the Sun sets in the 'West'; he can also occasionally be encountered making an appearance in the 'Eastern sector of the *Shamanistic* worlds.

Apart from their main connotations as regards regions in the Shamanistic Otherworlds, the names of countries employed by the Keltic Initiates would carry secondary meanings associated with Keltic cultural connections in early history. For example, *Greece* had associations with the mythical roots of the Gaels, in the Black Sea area and Thrace, from whence they migrated back to post-Atlantean Eirinn; *Spain* with the Phoenicians who shipped them back to Eire in this early migration; *Alba* with warrior Initiations by Skathach on the Pictish Isle of Skye; *Lochlann* as the home of the 'brother race' to the Wild Northern Picts.

As a fully trained Bard and storyteller, the Master would be expected to have memorized not only dozens, but even hundreds, of complete poems and Tales. Such that, if asked to, or if naturally he came to be discoursing, he could recite any one as required, faithfully from memory. Within early Keltic manuscripts are long lists of the title-headings of the Tales that made up such a Bardic repertoire; sadly, owing to the destructions, many of the actual Tales themselves have not come down to us. Thus we can only lament the literary treasures lost to the Keltic tradition, and make the very best of what has survived. When the tradition was in a state of cultural strength, it is said that an accomplished *Seanchaidh* could recite one or two Tales per night to an audience, and even after a whole year of such telling, would not have had to repeat any of the Tales. As there were no televisions, radios, record players, films or magazines, in these ancient times, the traditional Tales and poetry played a major part in the cultural education, entertainment and inspiration of the native folk; these stood alongside the mumming and festival plays, dancing and folk music. Not only did the Bards manage to weave enthralling atmospheres of wonder, mystery, fear, suspence, horror, excitement, sadness, hope, love, beauty and joy around these powerful Tales – but the listeners also readily played their part by entering into the spirit of the narrative with wholehearted relish. As these Tales (which were often in verse) were not just recited to the nobility at their feasts, but also by travelling storytellers in ale-houses, barns and cottages or crofts all around the countryside, the tradition came, down through the centuries and millennia, to permeate every strata of Keltic society. In course of time peasant *Seanchaidh* (untrained in the Bardic colleges) came to acquire quite extensive repertoires, from memorizing the faithful renditions of the Masters. Not only were the main storylines memorized by the peasant *Seanchaidh*, but also all the *kennings* and pieces of esoteric symbolism. This is proven by the fact that some of the later storytellers were able to give the symbolical equivalents (or explain certain obscure motifs) by quoting from parallel passages they knew from other Tales. Thus they *understood* what they were reciting. Eventually this sort of knowledge became almost common currency amongst the common folk, repeated in their milking songs, waulking songs, herding songs, supernatural ballads, and the customary verse to be employed at births, marriages and wakes (funerals).

As history came to show, it was crucial that this storytelling and Bardism had indeed permeated down into the custody of the peasant sages, for when the 'Ascendancy' destroyed the old Irish nobility, and when the artistic patronage of the Scottish Highland chiefs was crushed after the 1745 Rebellion, the Bardic colleges that had depended upon the old Keltic system were decimated in the process. Thus, in many areas, the learned farmers, peasant *Seanchaidh* and tinker Tale-tellers became the valued repositories, custodians and transmitters of our Keltic heritage. Padraic O'Siochfhradha describes a couple of these latter storytellers:

Muiris 'ak Gearailt, a prosperous farmer and shopkeeper, as a storyteller he could well hold his own with any; he could sing and dance better than most, and was very knowledgeable in Folklore and interested in it. He was a good talker and very lively and intelligent in conversation. Physically also, he was a big man – tall, broad-shouldered and stout with side whiskers; was fair with a ruddy complexion.

Whilst Michael O'Suilleabhain was:

A tall, loosely-built, rather gaunt man, he was thin and sallow-skinned, with a long, intelligent, and mobile face. He was a poor man, and lived a life of discomfort and hardship. Notwithstanding his poverty and poor clothing, however, he had a great natural dignity, and was always treated with respect by everybody.

I would now like to discuss a vital topic: language and power-words. In this department our ancient Keltic ancestors had one massive advantage over modern English speakers: all the elements of their speech were intrinsically linked to the creatures and things with which they interreacted in their environment; their language and the world constituted one jigsaw puzzle, which could be explored in a truly magical way. (Certain other 'sacred tongues', such as Scandinavian and Germanic, Sanskrit, Ancient Greek, Hebrew and Chaldean, were similarly formulated around Initiatory wisdom.)

The fact that 'English' is a hotchpotch and a pot-pourri containing the jigsaw pieces from about eight or ten seperate 'pictures' (Anglo-Saxon, Norman French, Gaelic, Brythonic, Norse, Flemish, Latin, Greek, etc.) makes it almost useless as a unified Shamanistic language from one master blueprint. The ongoing attempt at formulating and teaching 'the Queen's English' may have some small advantages where streamlined machine-age communication is concerned, but it becomes progressively weaker and weaker in its relationship with nature. The establishment's continuing linguacide affects not only the Ghaidhlig, Kymraeg and Kernewek languages, but also the regional dialects of old Albion, and will most certainly leave the speech of Britain immeasurably poorer. Make no mistake, the more you sever the links with nature-based tongues, and the more you discard power-words, the more your everyday speech will have little to do with the real environment and the spirit of the land upon which you dwell. Thus, although the bulk of this book is written in 'English' for ease of communication, it is woven through with many hundreds of power-words from Shamanistic speech. I am sure that, after you have read through the rich treasure store contained in this book, you will join those of us committed to halting the destruction of our native tongues (whether Keltic or Germanic) and the relearning and recultivation of them.

Some small positive steps that I have taken in this book to reverse the process of linguistic decay include accurate spellings according to the meaning-full original word-roots. This has involved the replacing of the Latinish 'c', which is weaker than the original Keltic and Indo-European 'k', 'kh', 'ch' or 'q' – e.g., KuKulain instead of CuChulain; and where letters have been unnecessarily doubled in later Keltic spellings these have sometimes been discarded and the simpler original re-employed – e.g., instead of '*collen*', it is better to have '*kolen*'.

To those detractors who say it is pointless to seek the old values, I say: '*Na Reys Gara Anvor Goth, Ragan Vor Noweth* [Ancient Cornish]. Leave not the old ways for the new.' And: '*Eur Feiz, Eur Lez, Eur Galon* [Breton]. One faith, one tongue, one heart. *Ar Ch'iz Goz, Ar Ch'iz Gwirion* [Breton]. The old customs are good customs.'

As regards Root Speech and the silent communications of nature, Martin Buber says in *Between Man and Man*:

To understand the 'say' that I am refering to is to understand Real speech. In the House of Speech are many mansions, and this is one of the inner. The effect of having 'say' 'said' to me is completely different from that of looking or observing. We may term this way of perception – 'becoming aware'. The limits of the possibility of dialogue are the limits of 'awareness'.

CHAPTER 3
De-Conditioning

When we have removed the strata of euhemerist fiction
and rubbish from the ruin, the foundations and
beautiful fragments of the once noble fane of Irish
mythology will stand clear to the sun.
WESTROP in *The Proceedings of the Royal Irish Academy* 35, C.No. 8.p. 140

The best Folk and Faerie Tales merge indistinguishably into the legends of Keltic mythology, and Keltic mythology has its deep roots in Indo-European spirituality. To trace the golden thread of wisdom down the silver wolf-trails takes a degree of skill; few care to make the required effort, though the rewards are indescribable. Many prefer simply to skim the surface, becoming passably satisfied with the superficial.

If you would like to be different and special, so as to try and grasp the inner core of the mysteries, then extensive deconditioning of what you think and see must be undertaken. For, most ordinary people, before treading the path to Initiation, are somewhat lost and submerged under many layers of conditioning. This conditioning is so extensive and pervasive that many items of what one holds to be our own beliefs and opinions and what governs our reactions to new situations fail to be perceived as alien accretions which have little or no relation to what our own inner self really thinks and wills. Thus the process of peeling back the many layers of false conditioning can also amount to a process of self-discovery, a Reunion with one's true nature.

Right from the moment of birth the conditioning begins. There are accounts by psychic individuals who can remember what the incarnational process felt like in this modern world – entering into a plastic, metal and high-tech room, full of glaring bright lights, harsh antiseptic smells, and masked uniformed strangers who try to orchestrate the proceedings. How un-natural. Of course some might say that such a reception for an incarnating human spirit prepares it for the kind of world he/she will have to deal with; perhaps, but it also starts to force him/her to accept the 'technological dream' others are weaving. No wonder there is a growing movement for 'home births', which take place under subdued lighting, with gentle music playing, and in comfortable (or at least familiar) surroundings – all these things are conducive to helping the expectant mother to relax and to deliver the baby when the time is right.

As soon as the child is old enough to be cosseted in arms or pushed around in a pram, it is instructed by adults (even if unconsciously) on how to see, perceive and understand its environment.

And what a world they see – a world gone square! As a manner of speaking, that phrase is true not only philosophically and socially, but also in the sense of a physical actuality. Houses and tower blocks are built in a rectangular or square format; doors and windows are invariably rectangular or square; and on Sunday another similar type of 'box' is visited – the church/chapel, where the regimented flock sit neatly in straight rows, listening or occasionally singing classical ditties. Outside, architectural embellishments, be they 'classical' or 'Georgian', are orientated around the straight lines and the main secondary shapes that they make.

Most street planning demarcates unorientated rectangular sections, with roads that bisect and flank such urban segments. Throughout our countries, the roads and railway lines are as straight and direct as we can make them (the 'planners' even try and make rivers follow suit, only to find out that they silt up and die if they are 'straightened out'). Computerized conveyor-belt production lines (of junk food or gadgetry) help to increase the already frenetic pace of efficient mass production up to an even more ludicrous peak. Then, to cap it all, the oil/gas/electricity is fed down long thin lines to keep the central heating on, so as to minimize the vagaries of the weather cycle; after all, the millions of clones want to watch the square box in comfort, whilst the kids fight another wave of Space Invaders on their square computer-screens.

By way of total contrast, in ancient North European society most dwellings (raths, duns, krannog mounds, chambered cairns, etc.) were circular in shape; the few long houses which were roughly rectangular were at least always orientated according to the four points of the circular compass; a few other dwellings (e.g., souterains/fogous etc.) were tunnel or cave-shaped. The people went to worship in open-air Megalithic stone circles (occasionally egg-shaped). There the folk, encouraged by the Druids, would sing 'rounds', and in following the designs of the Faerie Beings dance in circles, to the beat of round drums and the skirl of pipes. The ancient cross-symbol, Pagan/Keltic-Christian, was the cross-quartered circle. The holy bread/bannock/oatcake was naturally baked into a circular shape. Whilst well-respected God Kings such as Arthur (under the direction of Myrddin) brought these teachings into such things as his round table. When people travelled they learned the contours of their mother the Earth (some may not have thought that this was a pleasurable process, but at least it gave them a certain 'awareness' that most moderns lack concerning place and topography); the only straight pre-Roman roads were those special ones which followed the ley lines of geomantic energy, that had been sent between certain power-spots; rivers were left to snake their curving way across the countryside (it would have been held as strange to have wished it any other way). The priests, poets, chieftains, warriors, healer-women, farmers, clansmen and labourers all took part in the eight major festivals which marked the solar cycle (also adding lunar rites), and at the height and depth of this seasonal cycle the whole community would gather together to remind themselves where exactly they stood in the cycle – by rolling a blazing wheel down a steep slope.

Thus in essence the ancient Kelts were in harmony with the Gods and Goddesses that lay behind the circular processes of nature; whilst the present-day British and Europeans worship 'the false-god of the rectangle' (who cannot even help one to ascend to 'the Almighty God'). The full consequences of this deplorable situation should be seriously contemplated in relation to how it conditions the daily perceptions of every modern person, and their offspring.

It is obvious that the great Englishman J. R. R. Tolkien thought very similarly and, with a wry vein of sarcasm running through his words, wrote the following in his perceptive essay 'On Fairy Stories':

> Not long ago – incredible though it may seem – I heard a clerk of Oxenford declare that he 'welcomed' the proximity of mass-production robot factories, and the roar of self-obstructive mechanical traffic, because it brought his university into 'contact with real life'. He may have meant that the way men were living and working in the twentieth century was increasing in barbarity at an alarming rate, and that the loud demonstration of this in the streets of Oxford might serve as a warning that it is not possible to preserve for long an oasis of sanity in a desert of unreason by mere fences, without actual offensive action (practical and intellectual). I fear he did not. In any case the expression 'real life' in this context seems to fall short of academic standards. The notion that motor-cars are more 'alive' than, say, centaurs or dragons is curious; that they are more 'real' than, say, horses is pathetically absurd. How real, how startlingly alive is a factory chimney compared with an elm-tree: poor obsolete thing, insubstantial dream of an escapist!

Of course, it may be argued that the great bulk of the modern population would not want to do without any of the 'benefits' of this wonderful 'civilization', and that, even if it was deemed desirable, it would be impossible to reorientate society without generating massive confusion, disruption and fear. On both counts I would agree (but surely a self-undertaken catharsis is better than nuclear doom or ecological destruction). However, as there are very many good and useful commodities and services produced by technology, by all means let us retain those that are genuinely beneficial to human creativity. Such things excepted, we should stop manufacturing all the other next-to-meaningless gadgetry with which this society is cloyed and littered (and upon which is squandered all too much of the Earth's finite resources). In trying to retain perspective on our human situation vis-à-vis all the other life-forms that share this planet with us, it would seem to be crucial that individually and collectively we keep closely in touch with the seasonal cycles (otherwise, how shall we understand the feelings of the trees, birds and animals in relation to their physical environment). We should also retain an openness to learn from the ancient wisdom traditions, rather than mistakenly assuming that our present 'civilization' is in every way more sophisticated than and superior to those that preceded it. For, in the opinion of many (including myself), twentieth-century industrial society is like a hideous disease spreading over the skin-land of our Mother Earth, and if we don't take serious steps to heal our rampant despoilation – then the Earth herself and the Lords of Karma may have to retaliate against their deviant children (us humans) with a host of very drastic measures (even more troublesome than cancer or AIDS).

Now, what has all this got to do with Folk and Faerie Tales? Everything. For the beings and places in these Tales are related to sectors and qualities in a *circular* Shamanistic cycle; the Faerie giants often change themselves through a *circular* transformation process; heroes go seeking, or spells are laid down, for one year and one day (i.e., *a whole cycle*); the *Dun Sidhe* are often *circular* mounds; the whole Keltic Shamanistic framework is *circular* (containing spirals, helixes, cones and egg shapes, as well).

Another main area for cultural indoctrination and perceptual conditioning is in school (primary and secondary), colleges and universities. Stated briefly, the intellectual Ascendancy that gives structure and content to the curricula is committed openly (or otherwise) to retaining its preferred appraisal of history, the arts and sciences; whilst at the same time restraining the heretics from rocking the boat. The whole educational system is geared towards the former aim, and it always carries in its armoury various devices to smash, or immobilize, 'alternative thought'. This has relevance to all fields of learning, noticeably anything to do with psychic faculties; and, particularly here, every aspect of Keltic culture and spirituality. To understand the failings of the modern educational system, one has to look back at least to the medieval period, when education (what little there was) was carefully controlled by the Orthodox Church, backed up by a classical ethos (i.e., employing Latin and Greek, with associated cultural 'values'). This biased system continued, almost unchanged in its fundamentals, down into the Victorian and Edwardian eras, where it was still detectable in the English public schools. Some glaringly obvious remnants of this classical ascendancy's influence include the following: all medical and biological terminology is still in Latin; most scientific terminology persists to be in Latin; some archaeological terms are still couched in Latin; all the teaching terminology and the format of the dominant classical music departments are in Latin. As in each area of learning there will be intellectual *conditioning* passed along with the use of Latin, such a situation is nothing short of criminal, to those who care for their native British cultural heritage. Indeed, it borders on the sadly ludicrous that, in the British Isles, whose native tongues are *Keltic* (sec. Germanic), we are still employing an essentially foreign tongue within our teaching infrastructure. It cannot be stressed too highly that each language carries with it an inherent attitude of mind and image-making propensities. Thus, everywhere that one employs Latin one is handicapping the inspirational flow of the native British modes of expression and creativity. To use Latin, which has been linguistically described as 'the most grammatically "dead" of all the Indo-European languages", for descriptive terms for *living* things (plants, trees, birds and animals) is the most astonishing folly. By the end of this book you may, on the other hand, have come to gather how wonderfully alive and numinously fertile the ancient Keltic words are for all *living* things. Therefore, is it not about time we pressurized the 'Ascendancy' into abandoning a dead foreign language, for one of the truly living native ones?

We should briefly pause to ask ourselves some pertinent questions. How trustworthy or accurate does one suppose classical writers were in reporting about their enemies the Kelts or Germanic tribes? How accurate or honest were the fathers of the Church of Rome in describing the practices of the Druids, or of even the Keltic Christians (Brythonic, Pictish and Culdees) whom they set about to destroy? How trustworthy does one suppose classically trained Victorian scholars would have been in compiling an etymological dictionary of British topography (derivations of place names, etc.)? And finally how accurate (or even fair) are modern-day classicists whilst passing comment upon the old Keltic scripts (Ogham and Koelbren)? As Daniel Corkerry summed up this Ascendancy-bias:

> The first article in an Ascendancy's creed is, and has always been, that the natives are a lesser breed, and that anything that is theirs (except their land and their gold!) is therefore of little value. If they have had a language and literature, it cannot have been a civilised language, cannot have been anything but a 'Patois' used by the hillmen among themselves; and as for their literature, the less said about it the better. In the course of time the natives become tainted with these doctrines; and cry approval when the untruths of the Ascendancy are echoed from some distant place, as if at last a fair judgement has been pronounced, not recollecting that the Ascendancy have had for hundreds of years possession of the ear of the world and have not failed to fill it with such opinions as were opportune. What pains one is to come upon one Irishman who cannot speak either of the Irish language or Irish literature or Gaelic History except in some such terms as the Ascendancy in Ireland have taught him. In his case the Ascendancy have succeeded; they have created in him the slave-mind. They have won his thoughts and affections from his Native Country.

So is it surprising that we are struggling to liberate our awareness from under many centuries of classicist-biased conditioning? Ask yourself: why is the history of ancient Greece and Rome given a hundred times as much teaching space as the ancient history of the Kelts and Teutonic races? Why are our museums always packed with Graeco-Roman and Renaissance artefacts on display, whilst Keltic art treasures gather dust in the basements? Likewise, why is Graeco-Roman art and sculpture (not to mention, Byzantine, Chinese and French, etc.) given several hundred times as great a teaching platform than Keltic or Pictish art? Why is Keltic Folk music, generally speaking, not taught in British schools, whilst even jazz and blues are allowed a bigger place in the shadow of the dominant classical and operatic forms? Why is native Keltic religion and spirituality still a banned heresy within 'religious studies', whilst one can more easily learn about Hinduism, Buddhism, Taoism and Shintoism, and Islam? Where is there the remotest hint of justice (never mind proportional representation) in that catalogue of prejudice generated by the 'Ascendancy'?

An answer some people would give to such inquiries is: 'because these subjects and things are more popular'. Yes, I would reply, at this present time, but only after putting the cart before the horse – our Keltic culture, language and spirituality is on the intellectual periphery, and close to extinction, exactly because it has been for centuries continually squashed, debilitated, mocked and persecuted by the servants of the unsympathetic Ascendancy. And it does not stand a chance of long-term survival unless the intellectual balance of power at least shifts a little in its favour. This book (and others like it) will give a small hopeful nudge in that direction.

As an example of the layering of adverse conditioning, which can result in a totally distorted picture, I would relate the following. At Winlatter Rock there is a stone with carved footprint(s) in it. Originally this would have been a Pagan Initiation stone, upon which an individual would have stood to try and attune with the good Faerie Wildman being from Sh. North. The first layer of Orthodox Christian lies to be smeared over this sacred site was that the footprint(s) were described as being those of 'the devil'; latterly, however, when the Church had time to elaborate upon their fabricated conditioning, they said that the footprint(s) were made by a priest's feet, where he had planted them firmly to grapple with 'the devil' (who had appeared as a dragon from the North). Thus, as a modern-day reader, if one had only encountered the latter version of the Tale, then one might not have come to realize what a historical and spiritual travesty had been perpetrated around this site, through lying *conditioning*.

There are thousands of examples of such perverse conditioning; indeed, it is a wearisome task even to note them in passing, without trying to relate and expose them all.

With regard to the Keltic Folk and Faerie tradition, direct slander such as associations with 'devilish superstitions', 'black magic' and other such rubbish is often encountered. This is sometimes coupled with a no less destructive form of conditioning: ridicule, and the deliberate distortion of visual or conceptual imagery. Several great writers have addressed themselves to this problem before myself (notably, J. R. R. Tolkien and Anthony Roberts). This is what Roberts has to say as regards the distortion of Faerie Imagery in his book *Geomancy: A Synthonal Re-appraisal*:

> Fairies ... have also been portrayed from Shakespeare onwards as ethereal, delicate parodies of the more sentimental aspects of human nature. Coy, winged, transparently fluttering, they have flitted like brightly coloured insects across the narrowing panorama of conscious human imagination. But they were not always envisaged in this nauseating fashion. Once the very word 'fairy' carried a strange and terrible imagery, and they were credited with powers that contained the elemental fury of nature herself. The fairy races (for they were as diverse as the human species) were seen as the guardians and protectors of the magically charged monuments, mounds, stones and earthworks, that the giants had originally shaped and patterned. This is where they link with the geomantic vision. To study fairies in their correct perspective some of the veils that have been draped across their memory must be carefully removed.

I concur completely, and, in chapter 6, I present some authentic descriptions (verbal and visual) of what the true Keltic Faerie beings appear like to human beings who perceive them through the filters of the human 'form'. For, when one has the courage to discard most of the layers of inappropriate conditioning, one can approach a conception of these non-human beings that is reasonably true to their nature. In such conditions their luminosity has a chance to shine through the obscuring sheaths enough for us to draw close to 'seeing' our guides to the magical Otherworlds. As Anthony Roberts puts it:

> The fairies of the mounds retain a most cohesive relationship with their physical backgrounds; they are somewhat in context, both organically and metaphysically, with the central matrix of the magic. Whether they sparkle through myth, inhabiting shining palaces on mist shrouded hills, or whether they haunt the dark interiors of echoing, stone-lined barrow chambers, they radiate a meaning, an energy and a purpose that amplifies the vision of an advanced, living past. Even when the tales are totally parochial, a sense of charismatic power still drifts on the edges of recognition, creeping into the receptive brain on the strength of a partially deciphered memory.

The end result of discarding all the misnamed 'fairy tales', and all the many other layers of cloudy conditioning that can but weaken and confuse our psychic sight, is that we can not only perceive the physical world with a heightened perception, but that we can also begin to perceive the Otherworlds that interface with this material one. Then, being free of conditioning, and open to certain other modes of consciousness, one can start to receive certain profound communications, as Martin Buber has so brilliantly said:

> ... so I exposed myself to the distance, open to all sensation and perception. And then, not from a distance but from the air all around me, noiselessly, came the answer. Really it did not come; it was there, it had been there – so I may explain it – even before my cry: there it was, and now when I laid myself open to it, it let itself be received by me.

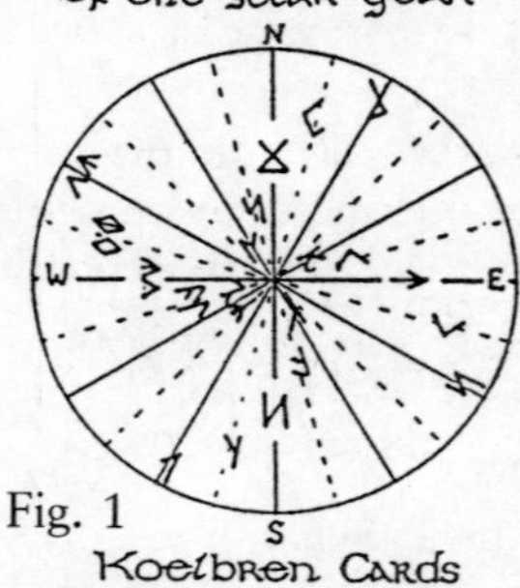

Fig. 1

The Shaman's Wheel Kaledon Naddair 19.10.85

Having woven the 'tops of the Trees' well together
I have recommenced the Strife that Gwyddion left us
the Eternal Battle at the Root of all things.
And like a Master Cartwright
I have shaped and placed
the Eight Spokes within the Shaman's Wheel,
and sent it spinning.
And like Odhin, with courage,
I have nailed myself upon its Cross-beams
its secrets to be winning.
And like Taliesin, with precocious speech
I shall mock the false and vainglorious posers,
For the Koelbren Song chants in a strict metre.
The Aisling-Vision
is born of a Warrior's striving
driven to the brink in searching
run to the ridge in hunting
there to make Myrddin's leap
into geilt Wisdom
the leap made
within the sable blackness of a Cave
within the green Shadows of a Forest Grove
within the dusken Sea-Coast Cove
within the brown eddies of a River Serpent
each leap a Quest into the Unknown
each a step in the Path of the Wildman.
And Keridwen, my darling Severe old Hag
has hounded me full-Circle for a Year and a Day
collecting the pre-arranged ingredients
for her Magic brew,
all this time Her Cauldron has been a-bubbling
preparing sustenance for the courageous
(for I've heard it shall not boil food for cowards).
So come forward those fearless enough to make the test
and push through the whining snivelling rest.
The Sprigs of the Arch-Diviner have been rightly ordered,
the potion is prepared to effect the transformation:
For one has to be strong enough to stand within the heart of flame,
Quick enough to see the web on a Dragonfly's wings
or catch the glint from Quetzecoatl's scales,
Dreamy enough to drift with the wash of Waves,
And slow enough to catch the meaning in a Toad's stare,
for that is the Way of the Sisters of Wyrd
to know the hidden laws that underpin the World.

CHAPTER 4

The Keltic Shamanistic Calendar

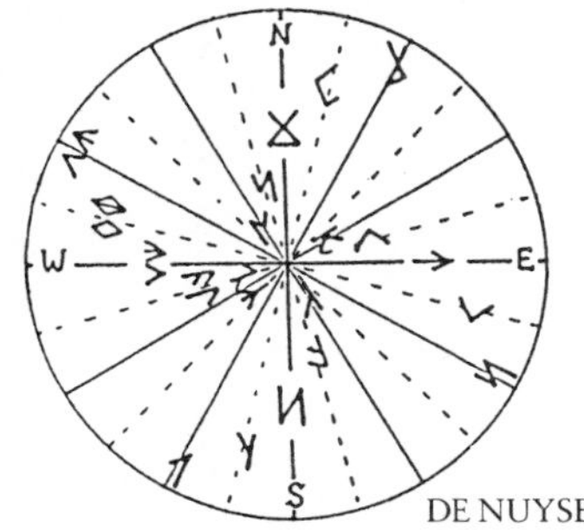

I recommend you to go by this road and no other.
Only take notice of the tracks of my wheel,
And, in order to give an equal heat overall,
Do not rise or descend too soon to heaven or earth.
For in rising too high you will be burnt by heaven,
And in descending too low you will be destroyed by earth.
But if your course remains set in the middle
The route will be plainer and the way more sure.

DE NUYSEMENT, *Poème philosophic de la Vérité de la Phisique Mineralle* in *Traittez de L'Harmonie et Constitution generalle du Vray.*

In any study of Keltic mythology, Folklore, Faerie faith and native Paganism, there is no more useful diagram than *the Keltic Shamanistic Calendar.* The reason for this is that it displays the ancient Druidical system of Shamanistic magic which provided the basis and major ingredients for all these subjects. When one comes fully to understand the principles that it is built upon, it is possible (as I have done) to grasp the internal significance of the eight seasonal festivals, ritual power-times, magical weapons, and the ingredients of other European religious mythologies. For those of you who would wish to read very thorough explorations of this calendrical system (and the Lore that supports it from the tradition) then I would recommend you to read my research articles in *Inner Keltia* Nos. 7, 8 and 9; plus my two-volume book *Ogham, Koelbren and Runic* (*Shamanistic Divination Scripts of Europe*); plus my forthcoming book on *The Keltic Shamanistic Calendar.* However, within the dimensions of this single chapter, excuse me if I merely summarize the teachings and evidence.

It is a known fact that the Ancient Kelts possessed a divinatory system of sprigs (small twigs cut from the trees in a *sacred* manner) marked with rune-like signs; in Gaeldom these were called *Krankar* (*Cranacher*), and within the Kymry the *Koelbren.* (*Krankar* from *Kran* = a tree, and *Kar* = a sprig/twig; *Koelbren* from *Koel* = an omen, secret message, and *Bren/Pren* = a tree-sprig, twig, lot or stick.) The Wheel at the top of the page shows these Krankar or Koelbren Signs.

Now, when the Druids were able to make detailed divinatory prognostications from these omen-marked twigs, they were (a) receiving and extrapolating mystical and intuitive messages, and (b) decoding secret information contained within these Signs and their combinations. As these divinations were on many varied subjects, e.g., weather predictions, animal and bird omens, the right and wrong times for action (e.g., a battle, religious rites, tribal gathering) – plus what the directives of the Gods and Faerie Folk were, which direction one should travel in, and what one was likely to encounter, etc. – they obviously contained a rich potential for interpretive detail. This Druidical system, with its associated enciphered Shamanistic Lore, was in a strong position until the Roman war-machine invaded to crush and oppress our native Keltic culture. Later depreciations caused by the Church of Rome, the Graeco-Roman Renaissance, English Imperialism (e.g., in Ireland), and finally the ravages of the Puritanical Protestant Church, culminated in the slow, steady suppression of all branches of Keltic Initiatory wisdom. Thus it comes as no surprise to find out that, some time between the eleventh and sixteenth

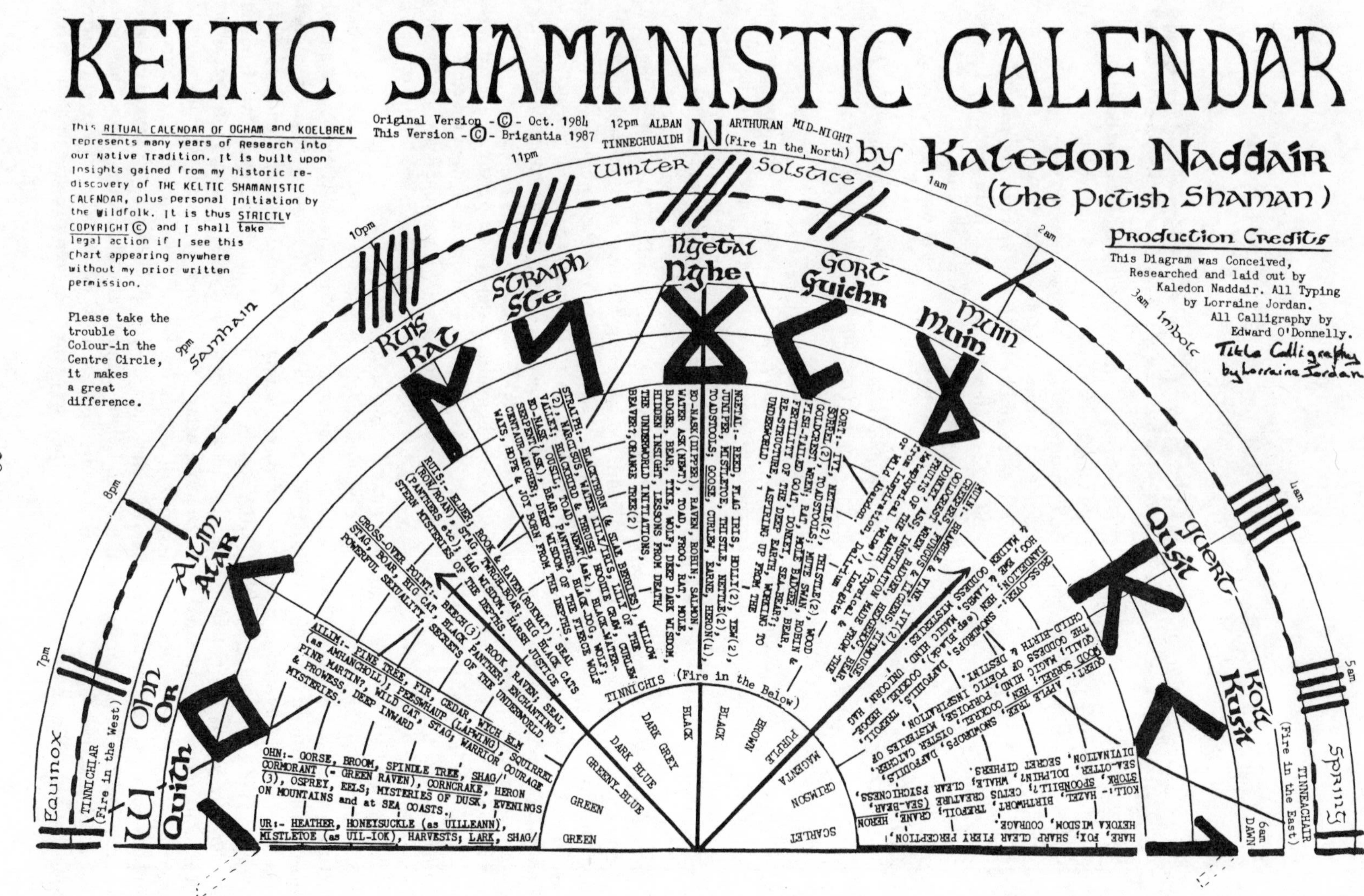
KELTIC SHAMANISTIC CALENDAR
by Kaledon Naddair
(The Pictish Shaman)
This RITUAL CALENDAR OF OGHAM and KOELBREN represents many years of Research into our Native Tradition. It is built upon Insights gained from my historic re-discovery of THE KELTIC SHAMANISTIC CALENDAR, plus personal Initiation by the Wildfolk. It is thus STRICTLY COPYRIGHT © and I shall take legal action if I see this chart appearing anywhere without my prior written permission.
Please take the trouble to Colour-in the Centre Circle, it makes a great difference.
Original Version - © - Oct. 1984
This Version - © - Brigantia 1987
12pm ALBAN ARTHURAN MID-NIGHT
TINNECHUAIDH N (Fire in the North)
Production Credits
This Diagram was Conceived, Researched and laid out by Kaledon Naddair. All Typing by Lorraine Jordan. All Calligraphy by Edward O'Donnelly.
Title Calligraphy by Lorraine Jordan
Winter Solstice
Samhain
Imbolc
Equinox
Spring
7pm
8pm
9pm
10pm
11pm
1am
2am
3am
4am
5am
6am DAWN
TINNICHIAR (Fire in the West)
TINNEACHAIR (Fire in the East)
TINNICHIS (Fire in the Below)
Ur Quith
Ohn Or
Ailim Atar
Ruis Rat
Straiph Ste
Ngetal Nghe
Gort Guichr
Muin Muin
Quert Qusit
Koll Kusit
UR:- HEATHER, HONEYSUCKLE (as UILLEANN), MISTLETOE (as UIL-IOK), HARVESTS; LARK, SHAG/
OHN:- GORSE, BROOM, SPINDLE TREE, SHAG/ CORMORANT (= GREEN RAVEN), CORNCRAKE, HERON (3), OSPREY, EELS; MYSTERIES OF DUSK, EVENINGS ON MOUNTAINS and at SEA COASTS.
AILIM:- PINE TREE, FIR, CEDAR, WYCH ELM (as AMHANCHOILL); PEESWHAUP (LAPWING), SQUIRREL PINE MARTIN?, WILD CAT, STAG, WARRIOR COURAGE & PROWESS. DEEP INWARD MYSTERIES.
CROSS-OVER POINT:- BEECH(3), ROOK, RAVEN, SEAL, STAG, BOAR, BIG CAT, BLACK PANTHER; ENCHANTING POWERFUL SEXUALITY, SECRETS OF THE UNDERWORLD.
RUIS:- ELDER; ROOK & RAVEN(ROKNAT), SEAL (RON/ROAN), STAG, TWRCH-BOAR, BIG BLACK CATS (PANTHERS etc); HAG WISDOM, HARSH JUSTICE STERN MYSTERIES OF THE DEPTHS.
STRAIPH:- BLACKTHORN (& SLAE BERRIES), WILLOW (2), NARCISSUS, WATER LILY/IRIS, LILY OF THE VALLEY; BLACKBIRD & THRUSH, HOODIE CRAW, CURLEW EO-NASK, OUSIL, TOAD, NEWT(Ask), BLACK-WATER-SERPENT(ASK), BEAR, PANTHER, BLACK-DOG, WOLF; CENTAUR-ARCHER; DEEP WISDOM OF THE FIERCE WOLF WAYS, HOPE & JOY BORN FROM THE DEPTHS.
NGETAL:- REED, FLAG IRIS, HOLLY(2), YEW(2), JUNIPER, MISTLETOE, THISTLE, NETTLE(2), TOADSTOOLS; GOOSE, CURLEW, EARNE, HERON(4), EO-NASK(DIPPER), RAVEN, ROBIN; SALMON, WATER ASK(NEWT), TOAD, FROG, RAT, MOLE, BADGER, BEAR, TYKE, WOLF; DEEP DARK WISDOM, HIDDEN INSIGHT, LESSONS FROM DEATH/ THE UNDERWORLD INITIATIONS, BEAVER?, ORANGE TREE(2)
GORT:- IVY, NETTLE(2), THISTLE(2), WOOD SORREL(2), TOADSTOOLS; MUTE SWAN, ROBIN & GOLDCREST WREN; RAT, MOLE BADGER, BEAR, FISH-TAILED GOAT, DONKEY, SEA-BEAR?; FERTILITY OF THE DEEP EARTH, WORKING TO RE-STRUCTURE, ASPIRING UP FROM THE UNDERWORLD.
MUIN:- BRAMBLE & VINE, IVY(2), CREEPERS, FUNGUS & LICHENS; TITMOUSE, GOLDCREST WREN, BADGER, HEDGEHOG, BEAR, DONKEY, ASS; INSPIRATION MADE FROM THE FRUITS OF THE EARTH, ('Wine'), (Physical & Metaphysical) Insights from Inspiration, Delirium or Wild Abandon.
CROSS-OVER:- SNOWDROPS, DAFFODILS, TREFOIL, DANDELION; HEN (esp. Black), COCKEREL, HEDGE-HOG, EWE & LAMBS, MAGIC HIND, UNICORN, HAG & MAIDEN GODDESS MYSTERIES.
QUERT:- APPLE TREE, SNOWDROPS, DAFFODILS, WOOD SORREL; HEN, COCKEREL, OYSTER CATCHER, QUAIL, MAGIC HIND, PORPOISE, MYSTERIES OF THE GODDESS OF POETIC INSPIRATION, CHILD-BIRTH & DESTINY.
KOLL:- HAZEL, BIRTHWORT, TREFOIL, CRANE, HERON STORK, SPOONBILL?, CETUS CREATURE (SEA-BEAR, SEA-OTTER, DOLPHIN?, WHALE, CLEAR PSICHICNESS, DIVINATION, SECRET CIPHERS.
HARE, FOX, SHARP CLEAR FIERY PERCEPTION, HEYOKA WISDOM, COURAGE.
GREEN
GREENY-BLUE
DARK BLUE
DARK GREY
BLACK
BLACK
BROWN
PURPLE
MAGENTA
CRIMSON
SCARLET

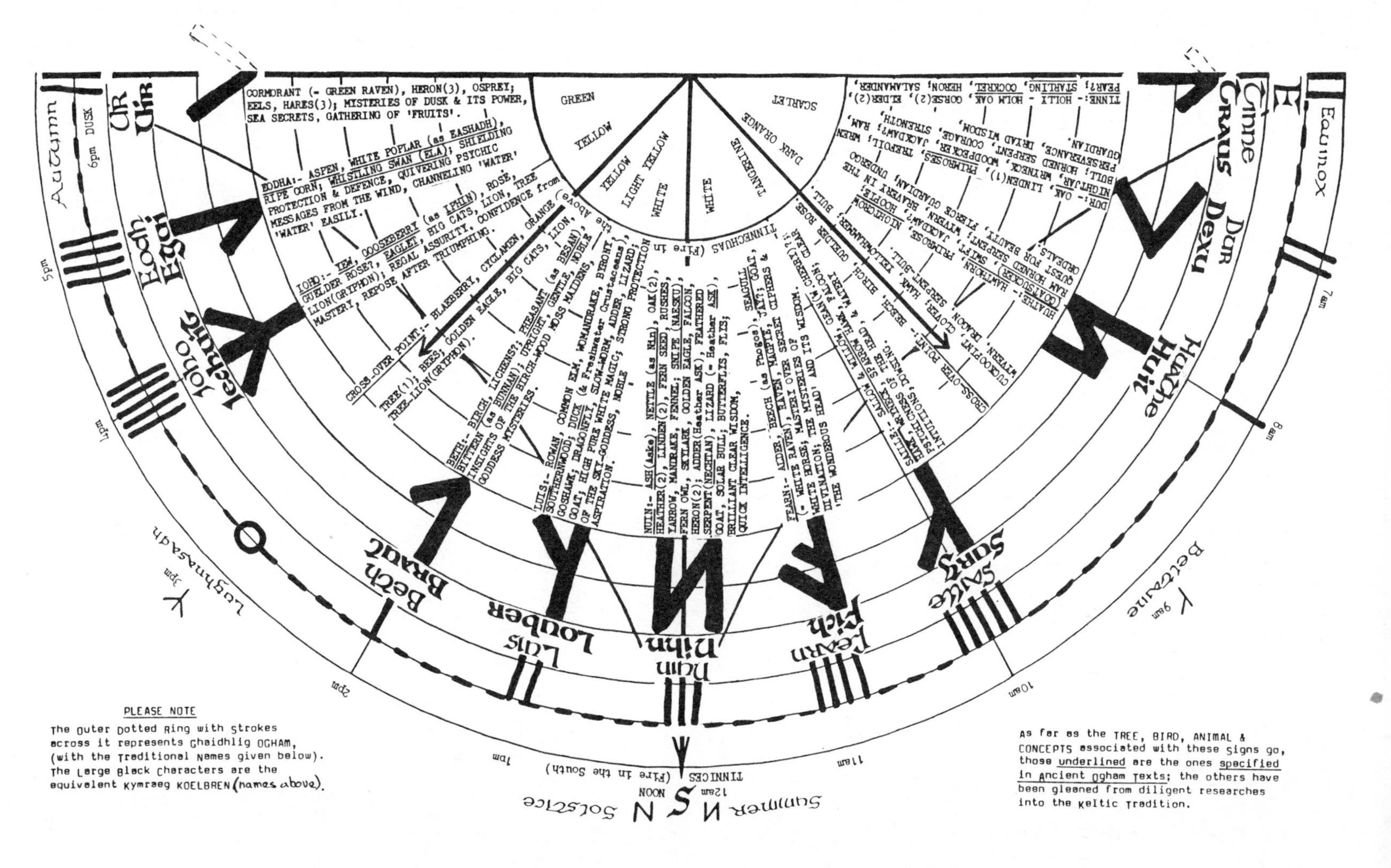
Equinox
Tinne
Traus
Dur
Dexu
Huathe
Huit
Beltaine
Saille
Sars
Fearn
Fich
Nuin
Nihn
Summer
Solstice
12am NOON
TINNICES (Fire in the South)
Luis
Louber
Beth
Bract
Lughnasadh
Ioho
Iechuit
Eodh
Egai
Ur
Uir
Autumn
6pm DUSK
7am
8am
9am
10am
11am
1pm
2pm
3pm
4pm
5pm
GREEN
YELLOW
LIGHT YELLOW
WHITE
TANGERINE
DARK ORANGE
SCARLET
TINNECHUAS (Fire in the Above)
CORMORANT (- GREEN RAVEN), HERON(3), OSPREY; EELS, HARES(3); MYSTERIES OF DUSK & ITS POWER, SEA SECRETS, GATHERING OF 'FRUITS'.
EODHA:- ASPEN, WHITE POPLAR (as EASHADH), RIPE CORN; WHISTLING SWAN (ELA); SHIELDING PROTECTION & DEFENCE, QUIVERING PSYCHIC MESSAGES FROM THE WIND, CHANNELING 'WATER' 'WATER' EASILY.
IOHO:- YEW, GOOSEBERRY (as IPHIN), ROSE, GUELDER ROSE?, EAGLET, BIG CATS, LION, TREE LION(GRYPHON); REGAL ASSURITY, CONFIDENCE from MASTERY, REPOSE AFTER TRIUMPHING.
CROSS-OVER POINT:- BLAEBERRY, CYCLAMEN, ORANGE TREE(1); BEES; GOLDEN EAGLE, BIG CATS, LION, TREE-LION(GRYPHON).
PLEASE NOTE
The outer Dotted Ring with strokes across it represents Ghaidhlig OGHAM, (with the Traditional Names given below). The Large Black Characters are the equivalent Kymraeg KOELBREN (names above).
As far as the TREE, BIRD, ANIMAL & CONCEPTS associated with these signs go, those underlined are the ones specified in Ancient Ogham Texts; the others have been gleaned from diligent researches into the Keltic Tradition.

centuries, the Irish sages seem to have lost knowledge of what the *Krankar* signs looked like, whilst preserving much valuable Ogham Lore; at the same time the Welsh preserved what the Koelbren signs looked like (using them as 'letters'), whilst losing the encoded nature and mythological Lore. The system remained in that fragmented disunity right up until 1984, when I was guided into reuniting the two main sundered halves.

The pronounced psychic gifts I had when as a youngster, I deliberately set about disciplining and harnessing to an in-depth training within the Western mystery traditions. This not only involved vast amounts of intellectual learning, but also physical (and inner) experiences at the ancient megaliths, petroglyph sites, power-rivers and magical woods. This resulted in certain very powerful Keltic deities and Wildmen making contact with me and slowly coming to act as my teachers. Although these beings normally exist in the Keltic Otherworld, they occasionally 'cross over' (or at least make their presence felt) in the 'normal' natural world. It was within one of these 'visits' that I was entrusted with the lost code that joined Ogham–*Krankar*–the *Koelbren* back together. This momentous event soon led on to knowing how the *Beth–Luis–Nuin* Ogham Alphabet fitted into a Shamanistic Calendar Wheel, and the significance of this reassembled lore for the European Initiatory traditions. Thus was the Keltic Shamanistic Calendar reborn.

On pages 28 & 29 is featured the most advanced version of this calendar I have produced so far. The outer ring features the Ogham strokes with their linked names in the *Beth–Luis–Nuin* Alphabet; and inside them are their matched *Koelbren–Krankar* signs; within this is Shamanistic Lore (that *underlined*) being specified in Ogham texts, the rest from research into our tradition conducted by myself and my colleagues); the colour circle in the centre is based upon Ogham Lore aided by my own insights.

As this Mighty Diagram is hard to take in at first viewing, and as the interconnections between all of its constituent elements are complex in the extreme, I feel it would be helpful and advisable to study it topic by topic, thus enabling us to grasp the principles upon which it is constructed.

First of all, let us look at the Keltic system of physical and metaphysical orientation. At its most basic (but still potent), it involves understanding the qualities of North, South, East and West; with the resultant Centre being the place of the *Axis Mundi*, linking the sky above to the underground below.

The Kelts cared about orientation. This is amply demonstrated both in the outer and in the internal alignments of the ancient monuments and stone circles. Their primal orientation was to the four directions: North, South, East and West, as well as to the important intersect at 'the Centre'. That this fivefold orientation was of supreme importance to the Kelts is shown by the fact that they organized whole countries in accord with the principle. This was reflected down through regions, townships, to the single house or croft. The individual Kelt also ordered his or her worldview accordingly, as an Irish riddle demonstrates: 'Where is the middle of the world?', the correct answer being 'Here' or 'Where you are standing' (in other words, each individual was regarded as being at the centre of their own universe). Thus each Keltic country contained within it devolving applications of this law of 'Centredness'.

Although the four directions of space and the four quarters had important qualities assigned to them, it was the Centre which commanded most attention. The Centre was the hub, the omphalos, the fulcrum, the balance, the creative essence, the resultant quintessence; it was the point 'betwixt and between' the worlds above and below the material plane.

If we turn first to Ireland, we shall find the clearest and most detailed example of this process in action. From time immemorial Ireland has been divided into four quarters: Ulster (N),

Munster (S), Leinster (E) and Connacht (W), with the Kingship anciently residing in the fifth province of Meath. This Central province was made up from a portion of the other four.

The Central fifth province of Meath was ruled from the King's Court at Tara (Temhair), and the very earliest record we have of Tara states that it was built on the site of a sacred hazel grove.

We read of the Sun God Lugh paying a visit to the King's residence at Tara on the day when there was 'a darkness over the earth' during Christ's Crucifixion. It was at this momentous time that the Sun God decided to recount the history of Ireland and its four quarters, thereby reaffirming the heritage of Ireland. He also chose to explain the qualities and characteristics at work in each of the provinces (refer to passages in Celtic Heritage by A. & B. Rees):

It was at Uisnech that the Mide (eponym of Meath), chief Druid of the People of Nemed, lit the first fire. The fire blazed for seven years, 'so that he shed the fierceness of the fire for a time over the four quarters of Ireland. From that fire were kindled every chief fire and every chief hearth in Ireland.' This custom came down into historical times in the form of a tradition that no one could light a Beltaine fire until the Ard Ri, the High King, had lit the first one on Tara Hill. In 433 AC St Patrick very knowingly usurped supremacy over the whole country when he lit a fire on Slane Hill (ten miles from Tara) *before* the High King Laoghaire lit his. St David committed a similar symbolic gesture a century later in Wales.

Fig. 4a

These five provinces were each further subdivided into five regions; it is related that Ireland was divided into twenty-five parts among the children of Ugaine Mor, a division which is said to have lasted for three hundred years.

Turning to the other Keltic countries we find that Keltic Gaul was also thus divided. Caesar testifies that 'on a fixed date in each year they hold a session in a consecrated spot in the country of the Carnutes which is supposed to be the Centre of Gaul.'

That Kymru (Wales) was likewise organized we can gather from the following quote (From Taliesin's *Kadair Teyrn On*):

Four Caers there are,
fixed in Wales,
their Rulers are quickeners of Fire (Rebellion?)

Fig. 4b

the great twelfth-century Bard Cynddelw echoes this

Bards are constituted the Judges of excellence:
and Bards will praise thee, even Druids of the Circle
of four dialects, coming from the four regions.
A Bard of the steep Mountain will celebrate thee,
even Cynddelw, the first object in the gate.

And in the Book of Taliesin 10, lines 20–21, we read:

Four chief sovereignties,
And the fifth not worse.

This principle continued into the medieval Bishoprics of Wales where we find: Bangor (North-west), St Asaph (North-east), Llandaf (South-east) and St David's (South-west). The Bishoprics met at the Mountain of Pumlumon (Pum-llumon, Five-peaks or Five-Beacons). Pumlumon symbolizes the whole. Extending westward from its top is a commote called Perfedd ('Middle').

Fig. 4c

Although we have no early evidence for Alban (Scotland) as a whole, we can still detect this five-fold process in its second stage of operation, the regional. For the Lothians (Loth-ians) were divided into *North* (Fife), *South* (part of the Borders), *East*, *West* Lothian, with a central *Mid-Lothian*. And within the capital of this Mid-Lothian, namely Dinas Eiddyn (Edinburgh), there lay (and lies) the famous '*Heart* of *Mid*-Lothian', at the Centre of Mid-Lothian.

It would be interesting to try and find traces of this law at work in Old Albion (for instance, is Essex, Wessex, Sussex and Middlesex a continuation from a Keltic system of county and land division?).

A clear example from a once strongly Keltic area is encountered when we read about Crockern Tor, which is said to be the precise Centre of Dartmoor, where the four 'quarters' into which it is divided meet. For that geomantic, ritual and judicial reason this small tor was selected to be the seat of the Stannary Parliament (of ancient tin-legislators). And upon the moot-days twenty-four members from each quarter gathered together in this place to attempt to make wise and honourable decisions, in keeping with the special spirit of the place. For it is said that upon dark, windy nights could be seen riding a mysterious horseman known as Old Crockern, whose bony old horse rattled over the tor's stones as it galloped by.

This process was not limited to the geography of physical orientation; we also find echoes of it in the mythology, Folklore and religion. For example, in Caer Sidi, the foursquare enclosure, which revolves four times; Otherworld four-square islands; pillar-supported islands shielded by four copper nets; the four spiritual cities from whence came the Tuatha De Danann; Keridwen's Cauldron, called 'Pair Pumwydd', the 'Cauldron of the Five Trees', etc.

The ramifications of this five-fold law are nearly endless. The physical and metaphysical orientation process interlinked with many other subtle laws to make the Keltic kosmos a coherent and well-ordered system. Depending on his or her degree of knowledge and awareness, the individual could come to grasp exactly how he or she stood in regard to the rest of creation. This would help individuals to understand the forces at work upon them, and how they could react or respond to those forces. Such a life-enhancing relationship with the elemental qualities of the four quarters would have heightened the individual's sense of direction. It would also have given him or her a greater appreciation of the characteristics of, for example, a snowy squall from the North, or a wet but warm wind from the West. Above all, our ancient Keltic forebearers were 'Centred', at least physically, which is more than can be said for most

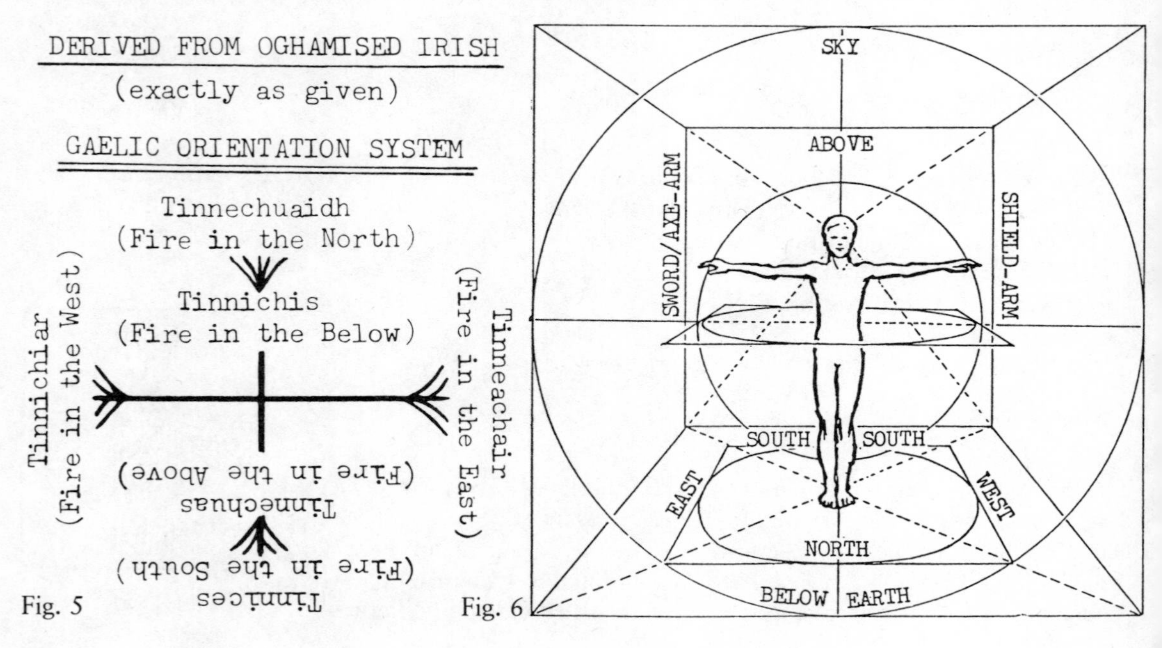

Fig. 5

Fig. 6

of their descendants today. There is nothing stopping us from relearning this ancient wisdom, except perhaps our modernist intellectual arrogance.

In the following pages there is much valuable life-study material that, if you learned and then put into practice, I guarantee would make you much more in harmony with the mysteries of nature, both physically and spiritually. Fig. 5 shows one of the last courageous attempts (in the seventeenth century) that the Irish sages made to preserve this wisdom for us. Whilst the native Gaelic culture was being crushed by the English ascendancy, planters and Anglophile Scottish farmers, the Irish Initiates set about creating a secret language in the hope of preserving fragments of Ogham Lore. The priceless word-store of Oghamized Irish lay only half appreciated until I rediscovered the Shamanistic Calendar, and devoted a chapter to Oghamized Irish in my two-volume book. *The Chart of Fire-Vortexes* can now proudly stand alongside the other Keltic orientation maps and help the individual find his/her place in the kosmos, cycle of festivals, and indeed within any magic circle. In Fig. 6 I have constructed a personal orientation map for warriors in these Northern lands – with our feet planted firmly in the soil to draw strength from our Mother Earth; our head tuning into the Sky Father's energies; for most, the magical weapon will be grasped in the right hand (which links to Shamanistic East qualities), whilst the shield is born on the left arm and hand (links with Shamanistic West qualities); thus we archetypally face North, which is upwards on the gradient of the land. For certain more Shamanistic practices, the shield (painted with power-glyphs and spirit-sigils) would be draped down the back, so that whilst in deep contemplation/trance, lying face-down on the ground, one would be protected by the motifs emblazoned on the shield. (Also known from Lappish, Slavic and Red Indian practices.)

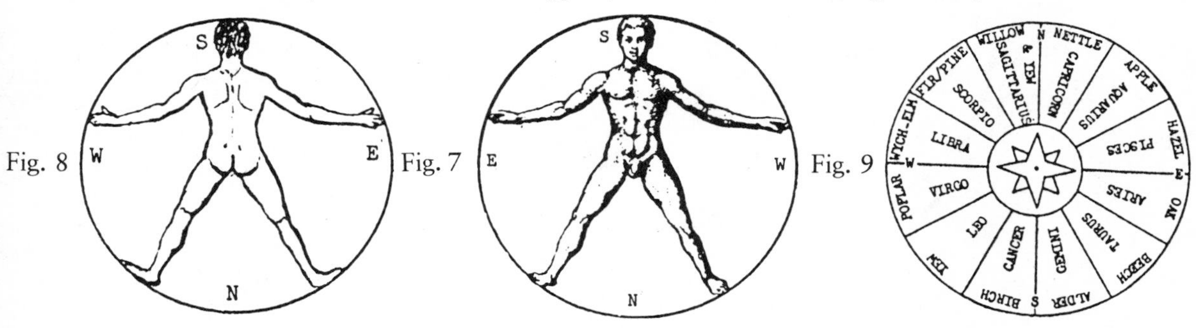

Fig. 8 Fig. 7 Fig. 9

Another system linked to the Shamanistic Wheel is where Shamanistic East is linked to emerging activity, whilst Shamanistic South is outward activity at its peak; Shamanistic West starts to descend inwards, whilst Shamanistic North is the peak of this introversion cycle. Thus the right hand/arm/leg, etc., are associated with active/outward/giving attitudes, and the left hand/arm/leg with mainly passive/inward/receptive attitudes.

If one has to lie down on one's back within a ritual circle linked with the qualities of the Shamanistic Calendar, then, for most general purposes, Fig. 7 is correct. Feet in Shamanistic North; head in Shamanistic South; right arm in Shamanistic East; left arm in Shamanistic West.

The other side of the coin, as it were, is shown in Fig. 8; this scheme one finds employed in Ogham's 'Fionn's Window' diagram, certain astrological charts, as well as the first illustration of the Qabalistic Space Cube/Sphere (Fig. 26 page 50). As these various orientational methods serve different purposes, it behoves us to learn the whys and wherefores of each, rather than throwing up our hands and saying, 'I'm confused', for such a response does not befit a magical warrior or warrioress.

Over two years after my historic rediscovery of the Keltic Tree Calendar, I noted with interest that J. Monard, in his booklet on *The Coligny Calendar*, makes mention of a Gaulish Astrological Tree Calendar (which I have illustrated in Fig. 9). Although much simpler in its ascriptions, it accords well with my Keltic Tree Calendar, as shown in Fig. 12. And, as Monard indicated, 'The Kelts used to name the Zodiacal Constellations not only by the noun *Prinnios* = 'arborescence/(tree) canopy/frondescence',

the Keltic Tree Calendar by Kaledon Naddair

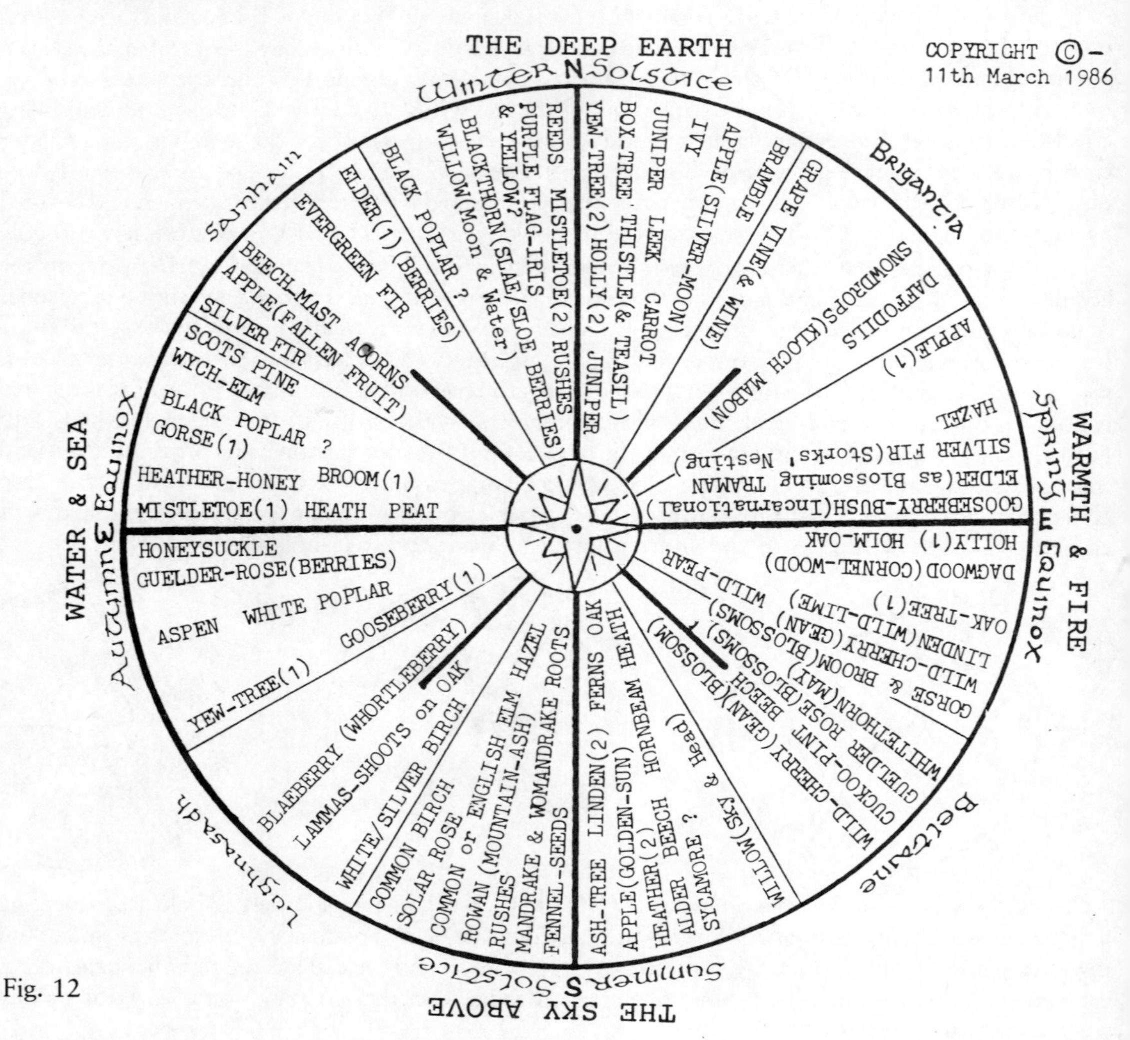

Fig. 12

but also gave to each one a tree-species name. Such names could vary with the climates, and the Picts of Kaledonia did not have quite the same nomenclature as the Galates of Anatolia.' Although there were small variations in ritual usage due to tree-species distribution in various geographical areas, one major Keltic (and even Indo-European) tree calendar can be discerned behind minor regional differences. Indeed Paul Freidrich, in his valuable book *Proto-Indo European Trees (the Arboreal System of a Prehistoric People)*, goes far in tracing the intricacies of this subject through linguistic evidence. Freidrich also inadvertently supplies much supportive information which confirms why certain trees had a particular ritualistic role within the Keltic Tree Calendar and what other trees were particularly associated with them (e.g., links between the ash tree, spears, Sky God and beech and hornbeam equivalents). It would seem advisable, therefore, if you spent a little while familiarizing yourself with the main and secondary positions of the trees in our Keltic Tree Calendar; for, as we shall find out in Chapter 7, trees often play a role in Folktales and are strongly linked to the Faerie Folk; thus, to understand their role *properly*, we should relearn the tree Wisdom of the ancient Druids.

Keltic Deities and Their Tree Totems

by Katedon Naddair

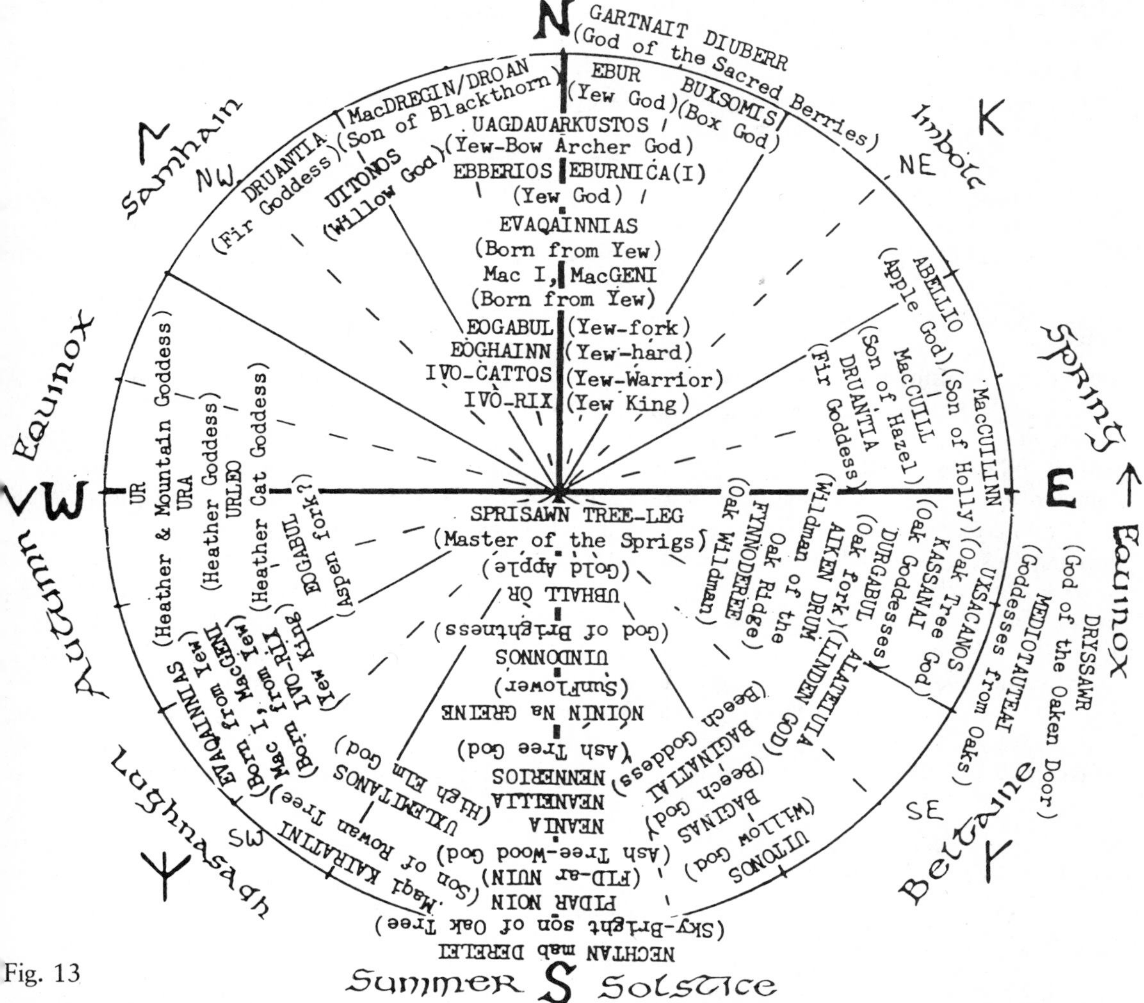

Fig. 13

With my grateful thanks to Monseur J. Monard for some of the Continental Divine Names, and to Mac Neil & other Early Scholars for Gaelic ones; all the Pictish material I translated, with a nod to Cinaeth Tucker for the meaning of 'Diuberr'. The resultant SHAMANISTIC CALENDAR given above is based-upon my own Ogham TREE-Cycle Discoveries.)

The Kelts (like their Cousins the Scandinavians and Phoenicians) were famous as a Sea-faring People, indeed the Keltic Galleys and Birlinns were better designed and built than the Vessels of the Roman Invaders. Thus it is not surprising to find that the Kelts preserved Esoteric Lore on the Qualities of the '4 Tides'. As Prudence Jones showed in her excellent Monograph 'Sundial and Compass Rose' (Eightfold Time-Division in Northern Europe)', Fenris-Wolf Pagan Paper No.3, 'Tide' (Tid) originally meant a Force or Quality that came from one of the 4 or 8 major parts of the Compass. The Pictish (and later Scottish) words Airt, Ġarth and Girth originally denoted Stations/Points on the Ritual Circle of the Compass/Year/Day.

Also associated with the Qualities of the Airts are The Winds, which carry Metaphysical as well as Physical Properties which effect all Humans and Animals. As modern-day folk have become more urbanite, we have also lost personal touch with the Qualities of the Winds. Our Ancestors were much closer to a symbiosis with these Qualities which were reportedly bestowed upon a new-born child in correspondence with what 'Wind' was blowing at its birth (see Fig. 14). Each of the 4 Winds have a distinct character. A piece of Winter Solstice Divination done on 'Dar-na-Koille', 'the Night of the Fecundation of the Tree', was that whatever Goath (Wind) was blowing would bring either: West – Fish and Bread; North – cold and flaying; East – snow on the Hills; South – fruit on the Trees; a sample of shrewd weather lore for December–January.

The various coloured 'rays' have long been held to convey specific qualities or healing effects; whether this is from coloured light, dyes, jewels, flower-blossoms or tinted stones (see Fig. 15).

Someone affected by the evil eye is given, as a charm, water to be drunk; for applying to the body, the water is treated by having coloured pebbles dropped into it. 'The charm is considered most potent when one stone is white, another black, the remainder being red, olive, or of greenish tint.' (In other words, with one stone from each of the four quarters.)

Presumably indicating a similar aim of ritual protection and orientation, we encounter white, black, green, red and multi-coloured oval stones in burials in the famous Carrow-More megalithic cemetery near Sligo. Whilst beneath a burial kist in the pagan cemetery of Ballan Hill, County Carlow, under an inverted urn, were three smooth round burnt stones; one was white, one black and the third *greenish* (ritually pointing the deceased towards the Otherworld West). Specific examples of the use of individual coloured stones also occur: according to Pliny, 'Jet has the power of banishing noxious serpents'; that accidental preserver of ancient traditions Bede also describes jet as having the power, when burned, of drawing away snakes. When we appreciate jet's position on the rediscovered Shamanistic Calendar as being at the Winter Solstice, it is clear that it functions as an opposite magical pole to adders and snakes, whose main station is at the Summer Solstice. Now, for the first time in millennia, one can truly appreciate the importance and function of the famous jet necklaces found in Pictland, and thus, contrary to academic scepticism, demonstrate that the ancients had a rhyme or reason for everything. In the Scottish Highlands, even until recently, a black stone would be taken in silence from a running tarn just after midnight and applied to a person suffering from mumps, whilst repeating a Gaelic rhyme. A similar procedure was followed with a green stone and rubbed all down a naked leg as a certain cure for hip disease.

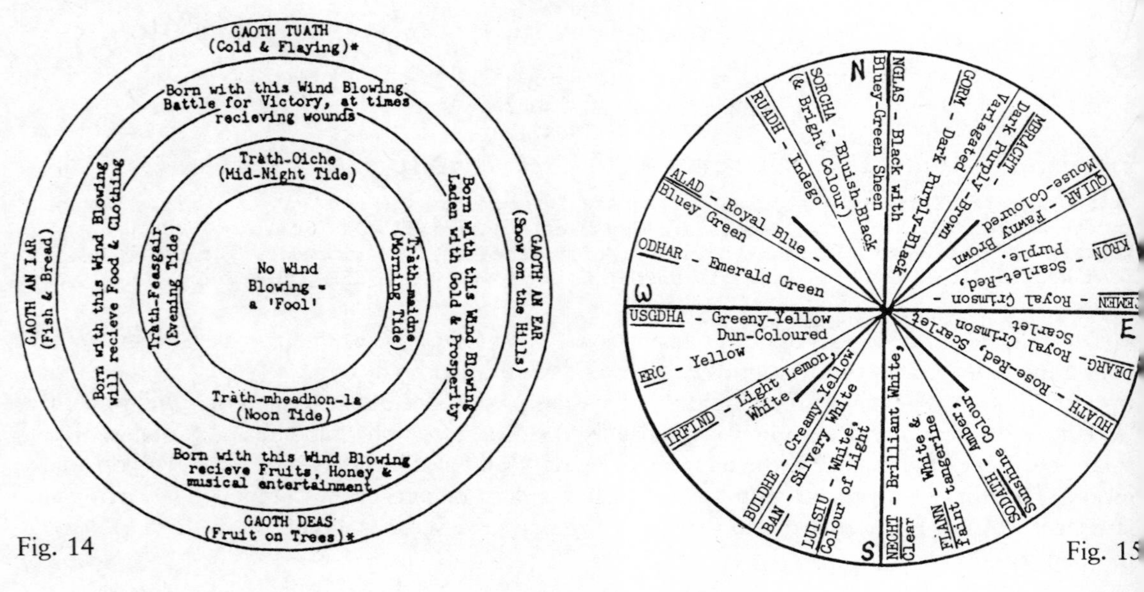

Fig. 14

Fig. 15

One of the first of the many sub-cycles within the Shamanistic Calendar I came to discern was that involving serpents–newts/lizards–toads/frogs. This small breakthrough was, I've no doubt, facilitated by the animals all being personal totems of mine. As each of these creatures is prominent within Druidical, witchcraft and Faerie Faith Lore, the insights thus gained are most valuable. As Alan and I have often found in such researches, the meaning of early Keltic root-words can be vital; it was just so in this case – for, from being miseducated into believing the River Esk took its name from the Anglo-Saxon for axe, I, by my own endeavours, discovered it was in fact named after the Keltic word *Ask*, meaning specifically here River Serpent. With further delving the nuances emerged: *ask* = *askr* = ash tree = white serpent = white adder = heather ask = lizard; and *ask* = black water serpent = black adder = water ask = newt; the polarizing in the North and South was clear. Having been immersed in serpent experiences since I was a child, and having had recent powerful serpent Initiations, the rest of the cycle was quite easily discerned. With a deal of further research into the extensive European Mytho-Artistic Wyvern (two-legged dragon) tradition, their position along with other 'worms', eels, sea serpents and such like became clear. The toad (puddock) is of course *the* prime totem for the element of Earth in the North; and its close relation with the frog stands for the rebirth of the Sun and the refertilization of the waters after the Winter Solstice. The natterjack toad, however, is a most significant exception to this grouping, as it quite likes dry summery weather, and is etymologically linked to the adder, thus natter = nadder. But of course all true Initiates of the Horseman's Society would know about that piece of Shamanism, thorns, polarities, *et. al.* (see Fig. 16).

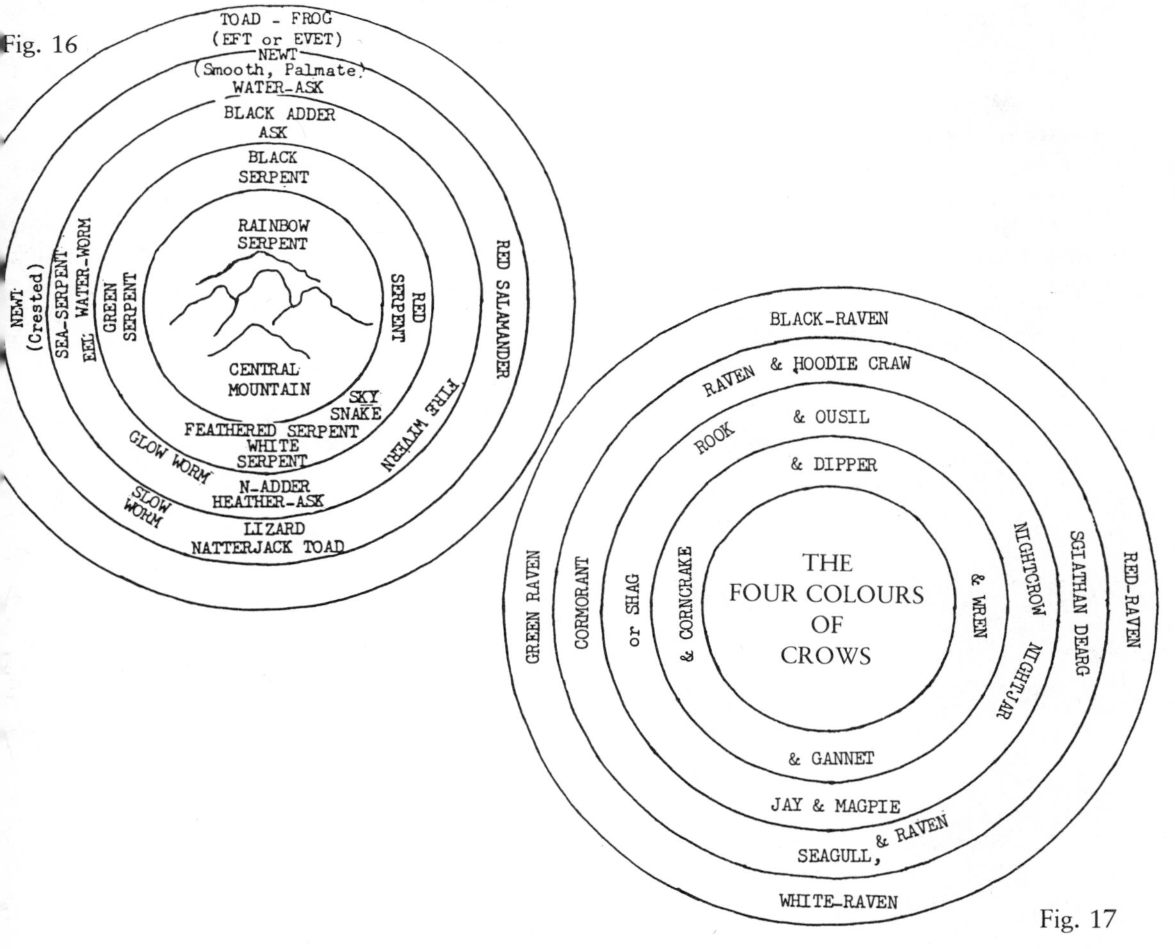

Fig. 16

Fig. 17

Since working on an esoteric Irish Folktale (No. 2 in a series by Keltia Publications), I had read of at least three different coloured ravens in the Keltic tradition – the normal black, common white, and rarer red (*Sgiathan Dearg*); whilst musing on the possibility of there being a mythological 'green' raven, I reconsidered all the personages connected with ravens and turned up a few surprises. For, from ravens/crows, I soon was led to certain affiliated real and natural birds. Black – *Bran*, *Kernun*, *Odhin*; white – *Bran Wen*, *GwynBran*, *Mor-Vran* (sea raven), *Odhin*; red – *Sgiathan Dearg*; green – *Mannanan*. Now *Mor-Vran* actually denotes seagull in Welsh, the seagull also being Odhin's sea raven, hence the white raven's; the magpie (which is physically partially white) is associated with Gwynbran and with the Astrological Sign of Geminii in the South, which is white. The nightjar is *the* bird for the *red* Eastern quarter, thus I smiled when reading that one of its other names is the night *crow*. The other red raven or red crow is the wren, which in Brythonic Scots is known as the *Cutty Vran* = the short (small) *Bran/* raven. The green raven is the cor-mor-ant, with its diet of eels; indeed it is called *Fitheach-mara* (sea raven) in Ghaidhlig, and *Mulfran* or *Gwyach* (sea raven) in Kymraeg. In an old Gaelic rhyme, the cormorant is reported to pass through three periods in its life-cycle: '*Seachd bliadhna na sgarbh, seach bliadhna na learg, agus seachd bliadhna na bhallaire bodhain*' = 'Seven years a scarf, seven years a speckled loon, and seven years as a cormorant of the rocks.' The shag, with its shiny green coat, is called in Kymraeg *Mulfran Werdd* (the green sea raven). Finally, as the period in the Shamanistic Wheel also involves the harvest on land, the corncrake (or landrail) features as another mythological 'green' raven, whose craking in a field foretold the misfortune/death of someone in the neighbourhood. The black raven of the Shamanistic North, in its Death Aspect, is the hoodie-craw; in its mountain wisdom aspect is the *ousel* (e.g., of Kilgwiri); in its dark river knowledge aspect it is the *dipper*, or *Eo-n-Ask* ('River Serpent Bird'), which runs along riverbeds under the fast-flowing water as 'the water craw' (in Brythonic

By now you will be starting to get an idea of what the Shamanistic Calendar contains, although I have presented only a tiny fraction of the relevant Lore. A fair percentage of what has been surveyed so far was preserved within the ancient Ogham ciphers – cycles of *trees*, birds, colours, skills and crafts and much more besides. My great achievement was to realize exactly how these Ogham cycles fitted into a Shamanistic Wheel, and indeed what the essential qualities of the different Stations within the Shamanistic Calendar were. How important a breakthrough this was can best be gauged by comparing it with one of the most serious failures – that of Robert Graves.

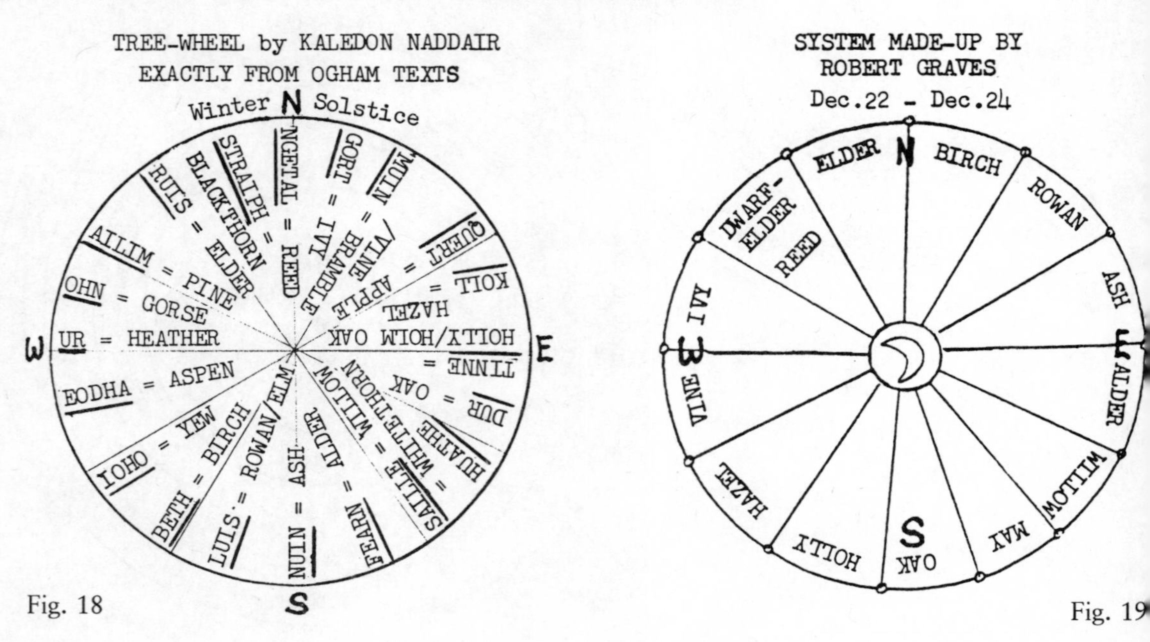

Fig. 18

Fig. 19

In my rediscovered Tree Wheel, the words underlined are the constituents of the main Beth–Luis–Nuin Ogham Alphabet placed exactly in the ancient order. The first group of five 'letters', Beth-Saille, occupy the Shamanistic Southern quarter; the second group of five, Huathe-Quert, are in the Eastern quarter; the third batch of five, Muin-Ruis, in the Northern, and the fourth group of five, Ailim-Ioho, in Shamanistic West. Thus are placed *all twenty* of the basic Ogham Alphabet. A few main features that we should note are: The Sky Father/Lord of Heaven and the Sky Goddess's ash tree is due Shamanistic South; the mountain ash tree or rowan, Brighid's Tree of White Magic, is right alongside in Shamanistic South, as is the gentle birch tree; whilst on the other flank is the alder of Bran's wonderous wisdom, and the sky willow (one species) used as an incense to promote clear thinking, and within Bach Flower Remedies is still employed to promote 'great optimism, realizes power of thought'. At the opposite quarter of Shamanistic North we find a lot of earth/ground-hugging plants like ivy, bramble, vines and blackthorn (and sloes), with reeds and elder being more associated with the Dark Waters. From other researches I've noted many of the winter-prominent evergreens – yew, juniper, box, holly, fir, mistletoe, associated with this Shamanistic North Station. In Shamanistic East, at the Spring Equinox, where the Dark Half of the Year (ruled over by holly) hands over to the Light Half of the Year (ruled over by oak), we do indeed find these trees side by side. Other Lore will be discussed in the section on trees in Chapter 6.

Turning to Graves's diagram (from *The White Goddess*), the first thing that should be noted clearly is that he chose only thirteen out of the twenty Ogham trees to concoct his false calendar. There is as little rhyme or reason in his choice of those particular thirteen as there is as little sense in why he left out the seven other major ones. Particularly noticeable pieces of craziness are that he has a dark evergreen holly around midsummer; whilst the Sky God/Goddess's ash is sequestered in March, a most insignificant time for that tree. Ivy is far away from its power station, as are most of the other trees. There are no longer clear groups of five; nor is the order-direction of layout the same – Graves has it *reversed.* Neither in observable nature, nor especially in Keltic mythological Folklore, does Robert Graves's system have any support. Being the aberrant invention of his own chaotic mind, it has only led well-meaning pagans into a disharmonious cul-de-sac. Indeed, far from assisting Goddess Worship, Graves's false pseudo-Ogham Calendar has crippled the growth of Keltic nature magic for some thirty to forty years. (For an in-depth analysis of these problems see my book on Ogham and Koelbren.)

In massive contrast to the chaos of the classicist Graves, when the key to the true Ogham and Koelbren Calendar was entrusted to myself for safe-teaching, it soon demonstrated its spirit-filled fertility and applicability within the native Keltic and European traditions. Not only have we the Keltic Shamanistic diagrams featured on the preceding pages of this chapter, but also new ritual calendars of the Irish, Welsh, Pictish and Gaulish deities; Shamanistic Wheels of the Faerie Folk and Otherworld creatures; orientation maps to the Keltic Otherworld regions, and the special times of the day/year when the 'cracks between the worlds' open to provide entry/exit. With all this having been rediscovered, we are drawing close to conceiving how the Keltic wise men and wise women understood the many worlds and beings they were cognizant of. Thus, our comprehension of Keltic mythology/Folk and Faerie Tales will be revolutionized.

The advances in our understanding of the ancient mysteries do not stop even there, for insights I gained from constructing the Keltic Calendar Wheels led me on to formulating three-dimensional models of the Scandinavian and Germanic mythological worlds and their inhabitants; Runic Wheels; calendars of Greek, Sumerian, Babylonian, Assyrian, Chaldean and Egyptian Pantheons, etc.

One of the most distinctive features of the Shamanistic tradition is its very close involvement with the trees, creatures and forces in nature (as distinctive is Orthodox Christianity's failure to work with the nature kingdoms). The following is an authentic account of a Siberian Yakut Shaman's magical workings:

> Only the gentle sound of the voice of the Drum, like the humming of a gnat, announces that the Shaman has begun to play. The folk gathered around scarcely breathe and only the unintelligible

mutterings and vocal noises of the Shaman can be heard. Gradually even this sinks into a profound silence. Then the music grows louder and louder and, like great peals of Thunder, the Drum roars and wild shouts rend the air; the Crow caws, the Grebe laughs, the Sea-mews complain, Snipes whistle, Eagles and Hawks scream. The music swells and rises to the highest pitch. The numberless small bells on the Shaman's garment rise, tinkle and clang. It is a whole cascade of sounds, enough to overwhelm all the listeners. Then sombrely the voice of the Shaman Chants his Inspired Teachings ...

In my booklet on *The Shaman and Ritual Drumming*, I explained many of the magical uses to which the drum was/is put. For our present investigations perhaps one of the most significant roles is where this round flat drum (which in the Keltic countries is called a *Bodhran* (pronounced bow-ran), is painted as a sort of miniature Shamanistic Calendar with power-glyphs or directional indicators included.

Fig. 20 shows just such a decorated Slavic gypsy drum (*Kovachaneskro Būklo*); on it are marked the eight directions: North, North East, East, South East, South, South West, West, North West, plus the Central point. The wood to make the drum-frame is cut on Whit Sunday (= Shamanistic East, strongest Station for the Drum God); it is covered with a specific animal skin, and then painted. In due course it is used for divination, being held flat in the hand; then between nine and twenty-one seeds of the thorn-apple plant (*Stramonium*) are scattered onto its surface; then it is gently tapped with a ritual hammer; and, depending on where the seeds end up in relation to the marked points, the answer to the inquiry is delivered. Should all the seeds come within the four main lines, all will go well, especially if three come within a, d, e and f. If two roll into the space between a and i, it is lucky for a woman; if between i and f, it is lucky for a man. But if nearly all fall outside of b, c, g and h, then the reading is unfavourable. The same sort of divinational procedures are used to discover whether certain individuals or animals will get well or not; and where stolen property is to be found concealed; and at what times important journeys should be commenced, etc.

The methods I teach for Keltic Koelbren divination are almost totally identical to these Lappish and Slavic psychic orientation maps.

Finally, a medieval occult equivalent to all this is given by the Master Fulcanelli on the hermetic alchemists' synthesis of all the natural laws to produce the *Philosopher's Stone* within the *Turning Wheel* linked to the *Rose of Transmutational Fire:*

> Thus *the rose* alone represents the action of the *fire* and its duration. That is why the medieval decorators sought in their rose-windows to translate the movements of matter, stirred up by the elementary fire, as may be seen on the north portal of Chartres Cathedral, in the *roses* of Toul (St Gengoult), of St Antoine of Compiegne, etc. In the Middle Ages, the central rose-window of the porches was called *rota* (the *wheel*). Now, *the wheel* is the alchemical hieroglyph of the time necessary for the concoction of the *philosophical matter*, and consequently of the coction itself. The sustained, constant and equal *fire*, which the artist maintains night and day in the course of this operation, is for this reason called the fire of the wheel. Moreover, in addition to the heat necessary for the liquefaction of the *Philosopher's Stone*, a second agent is needed as well, called *the secret of philosophic fire.* It is this latter fire, sustained by ordinary heat, which *makes the wheel turn* and produces the various phenomena which the artist observes in *his vessel.*

> 'I recommend you to go by this road and no other.
> Only take notice of the tracks of my wheel,
> And, in order to give an equal heat overall,
> Do not rise or descend too soon to Heaven or Earth,
> For in rising too high you will be burnt by Heaven,
> And in descending too low you will be destroyed by Earth.
> But if your course remains set in the middle
> The route will be plainer and the way more sure.'

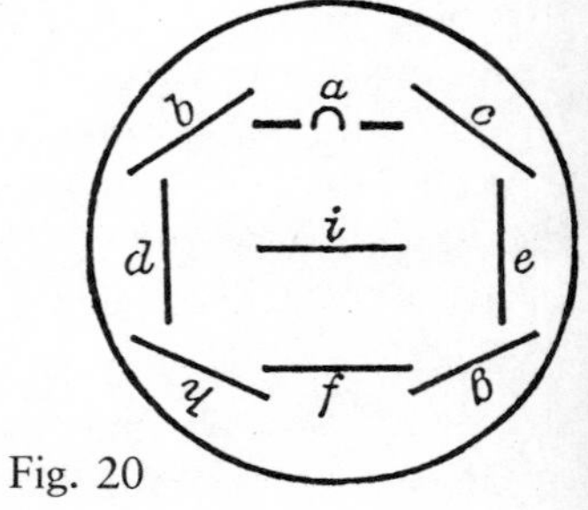

Fig. 20

CHAPTER 5

The Qabalistic Tree of Life and Jacob's Ladder Interpretive Frameworks

Top right: *Phoenician long-necked Gryphons flanking a Sacred Pillar-Tree. The other Illustrations are from Sumerian-Babylonian Cylinder Seals c.3500–2500 B.C.*

Rabbi Nachum pointed to 'The Great Almond Tree in the Garden of Eden whose leaves were letters, and whose branches were words.' Also to the apple tree, which 'is good to be eaten, fair to the sight, and desirable for the Understanding.'

The two main arboreal glyphs of the Qabalah, the *Etz Chaīm* (Tree of Life) and the *Sūlam Ya'aqov* (Jacob's Ladder), both have their roots in ancient Mesopotamian religious mythology. The deeper we investigate these primordial symbol-archetypes, the more we will encounter teachings similar (and on some items identical) to the Keltic, Scandinavian, Greek, Slavic, Vedic, Toltec and other spiritual offshoots from the Atlantean wisdom.

These sacred trees are commonly featured within the linked Sumerian, Babylonian, Assyrian, Chaldean, Akkadian, Hittite and Hebrew Esoteric Traditions; examples are shown in the Illustrations. For teaching purposes these would be styled as: (i) a fertile palm tree, (ii) the Sky Goddess Nūt's sycamore/apple tree, (iii) fronds with eagle feathers, (iv) a tree with sun-spiralling pine cones on it, (v) a wisdom-giving pomegranate tree, (vi) grape vine or other semi-naturalistic tree, (vii) a more stylized/abstract or metaphysical 'tree'. Within the later Qabalistic tradition it was this metaphysical tree-glyph that was employed most of all. Whilst the other Mesopotamian Initiatory traditions were crushed or

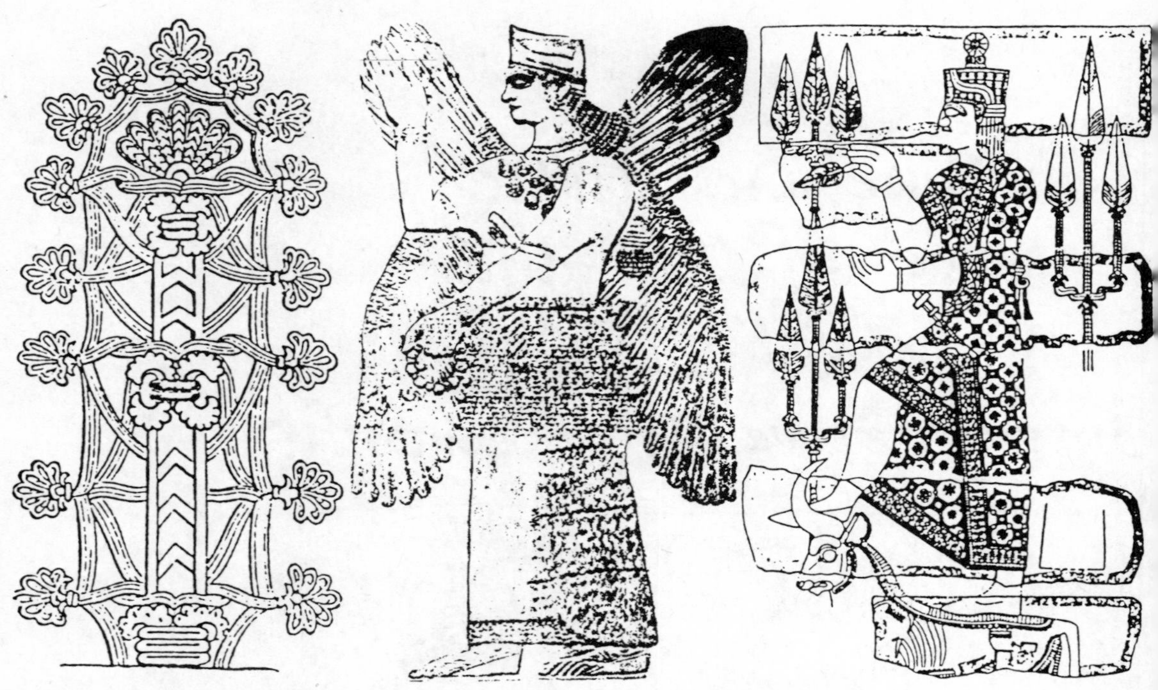

The two nine-sphered Pictish Trees of Life are symbolically linked to the nine-leafed ash-tree branch (*Yggdrasil*); whilst the one on the left features pine-cone motifs.

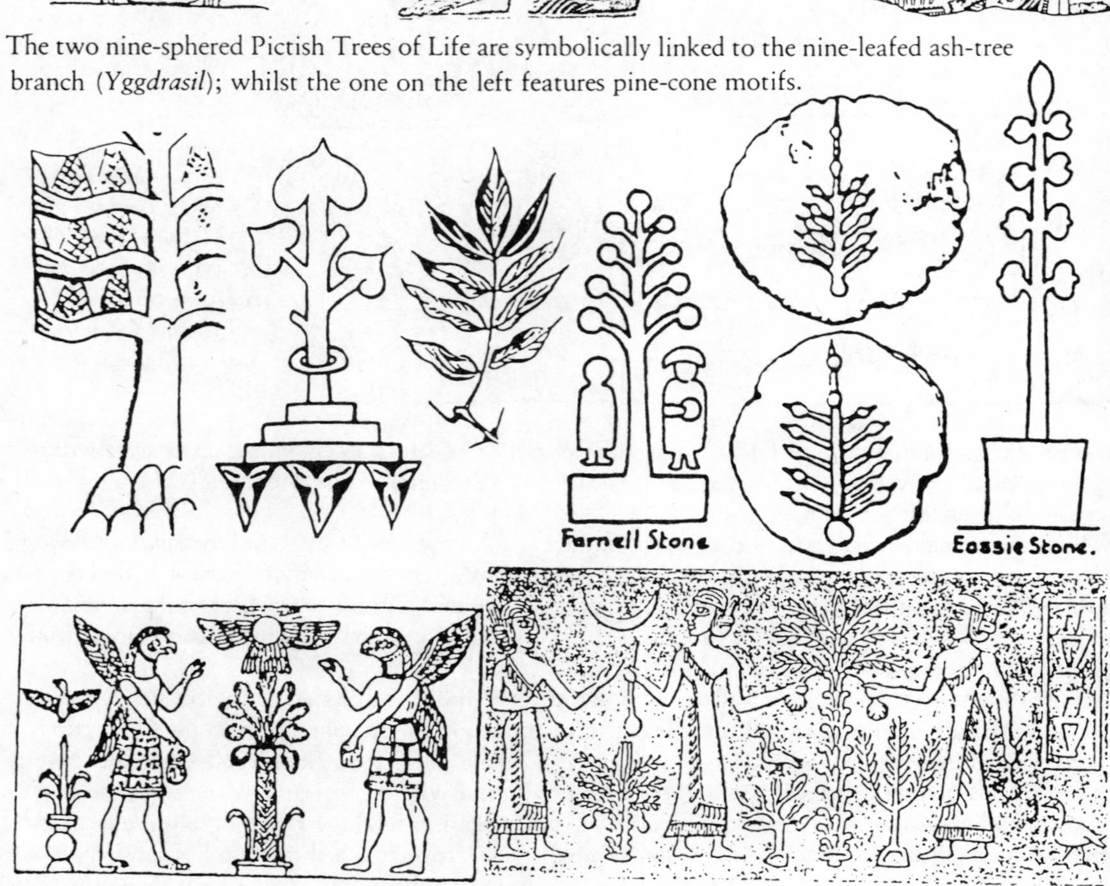

disintegrated under the stream of history, the Hebrew Qabalists preserved and developed the ancient Lore. The richness of the symbolism pertaining to the *Sĕphīrōth* (spheres, once fronds) in the Tree of Life can be gauged when one surveys that they were also called: *Pegai* (fountains, wells, springs, sources, Otherworld Beings); *Aumeqīm* (deep creative vortices, matrixes, bosoms, depths); *Auroth* (lights, shining spheres); *Kōchōth* (powers); *Mekorōth* (sources); *Ko'ach* (force, power, potency, essence); *Maroth* (mirrors); *Madregoth* (stages); *Neti'oth* (shoots, branches); *Ketharīm* (crowns); *Levushīm* (garments, coverings); *Aeon* (Greek = sluice of fire, fire-wheel, fire-dispenser, fire-being), also water-wheels, wheels, cups (containing the essence of the eggs); *Miqvaoth* (wells), etc.

In turn, the paths or rays that passed the energy (fire/water/life/consciousness) from one sphere to another sphere were called variously: pipes, conduits, channels (*Tzinoroth*), streams, branches, etc. Now all these multiplex terms were not just name-tags to 'fix' abstruse metaphysical contemplations, they were also accurate descriptions of Otherworld realities. With the space at my disposal I can only point to one or two insights and give their Keltic parallels.

The early Qabalist Joseph Gikatila wrote:

> In the beginning of Creation ... the 'well-springs' and the 'channels' through which everything in the higher regions flows into the lower were still active, complete and unhindered.

Then, throughout various levels of existence, there came to be a 'shattering of the lights' and a 'breaking of the channels' (*Shevīrat ha-Tzinoroth*), which allowed corruption, disease and disintegration to set in. Human history has sadly mirrored this process, and the environmental erosion, species extinction, pollution of the ecosphere, and the malaise of native spiritual cultures stand as distressing reminders of these principles in operation. Similar to an insight in the Book of Enoch – 'Ye have forsaken the Fountain of Life' – those treading the Keltic path have also forsaken the 'ladies of the fountains' (the *Gwyllion*), who once proffered their goblets of honey-sweet *Gwin* (inspiration) to those seeking Initiation into the mysteries of the lakes and mere-pools. In this case the Orthodox Church fostered fear of the 'water-witches' where there had once been love, trust and understanding; and the stealing and breaking of the cup–chalice–goblet, when there had once been the wholesome drinking from, and return of, these sacred Faerie objects. We need to relearn the respectful ways of approaching the guardians of the fountains.

The Wheel of Qabalistic Autiot (see next page)

After Abram entered into the Stream of Creative Principles, 'he looked, he saw, he explored, he articulated, he mapped out, he heaved, he combined, he structured, he raised his hand and Adon Hakol (the Lord on High) ... attached to his tongue *twenty-two Autiot* and revealed their foundation, and soaked them in water, singed them by fire, shook them by blowing, consumed them by the Seven (Planets) and guided them by Twelve Constellations.' (Translated by Carlo Suarés.)

After a great deal of deep and extensive research, I managed to reformulate the ancient Qabalistic Wheel, their magical orientation map. The characters around the outside of the wheel are the Siniatic petro-glyph forms, whilst those on the inside are the Hebrew characters redesigned by the Qabalist Ezra; both are known as the *Autiot* (signs, proofs, symbols, types and miracles). Allied to each of the *Autiot* is a tree, animal, object or quality. Carlo Suarés succinctly says that 'every letter is, in fact, an ideogram which symbolizes one aspect of kosmic energy'. Thus, when all twenty-two *Autiot* are fully understood, and their many-levelled meaning grasped in reality, then one could interact with all the forces at work in nature, humanity and kosmos.

After one has made allowances for the obvious differences in climate, the changing seasons, and trees, birds and animals, there is still a central core of metaphysical principles in common with the Keltic and other Indo-European Shamanistic Calendars. This residuum of principles obviously contains those that come closest to kosmic truths and natural laws; these are therefore of prime importance and interest.

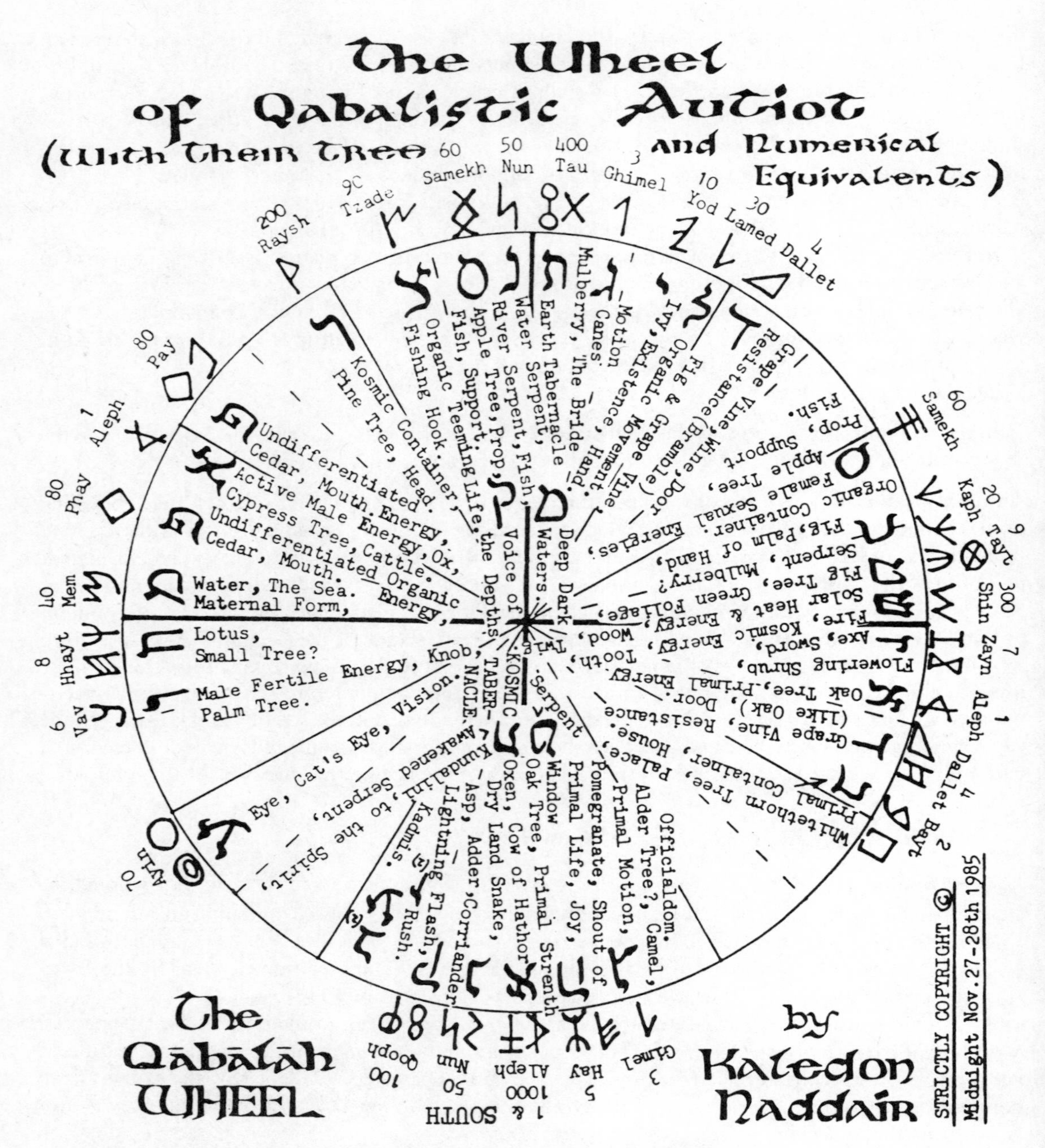

In the following quick synoptic journey around the Qabalistic Wheel, the key teachings are discussed, parallelisms with the Keltic Shamanistic Wheel should be fairly self-evident. (Here is an example of cross-cultural parallels – which should only be cited by the truly wise, for errors in such are serious. In the Qabalah, the feminine presence of God is known as the Shekhīnāh, and she is said to preside over the highest 'Holy Apple Garden', the trees therein being called *Etzperī*, from which may be derived the Greek mythological apple-tree island of the h-Esperides; this also has obvious links with the Keltic *Emhain Avallach* (apple-tree paradise), Avalon, and the seven apple trees (with their twenty Koelbren signs) that the Kymraeg seer Myrddin describes in his *Afallenau*; the comparison can be extended to

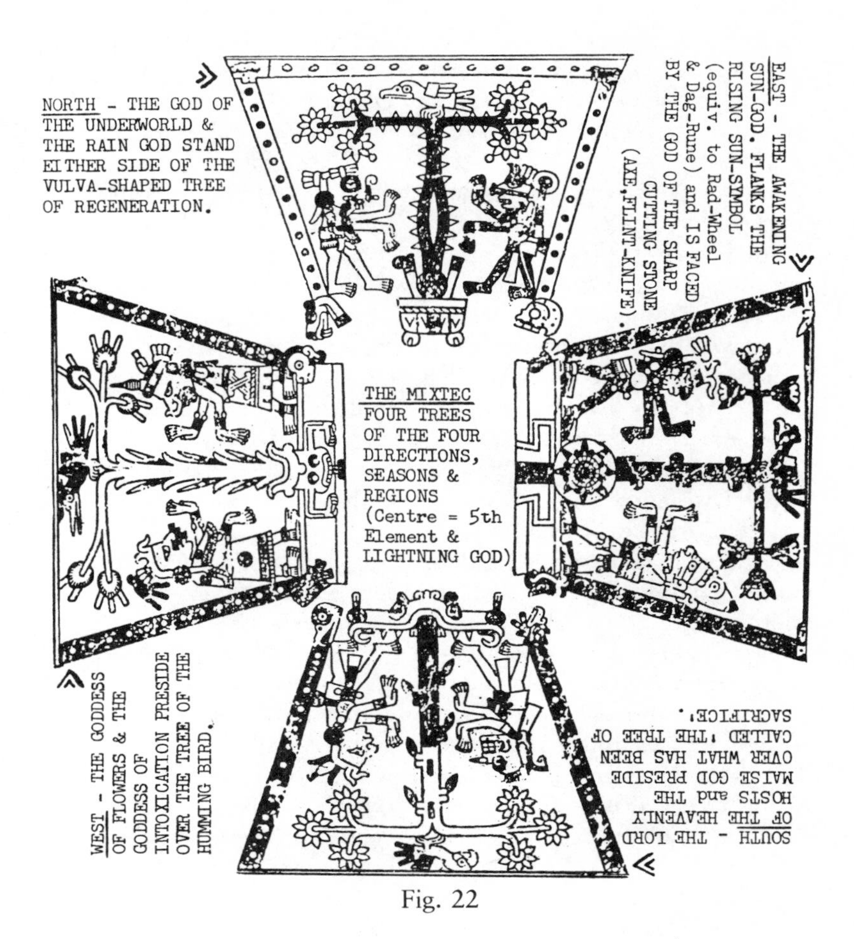

Fig. 22

This Diagram, formulated from one of the most Ancient Qabalistic Texts, clearly demonstrates that the Early Qabalists also used our 4 Quarters & 'The Above' and 'The Below' Orientation Map. I do not think Carlo Suares managed to allocate these Vortexes correctly to the Sephiroth, I would rather suggest an extension of my Diagram shown on page 49.

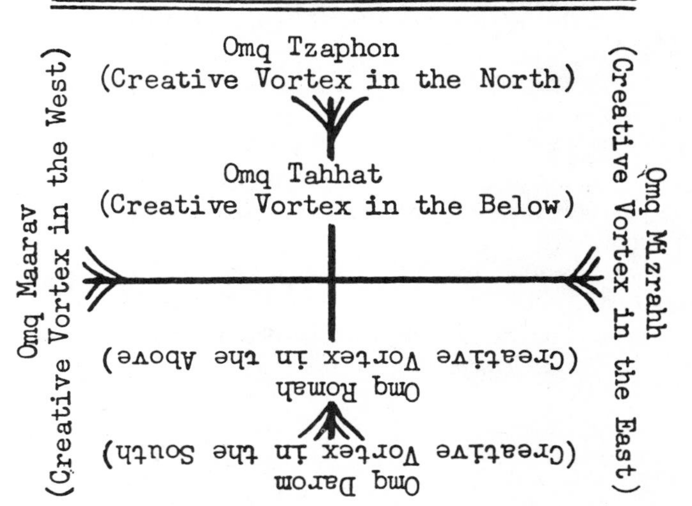

encompass Idun, the Scandinavian Apple Goddess (or Tri-Iduna, as she is called in Pictland), and Olwen, the Welsh Apple Queen. I could make similar mythological comparisons from many more of the Qabalistic *Autiot*, identifying the links with their Keltic Ogham and Koelbren equivalents.)

There are three 'mother letters' in Qabalistic Hebrew – *Aleph*(1) related to air, hence South-sky; *Mem*(40) related to water/sea, hence West; *Shin*(300) related to fire/heat, hence East; they combine to make *Tav*(400), the earthly tabernacle, resting place in the North. After a transformative process, this *Tav*(400) can be reborn skywards as the *Tau* of immortal life. In the early Siniatic form of this script there were two serpent forms for *Nūn*(50) – one a land/sky serpent, hence of midsummer/South, and another water/underground serpent of winter/North, both symbols for 'the self'. *Zayn*(7) is an axe or sword with sharp clarity, hence Shamanistic East. *Qooph*(100) is a kosmic aleph as a lightning flash and rush, hence from the sky above Shamanistic South. *Tayt*(9) is the ram's horned awakening serpent of spring (perhaps also a Shamanistic South aspect). *Dallet*(4) is a door which is an entry point in Shamanistic East; also, as material resistance (4), it has another Station in the North-east. *Hhayt*(8) is primal unstructured energy, as is *Phay*(80) in the organic level, thus both as amorphous fluids in the Shamanistic West. *Hay*(5) is a primal, pure expression of life, hence Shamanistic South, which is as transparent as a 'window'. *Yod*(10), traditional Hebrew symbol, was the hand which has five fingers as the ivy has a five-pointed leaf, both expressions of tenacious organic life. *Vav*(6) – as palm trees grow best with salt amidst their roots, I've placed it beside *Mārāh*, the sea. *Raysh*(200) I've placed approximately where the pine is in the Keltic Tree Calendar. Likewise with *Beth*(2), the primal receptive female container, corresponding to the May Queen; also *Samekh*(60), as Apple Maiden, is Shamanistic North-east, and North/South for the *Shekhīnāh* as the divine tabernacle presided over a mystic apple grove. *Gimel*(3), primal motion, and *Lamed*(30), organic movement, may well start the year with the ox-goad symbol for *Lamed*, being an exact equivalent to the Keltic *Gad* of Gort. *Tzade*(90) is the fish-hook to take the teeming life from the rivers of Shamanistic North. *Kaph*(20), as the palm of the hand, is what holds a weapon or tool firmly. *Ayin*(70) is clear vision from Shamanistic South-South-east. *Mem*(40) has a second aspect in the deep dark inland waters of Shamanistic North, and *Qooph*(100) is an echo-breath from the sky-spirit that breathes over 'the waters'.

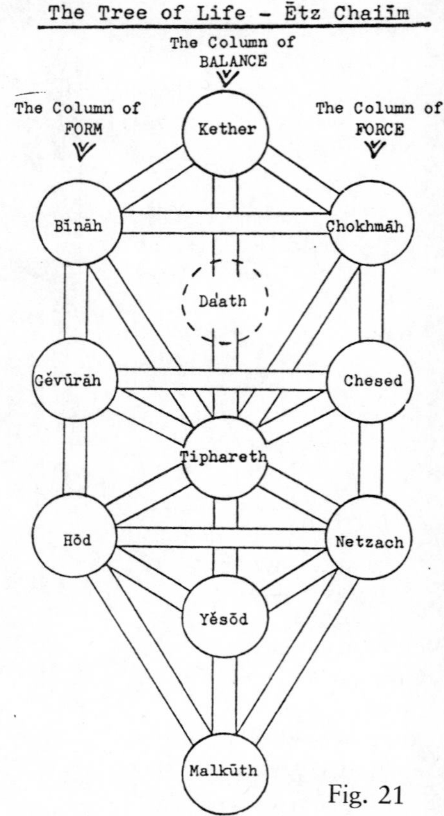

Fig. 21

The Wheel of the Autiot obviously provides the basis for the circular orientation map found within the *Sepher Yĕtzīrāh* (see page 45), which I have paralleled with its Meso-American equivalent.

We now turn to the Tree of Life diagram (Fig. 21). This is the primal, multi-purpose glyph used in the Qabalah; indeed, Jacob's Ladder (which we will deal with shortly) is in fact made up of four interleaved Tree of Life diagrams.

To get a basic grasp of the workings of a Tree of Life diagram is very simple. For instance, one can start with a few elementary laws (refer to Fig. 21):

1. The 'tree' is composed of ten circles (*Sĕphīrōth*), with one 'variable' circle (*Sĕphīrāh*).
2. There are twenty-two paths or channels that connect these circles (*Sĕphīrōth*) to each other.

3. The circles (*Sĕphīrōth*) form themselves into three vertical columns – the right-hand one is the column of force, the left-hand one is the column of form, the middle column is that of balance.
4. The lower one descends in the diagram, from top to bottom, the denser becomes the 'force' or 'form'.

Even with these four simple rules, I think you could start to use the Tree of Life diagram, but to use it to its full potential one has to learn many more factors and correspondences. Here are a few others that should be helpful:

5. Each circle (Sĕphīrāh) should be visualized as a sphere.
6. Each path should be visualized as a hollow tube or pipe.
7. To the three columns can be ascribed the basic qualities of fire (right-hand side); water (left-hand side); air (middle), holding the 'balance' between fire and water; with earth the confluence and product of the other three.
8. Alternatively, the four elements, fire, air, water, earth, are distributed as follows: fire to the highest region of the diagram, air just below this, water lower still, and earth at the foot of the tree.
9. All forms of consciousness, from the highest to the lowest, are primarily seated in the central column.
10. If necessary (for some metaphysical problem), each circle can be thought to contain a whole miniature 'tree', and within each circle of this miniature tree there is found the workings of an even smaller tree ... this process can be extended indefinitely.
11. The paths, pipes, channels, conduits, or whatever one may designate them, can be thought to perform the function of flow channels, through which the qualities of one circle can pass to another, thus helping to keep the whole tree in overall balance.

Once you feel you have mastered these eleven mainly structural laws, you may pass on to the twelfth law, which is perhaps the most important of all:

12. The *Sĕphīrōth* (spheres or circles), with their associated names (*Kether*, *Chokhmah*, *Binah*, etc.), always remain in the same relative position in the Tree; they also always continue to manifest that quality, law or attribute that is peculiarly their own. The qualities associated with each *Sĕphīrāh* (sphere, circle) are listed below; for the purposes of this book, the reader does not have to learn all the associated attributes, rather get an overall feeling of the *Sĕphīrāh*'s general quality.

1. *Kether*	–	Crown (hidden intelligence), hidden light, perfected wisdom, perfection, glory.
2. *Chokhmāh*	–	Wisdom (illuminating intelligence).
3. *Bīnāh*	–	Understanding (consolidating intelligence).
* *Da'ath*	–	Knowledge.
4. *Chesed*	–	Mercy (receptive intelligence), magnanimity, magnificence, compassion.
5. *Gĕvūrāh*	–	Judgement (critical intelligence), severity, discernment, courage, warrior-drive.
6. *Tiphareth*	–	Beauty (mediating intelligence), truth, love, compassion, harmony, devotion, honesty, balance.
7. *Netzach*	–	Victory (repetitive intelligence), cyclic rhythms, cyclic impulses, lower feelings.
8. *Hōd*	–	Glory (concrete intelligence), lower mind, reverberation.
9. *Yĕsōd*	–	Foundation (strength of intelligence), fertility drive.
10. *Malkūth*	–	Kingdom ('grounded' intelligence), basis.

If these twelve laws have been properly assimilated, then I feel confident that you now possess a workable (albeit surface) knowledge of the Qabalistic Tree of Life.

The Space Cube – The Space Sphere

A famous hard hazelnut (or should it be almondnut?) problem to crack within the *Sepher Yĕtzīrāh* is how are the *Sĕphīrōth* arranged within The Space Cube Sphere? Carlo Suares, in his book on the *Sepher Yĕtzīrāh*, had an attempt at constructing the Space Cube; sadly I think he failed miserably. With a degree more assurance, I think I have solved (or come very close to solving) the problem, as follows:

1. *'Aumeq Rōm* – Creative Vortex of the Above = *Kether*
2. *'Aumeq Rashīth* – Creative Vortex of the Beginning = *Chokhmāh*
3. *'Aumeq Achrīth* – Creative Vortex of the Ending = *Bīnāh*
4. *'Aumeq Tōv* – Creative Vortex of Gentleness = *Chesed*
5. *'Aumeq Ra'a* – Creative Vortex of Harshness = *Gevūrāh*
6. *'Aumeq Darōm* – Creative Vortex of the South = *Tiphareth*
7. *'Aumeq Mizrach* – Creative Vortex of the East (and West) = *Netzach*
8. *'Aumeq Ma'arav* – Creative Vortex of the West (and East) = *Hōd*
9. *'Aumeq Tzaphōn* – Creative Vortex of the North = *Yĕsōd*
10. *'Aumeq Tachat* – Creative Vortex of the Below = *Malkūth*

There is one thing in common between an Autiot Wheel, a Tree of Life/Jacob's Ladder, a Keltic Shamanistic Calendar, a Tibetan Mandala and a Navaho Indian sand-painting: they all purport to describe reality and its spiritual dynamics. Thus the question should naturally arise: are they compatible as conceptual frameworks? Or are they mutually exclusive in their diagrammatic format? As each is *sacred* within its own tradition, this is not a subject that should be 'played around with' foolhardily. Thus, the following diagram is the fruit of many years working with both the Keltic and Qabalistic traditions, and of more than two years of pondering over possible connections between their two main metaphysical charts.

I have a three-dimensional perspex sphere with the *Sĕphīrōth* fitted into place; this has served as a model for Figs 26 and 27. In Fig. 26 we view a Tree of Life straight on, with the upper spheres being more related to the sky, and the lower spheres being somewhat subterranean. In the chart shown in Fig. 27, we view a Tree of Life as though we were above it looking down, and the essential qualities of a sphere, inclining it somewhat towards Shamanistic South or Shamanistic North. It *may* be permissible to link them loosely to the eight Keltic festivals.

A simplified (but not simplistic) explanation of the attributions on the chart in Fig. 27 would be briefly as follows: (i) The basic aim is to see if the qualities of the *Sĕphīrōth* in the Tree of Life can be linked with the Autiot Wheel (which contains the four directions and the above and the below); and the same with the equivalent Keltic Shamanistic Calendar. (ii) Being one of the Mahezde Malkla, I decided to tackle the spheres on the central column first, starting at the bottom with *Malkūth*, which is the earthy tabernacle; the most densely constructed kingdom; the one nearest to contact with *Qlipoth* (husks of matter), associated with the element of Earth in Qabalah, hence its primal placing in the North of the Shamanistic Calendar. Next is *Yĕsōd*, which in the physical world is concerned with deep sexual and fertility drives, preservation, or strengthening a sense of ego and its 'image' in the world; the spiritual archangel assigned to *Yĕsōd* is Gavriel who, as Guide to the Dead and Underworld Traveller, has become associated with the Leader of the Wild Hunt and the Gabriel Ratchets (the *Kun Annwn*) such as hounds/geese, clammer their way over the midwinter skies before returning to the underworld. *Yĕsōd*'s planet is the Moon, which is also prominent at this time of the year. So all in all I have no hesitation in placing *Yĕsōd* near to Shamanistic North and the underworld in our calendar. *Tiphareth* seems like the 'central mountain', fifth, equidistant from the mountains at the four quarters. In traditional Qabalah, *Tiphareth* is associated with the element of Air and the sky; whilst also being the Sun sphere, the fire in the head/brain and the blood in the heart. Thus I would say that *Tiphareth* inclines towards the Shamanistic

South/sky/summer Station. *Da'ath*, the only semi-existent sphere, is probably halfway between *Tiphareth* and *Kether*. The sphere of *Kether* is always linked to 'the above', whether that is to the Sky Father in the Emperium, or to the Pole Star in the night sky, around which the constellations turn (for all of us in the Northern hemisphere). Within a circular orientation map, the best place to conceive *Kether* would be *above* the centre, although having Shamanistic Southern aspects. In the Keltic tradition this would link it to Nechtan/the Sky God's serpent of wisdom (Qabalah equivalent: Nechushtan), also to the Sky Goddess Noinia and Sky God Neania, worshipped in ash-tree groves.

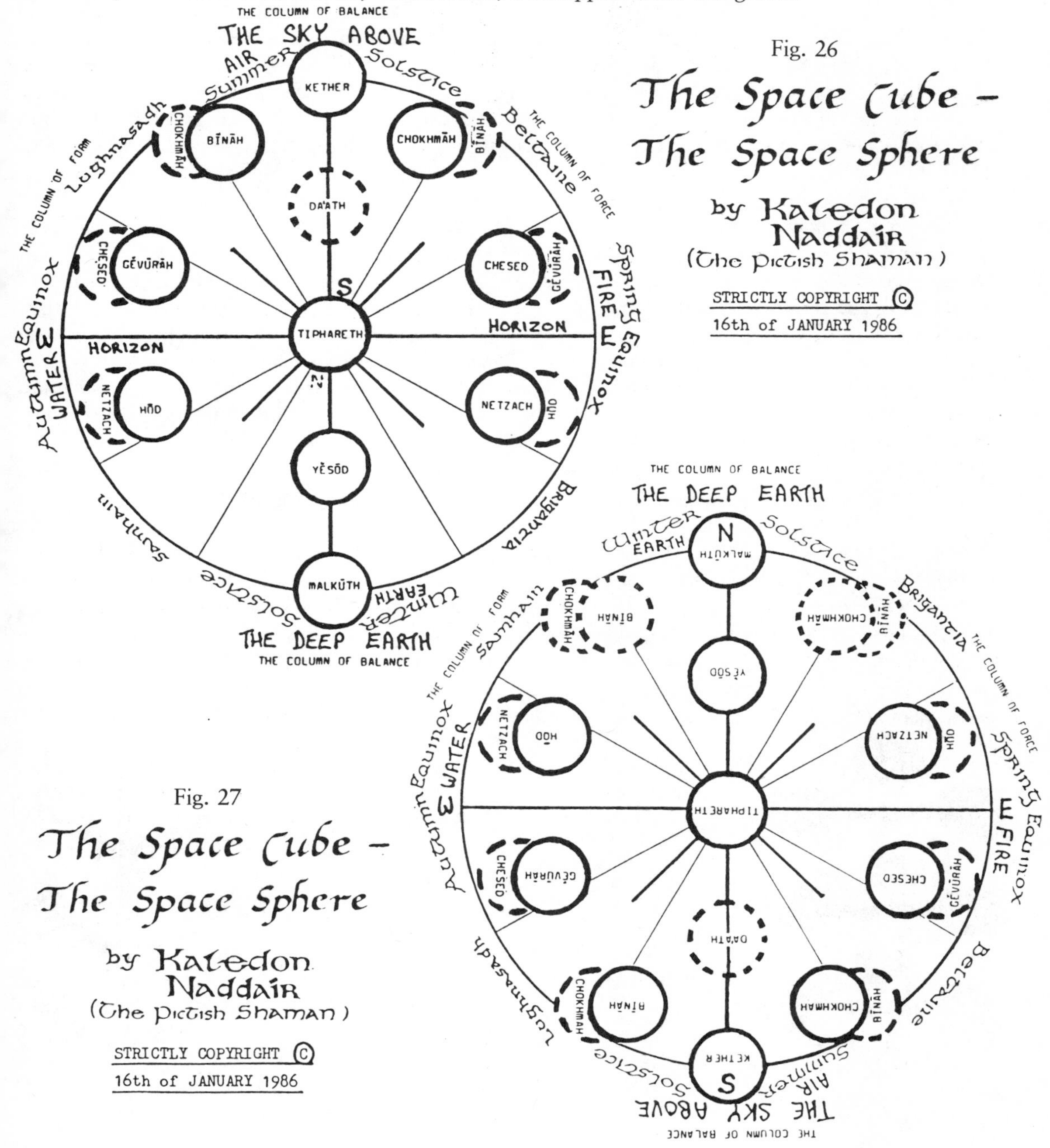

Fig. 26
The Space Cube – The Space Sphere
by Kaledon Naddair (The Pictish Shaman)
STRICTLY COPYRIGHT ©
16th of JANUARY 1986

Fig. 27
The Space Cube – The Space Sphere
by Kaledon Naddair (The Pictish Shaman)
STRICTLY COPYRIGHT ©
16th of JANUARY 1986

When we try to come to terms with the spheres on the side columns in a Tree of Life (re: the Shamanistic Wheel), it would seem advisable to note that they should work as pairs, and, where one side-sphere quality appears, its complimentary opposite will be likely to be evoked into being. Where we find *Chesed*, then *Gĕvūrāh* should not be far behind. Therefore, if *Kether* is associated with the forces at the height of the sky, then *Chokhmāh* and *Bīnāh* will be similarly situated, although on a slightly lower situation. Thus, I link *Chokhmāh* (wisdom) to the Keltic Gods Ogma Grianach (Sun-face), Lord of Ogham, and the Kymraeg equivalents of Gwyddion (in relation to ash tree) and Bran (in relation to alder tree), both wise Gods of the Koelbren Secret Ciphers; likewise I related *Bīnāh* to the high white magic of Brighid's rowan twigs (likewise the Goddess Rowena) and to the adjacent Silver/White Birch Goddess. Slightly Shamanistic South of Shamanistic East would be the Station of *Chesed*, linked to the strong and generous oak tree, but also to the gentler, more feminine linden, cherry and pear trees; the evoked *Gĕvūrāh* at this Station would link it to the Thunder and Warrior God Taran (and holly/holm oak tree – *tine/tan*, and fiery gorse). On the opposite side of the chart, slightly Shamanistic South of Shamanistic West, *Gĕvūrāh* might be linked to the warrior's yew-bow tree, and the gooseberry with its defensive prickles; and, further upwards, with the Storm and Warrior God's pine tree; the evoked *Chesed* here might find expression through the white poplar and the quivering aspen, as well as the gently sensuous woodbine. Slightly Shamanistic North of Shamanistic East, *Netzach* would find expression through the young attractive Goddess of Spring (in relation to Elder as Traman) and 'the Blessed Wild Apple Girl', and the erotic scent of gorse and broom flowers; the evoked *Hōd* may link to hazel trees, being associated with clear thinking and dowsing (also fir in spring). *Hōd*, in the Shamanistic West, may draw from the heath and heather, and perhaps the cleansing effects of wych hazel; the evoked *Netzach* (which seems very strong here in the Keltic Tradition) would be associated with powers of water and the sea, the diuretic properties of gorse and broom, and the more moody recalcitrant side of wych elm.
properties of gorse and broom, and the more moody recalcitrant side of wych elm.

The Qabalistic serpent-priests (the Na'assenes, Essenes) were known to conjoin in magical workings with the Angels of fire, air, water and earth, and the other Earth Mother spirits (the *Anunnaki* as they were anciently called), as well as with the angels of the Celestial Father (the *Igaga/Igigi*, the Heavenly Hosts). Although two of the most famous spiritual communities of the Na'assenes were on the shores of the Dead Sea, they still maintained a thriving use of physical and metaphysical tree symbolism in their religious compositions. Working with the nature spirits and herb lore earned them a reputation as effective healers throughout their own and nearby lands. It is also held by some that these Na'assene-Qabalists knew all about the seven psychic centres in the auric body of humans (known in the East as the *Chakras*). This would have involved them in beneficiently manipulating the seven levels or centres in the glandular, etheric and soul bodies, according to the seven levels within the Tree of Life.

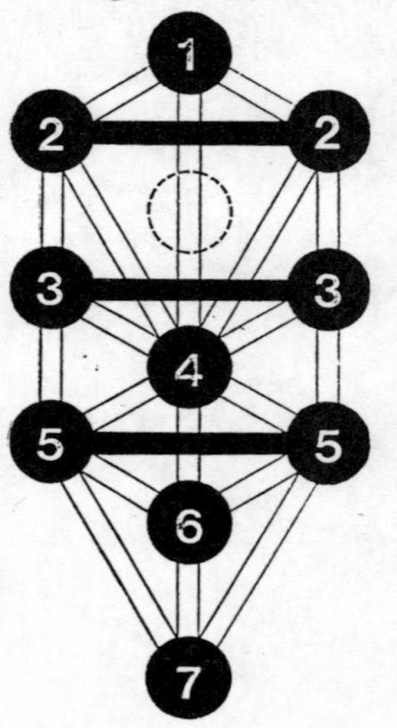

THE NUMBERED TREE (LEFT) DISPLAYS THE SEVEN PLANES OR LEVELS OF BEING WHICH HAS MANY APPLICATIONS WITHIN THE QABALISTIC WORLDS (e.g. The Seven Spiritual Palaces of Braiah; or the Seven Sky Regions, 'Heavens', of Yetzirah = ARABOTH, MAKHON, SHECHAQIN, ARAPHEL, ZEBUL, SHEMEI HASHAMAYIM, RAQI'A; or the Seven Earth Planes of Asayah; or the Seven Regions 'Below' midst the Qlipothic Husks.

THE TREE OF LIGHT (shown right) is otherwise known as The MENORAH or Seven-Branched Candlestick.

TWO OF THE 7 - FOLD CONFIGURATIONS INHERENT IN THE TREE OF LIFE DIAGRAM

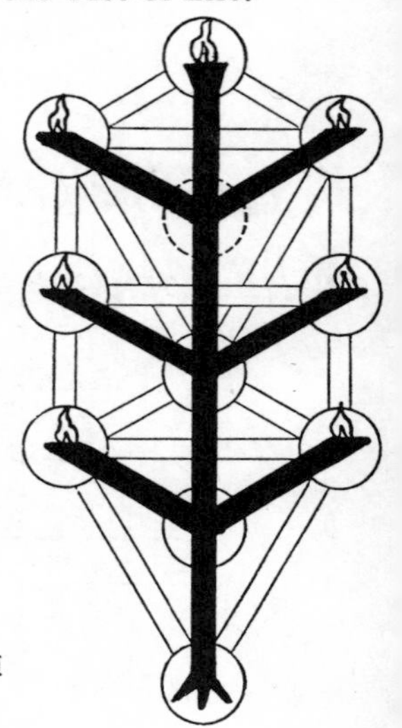

Jacob's Ladder – Sulam Ya'aqov

If we pass onwards and continue to survey the Qabalah's main teachings and diagrams, then pride of place should now be given to Jacob's Ladder – a superbly sophisticated metaphysical map. Thus, Fig. 28 can be seen to be made up from four intermeshing 'Trees of Life'; these represent different planes of existence, either in the world at large (the makrokosm) or in the individual human being (the mikrokosm). Let us tackle the makrokosmic dimensions first:

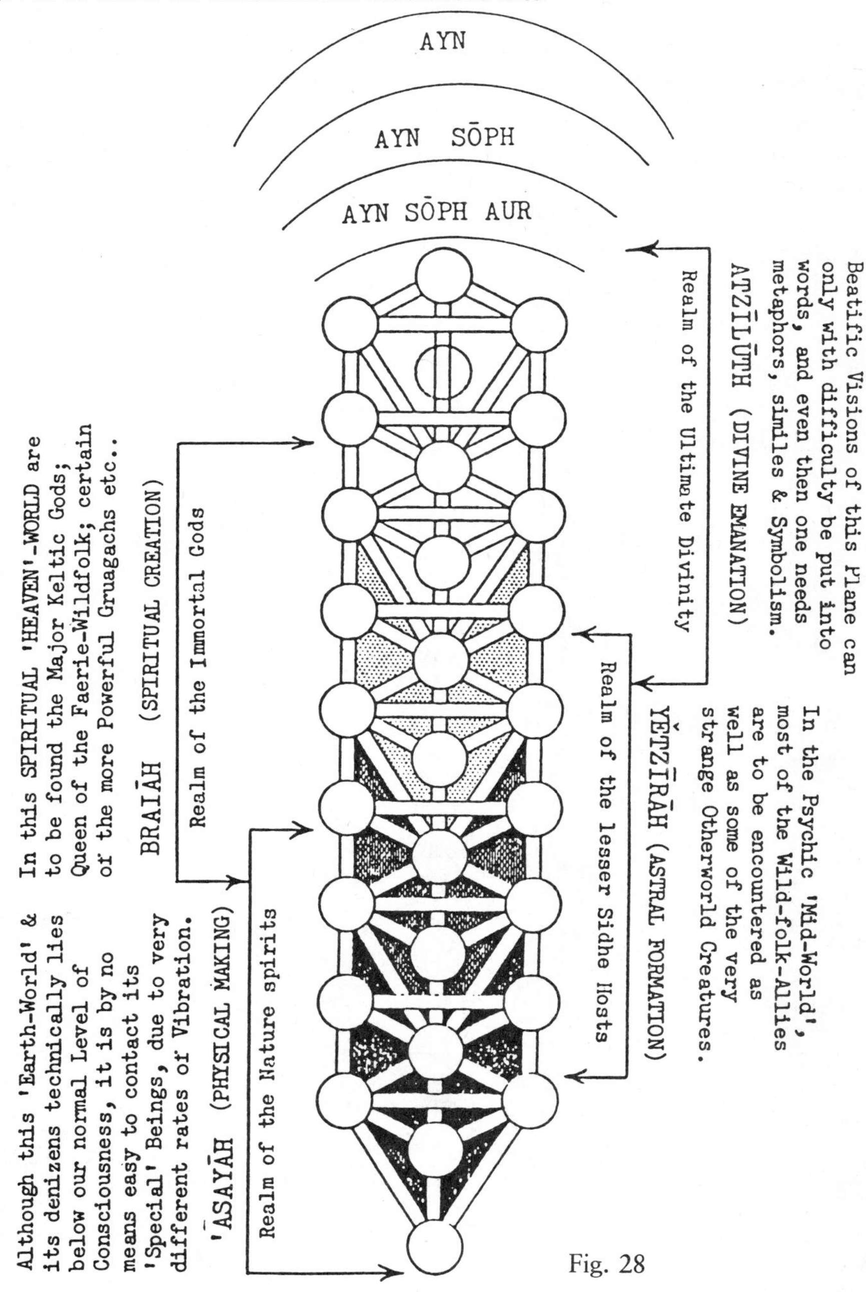

AYN
AYN SŌPH
AYN SŌPH AUR
Beatific Visions of this Plane can only with difficulty be put into words, and even then one needs metaphors, similes & Symbolism.
ATZĪLŪTH (DIVINE EMANATION)
Realm of the Ultimate Divinity
In the Psychic 'Mid-World', most of the Wild-folk-Allies are to be encountered as well as some of the very strange Otherworld Creatures.
YĚTZĪRĀH (ASTRAL FORMATION)
Realm of the lesser Sidhe Hosts
In this SPIRITUAL 'HEAVEN'-WORLD are to be found the Major Keltic Gods; Queen of the Faerie-Wildfolk; certain of the more Powerful Gruagachs etc..
BRAIĀH (SPIRITUAL CREATION)
Realm of the Immortal Gods
Although this 'Earth-World' & its denizens technically lies below our normal Level of Consciousness, it is by no means easy to contact its 'Special' Beings, due to very different rates of Vibration.
'ĀSAYĀH (PHYSICAL MAKING)
Realm of the Nature spirits

Fig. 28

1. The World of *Atzīlūth* – the World of *Emanation*, which, to the Hebraic Qabalist, contains the ten divine names or aspects of the Almighty GOD: AHYH, YHVH, Elōhīm, El, Yah, YHVH-ELOHIM, Yhvh Tzābāōth, Elōhīm Tzābāōth, El Chai Shadai, Adōnai Melekh. For the Christian Qabalist, these are simplified into the Father, Son (Christ) and Holy Ghost (the *Shekhīnāh*, feminine bride to Christ). It is worth noting that the *Shekhīnāh*, Presence of God, is often styled as a mighty divine eagle – which might be similar to the 'divine' eagle in Don Juan/Castaneda's writings, and also with Zeus, Ahura Mazdah, Lleu and other major pagan Gods that are symbolized as eagles. The World of *Atzīlūth* can be seen to hold the primordial, original Tree of Life (and perhaps the Golden Tree in Keltic Mythology). *Atzīlūth* is also called Adām Qadmōn (the primordial man). In certain branches of the Kymraeg (Welsh) tradition, the universal spirit is known as Kelu, and the highest world as Keugant, both possibly Atzīlūtic. This is the *Divine* World.

2. The World of *Braiāh* – the World of *Creation*, which contains the ten Qabalistic Archangels: Metatron, Raziel, Tzaphqiel, Tzadquiel, Khamael, Mikhael, Chaniel, Raphael, Gavriel and Sandalphon. For other religions it contains their gods and Spiritual and Creative beings, be they called Aesir, Ahuras, e.g., Odhin, Kernun, Thor, Mithra, Osiris or Vishnu. This world also contains the archetypes of everything that has come into Creation, including the archetypes for the planets,

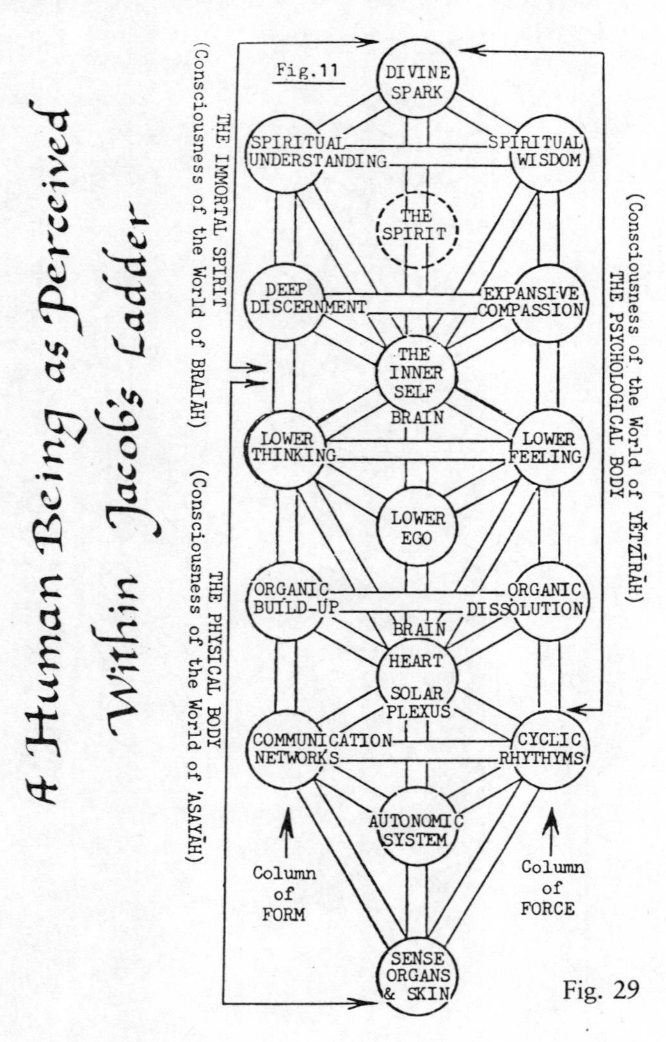

Fig. 29

sphere of the zodiac and the 'first cause'. This is the *Spiritual* World.

This World is known as: Tir nan m-Beo, Tir na n-Og, Tir Tairngiri, etc., in Irish; and Gwynffrydd in Welsh beliefs. It is the Keltic Heaven, where the immortal Gods hold sway and the Princes and leaders of the *Sidhe* are active as beings of light and great power.

3. The World of *Yĕtzīrāh* – The World of *Formation* which contains the ten Qabalistic Angel Hosts: Chaiōth ha-Qādēsh, Auphanīm, Aralīm, Chashmalīm, Serāphīm, Melākhīm, Tarshīshīm, Benai Elōhīm, Kerūvīm and Ashīm. In other mythologies or religious traditions, this World holds the Hindu Dyan Chohans; Greek Angelos; the Scandinavian Hamingjes, Fyljes, Valkyries, Giptes, Lios Alfar (and Swart Alfar?), the Keltic *Daione Sidhe* (Faerie Folk), Wildfolk, Brownies, Gruagachs, Dobies, Ekh-elphies, Leuchairpins, Bukka Gwidden, white dogs and other such power-beings. These 'Allies' will be contacted when one starts to enter into the Irish otherworld (*Tir N'Aill*) or the upper regions of the Welsh underworld (*Annwn*). Also within this region are to be found the subtle 'Prime Mover' (*Kether*), Aeon of the Zodiac (at *Chokhmāh*) and the seven 'Fate Spheres' (Saturn-*Bīnāh*, Jupiter-*Chesed*, Mars-*Gĕvūrāh*, Sun-*Tiphareth*, Venus-*Netzach*, Mercury-*Hōd* and the Moon to *Yĕsōd*). In the Western sense of the word, this is the *Astral* World.

4. The World of *'Asayāh* – the World of *Making*, which contains the physical and material solar system, as well as the zodiacal belt and the 'Asayatic Primum Mobile. On the Earth itself are to be found the four classes of elemental (etheric) beings associated with the four elements fire, air, water, earth; these beings fulfil their roles in the workings of nature. This is the *Etheric* and *Material* World. In the Keltic tradition, the invisible dimensions of the 'Asayatic World contain some of the lesser elementals, nature spirits, rock spirits, trows (trolls) and denizens of the lower regions of *Annwn*.

* Below these four Worlds lies the region of the *Qlipōth* (the lightless 'husks' or 'shells') – these are *chaotic* beings who seek to disrupt the natural order and destroy the very structure of Jacob's Ladder. (Humans are best advised not to contact them.) This region is that of the abyss, or 'pit' in Hebrew teachings, and the 'slough' in Greek.

Before we move on I should make clear how these four Worlds interleave, interface and interpenetrate with each other, as this will have an important bearing on this Keltic mythological study. Assuming that you have familiarized yourself with the Qabalistic names and positions of the *Sĕphīrōth*, then it can be seen from Fig. 28 that, for example, *Kether* of *'Asayāh*, *Tiphareth* of *Yĕtzīrāh* and *Malkūth* of *Braiāh*, all seem to cluster round the same point on Jacob's Ladder. In a sense this is indeed the case, but it must be remembered that each of these three *Sĕphīrōth* belongs to a different World (*'Asayāh*, *Yĕtzīrāh* and *Braiāh* respectively), therefore they are *qualitatively* each on a different level of existence. This may appear as just an awkward coincidence, from the point of view of a student trying to master the structural mechanics of this diagram; but in reality it is a fact of the profoundest significance, as this region (and the several others on Jacob's Ladder) are the transition, or crossover points, between the different Worlds that compose Jacob's Ladder. The main crossover points in the tree, reading from top to bottom, are as follows:

1. *Tiphareth* of *Atzīlūth*–*Kether* of *Braiāh*.
2. *Malkūth* of *Atzīlūth*–*Tiphareth* of *Braiah*–*Kether* of *Yĕtzīrāh* (this assumes the greatest importance for incarnated beings).
3. *Malkūth* of *Braiāh*–*Tiphareth* of *'Asayāh*.

Other minor interfaces can easily be spotted on the two side columns. It is a point to be remembered in connection with these regions of interchange that the *Sĕphīrāh* pertaining to the Higher World should have the greatest effect and dominance in this region, e.g., *Tiphareth* of *Yĕtzīrāh* should shine through and illuminate *Kether* of *'Asayāh*.

In the preceding summary I have concentrated on the makrokosmic aspects of Jacob's Ladder (as they are of central relevance to the subject matter of this book), but for those readers who are interested in the mikrokosmic aspects, i.e. those pertaining to the individual human being, I have included two further 'Jacob's Ladders' (see Figs 29 & 30).

1. Ancient Greek Initiates held that about 80 per cent of people were *Hylikoi* (men or women of earthly consciousness); on the whole I feel that still applies, with most modern people having their seat of consciousness in the triad of the lower ego, lower thinking and lower feeling. Their lives are filled with everyday concerns, materialistic motivation factors, petty schemes and lower passional loves, hates, fears and desires; all conditioned and influenced by social 'norms'.

2. Only about 19 per cent of people were/are held to be *Psychikoi* (men and women of soul consciousness); these true individuals have their seat of consciousness in their inner selves (following their incarnational destiny quite closely, availing themselves of psychic powers and intuitive insights and dreams); they also command profound intellectual powers and a clear grasp of the currents of deeper human emotions. Such individuals strive to ensure that there are creative, artistic, aesthetic, musical, or profoundly religious or contemplative dimensions to their lives. These individuals stand out from the crowd, not because they are loud or brash, but rather because they have a depth and strength of character that comes from creativity in fulfilment. (As *you* have chosen to read such obscure native religious material this far, you are, or at least are trying to become, one of the *Psychikoi*.)

3. Less than 1 per cent of any community are likely to be a *Pneumatikoi* (men or women of Spiritual consciousness); these shining lights amongst humanity have their consciousness seated in their immortal Spirit (thus probably *truly* recalling previous incarnations). Possessing a vast wisdom and understanding into the ways of human nature, often aided by uncanny Spiritual and psychic powers, these individuals push forward certain human frontiers of development (they include Sokrates, Pythagoras, Rabbi Aqīvāh, the Buddha, Plotinus, Valentinus, Paracelsus, etc.). Occasionally it seems that some work quietly as 'Hidden Masters'.

Human nature being what it is, most people would like to delude themselves into believing that they are something much more important, special, impressive or initiated than they really are. The sad fact of the matter is that, unless the Gods have laden you with lots of natural talents, each heightened level of consciousness has to be striven for with years of self-examination, filtering of lousy conditioning, cultivation of higher faculties, and the putting of the teachings into practice (whether this be on an individual path or within a *genuine* initiatory group).

I thank Thee, Heavenly Father,
because Thou has put me
at a source of running streams,
at a living spring in a land of drought,
watering an eternal garden of wonders,
the Tree of Life, mystery of mysteries,
growing everlasting branches for eternal planting
to sink their roots into the stream of life
from an eternal source.
And Thou, Heavenly Father,
protect their fruits
with the angels of the day
and of the night
and with flames of eternal Light burning every way.

From the Thanksgiving Psalms
of the Dead Sea Scrolls.

An Incarnated Human Being and their main Seats of Consciousness

The *Pneumatikoi* have their consciousness in *Ruach* (Immortal Spirit). The *Psychikoi* have their consciousness in *Neshamah* (Incarnational Soul). The *Hylikoi* have their consciousness in *Nephesh* (Lower Soul).

As a final note on these diagrams I would say that the Tree of Life and Jacob's Ladder should always be continually growing and living in the student's mind, and the point at which, in my view, the individual stops being someone 'studying' the Qabalah and becomes a true Qabalist is when he or she starts to *live* the Qabalistic teachings in their daily life, and when the various diagrams change from being an illustration in a book, or a chart on a wall, and become translated into the workings of creation all around them.

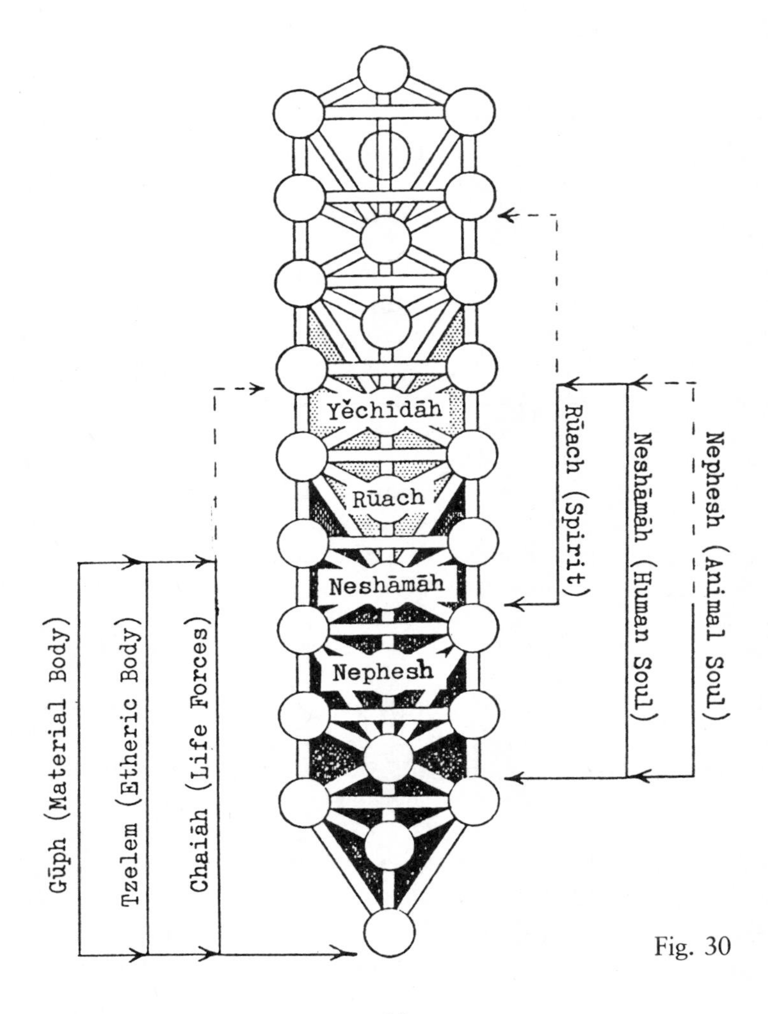

Fig. 30

CHAPTER 6

The Basic Ingredients in Ancient Folk & Faerie Tales

There are, I feel, only two useful approaches to the subject matter of this chapter: (a) to try to formulate a picture of the whole from what you understand of the fragmented parts; (b) to try to understand the place and role of each of the parts from your conception of the whole. The former method is that of empirical scientists, the latter method that employed by Initiated Seers. Of course, to the materialistic empiricist the 'alternative' method is inconceivable – but this book is living proof of its effectiveness, for in 1984 I was given the whole circular framework of the Shamanistic Calendar with all twenty Ogham signs in Station *before* I had a clear understanding of one tenth of the parts. Having been given an 'overview' of the Druidical principles at work within the whole, I found it not too difficult to work out the relative meaning of the rest of the constituent ingredients. Indeed, I was able to predict with a high degree of certainty what further items would be rediscovered to fit into position in the framework. To my view, that is the test of a true discovery, such that further research will only confirm the authenticity of the whole system by illuminating the purpose of more of the parts.

In orthodox science, on the other hand, be it archaeology, medicine, sub-atomic physics or anthropology, all we see is an endless number of 'models' being endlessly outmoded, changed and finally abandoned as untenable. Such a series of failures only points to a basically flawed and incorrect method of approaching areas of life. And the failure of inaccurate-to-life models will continue to haunt the probings of materialistic science. For example, modern medicine will never fully understand the workings of the human body so long as it refuses to deal with a complete human being as being made up of a physical body and an etheric-life body, psychic soul-forces, feelings and mentality, and an incarnated human Spirit, all woven together into an *interrelated whole*.

Similarly, archaeology has no hope of understanding the purpose of megalithic temples so long as it stubbornly refuses to accept the teachings of Shamanism, geomancy and Dowsing within the parameters of its all too narrow framework. And, in relation to the case in hand, academic anthropology and the misnamed 'comparative religion' hasn't the remotest chance of understanding the meaning and purpose of Keltic Folk and Faerie Tales so long as they resolutely refuse to accept the world view of the ancient Seers (the very individuals who formulated the earliest strata of myths and legends). Taking a Tale, putting it upon the operating table of analytical dissection, carving it up into its constituent 'motifs' (all neatly numbered –162*f*., etc., according to an international convention) is remote from the message that the sage-reciters originally wove into that Tale. Neither the dismembered carnage of academia nor the dry bones of anthropology can ever come near to understanding the life of a Faerie Wildman, nor the power in a living serpent river, nor the significance of a bird omen, nor the real meaning of a transformation into an animal totem – for all these items lie outside the perimeters of what the academics have decided is the 'real' world. But, in time, materialistic man will come to realize that 'There are more things in Heaven and Earth, Horatio, than are dreamt of in our philosophy.'

I fear environmental destruction will be widespread before such overdue realizations are given a place in modern man's world-view. In the meantime I shall offer the close-to-nature wisdom of the ancients, surveying each part whilst at the same time *always bearing in mind the whole to which it belongs*. The holistic system is, after all, the only true path to health.

As we are dealing with fundamentals, perhaps we should soberly ask ourselves the following questions. What constitutes 'life'? What are the characteristics of a living being? When does 'consciousness' arise? Of necessity such questions entail probing 'death': when can it be agreed that something is 'dead'? All branches of modern science would concur that rocks, stones, metals and jewels are lifeless, dead objects. At the same time, all branches of ancient science and spiritual philosophy (Druidical, Hindu, Qabalistic, Greek, etc.) would uphold the view that rocks, stones, metals and jewels are somewhat alive and have an attenuated form of consciousness. The former view has led to the unfeeling rape of the earth's mineral resources, often trampling over the cries of the Hopi and Aborigines. The latter view attempts to treat Mother Earth with a degree of respect, first asking permission to mine, then only taking what is environmentally wise – thus the rebellious children may not have too bad a karmic debt to repay.

In 1956 the Russian scientist N. T. Tchudinov began examining salt from the Beresniki Mines in the Ural Mountains. The salts were taken from deep underground sedimentary layers, estimated to date from the Paleozoic Era (laid down *c.* 250 million years ago). When Tchudinov treated samples with a solution of sodium chloride (an inorganic chemical compound), he noticed a quite remarkable phenomenon – impurities in the salt, existing as light green crystals, underwent a transformation, opening out to form a greenish-yellow substance, in the interior of which small green nucleii could be seen. Finally a regular-shaped bud arose, out of which grew a species of algae. In other words, primal organic plant-life had grown from inorganic 'seed crystals' that had been dormant for 250 million years. Naturally the Russian 'experts' he contacted were sceptical, but, when many came to observe the stringently controlled repeated experiments, eventually they all had to admit that these ancient life-seeds had indeed 'awakened' after a vastly long 'sleep'. More recently, H. J. Dombrowski succeeded in reviving bacteria from salt strata 180 million years old, taken from the mines at Zechstein, thus confirming the earlier discoveries of Tchudinov. Recent parallels can be noted in grains of wheat buried with the Pharoahs (a mere four thousand years ago), which were recently nurtured to sprout and grow into corn.

As the first two experiments conclusively demonstrated, the vital life principle in these 'seed crystals' had not entered from the material environment of the laboratory – in other words, the capacity to generate life had been stored *within* a substance for 250 million years, a substance that all normal scientists would catagorize as 'dead'.

Next the subject of 'consciousness'. There are well-documented cases of *live* toads or frogs being found encased in lumps of sandstone/limestone/coal, indeed actually forming part of a sedimentary layer in a Mine. Most scientists prefer to dismiss such reports; some theorize that a 'nutritious water' could have sustained the imprisoned amphibians indefinitely. Progressive as this line of thinking is, it does not really provide an explanation of the enigma.

There are also some fairly common examples of similar phenomena which I myself have witnessed. In hard winter one can occasionally find toads, frogs and newts, frozen stiff, encased in a large block of ice or attached to a log or dirt-track. If at this point you split the block of ice apart and attempt to take readings from the toad with regard to such things as respiration, brain activity or biochemical metabolism, there will be none; by normal standards, the toad would be classed as 'dead' – indeed, toads, disturbed in this way, almost certainly would not reawaken. However, if Nature is allowed to take her course, and the block of ice is allowed to melt *naturally* in situ, or the toad defrost from the log *naturally* in situ, then often the amphibian not only regains *life* after a few days/weeks, but also obvious *consciousness*.

The two essential questions here are: (a) Does the deactivated toad retain a spark of life within some secret area of its being, such that it can reanimate itself when the time comes? Or (b) Is the individual toad actually dead, whereupon its tiny spirit temporarily discarnates to join the toad-spirit or earth-elemental on another plane of existence, later to be sent to reactivate its old body when the physical conditions have improved?

To answer either of these questions fully would take scientists beyond the parameters of orthodox investigation. Cowardice prevails and such subjects are generally avoided. One wouldn't want to rock the boat; after all, it might jeopardize funding (money, money, money), and few relish becoming impoverished scientific heretics. There is, however, one branch of scientists who could at least approach facing such questions: the more progressive sub-atomic physicists – over the years individuals from this fraternity have embraced the teachings of Hindu or Qabalistic metaphysics along with their ever advancing tenets of physics (to such individuals I take my Heeland bonnet off in respect).

As for the subject in hand, unless we properly understand 'life', 'death', growth', etc., we cannot properly understand the essential ingredients and happenings in certain Folk and Faerie Tales. Time and time again in Folktales we encounter things or beings 'crossing thresholds', 'passing through barriers', 'undergoing magical transformation', from being long-dead coming back to life and consciousness, stones activated to move.

The physical world and the world of Shamanism, magic and alchemy are intimately interwoven, after all only frightened orthodox scientists, doctors and archaeologists, etc., (frantically trying to maintain the bullwarks of the 'reasonable') and the head-in-the-sky, spaced-out mystics don't want their two disciplines to explore a common frontier. The ancient seers and storytellers would have laughed at such a prevaricatory attitude.

To the Qabalists and other ancient sages, material substances (such as the stones, metals and jewels of '*Asayah*'), whilst not being as alive, mobile or conscious as organic beings further up the ladder of existence, nevertheless did possess faint sparks of spirit-fire and rudimentary consciousness. In her book *Flight of the Seventh Moon*, Lynn Andrews recounts an alleged discussion with a Cree medicine woman, who described to her how rocks had seven modes of sense or being, including 'making a cry', 'rock-sight', scent, taste, touch, feeling and awareness. Knowledge of these different 'senses of stone' has been preserved in various traditions, e.g., psychometry, crystal-gazing and gem-healing. The ancients held that each planet vibrates at a certain frequency to produce its characteristic 'note' of sound. The Qabalist Carlo Suares has explained this as the material container (*kaph* 20, or *raysh* 200) being gently vibrated by the constant stream of kosmic radiation passing through it, or impinging against it. Naturally enough, a similar process is at work upon every material object on earth – only normal human hearing is not aligned to pick up these subtle, low sounds. Top American and Russian scientists know this to be true, having (in typically perverse fashion) designed a low-frequency sound-lazer capable of shaking apart the walls of buildings or the metal of tanks.

With the recent revolution in understanding of the information-storage capacities of quartz crystals, silicon chips and mica sheets, one would expect a begrudging acknowledgement that the ancients did indeed know the special qualities of such substances – but orthodoxy is a jealous beast and is tardy with its praise. It is my contention that what modern science knows about quartz and silica is only a tiny fraction of what the ancient sages knew (the difference being that the wise men employed it for more *spiritual* purposes).

Quartz can sometimes crystallize in hexagonal crystals that have special properties: the molecular structure is in a spiral form and the quartz expands slightly when touched by a small electric charge; thus, if the quartz picks up the small electric charge of an adjacent stone whilst under pressure, the charge will divide into positive and negative on the opposite sides of the crystal. On one level of keltic art symbolism, spirals represent the expansion and contraction of special substances and the energy transferance generated therefrom. The ancient sages used quartz consciously in standing stones in megalithic complexes, in white godstone pebbles in cairn burials; quartz chips to neutralize a diseased geomantic site and used thin outer layers of quartz on some of the Pyramids, etc. I have even been guided to quartz crystals at the bottom of certain 'cup marks' by a rock-spirit Wildman, when I needed to be taught a little more of the ancient Druidical wisdom.

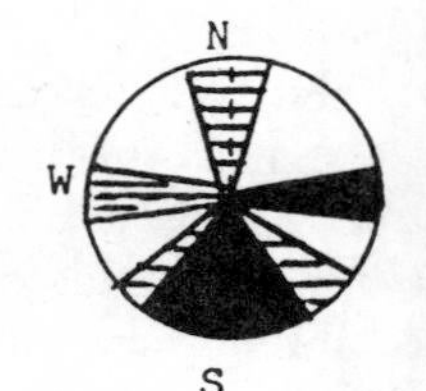

QUARTZ, SILICA, MICA, CRYSTAL.

Everything the Initiates did was according to deep knowledge. Sadly, modern archaeologists, in their plundering 'digs' or, even worse, 'back-filling', do not leave quartz (and other substances) where the Initiates intended it to lie; conversely, white or red granite chippings (including quartz) are sometimes laid to tidy up the appearance of a site regardless of their geomantic suitability or, more likely, unsuitability (not to mention the *iron* fences cemented into place).

As you can see from the miniature Shamanistic Calendar shown alongside, jet has almost the opposite qualities to quartz. The black shaded area indicates its Shamanistic Station and hence often its 'power time' in the year or day; the part shaded with horizontal hatching shows areas of secondary or lesser influence. Jet is a none-too-hard black stone which, according to Pliny, 'has the power of banishing noxious Serpents'. Also Bede (the begrudging relator of Old Lore) describes jet as having the power, when burned, of drawing away snakes.

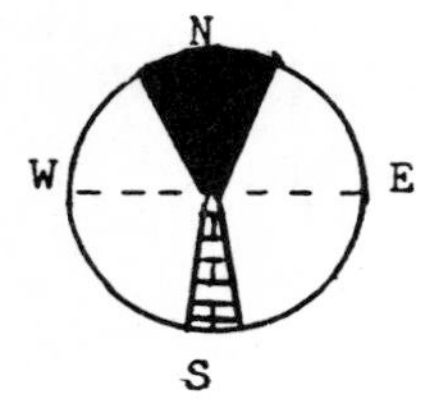

JET-STONE

When we appreciate jet's position on the rediscovered Shamanistic Calendar as being at the Winter Solstice, we realize how it functions as an opposite magical pole to adders and snakes, whose main Station is at the Summer Solstice. Now, for the first time in millennia, we can truly appreciate the importance and function of the famous jet necklaces found in Northern Pictland, and thus, contrary to academic scepticism, the Ancients had a rhyme or reason for everything. In the Scottish Highlands, even until recently, a black stone would be taken in silence from a running tarn just after midnight and applied to a person suffering from mumps, whilst repeating a Gaelic rhyme.

Similar Lore could be presented for each and every 'stone of worth' (e.g., flint 'airteine', 'fire-stone') in the Keltic tradition, but that would take a whole book in itself. We can begin to arrive at something of an overview if we survey the 'compass rose' that comes from T.C. Lethbridge's Dowsing Experiments (see Figure 00). Lethbridge calibrated the length of his pendulum in inches, when it responded to the edge of an energy-field of an object; this was termed the 'rate', corresponding to the radius field-strength on the horizontal to the object. After many thousands of experiments, Lethbridge arrived at such circular charts, which stand as sort of Shamanistic Dowsing Calendars. Lethbridge's actual methods and results have been triple-checked by later dowsers, incluing J. Havelock-Fiddler, and from my knowledge of the Shamanistic Calendar I have found at least a 60 to 80 per cent correlation between the two systems (which is not at all bad).

Whilst there are some notable anomalies and puzzles still requiring answers, such dowsing charts need our respectful attention as containing possible insights into the wisdom of the ancients. For example, Lethbridge noted that graphite reverses the sex rate of anything that it is placed beside in dowsing (not biologically); this is interesting, for both in the Keltic and Red Indian Traditions the Shamanistic East is the Heyoka quarter where, in ritual dramas, the costumes and sex roles of the participants would be temporarily reversed (e.g., medieval jesters, fools; Morris 'fools', April Fools' Day, etc.).

As yet the calibrated energy 'rates' (field-strengths) that Lethbridge and others have dowsed, have eluded detection by modern machines – but that proves little other than the limitations of our technology. As you will read later in this chapter, Lethbridge also dowsed corresponding 'rates' for plants, trees and human thoughts and emotions impregnated into bones, skulls, tools and Weapons. This goes a long way to confirming the ancient belief that individuals

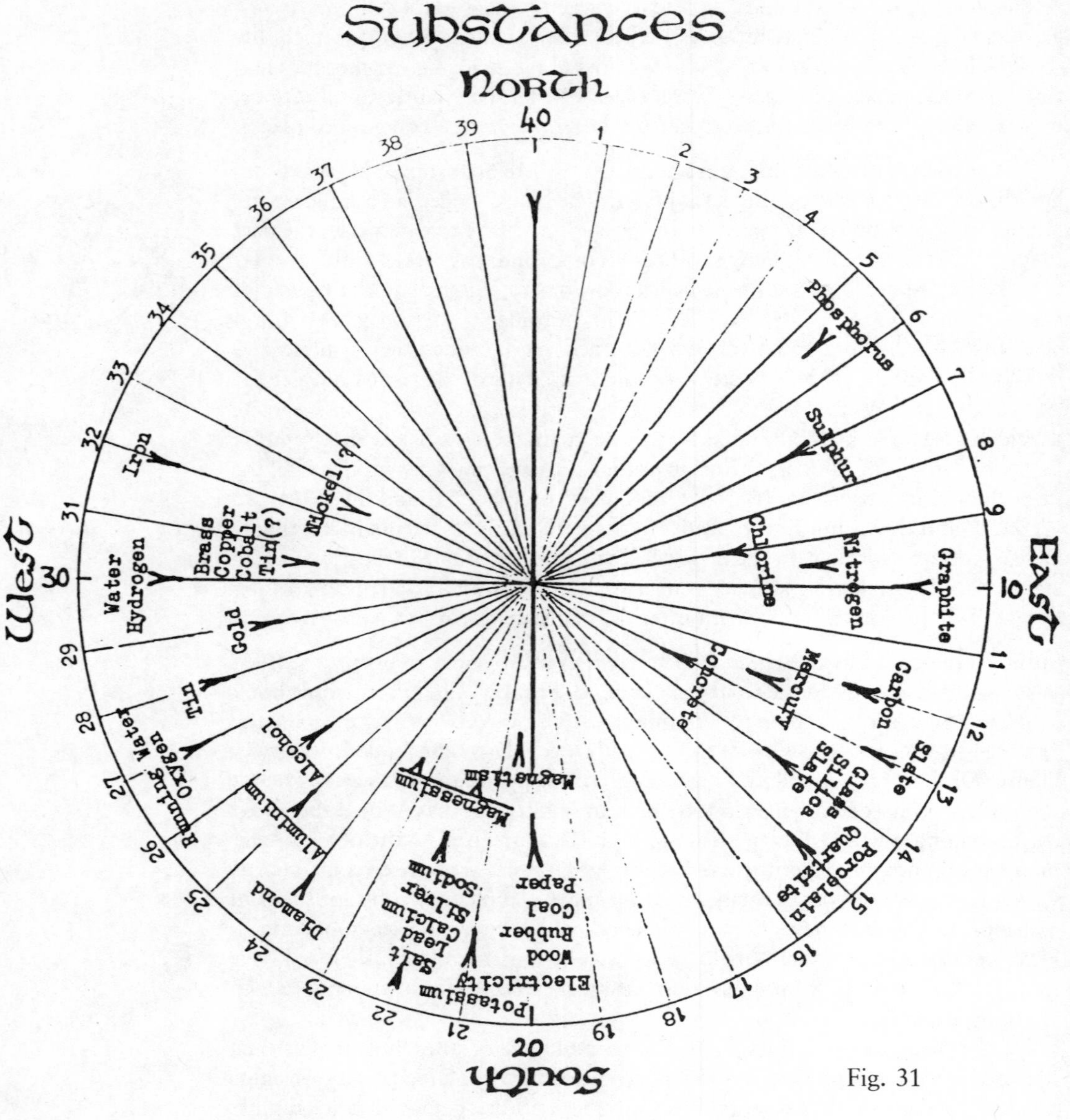

Fig. 31

could leave an essence of themselves in their bones (or the stones they lay against) or in their prized weapons or jewellery. (This was why the weapons of certain mighty warriors were either coveted or smashed up, depending on whether one wished to acquire or dissipate the 'magical charge' contained within them.)

In the Qabalah, 'the fire, essence of life stored within the bones and skull' was called *Habal de Garmin*, and in the Keltic tradition it was called *Gille Dubh mac 'Ille Chnamhlaich (Teine)*, as 'the Black Lad, Son of the Bones (Fire)'. The word *Knamhlach* conveys the sense of 'smoldering embers of fire', or 'latent life-spirit', and should remind you of the qualities discussed at the start of this chapter. In certain Highland Tales this *Gile Dugh mak 'Ille Knamhlaich (Teine)* could become reactivated in a certain capacity long after its owner had been laid in a grave. In one tale it affected the child of a certain woman at the sacred pagan site of Kilmallie (where a very ancient ash tree stood – fifty-eight feet in circumferance at its fall in 1746).

With such inner essences and energy rates in mind, let us progress to the trees, birds, animals, Faerie Beings and ritual weapons or treasures that feature in Keltic Folk and Faerie Tales.

As you will shortly be seeing many more of these miniature Shamanistic Calendar diagrams alongside each tree, bird, animal, etc., I should briefly explain their purpose and how they came to be formulated.

Their intention is to provide basic understanding at a glance and a quick *aide memoire*. For example, you could be reading some old Keltic Folktale (exterior to this book) and you may wish to find out what symbolic meaning a bear/heron/elder tree might have; all you need do is to turn to the relevant section in this book, glance at the miniature Shamanistic Calendar and return to reading your other Tale with a clearer idea of what is going on.

These small diagrams were found to be visually very effective in earlier booklets and sets of Koelbren cards that I have designed. As far as their Shamanistic accuracy is concerned, they can be counted on to be very dependable. For about 80 per cent of the trees and birds, the main Shamanistic station is based upon an Ogham cipher. (This main Shamanistic station, which is shaded in black, may also be a 'power time' for the item, either during the twenty four hour daily cycle, or within the cycle of the year.) The other 20 per cent of trees and birds, and all the ascriptions for animals, treasures, ritual weapons, etc., I have allocated myself, soundly basing such ascriptions upon Lore gleaned from the Keltic and Indo-European mythological traditions. After witnessing the disastrous confusion generated by Robert Graves and the like, I did not engage upon this task lightly; all my ascriptions have been triple-checked against the teachings of the ancient Initiates before being committed to print. Thus, although more areas of secondary importance (shown as cross-hatching) may appear after further research, I feel confident that well over 95 per cent of the main Shamanistic Stations (shaded in black) will remain unchanged, their accuracy well supported by further discoveries of Keltic Druidical wisdom.

Tree and Plant Shamanism

Without trees and plants to reprocess carbon dioxide back into oxygen, humanity could not breath upon Planet Earth. Without the produce of the vegetable kingdom (even via animals), humanity could not eat upon Planet Earth. These two facts alone should be enough to convince anyone of the massive importance of trees and plants for each of us. Lack of awareness is only half of an excuse for the hack and burn policy of the Romans, the tree-genocide of the 'planters' in Eirinn, the decimation of Koed Kalydon in the Highlands thanks to the English and the aristocracy, the widespread green-to-grime forest-stripping in the medieval and industrial eras – but we cannot plead ignorance nowadays, only a money-orientated greed. None of us can idly stand by and watch as the tropical rain forests are destroyed through craziness, or vast tracts of Scandinavian and Germanic forests (e.g., the Black Forest) are wiped out by acid rain, or British trees weakened by pollution, then destroyed by insects (first elm, then next yew, oak, sycamore, beech and chestnut – for in one way or another these things effect our quality of life (and will ruin that of our children's).

That trees and plants also provide herbal medicine, psychic healing, and guidance into the Magical Otherworlds is a further demonstration of how important they can be for our health and Spiritual well-being.

The Keltic Druids, priestesses and healer-women had a profound grasp of all the characteristics of trees and herbs, and, as discussed in chapter 00, encoded this wisdom into an Ogham cipher. From my analysis of the Keltic Tree Calendar etc., it should be very clear that this had a direct correlation to actual nature. Apart from Ogham ciphers, Keltic mythology (e.g., *Kad Goddeu*), Folklore preserves many of the beliefs and practices of Tree Lore and Plant Shamanism. And it is into that treasure trove I would now like to guide you, following the Tree Wheel (of Power Stations) from Shamanistic North to Shamanistic East to Shamanistic South to Shamanistic West to Shamanistic North.

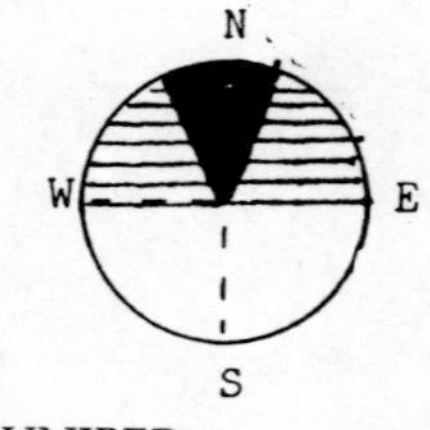

JUNIPER or 'MOUNTAIN YEW' AITEAL

In the Keltic as well as in other Indo-European cultures, the juniper tree is associated with purification, particularly around the death and rebirth of the Sun at the Winter Solstice. As we read in this Folk practice from Alban: 'After sunset on Hogmany, bands of young men carrying axes and ropes set off to the hill, whence they returned with loads of juniper. This was ranged round the fire to dry overnight. A member of the household was also sent to draw a pitcher of 'magic water' from the 'dead and living ford'. Early next morning the household assembled, and each member took a draught of the water. The head of the house and his assistant then went from room to room, sprinkling the rest of the water on the beds and on any remaining occupants. This done, all windows, crevices and keyholes were carefully stuffed and the performers of the rite seized branches of the dried juniper, set them alight, and carried them through the house. The fumes spread over the low ceilings and gradually concensed into a thick cloud. This odoriferous fumigation caused sneezing, wheezing, coughing, and hiccoughing, and even drew cries of suffocation from the children. When the fumes were deemed to have accomplished their work, fresh air was admitted, and the women of the house, 'having vented the most latent embryo of disease in a copious expectoration', as one participant has described it, administered a restorative from the whisky bottles. Whoever contrived to greet his neighbour first was entitled to a gift. The fumes were washed away and they all sat down to their New Year breakfast.'

A very similar practice was conducted by youths with flaming torches who went into one of the Pictish Intiatory caves at East Wemyss to collect 'the flower of the Well' (magical well-water) on New Year's morning. In this way a propitious start to the young year was obtained.

Juniper berries are still used widely to cleanse and purify the human digestive tract.

In Greek mythology branches were sacred to 'the Furies' as messengers of the Gods' justice. This is paralleled by German Lore, where a Wildwoman spirit of the juniper tree was approached by someone who had been robbed; a branch was held down to the ground whilst the juniper Faerie being made the thief declare himself or make amends. (This ties in with the concepts of truth, right versus wrong, etc., associated with the *Lia Fail*, 'speaking sod of turf', and the better Sagittarian qualities.)

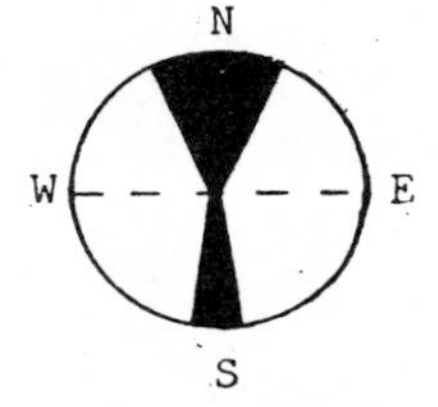

REEDS WATER IRIS & LILLIES NGETAL

The main plant power, respectfully designated 'a tree' in Ogham and Koelbren sources, is *Ngetal*, the reed. It may well be difficult for us in our devastated post-industrial country, drained of its ancient marshes, which have been sacrificed to that ever-voracious monster 'progress', to conceive of the part once played by reeds. One needs to repicture the extensive fens, marshes or the thickly reeded surrounds of lochs to appreciate the mystery and magic of a wind-blown expanse of reeds. In such an environment, often more than man-high, lateral vision may be obscured, whilst, above, the wind passes over the reed-tops ne'er stirring what is beneath; thus all attention is turned to what is on the muddy or watery floor. There is a quiet, secretive, inner attention and strength here, spiritual wisdom sometimes following. One should remember that both Taliesin and Moses were taken from the reeds at birth, and Christ later given one as a sign of Kingship (as it was the Royal insignia of Egypt and the Middle East). Thus, Christ's often misunderstood question regarding John the Baptist – 'What went ye out into the winderness to see? a Reed shaken in the wind [*Ruach*=spirit]' – contains great depth, for Christ's main Station is at the Winter Solstice, whilst John the Baptist's is at the Summer Solstice – St John's Day. Other reeds are not really shaken, as the proverb attests – 'Oaks may fall when reeds stand in a storm'. The reed has many other powerful associations in mythology, for Prometheus is said to have stolen the fire from heaven in a reed stalk (more likely a rush-pith in my view, or in a fennel stalk according to others – both at the Summer Solstice, place of the lightning flash); in a Greek myth, *Syrinx* ('Reed') was changed into a reed to escape being violated by Pan, who, however, cut several of the reeds down to make his Pan-pipes (which contained the harmony of the seasons).

One of the many Gaelic names for the reed is *Gaothaiche*, meaning hollow, mostly filled with wind (spirit), which connects it to *Gaothaire* (ean) the mouthpiece (chanter) of a bagpipe, which is of course a reed. Therefore, we realize that the Pictish and Keltic bagpipes are mythological equivalents of Pan's reed-pipes. When the Burdoun, the Drone of the Bagpipe, ascends into some wild or plaintive playing, I am often stirred to my deepest being. The Faerie Folk Wildman who presides over this Shamanistic Station is a black or dark giant, often sporting cloven goat's feet (like Pan) and very fond of playing wild reels on his bagpipes (see 'The Towzie Tyke' poem). With such a set of characteristics this Wildman (also of the black goat-man, Capricorn) came under heavy attack from the ignorant simpletons of the Church, who labelled him with such misnomers as 'Satan' , 'the devil'. These short-sighted Christian bigots have thus crippled themselves to responding to Christ as the Piper, the Lord of the Dance, when he begs us all 'dance, dance wherever you may be,' – a good recommendation for a Faerie reel or a Morris hey, in my book.

Intimately associated with the reeds Shamanistically are the *Bileag-bhaite* (Water-lily) and the *Seg* (yellow flag iris), for apart from the obvious water connection, they fit into the colour-dye cycle perfectly: water-lily roots giving a dark blue or black; iris root – black; and flag iris root – black or dark grey. The lily of the valley is associated with death, sorrow and the Underworld in Folklore, whilst the water-lily is known as the Sun-vessel for its night-crossing through the underworld sea. Dr Knight Dunlop, through a long period of observation, found a definite correlation between the phases of the Moon and the blossoming periods of irises. He states that the plants stand bare-stemmed or nearly so during new and full moons, thus proving a long-held belief of Folklore and astrology. (Narcissus = Sagittarius) Narcissus in Greek mythology was associated with Pluto and Proserpine, as well as with the Three Fates; whilst the iris was dedicated to Juno. The iris (which means 'rainbow' as well as a part of the eye, left or right) was to be found at either the North or South end of the Scandinavian 'Rainbow Bridge'.

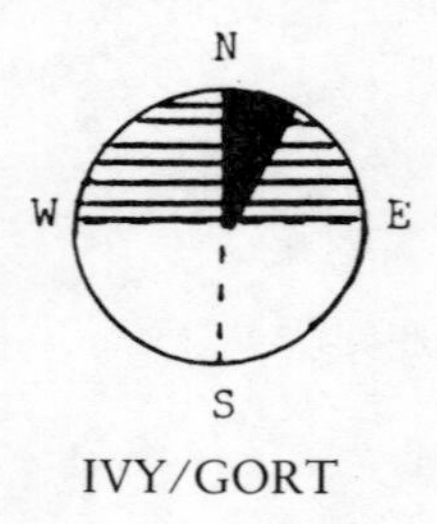

IVY/GORT

The ivy has essentially a twofold signficance: (a) it is the strangler and bringer of death to other forest trees; (b) it is a symbol of the tenacity of green life holding on through the darkness and remaining luxuriant into the New Year – hence a token of rebirth and regeneration. Both these motifs appear in old Folksongs where murdered lovers meet again after death over their graves, thanks to an arch of ivy joining both graves (e.g.., Tristram and Iseult).

The ivy (usually female) and the holly (usually male) are paired in the well-known Folksong lines:

> The holly and the ivy when they are both full grown
> of all the trees that are in the wood the holly bears the crown.

Hence, Holly Men and Ivy Girls contended in a Yule custom against each other, where they played a competitive game of forfeits based on singing songs to each other which often contained jibes and bawdy teasing. As a symbol of rebirth, ivy was carried in a basket, representing Bacchus born by Selene when she was thrown into the river in a basket (similar to the experiences of St Kentigern/ Mungo's Mother, Taliesin, Moses, etc.).

Ivy flowers are the last to be sucked by bees, and the ivy berries form a providential supply for birds long after winter frosts have spoiled the remaining haws (these two seeds are in turn spat out by the birds, which assists in spreading the species). Water in which ivy leaves have been steeped is known to be beneficial for sore eyes; a solution of ivy leaves is also known to clean *black* silk.

Chewing ivy leaves or berries can have a twofold effect on humans: it can make you temporarily deranged; or, if you have previously drunk a lot of alcohol, it can help clear the muddled mind. So we can understand the Bassarids waving fir branches spirally wreathed with ivy for Dionysus, for the pine/fir cone, tipped thyrsus (Initiation wand), was also twined with ivy. Of similar significance must be the ivy-leaf symbol portrayed on early Keltic coins; for the bindwood snake that spirals round trees Sunwise also leads to the Lord of the Forest.

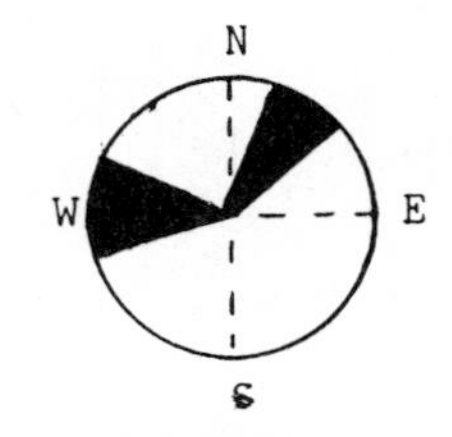

BRAMBLES
BLACKBERRIES
MUIN

In October 1984, when I made the breakthrough into rediscovering the secret code of the Koelbren and Ogham cycle, one of the tree placements I initially found hard to understand was that of the bramble/vine stationed near the end of January. However, crediting the ancients to be wise and myself as yet only partially enlightened, I decided to accept the order as given in the Ogham Alphabet, and pursue my researches to discover the *raison d'être* for such an arrangement. This confirmation has now come.

One of the bramble's alternative names (*Orir*), which places it just before the Autumn Equinox, a time when its fruit is abundant and free to be gathered. However, from the last day of September onwards, brambles become *wapp*it, and one shouldn't gather or eat them 'because of the Faeries'/'*a cause des Fees*' (as they say in Brittany) – they have now become a taboo Faerie plant-totem. The 'Dark Man' is reported to go into them around 11 October. Nearer the Winter Solstice it has a death aspect, being reported as one of the plants of which Jesus of Nazareth's Crown of Thorns was made (*Hepthorne* is another name for the briar, and the Gaelic *Dris* or *Dreas* can mean a briar, bramble or thorn-bush.) One of the miracles accredited to St Kentigern is his producing bramble fruit in midwinter; this is interesting in respect of this Keltic saint's birth and his Shamanistic connections. St Kentigern was in fact simply carrying on an ancient Keltic Shamanistic practice of knowing where a Seer could find ripe bramble berries in January and February, as is recounted in Tales such as *Smeuran Dubha 's an Fhaoillteach* ('*Bramble Berries in February*') – the location sometimes being where giants stacked dead bodies.

Also worth pondering is the following profound nursery-rhyme (which, as often, preserves some Ancient Lore):

There was a man of Thessaly,
And he was wondrous wise,
He jumped into a bramble bush
And scratched out both his eyes.
And when he saw his eyes were out,
With all his might and main,
He jumped back into the bramble bush
And scratched them in again.

Brambles have several healing traditions attached to them, including this: 'One dips *nine* bramble leaves in spring water and then applies the lotion as a charm against a scald.' Also, if you were ailing (or if your horse's hoof had been run over by a shrew) you had to be passed through some natural aperture or arch with brambles on both sides:

T.C. Lethbridge, that redoubtable pioneering researcher, dowsed the bramble to be in exactly the same position as that accorded to it in the Shamanistic Calendar I rediscovered.

As ever in this study, much can be gleaned from etymology. Variant names include: *Cruban-na-saoma* (dwarf mountain bramble); Scrogs (thorns, bramble briars); *Brylies* (*bear*-berries, note totem connection); roebuck-berry (the stone-brambleberry – this supports the Keltic legend of the Goddess Deer being entangled in the thorny thicket); and, most importantly, Garten-berries (brambles), which take their name from 'Lady Garten's Berries' – Lady Garten is the Pictish Goddess depicted as riding side-saddle on a small horse (a *Garron*). Lady Garten also presides over this quarter (*Garten, Girten*), girth originally meaning the diameter of a sacred enclosure, circle or round. Her small *Garron* horse stands between the mighty stallions and black kelpies of the Winter Solstice point in our calendar, and the horses and unicorns of Brigantia (the Horse Goddess). Her bramble berries connect through bears to Arthur, Myrddin and other Wildmen Shamans. With the Goddess presiding over brambles it is no wonder that: 'A great dowry is a bed full of brambles' and sweet is the wine of inspiration from *Muin* the Bramble.

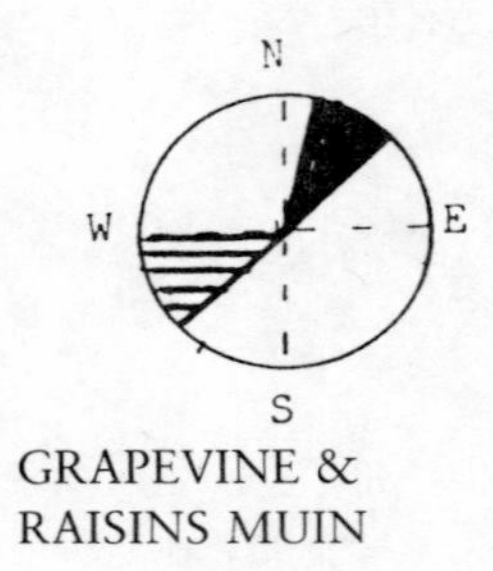

GRAPEVINE & RAISINS MUIN

The 'tree' paired with the bramble in Ancient Ogham is the vine. It is, I think, highly significant that T.C. Lethbridge dowsed these two bushes at exactly the same point, which matches their Station in the calendar. In the Keltic countries it was often the dark evergreen-leaved creeper similar to the ground or wall ivy that was mant. However, sometimes the *Dearc-fiona* (grape) or *Dearch-fhrangach* (currant) is meant as the provider of a form of mead. George Ewart Evans, in his fine book *The Pattern Under the Plough*, relates that 'the best place to bury the [foal's] placenta is under a grape-vine' (probably to promote healthy life). The grape vine also has a Station in the summer months, as can be seen from Wildfolk tapestry illustrations. Thus, not surprisingly, the vine is sacred to Dionysus–Bacchus (Bucca, Pukka, Puck – Lord of the Faerie Folk). Christ is also often represented as standing between grapes (inspiration) and thorns (suffering, yet sometimes cautionary protection).

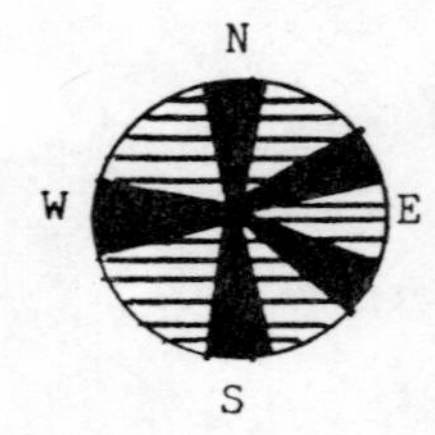

APPLE TREE QUERT

The apple tree was mightily important to the Kelts. As one of the seven chieftain trees it features prominently in every strata of the mythology and folk customs. It has several times of ritual significance throughout the year: blossom – spring (fertility); fruit – autumn, *Samhain* (divination and death); and bare trees being wassailed at mid wintger (as the Old Wise Apple-tree Man). For the present I will focus only upon the spring Lore.

In the sacred hunt, the apple tree is the shelter of the hind and the unicorn; it thereby acquired the epithet *boiscul* – 'shelter of the hind'. The hind that Herakles followed hid under a wild apple tree, later leading him to the Hyperboreans. Apple blossom is a herald of spring, and as such is a token from the sexually arousing young Goddess. An apple fertilized Rerir's wife, Ljod (East Wind, daughter of a frost giant); an apple was given by the Goddess Goda to the sacred King at the Spring Festival in Northern Europe (just as the Queen of Faerie gave Thomas the Rhymer an apple to confer the gift of rhyming prophesy, which relates to the Welsh Goddess Awen and Myrddin's Avallenau). The wild apple tree is associated with Olwen; other Apple Goddesses are the Scandinavian

Idun (perhaps the Lowland Scottish Tri-Iduni, the Triple Idun) and the Qabalistic *Shekhīnāh* that presides over the Apple Groves of Paradise. Melus, the priest of Aphrodite, was turned into an apple tree, just as certain giant Kings in Irish Folktales have their souls contained in the midst of an apple. On another track, apple trees are often planted near the house for protection: lightning, it is said, cannot split the apple's trunk, and Thor's hammer cannot touch it.

Often when the apple appears in the Bible, or elsewhere, there is implicit sexual symbolism (see, for example, the Song of Solomon 2, 3 and 5), for the Young Maiden of Spring is developing into the lusty Hare Goddess.

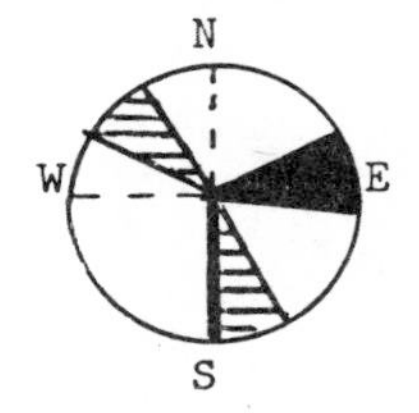

HAZEL TREE KOLL

Kuil or *Koll*, the hazel tree, is another of the chieftain trees, for the wanton felling of which the Kelts maintained the death penalty (compare that reverential attitude to the wholesale slaughter from the Roman and Anglo-Saxon periods down into the present). This tree has several mythological aspects: the ancient dripping hazel, having no leaves, dripped a poisonous milk and was inhabited by divinatory vultures and ravens (Fionn made a 'shield' of its wood for satiric poetry); the nine hazels of knowledge hung over Connla's Well and dropped their nuts into it to feed the salmon of wisdom; the Keltic God of Love, Aengus, carried a hazel wand (Jove in amorous mood pursued Luturna, who hid in an hazel tree); Irish Heralds, wise Druids and early Bishops all carried hazel wands to gain them a quiet hearing (as did the Faerie chains); hazel was the tree of Thor and related to fire, perfect for its place in the Shamanistic Calendar). The hazel's uses in dowsing for locating hidden springs, metal or buried treasure are well known; new to some may be its ability to make a Shaman Druid invisible (like fern-seed, to which it is related). Hazel, along with hawthorn, were the two trees which stood outside the Green Knight's (the Holly King's) Castle, further supporting our Koelbren cycle. (It is perhaps significant that, in Irish, *Cuilen* (*Kuilen*) can also mean 'the wood of the holly tree'.) Finally, in confirmation of an idea of mine touched on elsewhere, Bob Robin reputedly lives on a hazel twig. Thus my equation of Robin = Holly King, and Wren = Oak King stands evermore clearly.

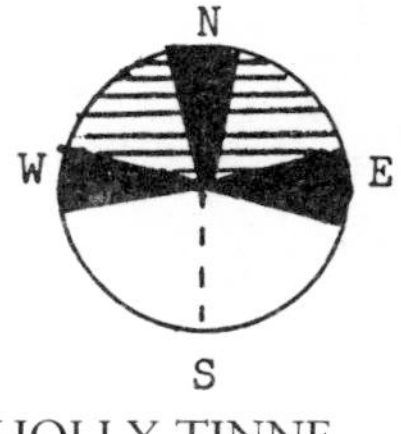

HOLLY TINNE
TARAN

The most important tree at this stage in our journey is the holly. Its name *Tinne* means fire, for from *Tindi* we got tinder, which is the wood turned into charcoal/coke (to make swords and axes) in olden times; the Gaels call it '*Smir guali*' – 'fires of coal'. It was also *Is Cuileand in tres fidh roith in carbait*, 'One of the three types of wood used in chariot wheels', (warrior, Thunder God connection). Another use is revealed in its Cornish (Kerneweg name '*Gas-tann*' (green sacred tree), used to mean the evergreen holm-oak – the English verb 'tan' is derived from the use of its bark in tanning. This word-root is also the name of the God that presides over the tree – Tannus or Taranis is the Gaulish Thunder God, Tina is the Etruscan Thunder God, Taran is both the Pictish and Gaidhlig Thunder God, Thunor or Thor is the Scandinavian; the holly, holm-oak and oak are the three trees intimately associated with this God in the native mythologies. Holly was planted near the house to protect it from thunder and lightning; old fen builders liked to use holly wood for making the external door sills, believing that no malignant witch would dare to cross it to work mischief within the dwelling. That important Wildman Giant, the Green Knight in the *Arthuriad*, is the Holly Giant carrying a holly club (his daughter/Queen sits under a green *hollen* dressed in scarlet); the Green Knight comes to remove idle boasting and to test the knight's true courage by facing a possible beheading with his mighty axe. In the Irish myths, Ku Roi (Cu Roi) fulfils a similar role, testing Kukulain and his Fianna (Ku Roi is also a Heyoka Master). Saturn's club was of hollywood, and an ass was sacrificed at the mid winter Saturnalia, killed with holly. In Hector's dream (Quest of the Holy Grail 8) Lancelot wears a robe spiked with holly and sits on an ass. The holly (↑) is connected with the T-sign and Christ's Crucifixion (Christ had earlier ridden an ass). In Malory 4, 25, Sir Marhaus brings happiness and riches by symbolically killing the giant who sits under a holly tree (possibly the Green Knight again?). In the Initiatory mysteries, rebirth and rejuvenation often followed a symbolic death; thus 'from under the dark ilex tree [holly/holm-oak] the fountain sprang up, into which Byblis was changed'. As I have already mentioned Ku Roi's testing of Ku/Kulain, it is important to know what these Initiatory titles mean: Ku = dog, hound; *Roi* = king; *Cuilen* = pup, whelp, cub or kitten. Ku Roi therefore means 'king dog', and Kukulain means 'dog pup'. The red dog stands in the East, the place of the back-to-front Heyoka power and the reversible sacredness of the dog as totem sacrament.

GORSE FURZE WHIN TINNE or OHN

The significant bush gorse/furze/whin has two main Stations: as *Tinne* (fire) at the Spring Equinox, and as *Ohn*, just after the Autumn Equinox. Many things about this 'tree' relate to purification and testing, for it was traditionally burned in the autumn, the fire burning away the old dry spines to promote new growth in the spring which sheep could feed upon. Infusions and distillations from new blossoms can be used for a diuretic purifier. As an expression, 'to tak' through the whins' came to mean 'to be severely reproved'. This may well derive from an Otherworld journey prominent in Keltic and Scandinavian mythology, where unless the discarnate spirits had previously fashioned a pair of *Hel/Annwn* shoes they would have a painful journey over 'the Muir o' Heckle-pins', 'the Whinney-Muir'. This Otherworld moor of whin bushes with their spines is described in 'The Lyke-wake Dirge', where 'if hosen or shoon thou ne'er gavest nane, the whins shall prick three to the bare bane'. The heckle-pin was the steel comb used by weavers to remove impurities from wool. Whilst its essential character is of harsh purification, we should not overlook a much gentler side of the bush's nature, for when it is fully in bloom (May–June) its rich yellow flowers have a heady erotic scent. This is fitting, as the gorse/whin shelters the lusty Goddess's hare totem.

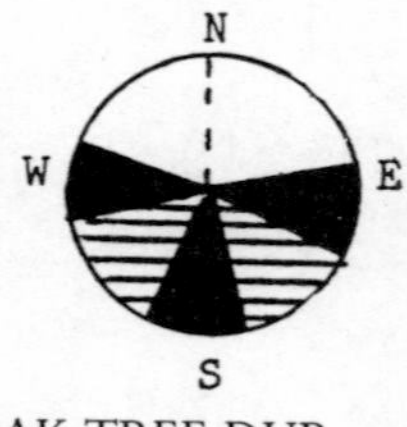

OAK TREE DUR or DERWEN

In Keltic Druidism there can almost be no more important tree than the oak. For the oak's Keltic name is *Dur, Daroch, Der, Derwen*, etymologically linked to the root of Druid, and the Druidical knowledge – *Druis*. In Gaelic, *Draoidh* is the word used for a wise man, magician or Druid. Another root meaning of this word *Dur* is 'door' (*Doirseach/Dorus* = 'full of doors'); the secret 'oaken door' features prominently in the mythology, appearing in Taliesin's poems several times. Through this magical door lay Initiation by the Faerie beings, the Wildfolk. There are three reasons why the oak should be singled out for this distinction: (a) the nature of the tree itself, being related to the Sky God; (b) the East being the entry point in the circle; (c) the fact that most of Britain, Eireann and Breizh was anciently covered in extensive oak forests (which contained the Wildfolk). As I have investigated in my article in *Inner Keltic*, No. 7, some of the names for the Wildfolk are connected with this tree; e.g., the Manx *Phynnoderee* is derived from the Irish Gaidhlig *Fionnadh-doiri* = 'Hairy Man of the Oak Woods'. This knowledge is preserved in the old English rhyme 'Faerie Folks are in the Oak Woods'. Also, the primal tree spirits in Greek mythology are 'the Dryads', 'oak-tree spirits'. And Shakespeare tells us that the spirit of Herne the Hunter walked round an oak in Windsor Forest. This tree is sacred to many powerful Gods and a few Goddesses, as follows: Thunder/Sky/Fertility Gods = Taran (Keltic); Thor (Scandinavian) who is reported to have had a red beard, red hair and red eyebrows; Indra (Vedic); Jun-Pater, Jupiter (Greek); Yahweh (Hebrew); Ukho (Finnish); Goddesses = Kirke (Circle), Rhea, Kybele, Artemis (Greek), and other figures – Balder, the Erinyes and Kikonian Maenads. We find an important Keltic account in 'Sir Gawain's Marriage', where King Arthur (who has his royal seat at Kaer Luel, Carlisle) says, '... as I came over a moor, I saw a lady where she sat, between an oak and a green hollen, she was clad in red-scarlet.' This lady may well have been Keirddylad, for whom the Oak Knight and the Hollen Knight fought every Beltaine, and are held to continue to do so 'till the end of creation'. Oaks were also oracular as regards the Sky God's wishes; e.g., the oaks of Dodona spoke for Jupiter: 'The high oak trembles and branches moved without wind' (Ovid, *Metamorphoses*, ll. 7629*ff*.). Another link with the Sky God is that oak trees should be felled with a double axe only.

The Golden Fleece (note connection with Aries that Jason and the Argonauts strove for was in Kolchis and nailed to an oak, with linden trees nearby. In certain traditions the female partner to the male oak for the Light Half of the Year is the linden tree (lime). This esoteric teaching the Greek Mystery Schools preserved in the following Tale: 'Philomon, who, in his poverty, had entertained Jupiter and company unawares, was changed into an oak (at his request) instead of dying, beside his wife Baukis who was changed into a linden tree.' (Ovid, *Metamorphoses*, ll. 8620-8724) In other myths it was reputed to be the first tree created, from which the human race sprang (see also the ash, alder and rowan). The Arkadian Greeks even called themselves *Eggenoi Dryos*, 'Sons of the oak'. The ancient Druids had their teaching centres in the midst of oak groves, and the early Keltic saints such as St Kentigern, St Brigit and St Columba recommissioned such sites for their own establishments. The oak's Shamanistic Stations are, in order of importance: mid-April, around the Summer Solstice (21 June), *Lughnasadh* (1/8 August), and during the autumn for the acorn mast. The first period is its key position on the Koelbren cycle; this is also when Kernunos raises up the ram's horn serpent power. As regards felling trees, Herbert L. Edlin quotes the earlier Moses Cook (1675) as writing that: 'December and January is the best time to fell timber, but the *oak* in *April* if you would have the *bark*, when the Moon is decreasing, *and the wind not East*.' Herbert concluded, 'Even in our times oak bark will only strip easily in *April*. Gilbert White, the famous naturalist, thought that this was due to the sap flow; 'so oaks may be barked while the leaf is budding; but as soon as they are expanded, the bark will no longer part from the wood, because the sap that lubricates the bark and makes it part, is evaporated off through the leaves'. Others disagree and maintain that the phenomenon is a (Shamanistic) mystery. The Tarot suit related to this quarter is wands, elementally fire, related to clubs in my set of ascriptions (see *Inner Keltic* No. 9); in medieval German packs of cards oak acorns replace the (oak) clubs of the Warrior God–knight–hero. Oak-apple Day was celebrated long before an English King may have hid in such a tree to escape his pursuers – early records show it being held on 29 May, then later it was transferred to Whitsun (White-Sun-Tide = 10 June). In East Anglia, village children wore oak leaves or oak apples on 29 May; if they neglected to do so, they were pinched or stung with nettles by their companions. '... A special Whitsun song was sung in the last century by men who used to place a twig of oak on each house as they went along.'

The Summer Solstice is the flowering period of the oak, a magical time of transformation and invisibility – Taliesin included oak flowers in several of his Shamanistic transformation or creative poems. By midsummer, oak leaves may be considerably nibbled or stripped by chaffers, but soon afterwards the trees have a spurt of growth and send out young green foliage at the end of long thin stalks; in Alban this is called 'Lammas growth' or 'Lammas shoots', for it is most noticeable around *Lughnasadh* (Lammas – 1/8 August).

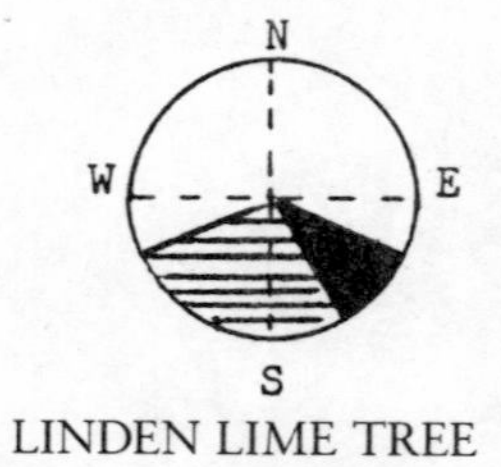

LINDEN LIME TREE

Next in rightful order comes the linden tree (lime), which is the feminine partner of the male oak. In Greek mythology Dryads (oak-tree spirits) were 'wedded to' linden trees. *Philyra* ('linden' in Greek) is the mother of Cheiron the Centaur (who is associated with the erotic wryneck – the serpent bird); now it so happens that the German *Lind* means 'serpent'. Another East connection appears in the Tale of 'Reynard the Fox' (the red dog), where the hen Copper is buried under a linden tree. Being linked with the oak it was planted as a protection against thunder and lightning. The 'short hare', the rabbit, also shows deference to this tree by not knawing its bark. Nor is its wood eaten by worms due to its serpent-power connection. Linden trees have strong fertility associations: it was a favourite among the love poets of Germany and France, providing fine cover for spring and summer's lusty frolics; its leaves were thought of as tender, charming and graceful as a lady's hands and skin; and with its delicate fragrance it was sacred to Frigga. Whilst in Greece it was often a substitute for the mountain heather (its Shamanistic opposite) and linked to Aphrodite. This delightful tree has many more virtues: in the South of France an infusion of the blossoms of the lime tree (*Tilia*) is held in esteem as a remedy for coughs, hoarseness, fevers, etc; its tissues were also used as antiseptic wound-dressing in wiser times.

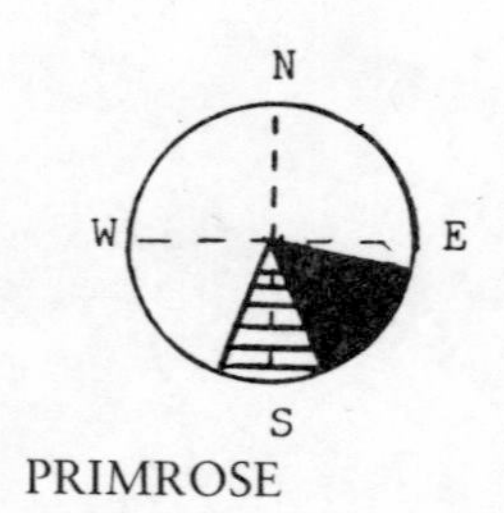

PRIMROSE

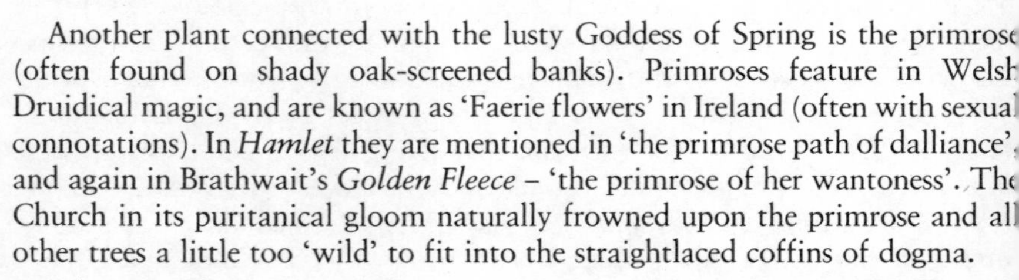

Another plant connected with the lusty Goddess of Spring is the primrose (often found on shady oak-screened banks). Primroses feature in Welsh Druidical magic, and are known as 'Faerie flowers' in Ireland (often with sexual connotations). In *Hamlet* they are mentioned in 'the primrose path of dalliance', and again in Brathwait's *Golden Fleece* – 'the primrose of her wantoness'. The Church in its puritanical gloom naturally frowned upon the primrose and all other trees a little too 'wild' to fit into the straightlaced coffins of dogma.

'The trees that 'grow of their own accord' may be a survival of the once wisespread belief that hawthorns originated from lightning and gave protection from being struck by it.' However whitethorns arrived here, they were widespread in Britain from before the Boreal Period (7000–6000 BC), as scientific 'pollen counts', etc., have demonstrated. Their remains have been found within megalithic grave burials and within the deepest strata of Keltic mythology – thus Graves's stupid statement that 'the Hawthorn Cult was introduced into the British Isles in the late first century BC' (W.G.) is a total travesty. Likewise his ignorant and perverse statement that there was 'a taboo against marriage in the hawthorn month' (W.G.), further saying that both this tree and the Blackthorn were 'unlucky'. This is massive insult to the lusty Keltic Goddess of Spring. Graves used scraps of Graeco-Roman Folk custom to foist upon the Kelts his incorrect theories, as he at the same time ignored a lot of Greek mythology and widespread Keltic tradition – e.g., at marriage ceremonies on the Greek island of Delos, 'Singer and dancers appeared crowned with oak, myrtles and Whitethorn.' Often the Greek bridal wreath 'was of hawthorn blossoms' (may). The beautiful Kymraeg Goddess that presides over May-time marriages was Olwen, who was liberated by Kilwch (grandson of Prince Kelydon) from Yspadden Penkawr (the One-eyed Wildman Hawthorn Giant). That May and midsummer were the two favourite times for such bondings or unions is copiously demonstrated from within the Keltic and European Keltic traditions. The very scent of may blossom has been compared to the scent of female sexual issue. Athenian brides wore garlands of hawthorn, and it was draped upon the alters to the marriage divinity, Hymen. In Britain and Ireland newly married couples used to dance around fairy *thorn trees*. British girls also used to go out very early on Beltain and gather may blossom, which was carried quietly, respectfully back home, lest they wouldn't get married that year.

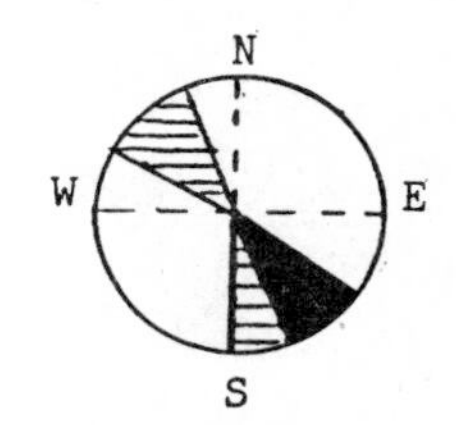

WHITETHORN
MAY or
HAWTHORN
HUATHE

That thorn trees (which sometimes live for 300 to 400 years) were dwelling places for the Faerie Folk is well supported by the number of prayer trees (often old thorns with devotional rags attached) in rural areas.

Another aspect of thorn-tree worship (like that of the oak) is it was conceived of being associated with a 'doorway' into the Otherworld, thus those planted outside the door or at the end of the house were called 'AuchinDorus'. Similarly, it was sacred to the Goddess Carnea, whose son/husband was Janus (the Door god); later it was his role to keep out Carnea, who became his mistress – Iana, Iuno – the Door Goddess. As the hawthorn is twined with the hazel outside the Holly-Oak Knight's (Green Knight's) dwelling, it might just be that all trees of the Eastern quarter have a connection with a mystical 'door'.

The willow, sallow and osier are closely related physically, and are similarly bonded within the Folk traditition and mythology. The Ogham name for willow/sallow is *Saile*, which quickly became anglicized into Sally, as in the song 'Sally Gardens'. The Welsh is *Helyg/Helygen*, whilst Brythonic terms are *Saugh/Sauch/Saughen* (from which is perhaps derived the Scottish surname Shaw, although *schaughs* is a term also generally used for the trunks of trees, and even the thick stem of some plants). *Willan* is another term, and *Willie-wain* means a 'willow wand'. The tough and pliable young 'withies' were used for making baskets, thatch support, and stockading. These basket-sieves (which were used for winnowing corn) also had a magical function, for, during the North Berwick witch trials, witches confessed to going to sea on their 'riddles' during their Esbats. The bark of certain kinds of willows was used in this country (and by the Red Indians) as a head-clearing and uplifting incense. Much has rightly been written about the willow's connection with water and feminine moon-magic, but let us not forget its solar associations, for the young sun God was often lifted from a coracle (the frame of which would be made of willow) lodged in the rushes. The Keltic Sun God Belin is also linked to the willow. In the eighteenth century it was the brides-men that carried osier wands in the marriage procession as it walked Desuil around the Church.

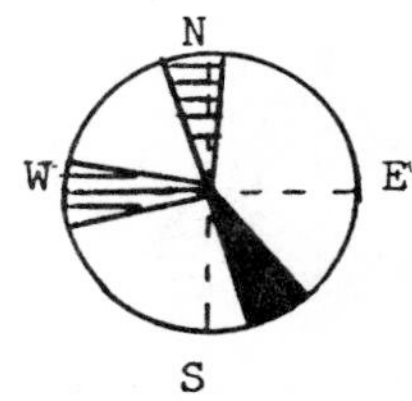

WILLOW SALLOW
OSIER SAILE

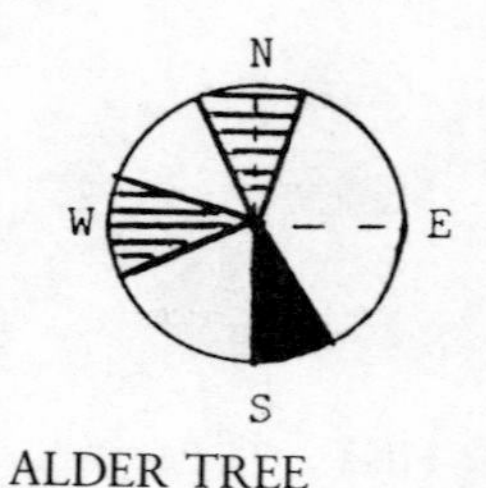

ALDER TREE
FEARN

Fearn (the alder, aller, eller, howler) is Bran's tree. This primordial God of Prydain is also known as Bendigeid Vran ('Bran of the Wonderous Head'), which alludes to the Sacred Head Cult over which he presides. After Bran's mythological 'death' he instructed his companions to bare his head, with them sitting it atop a pillar, wherefrom it would provide them with wise council. Eventually it was buried under the White Mount in Kaer Llyndain, where ravens have been ever since. Within the Keltic tradition 'sacred heads' often appear staring up from the bottom of a deep well, immersed in, and sanctifying, the inspirational waters. Thus the wood of *Fearn* (alder) is remarkably durable under water, taking far longer to rot than virtually any other wood. Because of this ability, alder wood was used to make support piles for *Krannogs*, watermill wheels, house foundations, canal lock-gates; milk pails (related to White Cow Goddess); also for whistles and musical pipes. To think it was solely associated with water would be to underestimate this great tree, for its use as charcoal connects it with smiths' and potters' furnaces. Thus it was sacred to Phoroneus, an oracular hero (like Bran) and inventor of fire; it was also linked to Astarte and her son, the Fire God. Why it was related to the dogwood (*Cornel*) can now be understood. Felling an alder is reported to bring fire to a house (via the agent of lightning, I wonder?). In the *Angar Cyvyndawd* the question is asked, 'Why is the Alder of reddish-purple colour?' When one realizes that cut wood turns red like blood, and the bark gives a red dye, and the twigs brown, one starts to see the answer.

In an Irish legend 'The first man was created from an alder tree and the first woman from a mountain ash [rowan]; in Sandinavia, the couple came from an *Aske* (*Askr*, ash) = man, and *Emba* (rowan) = Woman. *Yggdrasil*, the kosmic ash, is stationed at the South, flanked by the male alder and female rowan in our Shamanistic Calendar. On Kalypso's Island it is mentioned along with the willow as a tree of resurrection.

That Bran's bird totem is the 'raven' shall soon command more significance.

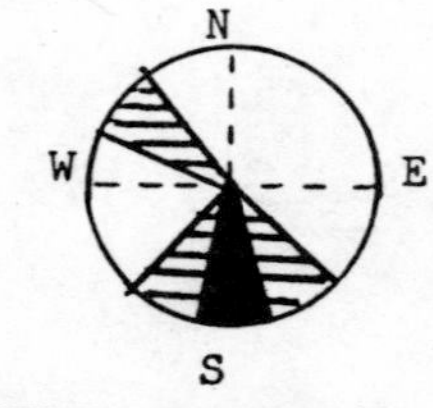

BEECH PHOGOS

In some of the Ogham source texts, beech is called *Phogos*, which may well relate it to bright white light, and thereby Finn, the God of Southern white luminence. As the '*F*' of *Fearn* equates with '*Ph*' there is a sonorious link with *Phogos*. From Greek mythology we encounter beech trees on Jupiter's (Jun-Pater, the Sky Father's) Alban mountain. Also, Diana's husband, the 'King of the Wood' (beech), is the focus of a sacrificial ritual in a grove on the Alban Hills. Now the use of Alban could be coincidental, but I think not, for Alban derives from the root Alb/Alp, which means 'white', and can be found wherever the Aryan peoples have wandered in their naming of topographical features. Having spent much time since I was a child in a primordial sacred beech wood, my psychic impression of this noble tree has always been of an upright, dignified, clear light and strong, tender friend of man. I feel as much at home calling it 'the Mother (or Queen) of the Wood' as 'the King'.

Flower buds are formed abundantly only in hot dry summers, so that beechmast years only follow on from such conditions. Anciently beechmast was used as a food in times of need, as well as providing abundant fodder for many woodland creatures and the herds of swine turned out into the oak and beech woods in the autumn (another time of prominence). The beechmast or 'buck' features in the etymology of Buckinghamshire, Buxton, etc. 'Beech' was also a popular kenning for 'literature' or 'books', for many of the writing tablets were made of beechwood.

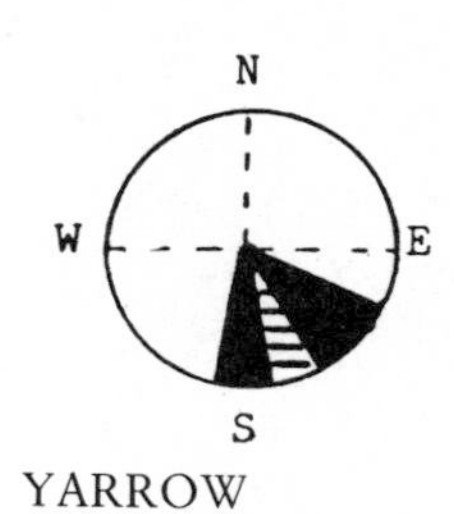

YARROW

Apart from its Beltaine Station, this magical plant was also collected on the Summer Solstice (St John's Day), the belief being that the bunches would keep illness away. An Orkadian witch, Elspeth Reoch, used to cure people with the herb melefour (millfoil = yarrow); this was one of the 'crimes' she was tried for in 1616. The Beltaine divination practice was where young lasses went out to a yarrow patch, bent down, closed their eyes and pulled what came first to hand, repeating the words:-

O its a bonny May mornin,
I cam t'pu the yarrow;
I hope before I go,
To see my marrow,

(or, sometimes:)

Good morrow, good morrow,
To thee, braw yarrow,
And thrice good morrow to thee;
I pray thee tell me today or tomorrow
Wha is my true lover to be.

They then opened their eyes and looked about in all directions as far as the eye could see. If a man was visible, the girl who spied him was to get a marrow that year. In some districts they went out on the first night of May (again in silence), carried the yarrow home, and went to bed without speaking a word. During the night the future husband would appear in a dream.

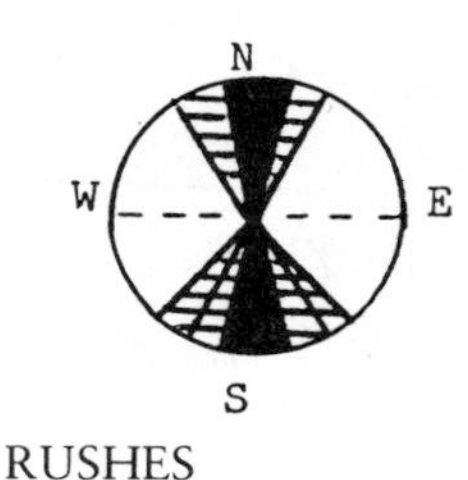

RUSHES

The several kinds of rushes have literally dozens of Keltic names, a few of the most interesting being: *Bog-luachair* for bulrush (Luachair means 'wind', also 'being of light', as in *Luachair-pin* = leprechaun); *Bull-segg* for reedmace (and gelded bull; see also Seg-purpoise); *Toad-rush* for coe grass; *Eireaball-cait* for cat's tail or reedmace; *Seave* for rush (Old Norse = *Sef*); *Thrush* for rush. The soft rushes which in olden times were made into rush-lights were best gathered at midsummer; beeswax was sometimes mixed with the grease to enable the soaked rushes to burn longer and cleaner through the winter nights. In far-off days, when the Church was marginally more in touch with nature, this was the time of the year when cartloads of rushes were gathered to strew the floors of all churches through the wet and muddy days to come. At Grasmere in Cumberland, a traditional rush-bearing ceremony is still held, with young maidens dressed in green dresses, white blouses, yellow flower circlets, and bearing the green and yellow rushes on a white sheet.

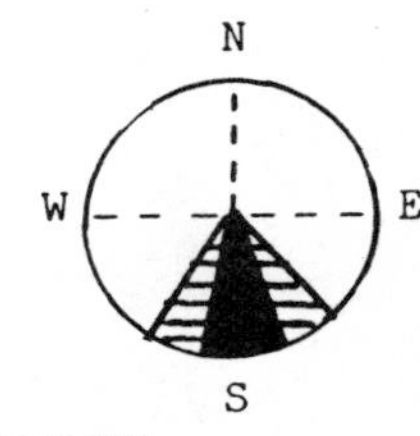

FENNEL

In herbalism, fennel is described as mercurial (remember Hermes–Thoth). Fennel seeds were used at Summer Solstice rites to render the magic worker invisible. As an infusion in tea it works powerfully on the faculties of consciousness. In British Folklore it is described as being a favourite food of serpents/adders, since it cures their failing eyesight and aids the sloughing of their skins (by rubbing against it). Prometheus is recounted as having carried the stolen fire in a (giant) fennel stalk. Fennel stalks were later religiously used to carry the new sacred fire ('needfire') from the sacred bonfire to the household hearths after the yearly, or half-yearly, ritual extinction.

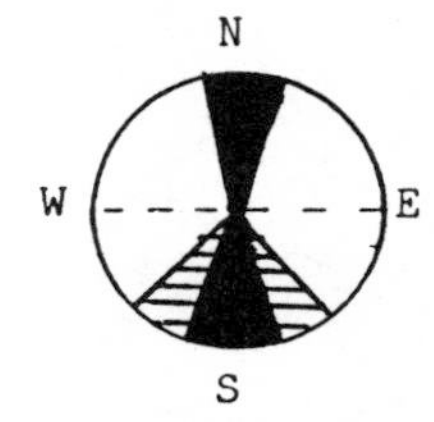

FERN RAINECH or NGETAL

The Shamanistic Station of the fern is proclaimed loud and clear in traditional Lore: 'Fern seed obtained on Midsummer Eve was believed to possess great power and protected the possessor from all evil influences. The gathering of the seed was dangerous, for the Faerie Folk were jealous of mortals who acquired it. "Only on Midsummer Eve," it is said, "can it be gathered from the wondrous night-seeding Fern. On that one night it ripens from twelve to one, and then it falls and disappears instantly ... It has the wonderful property of making people invisible".'

As in the saying 'We have the receipt of fernseed, we walk invisible (IH4, 2, 1).' These seeds at mid-summer are said to 'blossom' like gold or fire, and are also accredited with inspiring prophetic dreams or reveries (three grains of them could summon any living creature). This 'royal' fern features prominently on Wildfolk and medieval Goddess tapestries.

The fern was associated with thunder and lightning, and cutting, burning or even pulling a fern may cause rain to fall. The fern being totemistic to lightning, it was held to protect houses against being struck by lightning. Intimately bound up with its associations with the lightning serpent and the fern's links to adders (which they attract) and the decoctions and poultices made from it to treat adder bites (homeopathic). St Patrick, that curse upon Eirinn's ancient faith, in his usual style cursed all ferns as a harbourage for the Druidical adders. Another piece of Lore worth noting was that: 'On Midsummer Eve; cut away all but 5 of the unrolled fronds, and the result will look like a gnarled hand; it must be smoked and hardened in the bonfire, and then will protect the household, cattle, etc., against demons and witchcraft.' The nightjar (or fern owl) feeds off the fern-chaffer, a winged beetle linked to the oak-tree cycle in May and at the Summer Solstice.

To a lesser extent, the fern had a Shamanistic North Station: carrying seeds in the hand at the Winter Solstice helped to find underground treasure troves of gold, etc. We can thus understand how in old Ogham lists it (along with the dark seed-pods of broom, 'dead men's rattle') was ascribed to *Ngetal*; and in Greece linked to Hades–Pluto (especially maidenhead fern).

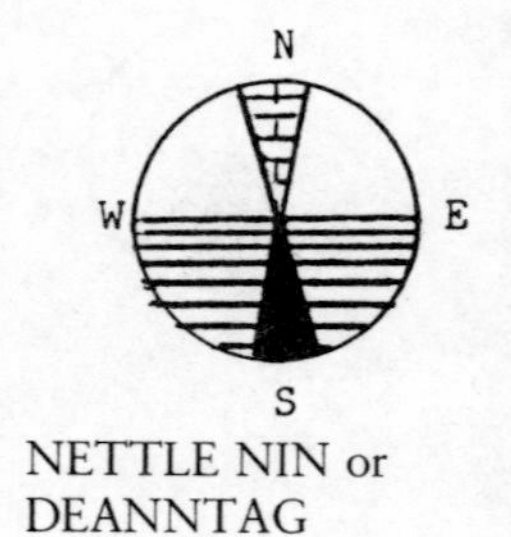

NETTLE NIN or DEANNTAG

The main Shamanistic Station of nettle is South (midsummer), with a secondary role in Shamanistic North (midwinter/earth). This was encoded into its Ogham name *Nin*, linked to that for an ash tree, *Nuin*. Nettles are also connected with thunder and lightning (protective). It is held that the Great Serpent lord imbued this plant with a little of his poison; it could therefore be called 'the Adder of the Plant Kingdom' (a phrase coined by myself). The pain from its stings is far from being 'bad'; indeed Edward O'Donnelly related that a famous painter suffering from severe rheumatism was brave enough to strip naked and roll in a nettle clump on several consecutive days, thereby effecting a complete cure. Less desperately, young nettle leaves chopped into salad was a widely used spring tonic, and nettle herb tea is still used as a diuretic and purifier.

'According to the gypsies, nettles grow chiefly in places where there is a subterranean passage to dwellings of the *Pçuvus* or Earth-fairies, therefore it is consecrated to them and called *Kásta Pçuvasengré, Pçuvus*-wood. Hence the gypsy children while gathering nettles for pigs sing:'

Cádcerli ná pçábuvá!	Nettle, nettle do not burn,
André ker me ná jiáv,	In your house no one shall go,
Kiyá pçuvus ná jiáv	No one to the Pcuvus goes,
Tráden, tráden kirmorá!	Drive, drive away the worms!

We have now arrived at the mighty Sky Father's ash tree, one of the most important trees in Indo-European mythology, and hence in our ritual calendar. It is reputed to have sprung up from the blood of Uranus's castrated genitals. In Apollonius of Rhodes' *Argonautica* we can read that Zeus fashioned the 'Bronze' race of men from ash trees. Similarly, in Scandinavian mythology the First Man (*Aske*) was made from an ash tree (*Aske*), whilst the First Woman (*Emba*) was made from an elm/alder/rowan tree. As a latterday echo of this belief, Pennent, in his tour through the Scottish highlands, noted the following custom: 'In many parts of the Highlands at the birth of a child, the nurse puts the end of a green stick of *ash* into the fire, and while it is burning receives into a spoon the sap or juice which comes out at the other end and administers this to the new-born babe.'

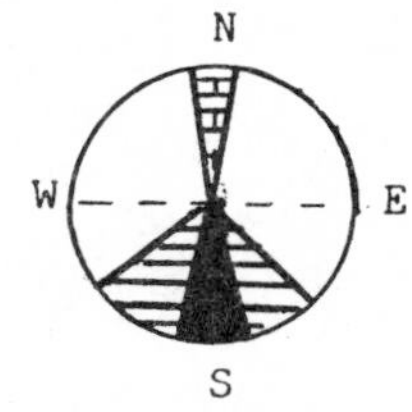

ASH TREE NUIN, UIN or ONN

Ashe-Ygge-Drasill–'Ash tree that is the horse of Ygge [Odin]' – is famous as the Shamanistic vehicle that Odin hung upon whilst he grasped the essence of the kosmic laws, the runes (see my book on the runes). This sacred ash *Yggedrasil* had an eagle in the topmost branches that saw everything that happened in the world, a cockerel–tree-serpent called Vidofnir in the lower branches, and a squirrel called Ratasok that ran up and down from the roots to the crown bearing news of what was going on in the worlds of men, elves and dwarfs – if these are not Shamanistic conceptions, then nothing is.

The early Kelts also shared this reverence for the sacred ash tree – three of the five sacred trees of Eirinn were ashes (the two others being a yew and oak); indeed the one in the Shamanistic centre of all Ireland was the Ash Bile Uis-nech in Co. Meath. In the Far East the Banyan trees was used as a ritual equivalent. This tree wisdom has left a strong imprint on Indo-European word-roots: *Ask, Esk, Isk, Usk, Us, Os, Oks* and *Uin, (N)uin, Nion, On* all denoting ash or South/North totemistic concepts (lizards, adders, snipes, newts, etc.). The Gaulish Goddess On-Niona, worshipped in ash groves, has a name compounded of *Onn and Nion*, which conveys the feminine aspect of this 'Venus of the Woods' (ash tree in Middle Welsh is *Onn-en*). Cognate with this are the Irish words *Uinde*, 'act of seeing, beholding', and *Uindim*, 'I see'; (cognate with Hb'Ayin) also the Oghamized Irish word for 'heaven', *Nionon* (*Nion-on*). In Icelandic *Aske* means 'blaze of the great fire', whilst the Italic *Fraxinus* denotes 'great fire-light'.

The old Shaman Druids carved magical images (*Alraun*) from ash-tree roots, which were denoted as a type of 'mandrake'. When making a divining rod from ash wood it was best to cut it on the Summer Solstice (St John's Day) – such a Druid ash-wand with spiral decoration was found on Môn (Anglesey). It was also held that those who ate the red ash buds on Midsummer's Eve (St John's Eve) would be rendered invulnerable to black witchcraft. Whilst the besom, used by white witches to fly (astrally) through the sky, was made from an ashen pole, with birch twigs and osier bindings. Like the oak, the ash tree was believed to attract lightning, and was thus used in sacred-fire/rain-making ceremonies. In many areas (e.g., Somerset) the wassailing bowl was 'made of the good ashen tree', or it was of 'white maple'. And to call back the Sun God, the Yule log or ashen faggot was a bundle of bound ash-logs used at the Winter Solstice.

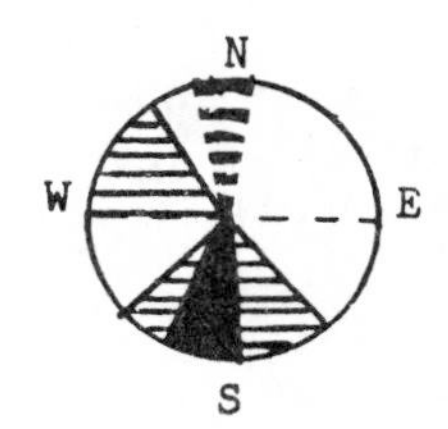

ROWAN MOUNTAIN-ASH TREE LUIS

The rowan tree stands as a somewhat feminine equivalent to the ash as a type for the kosmic tree, hence it is known as 'the Lady of the Mountain'. Its Ogham name is *Luis*, cognate with *Loise*, meaning radiance, brilliance, glory, blaze, flame, glow; this does not refer simply to its flame-red berries, but rather to the Great Power of White Light it radiates (perceived by those with psychic sight). Thus it is not surprising that it was glossed *Li Sula*, 'Delight of the Eye'. Some of its other names are *Roden, Royan, Rown* or *Ran* tree (Scandinavian *Reynie*); these are said to derive from the root for red, *Ruidh*, but the other meaning of *Ruidh, Rod*, is 'wheel', and that makes every bit as much sense. It would thus be significant that *Roks* (Spinning wheels) and spindles were commonly made of rowan wood, the wood being gathered between Beltaine and midsummer.

As the archetypal tree, this 'Lady of the Mountain' has its main Station at the height of summer – this is reflected in the Highland version of the Tale of Fraoch (given in the Dean of Lismore's book). The rowan tree is a Keltic Tree of Life, guarded by a serpent, bearing special fruit every month and every Quarter, the red berries staving off hunger month by month. Similarly, when 'He [Diarmuid] went on walking the plain, and as he was looking about him, he saw a great tree [rowan] with many twigs and branches, and a rock beside it, and a smooth-pointed drinking-Horn on it, and a beautiful fresh well at its foot.'

At its opposite Station of the Winter Solstice the *Reynie* (rowan) covers itself with lights (the stars) which the strongest wind cannot put out, according to Icelandic legend. Another Scandinavian legend relates that Thor was in danger of being swept away in the strong current of the Otherworld River Vimar, when he managed to grasp onto a mountain-ash tree, and ever since then the rowan has been held in sacred respect by the worshippers of Thor. The autumn rowan berries are still regarded as sacrosanct by the Finns.

The rowan pre-eminently, above all other Keltic trees, was linked to high pure magic (Druidism, Shamanism or white witchcraft). It was thus named '*Fid na nDruad*', 'the Druid's tree'. The three fiery Arrows of Brighid (Bridhe) were said to be of Rowan wood, which might relate to the triple-arrow sign of Awen /|\ – knowledge and inspiration. These were directly linked to the wisdom of the Koelbren and Ogham ciphers, as we hear: 'Then Menw ap Teirgwaedd took the three rowan-rods growing out of the mouth of Einigan Gawr [Kymraeg God of Wisdom], and learned all the kinds of Knowledge and Science written on them, and taught them all, Except the name of God which has originated the Bardic secret, and blessed as he who possesses it.'

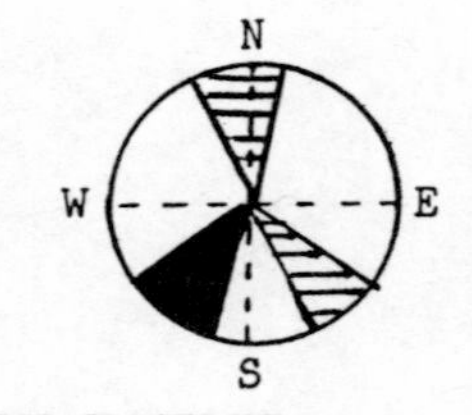

BIRCH TREE COMMON (BEITH, BETH) & SILVER (BEITH GHEAL)

In nearly all the Indo-European tongues the word for birch derives from a root meaning 'bright', 'shining' (similar to the word-cognate with roots for ash and rowan). Examples are: Old Norse *Bjork* (*Bjarte* = bright); Old High German *Birihha* (cognate with *Beraht* = bright); Latvian *Birkstis* (glimmering); Late Vedic *Bhurja* (cognate with *Flagro* = flame, give out light); Avestan *Braz* (to Shine, Glitter (related to Greek *Phlox, Phlego* = to give out light). As before, I do not think this refers just to the beautiful bright-coloured bark of the silver birch or the white (alba) birch; rather, essentially, to the inner light it gives out.

That birch was one of the two or three trees employed as 'the Kosmic Tree' (mainly of Shamanistic South Station) is amply demonstrated by the fact that it was used for Maypoles (*Axis Pillar*) in Keltic and other regions, and as the Shaman's sky ladder in Siberia and Lapland (and North America). It is thus significant that the birch as the pillar of existence should have cognate words in Gaelic, such as *Bith* (existence, world), *Bith* (enduring, constant) and *Bithe* (womanly, feminine). In this light may be understood the Scandinavian legend that it would be around a birch that the last world battle for existence would be fought. Birch was the wood used for the first Ogham inscription in Ireland which was a note to Lugh (the Sun and Spear God) about his wife being taken into Faerie. As Lugh's totem animal is the big cat, *Lug* (lynx, mountain lion), it is worth nothing that: '*Cloimh-chat* – catkin, cat-wool, inflorescence of the birch, beech, willow, etc. The catkin wool was twined into a three-ply cord, and that into a circle, to safeguard against unseen powers.'

At Whitsun (June), Russian girls used to sing, 'Rejoice, Birch Trees, Rejoice, Green ones! To you go the Maidens! To you they bring pies, cakes and omelettes.'

The festival fires were of oak, but on Beltaine twigs of birch were used for the kindling. The Maypole was also usually required to be a birch tree, and in Wales a living, standing birch tree. Traditionally the Mayday love-making frolics took place in a birch forest. [Dedicated to the Scandinavian Fertility Goddess Frigga, Frig-off, etc.] In a tale from Dumbartonshire a young Princess runs away to a birch forest where she meets and falls in love with a noble Elven Prince. Whilst the famous lovers Diarmid and Grainne sheltered in huts made of birch branches, when pursued through Argyll.

Several sexual allusions (including that to the cuckoo's nest) are made by Iolo in these famous lines):

Is it true, the girl that I love,
That you do not desire Birch,
The strong growth of Summer.
Be not a nun in Spring,
Ascetism is not as good as a bush.
As for the warrant of ring and habit
A green dress would ordain better.
Come to the spreading Birch,
To the religion of the trees and the cuckoo.'

In the pack of lies that Robert Graves tried to pass off as a Celtic Tree Calendar, he placed the birch in January, ignoring all the above noted summer, sun and sky symbolism (even the wet-loving common birch has these roles).

Like other white magic trees, its wood was employed to ward off black witchcraft, by making cradles; also, birch rods were used to drive out bad spirits from delinquents and lunatics. In Folksong birch is often associated with a return from the summer lands, 'Heaven':

At the Gates of Paradise that Birk grew fair enough.

Or linked to summer roses:

That bonny snoode of the Byrk sa green,
And these Roses the fairest that ever was seine.

The first of the yew's two main Shamanistic Stations is at *Lughnasadh*. In this context we must remember that it was often employed for Ogham staves. Also yew, as the commonest wood used to make long-bows, was fitted with birch-shafted arrows and eagle-feather flights (Lugh/Lleu's totem bird), beeswax and silken strings. The pioneering dowser T.C. Lethbridge dowsed yew wood in almost exactly the same place on his compass-rose diagram (see page 00) as it is in this Ogham Wheel. Finally, the Irish Keltic Yew Divinity, Fer h-I, 'Man of Yew', was associated with the Druidical power to render invisible (*Fath-fith*); as is noted in the Book of Leinster: 'Fer Fith was found in his Yew.'

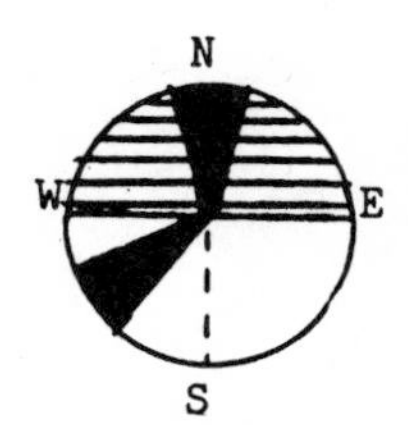

YEW (1) IBAR, IODHA, EBUR, I.

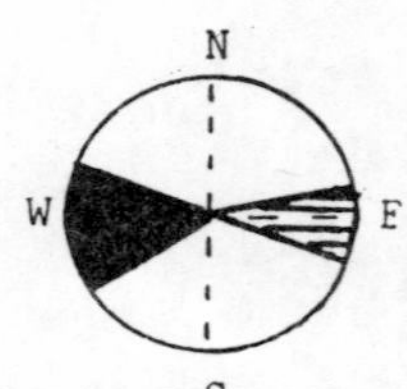

GOOSEBERRY IPHIN, IFIN, KRANN-SPIONAN

Goose gogs (the Egg-shaped fruits of this tree or bush are ready from *Lughnasadh* to the Autumn Equinox – this coincides with the powertime according to the Ogham Cipher. The Wildwoman 'Gooseberry Wyfe' could take on the appearance of a giant hairy caterpillar in British Tales (exactly the same is recorded about the Slavic gypsy '*Wolos*' being). The Gooseberry Wife may also be noted as the stork who brings each child into incarnation and deposits it 'under the gooseberry bush' = Shamanistic East (possibly other spiny thorn bushes as well, e.g., gorse).

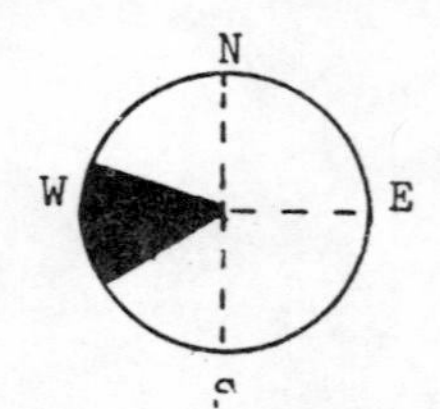

ASPEN WHITE POPLAR EODA, EBAD, EASHAIDH

The Ogham Station (water, sea and sunset) of these two trees is amply supported by Indo-European Lore. It is called 'the shaking ash' (= Shamanistic West, *Ask*); the biological purpose of the shaking of the aspen's leaves is to evaporate vast quantities of water which the tree channels. (Poplar bark was used as a urinary cleanser in herbalism.) In Irish *Ebad* (aspen) was called '*Snamchain feda*, "most boyant of wood", "fair-swimming wood" to wit, that is the name for "the great raven" (*Don Bran More*)' = *Muir-fedach* = sea raven = cormorant, shag. 'E' is also a name for the salmon at this Ogham Station, and Eonask the dipper (or water-craw).

In Keltia aspen and poplar wood was made into shields; in Greek '*Aspis*' actually means '*shield*'. The Indic '*Sphya*' means 'front oar' or 'punting pole' and is cognate with Persian '*Fah*' = 'oar, paddle'.

The Wildfolk Faeries were believed to frequent aspen trees and to give omen-messages from the quivering of the leaves in the wind. In Greek mythology Persephone had a grove of poplars in the Far West (sunset), and the Death Goddess had a grove that grew on Kalypso's Island of the Blessed. Whilst the Ancient Irish *Fe*, or measuring rod, used by coffin-makers on corpses was made of aspen as a symbol of hope. This tradition was strangely perverted by Church leaders in the Western Isles, who repeatedly cursed the poor aspen tree for allegedly being the wood of the Cross. Whilst in nature, during the severe Siberian winters, aspen does a kindness by providing food for deer, bears, rabbits, etc., in the form of its seeds, buds, twigs and shoots.

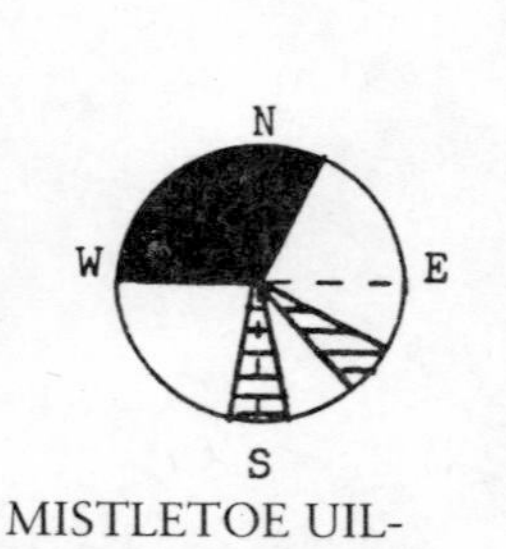

MISTLETOE UIL-IOK UKHELWYDD

The mistletoe was called '*Druad-lus*', 'the Druid's Plant', because of its sacredness in the eyes of the Keltic Shaman Priests. As the Kymraeg word *Ukhelwyl* means 'high festival', mistletoe was obviously the 'wood' (*Wydd*) of the High Festival (Alban Arthuran?). Other variant Irish Gaelic names include: *Rug Oarak, Oruiolur, Ireal-oar*. The clusters of these writhing green plant-serpents have a complex and ambivalent nature – mistletoe graces its host tree, but later can sap and kill it. It was called 'the thunder besom' in Switzerland, and was widely held to be deposited on the branches by a lightning flash (hence by the High God). The physical agent of its spreading is the mistle thrush (storm cock, thunder cock, thristle cock).

As mistletoe does not grow readily on the oak tree (though it is most sacred on such, it has been said that the Druids especially grafted it upon certain oak trees. In its Keltic and West European forms it is more commonly found upon poplars, apple trees, ash, whitethorn, willows, rowans, lindens, pear and maples (mostly Shamanistic summer trees). It is considered as the spermatozoa (semen) of the spirit of the host tree; indeed, the Aborigines say that spirit children are contained in bunches of mistletoe, equivalent to the Keltic Wildfolk.

Its sacred use goes back to the Bronze Age (and probably long before), for within a tumulus at Gristhorpe was bound an oak coffin containing a human skeleton covered with oak branches and decayed vegetable matter identified as mistletoe. And, against the scepticism of modern botanists, the mistletoe anciently grew North into the Highlands of Alba, for there is an historical tradition that a member of the Hays of Errol (in Perthshire) would each Samhain walk thrice (*deasuil*) round the 'ancient oak' and cut a sprig of mistletoe from it with a new *Dirk* (dagger); the berries were accredited with much good magic (for they were held to have fallen from the lips/genitals of Thomas the Rhymer, a thirteenth-century sage).

The *h-Uil-Iok* (*Hwl-Iog*), 'all-heal', was much employed in Folk medicine, e.g.: 'A powder made of the mistletoe given in doses of three grains at the full of the Moon to persons troubled with epilepsy, prevents fits; and if given during a fit it will effect an immediate cure.' It was also used as a liniment to dispel stiffness, a cure for stitches of the side, a panacea for 'green' wounds (gangrene) and a nerve-tonic. It has the ability to relax the motor nerves and muscles; also, if the sample is potent and the imbiber correctly prepared, it can aid the psychic 'watcher' state of consciousness (as I can testify). A decoction of mistletoe was given to promote the discharge of calving cows; in Worcestershire farmers took the Christmas mistletoe bough from the wall and gave it to eat to the first cow that calved after New Year's Day (giving good luck to the whole herd).

The Druids, when guided by a dream, went to a sacred mistletoe-bearing oak, and one of their company climbed into the branches, where he would adopt a Wildman stance (one-legged, one-armed) and with one stroke of his golden sickle (*Aurea*) send a bunch of mistletoe tumbling down to the white linen sheet below; this was done in and around the Winter Solstice, preferably on the sixth day of the Moon. Some say the sickle was a brass/bronze implement (*aera*) – but the Gaelic alternative names support 'gold'.) The '*Dour-dero*', 'vigour of the oak', was held to assist the Sun God to be reborn after its weakest winter period.

In Scandinavian myth the mistletoe was once slighted, and in revenge became the arrow that killed the Sun God Balder; but, when Balder was later resurrected, the mistletoe was reinstated and dedicated to the Goddess of Love, Frigga. The semen-like berries were worn as an amulet to promote conception in women; when the branch was kissed under at New Year; and it was one of the branches in the Beltaine fertility bundles.

Heather has two main Shamanistic Stations:- one at the height of summer, where it does indeed shelter the adder and lizards (heather *ask*), reflected in the practice of Clan Donald chiefs who all carried into battle 'a bunch of wild heather [ling] hung from the point of a quivering spear'; the second Station is at Shamanistic West (its Ogham place) – here after the late summer blossoming of some species, the bees gather and make their beautiful heather-honey. Apart from being a prime ingredient in mead, it may well have been a constituent of Pictish barley ale: According to C. F. Lloyd in *Elixirs of Life* (1947), 'The ancient Picts were said by Boethius to have made a beer from the flowers of the heather. The secret of heather beer is said to have died with the Picts. There is a tradition that two survivors, father and son, preferred to die rather than to yield the secret to a victorious enemy.' This is preserved in the Pictish and Brythonic word for beer/booze = *Grog*, cognate with Kymraeg *Grug*.

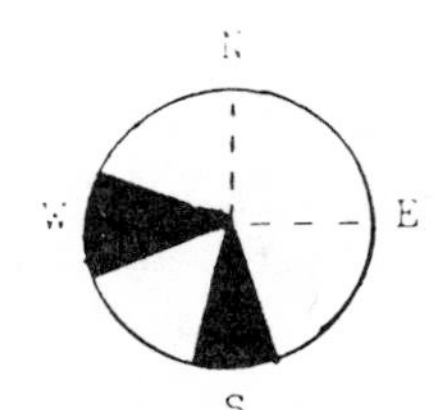

HEATHER H-ADDER UR, URA, GRUG-MEL LING, HEATH.

Anciently, rough ropes were twisted out of heather, and tightly packed branches were formed into springy fragrant mattresses. The 'sprig of tufted heather' (*bar Gaganach Fraoch*) is linked to the Wildman (*Gogan*) with the tufted hair; whilst the feminine Keltic Heather Goddess was Ura, in Gaul called Uroica (cognate with Greek *Ereike* = heather). Finally, in Bach flower remedies, heather is described as 'generous, understanding, willing to help others' – no wonder a sprig of heather is considered 'lucky'.

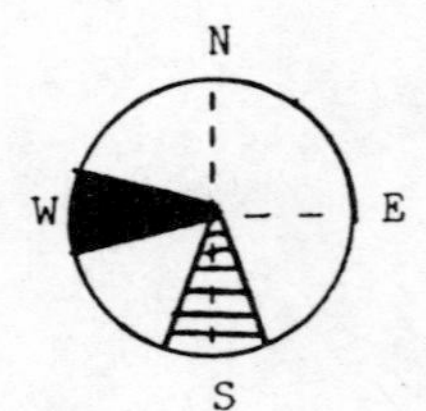

HONEYSUCKLE
WOODBINE
UILLEANN
DUILLIUR-F.

In the Ogham sayings honeysuckle is known as '*Tutmur fid Uilleann*' – 'a juicy wood is the woodbine'. This 'mother of the wood' was believed to give young girls erotic dreams, so prudish mothers in the Fenlands banned it from the house (else 'a wedding would follow shortly' – we know what would have preceded that!). It was called 'luscious woodbine', for the sensuous snake-twinning of two pieces of woodbine together denotes the amorous embrace of two lovers. As the great Bard Burns said, 'Aft hae I rov'd by bonie Doon, To see the Woodbine twine.' As I write this, it evokes memories of the corner of a wood (near my birthplace) which was hung with great curtains of honeysuckle traceries, possessing a degree of Faerie peace and beauty.

Its name *Caprifoyl/Caprifolium* links it with the lusty goat of Pan, for goats ate it with relish and its leaves were said to resemble goats' ears. Its Anglo-Saxon name is *Barebind* or *Baerbine*, linking it with wild barley, which it may have grown beside in clearings and hedgerows (it was also perhaps used in beer-making). Finally, this plant is known as 'evening pride'.

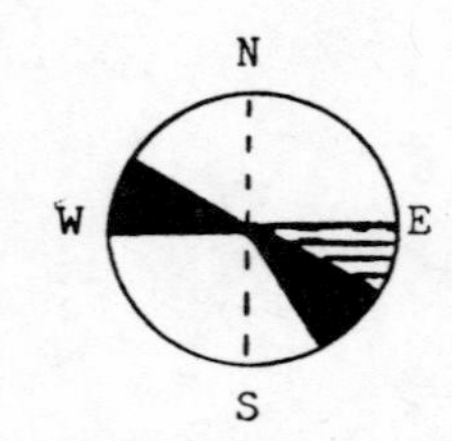

BROOM OIR,
BEALADH ng-GETAL
Luth-legha

This is a Faerie bush and has hidden magical powers when used with knowledge. Its first power Station is when its erotic and heady smelling blossoms waft over sunny braes in spring. An example of its magical use at this time is preserved in the ballad 'The Broomfield Hill', in which a young lady has for a bet arranged a tryst with a male suiter, but has second thoughts and wondered how she can keep both her word and her maidenhead; she consults a Wise Wyfe (witch), who tells her that, if she creeps up to the trysting place she'll find the young man asleep in the sunshine, then she should:

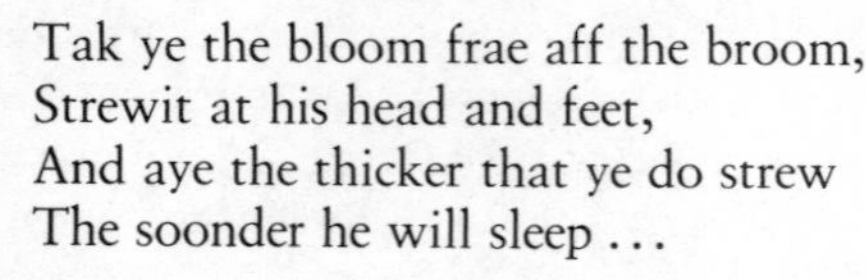

Tak ye the bloom frae aff the broom,
Strewit at his head and feet,
And aye the thicker that ye do strew
The soonder he will sleep . . .

The lady leaves a token to show she has been, and leaves to collect her wager. This sleep-inducing quality of broom is echoed in this ancient Kymraeg verse:

Bright the tops of the broom; let the lover make suggestions;
Very yellow are the clustered branches;
Shallow ford; the contented is apt to enjoy sleep.

The flowering branches were used as a house decoration at the Whitsuntide festival and at Beltaine, but should not be employed as a brush whilst in flower. The young buds of the flowers were also eaten as a salad delicacy in medieval times. Before hops were commonly used here, the tender green tops were employed to give a little sharp or bitter flavour to beer, and make it more intoxicating as well. Both the flowers, ground seeds and decoction of twigs were/are used in herbalism, mainly as a diuretic and stimulant of the liver, etc. – it was called in Gaelic '*Luth-legha*', a physician's strength and healer's help.

Broom was also known as *Kow*, *Kowe*; this primarily denoted a 'branch', hence it was applied to the besom (= thunder broom/brush), and to a Wildman

(*Kow*) of strong temperament 'to overbear', 'to scare'. (It was also dedicated to the God Mars.) This name is preserved in the place (and song) 'The Broom of the *Cow*den Knowes' (= broom-covered knolls) anciently adjacent to Glasgow. A final Shamanistic West connection is that broom will flourish within reach of sea spray and, like gorse, it is a good bush to shelter grasses and flowers whilst they are trying to become established at the seaside.

With the likes of the Black Wood of Rannoch standing as a living relic of the ancient British pine forests, we yet have living channels to tap into the old wisdom (but for how long, in the face of industrial pollution of the atmosphere?). The pine cone ('tree egg') is formed in a spiral sun-growth pattern, and thus was ideally suited to act as the magical 'conducer' at the end of the Initiate's ivy-twined Thyrsus rod.

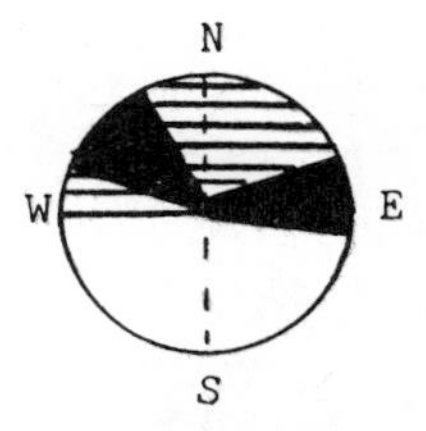

PINE AILIM GIUS OCHTACH

The Ogham saying '*A diaiu Ketlapra gach pip-lachtad gach mairb*' means 'Ah! is the first thing we utter on entering life and the last when we die' – curiously enough, this idea is supported from the Lore of other Traditions: storks (our Shamanistic incarnation guides) prefer to nest in pine or silver fir trees in early spring: 'As for the stork, the fir trees are her house' (Ps. 104, 17); in Russia at spring marriages (and generally) a decorated pine bough was presented to brides; at his death Attis was believed to have transformed himself into an evergreen pine (or fir) tree – then, 'Violets were believed to have sprung from Attis's blood, and for the Spring Festival of Kybele, a pine tree was cut down, shrowded and decorated with violets, and carried into a Phrygian sanctuary.' Whilst in Egypt. 'Tradition fostered a ceremony in which a pine tree was cut down and the centre hollowed out into a hole in which an image of Osiris was placed.' In Greece 'They associated the pine with the nymph Pitys, who was cast down from a cliff by Boreas, the jealous North Wind.'

In Keltia the Scots pine was equated with heroes and the arts and skills of the warrior class, and it was one of the Chieftain trees. (In the Bach remedies, pine (and larch) gives the qualities of 'persevering with humility and not dwelling upon mistakes made', the mode of a warrior.) This tree had its own special type of Wildman Faerie Being, as I felt in an old wood in Argyll (until all the trees were cleared three years ago).

Mythologically the fir is almost identical to the Scots pine, although perhaps marginally more feminine. It is sacred to Artemis of Childbirth, and appears as a birth-tree in nativity contexts. Dionysus was born from a fir (and to whom the Thyrsus was dedicated). In Alban the mother and newly born child were purified by having a blazing fir torch whirled three times around the bed. The fir is also sacred to Poseidon–Neptune and was used to make oars and parts of ships: 'They have made all thy ships' boards of fir [or cypress] trees of Senir' (Eze. 27.5c).

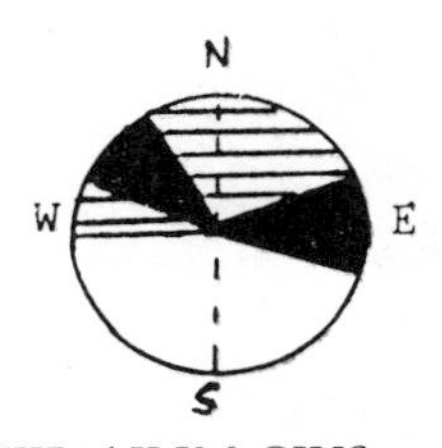

FIR AILIM GIUS

Like the palm tree (also *Ailim* in Irish), it thrives in a sandy soil, with sea breezes and salt spray. Fir cones open up to indicate hot weather, but close in when rain is on its way. *Beoir* (spruce beer) was made from the spruce. The fir is linked to the boar that killed Attis at the period known to the Kelts as Samhain (the Faerie animal for this festival being the boar, see page 00); (T. C. Lethbridge dowsed both pine and cypress around this point in the Wheel). The Gallic Fir Goddess was Druantia (Pictish Droan?). Finally, some hold that the 'Fir tree was the original Yule/Xmas tree. In the Hartz Mountains of Germany young girls danced around a fir tree to prevent the escape of a spirit being who was concealed in its branches. Until he gave them presents he was not allowed to leave.

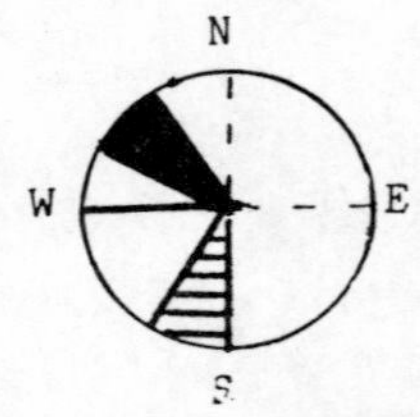

WYCH ELM WYCH
HAZEL
AMHANKHOLL

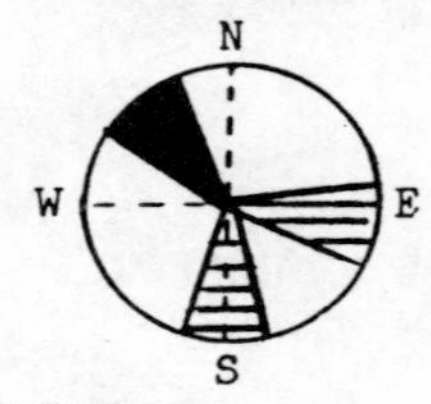

ELDER
RUIS
TRAMAN
BOUR-TREE
SKAW
SKOBIE

Uprooted fir trees were also the traditional weapons of Centaurs [Sagittarius].'

The Station of the common elms is Shamanistic South, around the rowan's position in midsummer (where T. C. Lethbridge dowsed it), whilst under the rougher wych elm was a favourite place for witches to meet. In general, it is a tree of purification (soaps and skin-cleansers are made from it). Also, the handles of mill bills or mill picks were made out of wych elm; these impliments were employed to chip the grooves across a mill stone, etc. Elms are a favourite host tree for rookeries (the Samhain totem bird).

The elder has rich and complex Folk and Faerie Lore associated with it. Its main Shamanistic Station in the Ogham Wheel is at *Ruis*, over the Samhain and November periods, when the dark clustering bunches hang from this tree (and were/are gathered to make into the excellent elderberry wine). Anciently, the hard wood was polished and made into fishing rods. Before anything is taken from this Faerie tree, permission must be respectfully asked from 'the Elder Moeder' (*Hylde-moer*), a female/male Wildfolk tree spirit. We read that: 'Elder trees were always thought of as fairy trees in the Isle of Man. There wasn't a house or farm that didn't have its "tramman tree" planted by the door or in the garden "for the fairies". It was said that they would desert a farmer's house where the elder trees had been cut down. This must have happened only very rarely: no one would cut a branch of the tramman, let alone the tree itself, but if it was done, the fairies grieved. "The old trammans at Ballakovg were cut down, and the fairies came every night to weep and lament."'

In Ireland it was held that witches' broomsticks (used as magic psychic 'horses') were made from elder branches. This would link with the Slavic gypsy practice of weaving wreaths of elder sprigs, to be worn around the head on Walpurgis Night (Samhain) so that they could see the sorceresses as they swept along through the air on their brooms, dragons, goats and other 'strange steeds'. The St Margaret's Well (previously a pagan fountain) was believed to have gushed forth where a magical hart vanished in front of King David I (at Samhain?); beside this fountain there grew up an elder tree.

The ancient Lithuanians worshipped Puschkeit, 'the lord of the Underworld', at dusk, leaving offerings under an elder tree. Among the Slovaks, magical puppets were made out of elderwood; these were called *Pikuljk* (from *Peklo*, 'the underworld'), and as 'jumping jacks' embodied such elder spirits. The Slavic Frau Holle (or German Frau Ellhorn) was the Goddess of Death and Underworld Initiations. In the very old Jewish cemetery in Prague, many elder trees were found which had grown up from twigs planted in the graves (in the Tyrol, little twig crosses were planted in the graves, and in Britain the handle of the hearse-driver's stick was made of elder wood). Thus we can understand why at the ritual killing of King William Rufus, the archer was posted under an elder tree. (There may then be something in the belief that Judas hanged himself on an elder tree on the Winter Solstice; or it may be attempted adverse Christian propaganda.)

Taking a brighter tack, the hollowed-out stem of elder branches were used as whistles; or as a pluff, bellows to blow up a fire. Chewing an elder twig was held to relieve toothache; elder branches hung up in the entrance of a cowshed keep away flies. The wood of the main stem is hard and yellowish and was used as a substitute for box wood (Shamanistic North); in East Anglia an eye ointment was made from elder leaves, and from the blossoms good skin-fresheners and cleansers are still made by herbalists.

'... some inhabitants of the Cambridgeshire village said that the elder tree afforded protection against lightning and that it was particularly lucky to have a tree growing in or near a farmyard, because it kept away evil spirits and promoted fertility among the stock'. (The Irish planted the *Kraob Troim* or traman trees beside many houses for the same reasons.) This all points to its midsummer Shamanistic Station. Likewise in the Fenlands adders were meant to congregate around elder roots and could become unwelcome guests in a house if someone had brought into it an elder branch. Finally, in several parts of Britain it was believed that, if you spent/slept Midsummer's Eve under an elder tree you could be fortunate enough to see/dream experience the King of Faerie.

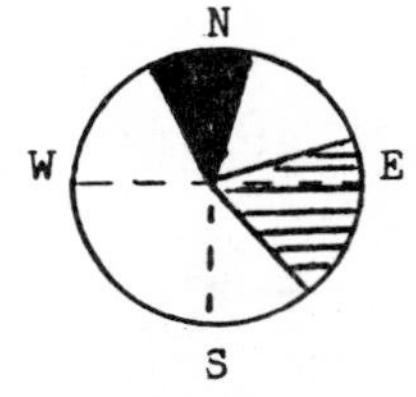

BLACKTHORN
STRAIPH
DRAIGEAN
SLAE, SLOE

In the Ogham sayings, Blackthorn is called '*Morad Rune*' – 'the Increaser of Secrets' or 'the Rune of the Great Wheel'. This related to the 'Crown that was woven from blackthorn and mistletoe on New Year's morning and hung up as a luck-bringer. 'In Worcestershire a crown of blackthorn was made before dawn on 1st January, baked in the oven, then carried to the first sown field and burnt, for its ashes to be later scattered over the furrows.' Also on 1 January, folk in the North of England used to construct a blackthorn globe and stand in a circle hand in hand around the central bonfire, chanting in monotones 'Auld Cider', prolonging each syllable to its limit (this was a fertility blessing on the sacred apple trees and their cider).

Its Shamanistic North Station of December covered the collecting of the sour-ripe blue-black drupes (the *Slaes*) and the commencement of the making of potent 'sloe gin'. In a slightly less jovial role, blackthorn branches were and are used for making the *Shilelaighs*, 'fighting sticks'; other names for the cudgels being *Rowng/Rung*, and *Kud* if a short version. Esoterically and physically this is in keeping with the blackthorn's fierce, stroppy and fighting-sharp thorniness (as anyone who has tried to crawl through a dense blackthorn thicket can testify).

In some Irish Folktales the hero is pursued by an aggressive Giant, and is instructed (by his female guide) to take 'a twig of a sloe tree' and 'throw it behind thee', Then: 'No sooner did he that, than there were twenty miles of blackthorn wood [left behind him] so thick that scarse a wheasel could get through it'; and thus was the giant slowed down until he went back and got his axe. Blackthorn spines may also have been dipped in poison to become the '*Bar an Suan*', 'pin of slumber'. It is also held that witches carried a blackthorn stick, 'the black rod', which may explain why, when witches were burned, blackthorn branches were thrown on the pyre.

The blackthorn has a secondary Station of Shamanistic East; this corresponds with March–April when, whilst braving the cold North-east winds, it puts out its blossoms upon otherwise bare branches. These blossoms have a strange potent scent, sweet yet musty and slightly erotic; at this time of the year it is known as 'the mother of the wood'. This Shamanistic Station may also explain its epithet *Tresim Ruamna*: '"*Tresim Ruamna*" – "Strongest of Red", to wit, that is Str with him in Ogham. Straif, sloe, blackthorn for the sloe red for dyeing the things is stronger, for it is it that make the pale silver become azure, making it genuine(?) silver. It is it which is boiled through the urine into white gold so as

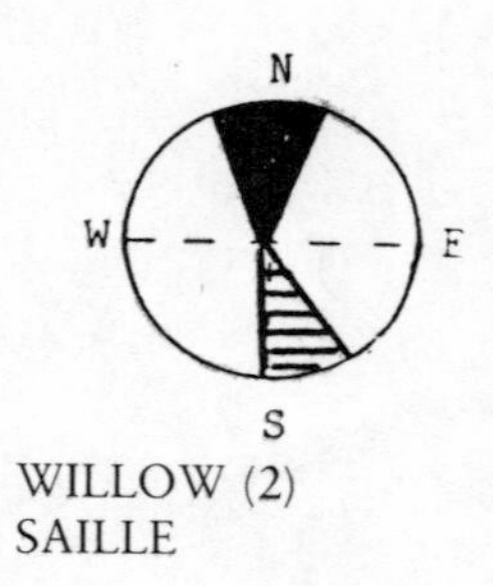

WILLOW (2)
SAILLE

to make it Red.'

I shall briefly mention the second midwinter or Shamanistic North Station of the willow, when 'the Moon owns it'. This is a Shamanistic darker watery aspect. The gypsy girls of Transylvannia believe that certain festival days were propitious for divining about their future husbands and the like, thus: 'On New Year's Eve they throw shoes or boots into a willow tree, but are only allowed to throw them nine times. If the shoe catches in the branches the girl who threw it will be married within a year.'

A British custom still maintained on 6 January (from Old Calendar) is the rough game of 'the Haxey Hood' – the leader of the players is the King Boggan (Chief Wildman) or Lord of the Hood, who carries a wand as badge of his office (it is made from a roll of thirteen willow sticks bound together with thirteen withy bands). This symbolizes the reborn Sun, which is contested for by all the men dressed in the traditional scarlet flannel coats and hats wreathed in red flowers. (The red gear giving fire power to the still weak Sun.)

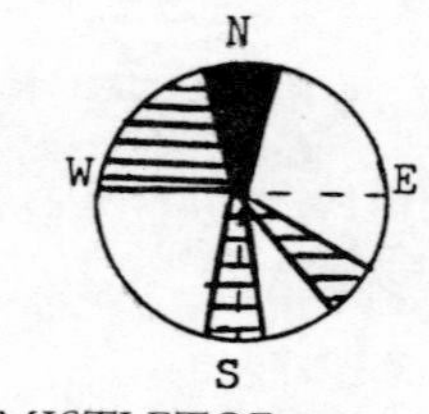

MISTLETOE
UIL-IOK
UKHELWYDD
MISSELTAN

Just a reminder that the mistletoe peaks in power at the Winter Solstice (Yule), due Shamanistic North. As this festival was anciently the real New Year (being the turning axis point in the Sun's cycle), when we read of customs, transferred or misappropriated to Christmas or 'New Year' (1 January), we should mentally reallocate them to their true Shamanistic place in the cycle. Although Church orthodoxy generally sought to obliterate all the nature-based pagan customs, one was preserved in several churches: at York Cathedral a branch of mistletoe was ceremonially laid upon the high altar, and remained there for the twelve days of Christmas. During this time a universal pardon was proclaimed at the city gates (this echoes the Keltic law that warfare had to cease when the Druidical mistletoe was employed in the Solstice Festival). In the Collegiate Church of Wolverhampton, mistletoe which had been lain on the Christmas altar was then distributed to the people. Records show that the Staffordshire churches of Bilston and Darlaston both used mistletoe and evergreens in such a manner.

It is known that anciently a 'First Foot' carried an evergreen branch in one hand and a sprig of mistletoe in the other, and upon entering a house in silence would place the evergreen on the fire, and the mistletoe above on the mantlepiece before turning to greet the building's occupants. Also, on 1 January, farmers burned a spherical globe of mistletoe and whitethorn which had been carefully kept for a whole year, and then scattered the fertilizing ashes onto the field that was to be first sown with wheat. Thereafter the 'Auld Cider' ritual was enacted.

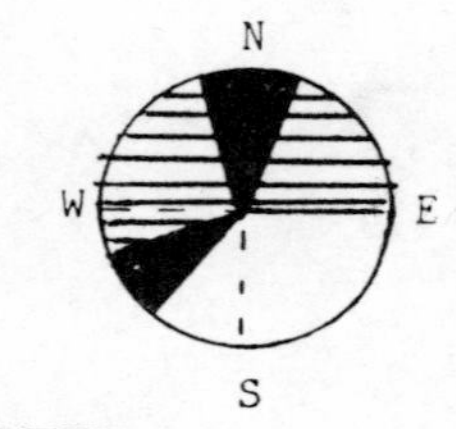

YEW
Y, I,
Ibor

At the Shamanistic North midwinter Station, all the dark evergreens stand in pre-eminence: the holly, ivy, box, pine, privet, juniper and yew. In the Keltic (Alban Arthuran) and the Scandinavian Festival of Yule-tide, an evergreen tree was decked out with lights and sparking objects; in the Roman Saturnalia a pine tree was loaded with images of Bacchus; in Greece the Feast of Light featured a decorated tree; and in the Hebrew Feast of Chanūkāh the 'Tree of Light', the Menorah, was prominent. (These are all types for the midwinter kosmic tree.) In this context we should remember the Greek practice of sacrificing a black bull to Hecate; the animal had been wreathed with yew, and its blood was offered to the harsher spirits of this festival. The yew tree is said to 'like the cold of the North Wind', and is associated with the Faerie Wildman Fer h-I, 'the Man of the Yew', or 'Fer-Fith', who could weave a Faerie darkness and through it disappear! (See page 186.) The Wildman Dobie of Mortham inhabited the dark yew grove in the vicinity. And the Irish Initiate Suibhne Geilt disappeared into a large yew tree at Ros Bearaigh in Glenn Earkain. Thomas the Rhymer and the Fingalians are meant to be residing within Tom na h-Iubhraich (knoll of the yew tree) near Inverness, where the Faerie guardians protect them until their return.

Finally, the Pictish God Gartnait D-iuber has totems in yew berries *Dearkiubhair*, and hence with the arrows (*Diubarkan*) dipped in poison made from fermenting yew needles and yew berries, and to the yew bow (*Ibhar*) that fired them. Thus to the zodiacal sign of Sagittarius, which leads up to the Winter Solstice, and the Scandinavian God Orvandel-Egil (and his son Ulle = Yule) who lived in *Ysete Ydalir*, 'the Chalet in the Dales of the Yew Bow'.

Bird Shamanism

Birds not only possess the power of physical flight, but they can, under the right circumstances, teach humans out-of-the-body psychic flight, as well as the divination of signs and omens. In such capacities they appear in many many Folk and Faerie Tales. This chapter surveys the Keltic Wheel of Birds from Shamanistic North around the year Sun-wise.

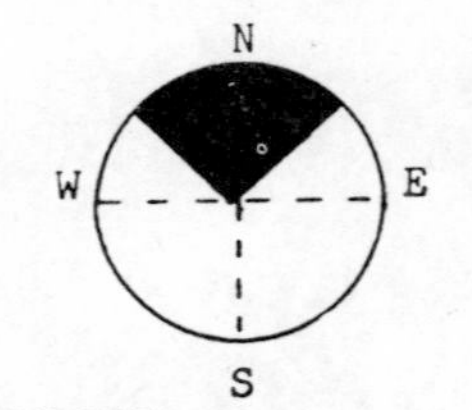

GOOSE
NGEIGH
DRAK
RUDHE

In Ogham, the name of the goose is *Ngeigh*, linked to the reeds (*Ngetal*) present in its habitat. A flight of geese is a gaggle, and a young goose in Old Norse is *Gagl*, both from the word-root *Gag* for 'wheel' and 'egg'; the *Rudhe* prefix also is tied to the *Rud/Rod* word meaning 'wheel'. The goose, in its various forms, was an immensely popular ancient totem for the Kelts. The primal goose and gander were creators; their golden egg was the Sun. In the Shamanistic Calendar its main period of influence is from Samhain (1–8 November) through St Martin's Day (11 November, when the wild geese migrate), through the Winter Solstice (wild hunt and snow goose) to the rain-bringing sign of Aquarius.

One of the main Gods who invented and presides over the secret science of the Koelbren is Gwyddion – it so happens that the root of his name '*Gwydd*' means both 'tree' and 'goose'. Thus Gwyddion as the primeval gander/drake/*Rak* presides over the Koelbren, which would be later written with a goose-quill pen. (In Egypt the goose is sacred to Osiris–Thoth, Scribe of the Gods.) Old wise Socrates even took oaths 'by the goose'. There were several carvings of a goose related to a powerful wild male deity in pre-Roman Gaul (e.g., at Roquepertuse in Gaul). Taliesin may well have been pointing in a similar direction when he said he wasn't sure if he was flesh or fish (goose or salmon, as reported of the barnacle goose – see the above Pictish stone). Other Pictish geese glyphs are to be found at Tillytarmont, East Wemyss Caves and possibly Aberlemno, the Picts being *the* Masters of Shamanistic art. The high-flying honking geese are often associated with the *Cwn Annwn* or Gabriel Ratchets which yelp across the dark midwinter skies with the wild host. Similarly the snow goose is the Goddess, for when she ruffles her feathers in blustery flight, down comes a snowstorm (the snowflakes being her numerous loose feathers). So the traditional Highland Christmas meal of a goose is either a deliberate Christian device to break an ancient taboo or the pagan-sanctioned ritual feast on sacred goose flesh. Apart from being a transformation-mode for witches to enter into, goose-form was one of the vehicles of enchantment used in Faerie (e.g., the Faerie Queen Aine transformed the Earl of Desmond's son into a goose as punishment, as she had previously done to others).

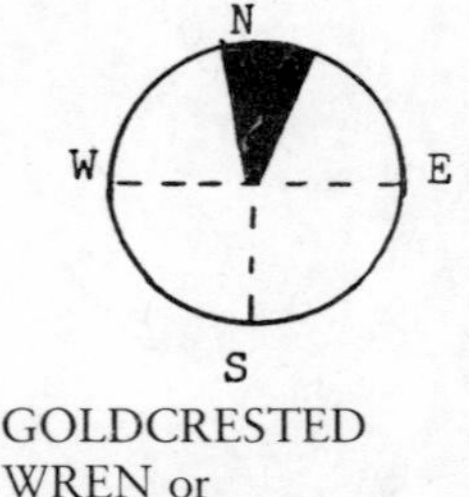

GOLDCRESTED
WREN or
FIRECRESTED-TIT

Originally the goldcrested wren was chosen to represent the death and rebirth of the Sun at midwinter. This was an excellent choice in living symbolism, for this tiny bird has a fiery crest and flits about in the evergreen fir trees, making 'a very tiny, high-trilling song like the tinkling of a fairy bell, often difficult to locate' (Q. Vere Benson). In course of time this role was transferred to its cousin, the common wren. One of the most important ritual ceremonies of the Keltic Cyclical Year revolved around 'the Hunting of the Wren' at the Winter Solstice.

In ancient Ogham the wren is known as *Druen*, and is linked to *Dur*, the oak, in the Beth-Luis-Nuin Alphabet. It is known that the Keltic Calendar was basically divided into a Light Half and a Dark Half; the Oak King ruled over the Light Half from just after the Spring Equinox, through summer to the Autumn Equinox; the Holly King ruled from just after the Autumn Equinox, through winter to the Spring Equinox, where the Green Knight and holly have their Stations; after a symbolic fight the cycle is handed over to the oak once more.

Now, if the wren is linked to the oak, should not this mean that it too rules over the Light Half of the Year, with the robin ruling over the Dark? Several things seem to support me in this theory, most importantly: the old Brythonic name for the robin (preserved in many regions of Alban and Albion) is *Ruddock*, from *Ruad-ok* meaning 'Red-ok', or from *Rud-ok* meaning 'Ok of the Wheel'. The robin is actually a member of the thrush (*Smoltach*) family, which in Ogham is related to *Straiph* (the blackthorn) in a Shamanistic North Station. Thus the robin and his lads hunt the wren at the Winter Solstice, or just after, looking in an ivy bush for 'the King' (the ivy is at this Station). The wren is beaten with birch branches (a tree from its own high Station). Sometimes the wren is described as being caught in the furze; perhaps this is an echo of when it Shamanistically ceases to rule at *Ohn* (gorse, furze), just after the Autumn Equinox, exactly opposite its initial position at *Dur* (oak). The opposite side of the coin is when the dunnock (the hedge sparrow) kills cock robin with his bow and arrow. When the wren is finally caught and killed just after the Winter Solstice, in Somerset he is carried about as 'the King' enclosed in a box with glass windows, surmounted by a wheel from which are appended various coloured ribbons (strikingly similar to the colour wheel at the centre of the Shamanistic Calendar). The 'King' (wren) is symbolically so large that he/she has to be carried on a cart pulled by six horses (six months), and seven cooks boil him/her in a 'brewer's big pan'. The relationship between these two birds is very close – they are sometimes described as being husband and wife, and on another occasion, when the wren flew to the Otherworld/Heaven to fetch fire for mankind, it returned in a blaze and the robin saved it.

In another rhyme, the robin lives on an hazel twig (which is just before the Spring Equinox, just as the Green Knight is connected with a holly club/tree at this Station. Although 'Jenny' is a female name within the witchcraft tradition, the Wren also has male associations, in that Taliesin said, '*Wyv cerdoliad; wyv saer mal dryw*' 'I am a musician, an artificer like the Wren', obviously alluding to its song being treated as augury by the Druids (who kept tame ones).

Although this complicated mystery may not be fully resolved, at least the ingredients are much more clearly perceived thanks to the Shamanistic Calendar.

As the masters of Ogham took great pains to differentiate between the whistling swan just before the Western Station, and the mute swan just past the Northern Airt, we should attempt to sharpen our perception to disentangle such threads within Keltic mythology. Thus I shall present a little of the relevant Northern Quarter Swan Lore as follows: Why should a swan be depicted with a crown and with a golden chain draped round its neck? Consider the following passage turned up by Alan Miller: 'According to a Herefordshire tradition, a fish with a golden chain around it was caught in the River Dore, and afterwards kept in the spring whence the river flows. At Peterchurch, in that county, is a sculptured stone bearing a rude representation of the fish and chain in question.' Further, why does Merlin – a Wildman, bears, dogs, etc. – have a chain attaching

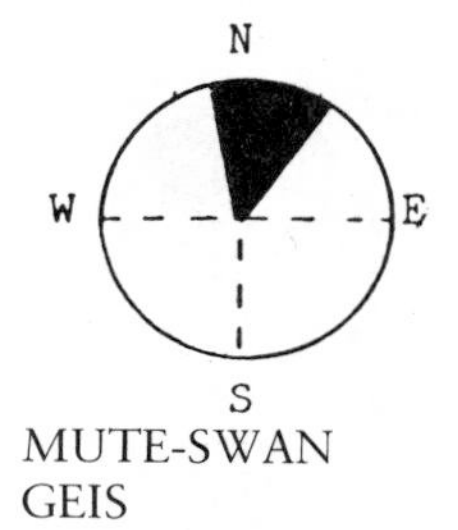

MUTE-SWAN GEIS

them to a Goddess figure? Probably for exactly the same reason that the Irish Bards carried precious chains (which, when shaken, gained them immediate silence): because they were a sacred symbol from Faerie, occasionally carried by a *Ban Sidhe* visitor to our world. The female denizens of Faerie sometimes appeared as swan maids with their magical swan-feather *Kokhuls* (coverings), whilst their male equivalents are the swan knights prominent within the more profound strata of the Arthuriad. Swans often appear as guides of the dead, taking them to the Far Northern Otherworld, through the 'swan veils' (e.g., the roles of the Valkyries). In legend, swans also pull the sun bark across the Underworld Sea during the night (cf. *Lohengrin*). On a larger scale (that of the ritual year), Apollo's chariot was drawn by swans when he flew to the land of the Hyperboreans (the people that live 'behind the North Wind'), which was both the country of his birth and of his winter residence. In the ancient Keltic Folksong 'The Swan Swims Sae Bonny O' a woman is tricked by Jean, her jealous (over a man) sister, into going to the banks of the stream to listen to the blackbird change its tune, whereupon putting her fit on the *stane* she is pushed into the stream and drowned. She is transformed into a swan maid who is washed up dead at a miller's dam, so he decides to make a fiddle (in older versions, a *Clarseach*/harp) out of her body, which when played recounts who committed the murder. This parallels stories of mute swans only singing when they are about to die. It also explains why Apollo's lyre had a swan's head, neck, feet and feathers carved upon it. The Three Norns (Fate Goddesses) who were also primal muses are connected to this mythopoetic motif, for they appear at one Station as three swan goddesses; at another, as three cranes/herons. (In this context should be remembered the *Geasa* or 'Fate bonds' laid upon us as sort of Shamanistic taboos which we break at our karmic misfortune.) Another death aspect appears in 'The Ballad of the Chevy Chase', where 'The swan feathers that his arrows bore, With his heart's-blood they were wet'. Similarly, Cycnus (*Cygnus* = the swan), the 'invunerable' (like Balder) son of Neptune, was strangled by Achilles (= Balder), thereby turning into his swan form.

The swan has, however, one aspect as a love totem, being the form into which many lovers in Keltic mythology change, or are changed into (e.g., Midir and Etain, and Zeus and Leda). The swan is also a wise bird (in the context of augury and 'philosophical mercury' in alchemy); as king of the water birds, it is the only bird the eagle thinks it worthwhile to fight. A relationship with the Sky God is hinted at in the legend that swan's eggs are hatched only during storms, the thunder and lightning breaking open the shells. All in all, a richly significant bird in our Shamanistic Tradition, well worth deep attention, respect and protection (for Britain lags far behind Eirinn with her awe-inspiring flocks of hundreds of swans gathered in Galway Bay and other such places).

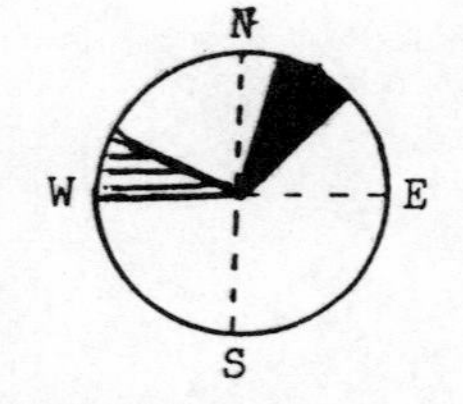

TITMOUSE
MINTAN
MIONDAN
KAILEACH

In the Ogham ciphers the great tit, blue tit, coal tit, etc., were all related to the bramble and vine's Station. A couple of the Keltic names for these birds linguistically confirm this positioning: in Scottish Gaelic *Kai* (also jackdaw), *Kailleach* (hag or old woman); *Kaileach-khean-dubh* ('old wife with the black head'); the Kymraeg *Gwas-y-Dryw'* means 'lad/servant of the Seer/Druid' or 'servant of the wren'; in Irish Gaelic it is called a 'grass moth'. Some of us may well remember this harmlessly mischievous bird removing the cream off the tops of milk bottles early in the winter mornings, and other such ingenious and acrobatic tricks.

Hens feature prominently in Keltic rituals from Brigantia (1 February) through to Easter eggs (also related to hares), etc. And the cockerel obviously has a key role, as it greets the dawn. One of the totem forms of the Goddess Keridwen is that of a high-crested black hen. It is therefore not surprising that formerly one of the commonest pastimes engaged in at this festival was cock fighting. The young lads would bring their cocks (called 'stags') to school, and the owner of the *Coileach Buadha* ('victorious cock') was elected Candlemas King. A ritual oatmeal and egg dumpling shaped like a cock called the *Fastyn*, *Festy* or fitless cock, was eaten on Fastern's E'en. Further to this, there was divination by dropping an egg into a glass and reading augury from the shapes made by the albumen. Another form of divination involved young girls chasing crows (the hag's winter bird), the direction in which the crow flew indicated her future home and husband.

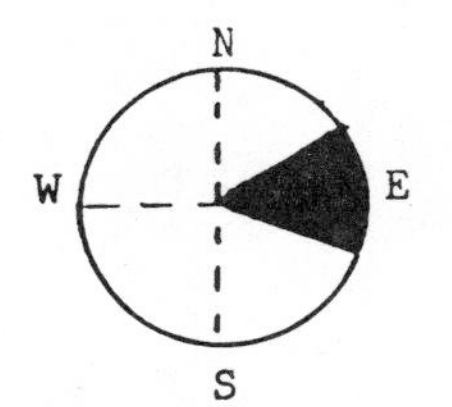

HEN & COCKREL
QUERT

Another bird sacred to the Goddess at this time is the oystercatcher (called variously ester, scolder and sea piet and 'Brigit's bird'); the oyster itself is termed a 'horse muscle'. The Goddess Bird of March and onwards was the returned (resurrected) quail, whose meat was reputedly an aphrodisiac. Zeus coupled with Leto whilst both in quail form. Lascivious quail celebrations were held in honour of the Spring Goddess. Iolus revived Heracles by holding a quail to his nostrils. And the courage and fighting qualities of this bird were further exploited in quail fights (similar to cock fights in Keltic lands).

The tribe of birds – herons, cranes, egrets, spoonbills, benu birds, storks, pelicans, etc., are exceedingly important throughout the whole of European mythology. Even allowing for loss in Lore over the passing centuries, there is still a voluminous amount, as my nine-page article in *Inner Keltia* No. 6 demonstrates. Therefore I shall make a small selection pertinent to our Ogham investigations.

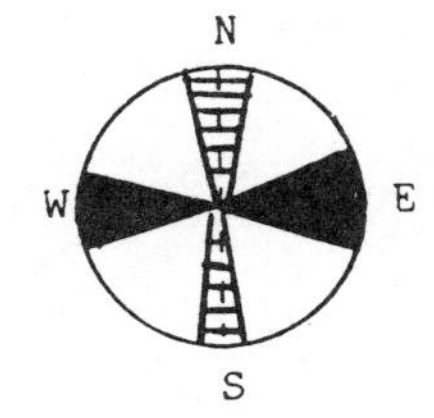

HERON or CRANE
KOR

Kor, Corr (from the root *Kern*), the crane, was resident in Britain until the 1660s, when it came to be hunted out of existence for its flesh, which was considered a delicacy in the Middle Ages (a sad turn-around from the ancient Keltic period, when it was strictly taboo and exceedingly unlucky to eat it). Herons and cranes were often hunted with falcons which pursued them in furious zig-zag fashion – it then became fashionable to ornament a knight's dress with heron feathers, especially whilst on a falcon hunt. Frigga's crown had heron feathers on it to symbolize that she knew of everything that transpired on Earth, but remained fairly silent about it. Keltic Druids kept their Koelbren lots, their Ogham *Cranachann* within a crane/heron-skin bag. In general, these birds are sacred to the female Muses – 'Fowles that to the Muses' Queen we vow' and the presiding male Gods – Gwyddion, Ogma, Odhin, Thoth, Hermes, and equivalents. Cranes and herons standing by the waterside are reportedly the first birds to greet the dawn, perfect for their Shamanistic Station. They are also renowned for predicting rain and storms. This tribe of birds at the highest level of symbolism are related to a Creator God in traditions from China, the South Seas, the Middle East, throughout Europe, to the North American Indian. In turn, through being related to the Young Goddess of Fertility, the crane in Ireland has become known as *Siothlagh a' bhoga* ('Sheelagh of the Bogland'), a euphemism for a whore or promiscuous woman. From a more noble viewpoint these birds are related to the God and Goddess that preside over the mysteries of reincarnation, and as the stork it is the bringer of all incarnating human spirits.

As part of the reverse process, herons/cranes can augur death and act as guides to the Underworld – they are portrayed on church carvings sucking the breath/ spirit from dying people, to carry it away; indeed, herons are reported to have come originally from the Underworld, where they were guarding the King's treasure. Often three of these birds appear together in symbolism (e.g., the three egrets on Gaulish carvings of Esus, the Axe God or the Bull Sun God; also Mannan's 'come, stay, go' three-cranes) all pointing to the Three Fates, the Sisters of Wyrd.

In conclusion, the triple kerns can be found operating at the quarter points (North, South, East, West), but most noticeably the East; nesting storks are held to be protection against fire in Scandinavia.

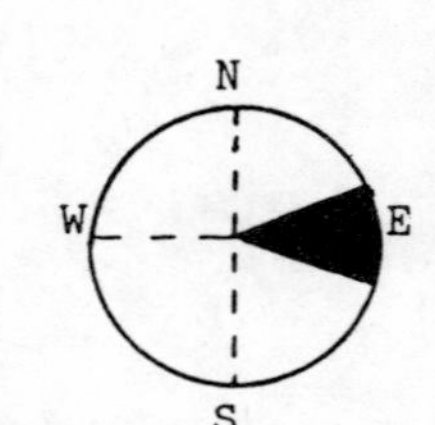

STARLING
TRUIT
SUGGE
STUCKIE

The bird linked to *Tinne/Tan*, the holly, in Ogham manuscripts is *Truit*, the starling. As *Truit* is alternatively found as *Truith* or *Druid*, certain researchers have conjectured that the Initiate of Faerie, Thomas the Rhymer, known as True Thomas, was originally *Drui* or *Druid* Thomas. This is plausible when we remember that the Druids kept both starlings and wrens (*Druen*) as birds of augury. Further, as a bird name, *Druid* can also occasionally mean a thrush or blackbird, the blackbird which reportedly sings atop a holly bush at the approach of spring. In Folklore there is a reported rivalry between the starling and the swallow. In the Folk tradition the swallow brought fire to humanity from the underworld; it thereby scorched its reddy-brown throat, and still has smoke-blue wings as a result. Now it is only thanks to the Shamanistic Calendar that we can, after many hundreds of years, appreciate the profoundity of such teachings:

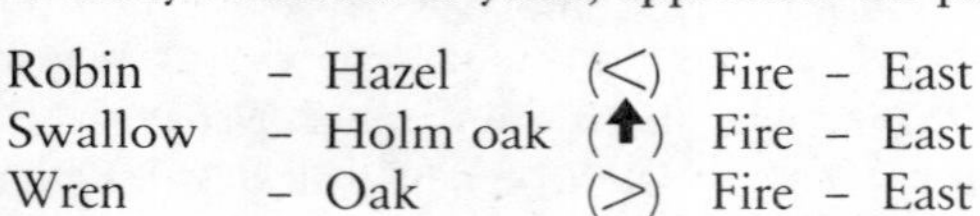

Robin	– Hazel	(<)	Fire – East	The three birds
Swallow	– Holm oak	(↑)	Fire – East	that stole fire for
Wren	– Oak	(>)	Fire – East	humanity. Beside each
				other here.

At long last we can start to appreciate the mythopoetic rationale that supports all our ancient mythologies – the Koelbren Wheel is the key to all. Iduna, the Apple and Fertility Goddess of the Scandinavians, was changed into a swallow when Loki (spirit of fire), in the shape of a hawk, released her from Thiasse (in eagle form) who was trying to rape her. A spring fertility song sung by groups of Greek girls was called a 'swallow song'. The swallow was Aphrodite's totem bird, its five eggs held to be symbolic as well. In Christian mythology this bird is a symbol for the incarnation. Unfortunately and paradoxically the Church bigots had to slander the opposition at the same time by branding the swallow 'the devil's bird' (because it has 'a drop of devil's blood below its tongue/beak') or 'witch-chick' – if we replaced 'devil' with 'Wildman', we would rectify the perverse conditioning. Although perhaps factually erroneous, the old rural belief about swallows hibernating through winter in holes in cliffs or at the bottom of ponds, to re-emerge in spring, is nevertheless mythologically intriguing. In Folklore they are reported to be able to indicate (by flying low) when a thunderstorm is approaching. Finally, like several other medicine birds and animals, the swallow is meant to contain a precious magical stone, with which (aided by swallow-wort) they improve the eyesight of their young.

As we have already discussed the Wren (*Dreadhan*) and Robin Lore in some detail, I shall pass onto another quintet of birds that stand at this Shamanistic Station: the cuckoo, wryneck, woodpecker, hoopie and nightjar.

One of the strongest power birds we have is the nightjar. It has over twenty other significant names, such as eve jar, eve churr, fern owl, dorr hawk, night raven, dog hawk, jar owl, night char, night crow, dawn crow, moth eater and wheel bird, and perhaps whip-poor-will. Contrary to the opinion of sceptical naturalists, these names have deep Shamanistic relevance (if not a physical basis within 'ordinary nature').

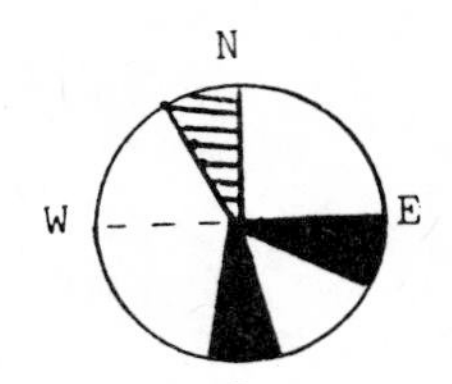

NIGHTJAR
NIGHTCROW
HADAIG

About the only time this discreet bird can be easily observed is around dawn and dusk, for during the day it lies well camouflaged at the foot of an oak tree, or amidst the ferns and undergrowth. This bird is intimately bound up with the oak, and its two main positions on our Shamanistic Calendar mirror this – May and at the Summer Solstice. As usual with the deeper aspects of Shamanism, this receives confirmation from within observable nature, for this bird feeds off a kind of chaffer called *Scaraboeus melolontha* in May from off oak trees, and also upon *Scaraboeus solstitialis* at midsummer, also from oak trees.

It is perhaps worth noting that the night crow's eggs are often preyed upon by its close totem associates – magpies, jays and crows. This *Bran y Nos* (raven of the night) may well also be the red raven of the Eastern Quarter as I put forward earlier. It also has connections with the Thunder God through its thrumming purring call, as Gilbert White relates in his classic book *The Natural History of Selborne*: '... one of these churn owls came and settled on [the Hermitage] and began to chatter, and continued his note for many minutes; and we were all struck with wonder to find that the organs of that little bird, when put in motion, gave a sensible vibration to the whole building!' Some naturalists are perplexed as to why this extraordinary bird should be termed a 'fern owl' or 'churn owl' when they observe that it has no outward similarities (apart from being nocturnal) to the owl – I am tempted to deal with this question as did Agnes Whistling Elk, the Cree 'medicine woman', in Lynn Andrews's excellent book *Flight of the Seventh Moon*, for, when Agnes handed Lynn an 'eagle' feather, Lynn protested that she would not be duped into believing that what was obviously a turkey feather was an 'eagle' feather. The argument was ended when the Wise Woman Agnes explained that in Cree Indian mythology the turkey was known variously as the 'south eagle', 'giveaway eagle', or 'buffalo eagle'. In a similar fashion we can understand that the nightjar is referred to within Keltic Shamanism as the fern owl, the red raven or the goat-sucker; being mirrored as 'the toad bird'.

Following on from the dor hawk (*Dur*, door), dog hawk (the nightjar), we arrive quite naturally at the hawk itself. As there are many species of hawk, this bird has quite a spread of influence on our Shamanistic Calendar, but by focusing on the archetypal we can narrow the range. In Egypt it was related to the East Wind (and Horus); elsewhere it is described as 'the flashing and exploding fire-bird' and generally related to the resurrected Sun God or his son – 'I [the Sun] have risen like the mighty hawk that comes forth from its egg.' Within the Keltic Arthuriad the equivalent solar hero was Gawain, or, more properly, Gwalch Mai (the Hawk of May).

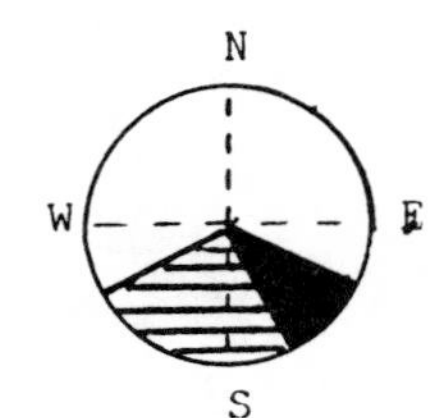

HAWK
SEG(S-Og)S-OK
An t-Eun Fionn
(The Bird of Finn)

One of the hawk's reputed abilities was to be able to metamorphosize itself into a *Gowk* (cuckoo) at will. The hawk, or falcon (close in symbolism), appears associated with the Wildfolk in medieval European tapestries, often being used there for hunting purposes. Within the calendar we progress from the red East through Beltaine to the white South – or, as is written in the Qabalistic book of

Job 39, 26: 'Doth the hawk fly by thy wisdom, and stretch her wings toward the South.' Here it becomes the Arthurian Knight Galahad or Gwalch-y-Had (Hawk of Summer, or Hawk of the South/White). The equivalent bird in Germanic mythology is *Vedfolnir*, the hawk, that sat between the eyes of the white eagle in the sacred ash tree, *Yggdrasil*.

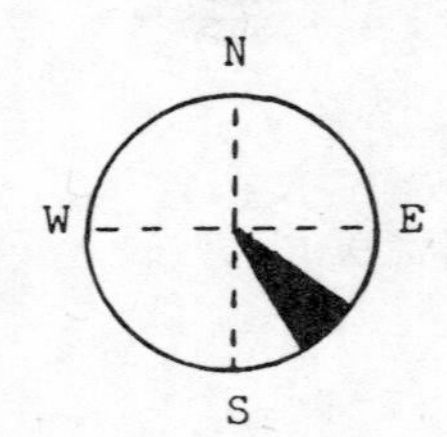

YELLOWHAMMER
BUIDHEAG
BUID-OK
PENFELYN
WRITING-HAWK

A shy and gentle little bird which may well have a totem relationship to the pagan God of the Wilds (slandered as the Devil by Churchite detractors) is the yellowhammer. 'In the North of England, the yellowhammer was popularly believed to drink a drop, but, according to some, three drops of the devil's blood every May morning.' This interesting bird is also closely associated with the serpent power in the following extract from Welsh Folklore: 'The snake was popularly believed by us to have another servant, and that was the yellowhammer (*Penfelyn*), a shy and retiring little bird which haunts the furse bushes of the open heath ... for he was credited with carrying food to the snakes, indeed, in some districts credited with feeding them with his own young – did not his very eggs bear snake-like marks! As children, we became uneasy when he was about, for we feared it indicated the presence of snakes.'

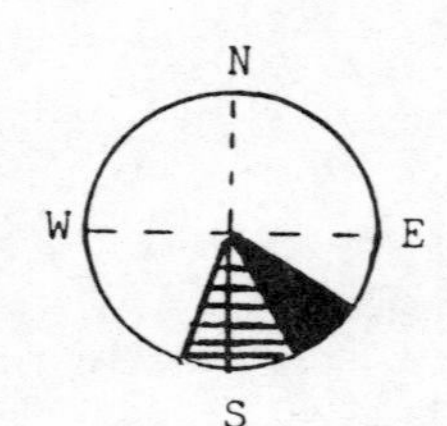

CUCKOO
GOG, KOG
GWKW, GOWK

In the speech of Brythonic Alban *Gowk*, *Gouk*, *Gukkow* and *Golk* are all ancient names for the cuckoo, related to the Kymraeg *Kog*, *y Gog* or *y Gwkw*. Thus, April Fool's Day in Scotland is known as '*Hunt-y-Gowk*' ('Hunt the Cuckoo'). This bird above all others stands for wanton lustiness, as it lays its eggs in the nests of others, notably the dunnock (*Sugge* or *Stuggie*), pipit, robin, woodpecker, etc. Also, it is a noted fact that many more male *Gowks* arrive in this country in April, and it is they that produce their characteristic call *Guk-koo, Guk-koo*. It is easy to see why Zeus pretended to be a bedraggled cuckoo to trick, ravish and then marry Hera. In the mythology it is associated with a couple of (femininish) fruit trees – orange and cherry. It was linked to the scent of the orange-tree blossoms (a common ingredient of bridal bouquets); women wishing to know about a future husband could address a cherry tree as follows: 'Cuckoo, Cuckoo, Cherry Tree, how many years before I marry?' whereupon the cherry tree would make the answer. Like other birds of this Thunder God Station, its movements and song were observed as portenteous of rain. It was a reputed guide to the Underworld, and as it roosted in holes in the ground and hollow trees it was identified with the Faerie Folk.

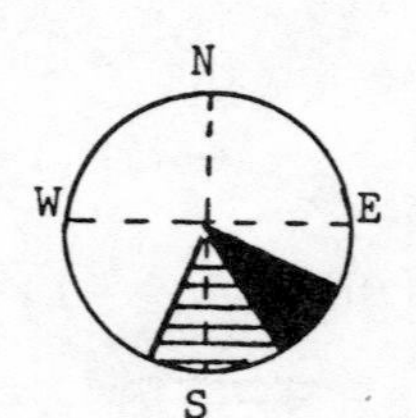

WRYNECK
SNAKE-BIRD

The wryneck, snake bird or cuckoo's mate is an uncommon spring migrant to Britain. This extraordinary bird lies flat along a branch, and when it is angry erects its crest, writhes its neck about, hisses like a snake and darts its tongue in and out. A 'medicine' bird if ever there was one. Coincidentally, it has ▽ or > markings on its (neck) feathers (Koelbren position >). It is a bird of female eroticism, being sacred to Aphrodite; it was used as a love charm, being tied to the four spokes of a wheel, incantations were made over it (then, it is to be hoped, it was released!). The bird is also reported to twist its neck towards a murderer.

Like the woodpecker, to whom it is related, it avidly eats ants whenever it can (the ant is another Shamanistic power-giver). It is known to prefer nesting in willow trees, where it lays its white eggs, thus also linking it to a more Southern Shamanistic Station; this is echoed in the Greek myth in which the Pierides, who challenged the Muses, were turned into wrynecks or, alternatively, magpies.

In the *Quarterly Review* of July 1863, we read: 'In Bavaria the hoopie is said to play the part of attendant to the cuckoo. It was believed that the plantain was once a maiden, who, watching by the wayside for her lover, who was long in coming, was changed into a plant, and once in seven years she becomes a bird, either the cuckoo or the hoopie, or, as it is called in Devonshire, the "dinnick", the cuckoo's servant.'

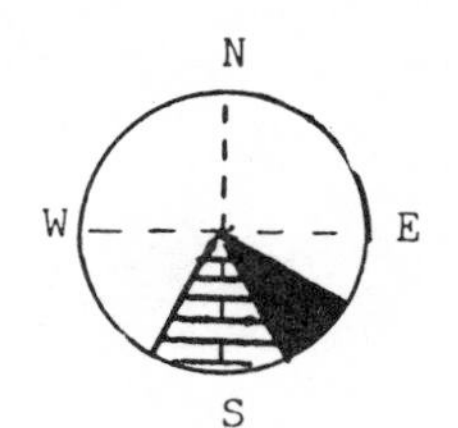

HOOPIE
DINNICK
(DIN-OK)

The *Specht* (*an Snagan-daraich, an Lasair-choille*) or woodpecker, like the cuckoo and the wryneck, has strong erotic symbolism in that it 'hammers its bill into the cracks in trees' – this motif has been used in Scottish bawdry and European Folksong. Being a many-faceted character, the woodpecker announces summer rains by hammering its bill on oak trees, and generally indicates rain and storms; Grimm said it could tell one where treasure was hidden; further, it allegedly knows the medicinal herbs and where they are to be found, but it guards them and threatens to peck out the eyes of potential thieves.

Its habit of climbing trees spirally has been felt indicative of a knowledge of the post-death journey up the Tree of Life. Several Gods and Goddesses are associated with the woodpecker, notably Zeus, who changed himself into one; also Pikus ('woodpecker'), son of Saturnus and father of Pan (a 'tamer of horses'), was changed into a woodpecker by Kirke for spurning her love. In the magnificent European Wildfolk tapestries, the green woodpecker often appears in the background on some tree adjacent to the lady-Goddess. Generally speaking, it is felt to be an incarnation of a forest spirit, and wise in woodland ways, well worth listening to with an open ear.

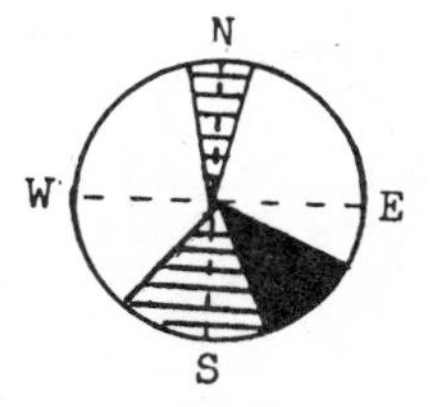

WOODPECKER
SNAGAN-DARAICH
OAK-CREEPER

Just after Samhain 1981, when I wrote the poem 'Mon (of my Heart's Desire)', I insisted on addressing Morvran as 'Raven-God of the Sea', and in the notes as sea raven (see *Inner Keltia*, No. 2). For this small visionary insight I was squarely criticized by less than well educated academics. As has often been the case, the reborn Druidical knowledge has since triumphed completely, for in old Kymraeg, Morvran means 'seagull' (sea raven)! Also, Odin's white sea ravens were seagulls. Warriors who died in battle, as worshippers of Odin, were transformed into seagulls, as we read: 'Seagulls, too, were battle birds but in a different sense. They were the spirits of men killed in action, ever wary, ever on guard, the bright red spots on their beaks the symbol of their wounds.' Furthermore, a remarkable piece of Irish Lore vindicates my intuitions totally. Ravens with white feathers were popularly believed to be birds of good omen in Ireland. Toland in his *History of the Druids* states how he was in Dublin in 1697, and while walking to the village of Finglass, he came upon two acquaintances who were engaged on some business transaction. They were overjoyed on seeing a raven hopping nearby with white feathers in its wing. The favourableness of the omen was apparently increased when the bird flew off to the South of the observers, and with much croaking. The men informed Toland that it was an invariable sign of good fortune to see a raven with white on its wings, flying on one's right hand and croaking simultaneously.

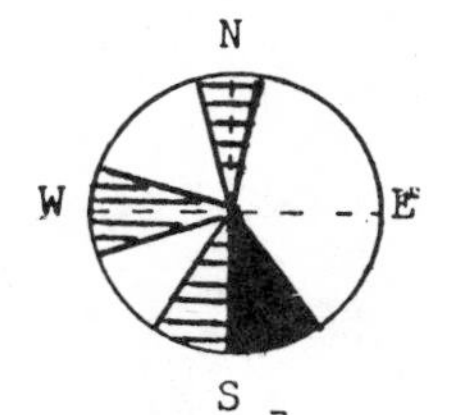

SEAGULL
FAELIN
MORVRAN

A later piece of Scottish Gaelic Lore adds that 'black-headed gulls are the messengers of the angels'. 'But the following story which Artemidorus told about the crows is still more fabulous. He says there is a harbour on the ocean coast called "Two Crows" and that in it may be seen two crows with their right wings partly white; people who have disputes over certain matters come there and put a plank up on a high place and place barley cakes upon it, each man

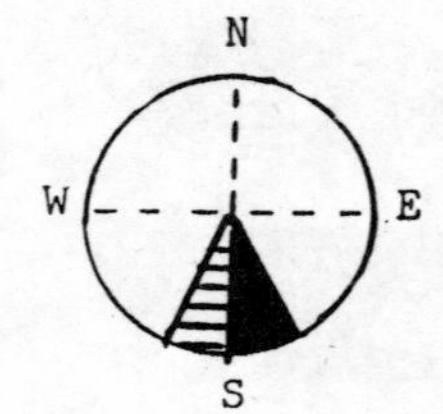

MAGPIE
PIODEN
PYAT
'SNAG-BREAK'
('Two-tone Ambler')

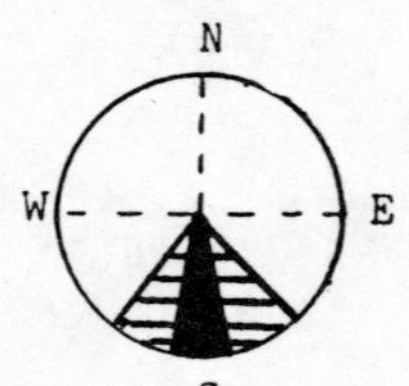

JAY, GAE*,
JAY-PYET
(*GAE = SPEAR)

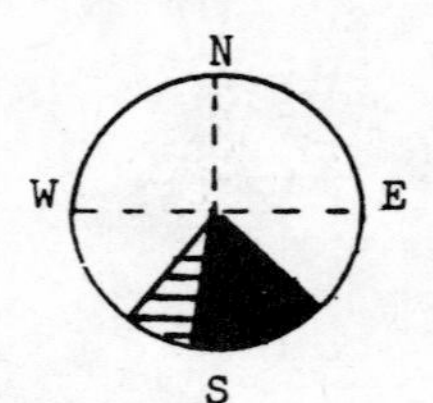

SWIFT
AIGNE-DUBH
(BLACK-CHARACTER)
GWENNOL-DDU

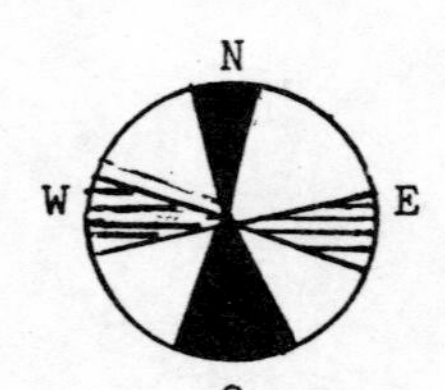

SNIPE
NAESKU
(N-ASK)
NECK, NEX
RUDE-KOKE
BOK-SAIK, Ys-NIDEN

separately; the birds fly up and eat some and scatter the others; the man whose barley cakes are scattered wins the case.' Apart from black ravens with white patches on their wings, and seagulls with black heads, etc., there may be two other land-birds linked with the white raven. We may also quickly note that the gannet is known in Kymraeg as *Mulfran-wen* (white sea raven) or *Gwylanwydd* (white goose).

The English word mag*pie* preserves a trace of its earlier Brythonic name *Pyat*, and the Kymraeg *Pioden*, *Pia*. 'In Sweden tradition says that sorcerers on Walpugis [Beltaine] Night ride to Blocula and there turn into magpies.' In Greek myth the Pierides, who wanted to compete with the nine Muses, were changed into magpies. (This may have a connection with magpies laying nine eggs.) These birds are known to try to imitate human speech, and Pliny believed that they secretly ponder the meaning of the words, and die of shame when a word is too difficult for them. The well-known nursery rhyme 'One for sorrow, Two for mirth, Three for a wedding, Four for a birth . . .' preserves a degenerate hint of a once-upon-a-time more profound observation of magpies for divinatory purposes. Their 'unlucky' reputation is just another unwelcome relic of Christian slander which we would do well to reject; personally, I have always held an immense affection for these birds.

Magpies have long been associated with Geminii in astrology. Their habit of collecting brightly coloured bits and bobs, as well as jewellery, gold rings and semi-precious stones into their nests, speaks to me of a relationship with the rainbow serpent, bejewelled Quetzecoatl.

Intimately associated with the *Pyat* (Magpie) is the Jay-*pyet*, *Ja*, *Gae*, or *Sgrech y Coed* (screecher of the wood) – the jay. A piece of Christianized British pagan Lore relates that as the Sun rises to its height at noon every Friday, all the jays go underground to speak with their Woodland Lord (wrongly slandered as 'the Devil'). Thereupon they relate all the things they have observed within the last week, and return to Upper World by dusk, their beautiful blue wing feathers assisting their return. Like the magpie and jackdaw, the jay can be taught to speak when tame, and it is also fond of brightly coloured 'little treasures'.

This spirit of the air even sleeps on the wing at very high altitudes. The swift has long been respected as a weather prophet (it has been known to vacate an area whilst the approaching storm is more than 800 miles away). As a result of its success at prediction, it has been named 'the Thunderbird', 'storm swallow' and 'rain swallow'. One of the more sympathetic Christian naturalists, Reverend Graham, wrote about the swift: 'It is an Ethereal Songster. To me he is the Spirit of Summer in sound.'

Shamanistically related to the swift is the snipe, which is the lightning bird whose zig-zagging flight was meant to presage the storm. In spring and early summer it also makes an extraordinary 'drumming' noise with its tail feathers as it hurtles like a gannet down through the air. (It is an insensitive person who cannot relate to the magical quality of this phenomenon, if one is fortunate enough to hear and witness it; I know it is one of the most potent experiences of my youth.) This drumming or bleating noise has Shamanistically linked it with the goat, hence its name *Ean-ghabhrag* (bird-goat) or *Gabhar Athair* (goat of the air; just as a goat is raised into the sky at Puck Fair in Eirin); heather-bleat; also heron-*bluter*, and horse-*gok* (all of Shamanistic South Station). Two of its names – *Rude-koke* (kog of the wheel) and wheelbird – relate it directly to the key axis point in our Keltic Wheel. As the snipe for the most part is a shy retiring bird of the reedbeds, it has a nocturnal significance as well; indeed some less observant people only spot it in flight at dawn or dusk.

It would become too complex to explore the Shamanistic differences between the sea/shore lark, wood lark, tit lark (meadow pipit), etc., so I will focus on perhaps the most important member – the skylark.

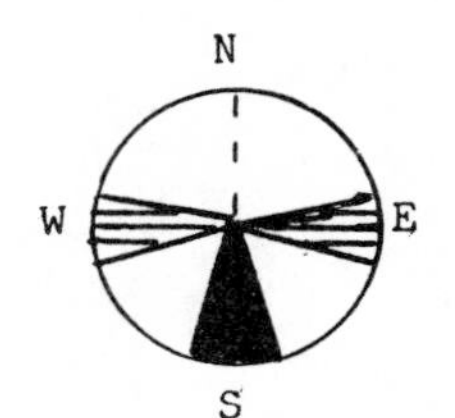

SKYLARK
BIGEAN-MOR
(GREAT LITTLE
(BIRD))
LAVER-OCK
LUATHARAG
(Swift-Ag)

The phrase 'up with the lark' reflects the fact that it is one of the first birds to greet the dawn (Shamanistic East). As it often retires into the heather (especially at dusk) the lark also has a Shamanistic West Station; but pre-eminently it is a bird of Shamanistic South, as it climbs the ladder (*Aradh*) of air into the sky. There it delivers its tireless teachings of Awen in wise song-sayings (*AgRadh*), as I poetically described it:

Skylarks climb into the radiant heights,
to shower-down honey-throated song-schematas,
in an untiring, unhurried, yet insistent flow
But gone are those who had the Gael's birthright –
a hearing so attuned to the bird-speech-formulas,
that they could translate their Teachings, contemplate them, and *know*.

Yes, this sweet Pibroch of the sky eludes the comprehension of almost all modern folk, whose sensitivity has been dulled by technology's unremitting buzz.

Because hawks and falcons are closely related, it is understandable that in mythological symbolism their roles overlap. But pre-eminently the 'bird of nobility' is the peregrine falcon; that is why it was given the name of the Sky God's totem weapon *Lannair* from *Lann* meaning a 'spear', 'lance' or 'blade'.

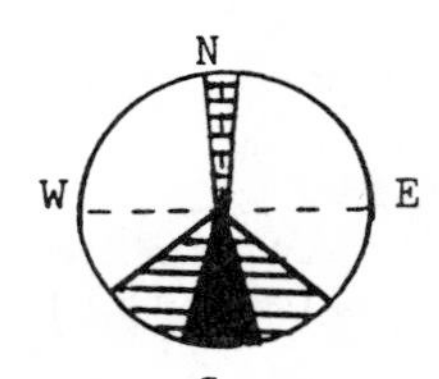

FALCON
LANNAIR
GLAS-EUN
GWALCH-GLAS
SEOG (equiv. SEG)

In Folktales such as 'The Lay of Yonec', the hero takes the shape of a great falcon to become the lover who rescues a lady shut up in a high tower. The Arthurian Grail hero Galahad takes his name from *Gwalch-e-Had*, 'hawk of the summer'; in general it is associated with Gods of Sun, Light and Sky, such as Horus, Harakhte-Ra, Apollo, Freya, Frigg, Loki (as fire spirit) and Siegried. A falcon perches on an eagle's head on the highest branch of *Yggdrasil*. Its eyesight is of the keenest (related to Qabalistic sign *'Ayn*), and as it preys with speed and alertness, it can be said to have the qualities of *Tiphareth* and *Kether* in its world of operation. As it nevertheless kills, it is an emissary of death in its purest form; it is thus found on Kalypso's Blessed Island of the Dead, and is also associated with the Goddess Kirke (it calls 'Kirk-kirk'; more probably, though, this relates to *Korak*, 'raven'); thus came its rulership of Sagittarius and its relationship to the kite (puttock) and its *Glas*, 'grey-black', name.

In all the world's mythologies, the eagle is revered as a sacred and powerful Bird. One of its Gaelic names, *Iolair*, comes from *Iul* and *Adhar* meaning 'guide to the air'; another is *Suil-na-Greine*, 'eye of the sun', (related to Qabalistic *'Ayn*). It is further honoured by the phrase *Righ na h-Ealtain*, 'King of the Bird World'. It therefore can be understood why Scottish clan chiefs were entitled to wear three eagle plumes in their bonnets (likewise Princes in Faerie Wildfolk tapestries).

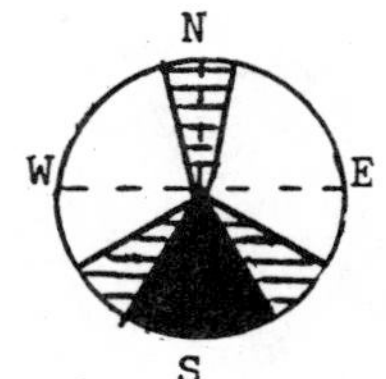

EAGLE & Eaglets
(Golden Eagle)
AGUIL, ACHILL
IOLAIR

Its Shamanistic qualities are well expressed in a poem extract from Percival:

Thou sittest like a thing of Light
Amid the Noontide blaze,
The Mid-day Sun is clear and bright,
Yet it cannot dim thy gaze.

Eagle form was one of the guises Druids were known to adopt; indeed, a gathering of three-score eagles (Druids) on an island in Loch Lomond is recorded; the Druids met there each year at Beltaine to augur the omens for that year. Similarly there is a Welsh saying that when high winds prevailed 'the eagles are creating whirlwinds on Snowdon,' obviously relating to the weather wizardry of the Druids in their *Kaer* in Snowdonia. Thus, when we read that the 'grave' of King Arthur in Snowdonia is guarded by a pair of eagles bearing chains, the significance is clear.

The Keltic Sun and Sky and Light God Lleu (Lugh or Lugos) was known to have adopted an eagle form and sat up in an oak tree. In early Greek votive art Zeus is represented simply as an eagle clutching thunderbolts and lightning flashes (similarly, Indra, Ahura-Mazdah, Yahveh, etc.). Indeed, the Greek Eagle-*Logos* (creator of the Kosmic Laws) finds echoes in St John the Baptist, John of the Fourth Gospel, the Chaldean eagles, Phoenixes and Chaldriki; the Qabalistic *Shekhinah*; and the 'eagle' discussed in Castenada's 'The Eagle's Gift'. (* The two-headed eagle is linked to Geminii, and its talons to the pincers of Cancer in astrological Lore.)

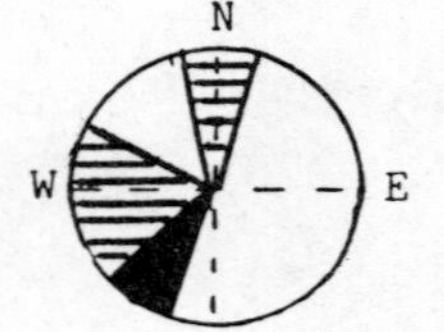

WILD DUCK
LACHU
LACHA-FIADHAN
KRAN-LACHA

In the Ogham Alphabet the duck (*Lachu*) was considered a 'lucky' bird and related to the rowan (*Luis*) Station. Sailors and voyagers held it a good omen to see a duck before they commenced a journey upon the *Linn* (loch, river, sea). For indeed, '*Cha chudthrom air Loch an Lach*', 'The wild duck does not burden the loch.' In certain Keltic areas it was held unlucky to steal and eat ducks' eggs, especially if the eggs were removed from the nest after dusk had fallen. This is probably because the wild duck was sacred to the Goddess Sequana (G'ess of the Seine) and other such Water Goddesses.

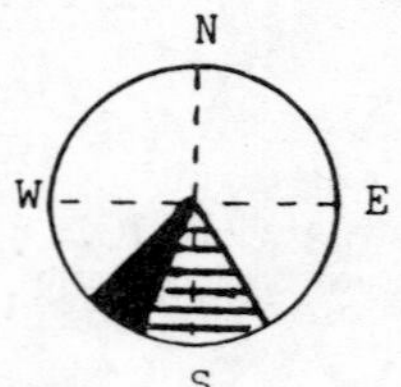

PHEASANT &
GOLDEN Ph.
BESAN

This beautiful game bird fulfils a similar symbolic role to the peacock of other traditions, the males being gloriously highlighted with radiant hues. The female, although more browny-cream coloured, is very fertile and raises large families.

There is enough Lore to show that the bittern was once a sacred bird to the Kelts and other peoples, but sadly it has been hunted and persecuted almost out of existence in Britain. During the breeding season (spring and early summer) the male bittern makes a strangely weird sound described as a loud boom or drumming, which can be heard over a mile away. Its early arrival was held to be a good spring omen (like that of the Storks), thus the Northumberland saying:

You may knaw there's nae mair Winter te cum
when the Bull o' Prestwick beats his drum.

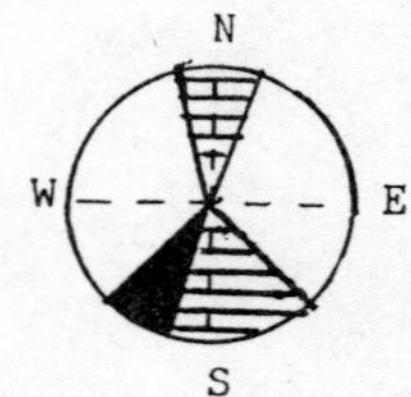

BITTERN
BUNNAN
KORA-GHRAIN
HERON-BLUTER

Its Old Keltic name was *Bo-tarvos*, 'bull of the marshes' (for it roars like a bull when sexually aroused. This name is echoed in the Latin *Botaurus* or *Botaurus Stellaris* (starred/speckled bird bellowing like a bull); Gaelic *Bo'ithre*; Gaulish *Butor*; Anglo-Saxon *Botor*; Highland *Bubaire/Boobrie*; French *Boeuf du Marais*, 'bull of the marshes', or *Taureau d'Etang*, 'bull of the pond'. In the O.T. it is a symbol for an area of habitations returning back into swamp: 'Yea, Pelikan and bittern shall roost on the capitals' (Zeph.ii.14). In its Highland

Gaelic form of *Bubaire/Boobrie* it becomes associated with a gigantic and voracious Otherworld creature.

I and a group of associates were fortunate enough first of all to hear and then to see quite a few Bewick swans in the middle of an inland loch in West Lothian. Their deep, ringing, bugle-like call-notes sounded as if they were being produced by a herd of animals. Their normal habitat is sea inlets and salt-water lochs, and they feed on seaweed and shellfish; these facts determine their Shamanistic Station in the Ogham Wheel.

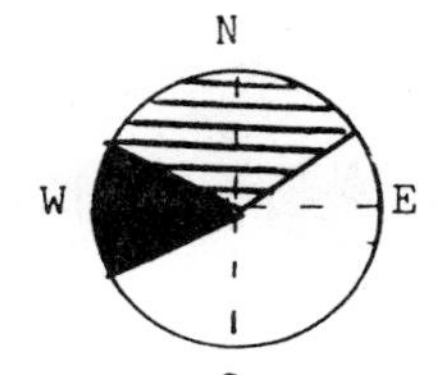

WHISTLING SWAN ELA, EALA. BEWICK & WHOOPER

In 1984, when I was in the midst of rediscovering the Cipher to the Ogham Alphabet and hence the Ancient Keltic Shamanistic Calendar, one of my most interesting insights was that the cormorant/shag was at one and the same time the heron/crane of the sea and the sea-green raven associated with Shamanistic West. The above list of Keltic names for these birds provides ample linguistic proof that this is indeed so. A little further delving shows that the cormorant (black) and shag (green) also share several of the Ancient Keltic 'raven' words, e.g., *Veipa*, *Vip*, *Fiag*, *Fiach*, *Gwya*, *Gwach*.

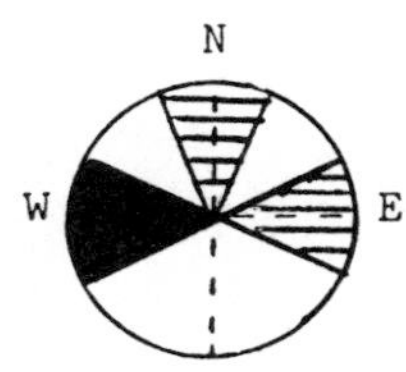

CORMORANT, SHAG ('GREEN CORMORANT') (HERON/CRANE OF THE SEA), MULFRAN, ODAR-SCRACH (GREEN-SCREETCHER), MOR-BHRAN, MUIR-VRAN (RAVEN OF THE SEA), BALAIRE, KAILLEACH-DUBH (BLACK HAG), BHUTHAIN, SGARBH, VEIPAKS, GWYACH, KRON (Crane), FITHEACH-MARA or FAIRGE-MARA (SEA RAVEN).

As regards Shamanistic Station, the Ogham Alphabet gives for the *Ohn* (gorse), *Oir* (broom) Station (one cog after due West) the bird *Odar-scrach*; now *Odar* is esoterically 'green' and *Sgrech* is 'screech' in the sense of the cry of a prophetic bird. The most noted 'screechers' are the herons and cranes (*Kor*) of the *Kol* (hazel) and *Kron* (reddy-brown) Station (one cog before Shamanistic East); thus the cormorants and shags stand as their exact Shamanistic opposite. These sea-coast 'screechers' have their inland equivalent in the *Korn-scrake* (corncrake), as will be discussed shortly. But finally let us read about the 'green' heron's battle with the 'green' serpent, from W. H. Hudson's eye-witness account:

'One day when sitting on the bank of Beaulieu River in Hampshire I saw a cormorant come up with a good-sized eel it had captured and was holding by the neck close to the head, but the long body of the eel had wound itself serpent-wise about the bird's long neck, and the cormorant was struggling furiously to free itself. Unable to do so it dived, thinking perhaps to succeed better under water, but when it reappeared on the surface the folds of the eel appeared to have tightened and the bird's struggles were weaker. Again it dived, and then again three or four times, still keeping its hold on the eel, but struggling more feebly each time. Finally it came up without the eel and so saved itself, since if it had kept its hold a little longer it would have been drowned.'

In the Ogham Wheel, the corncrake is also known as the Odorscrach, around the Autumn Equinox Station. This makes sense, for when the harvest cleared the cornfields the corncrake would be flushed out, exposed and hence more noticeable. From a deeper point of view, the screech (or crake) of the land rail was considered an omen-cry; it was accredited with strong invocatory powers to the Heavens, particularly if it made a frequent rasping note – then rain would be shortly due.

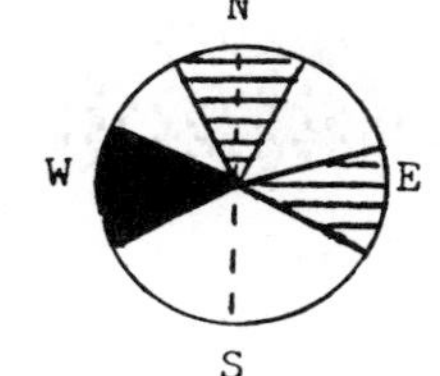

CORNCRAKE; LANDRAIL KORN-SGRECH ODAR-SGRECH, GARA-GART, GARTAN

In the North it was/is considered a blessed bird; it was supposed to lie torpid in winter, even dwelling under water (true, Shamanistically), whilst in spring its first cries were held to denote that all hard frosts were over. If a land rail was heard craking in a field nearby, someone in the neighbourhood was going to get ill or die. The water rail spreads the symbolism round to Shamanistic North (see the Pictish Goddess 'Lady Gartan').

The mighty fish-eagle was anciently known as the *Earn*, or *Erne*. The power,

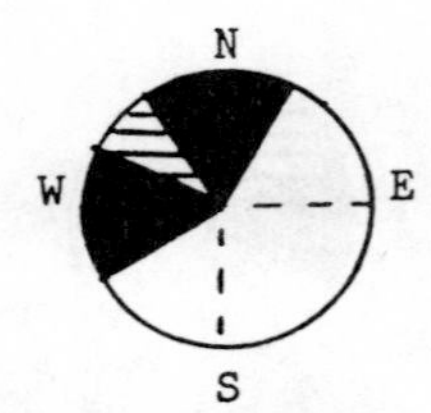

OSPREY & SEA-EAGLE
ERNE, EARN
A t-Eun Fionn

might and utter dignity of this noble creature can be gathered from photographs. Much is made of the golden eagle as a tourist attraction in this sadly exploitative world, but the fact remains that the *Erne* has in fact a much greater wing-span and seems to have been as, if not more, important mythologically. The Pictish eagle glyph, carefully pecked onto the Picts' symbol stones, is demonstrably that of a fish eagle; likewise, some of those illustrated in Illuminated Gospels, also those 'ghost' (spirit-form) sea eagles and fish in the panels of a ritual horn (Danish).

The language of a whole Pictish region (Ern) took its name from what could have been one of their major tribal totems; other lochs and placenames in Alba and Eirinn show their obvious derivation. Recent archaeological investigations in Orkney and Shetland have proved that this area was once the centre of a powerful fish-eagle cult for several thousand years (see *Tomb of the Eagles*), and they also show the Pictish inhabitants of around 3500 BC to have been in advance of their Mediterranean counterparts as regards burial architecture, etc. The recent reintroduction into the Western Highlands of this Sea-King/Queen of Birds marks a significant physical and symbolic return, nesting as it does often on high pine or fir trees.

PEWIT, LAPWING
AIDHIRKLEOG
PEES-WHAUP
TUQUHEIT
ADHAIR-KIN-LUACHRACH
PLOVER,
KORNIKYLL

In the Ogham Ciphers the *Aidhirkleog*, the lapwing, is linked to *Ailim* (the Scots pine) and *Amhancholl* (the Wych Elm), also to *Arathar* (the plough, used in autumn on some fields, behind which the pewits would flock, as they do in spring). The ploys of the adults in springtime, feigning injury to lure away raiders from the nest site, has contributed to the bird's reputation for secrecy and bravery. Magical stones, called *Quirins*, found in pewit nests, were valued by sorcerers for locating hidden treasures (this stone has Sh. North qualities).

Being placed in the Ogham Wheel just before Samhain would associate it with Underworld mysteries and Faerie secrecy and kunning, as Otta Swire has commented: 'Perhaps it would pay to consult the green plover, for once he was a king of the Underworld and he still knows all about subterranean rivers and lakes and can find water under any dry and arid land if he so wishes.'

This bird is associated with the darker aspect of Bran at Samhain, as are rooks (*Roknat*), the Ogham cog flanking this festival on the other side. Zeus, in the form of a lapwing, mated with Lamia the Underworld Water-serpent Goddess. Finally, its cries are associated with departed spirits, as is the *Whaup* (curlew), the big brother of the *Peeswhaup* (*Kornikyl*-lapwing).

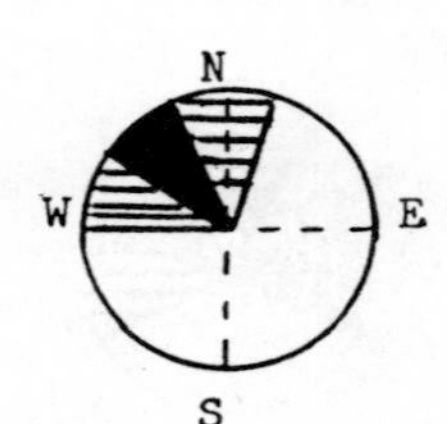

ROOK
ROKNAT
SIONNACH, BADB
TEATHRA
BRAN-BIGWEN
Swedish K-RAKA

In the Ogham Wheel, the bird linked to *Ruis* (the elders') Station was *Roknat* (the rook): 'Rooks traditionally bring good luck, so country landowners at one time liked to maintain a rookery on their estates. The birds were protected and anyone who killed one was severely punished.'

Sadly, in this century, many thousands of these birds (and other 'crows') have been shot by hooligans and misinformed farmers. This, together with the decimation of elm and wych-elm copses (by DED), has significantly reduced the number of Rookeries. In autumn 1986 I and three friends were fortunate enough to observe one of the much debated 'crows' parliaments', in this case of rooks and ravens, in a rough field in East Lothian. As far as I am concerned, it would be a stupid and unaware person who didn't realize that there was meaningful communication taking place between these hundreds of birds, who were standing in a perfect circle, with sentinels posted on the periphery. My Druidical group and I have also been present at significant sites, where a swarm of rooks have arrived right at the power time of dusk or dawn – thus we know these birds to be wiser than is ever credited by the unenlightened.

Of course, that is not saying rooks (and other crows) are 'nice', 'gentle' or 'sweet' birds. Far from it – the saying '*Cho garbh ri Rokas*', 'as rough as a rook', is very apt. They harry the nests of the pewits, peck out the eyes of dead lambs, and generally scavenge. Anciently they were sacred to the Battle and Death Goddess Badb, Macha, or the Morrigan, 'Macha's fruit crop', being the heads and corpses of slain warriors (such as Odin, Bran, Arthur, Owein and Tethra).

A crow is said to have twenty-seven different cries, each corresponding to a different action. In Shetland Folklore, a girl retrieved from Faerie enchantment as a rook/hoodie, was re-aligned with human characteristics except that she pronounced the letter 'r' with a peculiar croak; this was termed *Corbieing*, 'talking like a crow'.

The windy and wet weather of autumn (more so than in spring) is said to make the rooks *gang gyte*, 'go crazy', flying to a height and then performing somersaults and various acrobatics solely for their own and their associates' pleasure.

As it is a very sacred and important bird, it should not come as a surprise to discover that the Keltic word for the raven spreads back into Indo-European roots. Proto-Keltic *Vip* (Pictish *Vip*, *Vep*, *Uip*), *Viipo*, *Veip* (crow), *Vepo*, *Vipio*, *Veipak* (crow-like), thence Kymraeg *Gwyach* (and *Gwya*); Irish Gaelic *Fiach Fi(p)ach*; and with a 'p' shift to a 'th' we have the Highland Gaelic *Fitheach*. It appears as a name element in several Pictish deities and divine Kings and Princesses, as follows: Vepogeni ('raven's offspring'); Uip (raven); Vippoig-namet (Uipo-Ignauit, Vip Ogmemet); Uiipotalo ('raven-browed', i.e., dark haired/brooding), a Pictish Princess (3); and from Europe Vepi-sona ('raven-voiced').

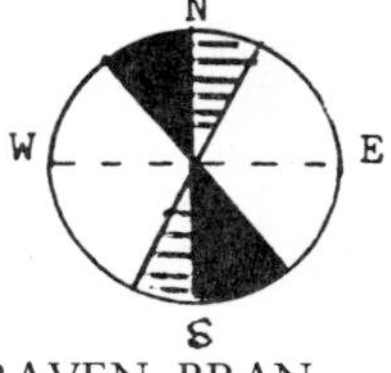

RAVEN, BRAN
VEIP, FIPACH
KIG-FRAN
LUGOS, LUGI

The Kruithni (Picts), the Kymry (Welsh) and the Brythons (of Albion) all shared raven-totem knowledge; witness the mighty Ravens versus men, employed in the Battle that went parallel to the *Gwyddbwl* (Shamanistic 'chess') game between Arthur and Owein in the Mabinogion. As Arthur is the 'Bear-man' (Arth-ur) related to the Pictish Deo-ard (Bear God), it is interesting to consider the Irish name Art-bran, normally translated as 'Priest of the Raven' but ambiguously stronger as 'Bear Raven'. It is worth noting here the widespread tradition that Arthur, after 'death', became a raven or, in the coastal parts of Kernow, a cough. This is why in Somerset men doffed their hats to either of these birds as a mark of respect. To dare to shoot one of these birds was a heinous crime and a direct affront to Arthur himself. ('Bran' spreads even further afield, e.g., Slavic *Branu* = raven.) Bran's head was eventually intered in 'the White Mount' in Kaer Llyndain, which echoes the fact that the Gaulish city of Lyon had as its totem-bird the *Lugi* or *Lugos*, 'the white raven'. (Londoners should not, therefore, crow about any exclusiveness; we are dealing with essentially Shamanistic and Otherworld teachings here.)

Now, most of the raven's qualities are of Shamanistic North-West-to-North, e.g., 'What is blacker than the raven – only death,' and the Triad:

The Calends of winter, it is hard and dry;
Very black is the raven, quick the arrow from the bow;
At the stumbling of the old, the smile of the youth is apt to break out.

Badb (wife to Tethra) was the Raven War Goddess, Baobh was a Gaelic riv nymph, whilst Baobhachd meant 'the croaking of a raven' (hence 'boding'). fierce old raven guards the underground gold in Chaw ('raven') Gully Mine i Cornwall. The seven ravens in Slavic mythology may well correspond to th seven whistlers (*Whaups* = curlews) in Brythonic myth. (See also Odin an ravens as the Yuletide Father, and the Greek Raven God Kronos (*Kravn* = to cry croak), and Goddess Kirke (from *Korak* = raven).) Perhaps of relevance here 'the raven stone' or 'stone of victory', which certain individuals in the know hav obtained from ravens' nests to aid them in discovering secret treasures and th arts of prophecy (e.g., the pebble that the Brahan Seer had).

As already mentioned, there is a mythological 'white raven' aspect whic relates it to Shamanistic South (*Fearn*, alder) and hence to the Gods Bra Lughos, Gwyddion, Apollo, Aeskulapius, Odin (seagulls = light), Mithra, eve Yahweh, Noah and Elijah.

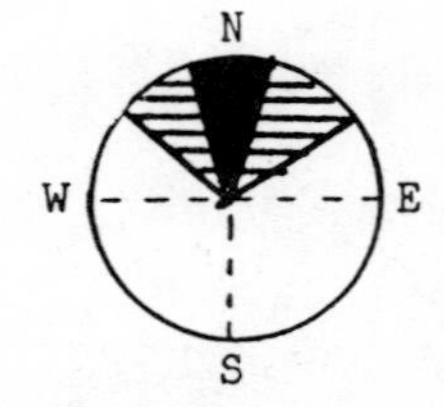

HOODED CROW & BRAN-LWYD & PEWIT-GULL

As if some of the name associations already cited were not startling enoug the following took even me by surprise, for the Brythonic/Pictish name for th hooded crow is 'the pewit gull', in other words 'the Underworld gull'. As yo might remember from Fig. 17, page 37, the seagull is mythologically 'the whit crow', so the perfect Shamanistic inversion is to call 'the hoddies that aye croa for doom' 'the peeswhaup gulls'.

Hoodies (hooded crows) are Shamanistically at the black Northern quarter battle, death and dark augury. There is a very old Scottish Folk song, 'The Tw Corbies' ('The Two Hooded Crows'), in which a knight has been murdered b his lady; the corbies know of the act and are feeding on the corpse. Oth instances of their uncanniness are less unpalatable to our refined moder sensibilities. As a footnote we should mention that jackdaw = *Kai* (as i Arthurian *Kay*) and Cornish chough (Arthur's bird).

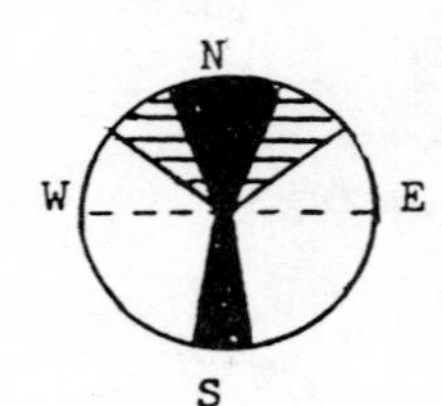

CURLEW
WHAUP, AWP
KRITH-EUN
KRUITEACH-MARA
GYLFINIR,
KA THAICH
KWRLIG, 'GREAT-PLOVER'

This is a dear Shamanistic friend of mine, and I totally endorse Robert Burns words: 'I never hear the loud solitary whistle of the curlew on a summer noo or the wild mixing cadence of a troop of grey plover in an autumnal mornin without feeling an elevation of soul like the enthusiasm of devotional poetry Indeed, the eerie call of the *Whaup* once literally caused a magical transferenc of me once (in July 1984), as I related in my poem 'The Curlew Call'.

In various parts of Britain, curlews were associated with 'the seven whistler (giving warning prophesies) and the Gabriel Ratchets (the geese/hounds c Annwn that fly over the midwinter skies). Also 'Whaup' was the name of Pictish Wildman Goblin who sat upon the roof tops at night and carried off th discarnating spirits to the Underworld. Hence in Shetland and elsewhere it wa taboo to eat its flesh or eggs (best not to annoy the death spirit's emissary).

Its 'Krith'-Bird name is usually related to its 'shaky' way of walking, but I fe it is as much to do with the Shamanistic shape (*Kruith*), totem-form that i embodies for the Kruithni (the Picts), with their many totem-tatoos.

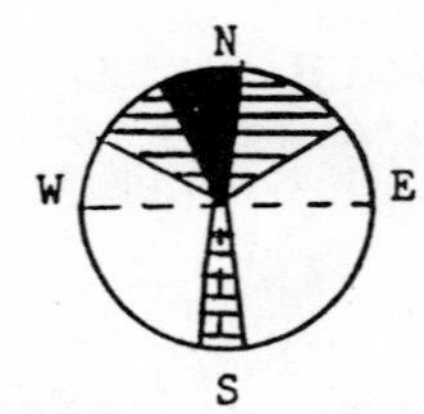

THRUSH
STMOLACH
SMEORACH
KULLIONAG
(= Holly-Bird)

Next in our journey around the Ogham Wheel we come to the mighty thrus tribe of Birds. Those such as the song thrush, mistle thrush, blackbird, robin black redstart, stonechat, redwing, fieldfare, ring ousel and water ousel are fairl easy to identify as being of Shamanistic North nature; more difficult to place ar the wheatear, redstart and whinchat, as they are summer visitors to Britain.

As these birds often play a part in Keltic Tales and Legends, e.g., the Faeri Wildman called Lun Dubh Macsmola (Blackbird Son of Thrush), it i nperative that we first of all understand their Shamanistic qualities, for only ıen can we understand why the Wildman was so named, and only thereafter ın we understand the essential message of the Tale – so far, academics have ıiled miserably on all three levels understanding.

In Carlos Castaneda's book *Journey to Ixtlan*, is an account of a sorceress, 'la ;atalina', who adopts the appearance of a giant blackbird. This parallels giant ıagical blackbirds described in the Otherworld voyages (*Imrama*) of Irish Seers, lus the ousel of Kilgwiri in the Mabinogion, etc.

The mistle thrush (thristle cock or linnet ousel) has quite pronounced ıaracteristics: 'On New Year's Day [in InverLeith Park, Edinburgh], the pair 'hich annually consume the red berries off the two old yew trees in front of the ıanse made their appearance. With mysterious regularity the mountain thrush rrives as punctually as if he kept a diary.' Also, a correspondent of Reverend Villiam L. Sime reported 'a great chorus of birds [thrushes] in the North of eland last Boxing Day.' When we remember that the Mistle-Thrush is a main ɔreader of Mistle-toe, the Yuletide plant the totemistic elements become ıterwoven.

Apart from the thrush, two other birds of this Station are the blacksmith's lackbird and the ousel, all using a stone or rock as an anvil on which they ammer and pound open, say, a snail shell. It should be noted that a folk rhyme as the thrush singing at the funeral of Cock Robin. A Pictish tribe of the North-ıst – the Taixeli or Taizeli – take their name from the Kruithnig word for histle' – *Taixel*, *Texel* (to *Tiksel*, then *Thisel*). As Cinaeth Tucker so erceptively pointed out in his commendable booklet *The Orphans of History* No. 1) kindred words are traceable in all the Scandinavian and Germanic ɔngues: Frisian *Tiksel*, Anglo-Saxon *Thisl*, Gothis *Theislo*, Old High German *ihsmo*, *Dehsmo*, *Dihsila*, *Deichsel*. The transported form of *Thristle* is also 'orth remembering, for *Thris* is the root of 'thrush'. And mistle thrushes spread ıistletoe, sacred at and near the Winter Solstice. Thus the thistle is a very ncient plant-totem within Alban, contrary to the Anglo-Saxon lies. *Tiksel* has secondary significant meaning as the 'pole of a cart', used for the constellation f The Bear, also known as *Wodens Wagon*, Anglo-Saxon '*Woenes Thisl*'.

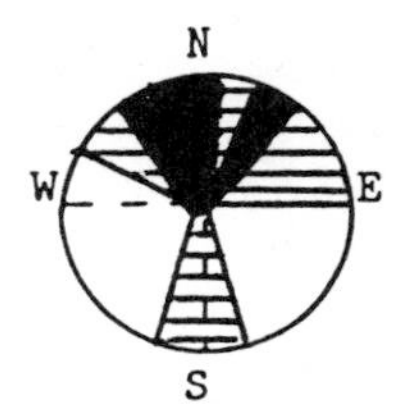

BLACKBIRD (LON-DUBH) DRUID-MHONAIDH DRUID-DHUBH (Dark-Druid) REARGAG

The Sage Thomas the Rhymer calls the blackbird the '*Throstle Kokke*' and elates that the male bird got its yellow beak from having dug its beak into a ıass of gold in an enchanted cave. As has already been noted, the Orthodox ;hurch, disapproving of anything that was not pristine white, alleged that 'the)evil' appeared in the form of a blackbird to tempt St Benedict. (Thus will the visdom of the Chythonic Powers remain distant from them.)

Several naturalists have recorded the blackbird singing into the midnight hour ɔower-time): 'At 8 p.m. I was surprised at hearing a number of blackbirds in ɔng. After a time the singing ceased, but going out again at midnight it had ecommenced, and in various directions I could hear a dozen or more birds in full horus' (Gilbert White). 'I was greatly surprised to hear one [blackbird] singing ıst night between 11 p.m. and 12 p.m. . . . it was a beautiful moonlit night and ery still' (B. M. McNab). Thrushes, blackbirds and robins are all known to ommence singing around 2 a.m. and sporadically to continue in voice to certain pecial late performances.

Fieldfare: *Liath-ruisg* (grey-stripper of tree's berries), *Siokan*, *Sogiar*, screech hrush, grey thrush. 'The fieldfare and redwing nest among the pines and firs of

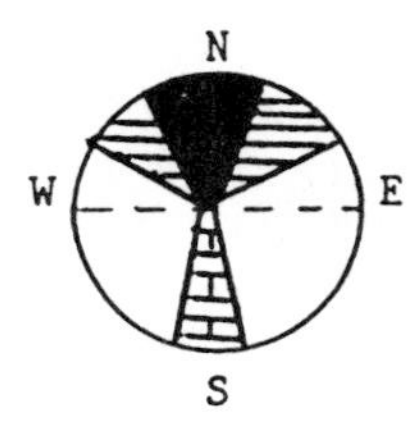

RING-OUSEL, DUBH-CHRAIGE (BLACKBIRD of the Rocks) DRUID-DHUBH (Black Druid) GOBHA-DUBH-NAN-ALLT (BLACK-SMITH OF THE HEIGHT) REAR-GAGAN, RING-BLACKBIRD MWYALCHEN Y MYNYDD (BLACKBIRD OF THE MOUNTAIN)

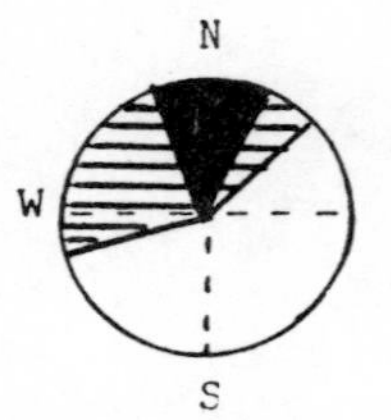

EONASK – BIRD OF THE SERPENT RIVER
THE WATER OUSEL,
DIPPER, WATER-CRAW,
BOG-AN-LOCHAN (WET ONE OF THE SMALL LOCHS)
GOBHACHAN UISGE (SMITH OF THE WATER)
GOBHA-DUBH NAN ALLT (BLACK-SMITH OF THE WATERFALL)
ESK-COCK
WATER-CRAKE,
WATER-THRUSH/BLACKBIRD

Norway and Sweden, and arrive in Britain in large flocks in the winter.'

Waxwing: an uncommon winter visitor to Britain is called 'the death bird' (*Sterbe-vogel*) in Switzerland and regarded as a bringer of serious omens.

Wheatear: *Klacharan* (stone bird), *Tinwen Y Garreg* (white-tail of the stones), *Bogachan*. In County Kerry, the wheatear is called 'the cunning little old ma[n] under the stone' and is associated both with toads (who are meant to hatch ou[t] its eggs) and with the Lord of the Underworld. (Thus similar to the stonecha[t] and yellowhammer.)

In the Mabinogion, those seeking the whereabouts of Mabon have to go an[d] speak to the Wise Old Ousel of Kilgwiri (Sacred Enclosure of Truth), up on hi[s] mountain.

In the autumn and winter, ousels can sometimes be found in the company o[f] mistle thrushes, feeding on haws and yew-tree berries, whilst very early in th[e] spring they are seen eating the ivy berries.

This truly remarkable and Shamanistic bird is renowned for running up an[d] down riverbeds, foraging for food, completely underwater. Last century dipper[s] were slaughtered by the hundreds in the stupid and mistaken belief that the[y] seriously ravaged fish eggs and fry (more scientific studies have shown that to b[e] false).

Now, although the shooting and nest-harrying has almost stopped, they ar[e] being slowly poisoned by river pollution – a situation that creates a bad karmi[c] debt for Western man. For if we are out of harmony with the river serpent's bird[s] we are out of touch with much deep and vital wisdom. 'The Indo-Europea[n] Aino people believe that the heart of the water ousel is exceedingly wise and tha[t] in speech the bird is most eloquent . . . Therefore, whenever he is killed, he shoul[d] be at once torn open and his heart wrenched out and swallowed before it ha[s] time to grow cold or suffer damage of any kind. If a man swallows it thus he wi[ll] become very fluent and wise, and will be able to argue down all his adversaries.'

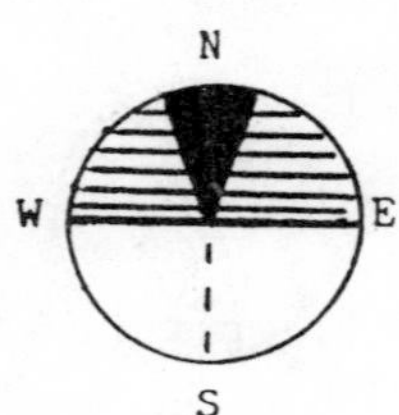

OWL,
TYLLUANWEN,
KAILLEACH-OIDHCHE (Hag of the Night)
KAILLEACH-OIDHCHE-GHEAL (Hag of the Night-Moon)
SEAN-EUN (Old Bird)
GWDIHW,
MULCHA, HULE (A.S.)
ADERYN-Y-KORFF (BIRD of the Corpse)

To many, the owl is a hated bird; others think its dark augury should b[e] treated with care; some worship it as the wise servant of the Hag Goddess[;] personally I take the middle view.

There is an old Tale that says that the owl is a servant of one of the te[n] Underworld Kings; another says the owl is an old weaver who spins with silve[r] threads, another says it is a death messenger if it flies down a house chimney an[d] beats against a window. The owl was sacred to Blodeuwedd, Pallas Athen[a] (Goddess of Wisdom), Kalypso, Lilith, Hekate (Death Goddess) and Asklepiu[s] (God of Sacred Science).

We have arrived at the deepest aspect of Shamanistic North, and have complete[d] our journey around the Keltic Wheel of Birds. You have at your disposal the key[s] to understanding virtually any bird you are likely to meet in Keltic Folktales. W[e] shall now progress to the Wheel of Animals.

Animal Shamanism

Out of the hosts of incarnated beings there are perhaps none closer to humanity than the various animal clans. It should therefore come as no surprise that through human history there have been innumerable Tales of companionship and at-one-ment with animals. It has also long been held that each of us has a special totem-animal (or various animals) to help us on the different planes of existence. One of the aims of Shamans and magicians has been to discern what their particular totem-animal (*Nagual*-beast) is; and to seek to establish magical contacts with it, thereby to aid them in their inner quest. Once the experienced Shaman has come to know and work with his/her own power-animals within a more general system of animal-totems, then he/she is in a position to advise others on their possible totems.

As an Initiate of the Keltic mysteries, I have come to reformulate the Shamanistic Calendar, which, as can be seen from pages 28 & 29, contains a fairly complete, accurate and compact system of animal totemism. Thus the reawakened Druidical wisdom stands in marked contrast to the bumbling, blind ignorance of academia, e.g. Katherine Brigg's statements: 'It will be seen that fairy zoology is not easy to bring into a compact system' . . . 'the whole subject presents as rich a tangle as any aspect of fairy belief'. Which is just another way of saying that she hasn't the slightest clue about native animal totemism – so much for the 'experts'.

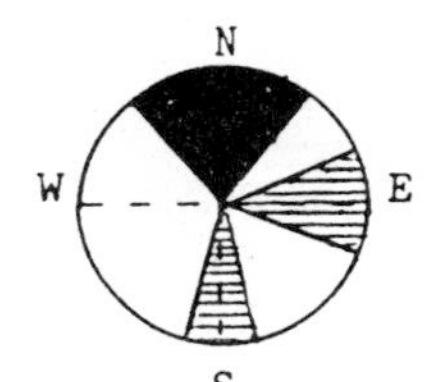

TOAD
PUDDOCK
PADDO
TAID
NIKIR

As this animal is of prime significance as *the* Earth elemental, one of the most ancient and persistent phenomena associated with the toad are the reports of its being found alive within solid blocks of sandstone, cracked open from a piece of coal deep underground, unearthed from long-buried and sealed tombs or from bricked-up walls. A typical report from a geomantically powerful area of Lowland Alban appears in the following nineteenth-century account:

'A few days ago, as two colliers were working coal in a pit in the neighbourhood of Bathgate, Linlithgowshire, they were astonished, on breaking a large piece of coal, to see a living frog skip nimbly from it. The niche in which it had lived was perfectly smooth, and of the exact shape of the frog. The hind legs of the animal are at least twice as long as those of an ordinary frog, the forelegs almost gone. It is of a beautiful bronze colour. It leaped briskly about the moment that it was liberated from its dark abode. How many generations it may have been shut up from light and air it is impossible to say; certain it is that although diminutive in form, and with great brilliancy of eye, it is a very antediluvian-looking customer.'

Another power that Toads possess in in effecting the Earth's fertility strongly. In the old days this fact was known and respected; latterly however it came to be mocked in the parodies of witchcraft found in popular literature. One description of the Keltic Earth Goddess (Luxuria) had her standing with a fox between her legs and a toad hanging from each breast. From one of the sordid

Scottish witch trials comes the following account: 'In another ritual they yoked toads to a plough with harness of dog-grass. The plough's blade was the horn of a ram. The "Dark Man" and John Young drove it twice round the farmer's field, with the coven following and praying to the "Dark Man" that they should get the fruits of the land, and the farmer a crop of thorns [bramble-briars?] and thistles. And so it worked out.' Whether this ritual was worked for good or ill, at least it can be seen that the practice involved the right Shamanistic ingredients. It is also apposite to note that Pliny said that the most awe-inspiring toad is the horned bramble-frog associated with witches. The paddock is reported as a witches' familiar which cries out to warn its master of danger. From the Elder Initiatory Tradition it made its way into Heraldry, where it was initially honoured e.g., the three toads on the ancient crests of Gaul/France.

(W. H. Barrett recalls that 'The milky sap of the sow thistle was believed in the Fens to be used, mixed with toad spit, by witches for drawing a crooked cross, or *Flyfot*, on their bodies to render themselves invisible.')

To conclude, mention must be made of the famous toad-stone 'bufonite' – a dark grey or light brown stone coming from the heads of very old toads, and to be taken from them when they are dying. Two early accounts of this power-object are as follows.

Fenton (1569): 'There is to be found in the heads of old and great toads a stone they call Borax or Stelon which being used as rings give fore warning against venom.' These rings were said to bear a figure resembling a toad.

Brewer's Phrase and Fable: 'A toad-stone, called crepandia, touching any part envenomed by bite of a rat, wasp, spider or other venomous beast ceases the pain and swelling thereof.' In the Londesborough collection there is a silver ring of the fifteenth century in which there is one of these toad-stones. The stone was supposed to sweat and change colour if there was poison in the vicinity.

This 'precious jewel in the head of a toad elemental' is on a Shamanistic par with the pearl in an old fox's head, the pearl that the otter transports, and the Druidical Serpent Glain, and suchlike powerful 'medicine stones'.

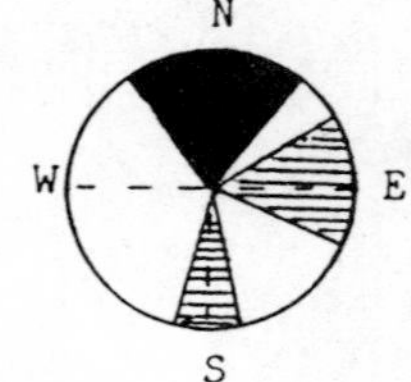

FROG
PUDDOCK

In the Ancient Mystery Schools there was held to be very little difference in magical role between the toad and the frog. Thus frogs are still called puddocks in rural parts of Alban today; also the name *Paddle Doo* (*Puddock Dubh* = black/dark frog) was applied, as well as *Cnadan* in Gaidhlig. Similarly, frog-stones are lucky yellowish stones having the shape of a frog, found near large ponds/lakes. The stonechat is mentioned as 'the waddling stonechat, the frog's grandchild', the toad previously reported as hatching out the stonechat's eggs. As to the puddock-ride or frog spawn, gypsies have long recommended it as a cure for rheumatism; and the famous physicians of Myddfai from North Carmarthenshire used a frog's tongue 'to oblige a man to confess what he has done wrong. Take a frog alive from the water. Extract its tongue and put him back again in the water. Lay this same tongue on the heart of the sleeping man, and he will confess his deeds in his sleep.' At least until the turn of this century, green tree-frogs were used in Germany as barometers: 'They are placed in tall bottles, with little wooden ladders. The steps of the ladders mark as it were the degrees: the frogs always go up to the top in fine weather, and lower down at the approach of bad weather.'

At Acton Barnett in Shropshire there is an ancient healing spring of great virtue, wherein the spirits of the well appear as frogs, the largest of the three being addressed as the Dark God (reminiscent of the three toads in French heraldry). In other ancient civilizations the frog has also been revered as a symbol of fertility, rebirth and regeneration – as such, the Egyptian Mother Goddess Heqet (Hekit) is a Frog Goddess; likewise several of the primeval male Gods of the Nile had frog heads, including Keh. In Egyptian mythology the frog is paired with the Water Serpent (Nau), as it is in African, Greek and Keltic. Thus the mythozoomorphic truth shines on.

Although not active during winter, the reason why newts are linked to Shamanistic North is that during their waking life they prefer to go foraging for food during the evening, night and early morning. On grey days they will move about enjoying the cool and wet; whilst on hot sunny days they will be found hiding under stones or a few feet under water. Thus, in virtually every aspect, they are exactly opposite to lizards, who are the heather-asks of summer.

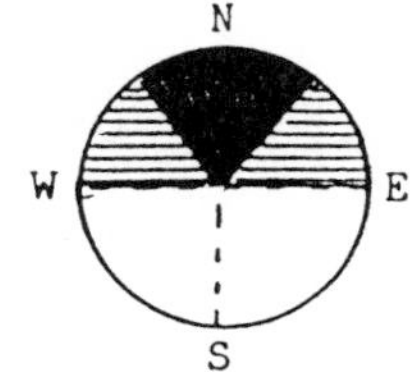

NEWT
(WATER) ASK
AWSK, ESK

Some say the Saxon (?) name for this creature is the *Efete*, *Eft* or *Evet*; with the article '*an*' in front this became *aN-evet*, then *Nevet*, then our newt. It is also worth noting that *Eft/Evet* appears as a Keltic Faerie word.

It is a sadly forgotten fact within our native tradition that many of Britain's great rivers were/are living water serpents; knowledge of this is preserved within their ancient names: *Ask*, *Usk*, *Isk*, *Esk*, *Eks*, *Exe*, *Oos*, black adder, white adder, river adder etc. This has been confirmed by the pioneering research of Viktor Schauberger as regards living serpent rivers and their deteriorating environment. As glyphs representing river serpents appear on Pictish symbol stones, and as beings from these rivers frequently appear in Folktales, we should seriously attempt to understand what lies behind such matters. Nor is it just of past pseudo-antiquarian interest, for sightings of 'black dogs' (and the like) are still being reported in or near certain rivers.

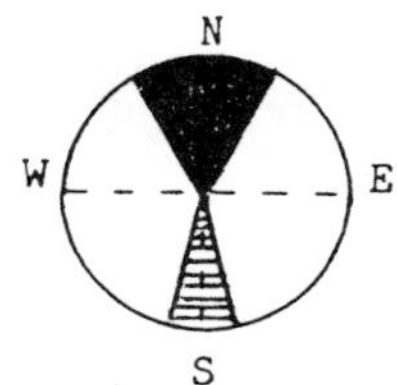

BLACK ASK
RIVER-SERPENT
WATER-SERPENT

By far the most important fish at this calendrical point is the salmon of wisdom (*Bradain Sikir*, *Eo-fis*) which swims in the Pool of Inspiration and Foreknowledge. His Kymraeg equivalent is the mighty salmon of Llyn Llywn who was so ancient and powerful that he gained a truce with the eagle of Gwern Abwy, who agreed to take fifty fish spears out of the venerable salmon's back for him. A similar wise salmon swims in the Scandinavian Mimer's fountain with the three Wyrd-Sisters–swans circling around on the surface of the water amongst the reeds. As Viktor Schauberger has shown in his brilliant book *Living Water* (Turnstone), there is a special reversed current which flows against and through the normal stream of water (river serpent); the wise salmon know of this and utilize it, especially to assist their prodigious ascents of waterfalls and rapids. As a totem connection, some of the Keltic Faerie Folk are reported to wear salmon-skin caps. From Christ training his Initiates to be 'fishers of men' to the rich Fisher King in the Arthuriad, this numinous symbol is of great importance. One variant of the *Ngetal Koelbreni* is actually in the shape of a salmon/fish, as were Scandinavian, Slavic, Middle and Far Eastern hieroglyphs. Bearing these associations in mind, we can perhaps appreciate the profound significance of the Pictish salmon glyphs. Still redolant with meaning in the face of academic scepticism, lies and degradation, their wisdom swims on.

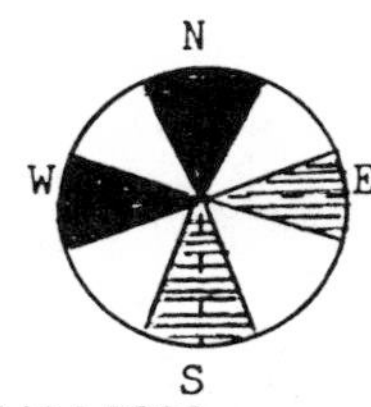

SALMON
TROUT
BRADAIN-SIKIR
EO-FIS

The *Dobhran-leathann*, the industrious beaver, may have a place around this Station. Its good nature and wisdom make it one of the more charming fish-farmers I know. Sadly it was persecuted out of existence in Britain by the twelfth century.

Two small, nocturnal, underground burrowers or explorers deserve a mention: the *Moudiewark* ('earth thrower'), better known as the mole these days, and Mr Rat. The *Moudiewark* is associated with death because it tunnels through graves, etc., but also with the dark wisdom of the Underworld, and the fertility which it brings to seeds with its front paws. Rats are secretive messengers for the Lord of the Underworld (note them on Gaulish statues to Kernunos in his Chythonic aspect).

There is one aspect of bull symbolism that places these animals in Shamanistic North as full of strong, heavy, earth forces and fertility. Black bulls were sometimes sacrificed around the Winter Solstice in relation to the Underworld deities. On a more mundane level, as food stocks would be run down during winter, ancient people used to slaughter some of the oxen at a 'mart' to provide some required meat; poorer peasant farmers used simply to drain off some of the animal's blood, which was then mixed with oatmeal, etc., the forerunner of the now more degenerate black puddings.

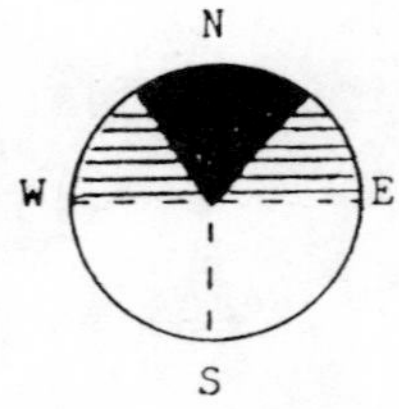

BADGER
BROK
BREAK
STIALL-CHU
(LARGE-STRIPED-DOG)
BORESON
(SON OF BEAR)
MOCHYN BYCHAN

Another animal of the Earth element, nocturnal habits and Shamanistic North Station is the *Brok* or badger. Some think its name is derived from being parti-coloured or striped, hence *Breac* in Gaidhlig; but notice of the old '*ok*' word-ending should be taken. That the Druids knew about its Shamanistic properties is demonstrated by the fact that a Pictish Druid was called Brokan or *Broichan* in Gaelic. Also, when five of the sons of Konal were foolish enough to dig into and destroy the Fairy Knoll of Grian's father, they were turned into badgers for their crime, by the sorceress. The 'kicking of the badger-in-the-bag' episode in the Mabinogion also brought serious repercussions. In a more positive vein, Keltic warriors knew that the very best healing salve for wounds was badger grease.

Badger sets (called *Brok-lann* in Gaelic), if left alone, can become very extensive and some have been known to be over one hundred years old. Badgers scrape tree trunks (especially elders), some say to sharpen their claws. They also dig up and eat tubers, bluebell bulbs, clover, wild fruit and rosehips; and quantities of earthworms, beetles, wasp grubs, honey, occasional hares, rats or partridges; and their favourite dish, a nice fat hedgehog. This is Shamanistically interesting because the hedgehog is one of the totem-creatures of Brigantia: The clan MacIvor make a pact with the serpents (reawakening from their underground retreats) not to harm each other; the MacIvor clan also wore badger heads and skins as totemistic gear.

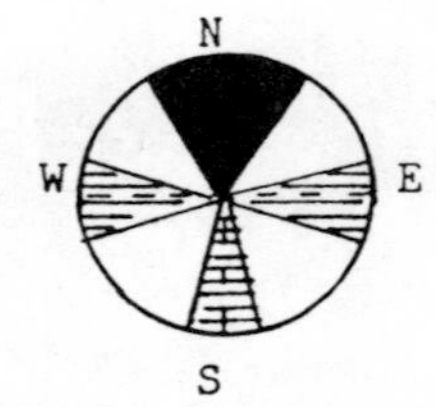

WATER-GOAT
SEA-GOAT
GOAT-DOG-MAN

Although this creature does not exist physically, it still plays a major role in the Faerie Traditions of Keltia, Europe and elsewhere. This is echoed in early astrological Lore about the water goat of Capricorn (an Earth sign). This dark or black water goat stands at the completely opposite Shamanistic Station to the ordinary goat of midsummer. The water goat's Ogham Station is *Gort* (ivy), thus it becomes significant that ivy leaves were used to cure sick goats. Like so many other items of ancient symbolic wisdom, the dark or black Wildman with goat's hooves, horns and beard, often found playing the bagpipes at Faerie revels, was slandered into the role of 'the Devil' by Orthodox Church theologians (see the poem on *Towzie Tyke* in the Pictish Shaman No. 1).

In the ritual calendar, 'Ground Hog Day' is 2 February, in other words Brigantia, Candlemas. On this day hedgehogs reputedly emerge from hibernation (but if they see their shadow cast by a precocious Sun, they will retire to their fastness pending a period of bad weather for six weeks or so).

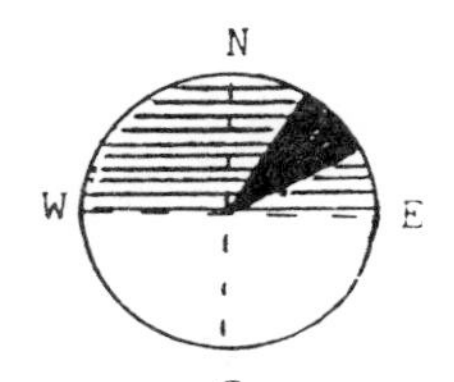

HEDGEHOG
HURCHEON
HURCHAM
URCHIN

The hedgehog (*Hurcheon*, *Herison*, *Hurcham*, urchin, woodchuck) is itself a diminutive solar boar, its bristles being the rays. It thus stands in a strangely ambivalent relationship to the snake/serpent/adder, whom it occasionally eats, for the male serpent (MakIver) briefly emerges from its winter sleep to greet the Goddess. In turn, the *Hurcheon*'s greatest enemy is the fox, which reportedly rolls it into any nearby water to force it open. Another decidedly more curious but highly significant story, as vindication of the Koelbren Cycle, is that it reputedly shakes the vine, rolls on the downfallen grapes and then makes off with them. (Although this activity would happen at a later time in the year, we nevertheless have the *Hurcheon* closely linked to its nearest tree-totem.)

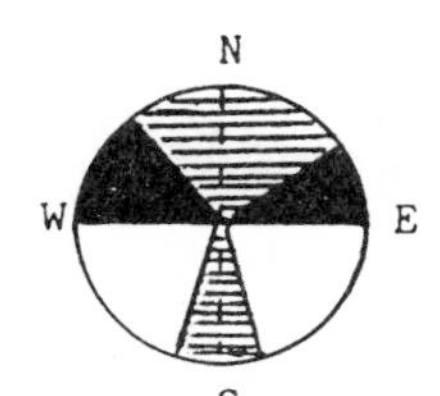

PORPOISE
DOLPHIN
CETUS-CREATURE

When the ancient star-gazing priests looked up to the star-draped dark heavens, they named certain clusters of stars, I've no doubt, according to a spiritual emission issuing therefrom. The one below Pisces in the firmament they called 'Cetus', which covers dolphins, porpoises and small whales; curiously enough, early illustrations of the 'Cetus' figure have two front paws shown.

In Traditional Lore, the New Year Child was often brought in by a dolphin (often a mount of 'mer-maids') to her myrtle-wooded grotto where, after going through some Shamanistic transformations, she agrees to let Peleus seduce her, thereby to produce Achilles. Similarly, Ino, fleeing Athaman, dives into the sea with her son Melicertes; thereupon the two of them became deities, her Son receives a new name, Palaeman, and rides a dolphin steed. Amphitrite, Leto, Deme Fer and Apollo were also famed for riding/adopting a dolphin form. The dolphin's great intelligence and friendliness to man is well known – they have often been reported saving human lives (but they drowned a monkey who pretended to be human: Aesop's Fable 50).

Dolphins/porpoises are also related to Venus–Aphrodite who comes rising out of the sea in a pearl of wisdom-bearing, oyster shell. Thus we may start to understand why dolphins are generally connected with erotic dieties; the Scottish word for a porpoise being a *Pallach*, 'a lusty person'. In this vein Shakespeare says, 'his delights were dolphin-like' and inquires, 'Why, your dolphin is not lustier.'

The dolphin's natural enemy is the shark species, the most directly opposite variety being the dogfish; thus it is paradoxical that one of its alternative names in Scottish is 'the louper dog' (in relation to leaping and otters). Other names include '*Mereswine*', 'sea hog', 'gairfish' and, most interestingly, '*Willie Powret Seg*' (from Fife). Within art symbolism a cousin appears as the Pictish 'Cetus' figure, one of the first depictions of this being from the Initiatory caves at East Wemyss in Fife.

Thus the porpoise's two main Shamanistic Stations may be in the Shamanistic East (at Pisces) and from Shamanistic West–North-west (around Samhain). That they were important within the Druidical science is confirmed by their jawbones being used as Ogham staves and as Runic Seasonal Calendars.

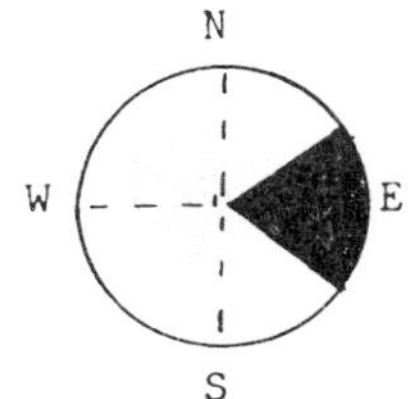

SALAMANDER
(FIRE-LIZARD)
A'CHORA
CHAGAILT
(VOICE OF THE
HEARTH-FIRE)
(VOICE OF THE
FURNACE)

This Otherworldy creature should not be confused with the species of newts, very inappropriately termed (fire-bellied) 'salamanders' by un-Shamanistic naturalists. This elemental being of fire is depicted on early medieval manuscripts as dark in colour with lighter spots along its body. Its Gaelic name exactly supports its Shamanistic Station, for *Kor* = crane/omen-speaker, *Gor* =

heat, fire, flame; *Kol* = hazel (fire tree): all are Shamanistic East. Thus, as East (and South) are the Shamanistic quarters for gold, one can understand why the ancient alchemists worked with salamanders to turn mercury into gold. The Scottish Gaelic for the salamander is *A'Chorra Chagailt*.

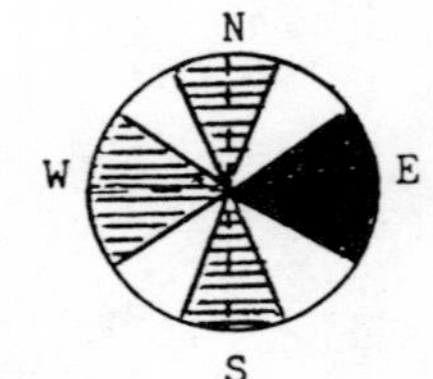

HARE
KUNIE
KEINACH
MIL-KHU
(Hound of the Plain)
FURZE-CAT

The hare is massively important to the Shamanistic Traditions as the Shamanistic East quarter totem. And as far as my calendar goes, I could wish for no clearer confirmation than the fact that within eight mythologies and over twelve languages its associations with dawn, East, red, fire, Spring Equinox and fertility are explicitly stated. The world over, it is encountered as one of the commonest witch familiars; witches can shape-shift themselves into the astral form of the hare. As they were such important totem-animals, there was for a long time (in Keltic lands) a strict taboo against killing hares. John Layard (in his commendable book *The Lady of the Hare* quotes A. H. Krappe as saying: 'As late as the nineteenth century the peasants of western Brittany could hardly endure to hear the name of the animal. In parts of Wales hares were not killed down to the reign of Queen Victoria; in the south-west parts of England the peasants, as late as the last century, would eat neither hare nor rabbit. The peasants of Kerry, Ireland, are even now said to abstain from hare.'

It is probable that the Ancient Kelts lifted the taboo on pursuing the hare at the Spring Equinox and perhaps Beltaine so that it could be ritually hunted to 'make the give-away' of its numinous flesh. The year-round wanton slaughter of the hare and other totem-creatures has, I am certain, contributed to the spiritual impoverishment of the native Keltic Cultures. When next to nothing is treated as sacred or shown reverential respect, then the Gods must (in obeyance of the kosmic law of justice – karma) withhold many of their blessings.

In Kymraeg the hare is *Keinach* (*Ceinach*), with the 'short hare', the rabbit, being called *Kwnigen*, *Kuning* (*Cwningen*), slightly anglicized as *Kunnie* (*Cunnie*, *Conie*), *Kuning*, *Kinner*, *Kinnin*; all these Brythonic words stem from the important root *Kwn* or *Kun* = dog, hound. The Gaidhlig name is also of interest, being *Gearr-fhiadh* ('short deer'), which links it to three of the epithets listed in the famous Anglo-Saxon 'Addresse to the Hare': 'The stag of the stubble, long-eared', 'The stag of the cabbages, the cropper of herbage', 'The stag with leathery hornes'. In the same poem of ritual hunting, the hare is addressed as '. . . the cat of the wood, the starer with wide eyes, the cat that lurks in the broom, the purblind one, the furze-cat', which is a quite remarkable identification, but one which accords with ancient cult practices. As hares are known to hide in cornfields until the very last stage of reaping, it is not surprising to hear of the last sheaf being called 'the hare', and reaping it being described as 'killing the hare', 'cutting the hare', 'cutting the hare's tail off'; more notable is the usage 'We have the cat by the tail', used by French reapers for the last bunch of standing corn. All this happens during the period of the cat tribe's ascendancy, at the hare's opposite Station – the Autumn Equinox.

In the mythologies we encounter Shamanistically 'black', 'red', 'white' and 'green' hares. One Chinese writer tells of a black hare, saying, 'The black hare is more uncommon than the white hare. It comes from the North Pole bringing greetings from the Moon Goddess.' In other ancient Chinese writings a red hare appears in company with the phoenix and the unicorn, all harbingers of peace and prosperity. White hares are featured; they are not just albino or winter-coated mountain hares. Many green hares are met with as jade amulets for luck and protection. (The apparent preponderance of white hares is deceptive, for to our dimmed human vision all Otherworld hares will have a whitish astral light around them; their true Shamanistic colour has to be discerned from within this light. For, overall, the hare's main place is in the red quarter, the East.) The richness of this particular totem is partially due to the diversity of its symbolic values. For instance, apart from being intimately associated with the Moon, it is also linked to the dawn-rising Sun God/Goddess at Easter. As it is described: 'The east is summoned in his name, the door opens in that direction, and there, at the edge of the earth, where the sun rises, on the shore of the infinite ocean that surrounds the land, he has his house and sends the luminaries forth on their daily journeys.' In some of the oldest accounts of North American Indian beliefs gathered by missionaries, we encounter the Hare God's residence as being 'towards' the East,' sometimes located on an island in a lake or the sea. In Europe we have the charmingly illogical Folk belief that male hares lay the Easter eggs. Also, in England, 'A custom called "hunting the hare" survived late into the eighteenth century.' Whilst in Egypt the hare is portrayed as greeting the Dawn. Comparative linguistics and etymology fully supports all these interwoven meanings: the name of the Anglo-Saxon Hare Goddess Eostre is preserved in the name of the Christianized festival of Easter (it being previously Anglo-Saxon *Eastren*, Old High German *Ostarun*). Jacob Grimm describes the Goddess Ostara as 'the Divinity of the Radiant Dawn'. Old Norse *Austr*, like Lithuanian *Aušra* and the verb *Aušta* (which means 'day is breaking') are all cognate with the Sanskrit *Usra*, meaning 'dawn'. Thus we get Sanskrit *Usra* meaning 'dawn' becoming Old Norse *Austr*, meaning 'East', which has dropped the 'r' in the common English pronunciation of our word 'East' when referring to the point of the compass, but has retained it in the name of the Easter festival. Sanskrit *Usra* is also cognate with the Hellenic root *Ausos*, 'dawn', and the Old Latin form *Ausosa*, which (since Indo-European 's' between vowels turns in classical Latin into 'r') becomes the classical Aurora, the Goddess of Dawn.

'In many parts of Cambridgeshire a hare running through a village street is taken to be a sign of an outbreak of fire in the near future.' A case in point is quoted by John Layard: 'A curious point arises in connection with a fire at Fordham. It is part of the old Cambridgeshire folklore that a fire always follows if a hare runs down the main street of a village. The week before last a hare did run down the main street of Fordham. It was pursued by Mr Richard Nicholls, a septuagenarian, and it was killed in a shed within three yards of where the fire broke out.'

'Sakka is one of the names given to Indra, who, as a Sky God of Lightning, Thunder and Rain, and also a War God, could be compared with the German Wotan or the Norse Thor, and with the more terrible aspects of Jove, such as Jupiter Fulgur or Jupiter Tonans. Indra is moreover one of the eight guardians of the world, whose place is in the east, which will be found to be of interest when we came to examine the connection between the hare and Easter. It is presumably in his capacity of God of Lightning that he spontaneously kindles the fire in which the hare–Buddha sacrifices himself. It is thus the Wise Sakka to whom the hare offers its body to eat, while he translated its spiritualized aspect associated with the self-sacrificing Buddha (by fire) into the Moon.' Q.

Other male Gods associated with the hare are the Egyptian Thoth, the Greek Hermes and the Roman Mercury. This is not just because as messengers of the

Gods they travel as fast as the hare; it is more that they are all light-bringers, culture-bringers, the givers of sacred writings and ciphers to mankind; and the East is the mythological Station for the Light- (and Fire-) Bringing God. The resurrected Osiris is linked to the hare, as is the risen Christ with the Easter hare.

The hare also has very strong associations with lusty sexuality, which the Church naturally tried to suppress.

'The well-known Cornish tradition says that if a young woman dies neglected after being betrayed by her lover, she haunts him after her death in the form of a white hare. The false lover is continuously pursued by the phantom.'

The more positive reverse side of this is where a 'Hare-man' is described as the best sexual partner in the Indian *Kamasastra*, '*Science of Sexual Love*'.

Hares' genitals were carried as a talisman to avert barrenness. Folk Traditions relate that 'eating hares' flesh for seven days would make anyone beautiful'. Pliny says, 'The people think that if you eat a hare your body acquires sexual attractiveness for nine days.' Philostratus in turn relates that 'the most acceptable sacrifice to Aphrodite is the hare for it possesses the gift of Aphrodite [i.e., fertility] to a superlative degree.'

A hare's foot if carried about in one's pocket averts rheumatism and cramp, and is a favourite with actors to promote the trickster's ability to play a 'role'.

I shall take my leave of noble '*Shagger*' (hare-*serd*), as the hare is addressed in the Anglo-Saxon poem, and leave you to contemplate the following excellent Irish Tale.

In the story of 'How the leg of Kian son of Maelmuaidh son of Bran was healed', a man slips his greyhound after a hare which, when cornered, turns into a beautiful young woman, having first rushed into the arms of her pursuer. She then leads him into a *Sidhe*, where she sleeps with him.

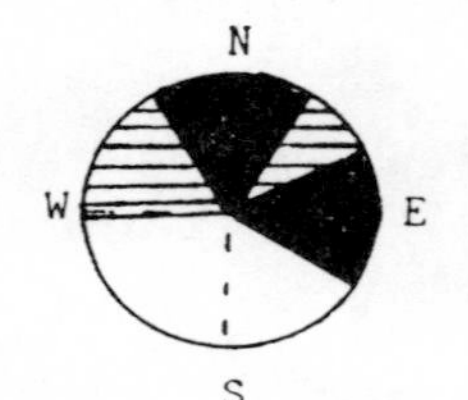

FOX
RED-DOG
RED-HOUND
(MADADH-RUADH)

One of the two main Shamanistic Stations of the Fox is in the red quarter of Shamanistic East. In this capacity it is famed for its *Kunning* (hound wisdom) and often plays the part of the wise trickster. This is preserved in its Gaelic name Madadh-ruadh (red/great hound/dog).

I could not possibly take my leave of the zodical sector of Aries without surveying the lamb, sheep and ram Lore. In the old days, when blood sacrifices were still made, white sheep were sacrificed to sky deities (or Zephyrs, 'spirits of the air', whilst black ones were devoted to underworld deities (or the Winter Storm God) and dispatched on ditches. They frequently appear in the mythology as the cattle of Sky Gods (symbolized by clouds). They have a connection with the East as well, for they are reported to rise at dawn and bow three times to the East.

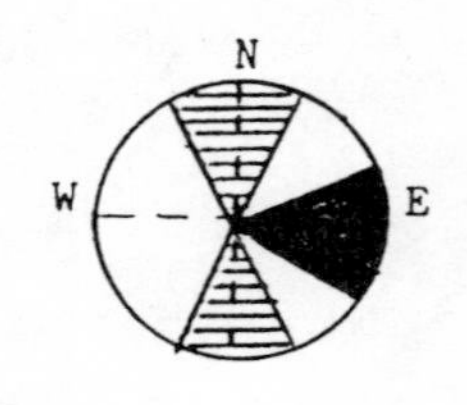

RAM
REITHE
WETHER
TUP, SEG

The *Reite* or *Reithid*, as the ram is called in Gaelic, features in Irish Otherworld Journey Tales. For example, 'In the story of the "Voyage of Teigue, son of Cian", Teigue and his followers come to an island which is populated by sheep as big as horses. One flock consists of gigantic rams, one of these having nine horns (three times three). This beast attacks the men furiously. Teigue kills it, and it takes him and twenty others to carry the ram.' These gigantic rams are reminiscent of the tup (as the ram is called) in the old Albion Folksong 'The Derby Tup', where the more than thirty-foot-tall ram – who had horns 'that grew so mighty high ... every time he shook his head they rattled against the sky' – had such a well-grown fleece that 'the eagles built their nests in it, you could hear the young ones cry'. The symbolic ritual slaughter of this ram-archetype is then recounted in the song where the flood of blood washes away the chalice holder, and various people make supplications for pieces of its gargantuan sacramental carcass. As the song is received as part of a Winter Solstice Folk play in Derbyshire, it may well be indicative (as Deirdre Green suggests in *Inner Keltia* No.5) of a death and rebirth of the Sun God motif with attendant recreation of the web of nature. As the tup also appears dressed up as a cow, bull or swine/ boar it perhaps has a little wider Shamanistic relevance. Similarly, 'Robin, son of Art' ('Robin Goodfellow, son of the Bear God') was the God of a Kilkenny Irish witch in the fourteenth century – it appears as a black dog or a ram. In the Book of Lismore there are mentioned wethers (castrated Rams?) which leap up out of a well, and in Irish mythological Tales a hundred and fifty Otherworld wethers having red ears and three horns appear. In yet others it is a stage in a totem-transformation process that a giant's soul goes through (see the Tales 'The Great Tuairisgeal' and 'The Young King of Easaidh' in chapter 7). Academic scholars usually greatly underestimate the importance of such giants – it would do them well to remember that the mighty God Jove (Jupiter) took the shape of a ram during the attack of Typhoeus. Further, Hermes, who leads the Graces out of an underground cave (which had been their winter residence) in spring, is often portrayed as carrying a ram, as Kernun (the Lord of the Forest) holds up a ram-headed serpent.

As a motif in symbolism, there is little difference between oxen, *Aurochs* (wild cattle) and common bulls, whilst the female cows have naturally more of a Goddess connection. The archetype for this symbol originates in the Otherworld, as do all the glyphs of importance; but, if we consider man's physical circumstances, we can appreciate how much he valued this beast of burden, for the ox was 'the primal driving force' – it pulled ploughs, carts, mill wheels, water pulleys, building blocks, hoof-threshed grain, etc. As the source of power it features as the zoomorphic glyph for *Aleph*, the first letter in the Hebrew Qabalistic Alphabet. In certain mythological accounts we encounter the twelve oxen of the Sun (months/zodiacal signs) used as standards. We also find them clearly linked to the four quarter directions: black = North (and underworld, i.e., sacrificed to Pluto); white = South (clouds, Sky God, etc); red-backed = East (fertility and War God); cream/green = West (sea divinities).

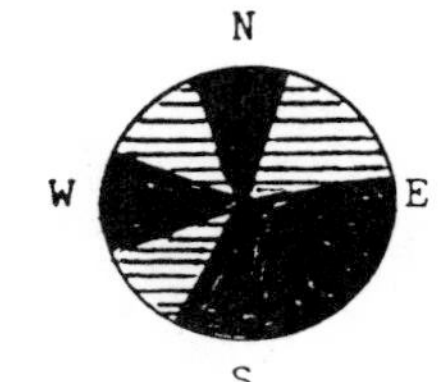

BULL
TARVOS
TARBH & COWS

Like the *Cwn Annwn* (the hounds of the underworld), the Otherworld cattle are often described as being white with red ears (white being the normal colour of an astral-light being). Curiously enough, cattle of this description also exist physically: 'The Ferrers, whose country seat is at Chartley Park, near Lichfield, have a peculiar breed of cattle on their estates. The colour of the cattle is white with black muzzles. The whole of the inside of the ear, and one-third of the outside from the tip downwards is red, and the horns are white, with black tips, very fine and bent upwards.'

Many Gods and Goddesses are symbolized as keeping or presiding over cattle/ cows, e.g., the Welsh Sun God Hu as a bull called 'the Mighty Hu'; Aneurin styles the solar divinity Beli Bloeddvawr 'the loud-roaring Beli' (note Beltaine connection); whilst Taliesin, being the master of much Lore, uses a Hebrew term *Becr-lled* (בקר לחט) meaning 'the bull of flame' (in all these, the bull's strength, tenaciousness and life-giving fertility are used emblematically for the Sun); Pictish petroglyphs (e.g., from Burghead), Gaulish votive carvings and

Brythonic ritual objects all point strongly to a Bull Lord called *Deiotarus* ('divine bull') in Keltic Galatia, *Donnotaurus* ('lordly bull') from Gaul, and the Irish *Donn of Cualnge* ('Lord of Cualnge') (The latter is part of a seven-stage Initiation process, see *Inner Keltia* No. 6). Of similar kosmic import is Mithras's sacrifice of the divine bull; other bulls are related to Osiris–Thoth, Pluto, Dionysus, Yahweh; Frey, etc. Goddesses associated with cows are: Boand ('She of the White Cattle'), Flidais, the Morrigan, Isis, Hathor and others.

That great mysterious Heyoka Tester Ku Roi appears as a cow-herd when carrying off Luchna's three white red-eared cattle which had three birds (transformed men) upon their heads (similar to the three egrets perched on the Gaulish Bull God's rump, middle and head). In Kymraeg mythology the solar cart or wagon was pulled by three *Yechen Bannog* (sacred oxen) which wore great brindled yokes, studded with a symbolic number of knobs. In early Greek mythology the killing of the oxen of the Sun caused Ulysses's shipwreck and the death of his companions.

In my *Inner Keltia* No. 6 article on four- and seven-fold Initiation I got closer to solving this process than any researcher had previously, but now, thanks to the Shamanistic Calendar, I have been able to detect a few of my previous wayward notions and have drawn very much nearer to fully decoding these recondite processes. The bull-herd, as a stage in a Shaman Initiate's magical transformations, is almost solely preserved within pre-Christian pagan writings, but there is one remarkable passage in Nash's *Christ's Tears over Jerusalem* (1613) – 'They talk of an Ox that tolled the Bell at Woolwich, and how from an Ox he transformed himself into an Old Man, and from an Old Man to an Infant and into a Young Man again' – which might hint at the retention of some vestigial Initiatory knowledge.

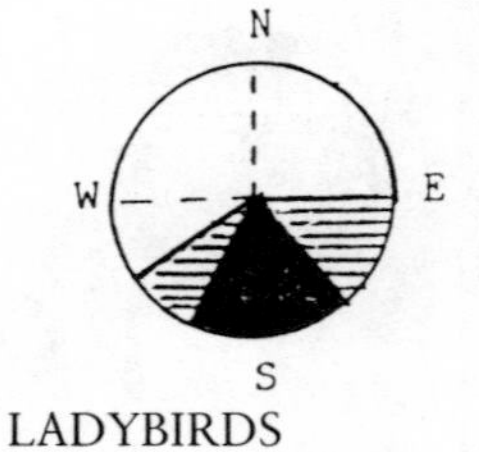

LADYBIRDS

Curiously enough, the ladybird is called 'the red-coated short-tailed cow' in County Meath, and 'lady-cow' in Shropshire, whilst our 'lady's bird' actually identifies it as a Goddess totem. Although functioning at many points within our ritual year calendar, the bull-ox obviously has a place of prominence within the astrological sign of Taurus (April–May), in the midst of which falls Beltain (the Teine, 'Fires' to the Sun–Fertility God Bel/Beli/Belin). It should thus come as no surprise that the bull is Bel's principal animal totem, and rules whilst the Sun mounts the sky.

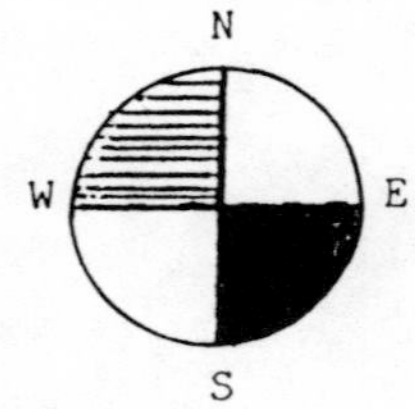

FIERY-WYVERN
(= Black Shading)
WATERY-WYVERN
(= Striped Shading)

Contrary to the opinion of those pompous, shallow researchers who say that the wyvern (two-legged winged dragon) only came into being with the advent of heraldry, Chinese, Toltec and Pictish equivalents were described many centuries before Christ – to say nothing of the immensely long period unrecorded by illustrated artefacts. For the wyvern forms a distinct transformation stage in the serpent-dragon cycle, as I briefly intimated in Fig. 16 in chapter 4. I have recently discovered that the cycle of ancient Chinese and Japanese geomantic dragons accords perfectly with my Shamanistic Calendar, which provokes some startling conclusions – see a future article in *Inner Keltia.*

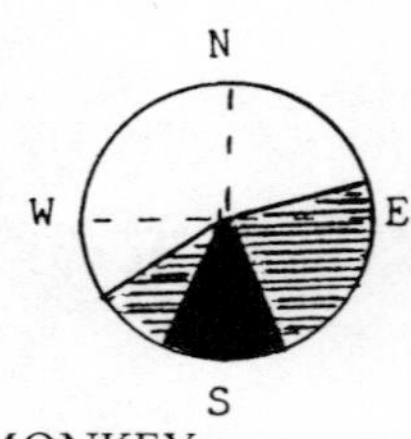

MONKEY

Within medieval Wildfolk and European Faerie Faith tapestries monkeys are often found in key positions – sometimes beside the Goddess. In probing mysterious happenings at a mill, a clairvoyant lady in 1853 distinctly saw 'a Lady like a shadow, with eyes but no sight in them' who was accompanied by various animals: 'One is like a Monkey and another like a Dog and another which was either a very quick Rabbit or a Hare.' In other words, the Goddess of Faerie (poorly described) and her totems.

Generally speaking, the monkey is linked to Hermes–Thoth, and is found in such a role within alchemical treatises.

At about the beginning of July occurs the period called 'the Dogs' Days', where all dogs were muzzled to minimize the spread of disease, which was reputedly caused by 'high' dogs responding to the rising and setting of Conicular (the Little Dog Star) in coincidence with the Sun.

Apart from *Y Draig Koch* (the red dragon), the other animal totem of the Kymry is the goat, for the mythic progenitor of the race was called *Gower* (i.e., *Gobhar* = goat). Goats were the totem animals of several Highland Clans, notably the Kummings. As might be expected, goats were sacred to various Keltic Gods and Faerie Wildfolk, e.g., Bwkka, Bukka, Puck, Glaistig, Uruisk, etc.; and to many other pagan divinities: Ashtoreth, Seirissim, Athene, Pallas, Venus, Mithra, Britomartes, Thor, Goda, Frigg, Hera, Juno Sospita, Osiris, Dionysus, Tammuz, Bacchus, Faunus, Zagreus, and of course the great Pan. In Norse mythology the she-goat Heidrun (sky) yielded enough milk every day to sustain the Einheriar dwelling in Valhalla. This is similar to the cornucopia of Amalthea. And the Gaelic:

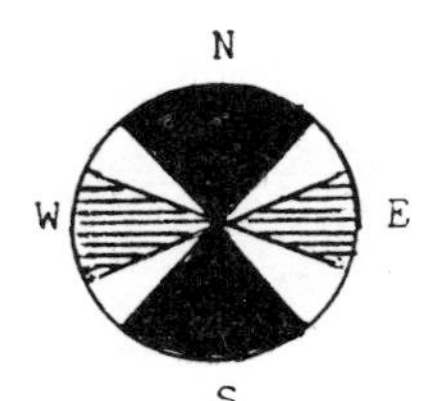

GOAT
GABAR
BOK
KUL-BHOK
BWKH-GAFR

Bainne nan gobhar fo chobhar 's e blath, 's e chuireadh an spionnadh 's na daoine 'bha.

'Tis the milk of the goat foaming and warm
That gave the strength to our sires before born.

In the Swedish May play *Bukkerwise* the Goat God (or his priest) was mated with the Goddess; likewise in the Broken May-eve ceremonies a goat was sacrificed to the Goddess. In Eirinn, the Puck Fair is still held every July/August, during which a goat decked in royal purple is hoisted into the sky within an enclosure (*Gabhar-lann*) filled with foliage to eat. The gold-crowned goat thus presides over this ancient pagan fayre. Exposure to the winds in this way would be quite appealing to the goat, as we read:

Gobhar Gaoth ann an aodann kreag.
Goat Wind in the face of a rock.

Miann Goibhre, Gaoths dol 'an aodann kreag.
A Goat's desire, Wind and climbing up a crag.

One derivation of the root word for goat is the Aryan *Ghaida* or *Ghid*, meaning to 'sport, play, frisk or dance'. Another Keltic root, *Gamra*, *Gabr Gafr*, *Gamh*, is related to winter. Both these derivations come together in some of the dancing Faerie Beings and mimicking Initiates, as I discuss in p. 136–168. Fairies are reported to comb goats' beards every Friday, indicating a possible link with Frigga, the Goddess of Fertility. Russian wood-spirits (*Ljeskhi*) are believed to appear partly in human shape, but also with the ears, horns and legs of goats. It is recorded from Postbridge on Dartmoor that a headless white goat occasionally jumps out from a boundary hedge to scare horses and their riders in broad daylight.

The renowned fertile and sexual capacities of the goat obviously contributed to its prominent place in all nature-based religions. Certain Goddesses (or their priestesses) were pictured as riding naked upon their totem-mounts. There is a Gaelic saying:

Tha suilean nan gobhar an ceannaibh nam fir a' taghadh nam ban.
Men have goats' eyes when choosing their woman.

Which is counterbalanced with:

Bidh suilean ghobhar aig na mnathan a' gleidheadh am fear dhaibh fhein.
Women have goats' eyes in keeping their husbands to themselves.

Goats as is generally known are very keen-sighted.

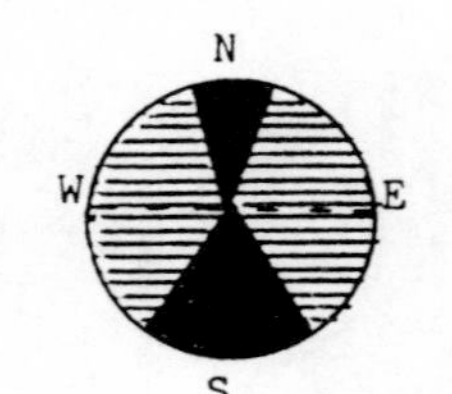

ADDER, NADDER, SUMMER & SKY SERPENTS, NEIDYR, NATHAIR, NATHRACH, NECHTAN

Being something of a serpent-priest, I have gathered enough serpent Lore to write a whole book on this subject. For the present, however, I present only a small relevant selection. The modern reader should not naively suppose that just because adders and other European snakes are becoming scarcer in the wild their importance has correspondingly decreased – for Inner Plane experiences still tend to arise when required. I myself have undergone several major Initiatory contacts with Otherworld serpents of a beautiful or staggeringly frightening nature. And, as Don Juan and Carlos Castaneda assure us that one of the best totem-guides we can have is a serpent (for those of us that it is right for, that is), we should relearn how to seek contact with them. That brilliant naturalist W. H. Hudson, in *The Book of a Naturalist* p. 21–22, has some sound advice to 'adder seekers'. In their search many people all over the world will suffer from the debilitating effects of Orthodox Church conditioning against serpent magic; these perverse shackles should be consciously shaken off. To aid this process I would suggest that you read Lyall Watson's book on Adrien Boshier called *Lightning Bird* (Hodder and Stoughton, 1982).

In Keltic mythology certain heroes have serpent guardians. For example, Keneu Menrud ('red mark') had a *Neidyr* (serpent) about his neck for a year; Konal Kernach had a serpent-being coiled around his waist which helped him in battle in the *Tain Bo Fraich*; Karados (Karadawg) similarly had a serpent wrapped around his arm.

Giraldus Kambrensis mentions a Pembrokeshire well which contained a golden torc, guarded by a large serpent, which bit the hand of anyone who tried to steal the torc. (For my own visionary illustration of a torc-guarding serpent see the cover of *Inner Keltia* No. 8, and a more recent Summer Solstice banner I designed for my Kaer Eidyn group). The Maiden's Well in Aberdeenshire, Pictland, and Grinston Well, Brawdy Parish, Pembrokeshire, are meant to contain a winged serpent which curls up in them at night. On the other side of Atlantic the ancient Creek Indians believed in a miraculous horned snake which would at times appear at the surface of a local waterhole (well). More generally, in Hopi Indian Folktales it is said that the waters of the world come from the breasts of the great snake.

In central American mythology there is a tale in which a Princess (who is normally enchanted as a white snake) is allowed to appear in her human guise at Midsummer's Eve once every quarter of a century (possibly a symbolical number of years). Elsewhere the Sea Dragon Kings live in underwater palaces, drawing energy from pearls and opals, etc. Four of the five serpent kings represent the cardinal points, and the Chief represents the quintessential element (the *Akasha*) in the middle. (For the Keltic five Serpent Kings see Fig. 16 in chapter 00.) A piece of serpent Lore from Glamorgan in Kymru relates that anciently in the woods of that area mighty winged serpents whilst coiled up at rest 'looked as though they were covered with jewels of all sorts. Some of them had crests sparkling with all the colours of the rainbow' (Marie Trevelyan, *Folklore and Folk Stories of Wales*). In my decoding of certain European Wildfolk tapestries, I pointed out that certain combats between Wildmen and totemistic creatures (e.g., wyverns) should be understood in a symbolical Shamanistic light; likewise, in one remarkable passage which chronicles Finn's triumphs over mighty serpents in many of Eirinn's lochs, rivers and glens, we should recognize the grappling with a serpent spirit (Shamanistic ally), which may only be 'killed' symbolically.

In Keltia the primal male God was Kernunos, who on the 'Gundstrop' Cauldron is shown holding a ram-headed serpent (*Nech*) in one hand and a gold torque (*Naesk*) in the other. The Kymraeg Sun God Bel/Belin/Belinus is sometimes figured as a mighty serpent, chief dragon (*Pen* dragon) or serpent bull. When Diankecht (Physician God) slew Meiche (the Morrigan's son), in his chest were found three hearts, which were three serpent's heads, and if they had been allowed to grow they would have caused havoc in Eirinn. In Scandinavian mythology the serpent of wisdom is called Faffnir, whose roasted heart provides illumination, just like Finn's/Gwionn's roasted salmon in Keltic myth. The great Odin disguised himself as a serpent/eagle, as did Loki; this parallels Zeus as the 'good serpent' (*Agathos daimon*) and Typhon as the 'evil serpent' (*Kakos daimon*). Hermes–Mercury–Asklepius (Physician God) was always closely associated with the serpent powers. Likewise Kadmus ('inventor' of the Greek Alphabet) and his wife Harmonia in leaving Thebes went to reign over a tribe of Eel-men in Illyria and became transformed into mighty serpents. The Serpent God Erechthonios (serpentine from the waist down) was placed in charge of Minerva's sacred olive tree near the Akropolis. (The Chinese God Foki was also depicted with a serpentine tail.) Kekropes, the first King of Athens, was supposed to have been half man and half serpent; and Kychreus, after slaying a great serpent on Salamis, had to appear himself in a serpent form. Medusa, as Moon and Earth Goddess, was conveyed in a serpent-drawn chariot (see also Hekate, Dionysus and Demeter). Alexander the Great's mother was reported to have conceived him after sleeping with one of her totemistic house serpents (some say this was Jupiter–Amon). The Akkadian God Hea appears in a serpent form, once linked to a seven-headed form (just like the seven-headed cobras associated with the Naga Kings of India). In the Pelasgian creation myth, Eurynome, the Goddess of All Things, rose naked out of chaos, caught hold of the spirit of the North Wind (Boreas), rubbed it between her hands, and thus the great serpent Ophion was created; he in turn fertilized Eurynome. (Similarly, Zeus in serpent-form coupled with his mother Rhea, who was also serpentine at the time.)

Various Sun Gods were either serpentine or closely involved with such, e.g., Apollo, Pythius and Helios (who is reported to have married Ops and then fathered Osiris, Isis and Typhon). The primal Earth-mound (first 'matter' created), the *Omphalos*, often had a great serpent coiled around it, as Ophion coiled around the world-egg. The Babylonian Earth God Ea-en-ki, in serpent form gave humankind knowledge of the world's order, but made death necessary so that man could be reborn. The African creation myth has the great serpent's seven thousand coils setting the stars and planets in motion. He brought life to Earth and still can be seen moving in the current of a river, arching over us in the form of the rainbow and flashing down within the lightning. He is held to rest within a cave deep underground. Toltec and Mayan Lore is richly endowed with serpent deities. In case any semi-Christian reader is wondering how this pagan Lore may harmonize with true Christianity, St John 3.14 should be borne in mind: 'Even as Moses lifted up the Serpent [*Nechūshtan*] in the Wilderness, even so must the Son of Man [Christ] be lifted up.' This identification is confirmed in the better Christian gnosticism, where Christ's Crucifixion is depicted as the serpent Nechūshtan–Christ being nailed to a Tau–Cross. Thus Christians should implement Christ's own recommendation: 'Be ye therefore wise as Serpents, and harmless as Doves.'

The serpent of wisdom is connected with two other phenomena: lightning (*Dealan*), and the rainbow (called variously in Gaelic *Bogha-braoin*, *Bogha-bion*, *Bogha-frois* and *Bogha-uisge*). *Bogha* has a relation to the word-root *Bolg*/*Bolga*, meaning lightning/God.

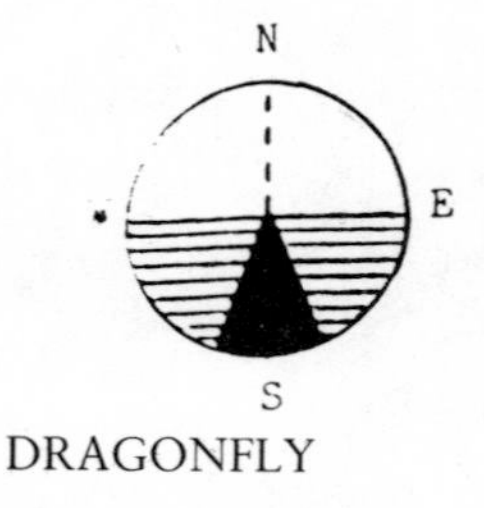

DRAGONFLY

Returning to the magical ingredients of our Shamanistic Wheel, let us look at the beautiful dragonfly. The associations evoked by this English name are fully supported by earlier Keltic terms for this creature, such as: *Gwas Y Neidr* ('adder of the air' or 'the snake's servant'), *Gwachell Y Neidr* ('long-thin flying adder'), both Kymraeg terms; and *Tarbh-nathair* ('serpent-bull') in Ghaidhlig. This is no Keltic flight of fancy, as the sceptics would whine, for amongst the Red Indians the dragonfly is known as 'the sister of the rattlesnake' and is said to hover near to them. A belief in Devon and Cornwall was that, where an adder lay concealed in the undergrowth, a dragonfly would hover above to warn or alert the perceptive walker.

When once out walking in the Strath of Kildonan (North-east Alban) on a blisteringly hot midsummer's day, I had a genuine psychic and physical experience with an adder and a dragonfly which convinced me of their Shamanistic interdependance (fully ten years ago, before I read such Lore). Thus, when I read that an elderly man from Wick (North-east Alban) said, 'It is very lucky to see a dragonfly skimming over a pool of water. If ever I do see one I always cross my fingers and make a wish – I was told to do this when I was a boy,' I would warmly support his counsel. Dragonflies are also meant to be able to point out good fishing pools by resting on a nearby bush as an omen.

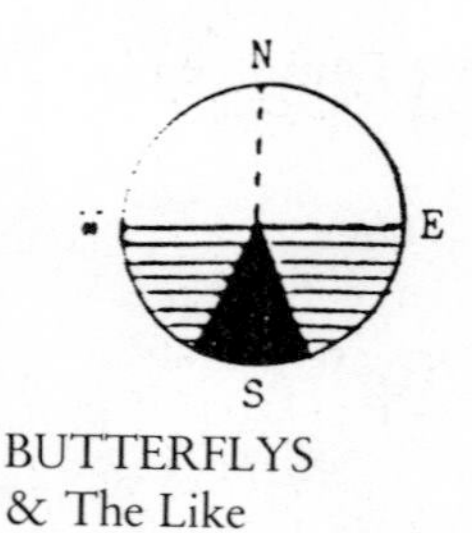

BUTTERFLYS
& The Like

With its prediliction for bright sunshine, it is not surprising that the butterfly has its ritual Station in the Shamanistic South of our Wheel. Apart from the physical creatures, butterflies also appear in Keltic beliefs as Otherworld guides and the vehicles for disembodied beings – their names include: *Dealan-de*, *Tarmach-de*; *Dearbadan-de* (each containing the Scottish Gaelic for deity, *De*); similarly in Irish Feilokan, Manx Follikan and the Breton. Amongst the Russians and Slavs, butterflies often appear as emblems of the soul, named *Dushichka*, a diminutive of *Dusha* ('soul'). The codexes of Central American MSS are also sprinkled with butterflies as the spirit forms of the Otherworld dead.

In Carlos Castaneda's brilliant books, Don Juan shows him one of the allies in a white moth form, and teaches him to reproduce its spluttering call-notes. Traces of a similar belief exist within Gaeldom where a little spectre, appearing as a white moth, was called a *Fuatharlan* – this having a more nocturnal role than the butterfly.

Pictland has beliefs similar to Castaneda's Otherworld guardian in the form f a gnat, for example the guardian spirit of St Michael's Well in Banffshire howed itself in the form of a fly that kept skimming over the surface of the vater off and on for hundreds of years, until the well's desecration in the late ineteenth century.

Finally a small piece of Welsh Lore: the fritillary butterfly is sometimes called he Snake's head' – *Britheg Pen Y Neidyr.*

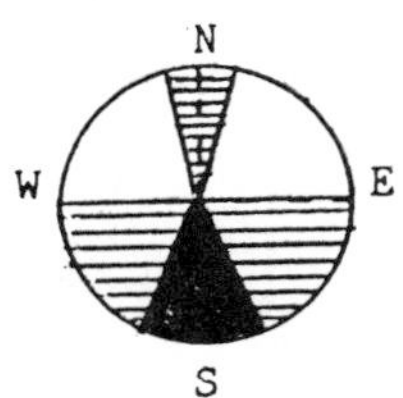

LIZARDS
HEATHER-ASK
ARK-LUACHAIR
LUACHAIR
LOCHRAG
ALP-LUACH

These beautiful and very dear friends of mine are Shamanistic totems of high ummer. Almost all the lizard's names in Gaelic and Kymraeg relate it to bright, vhite light: *Luachair*, *Lochrag* (Gdhlig) and *Lleufer*, *Louber* (Kym); this links it o the good light elves, the *Luachair-pin*, *Alp-luachra* and *Lios Alfar*; and thus o the Tree Goddess white magic, the *Luis*, *Loise* (rowan), as well as the nidsummer rushes *Bog-luachair*). With this creature being Shamanistically so ery good, it is alarming to see how adversely conditioned some people have ecome: 'There is no form in nature more repugnant to the eye than that of the izard, toad, and the serpent, shape not excepted, instinctive repulsion being the ule or condition indeed of most people to these members of the saurian tribe.'

In the Greek Hermetic tradition the lizard was sacred to Hermes–Thoth, who ad an Otherworld chariot drawn by lizards. This fits with lizards' associations o secret ciphers and their uses in good sorcery as described by Castaneda. A form f divination amongst the Ancient Greeks was to watch their movements upon valls, and interpret them with a seeing eye. All lizards have the relic of a third ye in the centre of their foreheads; in some species (e.g., the pine-tree lizard of America) it is even able to register changes of light. The lizard is sometimes lepicted upon the breast of Athene, the Goddess of Wisdom. Amongst the gyptian hieroglyphs it stood for 'kindliness and benevolence'. In Ireland it was eld that, if an individual licked a lizard all over, his/her own tongue could then eal sores in other people by licking the affected spot. Lizards are also strongly ssociated with the powers of vision, as is denoted by their Keltic names – *Ark*, *Arkan*, *Dearkan.*

As a final point, according to one line of thinking, snakes are simply lizards hat have discarded their legs, and birds are but lizards that have grown feathers nd climbed into the sky.

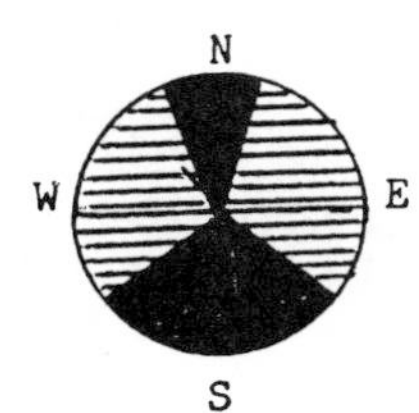

BIG CATS
LUG = Lynx or Mountain Lion
KAT-FIADHAICH (Wild Cat)
KATH WYLLT (Wild Cat)
LLEW (kym) LEO (Ir) = Lion
MOCHA = Black/ Brown Cat
GLASNEUNT, IACH, IARA
ONN-KHU = Leopard

Big cats were and are of great significance to the Keltic people. The God of Light and Warriorship was Lugh, Lughos or Lleu; he had as his totem *Lug*, the European lynx, the mountain lion (in medieval times the ordinary lion would ave been substituted within heraldry). Thus the lion, along with the unicorn, ppears frequently on the heraldic crests of Alban.

One of the Irish Kings was called Kairbar Kinn Khait ('*Karbar* of the cat's ead'); whilst one of the Pictish tribes, the Kati ('cat people'), took their name rom their totem and gave it to their province Kataobh ('cat country'), now nown as Caithness, which still today has many mysterious big-cat sightings. The Chieftain of Clan Chattan is called Mohr an Chat ('the great cat'); whilst a poem in *Silva Gadelica* preserves '*Ríg Katt Atuaid*' ('King of Cats in the North'). There are many places in the Highlands that take their name from big cats (*not* from the site of a battle), e.g., Teachait (*Teach a Chait*), Beinn-a-Chait near Applecross, etc.

Bridget, who is styled 'the daughter of the bear', is linked to a cat in a phrase *Kat firionn Brighid Ni Mhathghamhna* from an Irish Tale. The Scottish Gaelic saying '*Lath a Fheill-Bhrighde baine, bheir na cait an connadh dhachaidh*' means 'On Bridhe's Day, the cats will bring home the brushwood.' In another Tale of the fifteenth century, Merlin sets forth 'King Arthur's fight with the great cat' (Arthur = bear-man).

In one of the Irish Otherworld voyages, a little cat (*Kat Bec*) is encountered as a guardian of treasure; in maintaining its watch it turns into a flaming form and, leaping its way through a potential thief, turns him to ashes. As cats are also witch familiars, some very barbarous practices were employed, such as the *Taghairm* rite, where a cat was roasted alive on a spit to coerce other supernatural cats to deliver up their secrets; likewise live cats were burned in baskets in midsummer bonfires in Gaul.

There is already enough Lore presented here to belie Anne Ross's inaccurate statement 'Cats do not play a large role in Celtic Mythology.' Also, those who plod, plod, plod along within the ponderous and predictable avenues of thought will never realize why the *Kat-sith* (Faerie cats) of our ancestors keep reappearing up and down Britain, from Cornwall to East Anglia, from Gwynedd to Inverness. Sometimes the size of an ordinary cat but with unusual propensities, sometimes as big as an alsatian dog, sometimes appearing like a puma, sometimes like a black jaguar, the British big cat is still on the loose.

'A writer in *Notes and Queries*, H. Wedgewood by name, visited Mr Proctor in 1873–74 to ask him the truth about the Willington Mill ghost, and he told her that he had seen a tabby cat in the furnace room. There was nothing unusual in the animal's appearance, and it would not have caught his attention particularly had it not begun to move. But then instead of walking like an ordinary cat it wriggled like a snake. He went close to it and followed it across the room, holding his hand about a foot above it, until it passed straight into the solid wall.'

For more recent sightings I would advise reading Janet and Colin Bord's *Alien Animals*. Even I have seen one of these alien cats this summer, in broad daylight, whilst I was in Dumfries and Galloway discovering more new cup and ring mark sites. (1986).

The Keltic words for a lion/mountain lion, *Llew*, *Lleu*, *Léo*, *Lug*, stem directly from an ancient Indo-European root, paralleled by the Old High German *Lewo*, Slavic *Livu*, and Greek *Lefon*; the root is *not* from Latin as the ascendancy would try and con us into believing.

The lion has mainly solar connections with Mithra, Herakles, Apollo, Ra and Samson; fire associations with Vulcanus, Vesta, Judah, Archangel Ariel, and more general ones with Dionysus (whose war chariot was pulled by panthers), Siegfried, Sir Galahad and the Lion Knight, and Jesus Christ, called 'Rabbi ben Panther' (see Hosea V: 14 – 'I am become as a Panther to Ephraim'). The Goddesses, Diana, Kirke, Kybele and Freya were also linked to Big Cats.

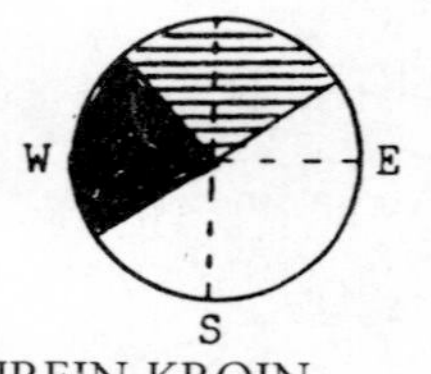

KIREIN-KROIN
SEA-SERPENT
UR-FEIST
MIAL-MHOR-MHARA
(GREAT SEA BEAST)
BLADMHIAL
(BEAST of the MOUTH)

As there have been thousands of sightings of sea serpents (which were not all mistaken killer whales, octopuses, sporting porpoises, etc.), I do not intend to survey the voluminous Lore. Rather I would refer those interested to certain books already in print on this subject. Two Gaelic sayings worth noting here are that it takes 'seven seals to make a meal for a sea monster' (*Seachd roin sath mial-mhor-mhara*); and 'An *Urfeist* of the sea must get a noble lady to devour every seven years.' (*Urfeist* is derived from *Ur* = original, greatest, man; *Piest* = serpent, worm, beast, monster.)

To a Shaman or Shamaness, this creature is a serpent, of the rivers, lochs and sea; anatomical distinctions take second place to magical characteristics.

Soup madé from the flesh of a conger was said to be a very good cure for many internal complaints. The oil was rubbed into stiff joints; the skin was used to defray the effects of rheumatism, as we hear:

'Until the end of the last century Fenmen and women protected themselves against attacks of rheumatism and allied disorders by wearing garters made from Eel skin. W. H. Barrett can recall from his youth the method of preparing them in the Littleport Fens. Only Eels caught in the spring provided suitable skins. After the heads and tails had been cut off the skins were removed in one piece and hung up to dry in the sun until they were quite stiff. Then the two ends of each were tied and the skins well greased with fat and rubbed with a round piece of wood until they were pliable again, when the ends were untied and the skins re-stiffened by the insertion of a 'stuffing' of finely chopped thyme and lavendar leaves. The skins were next inserted in linen bags which were buried in the peat for the rest of the summer between layers of freshly gathered marsh mint, as the water mint (*Mentha aquatica*) was locally known. This gave a mottled appearance to the garters. In the autumn the skins were dug up and a final polish was given to them, after the removal of the thyme, lavendar and mint, with a smooth stone. The garters, called 'yorks', were tied just above the knees, men knotting them on the right, women on the left side. Old women declared that in addition to their use as a cure and preventive of rheumatism the 'yorks' stopped mice from running above the garters when the wearers of them were working in the harvest fields.'

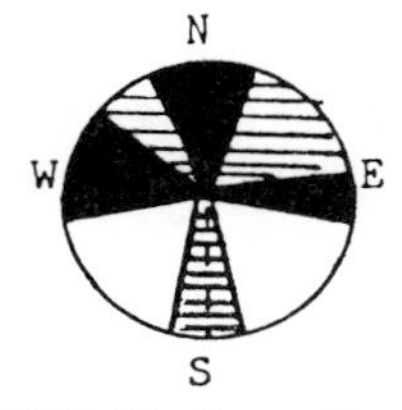

EELS (Ordinary & Conger)
EAS-KON or EAS-KU = Hound Fish
EASGUNN-MHARA = Hound Fish of the Sea (Conger)
KULLACH = VICIOUS HUNTER (lit. Sea-Boar)
GIOBAN, GEALOG = Sand Eel
BIOR-BHUASAN = Spear with pouting-lips
EASKANN-ABHANN = Freshwater Eel

As eels are mainly Shamanistic West (and Shamanistic North) in their Station, it is interesting to note that they are greatly disturbed by their Shamanistic opposite – springtime thunder. Thus, in East Anglia St Valentine's Day was used to prepare, and thereafter during thundery weather the Fenmen would go down to the rivers. If many eels were caught in fair weather, then thunder was soon due.

Conger and other eels feed mostly at night (on trout eggs, etc.), and during the day some congers can be heard 'barking' on 'grunting' in holes above the water's edge.

A widespread belief is that horse-hair placed under a stone of a stream in midsummer will, within a month, turn into very thin wriggling creatures; be that as it may, I once found in a pond a foot-long creature resembling a length of thick copper wire which I have yet to identify in books on pond-life.

As eels are so important Shamanistically, we should seriously consider the karmic message behind the recent death of 250,000 of them in the Rhine from factory pollution!

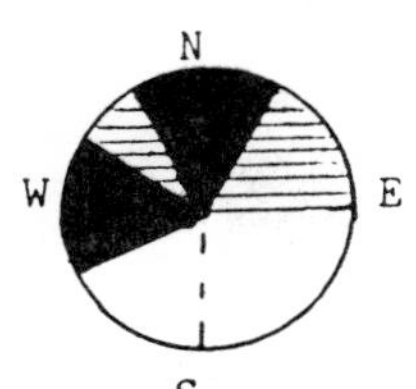

THE OTTER
DOBHAR-KU (WATER-HOUND)
MADADH-DONN (BROWN-DOG)
MADADH-UISSE (WATER-DOG)
ODHAR-CHU (DUN/SEA-DOG)
BEISD-DUBH = Black Beast
Tyke or Teak = Hairy Dog

The otter, which in every Keltic tongue is called the 'water dog' (Kymraeg = *Dwfr-ki (gi)*; Kerneweg = *Dofer-ki*; Brezhoneg = *Dour-ki*; Erse = *Dobhar-ku (chu)*), has two main Stations in our Calendar Wheel: in the North, and in the East, under Pisces and associated with the mysterious 'Cetus' creature. In European and North American mythologies the otter sometimes surfaces bearing a secret pearl or special stone in its paws, the treasured object of a quest. The skill and speed with which it catches the salmon (of wisdom) made it a natural choice for a Shamanistic otter-skin hunting-suit (invoking more than sympathetic magic). And, as you'll see from Tales in chapter 7, the otter features prominently in catching the Wildman's 'soul' in an egg/salmon.

Like the toad, the otter is said to possess a jewel in its head. The skin of an otter was worn as a charm against drowning; it kept harps dry when made into a large holdall (*Krot bolg*); and it was lucky to line the inside of a *Targe* (round shield) with otter skin. The 'master otter' is said to have appeared once at Dhu Hill (Black Hill), waited upon by about a hundred common-sized otters. (This Otherworld Chief of the Otter Clan is in South American terminology the Chief Nagual of Otters.) A white otter (or a dun one with a white star), which used to live in Sutherland, was also linked to this 'master otter.' In the Irish tradition otters were sacred to Mannanan MacLir, Lord of Deep Magic.

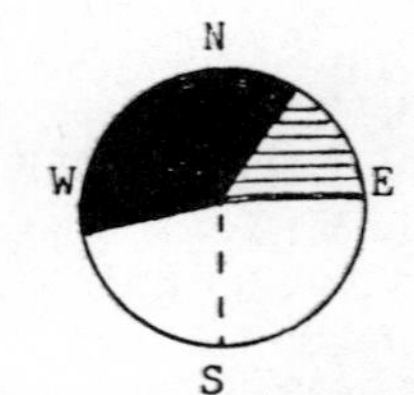

SEALS
KU-MARA = Sea-Hound
MOR-LUAH = Swift Dog of the Sea
KULLACH-KUAIN = Hound of the Waves
ROAN, RON, RON-MULACH & HRON
BEISD-MHAOL:
BOKA & PHOKA = Faerie
SILKIE, SELCHIE, SAEL

That the breeding season for grey seals is September, October and into November, perfectly fits their main Shamanistic Station from West to North. At this time many haul themselves up onto the skerries (rocky sandbanks) to breed in rookeries. The large seal brings forth its young at the start of October, whilst the lesser seal calves in the middle of June.

In the Faeroes it is held that, around the Winter Solstice/New Year, seals put off the seal skins (*Kokuls*) and become human folk again. They are known generally as 'the children of the King of Lochlann under spells' (*Mak Righ fo gheasaibh*; Lochlann = Shamanistic North); the Clan of MacKodrums were held to be descended from the seal-man tribe, or have it as totems: 'Clann Mhic Kodruim nan Ron,' 'Clan MacKodrums the Seals.' Such beliefs are preserved in the marvellous folksong 'The Great Silkie of the Sule Skerrie' (see the Corries' version on *Live at the Lyceum*). In Germanic tradition these Mermen and Merwomen were supposed to doff their fishy skins every ninth day. By name and nature they are related to the Sea Goddess Rann. In parallel traditions the Nereid Psamathe changed herself into a seal, whilst Menelaus hid amongst them in her seal skin to capture the elusive Proteus; they were totems of the Sea Goddess Thetis; and one of the disguises of the trickster Loki. Some Gaelic sayings are also worthy of contemplation:

Bu dual do isean an roin a dhol thun na mara.
The young seal takes naturally to the sea.

Seachd bradain sath roin.
Seven salmon, a seal's feed.

Sitheadh roin, aon de na tri sithidhean a's luaithe 's a chuan mhor.
The rush of a seal, one of the swiftest rushes [known] in the great ocean.

Is ann aig na roin tha brath.
The seals know. Said of the impossible.

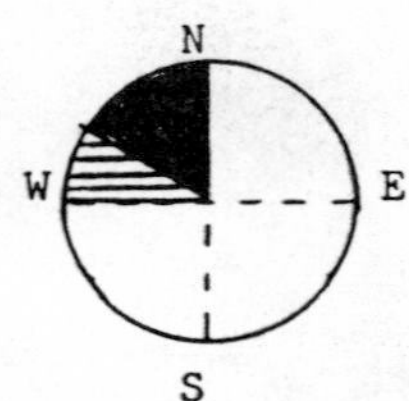

GRAMPUS – WOLF OF THE SEA
SPOUTING-BLUNT-HEADED DOLPHIN
ORKA, KANNA, KANACH KAN (Hound)
MADA-CHUAIN = Hound of the Sea-Waves
BECK-DOG, BUCKER (Faerie-Dog)

'The grampus is a sort of third cousin to the whale, and a first cousin to the porpoise. It bears the name wolf of the sea from its habit of assailing anything or everything living inhabiting the waters.'

The boar was and is one of the most powerful animals for the Kelts. On the whole it symbolizes the solar power during the Dark Half of the Year (on the duller side of the Equinoxes). Some of the most famous Keltic magical boars and sows are: Tork Triath ('King of the Boars'), which Diarmid fought in Alban/Eirinn; Henwen, 'the white ancient sow', guarded by Koll mab Kollfrewy; the swine of Pendaran Dyfed, in Glyn Kuch, guarded by Pryderi, son of Pwyll, Lord of Annwfn (the Underworld); the two magic pigs of Lubhdan, described to Fergus; the healing and wine producing pig of Tuis/Duis; Mukka Slangha ('the health-giving pig'), which had nine tusks in each jaw which, when it had been killed by Kaeilte, provided many warriors with magic food. Red swine (*Derga Mukko*) were encountered on an Otherworld island by Mael Duin. Subelino ('bright shining boar') resembles Frey's Gullinbursti. There were also the flesh-renewing swine of Assail (the Lightning God). One of the mightiest magical boars in the Gaelic tradition is Tork Forbartach, and in a Fenian Tale it is said:

'The description of that huge boar was enough to cause mortal terror, for he was blue-black, with rough bristles ... grey, horrible, without ears, without a tail, without testicles and his teeth standing out long and horrid outside its big head ... and it raised the mane of its back on high so that a plump wild apple would have stuck on each of its rough bristles.'

Its Kymraeg equivalent is the famous Twrch Trwyth, which the hawthorn giant Ysbaddaden Penkawr sends Kulhwch to encounter in the *Mabinogion*:

'"There is no Comb and Shears in the world wherein my hair may be dressed so exceeding stiff it is, save the Comb and Shears that are between the two ears of Twrch Trwyth, son of Taredd Wledig."'

Echoes of these fantastic legendary beasts can be seen in the Winter Solstice/Yuletide boar's head brought into banquets decked with bay and evergreens and with an apple in its mouth. Earlier in winter, October was the traditional boar-hunting season, after they had fed off the oak mast; whilst, at the end of winter, March was said to come in 'rough and wild' like a boar's head.

In Northern Europe a ghostly boar was thought to run with 'the wild hunt' through the stormy midwinter skies (whilst ordinary boars dislike strong winds which they try and avoid through foreknowledge). Pigs' bladders have been used in rituals since ancient times, and certain Morris fools still use them to belabour their fellows.

In other traditions boars and sows appear linked to Odin, who feeds the elect in Valhalla off Sachrimnir's flesh every day; Apollo (underworld form); Ares, Artemis, Mercury, Poseidon, Tammuz, Osiris, Diana–Persephone (underworld).

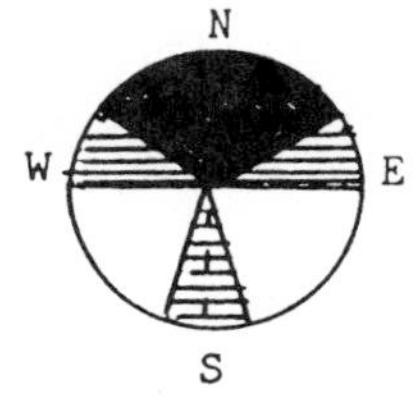

WILD BOAR
T-ORK (The Pig)
KALLACH,
ANTRELLACH
FIAKLACH-KOILLE
OG-KHULLACH
TORK-NIMH
(THE PIG, SACRED & VENOMOUS)

Of the four magical beasts of the Kelts, the stag ruled over the festival of Samhain. This makes sense according to nature too, for: 'The red stag cleans his new antlers in August–September. The rut follows quickly on the cleaning of the antlers, taking place from mid-September onwards, October is usually the big month. In certain years the rut will last well into November. Frost seems to play a big part in bringing it on.' Fertility is not indicated just by the antlers, for some stags never grow antlers. These beasts are called 'hummels' and because they do not have to produce horn marrow they grow heavy, and often become master stags. It was held to be very dangerous to encounter a wild full-antlered stag during the rutting season, for it could use its antlers with ferocious accuracy, as the old saying relates: 'If thou be hurt with hart [stag] it brings thee to thy bier, but the barbers [old physician's] hand will boar-hurt heal, therefore thou need'st not fear.'

With the stag ruts, harts and deer were all associated with the autumn and winter months, as is echoed in the Old Kymraeg triads:

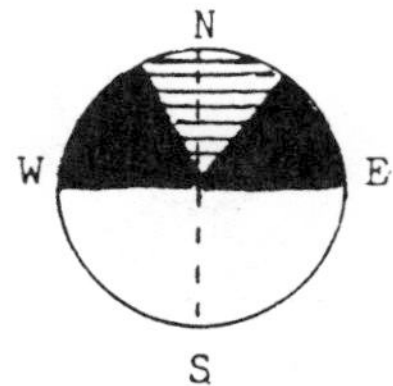

STAG, DEER, HIND
AG-ALLAIDH
(WILD-STAG)
AG-FEIDH
(FAWN-HIND)
LAN-DAMH
(ROYAL-HART)
BOK-EARBA
(ROEBUCK)
BODACHAN (YEAR-OLD BUCK)
BOK-DA-BHIORAIN,
BOISKEALL (MAGIC HIND)
AIRKHEALTRACH
(HIND)

Mountain snow – noisy the stag;
The waves wash the margin of the strand;
Let the skilful conceal his design.

Mountain snow – the hart in the forest;
Thoroughly black the raven; swift the young stag.
If one is free and healthy, it is strange there should be complaining.

Thus Pwyll (the King of the Underworld temp.) has a stag associated with him. At this time of the year the deer-herds were also held to be under the protection of the Kailleach Bheur, who along with her Wildwomen Glaistigs and Gruagaichs herded and milked them in the hills and forests. One account says that the Kailleach-mor-nam-Fiadh ('Great Hag Goddess of the Deer') is a giantess living among the mountains of Jura. This is paralleled by the Kailleach mhor Khlibrik ('Great Hag of Klibrik') who protected the deer from the disrespectful hunter who stooped so low as to use unfair bullets. The Gaelic hero–poet Oisin had been born from a mother who was strongly paired to a hind, thus it was *geassa* for him to hunt deer; likewise at the end of his life Oisin saw a stag (his *Nagual* animal) pursued by a white hound with red ears (*Kwn Annwfn*), and thus knew his death was nigh. Stags were also associated with winter rites and linked to Dionysus (by the Bassarids), Artemis, Diana, Kyparissus, Yggdrasil, and Kernunos of the Voseges. A biblical lover is described as 'like a young hart upon the mountains of Bether [through the night] 'till break of day,' (Song of Solomon 2:17).

Magic white stags are recorded from Ben Alder, and in Eire, where *Liath na dti mbenn* ('The grey-white one of the three antlers') was hunted down by the Fenian Kaoilte. (A real white stag was photographed some years back on Arran in the west of Alban. I have reproductions in Kaer Eidyn files.) The white hinds are more prominent from Imbolk through the apple-tree Ogham Station (see Fate and Birth Goddess) and on into spring, as R. L. Tongue recorded from a lady (from a Women's Institute) at Kilmersdon in 1962:

'In ancient times there were many kinds of deer that wandered in the forest near Kilmersdon, and among them sometimes ran a magical white hind. She was rarely seen, but any woodsman who saw even a flash of her whiteness was fortunate and happy for days. Many seekers tried to get a full view of her, but without success. But one May evening the Lord of Kilmersdon was riding back over Mendip, full of care, for there was a pestilence among his people, when, before him through the forest, sped the fairy hind. It led him on for more than a mile, and then it vanished, and with it went all his fears and heaviness. His heart was filled with great happiness all his life, and in gratitude he built the Lady Chapel at Kilmersdon Church to dedicate his joy to Heaven.'

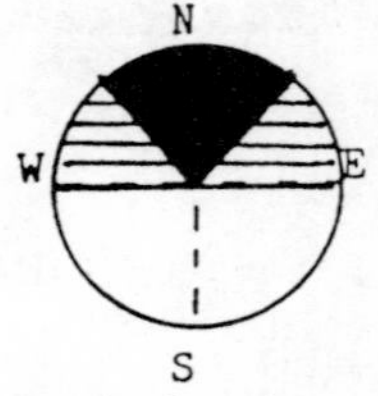

Also to be found at this Shamanistic Station is the REINDEER.

REIN-DEER (= 'Horse-Deer')
OS, OZ (= 'Horse-Deer')
BOIRCHE, BRAK, BRAKHE

A northern equivalent of the stag/deer is the Reindeer; even nowadays the pagan memory lingers in the Reindeer that pull the sleigh of the Yuletide father. *Os-muin*'s antlers (not tusks) were powdered into baked slingshot (*Tathlum*). (Note that *Muin* possibly relates to Ogham *Muin* Station, also reindeer relish feeding upon water lilies). The reindeer are herded by the Faerie Wildwomen, who have given us many songs such as this:

On milk of deer I was reared
On milk of deer I was nurtured

On milk of deer beneath the stormy-ridge
On crest of hill and mountain.

The presiding deity was the Wild Kaileach, who in the Loch Krew area was called 'Garbh Og', an ancient ageless giantess whose chariot (*Kar*) was drawn by elks, who dined upon venison, deer milk and eagles' breasts; she herself occasionally chased the mountain deer with a pack of seventy hounds (which each possessed bird names). Seasonally/periodically she 'set up her Kaer in a womb of the hills, at the season of heather-bloom' (Autumn Equinox) and then expired; only to be later born again from her own triple kairn.

Finally, it is encouraging to note the thriving herds of reindeer reintroduced into the Kairngorms around their friend Am Fear Glas Mor, the Wildman.

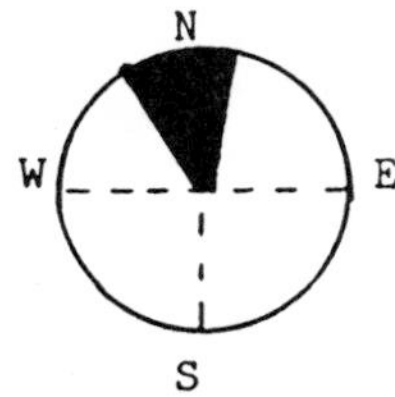

HORSES AT *Sh.*
NORTH
BLACK-HORSES
BLACK-WATER-HORSES

Horses have many places on the Calendar; that shown, however is perhaps the key point containing the wild, proud stallions and the centaurs of Sagittarius. One of the power-objects of the horseman's cult was the *Milt/Melt/Meld/Milch/Mummy* taken from a new born foal's mouth. In Alban (especially Pictland) this was called the 'pad'; *Pade* in Old Pictish means toad, paddock, frog'. 'Paddock ride' means frog's spawn; and 'paddock pipes' means marsh horsetail. Also a horse's field is still known as a paddock. The other main horseman's power-object was the frog's bone, which was actually taken from a certain type of toad's skeleton in a stream at midnight; this toad bone was held to resemble a bone/mark on the underside of horses' hoofs, called 'the frog'. After a specific rite this toad's bone had very strong Shamanistic powers over any horse. Toads/frogs have several sides to their characters, from the amorous and sexually lovable (Mr Froggy went a' courting and the handsome Frog/Toad Prince of Folktales) to the deeply contemplative eyes of a wise philosopher, fully conversant with the arcane mysteries (The Philosopher's Stone and toads in alchemy. I have been led to this wisdom by following the wolf-road of words and their ancient meanings. European mythology had four horses for the four winds coloured appropriately: North – black; South – white; East – red; West – green/bay. The original meaning of 'nightmare' was a dream/vision from the Horse Hag Goddess. In the middle ages, a bier was called St Michael's Horse, the Archangel Michael being the main guide for a discarnating human spirit. A horse makes a neighing sound; the gaelic for a goose is *Neigh*, a totem-bird for the winter solstice. The water horse, kelpie, *Ek-elphie*, Faerie horse is usually encountered as a black horse (or black-haired man) with staring eyes, sometimes with weeds in its hair and still wet from its nightly appearance from a stream/river/pool/lynn/loch. A special arrow was needed to dispel a kelpie; it was called a *Baodhag* ('fury of the quiver'), The various centaurs (horse-men) that are to be found in Pictish and Keltic carvings have not been borrowed or copied from classical versions (as the liars of the ascendancy's creed would have you believe); rather they are very ancient and native to our own mythology. The Keltic Horse (and Hound) God called Fal (or Phol) is also a God of Light midst the darkness – this Northern quarter being known as the Plain of Fal (truth and wisdom), containing the stone of Fal (the great *Lia Fail*, treasure of the Gaelic Gods – which is not under the coronation seat, nor anywhere on the physical plain). Perhaps the most widely known form of this horse-human is the centaur-archer Sagittarius, whose fiery arrows of spiritual aspiration shoot long and far.

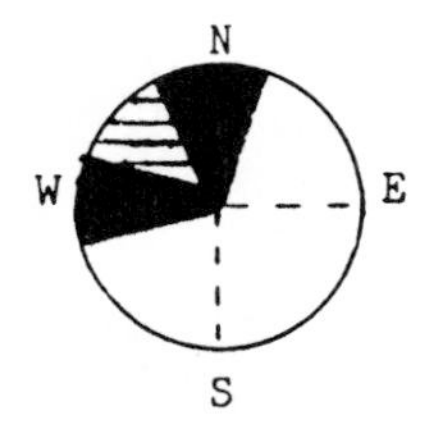

The water bull or *Tarbh-uisge*, as it is called in Gaelic, is an Otherworld bull form which inhabits streams, pools, wells and lochs. Its mythological close-cousin is the sea-bull. When one fully understands the water-serpent mechanics of how natural water currents flow (as Viktor Schauberger did), one will appreciate why the *Tarbh-uisge* is often called or seen as a serpent bull of the water. Although pollution of the environment (physical and mental) has affected the habitat of these creatures, yet within some wild localities and on the deeper planes of existence they can still be contacted.

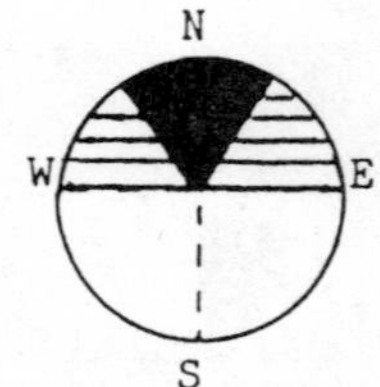

BEAR, ART, ARD
BEITHIR, BRAKH
URS, URSAN (male)
URSAG (female),
MATH-
GHAMHUINN
(= Stirk with Paws)
(thus MAHOUN an
Irish Giant rel. to
McMahons,
Mathesons)

The bear is in legend King of all the Animals of the North (dedicated to Donar and dark Zeus), the most famous Keltic equivalent being the God–King Arthur. The Gaulish Bear God was Artaois, related to the Kruithnaeg Deo-Ard (t). The Kaledonian bear was also a Shamanistic guise for the earliest Pictish Myrddin (Merlin) as a Wildman prophet. Likewise the Gypsy God who implements all changes of fate or fortune is the black Bear God known as Arty (or Art) – a piece of good luck being known as 'a gift from Arty'. The proud North European warriors often invoked their tribal and personal animal totems before going into battle. This would sometimes involve them dressing in bear skins and turning ber-serk and fighting furiously. The she bear in turn was sacred to the Keltic Goddesses Artio and Andarta ('powerful bear'); and to the Greek Artemis-Brauronia, the Arcadian Kallisto, and the Erinyes (the Furies); thus it is an animal of great grizzly 'medicine power' as our Red-Indian brethren would say. In the Gaelic tradition it is said that the *Kean mathon* ('head of the bear') was one of the seven signs or names of star clusters engraved on the shield of the Chief of Artha (Arthur). As bear-cult sites (including Votive statues and ritual jewellery) have been discovered throughout the Keltic lands, it is not surprising that people still encounter spectral/phantom bears (e.g., on Shipworth Common, in the Jewel Chamber in London, etc.), for they will still come through from the Otherworlds (as they do in Slavonia, Russia and North America).

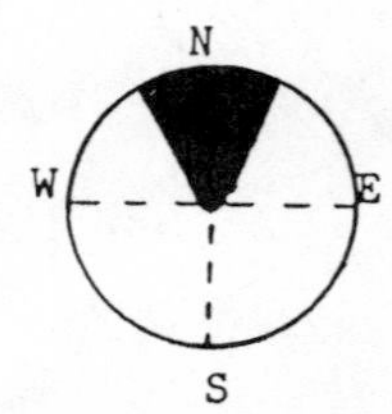

BIG BLACK CATS
KUGAR,
KUGARBHAD
(Male Wildcat/Hero)
KUGARBHAD MOR
RIGH
NAN KAT = Great
Kugarvad, King of the
Cats

As we have already mentioned, the spectral black cat (*Kait Sith*, Faerie cat, dark green with very long ears, and often seen standing up on its back legs like a Wildman) still haunts the British countryside, as does Kugarvad, King of the Cats in Europe and North America. One of the Shamanistic animals much lied about and insulted by the Church fathers is the red fox, the *Madadh-ruadh* or *Madra-rua* (red dog) in Gaelic. Although the main Station of the Fox may be in the red Eastern quarter, as that of the trickster, it also has its second most prominent quarter position in the North. There are several linguistic linkages that point to this connection: its old name in Alban is *Tod*, or *Tod Lowrie*, thereby connecting it to the 'toad' word-root. (Both later names – Lawrence, an Anglo-Saxon corruption, and Reynard, from Norman French, are less important mythologically.) In Gaelic it is called *Sionnach*, ('the reed of a bagpipe'), linking us to *Ngetal* (the reed); finally, with its wily speech, it is known to enrapture an audience of geese, later to carry one off. All three connections – reed, goose, toad – point to the black crack between the worlds at the Winter Solstice.

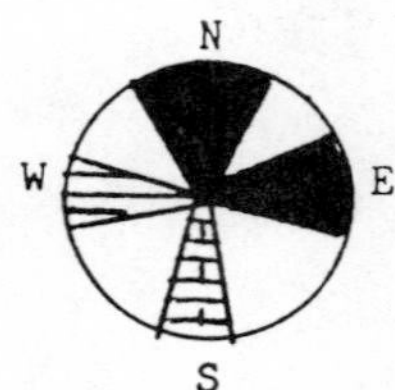

HUNTING
HOUNDS, BLACK-
DOGS, NASK,
NASG, NASG-KHU

Gabriel Rachets used to chase the discarnating humans (in the form of geese) across the night skies (especially in winter). Dogs were also depicted on gravestones in hope that the individual 'would obtain life after death'. In this function they probably appear on the famous Gaulish statues of Kernunos. Hekate, like Keridwen, appeared as a greyhound bitch and reportedly littered the first vine-stick as a symbol of fertility and rebirth (*Muin*, the vine/bramble, follows *Gort*, the ivy, as fertility after rebirth from the Winter Solstice).

Perhaps the most famous of the hounds at this Shamanistic Station is Finn's dog-dragon Bran ('Raven-Black'). 'One description of Bran gives him as being a *Ku-sith* [Faerie dog], as large as a two-year-old stirk, and of a very dark green colour [i.e., of *Ngetal*], ears were deep green, and his coat became lighter in colour towards the feet, his back was dark green, his sides almost black in hue whilst his belly was white or cream coloured.' In another version: 'A ferocious, small-headed, white-breasted, sleek-haunched hound, having the eyes of a dragon, the claws of a wolf, the vigour of a mountain lion, and the venom of a serpent.'

Other Keltic Deities linked to such dogs are: Nodens, Sequana, the King of Iruath, Kunobelinus ('Hound of Belin'), Kynhaval, Kynon, etc. From elsewhere: Hekate, Neleus, Anubis; Guardians Kerberus and Garmur.

The wise wolf, howling at the night moon, rules over the winter quarter (of purification or death) from Samhain to Imbolk. Thus it is particularly associated with my own Zodiacal Sign of Sagittarius, which in the Qabalistic tradition comes under the archetype of Ben-yamin, who shall 'ravin as a wolf' and later 'divide the spoil' between those he feels merit this honour. In Keltia February was called *Faoilleach* ('the wolf month, storm month, and month of bleak death').

The wolf stands beside the Keltic God Kernunos on the Gundstrop Cauldron. Odin is accompanied by wise wolfs in Scandinavian Lore; in Greece the Lykomanean Zeus had a winter wolf-form, and his son Apollo (the young Sun God) was born from the Wolf Goddess Leto.

'The benign aspect of the wolf is apparent in the belief that good luck will follow if (in the old days) a wolf crossed the path of a bridal party, and in the legend that a wolf faithfully guarded the severed head of King Edmund the Martyr, until his followers could find it.' It was reported that after his death King John roamed the countryside in the form of a wolf (perhaps it had been his totem-creature).

Associated with the wolf are the following clans: Mak Lennan ('Son of the Wolf'); Mak Tyre ('Son of the Wolf'); Mak Millan ('Son of the Wolf Servant' = Mak Gile Fholain) plus some septs of the Gordons (Gort-ans); in Kymru the evidence is not quite as strong (probably because the wolf didn't surive there quite as long as it did in the Highlands) but we do find the element *Blaidd* ('wolf') in several personal names: Bleidik, Bleddyn, Bleddri and Bleiddudd.

The Red Indians say that a Shamanistic drum made of wolf-skin can silence any other drum made of sheep or goat skin –such that no man can emit a sound from the other instrument whilst the wolf-skin drum vibrates ... thud, thud, thud – aaahowoo, aaahowooo, aaaoooooohooooo.

(=Black-Water-Dog), HOUNDS OF WINTER & UNDERWORLD & FAERIE DOGS WITH SACRED CHAINS; KWN ANNWFN, GABRIEL RATCHETS; SLUATH-BRACHE = Hounds of the Wind; FALPIE = FELPIE = VELPIE = HWELPA = WHELP = Hounds or Great Dog. STRIKER, TYKE, TRASHER, GREW, SOIDE-GLAISE, GLAS-KON (= GREY HOUND) MIL-KHU (= Hound of Plain), ABHAK (= AVANK?), ARKHU

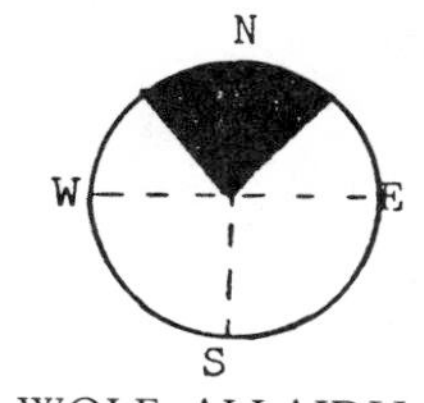

WOLF, ALLAIDH-MADADH (Wild-Dog or Dog of Wildness, Gaelic assoc. 'Wild, Ferocious, Proud and Haughty Dog'); LOARN = Wolf; KU-ALLTA (Dog of the Heights); KU-KOILLE (Hound of the Forest); KATH-WAL (or FAOL) = Dog of Battle, or 'Warrior Dog'; FAEL-KU = WOLF-DOG; MADADH-MOR (Great-Dog); KU-GEARR

Calendar of Mythological Objects Weapons and Sacred Treasures

by Kaledon Naddair © 22nd Oct. 1986
(The Pictish Shaman)

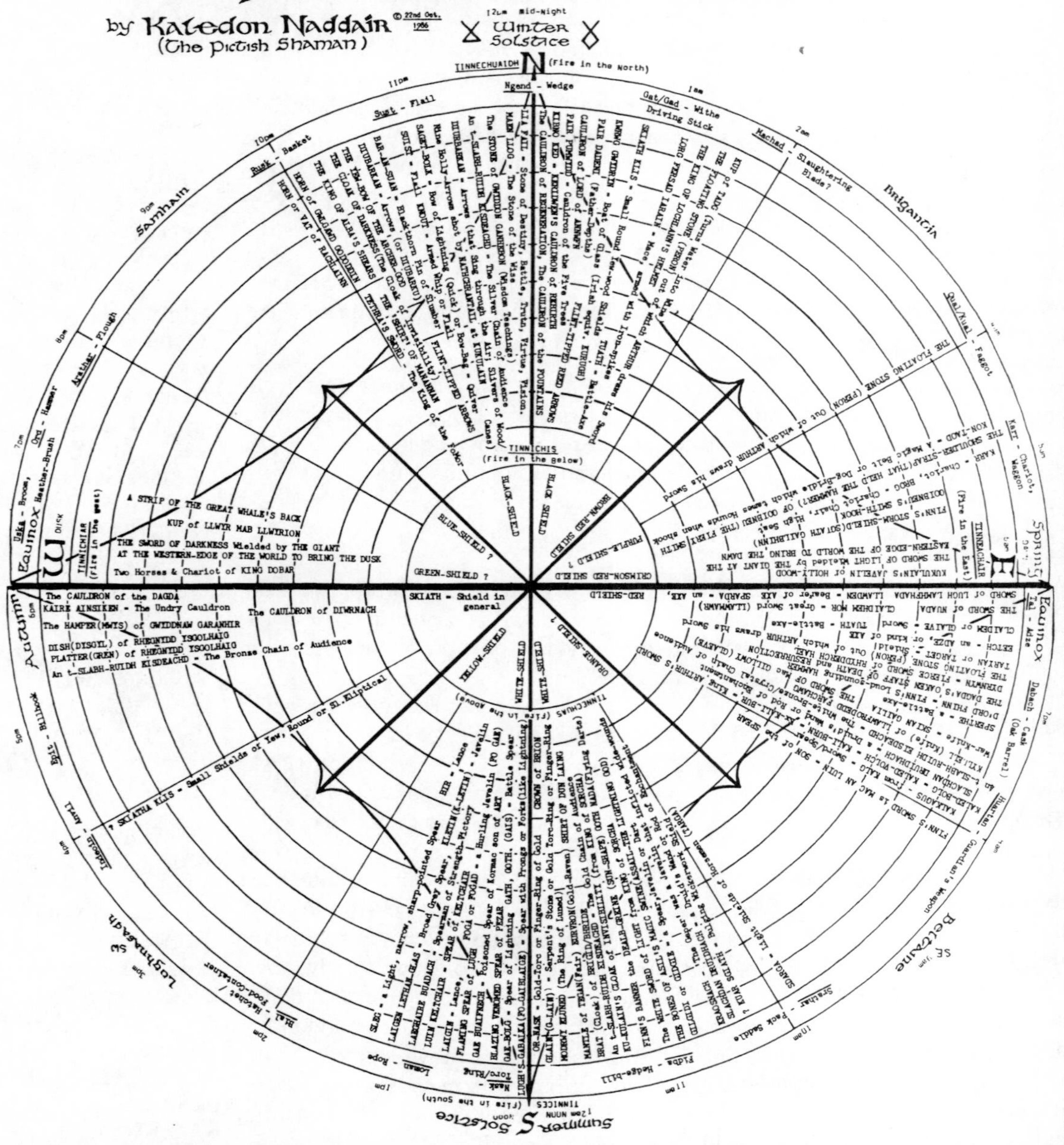

In the many years that I have been studying Keltic Mythology I became aware that the Sacred Treasures & Weapons of the Gods played a very important role in many of the Otherworld Adventures. After I was honoured to re-discover THE KELTIC SHAMANISTIC CALENDAR, it took a further 2 years of hard research since then to piece-together this Calendar of Mythological Objects. Certain precious Treasures such as the Sets of GWYDDBWL & FIDCHELL (Shamanistic Chess Sets) include elements (pieces) from all Stations within the Shamanistic Cycle (thus it would be wrong to place them in one position in this Calendar). Likewise, although one can place Keridwen's Cauldron at a certain place in the Circle, it should be remembered that it needed parts of many Tress, Plants & Herbs, gathered through a whole Cycle (1 yr + 1 day) to produce the Essence of Inspiration and Wisdom; to a lesser extent this can also be said to apply to The Dish of Rhegnydd Ysgolhaig, plus certain Magical Rings, Wheels & Circles. On the other hand, most Mythological Objects have a very precise 'Station' in the Shamanistic Wheel, as indicated above.

Mythological Objects Weapons and Sacred Treasures

On page 126 is one of my Shamanistic Calendars which synthesizes much of the Lore on mythological power-objects into a meaningful whole. Certain weapons or objects congregate around certain quarters of the diagram – e.g. spears in the Shamanistic South; swords and axes in Shamanistic East and South; cauldrons in Shamanistic West and North; and stones of wisdom in Shamanistic North. There are very good Shamanistic, metaphysical and occasionally practical reasons for this distribution pattern, and these should become manifest as I describe the main power-objects one by one:

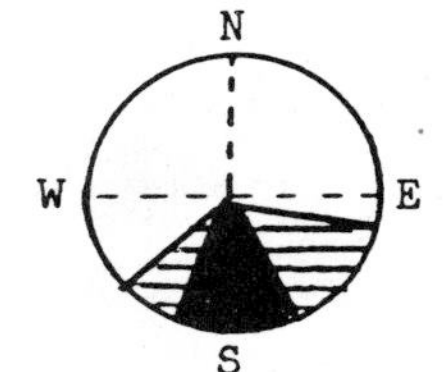

SPEAR (LANCE & JAVELIN), Gaelic = GAE, GAIS (LUIN, LAIGIN, LETIN, LEGE)

The Sky Father's ritual weapon is the spear or lance; the most famous Keltic God to wield it being Lugh or Lughos, a solar divinity. The Scandinavian Sky Father Odin had the spear as a totem-weapon after he pierced himself with it whilst hanging on the kosmic ash (similar to Christ on the Cross being pierced by the spear of Longinus). This connects with the flaming lance (*Pennon*) of the Grail legends and the hero Peredur of the long Spear (*Peredur Baladyr Hir*); this flaming lance is used to test Grail-seekers, and it also features in the procession of sacred treasures in the Grail Castle. Apart from such lofty symbolism, spears had a practical martial function; a cast of Odin's Ashen spear signalled the commencement of a battle, during which would be thrown and broken many such weapons. In the following two quotes the spears are unquestionably of a most ferocious nature:

'The lance [*Luin*] of Keltchar was carried with a cauldron of blood/venom before it, so that the weapon could be dipped into the liquid from time to time to save the head from burning the shaft or the man who carried it. One day Keltchar raised it up and a drop of poisonous blood ran from the tip, along the shaft, through Keltchar's body, and killed him.'

'O'Rahilly notes the spear of the gigantic MacKecht which was 'strong-red and oosy' (dubderg druchtach)/'dripping blood' (MacKecht ('Son of Power') assoc. with Dian Kecht Sun God and God of Healing at Shamanistic South).'

In certain Tales the fiery spear is associated with thunder and lightning; indeed it could be called one of the ritual weapons of the Lightning God. Like so much ancient wisdom it was enshrined in the sacred tongues and their root-words; to retrieve such gems from the depths of obscurity takes a keen mind. This is an attribute most Academic scholars lack; for instance, instead of focusing on the prosaic and near-irrelevant meaning of 'bag' for the Old Irish word *Bolg*, they would have been much wiser to have focused on the more pertinent meanings of 'lightning', 'flash', 'to shine', 'God'. Perhaps then they might have noted that KuKulain's weapon, the *Gae-bolg*, was a spear of lightning, as was his Father Lugh's *Gabalka* (*Gae-bolga*), which was a spear with prongs or forks like lightning (similarly, the *Fo-gai-blaige*).

This sheds a different light upon that bunch of Keltic Titans the Fir-bolg (Men of Lightning), whereas their Shamanistic opposites were the Fo-mors

(Under-sea Men) and the Fir-domnan (Men of the Depths). And, as T. F. O'Rahilly initially pointed out, thunder and lightning issues forth from Arthur's hard upright sword:

Kalad-bolg (hard, upright, activating – lightning flash)
Kalad-vwlch (hard, upright, activating – lightning flash)
Ex-*Kali-bur* (from hard, upright, activating – fire/lightning)

The link between lightning and the Shamanistic South Station is confirmed in several ways. For example, in the Brythonic speech of Alban, the South Wind is called Fuddy, whilst a term for lightning (*Dealan*) is *Fudder*. Spears were most often made of ashwood (though occasionally of hornbeam or beech). It so happens that these three trees are at the Shamanistic South Station in ancient Ogham ciphers, and all three trees are linked with the root-word for spear and Sky God in Indo-European philology! (Greek *Exya, Oxya,* ✓**Ask* = ash, beech, hornbeam or spear shaft; Greek *Oxys* = sharp, ash, spear; Latin *Ornus* = spear, mountain ash; Latin *Fraxinus* = ash, lance, javelin).

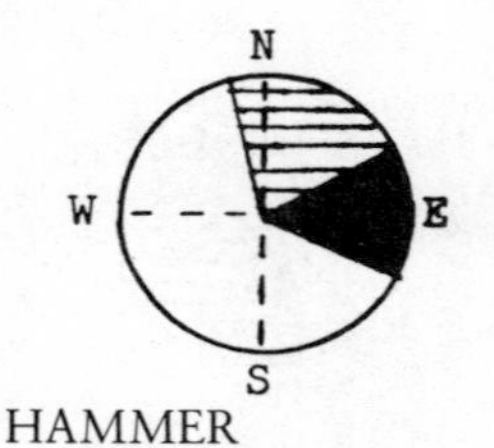

HAMMER
BATTLE-AXE &
SACRED AXE

When early man lashed a stone onto a stick with animal thongs, he had created a powerful hand weapon. Careful sharpening of the stone gave a cutting edge which was utilized in various crafts as well as in battle. There is ample evidence that from the most ancient times there was a religious and symbolic tradition that ran parallel to the militaristic one, which employed the sacred hammer and/or axe within the mysteries. From their non-manageable size and weight, and from the vast amount of time and care lavished upon the polished stone axes, we can discern their use as beautiful altarpieces and suchlike. These sacred stone axes were sometimes buried within a megalithic complex to confer the blessing of the Thunder God upon the Holy Earth. (Later, an axe symbol was pecked onto kist slabs for a similar sanctification.)

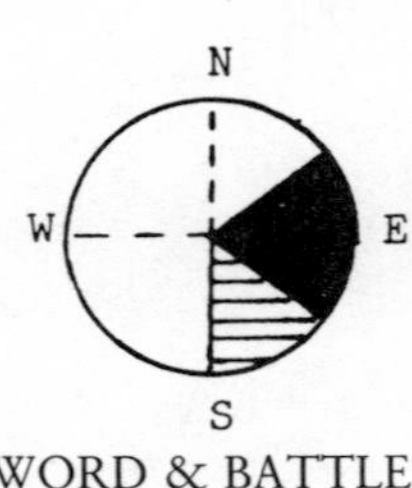

SWORD & BATTLE
KNIFE

Across the mythologies of the world there is a remarkable uniformity which gives the Thunder and Sky Gods the hammer/axe as a symbol – Gods such as Taran, Thunor (Thor), Indras, Zeus, Mithra, Logos, Hadad, Tengu. The sound of the *d-Òrd Fhinn*, ('the hammer of Finn'), was related to the sound of thunder; it also perhaps evoked the drumming of the war hammer off the totem-shield as a call to battle. In Orkney the *Dian-stane* ('power/fertility stone' linked to Nordic *Dynestein*) was a 'thunder stone', a round, holed piece of rock crystal/smooth stone or even a prehistoric stone axe which was always kept hanging on the side of the plough facing the Sun. In this way Taran or Thor could be invoked to drive back the frost giants and other forces of winter from the spring-ploughed fields. It was also believed that if thunder and lightning struck down in the open furrow during the spring ploughing and sowing, then a fertile life-force would have entered the soil and it would be a good year for the farm.

Miniature axes of polished stone or of bronze/silver/gold were employed as esoteric and metaphysical symbols within Keltic Druidism and other native faiths. These tokens were worn or carried as pieces of ritual jewellery (as I do), being awarded to an Intitiate who has gained a certain degree of perceptive intelligence, discernment, precision, clarity upon 'limits', and incisive power.

When the smithying skills of producing strong bronze/iron/steel swords out of the fire and forge came to prominence, this weapon gradually replaced the earlier axes. A practical reason for this was that a good sword could cut through the wooden haft of an axe, and it had a longer striking range. Esoterically the sword shared many of the attributes of Shamanistic East symbolism that the axe possessed, and it reached further into the realms of light and speed of Shamanistic South. This is reflected in certain solar swords of light, or in other zigzagged sword blades which represented the white lightning-flash (e.g., those wielded by Metatron/Mikhael/the Greek *Logos*). Ritual practices such as the Suabian and Keltic sword dances to mark various seasonal festivals should be noted, as should the marking of sword blades or pommels with the 🠉 (Tinne Koelbren sign) or the 🠉 (Tyr Rune).

Those simplistic writers who suggest the cauldron is but one symbol, and a Goddess one at that, are sadly distorting the very much richer Keltic esoteric tradition; for there are at least four distinct symbolic cauldron motifs, half of which are related to male Gods. They could be distinguished as follows:

1. Cauldron filled with the fruits of the harvest (barley, rye, turnips, leeks, onions), and slaughtered game and seafoods – e.g., the Dagda's, Gwyddnau Garanhir's, Ainsiken Cauldrons.
2. Cauldron containing the stored seeds to be planted for the next and future years' crops (this equates with the *Korn*, horn of the spermatic *Logos* given to the Earth Mother).
3. Cauldron that from a lower 'death' causes a psychic/spiritual rebirth within the magical Otherworld – e.g. the Cauldron of Matholwch, that of the Ruler of Annwn (Gwyn ap Nud).
4. Cauldron containing a carefully gathered and boiled essence of trees, plants and herbs (Ogham and Koelbren cipher), such that it produces remarkable mystical knowledge and inspiration. Keridwen's Cauldron is most famous in this capacity, into which Keridwen gathered the ingredients throughout one year and one day, in close consultation with the books of Pheryllt (teachings of the tree and plant alchemists).

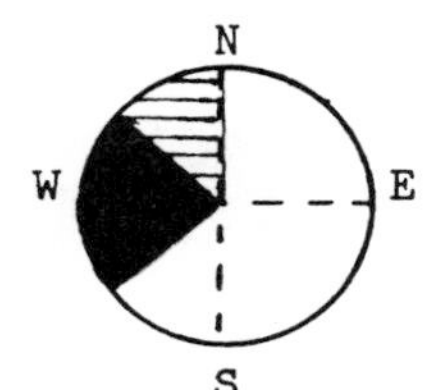

CAULDRON OF THE HARVEST & GARNERED FRUITS OF THE EARTH

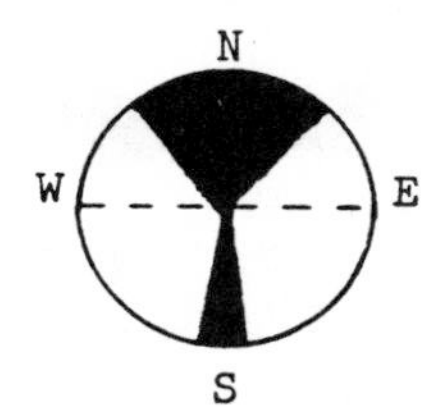

CAULDRON OF DEATH and REBIRTH, or SECRET INSPIRATION

As a footnote upon the Dagda as a Keltic God, certain simplistically minded commentators have described the Dagda as no more than 'the Good God' or 'the Oak God'. He is worthy of these names, but there is much more to his mythological 'character', e.g. his harp-playing, which contained the three strains of laughing, weeping and healing-sleep; his oaken staff which could deliver death to nine men from one end, or life from the other to resurrect them, as 'Lord of Great Knowledge' he was called Ruad Ro-fhessa; the Dagda, through his Folk the Tuatha Gods and Faerie Wildfolk, also have in their charge the fertility of the corn and the quality of milk, as they once proved to the Milesian Kelts, such that their descendants offered a tithe of milk and grain to the Wildfolk in respect to the forces of fertility. Thus the culmination of the Dagda–Oak God's six-month rule over the Light Half of the Year coincides with the corn harvest and the gathering of the fruits of the soil into his cauldron.

For the most part, horns and goblets share the same Shamanistic Stations of West and North with ritual cauldrons. But what they contain, and by whom they are proffered, makes a big mythological difference, giving them roles quite distinct from cauldrons. The goblets filled with the honeyed mead of inspiration were often found in the hands of the Gwyllion. These female Wildfolk Beings inhabit certain lochs, mere-pools, fountains and sacred rivers; their role is to act as inspirational Muses, guides to the psychic underwater realms, and sometimes as messengers from the World of Faerie. Mythologically there are 'nine' wave-maidens of the sea, and 'nine' Faerie maidens of the Sidhe mounds and kairns.

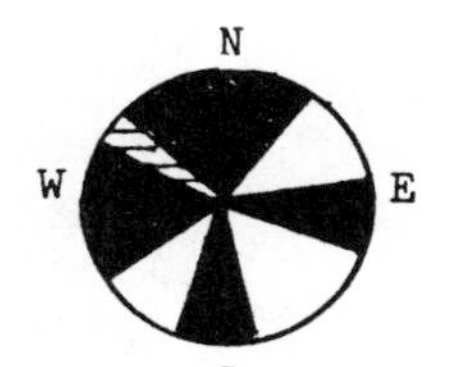

HORNS FILLED WITH LIQUID INSPIRATION, GOBLETS, CHALICE, CUP

In ancient times the more advanced humans, the Initiates of the Mysteries, participated within a harmonious relationship with the Gwyllion, such that these 'ladies of the lakes' were pleased to confer draughts of inspiration or healing from their goblets. There are also many Folktales from the North of Albion, Eirinn and Alban that describe how tired and weary travellers would fall asleep on a grassy knoll to be awoken by a beautiful maiden and restored with a goblet of refreshing wine/mead and occasionally a plate of barley cakes; after his unexpected repast, the horseman would respectfully return the precious goblet and platter before resuming his journey. Sadly, with the degeneration of the tradition, mankind broke good faith with the Gwyllion, certain Knights coming to steal the goblets – only to find that the Faerie powers had withdrawn their psychic and spiritual blessings in response to this abuse of custom. Also, as a result of Christian bigotry in the medieval period, the Gwyllion were mis-associated with the Welsh *Gwrachs* ('witches'/'hags'), who were in turn mis-associated with Churchite conceptions of 'evil'. This has produced yet another layer of false and debilitating conditioning which has sullied our own native spiritual tradition. Those who care for the truth above spurious bigotry must strip away such accretions and re-establish trust with our inspirational Muses. In this light we should remember King Arthur's good dealings with the Lady of the Lake and the three queens who nursed him on his boat journey to the Otherworld Avalon.

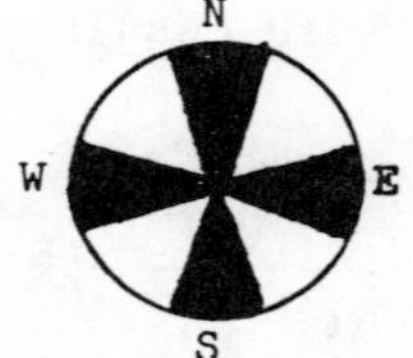

SACRED FAERIE CHAINS and HUMAN INITIATE'S COPIES FOR RITUAL USE

Another key object in our native keltic mysteries is the ritual chain. In several early Tales of Faerie we encounter messengers from the Otherworld bearing a magical chain as proof of where they had come from. When shaken (like the token branch from Otherworld trees) the sacred chain would produce remarkable effects such as sending a sweet sleep, easing the pain of mothers in childbirth and soothing the wounds of battle-scarred warriors. In Faerie Wildfolk tapestries from the Rhineland we see depictions of the leaders of the Wildfolk (*Sidhe*) wearing their golden chains as well as their Faerie bells (see illustration). The wise Druid Initiates of Keltia (in harmony with the designs of the Gods) came to make sacred copies of these Faerie chains for ritual use. At one time there may have been as many as two to three hundred ritual chains in use amongst the Initiates and Bards of the various Keltic countries; unfortunately very few of these treasures have come down to us. Two of the finest known examples that have survived come from my own heartland of Pictish Alban; these stupendous examples of stylish Keltic craftsmanship are constructed from circular links (*Ruidh*) heavily coated in silver, joined into a chain (*Slabh*) closed with a terminal ring which bears a couple of significant Pictish glyphs. (These sacred Pictish treasures now lie unappreciated in the National Museum of Antiquities in Edinburgh.)

While most academics still pretend that the function of these chains is 'a mystery' or fob off the public with red herrings such as 'slave chains for important prisoners', their true use is well attested in historical writings, as follows:

'Then it was that the herald of the palace arose, and whilst standing up he shook a 'chain of hearing' that he had. Hearing was accorded to him, both East and West, North and South, throughout the whole of that well-built mansion.'

'There are three chains in the palace, one of gold, one of silver, and one of *Findrinny* (white bronze?) which are shaken to seat the people at the banquet, and to secure their silence; but whoever spoke after the gold chain did it on the pain of his head.' (Dr D. Hyde, *Beside the Fire*)

As is intimated in the quotation from Hyde, there was a hierarchy of importance attached to the chains (*an t-Slabhruidh Eisdeachd*), such that the ones made of less precious metals were shaken first. These sacred chains were shaken (*Rithe*) by the Druid, Bard or, occasionally, the Chieftan if total silence was required so that an important announcement about a religious rite, tribal gathering, new law, local folk custom, could gain a respectful hearing. This practice worked because everyone at a gathering, whether a nobleman, warrior or serf, respected 'the chain of hearing' as in some way connected with the Faerie Beings and Keltic Gods, and to offend them was a serious matter. Thus no one would risk speaking after the third symbol was shaken, because he would have been ignominiously thrown out, physically punished and debarred from participating in religious worship. That was tantamount to being left without a Soul, without a channel into Spirituality, through having shown disrespect to a symbol of the Gods (even more widely notable in todays' sacriligious society). As a final example of the vast power ascribed to these chains of hearing, one reads in *Smeuran Dubha 's an Fhaoillteach*: that 'he did also receive [from the Giant], as well as the chain of audience. And the very first shake that he gave the chain, people heard it in the five provinces of Erin, and in the Bridge of the Hundreds of the Nobles.'

RITUAL SHEARS OR SCISSORS

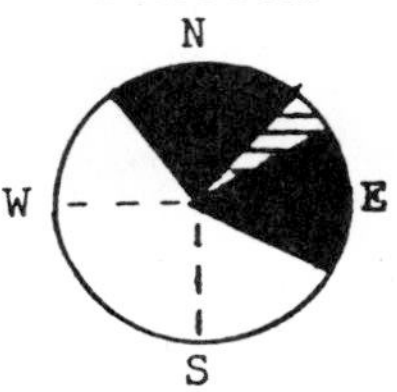

Ritual shears or scissors – craft implements, tools and, very occasionally, weapons – have two somewhat distinct symbolical roles. The first Shamanistic North role of shears is as the implement that cuts the light fibres, the threads of life, the silver cord, at the moment of death, such that the Soul and Spirit are forced to discarnate from the body. In this role we find the shears in the hands of Atropos, one of the three Fates in the Greek tradition. Similarly, the Roman Goddess Juno is depicted as holding 'the shears of death' on an early coin. As the classically orientated ascendancy in Britain has not cared to preserve our own native Keltic tradition with anything like as much fidelity, the Keltic evidence is as yet much more fragmentary; we can, however, surmise that 'the King of Alban's shears', mentioned as one of the treasures contained in the crane-bag of secrets, was used in such a role. As shears are wielded by certain *Ban Sidhe* (Faerie maidens), one would expect there to be a presiding Keltic Goddess, such as Keridwen's Death Goddess aspect, *Hen Widdon Ddulon* (ancient dark hag).

The other main symbolic role of shears relates to Shamanistic East and is slightly milder, being that of pruning, trimming, cutting back – but not resulting in death. In illustrations that bedeck the margins of medieval manuscripts and tapestries, figures such as 'the wild croppy tailor' wield shears. Sometimes the shears are used to remove the fleece of an animal, but more often to snip off the tail/ear/genitals of some misbehaving animal or human. This practice is reflected in certain Irish and British folk songs, in which a promiscuous wee tailor is making love to the adulterous wife of a warrior when the warrior returns and, after discovering the tailor in hiding, cuts off his two ears (or, in more severe versions, his two testicles) as punishment, hence leaving him 'croppy'. In marginal illustrations (e.g., in *The Metz Pontifical*) one often finds a male figure with shears in hand, chasing a hare, and later the hare spears this opponent and sometimes wields the shears itself. The symbolism becomes more understand-able when one remembers that the hare has strong associations with sexual promiscuity and lustiness (being a totem of the naked Fertility Goddess of Spring) – mad march hares and all that. The European hare with shears is linked to the hare wielding a knife in Egyptian art symbolism (see *Inner Keltica* No. 8 for more on such matters).

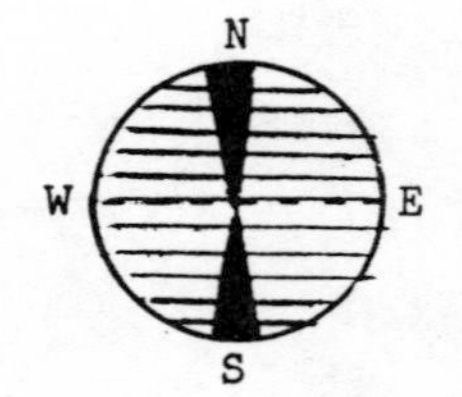

The RITUAL WHEEL

If this symbol was being used to represent the cycle of all the Shamanistic ingredients, then it would naturally have relevance throughout the whole circle, for it is indeed the wheel (*Rad, Rodd, Rit, Rhode, Rot, Ruide*).

Occasionally the Wheel symbol was more specifically linked with Sun/fire/lightning qualities, thus becoming a fiery solar wheel. As the Summer and Winter Solstices represent the height and depth of the Sun's power, a sun wheel features most prominently at both these ritual ceremonies. Thus, at the Summer Solstice in Germany the *Johannisfeuer* (St John's fires) are lighted and a blazing wheel rolled down the hill. Ancient Scandinavian rock carvings feature such sun wheels prominently, and in Keltia Banbha (Goddess of Ireland) gave 'the spell of knowledge and the King's wheel', for every Irish King wore a brooch in the shape of a wheel, which was carefully passed on to his successor. Thus, in the face of academic scepticism, we can see that Keltic jewellery was ritually symbolic as well as functional.

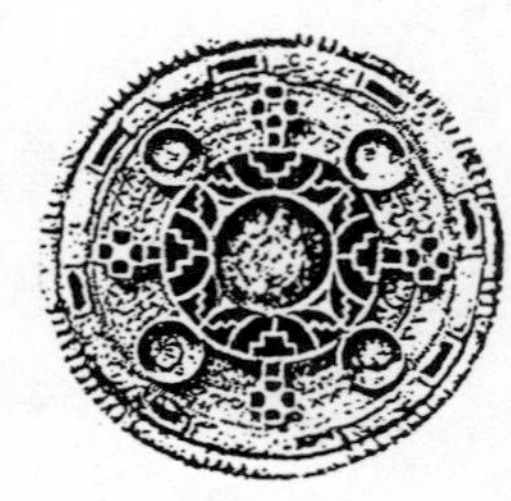

The Philosopher's Stone is a condensed essence of all the qualities within the Shamanistic Wheel, thus one could represent it by a small circle at the centre of the Shamanistic circle. However, due to this being elementally of a dense nature, it is predominantly associated with the Shamanistic Northern quarter, the quarter of Earth in the Keltic and European mysteries. A prime example from Keltic mythology is the *Lia fail* – the stone of destiny (truth, virtue, wisdom, vision, battle and death), which the Gods (*Tuatha De*) brought from the Otherworld city of Falias (*Fal* = truth). Parallel examples from the Kymraeg tradition are the *maen llog* ('stone of the wise') and the stone of *Gwyddon Ganhebon* (wisdom teachings) and *the Arthuriad*'s floating *Peron* stone.

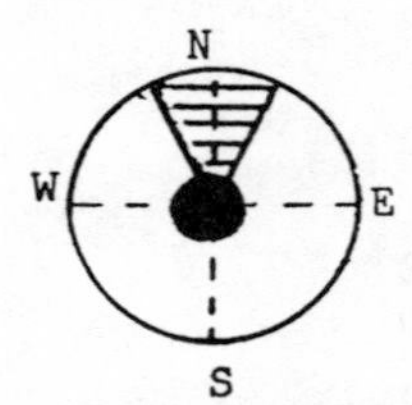

THE STONE OF THE WISE, STONE OF TEACHINGS

Apart from these mythological treasures, my researches into the Kymraeg system of Koelbren has led me to believe that the British Druids also perhaps inscribed a large circle on a slab of slate, within which they chiselled the Koelbren signs in their correct positions and other elements of a cipher code of wisdom teachings. Memory of this ritual object may be preserved in a line from the poet Kynddelw:

> *Mwyn Ofydd; Feirdd Eifaith Goelfain.*
> O Kind Ovate to Bards was his Large Stone of Understanding.

Several Irish, Scot-ic and Pictish Kings had a ritual stone/magic sod of earth that would proclaim/teach them the truth or wise judgement upon any problem. As I have discovered, it is possible magically to construct what I have termed a 'Touchstone of truth' inside one's psyche, if one knows the special techniques to do so!

In the Keltic Intiatory mysteries (as in other traditions) the soul body and/or spiritual body is sometimes described as 'the shirt of the self', 'mantle of light', 'robe of glory', etc. Thus, when a human or God being 'puts on' one of these very special 'garments', they might travel into the equivalent plane of existence and thus disappear or become invisible on the ordinary plane (to our physical eyes). There are many examples of such happenings within Keltic mythology, Folktales and Faerie Lore. This robe of light was conceived of as woven from strands of

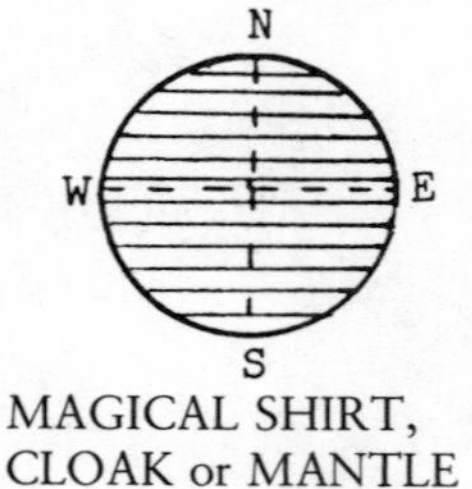

MAGICAL SHIRT, CLOAK or MANTLE

light (luminous emanations) spun out from the three Fate Goddesses. A contemporary Irish poet, Mícheál Ó Siadhail, expresses this belief in his poem '*Comaoin*' ('Compliment'), two verses of which read as follows:

I meask mhná na kruinne gile
Kasadh korrbhandia i mo bhealach
Aníos thríd an skafall sealadach
A tóigeadh idir am is spás.

Chuir na mná a gkomhairle in éindí,
Mná seo na kruinne gile,
Tharraing beirt nó thriúr an snáth le chéile
Is shníomh siad dhomsa léine.

Among the bright world's women
The occasional goddess came up my way
Through the temporary scaffold elevated
In between time and space.

These women their council took
These women of the bright world,
Two or three drew the thread together
And wove for me a shirt.

The identity of the God/hero/Faerie being and why and when he/she put on the magic cloak, would determine what Shamanistic Station the cloak had. Where the cloak (*Kokul*) is specified as being made from a particular bird or animal (e.g., swan feathers, eagle feathers, wolf/bear/fox/goat skin, etc.), then we can discern its Station thanks to my calendar.

The Gaelic *Slachdan Druidhach* (Druidical wand or rod of enchantment) seems to be paralleled by the Kymraeg *Hudlath* (*Llath* = rod; of *Hud* = appearances). The Shamanistic quality, and hence Station, of these ritual tools and weapons is very largely dependant upon which tree's wood they were made from e.g. a wand of rowan wood was employed for high white magic or spellcraft (related to Bhríde/Brighid or Kymraeg equivalent Einigan Gawr); an ash wand would invoke the Sky Father (Nonius) or the Sky Goddess (Nennia); hazel wand (psychic divination, fire in the head, related to Thor, etc.). Archaeologically or historically attested examples have been found made of the following woods: oak, rowan, hazel, ash, blackthorn, pine, willow, whitethorn, holly and yew – there may well have been other kinds. Cutting a branch of a tree and carving it does not necessarily produce a magical wand; it requires a Druid Shaman with a degree of personal power to engage a tree spirit or Faerie Wildbeing to act as a channel in the wand to the presiding deity.

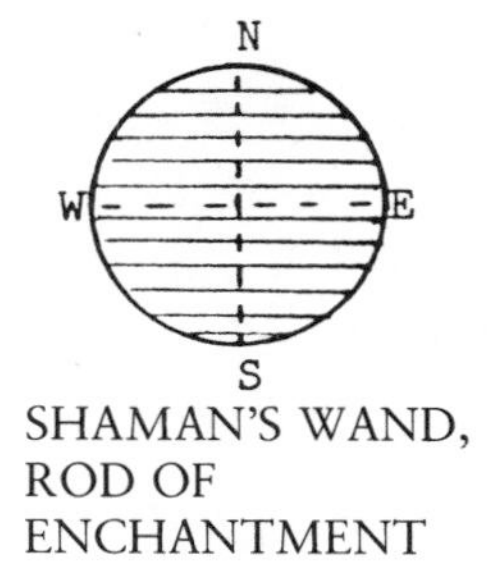

SHAMAN'S WAND, ROD OF ENCHANTMENT

If a wand or rod was conceived to convey essentially magical or psychic energies, then the ritual club was more especially notable as a symbol of strength and power. The club is more associated with masculine hero initiates and their Wildmen guides. There are therefore fewer types of wood that are ritually suitable. I have only heard of Keltic clubs being made from: oak, holly, blackthorn (*Shelaighlidh*), pine/fir, yew, and hawthorn. Further insights could be gained from investigating which types of Wildmen employ clubs and where,

RITUAL CLUB

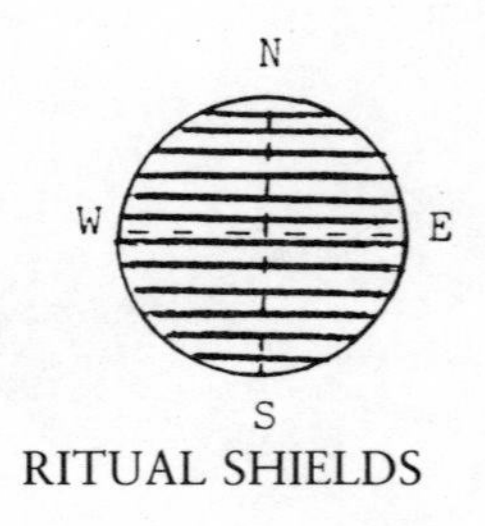

RITUAL SHIELDS

when and why. (Ritual staffs have some of the qualities of both wands and clubs, hence similar ideas apply to them.)

If held in the left hand or slung down the back, all shields have Shamanistic West and North connotations. However, this was/is modified by what colour the shield has been painted and what totemistic devices it bears. There is historical evidence that the Ancient Britons, Picts and Gaels had a colour coding for shields: scarlet/red was most associated with war, battle and fierce energy; reddy brown was the bear's bloody slaughter; black was the uncompromising fierceness of a wild wolf; whereas a pure white shield sometimes signalled a truce midst the conflict; yellow, orange, purple and other colours are recorded anciently. At a very early period, both personal and tribal totemistic motifs were also stained/painted upon the shields. Medieval heraldry is a degenerate (i.e., not psychically accurate) continuation of this practice.

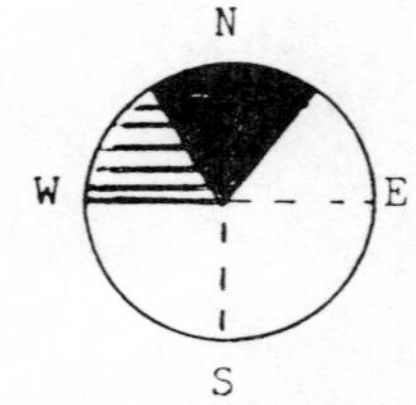

BAR-an-SUAN
PIN OF SLUMBER

There is evidence that the pin of slumber was initially made from a blackthorn spine dipped into a poisonous sleeping potion. The ingredients for the toxic poison may have included essences of foxglove, toadstools, broom seeds, nightshade/hemlock, box leaves, yew berries; it was also imbued with psychic magical energies. The pin was pricked into the victims' scalp whilst combing their hair or other such practice, thereafter sleep would follow shortly. In later times pins may have been made from bone or metal, but the ingredients of the poison and its effects are all distinctly of Shamanistic North.

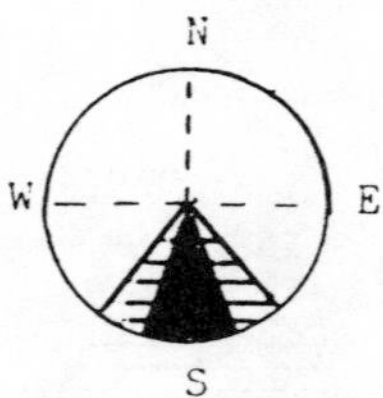

TORC (NAESK) OR
RING OF
INVISIBILITY

The torc (G. = *Naesk*) is pre-eminently a symbol of spiritual power, creative intelligence and immortal life. In this capacity it was carried by the deities, as the Egyptian deities carried the *Ankh*, and Chaldean and Assyrian Gods carried the sacred ring. In harmony with the mighty ones, the Keltic nobility wore gold torques, others wore silver torques, and the poorer folk wore torques of brass. As my decoding of the Ogham ciphers proves, the *Naesk* ring (torc) is related to Shamanistic South, midsummer, noon and the height of the sky powers. It is thus Shamanistically associated with the serpent ring (*G-lain*), and in turn linked to adders and midsummer (see Kernunos on page 163).

In esoteric Irish Folktales these magical rings, if operated in a certain way, can confer invisibility (as can fern seed). Some of the magical rings we encounter in Folktales are more generally associated with the whole wheel or circle of esoteric attributes – in this light we should remember the Kymraeg 'Ring of Luned' – '*Modrwy Eluned*' (ring of forms/constructions/ranks of structure) and Odin's magic ring *Draupnir*.

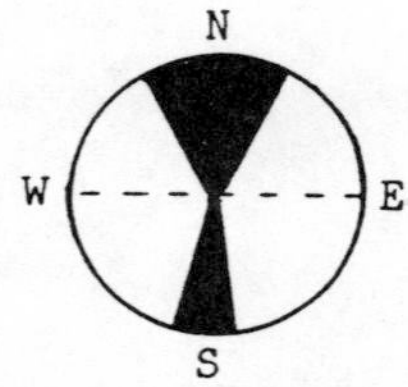

SLINGS and SLING-
STONES
(TATHLUM or
KAER-KLIS)

From the most ancient times Keltic warriors used slings. For sling-shot, apart from ordinary pebbles, concrete balls would occasionally be made from powdered bone and tusks and sand, mixed with poison ingredients, such that, if this baked-hard missile were to pierce the skin, it would leave fragments that would cause a festering wound. The ingredients of the ball (*Tathlum*) that Lughaidh (one of the *Tuatha De*) used to kill Balor (through his evil eye) are described as:

'The blood of toads and furious bears,
And the blood of the noble lion,
The blood [poison] of adders, and of *Osmuinn*'s trunks
It was of these that the *Tathlum* was composed.'

(*Os-muin* may refer to hairy mammoth/elk/reindeer.)

In another text a *Kaer Klis* (round missile) is cast at an enemy; as, in this case, its efficiency did not totally depend on its ability to cause physical injury (or on the effect of its poisonous ingredients), it was presumably magically charged as well.

Other ritual objects and weapons that we will meet in Folktales include:

A healing jewel (*Leug shlanaighearachd*): a 'stone of worth' that was usually dipped or steeped in a drink, which took on its healing virtues.

Great-sounding horn (the *Borabuigh*): the mighty horn of the Fenian warriors is described as circling round like a massive sea-shell.

Longbow and arrows: Often the bow was made of yew wood, and as such was related to the Archer God Ebur (Keltic) and Ulle and Orvandel (Scandinavian), all aligned with the zodiacal sign of Sagittarius and Shamanistic North-west to North. In very early times, when arrows were made of hardened reeds (*ngetal*) with flint tips and goose-feather flights (*Ngeigh*), they were linked to the *Ngetal* station of Shamanistic due North. In course of time, the reed shafts were replaced with wooden ones. Also, as arrows are basically darts that fly through the air, they have something of a Shamanistic South character.

As we have surveyed quite a wide range of power objects and weapons in this chapter, it will take you much careful thought to assimilate all the correspondences given. Once you have taken the time to learn the mythological ascriptions, it would be an interesting exercise to read some traditional Keltic Tales (which feature such objects) and see how much more you understand, thanks to the preceding investigations. Of course, this chapter need not be just an aid to understanding motifs in Tales from times past, for the proper use of symbolic ritual weapons and treasures still has a vital role within modern-day pagan rituals and Western occultism.

The Faerie-Wildfolk

'There has never been a merry world since the Fynnoderee lost his ground.' (Manx saying)

Who or what are 'the Faerie Wildfolk'? In what areas of existence do they live? How long have they been on 'our' planet? Well, answering those questions in reverse order: the more mighty of the beings of Faerie have been here since this planet has hosted life; indeed, they have been the unseen agencies behind most of the spiritual, psychic and physical changes in creation. The Chiefs of the *Sidhe* (Faerie Folk) are indistinguishable from some of the immortal Keltic Gods (being similar to others pagan deities and occasionally approximating to Qabalistic arkhangels as leaders of the angel hosts).

The power of the Wildman or Woman will dictate how much of an individualistic personality he/she has; some of the very minor Faerie beings have a corporate group-soul type of existence. Therefore, depending on the being's spiritual 'rank', and their 'role' in the makrokosmic scheme, they will be found to exist within the Spiritual (*Braiatic*), Psychic (*Yetziratic*), or Etheric (*'Asayatic*) realms or worlds. These beings function for the most part in a magical 'Otherworld' apart from us humans, only rarely materialising or manifesting themselves to our senses. Indeed, it is a sad fact that, in this urban and technologically fixated modern world, the consciousness and sensorial awareness of the average person is very narrow, clouded and aesthetically twisted. Our ancestors, on the other hand, living in an unspoilt natural world, unhampered by junk conditioning, had far more finely tuned physical senses and more opened psychic awareness; thus it should come as no surprise to read that they more often perceived these Otherworld beings, and with much greater clarity.

As the Faerie Wildfolk possess remarkable powers of transformation, they can appear in several main modes of manifestation. (1) A roughly human-like, tall (six- to eight-foot high), shaggy, broad and strong figure. Some Wildmen of the mountains (great Devas, as they would be called in the East), like Am Fear Glas Mor, 'the Big Grey Man' of Ben MacDuibh, have been seen as tall as between nine and eighteen feet in height; whilst certain brown men of moors/low hills have been perceived as stocky four- to five-foot figures. (2) An Otherworld creature, bearing some or no relation to earthly creatures, often with glowing eyes and a shining head or torso. (3) A faintly or strongly luminous amorphous being of light. (4) More rarely, in the form of an Otherworld Wheel-like, door-like or object-like being.

The Faerie Wildfolk can, and do, use things in physical nature as channels of manifestation, such as: certain rock strata; trees and plants; streams, wells, waterfalls, rivers and Lochs; mountain peaks/hills; caves and potholes; sea and seashore. Thus it is possible to roughly categorize them into 'clans', bearing in mind qualificatory factors arising from their Shamanistic Station.

I believe you will find accurate descriptions of some of these beings in Carlos Castaneda's books, therein called 'allies'; other descriptions from Irish mystics such as A. E. are quoted in Evan-Wentz's *Fairy Faith in Keltic Countries*; also, recent sightings and impressions of a mountain Wildman are related in Affleck Grey's *The Big Grey Man of Ben MacDhui*; other descriptions of my own can be read in *Inner Keltia* Nos. 7, 8, 9, and *The Pictish Shaman* No. 1; and a great deal more in my forthcoming book *The Faerie Wildfolk* (a guidebook and dictionary). For the present, the 'true to the tradition' artwork that fills this chapter should give you a visual impression of some of these ideas.

It is permissible to group approximately most of the Faerie clans into two main types: (1) the Light Elves (Alp-luachra, Leucharpins, Lios Alfar, White Boggarts), Shamanistic East through Shamanistic South to South West; and (2) the Dark or Swarthy Elves (Am Fear Glas Mor, Bukka-dhu, Black Boggarts, Swart Alfar), from Shamanistic West through to Shamanistic North to Shamanistic East.

On the whole, the Light Elves are of a gentler, friendlier, tolerant disposition, though they are perhaps harder to see in daylight (even psychically); whilst the Dark Elves are much more reserved, harsher, ferocious, sultry and intolerant in disposition. None of these beings are essentially anti-human, but by their very nature they are unhuman, thus they act according to their own modes. It is wise to seek contact only with those with whom your personal Shamanistic Station can harmonize (this particularly applies to the severe Dark Elves), otherwise the adverse effects could be like sticking your hand into the buzz-bars of an electricity sub-station: mental and physical burnout. This is unlikely to happen unless you have previously ravaged the laws of nature, for the Wildfolk would not deliberately harm you; rather you would be vulnerable to the unfortunate side effects of contacting a power-being unprepared (for if you have the right piece of equipment you can, after all, tap into an electricity sub-station properly to good advantage). 'Rough' contact with the Wildfolk powers can leave one 'wrecked' either physically or more especially psychically, slammed down, disorientated, or worse. However, as lessons of 'lesser deaths' and severe perceptions can teach much wisdom if properly assimilated, they should be courageously faced rather than avoided. In a 'testing situation' engineered by the Otherworld powers, most of the 'fear' that the individual may experience may stem from adverse Christian conditioning and reactionary emotions in reponse to fear of the unknown, and fear of the primeval and 'wild' in a comfortably civilized world.

It is a rare role of the guardians of the Keltic mysteries to rebuff the insincere

Left: Rhineland wildman and Dragon
Right: A wildman carved on the exterior of Peasenhall Church, Suffolk

desecrators; whereas those who show themselves genuine seekers, however new to the path, will be welcomed back into the wise ways. These 'easier' contacts with Inner Plane allies can heal, give scintillating knowledge way beyond normal human attainment, and suffuse one with vibrant joy, wonder and a spirit that just longs to be up and dancing. In fact, from my personal experience, a Wildman exudes a natural joy for, and in, *life*, and a warm fresh countryish humour; these qualities radiate out from his being in a way near impossible to capture in words.

Thus, instead of showing only fear, or a stern will to command (like the so-called 'ritual magicians'), if more modern-day folk showed *love* to our native spiritual guides, perhaps more of us would have a fulfilling Soul-life. It should be continually borne in mind that it is us humans who have to make amends by demonstrating that we do care about our natural environment; the Faerie Folk have always and only sought to heal and maintain its pristine life.

In ancient European society every aspect of people's lives was lived within Nature, and not apart from it. Thus the hunters, woodsmen, rustic farmers and herdsmen, not to mention the Shaman Druids, were much more intimately involved with the fertility powers (the Faerie Wildfolk) than modern-day urbanites. This is reflected in a vast number of Folktales, certain Folksongs and ballads, as well as in every strata of Keltic and European pagan mythology. What has been so badly translated into English as: 'giant', 'strong-man', 'wizard champion', 'water witch' or 'monster' is in nearly every case a much more dignified and powerful Wildfolk being such as a *Famhair, Keirthach, Kewach, Gruagach, Phynnoderee, Ur-uisg, Boggart, Ekh-Elphie* (*Kelpidh*). Even the native terms that have descended, almost unchanged linguistically, e.g. boggle (from *Bukka*), pixie (from *Pucca*), troll, dwarf, elf (from *Alph*) and fairy (from Faerie/Phairy) have sadly undergone a radical distortion in meaning from how they were originally conceived and perceived.

The slanderous devil-talk of the Orthodox Church, the diminutive irrelevance of Shakespeare's *Midsummer Night's Dream*, idle ignorant gossip, effete Victorian artwork and the distortions of Arthur Rackham, all have contributed to polluting our minds with grossly mutated visual images of the beings of Faerie and bogus babblings posing as 'Fairy Lore'. This puerile fantasy is unfit material for the impressionable imagination of young children, and it has no psychic or Spiritual teaching value for adult people. Far rather we should turn to the ancient teachings, which were much purer, and strive with all our intelligence to understand their wisdom more truly.

In Eileann Vannin (the Isle of Man), the much loved Wildman was known as a *Fynnoderee*, his name being derived from the Irish Gaelic *Fionnadh-doiri* ('Hairy man of the oak woods') or *Fionnadh-deorai* ('hairy aloof stranger'). This association with oak woods is natural when one considers that early Keltic Britain was covered in vast primeval oak forests, wherein the Druids held their schools of learning.

Another character who figures very prominently in Gaelic myths is the *Gruagach*. When translators encountered the *Gruagach*, they found difficulty in finding an equivalent English word, or even phrase. For *Gruagach* literally means 'hairyman', but because of the supernatural powers this Wildman holds he was sometimes translated as 'wizard champion' or, loosely, as 'giant'. That the *Gruagach* had many different roles and capabilities is vouchsafed by some of his epithets: *Gruagach na g-cleasan* = Gruagach of tricks (wizardry)/feats (heroic); *Gruagach casurlach donn* = brown bold-legged Wildman wizard (although *Donn*' could be a title like 'Lord' or 'Honoured One', as in Domnall Donn, the Lord of the Underworld and Blessed Dead); *Gruagach of Dun an Oir* = Wildman wizard of the Castle of Gold (solar). It is important to our understanding that, in the Tales featuring a *Gruagach*, he spends as much of his time in the magic Otherworld as in this world, and seems both familiar with and in control of its laws.

As a 'hairy man of the oak woods', the Wildman is mythologically linked to 'the oak tree spirit' which features in other Scottish Gaelic Tales (*Folk and Hero Tales of Argyll*, III):

The Strong Man of the Wood (*Keatharnach na Koille*), who hunted deer, one day went to cut a large oak tree, but, as he was cutting it, it fell and crushed him. Nevertheless he carried it home and threw it down at his door. He told his wife that he had just received his death-hurt and she was to plant the acorn he held in his hand from the tree, in the midden-heap before the door. He said that she was going to have a son, and that she had to nurse him with the sap of her breast and side until he could pull the young oak tree out by the roots. He died, and some time later she gave birth to a son, whom she nursed for seven years, and then gave him a chance at pulling the oak sapling out, but he couldn't do it. She took to suckling him another seven years, but he still failed. Finally, after another seven years' taking milk, he managed to uproot the oak tree and break it into pieces. The big lad had thus come into his full powers as a giant. He was sent off a-questing by his mother and he managed to do many wonderful feats, including overcoming a troublesome black water horse (*Ùsp*) and a big brownie (*Ùruisg*) in his travels.

Another Scottish Gaelic name for Wildmen was *Na Sàmhaichean*, ('the savages/silent ones'; this latter designation is meant to apply to their supposed lack of speech, their shyness and avoidance of noise; I would just like to point out that it is also an epithet of the *Daoine Sidhe*, the People of Peace, the Fairy Folk. A member of this type is a *Tuairisgeal*, a giant, of the kind called *Samhanaich*, who lived in caves by the seashore, the strongest and coarsest of any, and noted for its awkward and unshapely body. (*Tuairisgeal* seems to mean wild man, sower of confusion, and may thus indicate a link with the disorderly *liederlich* spirits in the German Wildfolk tradition).

In John Stuart Collis's book *The Triumph of the Tree*, we read that:

'Throughout the whole of Europe the Wildmen made a great impression. They were often clothed in moss and their long locks floated behind them in the gale. They announced their presence in the wind; they rode the tempest. When they 'fought' together they threw rocks at each other and used as hand-weapons the up-rooted trunks of pine-trees. The Wild Tree-women of the Tyrol were just as terrifying as these males: their enormous bodies were covered with hair and bristles, and their faces split across with a wide mouth.'

These powerful descriptions should I hope, dispel once and for all that pernicious error that confounded these mighty Wildfolk–Faerie beings with the tiny flower elementals, and further degraded them in Victorian times.

Also in *The Triumph of the Tree* we read that:

'Many Races, especially the Germanic and Scandinavian, believed that the express duties of certain wood-spirits consisted in looking after the forest, and shielding the trees from injury. They were coloured green, and their skin was of a mossy texture, though sometimes they appeared in the guise of men and women.'

The wood and moss damsels of the Oberpfalz region of Bavaria are described as being hairy, clad in moss, and having creased weatherworn faces, wreathed in long silken hair. These wood damsels were modest in their behaviour and are associated with the shrub trees of the underbrush.

At sowing time the farm workers of the Oberpfalz district threw a handful of linseed into the bushes as a gift for the wood damsels, and in Frankenwald they left three handfuls of flax for them at the time of the harvest. Thus did our more enlightened ancestors pay their dues to the nature powers, the Fairie Folk.

Several years ago at a certain point in my Initiatory training, a Wildman rock spirit communicated to me that my ancestors had used cup- and ring-marked sites as places of devotional communion with the rock spirits (*Fríd*) and offerings (of a non-violent sort) had been made into cup-shaped hollows in stones within old fields and farm steadings. This 'message', carrying as it did thunderously powerful authority (from one who should know), cut a swathe through the scores of irrelevant academic theories as to the purpose of these rock carvings. As has been shown time and time again, the Wildman's words have been vindicated in the evidence that my colleagues and I have turned up from research into ancient traditional practices. This is summarized below.

Faerie Wildwoman and Stone for Oblations.

The earliest Shamans, Druids and geomants knew well where all the magical power-beings of nature resided. Thus, at the places of Wildfolk manifestation (exposed rock faces with certain special energy characteristics), they carved cup and ring marks, upon which they and the common people proceeded to pour offerings of milk, etc., from their herds of reindeer, deer, cattle, goats and sheep. Certain of the cup- and ring-marked stones, located far out in the moors, would have been ritual sites for 'the Brown Man o' the Moors [Muirs]', offerings being made in respectful devotion with less emphasis on the fertility of herds.

Thankfully, records of these practices have been preserved right up to the present. In a book on supernatural beings we read about *Gruagachs*, male or female Wildfolk beings, that were wizard champions, animal herders and consultants on herbalism.

'[The *Gruagach*'s] main duty was to preside over cattle and take an intense interest in all matters pertaining to them. In return for her supervision she was offered a libation of milk each evening after the cows were milked. If the libation were omitted, the cattle, not withstanding all precautions, would all be found broken loose and trampling corn.' 'She frisked and gambled about the cattle pens and folds, armed only with a pliable reed, with which she switched all who annoyed her by uttering obscene language, or by neglecting to leave for her a share of the dairy produce.' 'A woman from the island of Heisgeir, off North

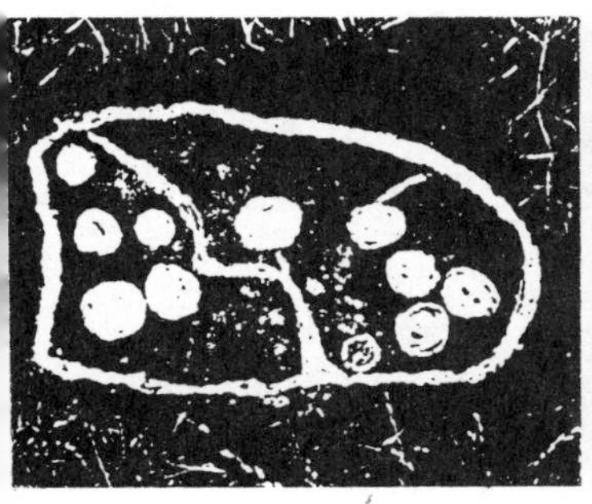

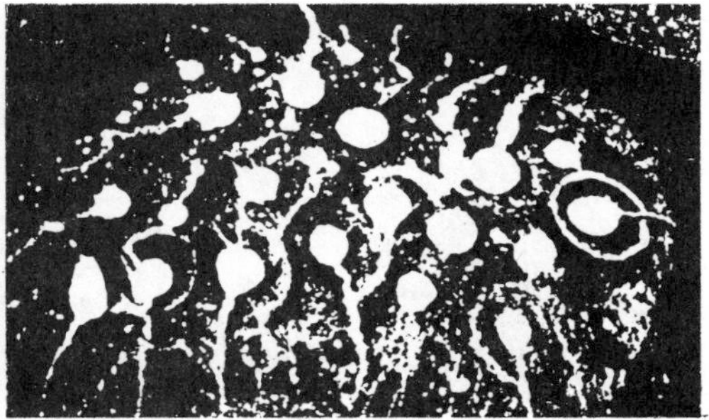

Oblation stones photographed by the author

Uist, once gave a graphic description of a *Gruagach*: she was seen moving about in the silver light of the moon, with a tall conical hat, with rich golden hair falling about her shoulders like a mantle of shimmering gold, while, with a slight swish of her wand, she would gracefully turn on her heel to admonish an unseen cow. At intervals her mellow voice could be heard in snatches of eerie song as she moved about.' (This is identical to how the Faerie maidens were sometimes portrayed in medieval German and French tapestries.) 'The following account is dated 1895 and concerns a *Gruagach* who frequented West Bennan in Arran. The creature lived in a cave known as Uamh na Gruagaich, and sometimes Uamh na Beiste, the cave of the Strange Being. She herded the cattle in the township of Bennan and no spring loss, no death loss, no mishap of disease ever befell them, while they throve, fattened and multiplied. Often the *Gruagach* was seen in the bright sunshine, golden hair streaming in the morning breeze and her rich voice filling the air with melody. She would wait on a hillock until the cattle arrived for her supervision.'

Below left: Cup and Ring marks in Dumfries
Right, top & bottom: Dobie-stone in Yorks

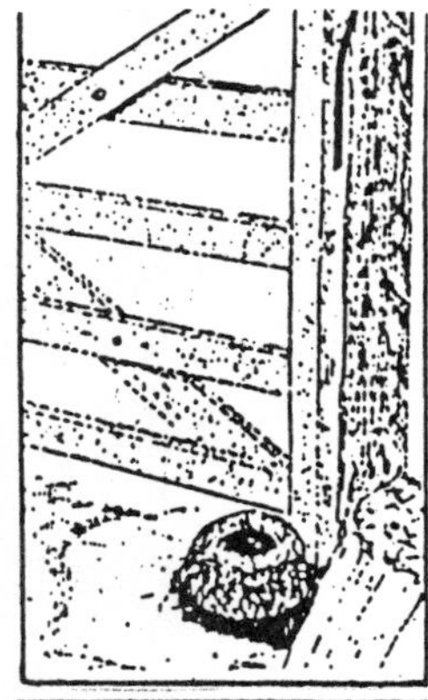

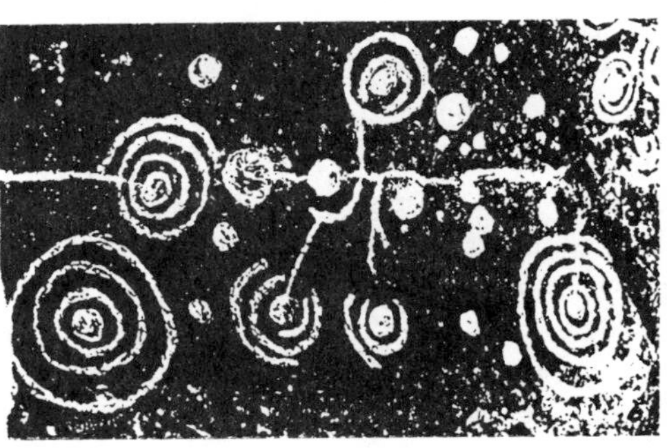

In Skye the *Gruagach* was a very tall thin woman with hair falling to her feet; she wore a soft misty robe, the effect being described as like 'a white reflection or shade'. She was linked primarily to the site, over a long time period, and not as much to its human colonizers. However, she helped the local families by caring for cattle and small children (so long as they allowed no dog near her). Like the Brownie of Old Albion, she was propitiated with a little tithe of milk or cream. At one time there was hardly a district in the Highlands or Lowlands of Alban which did not have a flagstone on which milk was regularly poured in devotion to these brownies.

At Gairloch there is a typical example of one of these stones called (in Gaidhlig) *Clach na Gruagach*. Of like derivation is *Tor Ban na Gruagaich* ('Fair High Place of the Wildwomen'), which is a round chambered Cairn at Halkirk in Caithness. 'Even so late as 1770, the dairymaids, who attended a herd of cattle

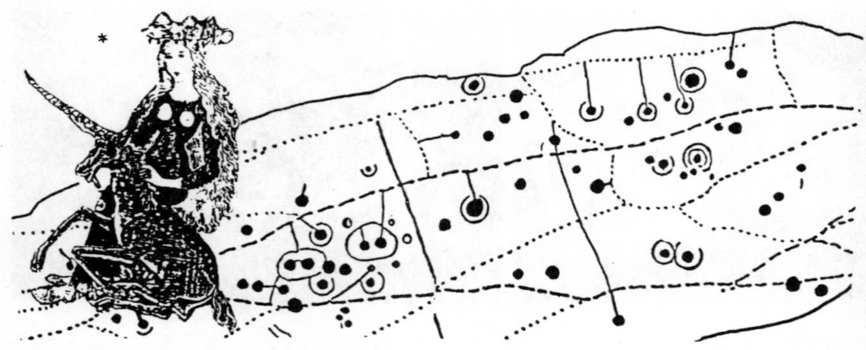

in the island of Trodda, were in the habit of pouring daily a quantity of milk in a hollow stone for the *Gruagach*. Should they neglect to do so they were sure of feeling the effects of the brownie the next day. (It is said that the Reverend Donald MacQueen, the then Minister of this Parish, went purposely to Trodda to check that "gross superstition".)'

A spiritual cousin of the *Gruagach* is the *Glaistig*, which is a half-woman half-goat Wildfolk being. Her name means 'black water spirit', and she was known to inhabit lonely lochs and rivers. *Glaistigs* are described as thin and grey in appearance, with long flowing yellow hair. She was sometimes clothed in a bluey-green covering. (This description of a Glaistig is identical to a medieval tapestry portrayal of a Rhineland wildwoman – as shown at the foot of page 165) Her charge was herding deer, goats and cattle, for which vocation she was thanked with a libation of fresh milk placed in a large cup-stone.

'On the Isle of Seil [North-west Argyll] it was the custom until a century ago that the youngest dairy maid on the farm had to go up the hill and fill a rather large cup-mark with milk each spring, for the Faerie Folk. If this was not done, there would be a shortage of milk and food that Autumn.' It is noted that special cup-shaped hollows in rocks 'can still be found today on the surface of some of the larger boulders situated near the older grazing grounds and many local place-names still commemorate her'.

Now if anyone still doubts that this was the main purpose of cup and ring marks, let me finally banish these doubts by relating that Montelius tells us (via Lewis Spence) that: 'In Scandinavia cup markings on cromlechs and standing stones were known as "elf mills" and are thought to have been used to contain offerings of milk, like the "brownie stones" and "*Gruagach* stones" of Scotland.'

So how did this priceless ancient tradition come to be almost completely forgotten and thoroughly denied by academics? The answer is quite a sad one, though the same one that is encountered throughout the rest of Europe. The Church of Rome and the later gloomy Presbyterian Orthodoxy, with the usual arrogant ignorance, set out to eradicate all such traces of 'gross superstition'. Of course, another way of destroying the ancient wisdom was to pervert it, so whilst the wise Pictish Christians respectfully used cup-marked stones as bases for their crosses (as in Meigle No. 1); the later Scot-ic Church in the Western Isles perverted the custom of turning a pestle thrice sunwise in the cups by insisting that the worshipper should leave a coin in the cup (these coins being collected periodically by Church officials). Thus was a pagan cup-stone, originally used to contact the nature powers, used to provide funds for the oppressor, the Church, who used the funds to further destroy the original harmony between man and nature. Within an atmosphere of Church and academic scepticism it is not surprising that the ordinary farm folk soon started to sever their links with the wise ones, as is recounted:

'A *Glaistig* forsook the township of Ach-na-Creige in Mull because of the trickery of a herd-boy. In the township cattle-fold, there was a large stone with a round hole in it, into which was poured some of the evening's milking. In return for this libation, the *Glaistig* would watch the cattle overnight. One evening a herd-boy poured boiling milk and went into hiding to watch the proceedings. The poor creature burnt her tongue so much that she promptly deserted her duties and the cattle of that township were never again watched over.' I don't think that the *Glaistig* would have physically burnt her tongue, but she would have become highly frustrated and aggrieved at the human-folk's growing wilful stupidity.

Another good Shamanistic purpose to which these *Klachain Aoraidh* ('worship stones') were put was to raise up a wind from a certain direction of the compass-wheel. (Bear in mind here Fig. 14, page 36.) An '*elph* cup' carved into a rock near Skallasaig in Kolonsay was called *Tobar na Gaoith Deas* ('the well (or creative vortex) of the South Wind') because the Chief of the McPhees could get a mild South wind whenever he wished by doing a small piece of magic with the rock spirits there. The Chief of the MacMhurichs (ancient hereditary Bards and Shamen) was even more accomplished at this Shamanistic operation, for at a basin-stone near his 'Bramble Knoll House' (*Tigh an Tom Dreis*) he could invoke a wind to blow from whatever *Airt* (quarter) he wished, by moving the elf-offerings out onto the corresponding side of the cup-basin (whilst doing the appropriate ritual). Only *Fear an Tom Dreis*, ('the Man of the Bramble Knoll'), had the ability to work with the stone of *Kuidh Chattain* ('food-share to the cats') in this magical way. The cats here mentioned could be merely domestic cats which came during the night to lap up the oblations of milk; but there is as much likelihood that large spectral cats were meant, the likes of which were the totems of the Clan Chattan, and gave their name to Caithness, and are still regularly 'seen' in Inverness-shire, Sutherland and elsewhere, as large black/white/puma-like cats with glowing red eyes. This theory receives strong support when we discover that a 'big cat' was one of the four major 'magical beasts' of the European Wildfolk cult.

Curiously enough, the bowl-shaped hollows, normally called dobby stones (after the *Dobie*, 'Wildman brownie', see two illustrations, foot of page 141) in the North of England are, in the following passage from Gerald Dodd's *Ghosts and Legends of Brönteland*, nicknamed 'cat troughs':

'In Brönteland I came across a farm which had a dozen Dobby Stones built into the dry-stone wall around the house. When asked if he knew what they were the farmer replied, 'Aye lad, they're cat troughs; we put milk in 'em for the cats; always have done.' When informed that he had been inadvertently offering sacrifices to the Old Gods he looked at me with a twinkle in his eye and said, "Well it don't seem to have done me any harm, lad, an' the cats ain't complaining, are they?"

Though knowing about Keltic examples, Gerald Dodd falsely ascribes this custom in the Pennines to the Scandinavian colonizers (but it was in use long before such invaders arrived); at least, to his credit, he got the usage exactly right:

'Testimonials to the belief in this northern elf by our ancestors can be found throughout the Pennines in the form of Dobby Stones. These stones can be found near the gates of many farmhouses; near stiles, doorways, any kind of entrance. They vary in size but can be recognised by the bowl-shaped hollow in the top of the stone into which our ancestors placed offerings of milk, porridge or oatcake to appease their local Dobby. The custom is Scandinavian in origin whereby our Viking forefathers made an 'alf-blot', an elf-sacrifice, to secure the good intent of the 'Landvaetts', the female spirits who safe-guarded the land. The Vikings also used honey, salt-water, wine and small dead animals as offerings.'

In Orkney, Shetland and the far North of Alban, the *Trows* (Faerie Folk) were also thought to preside over the welfare of the herds and fertility of the earth and crops. One type of *Trowie* Wildman was called a *Bu*-man (*Bu* also being the word for cattle), thus, in the old days, when a cattle byre was being constructed, care would be taken to ensure that there was an area of the underlying sandstone protruding through the floor, or incorporated into the wall, so that milk offerings could be poured into a carved cup/bowl/simple hollow in the stone surface; this was thereafter called 'the *Bu-stane*'.

In other parts of Britain this *Bu*-man was called a *Bu-kow*, *Bw-bach*, *Bw-bachod* or *Bwka*. In general this type of brownie was helpful and friendly and would assist with many of the farmstead/household tasks, often during the night. If his/her good faith was abused, or if the animals were mistreated, then the brownie could become obstreperous or openly aggressive towards the unwise humans. A fine example of this is recorded from old Monmouthshire, where a strapping dairymaid had struck up a working relationship with the *Boggart* spirit, such that for a nightly offering of milk or flummery he would assist with the chores. This amicable partnership lasted until one evening when, out of sheer cantankerousness, she put some stale urine (which was used for a mordant) into his bowl instead of milk. When she got up the next morning the *Bwka* attacked her and kicked her all around the house, roaring:

'The sheer cheek that the fat-arsed lass
Should give barley-bread and *piss*
To the *Bwka*.'

Fig. 31

After that she never saw him again. It was reported that he had moved to a farm near Hafod ys Ynys, where the servant-girl showed him more respect. We find traces of similar beliefs in practices of the Etruscans, Ancient Greeks, Slavs and other European cultures.

The illustrations on this page have been assembled from various corners of the globe. Figs. 31 and 32 are from Old Chinese and Tibetan manuscripts; Fig. 33 is an artist's impression drawn from sightings of the North American Sasquatch; Fig. 34 is a 'hairy saytor' from a Greek manuscript; Fig. 35 is Phoenician/Carthaginian from *c.* 600 BC. Allowing for differing ethnic cultures, the illustrations of Wildfolk have a lot in common with their Keltic and European equivalents. As mankind became more 'civilized'(?), the Greeks, Chinese, etc., started to portray their saytors as smooth-skinned human lookalikes, only preserving the tail to indicate their link to the nature kingdoms. This is symptomatic of humanity's woeful alienation from our natural environment.

As certain of the Wildfolk have guardianship over the beasts of the field and forest, it is no surprise to encounter some of the Greek saytors, Scandinavian wood-wives and Keltic Faerie Folk depicted with tails. Fig. 36 is a sixteenth-century Dutch depiction of the Faeries dancing in their magical ring; they have horns, hoofs, and one of them holds aloft a serpent (as does Kernunos in Fig. 82). The piper, as *Towzie Tyke* (the goat-dog-man) or *Am Fear Dubh* ('the Dark Man'), is a prominent Faerie musician and was sometimes reported as being perched atop a certain rock or boulder, skirlin' oot on his pipes.

Fig. 32

In the Keltic areas the Wildfolk contact-stones were not always horizontal base-rock carved with cup/cup and ring marks, for sometimes these power channels would be raised up as standing stones (with or without marks) or incorporated into a souterain or chambered kairn as a link to the Faerie guardians (as I discussed in my article in the *Pictish Shaman*). Thus these *Gruagach*/brownie/*Bodach*/*Wight*/*Dwarfie*/*Boggle-stanes*, as objects through which the Wildfolk could materialize, became local centres of the Faerie cult for early pagan worshippers. In this light we should remember Robin Hood's stone near Allerton, Liverpool, which had cup and rings and grooves upon it; and the *Clach na Gruagachs* outside most of the 'big houses' in the Western Isles, where the inhabitants used to supplicate the *Gruagach* Wildman for assistance in times of need or ill health.

In ancient times the seers and wise women perceived the Wildfolk beings in their various Otherworld forms. One of the strangest forms that our modern monorail 'logic' will find difficult to accept is of a one-legged, one-armed, one-eyed Wildman. A description of one such is given by an old Gaelic storyteller called MacPhie, about a being called *Direach Ghlinn Eitidh Mhic Kalain* ('Giant of the Bleak Moorland in Glen Eiti), son of Kolin (or off the hazel (*Kolen*) tree – related through Ogham to the heron/crane hence the one-legged stance). Anyway, it was seen 'with one hand out of his chest, one leg out of his haunch, and one eye out of the front of his face.' He was a good Giant, and a wood-cutter, and went at a great pace before the Irish King Murdoch MacBrian, who had lost sight of his red-eared hound, and his deer, and Ireland.'

Fig. 33

One is led to believe that the Irish King has been lured into an Otherworld at the mention of the red-eared hounds (otherwise known as *Kwn Annwn* or Gabriel Ratchets), hounds that often led Keltic questers into the underworld – as would the *Keirw Kwm Kych*, the *Eillid Chashion*, the Goddess's white-footed hind, after whom the hounds chased. Keltic Druids invoked the power of this type of Wildman when, standing on one leg, with one eye closed, and with one hand behind their back, they chopped off a bunch of sacred mistletoe with one blow from their golden sickle. Pictish Initiate Kings also called upon their spiritual guardians as they stood upon one leg in the Wildman 'footprint' whilst being ordained at the summit of the rock citadel of Dun-Add. KuKhulainn was also famous for using only one eye, one hand and one foot whilst magically cutting an Ogham spell. To dance or drum ritually whilst hopping on one leg is a well-known Shamanistic practice from Keltia, Scandinavia, Lapland, India, China, Brazil, Mexico, Australia and Africa: 'We find the one-legged dance playing an important part in the shamanist culture of the Chinese/Bronze Age, for example, in the dance of Yu. In a ritual dance youths imitated the magic bird Chang-yang by folding up one leg, dancing and singing, "Heaven will make rain fall in abundance. The Chang-yang beats on the drum and dances." (from *The*

Fig. 34

Fig. 35

Clashing Rocks) As did the Greek Melanesian masked men, for: " 'They do not need to walk on the soles of their feet as mortals have to do, but they hop about as is characteristic of gods.' In Greece *askoliasmos* (the Sacred Goat Dance) is much practised on the monuments by *Silenes* (Moon-Goat-Wildmen). On both black- and red-figured vases a characteristic dance-posture of satyrs and silenes is that described by Nonnos: 'Supported unflinchingly on the right foot, they straighten out the other to the tips of the toes, then bend the knee and cross hands.' "

Certain beings in the legends even took their names from this one-organed proclivity, such as *Unipeds, Mono-skeleis, Monokolai, Skiapodes*. In the *Táin* we find KuKhulainn confronted by a chariot drawn by a one-legged red horse; in the chariot is a red woman, the War Goddess, accompanied by a man carrying a hazel switch with which he drives a cow.

As an example of how, at a deep level, themes and characters link together in Keltic mythology, and as a demonstration of the importance of my Shamanistic Ogham key, please note:

Mac *Kolen* = Son of hazel, with one-legged heron stance associated with red.

Direach G. E. Mhic *Kalain* = Son of hazel, one-legged/armed/eyed Wildman, associated with red.

Ku *Kalain* = Hound-servant of hazel, adopted one-legged, etc., postures, associated with a one-legged red horse and

Kuilin red-crimson War Goddess and hazel-man.

Wildwoman
(with crown of Ferns)
riding upon a Unicorn

Fig. 40

Now let us turn to a famous one-horned creature, the unicorn, called in Gaelic *Aon-adharkach, Aon-Bheannach, Biasd-na-Skrogaig* (on Skye), also *Buabhall* or *Buabhull*. This 'beast of the towering horn' was reported to dwell in certain sea-lochs in the Western Isles and in certain meadows elsewhere in Alban). It was illustrated with just one horn arising from the centre of the forehead (as in an Intiation bowl from Ancient Keltic Rhineland). Although the unicorn could be described as an Otherworld horse with the third-eye centre activated into a cone of light, it would be wise to also note that it contains traces of also being: a goat (beard), deer, bull (*Bua-*), lion (long mane) and other lesser forms. After much

Fig. 36 Fig. 37 Fig. 38

crucial research it was my good fortune to rediscover the role of the unicorn and the other Faerie beasts as Keltic fire-festival totems.

That four-fold Initiation cycle is depicted in Fig. 41. Although identical in meaning and usage to the *Chaioth ha-Qadesh* (four holy living creatures) of the Qabalah, it was *not* derived from them; rather, it represents an Ancient Keltic parallel system. This finds proof in the following Ancient Gaelic passage recounting the Initiation of a mystical 'son' of the Goddess Bride:

Fig. 39 Wildman and Unicorn

Son (Initiate):
I will voyage in a God's name,
In likeness of deer,
In likeness of horse,
In likeness of serpent,
In likeness of King,
More powerful it will be with me,
than all others.

Fig. 41 The Four Keltic magical Beasts

In the twelfth-century. German epic *Orendel* we find this (interpolated) passage:

Stretched out under a linden tree lay
A lion and a dragon,
A bear and a boar,
As good to see as could be
There stood the Wildman
And I can tell you, that although made of gold
he looked as if he were alive.

Here the linden tree stands for the kosmic Tree of Life with the archetypal Wildman as its guardian and the beasts of the four festivals: boar (Samhain), bear (Brigantia), Dragon (Beltaine) and lion (Lughnasadh). Whilst in the sixteenth-century English Tale of Sir Gawain and the *Carl of Carlisle*, later renamed *Sir Gawain and the Green Knight*, Owain who stays at the edge of the Borders section of the Kaledonian Forest, he (the Giant-Wildman-Carl), keeps as guardians in the main hall of his castle a boar, a bear, a bull (Beltaine) and a lion. Similarly in the Danish song of 'Swend Vonwend' the giant lets his totemistic creatures play all over his enormous body – for he carries a bear under his arm, and a boar on his back, whilst deer and rabbits run along his outstretched fingers. Also in the fourteenth-century *Gawain and the Green Knight* the Wildman is found in the company of serpents, wolves and primeval bulls. And in the Welsh story *Owein* or *The Lady of the Fountain* a dark and shaggy giant, who is only one-eyed, declares that he is 'the Wood-ward of the Wood'. He is asked what power he has over the animals of the forest, and he replies disdainfully, 'I will show thee, little man,' and proceeds to give a demonstration. He strikes a deer with his club; and upon hearing its snorted warning the forest animals rush together from all sides, and stay in hushed obedience until the Wildman bids them go feed, whereupon they all bow their heads in passing as vassals to their overlord.

How Fig. 41, showing the four creatures (stag, lion, unicorn and gryphon) relate to the Initiation of Bride's 'son' can more clearly be seen in Fig. 42. In this diagram the four fire festivals are shown with their appropriate totemic

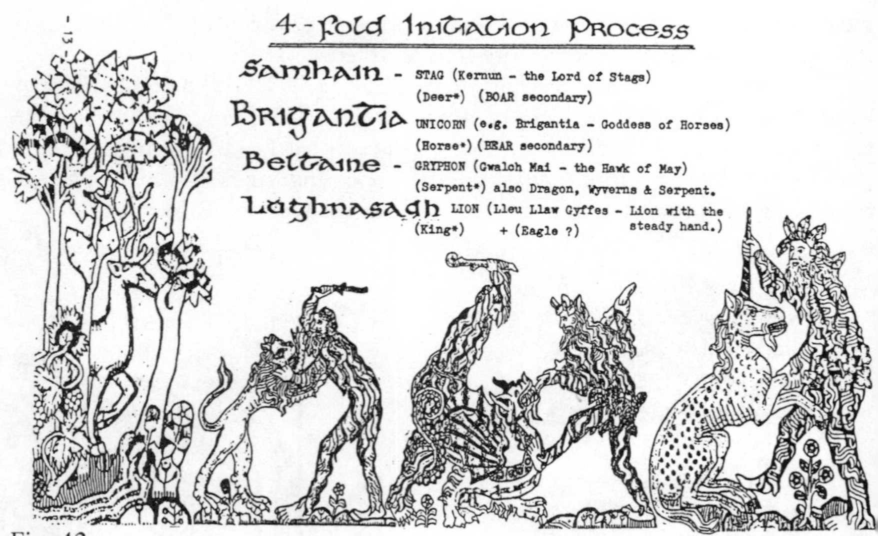

- 13 -
4-Fold Initiation Process
Samhain - STAG (Kernun - the Lord of Stags)
(Deer*) (BOAR secondary)
Brigantia UNICORN (e.g. Brigantia - Goddess of Horses)
(Horse*) (BEAR secondary)
Beltaine - GRYPHON (Gwalch Mai - the Hawk of May)
(Serpent*) also Dragon, Wyverns & Serpent.
Lughnasagh LION (Lleu Llaw Gyffes - Lion with the steady hand.)
(King*) + (Eagle ?)

Fig. 42

animals alongside, which in turn are strongly linked to particular deities prominent at these very festivals. Thus the Initiation of Bride's 'son' was probably consummated at the four fire festivals; it may also have been conducted on the Inner Planes at *Kaer Pedryvan*, otherwise known as *Kaer Sidi* (mystical castle) at the centre of the four primal zodiacal streams in the astral world of Annwn. (This gives us another angle on the Shamanistic and geomantic tattoos that the Picts emblazoned into their fiery blood. Note also the animals depicted on the Gundstrop Cauldron, which was used for Initiatory practices, although the outer panels may use a sevenfold form as outlined in my article in *Inner Keltia* No. 6.)

I have an intimation that the Wildman in his capacity as *Gruagach* Wizard-Initiator can lead us through this four-fold seasonal Initiation, as he is indeed depicted 'struggling' with these very totemic creatures. The 'struggle' is of the same ilk as that between the Holly King and the Oak King, where they symbolically 'kill' each other in an alternating cycle (the difference being that the Wildman 'masters' the creature to then ride upon it, use it as a vehicle for his expression). The overall master of all these creatures is of course Kernunos.

Fig. 43

Fig. 44a

Fig. 44b

Fig. 45a

Fig. 45b

The Four Keltic Magical Beasts

Wildman *Wildwoman*

Found riding upon, or associated with, the following creatures:

	Wildman		Wildwoman
(1)(a)	Stag (Deer)	(1)(a)*	Hind
(b)	Boar	(b)	*Boar
(2)(a)	Unicorn (Horse)	(2)(a)	Unicorn (Horse)
(b)	Bear	(b)	Bear
(3)	Dragon, Wyvern, Bull	(3)	Gryphon, Bull
(4)	Lion	(4)	
(5)		(5)	Phoenix Bird
(6)	Hound	(6)	Hound
(7)	Hare	(7)	Hare
(8)		(8)	Monkey
(9)		(9)	Cat
(10)	Goat	(10)	Goat
(11)		(11)	Donkey, Ass
(12)		(12)	Antelope (or long-horned Cattle)
(13)	Ram	(13)	
(14)	Heron/Crane	(14)	Heron/Crane
(15)		(15)	Sheep (Ewes)
(16)	Wolf	(16)	*(?)

*found on one late symbolic heraldic tapestry

In Irish a
Leomhan ohraobh
a Lion of the Tree
Fig. 46

Fig. 47

Top: A Phaerie from R. Topsell's Book (1907) Below: A Magic Beast from a Medieval Tapestry

N.B: In illustrations where the Wildman is shown *struggling* with a unicorn/lion/dragon certain writers have wrongly labelled these, e.g.: 'Wildman killing a lion'. This death fixation is an unfounded projection from the minds of these writers, as no real killing takes place; we are in fact dealing with a system of symbolism. It is important that we look at these symbolic struggles within the context of the whole system of the Wildman's totemic animals, and not in unfavourable isolation.

In some Tales the Wildman has his heart concealed in the body of some animal, which the hero (aspiring Initiate) must kill in order to rescue his lady – this same motif is found in one of the Irish Folktales (No. 3) by Keltia Publications as Booklets where the *Gruagach* (giant) is known as the King of the Golden Land.

Certain illustrations show the Wildfolk symbolically grappling with their magic beasts; in others Figs. 39, 40, 45b, 52 & 77, they are shown riding them whilst there is also reference to the creatures embodying their 'heart' (essence). I would like to draw your attention to 46 above, where the composite beast is actually described as a 'Phairie', thus exemplifying one of the stranger, totally animalistic forms in which the Faerie Folk can manifest themselves. This *Lamia* or Faerie has a humanish head, womanly breasts, front paws of a lion(?), back feet of a stag/goat, scales like a fish and the reproductive organs of a male animal. R. Topsell, who illustrated this 'Phairie', writes:

'This word *Lamia* hath many significations, being taken sometimes for a beast of Lybia, sometimes for a fish, and sometimes for a spectre or apparition of women called *Phairies*. And from hence some have ignorantly affirmed that either there were no such beasts at all, or else that it was a compounded monster of a beast and a fish.'

As beings of the watery Astral Plane, the Fairie Wildfolk are as relevant at inland aquatic sites such as lochs, lakes, mere-pools, fountains, rivers, ponds and wells as they are in relation to the sea and its environs. (Indeed, Menippus's *Lamia* seems to have been a water spirit, for she was first encountered near a fountain. The tradition of mermaids riding upon dolphins also has connections with the Pictish *Cetus* (porpoise- or dolphin-like) creature I have decoded; and other linkages to Swan Knights.) Thus mer-maids atop seaweed-covered rocks, with their mirror and comb in hand, can be as easily encounted as a lady of the lake, or, in another form, as the Queen of the Wildfolk – the Faerie Queen – the Pictish Goddess with her mirror and comb symbols.

According to Russian folk tradition when one of the unwise had the temerity to use an axe upon a venerated tree a loud cry would be heard coming from the trunk. And if it was felled, the people were sometimes appalled to see a serpent or a blue bull glide or rush from the falling tree. This remarkable piece of evidence surely shows the psychic powers of the Russian peasants! It also demonstrates that trees were perceived as channels of manifestation for Otherworld creatures and their masters, the Faerie Wildfolk.

Figs. 48, 49, 50 and 51 are part of a series of Wildfolk illustrations that Martin Schongauer copied from sources dated around 1450; they indicate a small interface between the European Shamanistic and alchemical streams. 49 perhaps shows the Wildman emerging from the Nigredo Cleft of Darkness (Moor's Head) towards dawn and Shamanistic East (hare). 51: although there are a few hound stations, a major one being: 'commencing the chase after dawn'. 50: the solar lion is mainly Shamanistic South to Shamanistic West; 48: the Stag ruts at Samhain, Shamanistic North-west.

Wildman hunts (to capture him for his knowledge of herbs and ointments), in dramatized form, are on record from Switzerland, Germany, Southern Tyrol, the Italian Alps, Austria, Eastern Czechoslovakia and Thuningia, Flanders and Venice. The Wildman in these dramas occasionally becomes a bear (totem animal for Brigantia, the Goddess Festival); at other times he is caught by young maidens who tie a red ribbon around him. In other plays he, as a bear, mates with a young maiden in a specially constructed bower – this drama takes place at the start of February – Brigantia!

In *Lestoire de Merlin* Merlin appears at court disguised as a stag; he reveals that only a Wildman will be able to explain the Emperor's dreams. He then disappears back into the forest, leaving instructions on how to capture a Wildman. All the Knights fail in this, and so finally Grisandoles, 'the most beautiful woman and the best in all [the Emperor's] lands and she a maiden', effects the capture of the Wildman (who is Merlin in another guise). Merlin then returns to the Emperor's castle and explains to the court, 'A maiden took me through her power and cunning, something which none of you men could have done with all your strength.'

Fig. 48

It is significant that only the choice maiden can capture the Wildman (Merlin), but only the Wildman has the wisdom to interpret the Emperor's dreams; the maiden could not – thus is revealed the crucial interdependence of male and female magic.

Not only does the above tale have an exactly similar schematic theme to the mystical 'hunting of the unicorn' (the most powerful male animal, yet the symbol of Brigantia), but the Oroborous serpent of wisdom puts his tail back in his mouth when we recall the true account of Merlin's genesis: his mother was a young maiden who lay down against a special tree in the enchanted Forest of Kaledon or Broceliande whereupon a Wildman came up and made love with her; Merlin was the fruit of their union.

Fig. 49

Thus is described the method of a personal Intiation process (which I have been through). For those that have ears let them hear.

According to the Vita Merlini (*The Life of Myrddin*): '*Merlin* prepared what must be regarded as a *charivari* for his wife Gwendoloena [Gwenhwyvar], after having sanctioned her marriage to another man. Merlin the Wildman appeared before the bride's house during the wedding night, accompanied by a great herd of deer which he had brought together in the woods. When the new husband incautiously put his head out of the window to see what was causing the fracas, Merlin overwhelmed by sudden jealousy, wrenched off the antlers from the stag he was riding and threw them at his rival, killing him outright.'

Fig. 50

In such passages we enter into both the heart of the Wildfolk tradition and the heart of the ancient *Arthuriad*. Indeed, it would be true to say that the earliest strata of the Arthurian cycle arose from the Kruithnaeg (Pictish) and Kymraeg (Brythonic Welsh) Wildfolk cults. In the beginning, 'the Green Knight' (and other 'colours' of knights) were giant shaggy wildmen; the green *Kapel* is actually a cave; Gawain and others of the court originally sought Initiation; Arthur was of the Bear God totem; Gwenhwyvar was a 'white spirit' and Myrddin (Merlin), as we have seen, was a very Shamanistic enchanter, sired by a Wildman, and riding upon a stag/bear/wolf just as the King of Faerie is depicted as doing.

Fig. 51

In searching for the origins of the Initiatory Keltic Faerie cult, early evidence comes in the form of certain of the Arthurian characters going 'wild', leaving knightly pursuits or even the battlefield, and heading off into the forest or mountains to be Initiated into their mysteries by the hidden guardians – teachers. In the Scottish Borders' Tale of Merlin's period in the Kaledonian Forest as a Wild man it was 'caused' by the loss of his two brothers in battle. Likewise the famous Welsh prophet Lailoken went *Geilt* and stayed in the Kaledonian Forest; his prophetic sayings are preserved in *The Lailoken Fragments*. The school of

Fig. 52→

Part of a Series of Wildfolk Illustrations that Martin Schongauer copied from earlier sources around 1450, they indicate a small interface between the European Shamanistic & Alchemical Streams. Fig. 49 perhaps shows

Tailiesin Initiatory poetry shows itself well versed in all the symbols and terminology of this tradition – not surprising, as it was based just south of the Kaledonian Forest in the old Brythonic Kingdom of Rheged. As the Carl of Carlisle, Owain stays right on the edge of the Kaledonian Forest where Gawain came to receive Initiation from him as the Green Knight (see below). Other Arthurian Wildmen are Lancelot, who spends years as a forlorn Wildman in the depths of the forests after his love-life has become emotionally unstable; *Perceval*, as '*le valet Sauvage*'; and Helias, who in the *Chevalier au Cygne* ('Knight to the Swan'), appears dressed all over in large leaves, unkempt and hairy. From the Irish tradition we also ought to remember Suibhne Geilt, who is reported as having gone 'mad', but of course a much fairer and more perceptive translation of *Geilt* would be 'wild'; for Suibhne became so sickened of the warrior's bloody slaughter that in mid-battle he received a spiritual directive to flee to the forest, there to live with the green powers, grow hair and feathers, and learn the secret ways of the mighty powers.

A more significant list of male Arthurian characters one could hardly gather, especially as Arthur himself features as the bear, husband of the Goddess Gwenhwyvar; and other figures such as Bors, Kai (Kay) and Loth play their part. Also, the importance of the Kaledonian Forest is plain to see – it stands as the strongest heartland of the Wildman tradition in Britain. It is thus fitting that my colleagues and I (individuals of Pictish and Brythonic attunement) should play a major part in reviving this tradition. An example of how the female Arthurian characters work is given in the following section from *Sir Gawain and the Green Knight*:

Gawain sets off to seek the green 'chapel' (cave in a forest), and he meets a friendly lord who puts him up over the Winter Solstice in his castle. Two ladies are there, one old and extremely ugly but highly honoured and surrounded with attendants. This old hag leads a young woman by the hand, and Gawain thinks the young maid is more beautiful than Guinevere. On New Year's morning the host goes off hunting whilst Gawain is still asleep in his bed. Into his bedroom this beautiful maiden sneaks, draws back the bedcovers and repeatedly tempts Gawain with her attractive body. He resists her and finally she gives him a magic green 'lovelace' to wear in her honour, and he puts it on over his armour. He then sets off once more for the green chapel, and at this cave he encounters the Green Knight, who puts him through an ordeal with an axe, which he survives only because he is wearing the green lovelace round his neck. Thereafter the Green Knight reveals that he was the lord of the castle, that he had sent his beautiful wife to tempt him, and that the whole test was contrived by the old lady, who is Morgan le Fay – Morgan the Goddess – Arthur's half-sister and Gawain's Aunt.

Shining through this Tale are aspects of the Keltic Triple Goddess, for in this instance Morgana is the ugly but wise old hag, with the giant's wife playing the more youthful and sexually amorous aspect.

It is a moot point whether in earlier, unchristianized Tales there would have been less chaste and 'pure' chivalry and more pagan sexuality, as in an early version of Thomas the Rhymer's encounter with the Queen of Faerie. One should never forget that during the Orthodox Church's bloody reign of terror the Inquisition butchered many lusty lassies believed falsely to be 'witches'. In a parallel case in 1691, in rural Sweden, a young man accused of having made love

the Wildman emerging from the Nigredo Cleft of Darkness (Moor's Head) towards Dawn & Sh. East (Hare); 51, although there are a few Hound stations, a Major one being: 'commencing the Chase after Dawn'; 50 the Solar Lions is mainly Sh. South–Sh. West; 48 the Stag rutts at Samhain Sh. N.W.

Fig. 53

Fig. 54

Fig. 55a

to a *Skogra* (Faerie Wildwoman) was condemned to death by the church.

Orthodox Church tradition which involved many thousands of monks and nuns remaining celibate could not come to terms with the better balanced marital relationships within the early Keltic Church (and hence persecuted it); it is easy to guess how much more vehemently the Church would have persecuted the Keltic Fairie tradition, which was openly sexually promiscuous. For example, we read in Diego de San Pedro's *Carcel de Amor* that the Wildman says, 'My name is desire, I am the principal official in the castle of love.' (In Fig. 55a he is represented as carrying an image of the Goddess, after whom the lover is drawn.) As the Wildman explains, 'With the beauty of this image he inspires affections and with those consumes lives, as can be seen in the prisoner, whom he is conducting to the prison of love.

Idiots travel this path stumblingly along, with eyes bedazzled; whilst the wise travel it, like the divine fool, with eyes open wide, perceiving the Goddess of Love.

One of the many interfaces between the European Wildfolk tradition and Keltic mythology can be found in certain of the medieval travelogues. These have previously been misinterpreted as wildly inaccurate accounts of journeys in far-off parts of the world; whereas they are as much accounts of Otherworld regions and their inhabitants. The choice of a geographically remote locale is a subterfuge employed by the esoteric storytellers: Greece, Lochlann, Spain and Sicily are employed by the Irish *Senachae*, and tropical foliage by the Rhineland Wildfolk tapestry-makers.

Thus the Wildfolk whom have been clumsily termed 'the riverine apple-smellers' subsist on the scent from certain wonderous apples – reminiscent of the Keltic Paradise of Emhain Avallach; the Isle of Avalon; the Greek Garden of the Hisperides; Idun's apples that fed the hosts in Asgard; and the Shekìnāh's Holy Apple Grove. Note these lines from the Middle English text *Mandeville's Travels:*

There is another island
That the men call Piktain
And the people of that region . . .
Never eat or drink
But everyone in that land
Holds an apple in his hand . . .
By whose scent he lives . . .
And on the Island of Dendros, I gather
That is next to it,
Men live on flesh and fish.

In the prose version we learn that the men of Dendros 'have skins as coarsely haired as beasts, except for the face. These people go as well under water as they do on dry land.'

The ability of these Wildpeople to travel over/through/under water is highly significant. The psychic Otherworld is otherwise known as the Watery Astral Plane, so mastery of this element befits an Initiate of this plane of existence ('the realm under waves' –*Rioghachd Fo Thuinn*). Of fundamental importance for our Wildmen research is that it takes them and locates them well into the magic Keltic Otherworld, with distinct links to certain other denizens of Faerie.

In ancient times virtually every Highland or Lowland clan seat had its Brownie or *Gruagach* guardian, and it was from this being that the clan received its 'slogan' (*Sloghorne, Slugh-ghairm* – 'cry of the Faerie host'). This slogan, or 'gathering-word of the clan' was also used as a watchword or warcry on the battlefield; in time it became 'a hereditary designation; appellation of a tribe; a peculiar quality viewed as inherent in those of the family'. The Wildfolk guardians occasionally appear on the clan's banner (and later, on heraldic crests), as well as plant/bird/animal totemistic devices. The noble families of old Europe maintained similar practices; indeed, close to three hundred European families have the Wildman on their coat of arms. In the course of time, however, the profounder levels of meaning to heraldic crests (which were current in Arthurian times) were lost and the Wildman/Wildwoman motif probably dwindled in significance, becoming merely a symbol of strength, courage, and of

Fig. 55b

Fig. 56
Fig. 57
Fig. 58
Fig. 59

Fig. 60

Fig. 67

Fig. 68

having achieved success from a rural family background. While the artistic symbolism remained alive in its profounder sense, it is bound to have permeated and influenced the European alchemical tradition, as the knowledge of Paracelsus and Fulcanelli demonstrates to us.

In medieval times, even after centuries of continuous opposition from the Orthodox Church, the Wildfolk cult continued to be maintained and celebrated in many strata of society. The behind-the-scenes Initiates orchestrated many hundreds of people to dress up in what were basically Shamanistic guises (see Figs. 61–66 and 67–70) and midst much ribald jollity act out Wildfolk ritual dramas. Even the participants' horses were decked out as the Faerie beasts shown in 45a and 45b. The major celebrations were held as carnivals (of much deeper import than the materialistic debauches we see today); other Wildfolk dances and plays were performed in the streets and village squares at the times of the pagan festivals: May Day (Beltaine), St John's Day (Summer Solstice), Harvest Festival, Yule (Winter Solstice), etc. Also, each of the craft guilds had its own special day on which all its members dressed up and acted out strange dramas which often contained distinct pagan wildfolk elements. For instance in Bullinger's *Chronica Tigurina*, written in the sixteenth century, the butchers of Zurich had the privilege (granted to them in 1330) of holding a masquerade on Ash Wednesday, where the bride and bridegroom were dressed in garments of moss and greenery, and would make sexually provocative jests and gestures to each other, finally to be thrown together into a fountain (The Fountain of Love). Secondary figures in this drama included a bear on a chain, a lion, fools and mummers in ritual masks.

In the neighbourhood of Sarrebourg, beside the Vosges Forest (Ancient Keltic Faerie heartland), the village shepherd was central in the lusty ceremonies, for he appeared attired as a Wildman on the first Sunday in Lent and proclaimed in a loud voice all the secret love affairs and engagements which were taking place in the community at that time, thereby giving them his pagan sanction.

A selective list of such events is given below:

Fig. 61 Fig. 62 Fig. 63 Fig. 64 Fig. 65 Fig. 66

1348: In Albion there is a reference to '*Capita de Woodewose*' in a masque of 1348, which indicates the employment of a Wyldeman disguise earlier than other records we have for continental Europe.

1392: This was the year of the disastrous '*Bal des Ardents*' in which companions of Charles VI of France were burned to death whilst performing a Wildman dance. This took place on 28 January – Brigantia!

Fig. 69

1431: For the coronation of the English Henry VI the Parisians erected 'a scaffold with a kind of forest upon it, on which three Wildmen and a woman fought a continuous battle, as long as the King and his noblemen were in attendance to watch it.'

1431: In Paris a performance included a forest grove on a scaffold and Wildmen dancing in it. The learned men of Bruges claimed these represented the first historic inhabitants of the region before the founding of their city.

1435: A Wildman dance in Basle, where the nobility from all Europe were in attendance at a Church council. Behind the musicians, twenty-three persons entered dressed as *uomini selvatici*, with their hair, half red, half green, falling to their feet.

1437: Charles VII of France entered Paris and there were 'in front of the city and at the Fountaine de Ponceau Wildmen and women who 'fought' with each other and went through several acts, and besides there were three very beautiful maidens impersonating Sirens [Mermaids/Goddesses]'.

Fig. 70

1438: The citizens of Valenciennes arrived on their annual visit to the tournaments in Lille 'all dressed up as Wild men carrying clubs and big sticks, their heads disguised with the skins of strange animals, which was astonishing to see'. At the head of the procession there were Wild men playing trumpets and horns, and a herald in a bear skin who carried the escutcheon of Valenciennes. Even the horses had been transformed into fantastic beasts by throwing over them the skins of lions, tigers and dogs and decorating them with feathers. The visitors were received by a delegation of their hosts all dressed in feathers and led by the King of the carnival in skins and plumage, his steed garnished with mirrors and peacock and swan feathers.

This Wildman Ritual Drama is still enacted in Oberstdorf in the Bavarian Alps. Herdsmen dressed in Wildman costumes Dance to celebrate the preservation of the Cattle through the Summer months.

Fig. 71

1450: In the Nuremberg Carnival one of the Wildmen wore a head mask and had little mirrors or pine cones hanging from the tufts of his shaggy apparel.

1496: In a pageant the citizens of Brussels showed fourteen Wildmen together with a Moorish woman and a fool.

1515: The Twelfth Night celebrations of 1515 for Henry VIII included 'Eight Wyldemen, all apparayled in green mosse with sleved sylke, with ugly weapons and terrible visages – there fought with eight Knyghtes and after a long fight the armed knights had drawn 'the Wyldemen out of their places'.

1534: Sebastian Frank in his *Weltbuch of 1534* describes a carnival of mummers, where, apart from men dressed up as Wildmen there were people who ran about naked, others crawling on all fours, and men impersonating storks, monkeys, and fools. The Wildmen's closest associates were bears.

1575: When Elizabeth I came to Kenilworth the Wildman actor came out of the wood dressed as of old in moss and ivy and bearing a small oak plucked out by the roots.

1610: At Chester the St George's Procession (end of April?) was headed by 'two Wildmen in ivy with black hair and beards, very ugly to behold, and garlands upon their heads, with great clubs in their hands, and with fireworks [associated with lightning] to scatter abroad to maintain a way for the rest of the show'.

1695: In 1695 a Wildman character in a pageant in Dresden walked between the mask of a stag and those of 'disorderley [*liederlich*] spirits who vexed people and beat them'.

With the Wildman dramas taking such a prominent place in the social calendar of so much of Europe, many inns, known as *Zum Wilden Mann* or *Du Sauvage*, acted as places of refreshment for the considerable number of participants in the ritual processions. Other visible vestiges from this period are the pagan Wildmen scenes which appear on the whitewashed walls of ancient houses in the Grisons.

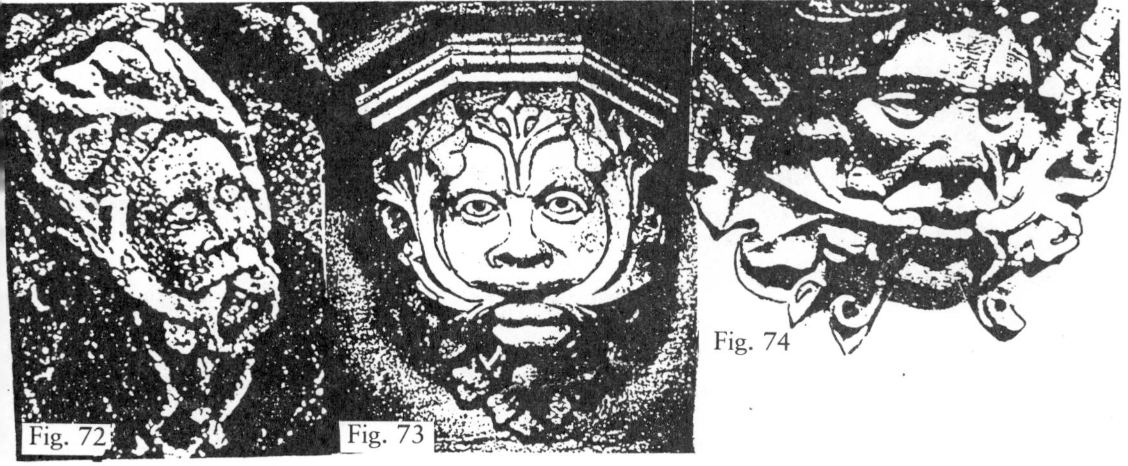

Fig. 72 Fig. 73 Fig. 74

What has been described as a *charivari* ('disruption of a marriage feast') was actually the ritual enactment of the presence of the wild horde by their human Initiate representatives.

As nearly all the participants in these Wildfolk dramas were so disguised as to be humanly unrecognizable, some of the highest ranking nobility and even royalty took part, letting their hair down as it were, and losing their accustomed image to be able to experience Shamanistic awareness. One of the most notable examples involved Charles VI of France:

Charles VI, whilst young, had an ecstatic vision in which he saw the Wildpeople riding through the woods upon their unicorns – their bodies were almost entirely covered with hair and, except for wreaths of ferns and leaves worn around their heads, they were completely naked. Charles inquired the Lore concerning these beings from his tutors. He was told not to seek for them on sunny days because they would hide in the shadows shunning human contact, but during thunderstorms and blizzards they would dance in the clearings and sing gutteral songs. In later life, Charles often travelled far into the depths of the forests searching for his much loved Wildmen. The only time he was to see one, however, was when he was dancing a serpentine dance dressed as a Wildman himself (as were five of his friends), as part of a drunken *charivari*. During the dance a real Wildman joined in, to make seven in the ring. This dance ended tragically when a servant accidentally set the six dancers' furry costumes on fire with a torch; the King was the only one to survive, thanks to his aunt's throwing a thick wrap over him to smother the flames. Thereafter Charles's interest in Wildmen became more obsessive, and he was deposed from power, being adjudged bereft of his critical faculties.

As I have pointed out in an article in *Inner Keltia* No. 2, another branch of the Wildfolk dance and drama was certain of the earliest Morris dancing teams. A strong similarity, both visually and ritualistically, can be noted between the antlered Shaman (61) from the prehistoric cave walls of Trois Frees, Ariege, the antlered Wildfolk participant in 62, the men of the Abbot's Bromley horn dancers in 75, the Wildman with stagshield in 48, the Faerie Wildman riding a stag in 77 (as did Myrddin) and the antlered Keltic God Kernunos from the Gundstrop Cauldron, 82.

Like many other Morris teams, Abbot's Bromley dance at certain times of the

ABBOT'S BROMLEY HORN DANCERS, STAFFORDSHIRE

Fig. 75

year which have long figured as festivals sanctified in Keltic Pagan tradition. The sets of horns the Abbot's Bromley men proudly bear are truly relics from ages past, for they are reindeer horns. Although reindeer may be depicted on one or two of the Pictish symbol stones, they are normally held to have died out in mainland Britain some time BC; thus either the Abbot's Bromley horns have been passed down from the remotest antiquity or they are later medieval imports from Scandinavia.

Two other human figures that embody elements from pagan fertility rituals are the Burry Man (76) and Jack-in-the-Green (not illustrated). The Burry Man is a character from South Queensferry on the banks of the Forth (a few miles North of Edinburgh), who, once a year, is dressed in a close-fitting white flannel suit which is then completely covered in burr thistles. Walking through the village carrying bunches of flowers, he was held to embody the fertility and luck of the district (though this symbolism has become confused of late). The Jack-in-the-Green is similar in that he is a man enclosed in a wickerwork frame which is completely covered with flowers and greenery, often only leaving apertures for the eyes and mouth.

The Keltic and West European countries are not alone in preserving traditional practices that link the Faerie Wildfolk and early forms of human dance, drama and Shamanistic ritual; for example, Greek monuments of the second and sixth centuries show men dressed as hairy satyrs; red-faced dancers with padded costumes, leaders wearing masks, others dressed in white tights as nymphs, men with pointed caps (Phrygian), false beards and draped with animal skins. And from early times the Greek *Kallikantzaroi* (Dionysian celebrants) rampaged around in the twelve days following the Winter Solstice; these ritual actors adopted many guises, some dressed as larger than human Wildmen with black shaggy hair; others decked in skins had a long thin tail with the legs of a goat or an ass. In the carnival before Lent in Skyros the young men danced through the town in hoods of goat skin (only having small holes for the eyes), with bronze bells jangling from their waist. On Cheese Monday a Thracian village hosted rites featuring actors wearing head-dresses of goat skin, fox skin

Fig. 76

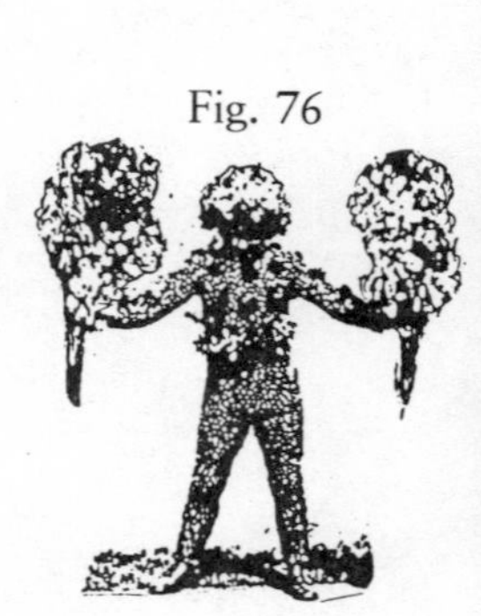

Fig. 77

Fig. 78

Left, *Fig 78*: Probably a quite accurate portrayal of what a Yuletide Drama-Celebration would have looked like in a Scottish or English castle-hall: a mixture of humour, dance and Shamanistic symbolism.

Fig. 79: A Knight spears a wildman through the throat to rescue the Damsel. Chivalric Christian piety or persecution of the native tradition of Initiation and its representative, the wildman?

Fig. 79

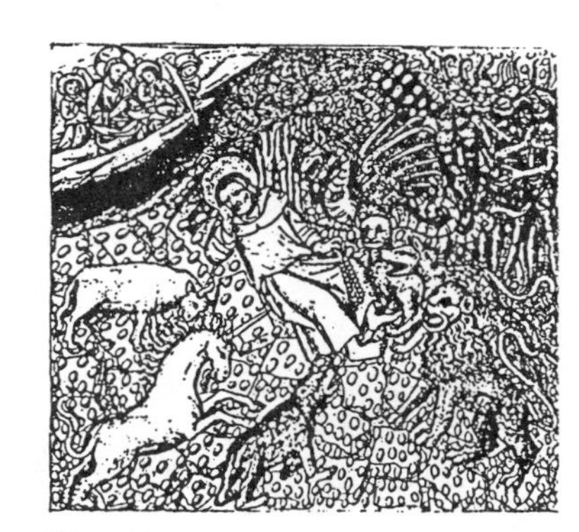

Fig. 80

Fig. 80: The patriarchal hierarchy of orthodox Christianity proscribed all creatures of the wilds as 'evil' and 'forces of temptation'. Thus a Native pagan Tradition was brought to near extinction (14c. miniature of The Life of St. Anthony Abbot).

or wolf skin. Another Dionysian dance ritual was called Askoliasmos (see Fig. 00), in which the Initiate danced or jumped on one leg upon a goat skin (which had been taken from the sacrificial victim). The line from Eratosthenes 'the Ikarians there first danced around the goat' can be understood to apply to this Shamanistic invocation practice. Also, certain 'hopping games', anciently played at Samhain and Yule, etc., have their distant origins in such rites. In Orkney and Shetland, Wildfolk actors known as *Skeklers* or *Grülicks* came out to dance and play music, especially during Yuletide (these islands having a strong Scandinavian influence).

The celebrations at Samhain (Hallowe'en) and Yule (Winter Solstice – New Year) tended to be more raucous, boisterous and fiercely 'wild' (see 00). This was not only in harmony with the weather conditions at this time in yearly cycle, but also with the Psychic and Spiritual changes, for the *Daoine Sidhe* (The Faerie People) were reported to change their *Lis* (Faerie fort) and other dwelling places at the times of the four fire festivals. Terence MacShane, a fiddler from County Antrim, whilst a boy, spoke with a local man called Paddy the Handyman who recounted that his grandfather had witnessed a fairy cavalcade (*Sluagh Sidhe*) at Samhain. It included the Faerie Queen dressed in ferns right down to the ground, and on her head was a crown of Ling; the King of the Faeries was dressed in rushes, in and out of which was woven strands of Ling. (From *The Witches Rune* album.)

The *Sluagh Sidhe* ('Faerie hosts in the wind') were perceived as riding furiously over hill and dale, mountain peak and forest, especially during the dark nights of Samhain and Yule. As Kernun, Herne or Odin, the leader of this wild horde can be equated with the crowned King of the Wildfolk, who wears a fine pair of stag antlers, and sometimes rides a royal stag whilst leading his Faerie hosts. This is borne out in European Folk tradition, for in the Tyrolean Alps the appearance of the *Schimmelreiter*, ('the rider on the white horse'), the wild hunter, Herne, leader of the host, was often expected during the celebration of a wedding feast (the God thus conferring his pagan blessing on the union). In the southern Alps the leader of the wild horde was known as the *Percht*. Worship of the Lord of the Forest and Mountains appears in accounts from all over the Keltic lands, Europe and Scandinavia, and from North America, where the wild huntsman was known as Heno, and who rode in the clouds, sending his thunderbolts down to split certain forest trees, whilst in the forest his one-eyed, one-limbed tree-spirits could run swifter than the black-tailed deer.

In this chapter I have attempted to present perhaps the most accurate sketch of the Faerie Wildfolk yet to reach print. Although reading it falls far short of actually experiencing contact with these beings, or seeing psychically as the Ancients Druids did, it will, I hope, have given you an idea of the characteristics and modes of existence of the beings of Faerie.

Fig. 81

Keltic Wolf-God

The main process that almost destroyed the once mighty Faerie tradition and well-nigh obliterated it from living memory came in three main phases: the cancerous spread of the Roman Military empire, the ecclesiastical dominance of the Church of Rome, and the artistic 'norms' set by the Graeco-Roman Renaissance. Down the centuries there have been innumerable attempts to belittle, deny, degrade, distort, falsely humorize and turn what we know as 'Faeries' into effete irrelevant whimsy.

Even recently, scholars who should have known better have illustrated their books on 'the fairy tradition' with pictures featuring naked (but not lusty), fat, lounging figures, the detritus of the Graeco-Roman art-style; or alternatively with the tiny flower-petal fairies twittering past on gossamer wings, the mere fancy of fools; whilst at the same time choosing to censor and ignore all the authentic Faerie Wildfolk art that strengthens this chapter.

In the days of the fire and brimstone ascendancy, the Church Fathers cursed and slandered most wild animals, reptiles, many birds and even some trees (only the 'pure', lovely and 'nice' have a place in their translation of God's creation). Many of the beings that should act as wise guides to human beings on their spiritual quest have been falsely termed 'devils' by the self-righteous and spiritually blind upholders of Orthodoxy. Thus, such Orthodox Churches became hollow shells, alien and rootless upon the lands they conquer (for they accept no ancient cultural ethos); they sit cut off and unattuned to the cycle of nature which ever turns all around them. The evangelical ministers and priests, having shunned the Spiritual Guides who could have helped them climb Jacob's Ladder became little more than pious social-workers gravitating into an ever more materialistic philosophy. They are a far cry from the biblical Initiates such as Ya'aqov (Jacob), who struggled through the dark night with the wild angel Aīysh (an emissary from the Elohīm) at the Ford of Yabōq, until this Wildman ally was obliged to give the secret wisdom of the Qabalah back to Jacob, renamed Yītzrael (Israel).

To those of us who would prefer native enlightenment to oppressive sightless authority, a life in harmony with the cycles of nature rather than one that seeks always to conquer and control them, a meaningful dialogue with the creatures that share this planet with us rather than to abuse and exploit them for human greed, to have friends within the magical Otherworlds rather than drive off such beings through a misplaced arrogance, the choice is quite clear: we must tap our sacred roots and relearn a system of native Shamanism. If we attempt this in merely an intellectual fashion, we will gain only intellectual insights. But if we take to this study our heart, mind, Soul-feeling and Spirit, then the enrichment of our lives will be immense.

In that spirit we should approach the Wildfolk poems that follow and the Folktales in chapter 7, always bearing in mind the more accurate conceptions of the Faerie Wildfolk, and we will thereby stand a better chance of receiving profound insights in return.

At a point in ones Spiritual Development, the Mighty Powers sometimes commandeer a personal Dream or Vision, re-direct it to a purpose of their own, and hence turn it into a Living Experience in an Otherworld Dimension of Reality.

< W77
KERNUNOS
(Lord of Animals)
VEDIC SHIVA W78
(Lord of Animals)

Fig. 82 right: KERNUNOS (Lord of Animals); right, VEDIC SHIVA (Lord of Animals)

The Wild-Man Came

14.2.1984 not so much a poem
more a retelling in loose verse.
by KALEDON NADDAIR

It was a church wedding,
for parents, family, and the like;
I was going through the motions
saying the hollow-word devotions,
whilst in my heart of hearts
I awaited the morrow
and our real marriage
in Keltic pagan bond.

When, into my dream-vision
a *Fynnoderee* came,
Wildman from the oak woods
breathing the moist balm
of forest depths
came, and stood, against a wall
to the side of the altar.

My heart leapt to see him
joy coursed through every limb
I laughed, embraced my bride
and danced like an idiot child.

People gazed at me as if I'd gone mad,
'cracked' under the strain –
of a 'difficult' marriage ceremony;
I just smiled elation, oblivious to their frowns
knowing that my brother from the wilds,
to their dimmed sight, remained unseen.

I turned to talk to him,
and he beckoned for us to go,
leave by a back door
and off into the forest green.

At the same time the priest
was concluding the proceedings;
I gazed round at the chapel walls,
statuettes of the Virgin (by dogma not a Goddess)
and endless hanging Christs with bleeding hearts
and all the Christians white-washed saved
and all the gaudy trappings of a pompous creed
and all the Catholics with their naive faith,
bewitched by a Church
that had murdered Christ's Gnosis, dead.

As a Christian of the Light, I spat, in disgust.

My eyes re-met the Wildman's,
we were at-oned.

I felt for my lady beside me
and the scandalous gossip she would have to endure,
So I turned to my love, and said,
'Remember in the hours we talked deep,
I said if at any time I was "called",
by rights I should have to go.
'Well, it's happened, yes even now.'
She kissed me; and, distraught, bid me go.
And so, arm in arm with my Wildman,
We danced through the fields,
and off into the old woods.

For a full week he taught me,
the secret ways of living things;
a wisdom devalued and lost,
by modern man in his technological lust.

I returned to my dear lover,
reborn from the Earth Mother;
closer to the source,
and closer to Christ.

Then, by a Keltic Shaman and priestess
we were joined in the old ways,
and our love waxed strong,
fertile and deep.

'For those who dance with the *Fynnoderee*
re-create a merry world.'

Kaledon Naddair
14.2.1984

"Through Another's Eyes"

I come not from this land cried I,
I come from the land where the secrets lie.

My people are not your people cried I,
for they are the people of forest, mountain and sky.

Your races migrate, change and die,
My people are immortal and never die.

You lost your way, pronounced us dead,
we wonder why, for we know that is a lie,
For we have never left these
mountains, forests, sea and sky.

I come not from this land cried I,
I come from the world where the secrets lie.

Channeled through Kaledon Naddai
24.3.198
Illustration by Bel Bucca.

The Dark Man Said Lorraine Jordan

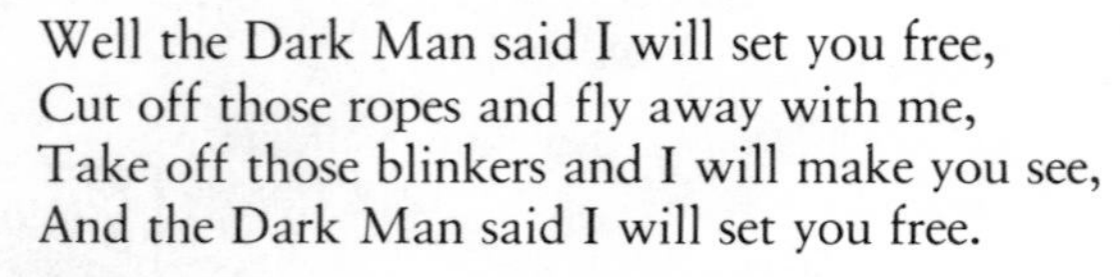

Well the Dark Man said I will set you free,
Cut off those ropes and fly away with me,
Take off those blinkers and I will make you see,
And the Dark Man said I will set you free.

And the Dark Man said I will make you feel,
He took me down to a muddy field,
Stood barefeet in the mud, and it felt so real,
And the Dark Man said I will make you feel.

And the Dark Man said I will make you wise,
Learn to see beyond the limitations of your eyes,
Speak from your heart, know the truth from lies,
And the Dark Man said I will make you wise.

And the Dark Man said I will make you whole,
Raise up the man and woman in your soul,
Balance your nature, make unity your goal,
And the Dark Man said I will make you whole.

And the Dark Man said I will set you free,
Cut off those ropes and fly away with me,
Take off those blinkers and I will make you see,
And the Dark Man said I will set you free.

24.6.198

The Dark Man of the Forest Door

The visitor from the Otherside
has returned again
bringing that old familiar restlessness
which no sop to true satisfaction can shake;
I feel a discontented churning of my psychic waters
as the wing-beat of my Spirit descends to draw near.
It comes to prepare my lower self
for another encounter with my *Gruagach* guide.

Though my ego seeks a release from this meeting
in each and every passing option.
the great brooding continues to grow
until nothing but its intended fulfilment
will cause it to abate.

I have thus been claimed for another trial.

So be rough with me, O Dark Man,
Mighty Giant of the hidden door.
turn me, push me, guide me,
as you have often done before.
For your hard manner is dearer to me
than any soft life of comfort and security.

Under your gaze, that racks my soul,
my thoughts are stripped down to their seed-cores,
my emotions are traced to their deep sources,
and my beliefs are taken back to their roots in truth.

What remains to me is always only Pictland:
its mountains for my aspiration,
its rivers and lochs for my purification,
its forests for my magical Initiation.

And it is from there you've come to test me

All my work-a-day interests drop away,
the chatter of pressing concerns
a rough hand sweeps aside.
I am left to still my centre
and wait . . .
wait . . .
to know if he will cross to my world
or I be drawn over to his.

I wait to see his eyes of dark-fire,
which sparkle with an agile cunning.
I wait to hear his gutteral, deep-throated laughter,
which pours scorn upon superficial city-humour.
I wait to draw near his mighty shaggy form
which radiates power all around.

He is my teacher
my heart leaps, the salmon-leap,
to follow at his leading.

I cry tears but seldom these days
only those young children of my yearning
and of my caring heart.
Self-pity I have long-since transmuted
in the alchemy of the will.
For my time is too precious to squander
on whatever lies outside of the quest.

So be rough with me, O Dark Man,
shake me free
from any remaining foolishness,
slap me awake.
For still I grope my way over the thresholds
and stumble half-blind through the dimensions.

Teach me your shape-shifting artistry,
Teach me protection as I carry my light aloft,
Teach me swift-travel along the inner pathways,
Teach me how to enter my beloved Koed Kaledon at will.

These you know to be the longings of my stilled centre,
O Dark Man of Kaledonia's wild places,
lead me home.

Kaledon Naddair
26 & 27/12/1987

Keltic Otherworld Regions

At the heart of the majority of ancient Folk and Faerie Tales lie ingredients with which most of us moderns are all too unfamiliar: magic, mystery and wonder. If we strip these ingredients from the Tales, in a false attempt at arriving at a clearer rational analysis, we will in the process destroy the very core of the Tales that we were seeking to understand. For one of the great achievements of the Keltic mysteries is the maze-like complexity and interwoven convolutions of its knotwork path; if you deny this mode of exploration, then you deny the voice of the Keltic Spirit. For if we, in every situation, insist upon applying the parameters of the lower rational mind, we will most assuredly never cross limits to awareness. We will thus never become at-one with the Tales, and never truly grasp their meaning. Sceptical rationalists will ask what is wrong with their method; to which I would reply: nothing, *as far as it goes*. But the operating laws of the magical Otherworlds far supercede the laws of physical existence as our limited five senses perceive them. Of course we can, if it is our bent, squash and crush the message of these Keltic esoteric Folktales into a materialistic mode and, if our blinkers exclude all opinions to the contrary, we may even be able to convince ourselves that our anthropological interpretations fit the story in question. But that is a sad counterfeit to accept in exchange for these truly magnificent route-maps to Initiation.

A few people have said that my investigations into this subject are no
objectively rational enough. I smile at this opinion for two reasons: my writing
are the most authentically rational explanations of Keltic esotericism yet pu
into print, and I could not remain coldly detached if I tried, for I am an Initiat
(of a certain degree) in the Wildfolk cult. Others find my writings on the Kelti
mysteries a sight too rational and analytic – to these good folk I would beg thei
tolerance in understanding that, in the face of so much deprecatory slander, th
worth of the Keltic wisdom tradition has, as far as is possible, to be prove
worthy of fulfilling human Spiritual aspirations.

As perhaps as many as half of all Ancient Keltic Folk and Faerie Tales involv
an Otherworld level of consciousness/being/journey into magical realms. Ho
the Kelts conceived of these Otherworlds is of prime importance to us.

Often the transition into an Otherworld dimension will occur through
physical channel. We could perhaps group these channels into the followin
categories:

(1) Standing stones, rock strata, clefts in rockfaces, caves etc.
(2) A special tree, sacred grove or magical forest.
(3) Unfamiliar hills, mountains and glen passes.
(4) Faerie mounds, *Lís*, raths, duns and rings in meadows.
(5) Fountains, rivers, lochs, mere-pools in moors, etc.
(6) The waves of restless seas to strange islands.
(7) The starry nighttime sky or the bright sunny daytime sky.

As you may have perceived, these channels parallel the channels through which
the Faerie Wildfolk operate. Something you may not have noted, but which w
must assuredly consider, is that in our concrete and plastic high-tech moder
world the urban orientation is inexorably polluting and destroying all thos
important channels.

Before we go further, I would like to clear up one point. Although I conside
it of very minor importance, its use as a pseudo-academic bolt-hole necessitate
its dismissal. Let it be clearly noted that in virtually none of the Keltic Folktale
that we possess is there the slightest trace of use of any psychotropic o
hallucinogenic plant substances. Although alcoholic inebriation and mushroom-
taking experimentation undoubtedly dismantle frontiers of perception, and
occasionally build bridges into other realms, on the whole this is the approach
of fools and is not required within the sober training practices of a genuine
Initiatory school. For the record, I have never taken any hallucinogenic
substance, nor have I ever been drunk during a magical rite; I have chosen the
harder but much more dependable path into the deeper mysteries. All my
experiences with the Wildfolk in Otherworld states of consciousness must be
assessed as the level-headed statements of a canny Scotsman.

As a result of the actions of the Church and classicist oppressors, many key
Keltic beliefs have been eradicated. We are left to piece together a jigsaw puzzle
in which many pieces are missing, and for which we do not know the original
painting. As a further complication we must always remind ourselves that the
ingredients are of an essentially sacred nature, and that they must be treated with
the utmost respect. Indeed, I would posit that no one without genuine
experiences of the Otherworlds should attempt to construct an orientation map
into (in this case) the Keltic Otherworlds: the ritual calendar that I have

reformulated on the following pages embodies not only a large amount of intellectual research but also the insights gained from personal explorations into other dimensions of existence.

In Ancient Keltic Folk and Faerie Tales, the items that require particular attention include:

(1) The orientation within a journey i.e., if a being came from, or went towards, the Shamanistic North, South, East or West.
(2) Colour indicators – i.e., if a character's clothes/knight's armour are described as black/red/white/gold/green, etc., or if we encounter, say, a red raven (obviously not an ordinary member of the species).
(3) The character and appearance of figures within the Tales – i.e., are they dark, sombre and sultry, or are they light, swift and graceful; and so on. (Assessing such factors was much more straightforward in ancient times, for the Tales were unpolluted; nowadays readers must be prepared to strip away layers of Church and classicist adverse conditioning before evaluating the character make-up of the main protagonists.)
(4) The area and means of departure of a journey – i.e., whether the main characters descend under a Lake, wander through a dense forest, disappear into yonder blue mountains, etc.

All these factors were deliberately employed by the ancient *Senachaidh* and Kyfarwydd to inform their discerning audience about the nature of the Shamanistic area of experience that the Tale was dealing with.

After long investigation and contemplation of such factors, I reformulated the Ritual Calendar of Keltic Otherworld Regions (on page 172 (and 173)). Thankfully I was able to cross-check many of the items in it with the ingredients of the other Keltic Shamanistic Calendars that I have reconstructed. Whilst in one respect this ritual calendar is a fine achievement, in another it has severe limitations, for putting so many fantastic and vast Otherworld regions onto a small chart in no way does these regions justice. Thus we need to make strenuous attempts at expanding this chart in our mind's eye, so that it can come more closely to approximate what it is attempting to describe. One of the first things we can do is to give it a vertical direction, as well as its apparent horizontal orientation. Although certain beings or regions may share certain of the qualities of a quarter in the Shamanistic circle, they may be worlds apart in power or spiritual rank. For example, one of the more minor Faerie Wildfolk beings may not be anywhere near as powerful as one of the mighty Keltic Gods; neither is 'the Glen of Toads' as spiritually lofty as the divine City of Falias, although they both lie in a Shamanistic Northerly direction. A visual model you may like to play around with in your mind is a spiral staircase turning up and down inside a lighthouse; also a pair of concentric cross-quartered cones, one pointing up to the heights, the other down to the depths, is a very useful metaphysical glyph (see Fig. alongside). Many things can be on this 'stairway to Heaven' with a Shamanistic Southern Station and yet be several turns of the spiral apart. (Of course, within the living kosmos, beings on different rungs need not always move in helixes to come into contact with each other; there are certain 'shortcuts'.) Another useful metaphysical glyph to bear in mind is the Qabalistic Jacob's Ladder, which we have already discussed (see pages 51–52).

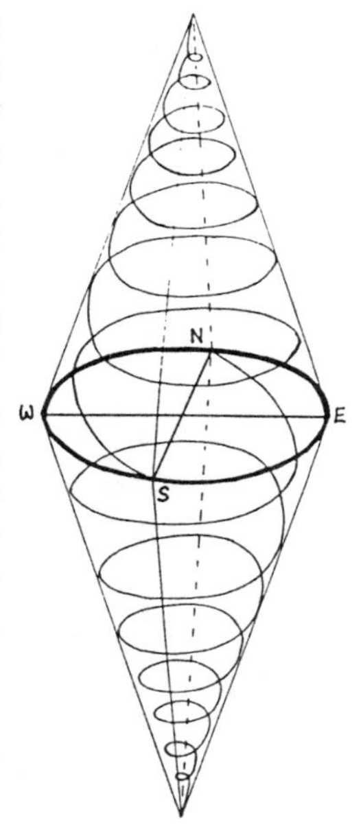

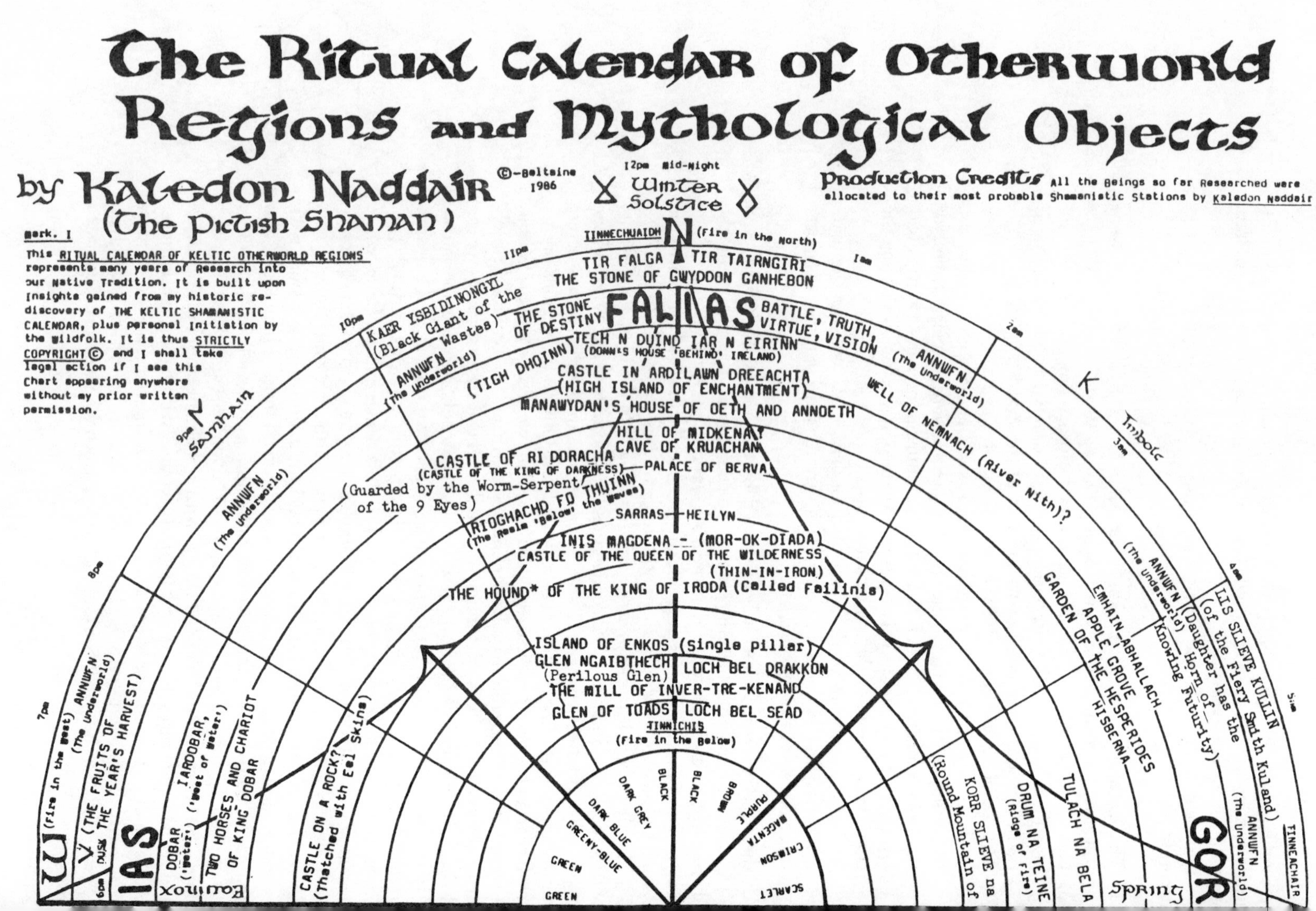

The Ritual Calendar of Otherworld Regions and Mythological Objects
by Kaledon Naddair ©-Beltaine 1986
(The Pictish Shaman)
Production Credits All the Beings so far Researched were allocated to their most probable Shamanistic Stations by Kaledon Naddair
Remark. I
This RITUAL CALENDAR OF KELTIC OTHERWORLD REGIONS represents many years of Research into our Native Tradition. It is built upon insights gained from my historic re-discovery of THE KELTIC SHAMANISTIC CALENDAR, plus personal initiation by the wildfolk. It is thus STRICTLY COPYRIGHT © and I shall take legal action if I see this Chart appearing anywhere without my prior written permission.
12pm mid-Night
Winter Solstice
TINNECHUAIDH
N
(Fire in the North)
TIR FALGA
TIR TAIRNGIRI
THE STONE OF GWYDDON GANHEBON
THE STONE OF DESTINY
FALIAS
BATTLE, TRUTH, VIRTUE, VISION
KAER YSBIDINONGYL (Black Giant of the Wastes)
TECH N DUIND IAR N EIRINN
(DONN'S HOUSE 'BEHIND' IRELAND)
(TIGH DHOINN)
CASTLE IN ARDILAWN DREEACHTA
(HIGH ISLAND OF ENCHANTMENT)
MANAWYDAN'S HOUSE OF OETH AND ANNOETH
HILL OF MIDKENA?
CAVE OF KRUACHAN
CASTLE OF RI DORACHA
(CASTLE OF THE KING OF DARKNESS)
PALACE OF BERVA
(Guarded by the Worm-Serpent of the 9 Eyes)
RIOGHACHD FO THUINN
(The Realm 'Below' the Waves)
SARRAS
HEILYN
INIS MAGDENA - (MOR-OK-DIADA)
CASTLE OF THE QUEEN OF THE WILDERNESS
(THIN-IN-IRON)
THE HOUND* OF THE KING OF IRODA (Called Failinis)
ISLAND OF ENKOS (Single pillar)
GLEN NGAIBTHECH (Perilous Glen)
LOCH BEL DRAKKON
THE MILL OF INVER-TRE-KENAND
GLEN OF TOADS
LOCH BEL SEAD
TINNICHIS
(Fire in the Below)
ANNWFN (The Underworld)
WELL OF NEMNACH (River Nith)?
11pm
10pm
9pm
8pm
7pm
6pm
1am
2am
3am
4am
5am
Samhain
Imbolc
Spring
Equinox
ANNWFN (The Underworld)
(Daughter has the Horn of Knowing Futurity)
LIS SLIEVE KULLIN (of the Fiery Smith Kuland)
EMHAIN-ABHALLACH
APPLE GROVE
GARDEN OF THE HESPERIDES
HISBERNA
TULACH NA BELA
DRUM NA TEINE (Ridge of Fire)
KORR SLIEVE na (Round Mountain of
GOR
TINNEACHAIR
(Fire in the West)
ANNWFN (The Underworld)
THE FRUITS OF THE YEAR'S HARVEST
DUSK
IAS
DOBAR ('Water')
IARDOBAR, ('West of Water')
TWO HORSES AND CHARIOT OF KING DOBAR
CASTLE ON A ROCK? (Thatched with Eel Skins)
GREEN
GREENY-BLUE
DARK BLUE
DARK GREY
BLACK
BLACK
BROWN
PURPLE
MAGENTA
CRIMSON
SCARLET

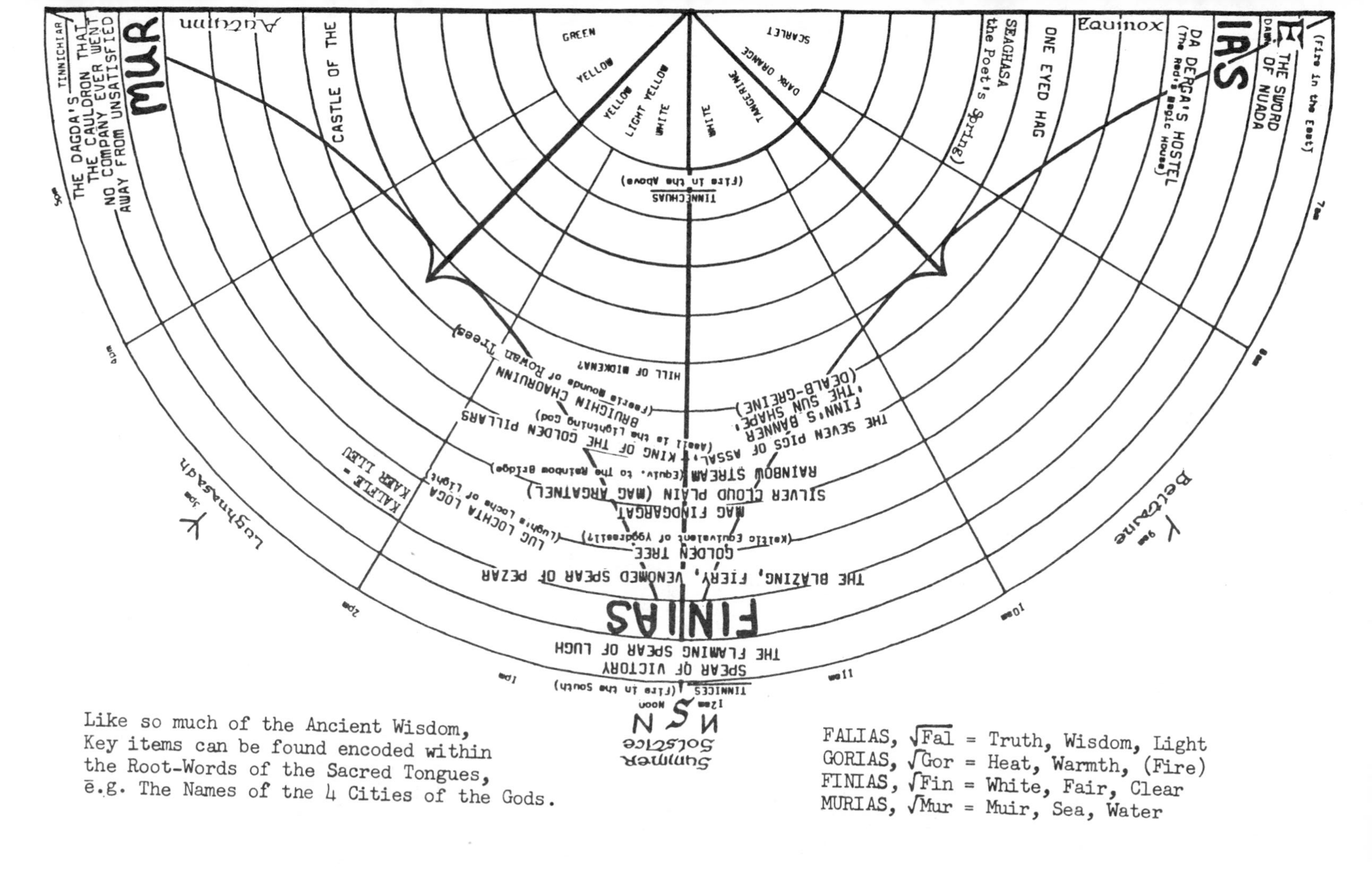

Like so much of the Ancient Wisdom,
Key items can be found encoded within
the Root-Words of the Sacred Tongues,
ē.g. The Names of the 4 Cities of the Gods.

FALIAS, $\sqrt{\text{Fal}}$ = Truth, Wisdom, Light
GORIAS, $\sqrt{\text{Gor}}$ = Heat, Warmth, (Fire)
FINIAS, $\sqrt{\text{Fin}}$ = White, Fair, Clear
MURIAS, $\sqrt{\text{Mur}}$ = Muir, Sea, Water

Although slightly inaccurate, it may be a permissible generalization to say that Keltic paganism has suffered a lack of useful metaphysical diagrams, because pagan writers were scared to make value judgements about things being higher or lower, greater or lesser in spirituality. This has led to an hotch-potch of ever increasing breadth on the horizontal. Until I made my calendar discoveries, this hadn't even been properly ascribed to Shamanistic quarters, far less graduated in significance. Furthermore, Hebraic Qabalah has suffered from many Qabalistic writers emphasizing an all too intellectual ascent up the rungs of the ladder, without realizing that even to do so necessitates a proper grasp of the plane you are attempting to pass through. This has left certain pseudo-Qabalists sadly out of touch with the cycles of nature and the creatures that share this planet with us. Thus, an overemphasis on the vertical ascent has often resulted in a narrow and unaware path.

I do not believe that these failings are intrinsic in either tradition; rather, I believe they are due to the various shortcomings of their practitioners. As can be gathered in this and other books of mine, I am making a concerted effort to rectify these omissions. I do not believe that one need borrow from another system to fill in the apparent gaps in one's own tradition. One can find enough vertical ingredients within Keltic mythology and Folklore if one has the inclination to look. And there have been certain leading Qabalists (e.g., R. Simon ben Yochai and Paracelsus) who have demonstrated that there is enough breadth in the Qabalah, if one has the scope of being to grasp it all.

Therefore, in summation, our metaphysical diagrams should be visualized in at least three dimensions. Other ingredients, such as time, colour, 'feeling' and power, can be added as one's inner experience. Eventually these ever more sophisticated, refined and extended diagrams should merge into the laws of existence all around you.

Figs E and F are ideas of my own on how to visualize a journey through Otherworld realms, such as one often finds described in Keltic Folktales. Usually in the Folktales (though not always), the stretches between the castles on knolls/islands are described as being great lengthy distances.

In certain of the best esoteric Irish or Welsh Tales I have analysed, the journey described clearly follows a path around the Shamanistic Wheel. Alternatively, there are a few Keltic Tales that display a clear, direct ascent through various dimensions into ever higher regions (as in Figs C & D). It is particularly in relation to such ascent journeys that I have placed Qabalistic ascriptions onto Figs. E and F. It will be easily noted that the way from *Malkuth* (of *Yetzīrāh*) through *Yesod*, *Tiphareth*, *Da'ath* to *Kether* represents a journey up the central column. Although it may appear as though the journey is along the level, it is the 'character' of the castle and its inhabitants that makes the qualitative difference between levels of being – just as the greatness of a human being should not be assessed by their physical height, but rather by the quality of Soul and Spirit that shines through their body. There are many other techniques of visualization required properly to follow the Tales of power composed by Seers, but it would perhaps be best if we encountered these 'in situ'. I shall therefore devote the rest of this chapter to excerpts from prime Keltic Folk, Faerie and mythological Tales that deal with Otherworld journeys or encounters.

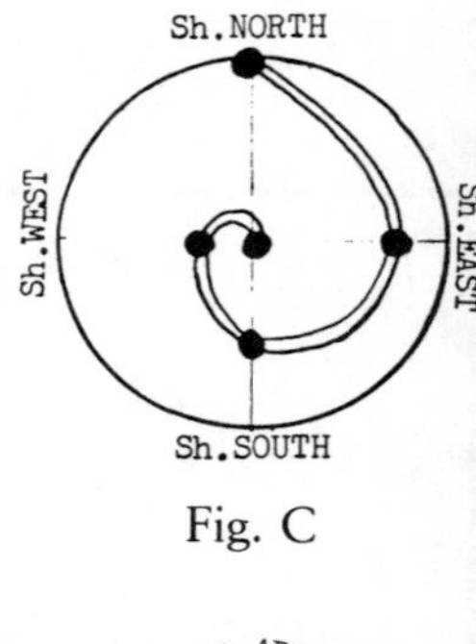

Fig. C

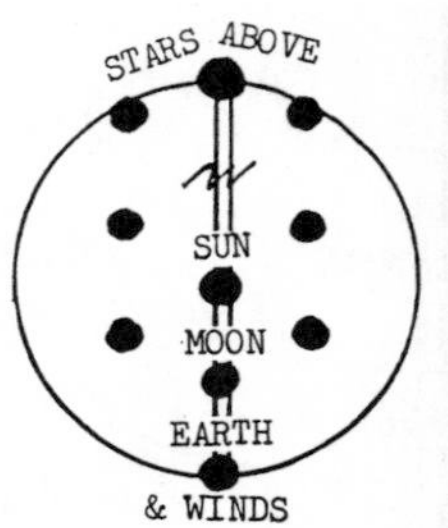

Fig. D

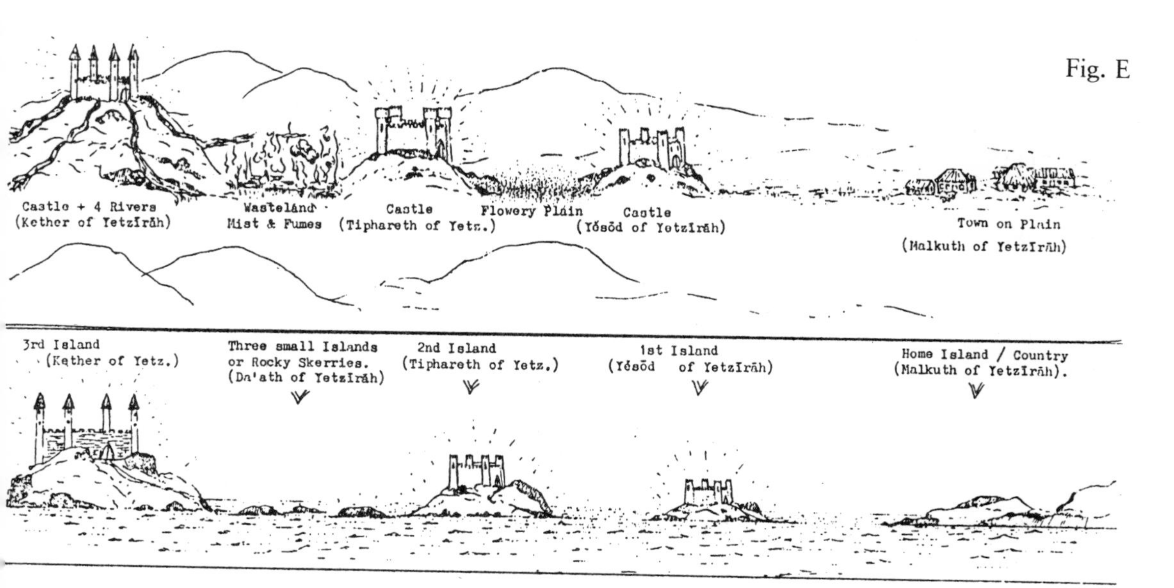

Fig. E

Fig. F

* *NOTE* – in the above Diagrams the distances between Islands/Hills has been deliberately foreshortened to facilitate depiction; whilst in Visionary experiences the distances between may seem like dozens or hundreds of miles.

'One morning Konn Ketchathach, High King of Ireland in the latter part of the second century, went up at the rising of the Sun (dawn) upon the royal Rath of Tara. By some good chance he put his foot upon a magic stone which has been brought originally to Ireland by the *Tuatha De Danann*. As soon as Konn's foot touched the stone, it cried out under him, so that it was heard not only by Konn and those that were with him, but all over Tara even, as far as Breg.' (Konn asked his Druids what the stone had prophesied; they could only give him partial insights and explanations.) 'As they were there, after this, they saw a great mist all round, so that they knew not where they went from the greatness of the mistiness; and they heard the noise of a horseman approaching. The horseman let fly three throws of a spear at them. The Druid cried forth, and the mysterious horseman desisted. Then he [Lugh] bade welcome to Konn and invited them to come with him to his house. They went forward until they entered a beautiful plain. Then they perceived a kingly *Rath* and a golden tree at its door.'

I thought that this extract, from a much longer Tale, would serve as a good stepping stone into greater dimensions. The 'magic stone', with its prophetic utterances, seems to be of the same lineage as the *LiaFail*, *Maen Llog* ('stone of wisdom'), Shamanistic North, and may have a distant relation to the stone that Paul Screeton stepped upon in the section on Toad Elemental stories (see page 187).

Although physical mists, which blur and take the edge of certainty away from our sight-clarity, can serve as a channel to Otherworld consciousness, there are also actual Faerie mists (which I have seen on several occasions). These mists are invisible to ordinary sight, but strongly visible to psychic sight. These special mists often act as a medium through which an Otherworld being can manifest; in this case it is Lugh, the Irish Sun God and Lord of Secret Lore (Shamanistic South).

After three testing casts of his totem weapon, the spear (Shamanistic South), Lugh invites the King of Eirinn back to his Otherworld dwelling. Lugh's circular royal fort has a golden tree at its entrance; this may well equate with *Yggdrasil* (kosmic ash tree) which stands beside Asgard, Odin and Urd's Thingstead of the Scandinavian Gods. This place I would expect to lie at *Tiphareth* of *Braiah* (inclining up towards *Kether* of *Braiah*).

Another key *Spiritus Locii* that we meet repeatedly in Keltic mythology is the Otherworld apple grove. A lot of important points emerge if we carefully look into what is said about this region. This first of all entails making more perceptive translations of source texts than academic scholars have managed so far. Indeed, it is a sad reflection upon the so-called 'advanced state' of Keltic research that the translations of Edward Davies (made more than a century ago) on certain points stand closer to the mark than those of modern 'experts'. We shall start with my radical and incisive translation of the first verse of Myrddin's *Avallenau* ('Apple Grove'):

The turning circle gave to no one at one unfolding [dawn]
A wheel [like that] given to Myrddin before he got too old.
Seven apple trees' short sprigs [stacked] as/in seven twenties
Through the mouth [speech] of mercy in the House of Judgements [Fate]
One ring of connections on high conceals them,
One wise-wife, head-heron, of their wooded slope [???]
Olwedd the Ancient One's [Olwedd's secret] grove is her cog [circle].

One of the most serious repeated errors of academics was to mistranslate the third line as 'seven score and seven [= 147] delicious apple trees'; this blunder ensured that they would not notice that what Myrddin is describing is identical to Taliesin's:

Seven score *Gogyrvens*	(7 × 20 apple-tree sprigs
Are there in Awen.	constitute Druidic inspiration.)

That Awen was an Apple-tree Goddess, as was 'Auld Goggie' (ancient Apple deity), and that the Druids took the twenty basic sprigs or Koelbren/Krankar/Ogham sticks for their Shamanistic divinations from an apple tree are strong and cogent mythological facts. Also certain is that the Druids and Bards used this circle of twenty Koelbren/Ogham signs not only to encipher their inspirational teachings but also as alphabetical letters, as well as for the basic counting division (a score) in Old Kymraeg. So we are in a position to understand Taliesin's comment:

Iaith ugain Ogyrfen y sydd yn Awen.	The language of twenty letters is in Awen.

We can now appreciate that the revelation of the seven apple trees (or seven-fold apple tree) and their stacks of sprigs stands as something of a Keltic parallel to Odin's grasping of the runes whilst he hung upon the kosmic ash tree (*Yggdrasil*).

The fact that in all subsequent verses of Myrddin's poem his address is to 'the fair apple tree' (singular) seems to support my contention that it was actually one sevenfold (i.e., seven-branched) apple tree that featured in his vision/experience. It is then readily understandable that Myrddin is in fact discoursing upon the Keltic archetypal Tree of Life.

A parallel is encountered in the Otherworld journey of that Irish explorer Maildun:

'When the ship came near to the island, Maildun caught one of the branches in his hand. For three days and three nights the ship coasted the island, and during all that time Maildun held onto the branch, whilst letting it slide through his hand. Then upon the third day he came upon an arrangement of seven apples on the end of it. Each one of these apples supplied the travellers with food and drink for forty days and forty nights.'

The piece of ritual jewellery shown in Fig. 00 centre, (from Faxo, Sealand, in Denmark) may illustrate Maildun holding this seven-appled branch; though it probably represents a Scandinavian Shaman *Goddr* (priest) standing beside a deity's head. The symbol underneath the runic inscription is also found on Pictish symbol stones, thus indicating another area in which the Keltic and Scandinavian traditions held teachings in common.

What Myrddin saw as the archetypal Apple Tree of Life may well have looked like the illustration shown in Fig. G, left, in which I have drawn the twenty principal Ogham–Koelbren sprigs within each golden apple (this parallels the Qabalistic teaching that within each *Sephīrāh* is contained a whole miniature Tree of Life and its guiding laws). In Fig. I, right, I have intimated that the secret of the groups

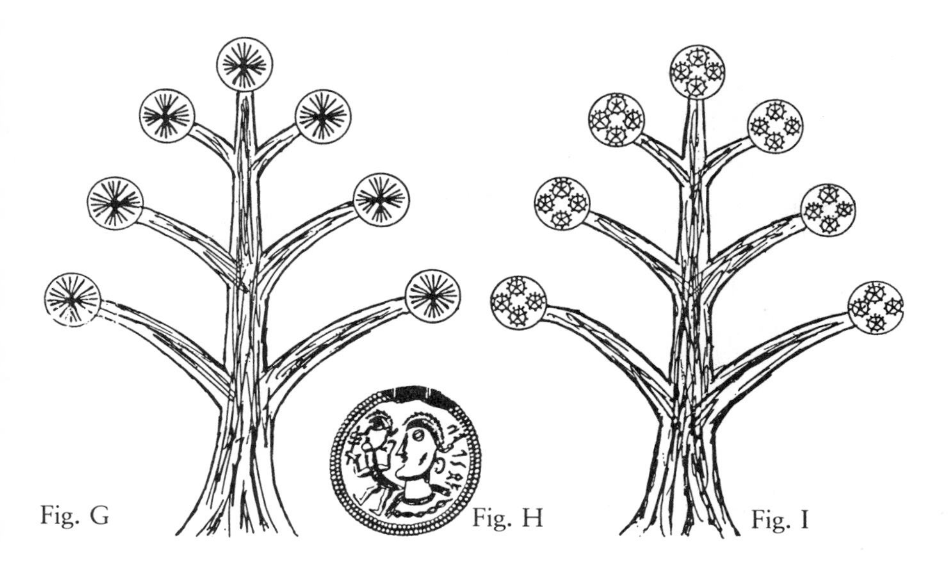

Fig. G Fig. H Fig. I

of five Oghams lies in the five-pointed star that is to be found in the core of every cross-cut apple. A possible variation would show each of the seven branches terminating in sevenfold fronds.

If we turn to the first part of the second verse of Myrddin's poem, we encounter a Faerie Wildman/ Wildwoman (*Gogan*) intimately associated with giving out teachings from this sacred apple tree. Edward Davies translated this being as a 'Goddess' or 'nymph'; other lexicographers equate it with the masculine Greek 'satyr'; others with a giant Wildman. Whatever its gender, all (except the most hardened sceptics) agree upon the being's supernaturalness. My translation is as follows:

Apple tree of sprigs, fertilely giving forth
Equal parts of dryly sweet and fresh green fruit.
Always lying hidden in the wood
Under the tree's truly broad and pleasant branches
The hidden Wildman–prophet tells the entire Tale
[so as] To agree 'signs' of divers colours for a [Ritual] day.

The 'signs' (Koelbren values) that this Faerie Wildman gives as 'divers colours for a [religious] day' could well correspond to the cycle of colour ascriptions I have discovered within the Ogham ciphers.

As an Initiate of these and similar teachings, Myrddin rightly considered them as sacred and thus worried that ignorant desecrators would not respect their preciousness. In Edward Davies's translation:

'Thou sweet and beneficient tree! not scanty is the fruit with which thou art loaded; but upon thy account, I am terrified and anxious, lest the wood-men should come, those profaners of the wood, to dig up thy root, and corrupt thy seed, that not an apple may ever grow upon thee more.'

This sad destruction of native wisdom Myrddin links to the activities of the Christian missionaries:

'But now, for fifty years, have my splendid treasures been outlawed. And a report has been heard this morning that the Christian minister has expressed his indignation against the authority of the small sprigs [Koelbren teachings] twice, thrice, nay four times, in one day.'

The course of history and present-day consumerist exploitation of the last remnants of native spirituality sadly confirm the accuracy of Myrddin's predictions. The only hope of restitution would seem to lie in the respectful (*vis à vis* sacredness) reapplication of those very teachings that were outlawed by the narrow-minded and psychically blind.

The sacred apple tree (or trees) that grew physically (or metaphysically) within *Koed Kelydon* (the great oak forest that stretched from Brythonic Kumbria, into the Borders and Highlands of Pictish

Alban) has its equivalents in many Otherworld Tales in Keltic mythology. For example, those specified by Lugh as part of the 'blood fine' given to the sons of Tuirin:

'The three apples I ask are the apples of the Garden of Hisberna [Hesperides], in the East of the world, and none others will I have. There are no apples in the rest of the world like them, for their beauty and for the secret virtues they possess. Their colour is the colour of burnished gold; they have the taste of honey; and if a wounded warrior or a man in deadly sickness eat of them, he is cured immediately. And they are never lessened by being eaten, being as large and perfect at the finish as at the beginning. Moreover any champion that possesses one of them may perform with it whatsoever feat he pleases, by casting it from his hand, and the apple will return to him of itself.'

The Irish King Konnla was once approached by a tall Faerie maiden (*Ban Sidhe*) who said she had come from *Magh Mell* (the Pleasant Plain) in *Tir-nam-Beo* (the Land of the Ever-living Ones). Korran (Konnla's Druid) thought it wise to repulse this enchantress by singing spells against her; as this was being done, she cast a special apple to Konnla, such that:

'All throughout the length of a month from that time, Konnla used no other food nor drink but that apple, for he thought no other food or drink worth the using. And for all he ate of it, the apple grew no smaller, but was whole all the while. And there was a great restlessness upon Konnla on account of the Faerie woman he had seen.'

Eventually Konnla sought for her in the magical Otherworld, which was the aim in his being given the alluring apple in the first place.

Even in the later somewhat Christianized Tale of *The Sons of O'Korra* we encounter a similar Otherworld region. In P.W. Joyce's translation:

'They rowed forward for a long time till there was shown to them a wonderful island, and in it a great grove of marvellous beauty, laden with apples, golden-coloured and sweet-scented. A sparkling rivulet of wine flowed through the midst of the grove; and when the wind blew through the trees, sweeter than any music was the rustling it made. The O'Korras ate some of the apples and drank from the rivulet of wine, and were immediately satisfied. And from that time forth they were never troubled by either wounds or sickness.'

A verse from a poem by Ragnall (son of Godrey, King of the Isles) discusses the Gaelic Emhain Avallach, equivalent to the Kymraeg Avalon:

An amaranthine place is faery Emain:
Beauteous is the land where it is found,
Lovely its rath above all other raths.
Plentiful apple trees grow from that ground.

Nor is this Otherworld apple grove perceived just by Keltic Seers, for the Scandinavian and Germanic Initiates knew of the Goddess Idun's apple tree(s) from which she fed the hosts of Asgard; the feminine 'aspect' of divinity, the *Shekhinah*, in the Qabalah presided over 'the Holy Apple Garden'; other parallels can be found within Slavic, Russian, Skythian and other Indo-European mythologies.

During the voyages of Tadg and his Irish companions, we read of more Otherworld arboreal regions:

"It is a beautiful country this is," said Tadg, "and it would be happy for him that would be always in it; and let you pull up the ship now," he said, "and dry it out."

'A score of them went forward then into the country, and a score stopped to mind the curragh. And for all the cold and discouragement and bad weather they had gone through, they felt no wish at all for food or for fire, but the sweet smell of the crimson branches in the place they were come to satisfied them. They went on through the wood, and after a while they came to an apple garden having red apples on it, and leafy oak trees, and hazels yellow with nuts. "It is a wonder to me," said Tadg, "to find summer here, and it winter time in our own country."

'It was a delightful place they were in, but they went on into another wood, very sweet smelling, and round purple berries in it, every one of them bigger than a man's head, and beautiful shining birds eating the berries, strange birds they were, having white bodies and purple heads and golden beaks. And while they were eating the berries they were singing sweet music, that would have put sick men and wounded men into their sleep.

'Tadg and his men went farther on again till they came to a great smooth flowery plain with a dew of honey over it, and three steep hills on the plain, having a very strong dun on every one of them.'

These three Otherworld duns (round forts) may have been arranged as shown in Fig. 00 with two further duns being described as lying North and South from them. In the text it is suggested that these three duns have past–present–future attributes. They are also made from various substances – gold, silver, *Findrinny* (a special bronze) and white crystal (or white marble) – the exact symbolical values of these substances can be pursued when we encounter them in more revealing situations. For example: 'An island with four fences of gold, silver, brass and crystal – which divide it into four parts, containing Kings, Queens, warriors and maidens, respectively.' (See Fig. J.)

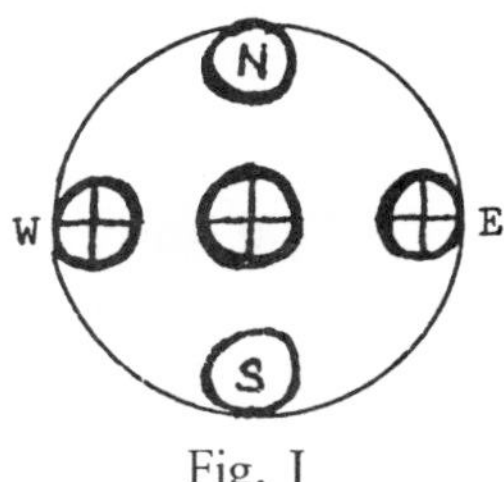

Fig. J

If we try to understand such an arrangement aided by the Keltic Shamanistic Calendar, the reasoning would proceed as follows. Gold is linked to Kings as silver is to Queens; this correlates with the peak of the Sun's power – noon – midsummer and Shamanistic South, complimented by the peak of the Moon's power – midnight – midwinter and Shamanistic North. As bronze is here linked to the warriors, one presumes it is in Shamanistic East, the quarter of the War God (the body of KuKulain's chariot was of copper); it also relates to the Smith God Kredne ('copper bronze'), who said, 'I will give them all rivets for their spears and hilts for their swords and bosses and rims for their shields,' from his forge (*Keardcha* = 'heat-producer'). That crystal and maidens are linked may well relate to the water-like quality of crystal, used to make precious goblets (hence Shamanistic West). (See Fig. K.)

Fig. K

(Thus would stand the basic reasoning; however, the whole story should be allowed even if it temporarily complicates matters, for, in an MSS Ogham cipher, soldiering is around Shamanistic North-east; whilst brasswork is due Shamanistic West – this is related to the esoteric quality of copper (associated with water) and tin (Irish *Ume*, dowsed by T. C. Lethbridge around Shamanistic West, its Ogham Station). Also there are certain ritual objects – crystal vats, purple-crystal trees, etc., which may be associated with Shamanistic East. The fact that it is an igneous and fire-affected substance has produced a debate between those that practise crystal-gazing about whether it is Moon-based psychicism or whether such quartz-like materials raise and focus the thoughts in a solar-light manner. For the present, I am confident about the gold and silver Shamanistic placements, and I will leave the brass and crystal placements to be decided by more in-depth research).

I would now like to tackle a subject that has unfortunately been marred by the inaccurate statements of certain pagan writers blinded by misplaced matriarchal sentiments. I am referring to whether or not the Kelts knew of and employed a twelve-fold calendrical and zodiacal system. Bigoted pagans hold that such a twelve-fold scheme is essentially Middle Eastern and was spread in the wake of Judeo-Christian civilization. This is not only naively erroneous, but appears ludicrous in the face of a great deal of native Keltic evidence. One does not have to be very clever at least to expect some sort of twelve-fold Shamanistic system, given the Kelts' predilection for triadic arrangements as applied to the qualities of the four quarters ($3 \times 4 = 12$). This is confirmed in Ancient Irish ritual practice:

'When Konaire proceeded to the Bull Feast of Tara, where he was chosen King, three Kings were waiting for him on each of the four roads into Tara with clothes to cover him. Also before his death at Da Derga's hostel, four sets of three men were stationed all round his room.'

This was far from being an isolated royal practice:

'According to Krith Gablach, twelve was the company of a King of a *Tuath* ('people province') and there were twelve couches in a royal house. In *The Wooing of Emer* we hear of a King of Munster and twelve under-Kings.'

We could hardly wish for a clearer delineation of the sub-divisions of a twelve-fold solar calendar than that found in the description of the construction of Brikriu's hall:

'It took seven of the Ulster champions to carry every single lath [stone hinge?], and thirty of the chief artificers of Ireland were employed in constructing and arranging the building. The hall contained the couches of the twelve heroes and it was built in the course of one year.'

(In other words, the seven weekdays (*Oka*); thirty days in the solar month; the twelve months in the one solar year.)

The King Konchobar also represents a ritual embodiment of the solar year, for his mother, Ness, had twelve foster-fathers; he became King of Ulster by being granted a nominal kingship for one year, and there were three-hundred and sixty-five persons in his household: 'That is, the number of days in the [solar] year is the number of men that were in Konchobar's household.'

In the Old Kymraeg Druidical Calendar, Beltaine is given as on the 1st of Mai, which was also the 8th/13th or whatever 'day of the Moon'; thus it is clear that the calendar of ritual festivals was organized according to the twelve solar months which encompassed the changing Moon cycle. The French scholar J. Monard has shown that the Gaulish Kelts worked with both solar and lunar cycles concurrently; the calendar sections which were solar-based and named were then linked up to the nearest orbiting Moon-month name (see his book on the Coligny calendar).

The Irish tradition of twelve winds from the various *Airts* of the compass, with their respective 'colours', is obviously older than the *Saltair na Rann* text in which it is embedded.

Also, on the Plain of Magh Slecht twelve carved stones were set in a circle to various deities; at their centre stood a golden statue stone which was dedicated to Krom Kroich, who was the Chief God of all Ireland before the coming of St Patrick.

That this twelve-fold division of a circle was also held to extend to the Otherworld is demonstrated in several Keltic Folktales, e.g. the hero in *The Bird of the Golden Land* has to lead his horse through the twelve stables of the castle of the King of the Golden Land, only letting it be attended to in the thirteenth. (This may be comparable to the thirteenth aeon in Gnosticism which lies behind/in the centre of the twelve aeons of the fixed stars.) A closer Keltic parallel occurs in the Tale of the Queen of Tobar Teinteachd (Well of Fire), where the Prince, after encountering twelve beautiful maidens in chambers in the tower, reaches the central, uppermost, thirteenth Chamber wherein dwells the Solar Queen resting on a golden couch, turning on golden wheels beside the matrix of fire (see pages 00–00).

As this Tale has all the hallmarks of genuine Irish Initiatory wisdom, we should note that in their thirteen Moon-month fixation, certain ill-educated pagans not only do a disservice to the Keltic tradition through their aversion to the equally important solar calendar, but in this case undermine an important aspect of the Keltic Goddess tradition.

That the Ancient Kelts employed a twelve-Sectioned horological, calendrical and zodiacal system only shows that they knew what every other Indo-European people knew and employed. For example, Aristotle noted that the Greek Athenians had distributed their four tribes in imitation of the seasons of the year. By dividing each of them into three *Phratries*, they had twelve subdivisions corresponding to the twelve months. Each *Phratry* was made up of thirty families of thirty men, as the months had thirty days.

Finally, let us note that (as the Rees pointed out) in Tibet, China and Madagascar, 'The twelve divisions around the cosmic square represent the twelve months of the year'.

The marvellous Fenian Tale of *The Pursuit of the Gila Deakair* contains many elements of Otherworld scenery and 'tactics'. Thus we'd be well served to survey it:

Finn and the Fianna had just commenced their Beltaine hunting season in Munster (South-east), and Finn, knowing the gods (*De Dannan*) were likely to work some magic whilst the hunt was in progress, asked for a sentinel to be posted on the overshadowing hill.

'Finn Ban Mac Bresal stood forward and offered to go: and, grasping his broad spears, he went to the top, and sat viewing the plain to the four points of the sky. And the King and his companions brought forth the chess-board and chess-men [*Fidchell*, a Shamanistic game], and sat them down to a game.

'Finn Ban Mac Bresal had been watching only a little time, when he saw on the plain to the east a *Fomor* of vast size coming towards the hill, leading a horse. As he came nearer, Fin Ban observed that he was the ugliest-looking giant his eyes ever lighted on. He had a large, thick body, bloated and swollen out to a great size; clumsy, crooked legs; and broad flat feet, turned inwards. His hands and arms and shoulders were bony and thick and very strong-looking; his neck was long and thin; and while his head was poked forward, his face was turned up, as he stared straight at Finn Mac Bresal. He had thick lips, and long, crooked teeth; and his face was covered all over with bushy hair.

'He was fully armed; but all his weapons were rusty and soiled and slovenly looking. A broad shield of a dirty, sooty colour, rough and battered, hung over his back; he had a long, heavy, straight sword at his left hip; and he held in his left hand two thick-handled, broad-headed spears, old and rusty, and seeming as if they had not been handled for years. In his right hand he held an iron club, which he dragged after him, with its end on the ground; and, as it trailed along, it tore up a track as deep as the furrow a farmer ploughs with a team of oxen.

'The horse he led was even larger in proportion than the giant himself, and quite as ugly. His great carcass was covered all over with tangled, scraggy hair, of a sooty black; you could count his ribs, and all the points of his big bones through his hide; his legs were crooked and knotty; his neck was twisted; and as for his jaws, they were so long and heavy that they made his head look twice too large for his body.

'The giant held him by a thick halter, and seemed to be dragging him forward by main force, the animal was so lazy and so hard to move. Every now and then, when the beast tried to stand still, the giant would give him a blow on the ribs with his big iron club, which sounded as loud as the thundering of a great billow against the rough-headed rocks of the coast. When he gave him a pull forward by the halter, the wonder was that he did not drag the animal's head away from his body; and, on the other hand, the horse often gave the halter such a tremendous tug backwards that it was equally wonderful how the arm of the giant was not torn away from his shoulder.

'Now it was not an easy matter to frighten Finn Ban Bresel; but when he saw the giant and his horse coming straight towards him in that wise, he was seized with such fear and horror that he sprang from his seat and, snatching up his arms, he ran down the hill-slope with utmost speed towards the King and his companions, whom he found sitting round the chess-board, deep in their game.'

When the giant reaches up to Finn and the nobles, he is asked his name, race and country of origin, to which he replies:

'As to where I came from, I am a *Fomor* of Lochlann in the north; but I have no particular dwelling-place, for I am continually travelling about from one country to another, serving the great lords and nobles of the world, and receiving wages for my service.'

Then the Wildman giant tells graphically how he lives up to his name of *Gila Deakair* ('difficult, hard to get on with, servant'), but having rightly gauged Finn's sense of honour he was duly given service.

Next, the *Gila Deakair* (pronounced Gile Dacker) let his old nag loose amongst the horses of the Fianna, whereupon it rampaged around the paddock kicking, butting, bashing and biting lumps out of the other horses until not one lay unmutilated. The nag now sauntered towards Konan Mail's horses, and to prevent further carnage he agreed to put a bridle upon it and lead it away. But the scrawny carcass proved to be massively strong and unbudgeable, so being persuaded that it needed a mount of the giant's weight upon it, Goll and fourteen others clambered aboard, thrashing it with their legs – but still it wouldn't move. The *Gila Deakair* took offence (staged) at how this wonderful beast was being treated, and so he loped and then ran off, with his nag galloping after him. As the horse's bony back was giving Konan and his companions a rough ride, they tried to dismount – but found to their dismay that they were magically stuck-fast by their hands, bottoms and legs. In this way did the giant Wildman, nag and passengers cut a swathe through the sea (which wet them not a spot) and forged their way off to an Otherworld island.

As the Wildman expected, this induced Finn and fifteen of the best Fianna to organize an expedition to search for these hostages. Finn was assisted by two special sons of the King of Innia ('inner centre'), the first, Feradach ('Man of Luck'), could create a fitted-out ship with three blows of his joiner's axe upon his *Krann Tabhall*, so long as those around covered their heads and did not look. (The word *Tabhall* has two main meanings. Academics have translated it in this context as 'sling catapult'. I see no sense in that here; rather, I would suggest *Krann* = 'tree', 'branch', 'wood' and *Tabhall* = 'writing board' or 'table', the meaning being that Feradach magically charmed the ship into being by applying discernment (axe) to the Krankar tree ciphers. There are recorded parallels of this Ogham practice which support this contention.) Feradach's brother is Foltlebar ('compass'?), who can track the Gila Deakair over 'whatsoever quarter of the world he may have hidden himself' within.

Finn and his companions reached the sea cliffs of a far-off (Otherworld) island. Diarmait O'Duibhne (Dermat O'Dyna) scaled the sheer cliff-face with the aid of his *Ga-derg* (red spear) and *Krann-boi* (creamy-coloured javelin) to jump from ledge to ledge. Inland he saw the beautiful country of Sorcha ('brightness'), with flowery plains, charming hills and groves of trees.

'Making no delay, Dermat set out to walk across the plain. He had not been long walking when he saw, right before him, a great tree laden with fruit, overtopping all the other trees of the plain. It was surrounded at a little distance by a circle of pillar-stones; and one stone, taller than the others, stood in the centre near the tree. Beside this pillar-stone was a spring well, with a large, round pool as clear as crystal; and the water bubbled up in the centre, and flowed away towards the middle of the plain in a slender stream.'

Being thirsty, Diarmait drank from a golden drinking-horn dipped into the well water.

'Scarcely had he taken the horn from his lips, when he saw a tall *Gruagach* [wizard-champion] coming towards him from the east, clad in a complete suit of mail, and fully armed with shield and helmet, sword and spear. A beautiful scarlet mantle hung over his armour, fastened at his throat by a golden brooch; and a broad circlet of sparkling gold was bended in front across his forehead, to confine his yellow hair, and keep it from being blown about by the wind.'

The *Graugach* ('Knight of the Fountain') challenged Diarmait to armed combat for drinking from his well without his permission. The two of them then engaged in a bitter and furious fight, until at dusk the *Gruagach* jumped into, and disappeared down, the centre of the round pool. Dairmait speared himself a deer in the nearby forest, cooked it on spits of hazel, then slept for the night. Upon the morrow, Diarmait had to encounter an even more wrathful *Gruagach* for having killed and eaten his speckled (fallow) deer unbidden.

'And again the two champions attacked each other and fought during the long day, from morning till evening. And when the dusk began to fall, the wizard-champion leaped into the well, and disappeared down through it, even as he had done the day before.

'On the fourth morning, Dermat found the wizard-champion standing as usual by the pillar-stone near the well. And as each morning he looked more angry than on the morning before, so now he scowled in a way that would have terrified any one but Dermat O'Dyna.

'And they fought during the day till the dusk of evening. But now Dermat watched his foe closely; and when he saw him about to spring into the well, he got near him and threw his arms round him. The wizard-champion struggled to free himself, moving all the time nearer and nearer to the brink; but Dermat held on, till at last both fell into the well. Down they went, clinging to each other, Dermat and the wizard-champion; down, down, deeper and deeper they went; and Dermat tried to look round, but nothing could he see save darkness and dim shadows. At length there was a glimmer of light; then the bright day burst suddenly upon them; and presently they came to the solid ground, gently and without the least shock.

'At the very moment they reached the ground, the wizard-champion, with a sudden effort, tore himself away from Dermat's grasp and ran forward with great speed. Dermat leaped to his feet; and he was so amazed at what he saw around him that he stood stock still and let the wizard-champion escape: a lovely country, with many green-sided hills and fair valleys between, woods of red yew trees and plains covered all over with flowers of every hue.

'Right before him, not far off, lay a city of great tall houses with glittering roofs; and on the side nearest him was a royal palace, larger and grander than the rest.'

The *Gruagach*, who was actually the King of Tir-fa-Tonn ('the land below the Water's Waves'), made off into his castle, leaving Dairmait to fight his guards. After scattering the ranks of these, Dairmait lay down to sleep, whereafter a 'Knight of Valour' offered him hospitality in his castle, and cured his wounds in a cauldron of herbs.

After being well treated, 'the Knight of Valour' recounted that he was in fact brother to 'the Knight of the Fountain', who, along with his son, had deprived the Prince (Knight of Valour) of his rightful share of the kingdom. Dairmait, aided by the Prince's warriors, goes off to fight the King of Tir-fa-Tonn.

In the meantime, after waiting many days, Finn and his companions scaled the cliffs and were met on the plain by the King of Sorcha, who showed them great hospitality in his palace. During the conviviality a messenger speeds towards them from the North-west saying that a hostile fleet had arrived to make war on the country. In thanks for his hospitality, Finn and his companions assisted the King of Sorcha and his army to drive off the attacking army.

The day after the fleet had been driven from the shores, Finn, his companions and the King of Sorcha were delighted to see Dairmait and a war-party troop over the hill. After news was exchanged, the Knight of Valour, now the new King of Tir-fa-Tonn stepped out of the troop, and by his Druidical Arts found out that it was one of the *De Dannan* Gods, Avarta ('relevant to existence'), the son of Illahan (of the many-coloured cloak), who had presented himself as the Gila Deakair.

After receiving directions as to the whereabouts of the Gila Deakair, Finn led off his small Fenian band in search again. After a long journey, they reached 'Tir Tairngiri, ('the Land of Promise'), on the far side of many seas, where they found that Konan Mail and the captives had been very hospitably treated, and that Abharta was amenable to a peaceful conciliation. After Finn and his men got back to Eirinn, Abharta (as the Gila Deakair) fulfilled his side of the bargain by taking a rough ride upon his own nag with fifteen of his choice warriors, watched by the Fianna, then to disappear by magic to the world from which they had came.'

In the preceding Tale the point I would like to emphasize is that one of the high Gods took on the form of an ugly *Fomor* in order to trick Finn and his associates, via a code of honour, into journeying into the Otherworlds. Trickery is often required, for us humans are often too stupid/foolhardy/scared to enter other dimensions in response to a plain invitation. I'm sure Abharta engineered getting the bravest and most skillful of the Fianna into the Otherworlds to effect changes in the balance of power, with human attributes being applied to the key pivots, and to defend these magical realms from the deprecations of exterior attacking forces.

A similar ruse, or trick, is unfolded upon Pwyll, Prince of Dyved, as he hunts in Glyn Kuch ('Red Glen'?):

'As he followed the dogs, he lost his companions; and whilst he listened to the hounds, he heard the cry of other hounds, a cry different from his own, and coming in the opposite direction.

'And he beheld a glade in the wood forming a level plain, and as his dogs came to the edge of the glade, he saw a stag before the other dogs, and lo, as it reached the middle of the glade, the dogs that followed the stag overtook it and brought it down. Then looked he at the colour of the dogs, staying not to look at the stag, and of all the hounds he had ever seen in the world, he had never seen any that were like unto these. For their hair was of a brilliant shining white, and their ears were red; and as the whiteness of their bodies shone, so did the redness of their ears glisten. And he came towards the dogs, and drove away those that had brought down the stag, and set his own dogs upon it.

'And as he was setting on his dogs he saw a horseman coming towards him upon a large light-grey steed, with a hunting horn round his neck, and clad in garments of grey woollen in the fashion of a hunting garb. And the horseman drew near and spoke unto him.'

Pwyll found out that this horseman was Arawn, a King of Annwvyn (the psychic underworld of *Yĕtzīrāh*), who came to ask his help, by exchanging places for a year. Pwyll agreed and Arawn led him to his kingdom, where he 'put his semblance upon him'.

There are numerous Otherworld regions described in other branches of Keltic mythology and Folktales, but to do the profundity of the subject matter justice would require a book in itself. Thus, for the present, I'll leave the Rainbow Bridge, Uffern, Druim na Teine, the Green Isle, House of Oeth and Annoeth, the Island on a Single Pillar, Kaer Sidi, the Perilous Glen and the Castle of the Turning Wheel as but names of mystery and power.

CHAPTER 7

The Interpretation of some Major Tales

Shamanistic At-one-ment with The The Toad Elemental

Linda Lees describes the following incident:

'In the few days leading up to the Spring Equinox 1986, the Kaer Eidyn Druidical Group had faced a series of external pressures and troubles from our social environment; this affected some members more closely than others. Thus, when five or six of us left Edinburgh to go to the nearby Pentland Hills to celebrate the equinox, there was a degree of strain upon us. It was actually the night before the festival when we left the city and, in the dark, walked up a tree-lined avenue to a cup-marked stone that we had planned to visit.

'On arriving at the stone, Kaledon moved the barrier aside and knelt down before the stone to do an attunement. The rest of the group stood within a few feet quietly watching. Around the cup-marked stone are a number of large trees, so it was very dark.

'Watching Kaledon kneel by the stone, I was in a very contemplative state of mind, as no doubt were the other group members. However, as I watched Kaledon squatting in front of me, his physical form disappeared, and in front of the stone I saw swirling black energy. The energy then vanished, and squatting where Kaledon had been I saw a huge toad. It was probably two or three feet high and the warts which I saw on its back were shining. Once again I saw the swirling black energy, then Kaledon reappeared in front of the cup- and ring-marked stone. He disappeared a second time into the black- energy swirl; but I saw no toad form clearly the second time.

'After a period of time, difficult to say exactly how long but perhaps about ten minutes, Kaledon stood up, and the group of us moved quietly away from the stone.

'As we walked away I looked around at the other members to see if I had been alone in what I had seen. My eyes instantly met Kirsty's and we both knew that "she had seen it too". Kirsty later described having exactly the same vision as me; and we both felt it had been a very healing experience, particularly for Kaledon and those of us who had actually witnessed it.'

When I spoke later with Lorraine, it became clear that she too had seen me disappear into the dark energy swirl, but without perceiving the toad form that emerged. I checked further and discovered that the two less psychic male onlookers had seen none of these magical happenings.

Most of what I myself experienced during my At-one-ment with an Earth elemental I will retain as a secret. Suffice it to say that it was indeed a very healing, calming and strengthening experience. I would also like to say that in all my experiences with the toad, frog and newt clans (both the physical creatures and their Otherworld forms) I have only had joyful healing encounters. I admit that those folk with a radically different Shamanistic Station might not have such beneficial experiences; but for those who can harmonize in the same way as I can the toad and newt archetypes can indeed be healing emissaries from the Earth Mother Goddess.

The Toad Elemental
1

This is how Paul Screeton described his encounter with an earth gnome in his book on prehistoric culture, Quicksilver heritage (Thorsons, 1974):

> The road into Carlisle from the massive marshalling yard at Kingmoor is narrow, and while walking down it towards the overgrown tump by an old empty mansion house, I had to step on to the verge as a car approached. Continuing walking through the grass that sunny afternoon I stepped on to a stone. I halted, looked down, and it glistened. It was quartz: it had been worked into a convex shape and was deeply embedded. I touched it for about half a minute and then walked a couple of paces. Then I saw something move a yard or so in front of me. The thing leapt like a frog and was frog-shaped, but about three feet high. It was brown but its form was hazy, difficult to describe, but the effect was not dissimilar to a television screen when the lines go crazy. I had the impression that what I had seen was an elemental and that I perceived it at the edge of my consciousness.
>
> It was an earth gnome, described by Geoffrey Hodson as lanky, sometimes solitary, and disproportionate to our senses. He regarded them as relics of Lemurian days and possibly representations of such times. In England they are always black or, as I saw, peat brown, but he, unlike me, found their atmosphere decidedly unpleasant.
>
> I never expected to see an elemental, though I was perfectly willing to believe in their existence.
>
> Two aspects of my experience are worthy of consideration, that is if my testimony is to be believed and that I did not have an hallucination. One is the fact that the experience took place on a ley; the second is the possibility that the quartz itself was instrumental somehow in bringing about the sighting, i.e. raising my consciousness while I touched it.

I respect Paul Screeton both as a writer on megalithic science and, in this instance, for having the courage to relate his extraordinary experience, which was similar to my own. Other points of convergence that should be noted are: (1) a stone, worked by our ancestors for a ritual purpose, played an important 'channeling' role; (2) the original site of the stone was geomantically significant – in my case the stone was originally by a knoll at the terminus of a sandstone ridge, in Paul's case the stone was on a ley-line to a tump by the ancient centre of Kaer Luel (Carlisle); (3) the experience was if anything beneficial.

Although perceiving how incredibly ancient some of these elemental beings can be, Geoffrey Hodson (perhaps because of his Eastern theosophical conditioning) failed to realize that in Northern Europe the wet, cold earth elementals have a vital role to play in the esoteric ecological scheme.

The Toad Elemental 2

In the following Irish account it is difficult to decide exactly what kind of an Otherworld being is being described. I have termed it a toad elemental, though it is also something like a yallery-brown in appearance. It is understandable that the young lad reacted in fear to this Otherworldly creature with glowing eyes – but, as Paul Screeton and I have demonstrated, more favourable reactions are as appropriate.

My father told me not once but several times of an eerie and unpleasant experience he had when he was a boy of about fourteen and was home for the Christmas holidays from his English school. He was playing hide and seek with his elder brother, Arthur, but the game was confined to the large square of the stable buildings, including the cow byres, granaries, haylofts, and all the rest. It was late afternoon and not yet dark outside, when my father, tiptoeing stealthily along a granary, heard a noise of trampling, plunging and snorting from one of the stables below. In those days there were two trap doors above the manger of each stable, one at each end, from which the men could throw down hay more easily.

Going quickly to one of the trap doors above the noisy stable, my father pulled it open suddenly, hoping to catch his brother, and thrust his head down through it before jumping down himself. But to his astonishment he saw the two horses in a mad panic of terror, trembling and snorting with fear as they tried to get as far away as they could from something in the manger at the far end from my father and, perhaps fortunately for him, right under the other trap door. Amazed, he looked across and saw, not twelve feet from his head, something that filled him with horror – a sight that he never forgot all the days of his life. For there he saw a crouching figure with blazing red, baleful eyes like glowing coals of fire. It was huddled in a compact ball, as a boy of his own size might look when squatting on his haunches. My father remembered only those awful eyes, the squatness of the body hunched in the dark corner of the manger, and one awful hand, a human hand, but how different! It gripped the edge of the manger and was a dirty greyish-brown. The fingers were all bone and sinew and ended not in human nails but in curved and pointed claws.

The boy's breath nearly stopped, and after staring at it in ghastly fascination, he hurled himself back into the granary again, slammed down the trap door, and raced for the house, calling to warn his brother first. Luckily, almost at his first shout his brother came and they both hurried back to the bedroom they shared, where my father told what he had seen.

Many years later, when I was nearly seven and long before I had heard this story, I was returning with my father one summer evening from the orchard, where he had been helping me to fill my pockets with good eating apples, for he knew all the best trees well. Twilight was just beginning and, having passed under the shadows of the big holm oaks, we reached the haggard; indeed, we were halfway across it, and I was firmly clasping my father's hand, when he suddenly stopped and turned and made the sign of the cross in the air with the spade which he always carried for cutting thistles.

He made the sign three times towards the dark shadows of the orchard, and as we walked on, I said, 'Daddy, why did you do that?' He hesitated a moment and then, clearly and impressively, replied, 'There are things there that it is better to keep at a distance.'

The Puddock Prince In The Well

This Tale was collected by Campbell in the Western Isles from a Mrs MacTavish of Port Ellen in Islay, and it was printed in his valuable collection.

There was before now a queen who was sick, and she had three daughters. Said she to the one who was eldest, 'Go to the well of true water, and bring to me a drink to heal me.'

The daughter went, and she reached the well. A *Losgann* (frog or toad) came up to ask her if she would wed him, if she should get a drink for her mother. 'I will not wed thee, hideous creature! on any account,' said she. 'Well then,' said he, 'thou shalt not get the water.'

She went away home, and her mother sent away her sister that was nearest to her, to seek a drink of the water. She reached the well; and the toad came up and asked her if she would marry him, if she should get the water. 'I won't marry thee, hideous creature!' said she. 'Thou shalt not get the water, then,' said he.

She went home, and her sister that was youngest went to seek the water. When she reached the well the toad came up as he used, and asked her if she would marry him, if she should get the water. 'If I have no other way to get healing for my mother, I will marry thee,' said she; and she got the water, and she healed her mother.

They had betaken themselves to rest in the night when the toad came to the door saying:

A chaomhag, a chaomhag,	'Gentle one, gentle one,
An cuimhneach leat	Rememberest thou
An gealladh beag	The little pledge
A thug thu aig	Though gavest me
An tobar dhomh,	Beside the well,
A ghaoil, a ghaoil.	My love, my love.'

When he was ceaselessly saying this, the girl rose and took him in, and put him behind the door, and she went to bed; but she was not long laid down, when he began again saying, everlastingly:

A hàovaig, a hàovaig,
An cuineach leat
An geallug beag
A hoog oo aig
An tobar gaw,
A géule, a géule.

Then she got up and she put him under a noggin; that kept him quiet a while; but she was not long laid down when he began again, saying:

A hàovaig, a hàvaoig,
An cuineach leat
An geallug beag

A hoog oo aig
An tobar gaw,
A géule, a géule.

She rose again, and she made him a little bed at the fireside; but he was not pleased, and he began again saying, '*A chaoimheag, a chaoimheag, an cuimhneach leat an gealladh beag a thug thu aig an tobar dhomh, a ghaoil, a ghaoil.*' Then she got up and made him a bed beside her own bed; but he was without ceasing, saying, '*A chaoimheag, a chaoimheag, an cuimhneach leat an gealladh beag a thug thu aig an tobar dhomh, a ghaoil, a ghaoil.*' But she took no notice of his complaining, till he said to her, 'There is an old rusted glave behind they bed, with which thou hadst better take off my head, than be holding me longer in torture.'

She took the glave and cut the head off him. When the steel touched him, he grew a handsome youth; and he gave many thanks to the young wife, who had been the means of putting off him the spells, under which he had endured for a long time. Then he got his kingdom, for he was a king; and he married the princess, and they were long alive and merry together.

The Toad Man

The following Breton Tale was collected in 1869 by F. M. Luzel from Barbara Tassel of Plouaret in Breizh; it was admirably translated into English by Dr Derek Bryce, and appears in his book Celtic Folk-Tales *(Llanerch, 1985). The Breton version shares a fair amount with the preceding Scottish Gaelic Tale, but also preserves some valuable features in its own right.*

Once there was a good man who had been left a widower with three daughters. One day, one of his daughters said to him; 'Would you go and fetch a pitcher of water from the spring, father? There's not a drop left in the house, and I need some for our stew-pot.'

'With pleasure, daughter,' replied the old man.

And he took a pitcher and went to the spring.[1] As he was leaning over the water filling his pitcher, a toad jumped up and stuck itself fast on his face, so fast that all his efforts to loosen it were in vain.[2]

'You won't get me off, until you promise to give me one of your daughters in marriage,' said the toad.

He left his pitcher by the spring, and ran back to the house.

'God'! What's happened to you, father?' exclaimed his daughters on seeing the state he was in.

'Alas, poor children! This animal jumped on my face, just as I was getting water at the spring, and now he says he'll only let go if one of you consents to marry him.'

'Good God! What are you saying, father?' replied the eldest daughter. 'Marry a toad! It's horrible to look at!'

And she turned away and went out of the house. The second daughter did likewise.

'Ah well, poor father,' said the youngest, 'I'll have him as my husband, for in my heart I can't bear seeing you stay in that state.'

Straightaway the toad fell on the ground. The wedding was fixed for the next day.

When the bride went into church accompanied by her toad, the vicar was quite taken aback, and said he would never marry a Christian to a toad. However he ended up uniting them, when the bride's father had told him the whole story, and promised him lots of money.[3]

Then the toad took his wife to his castle – for he had a fine castle. When it was time for bed, he took her to her room, and there he took off his toad-skin[4] and revealed himself as a handsome young Prince. Whilst the sun was above the horizon, he was a toad; by night he was a Prince.[5]

The young bride's two sisters came to visit her from time to time, and they were quite surprised to find her so happy, laughing and singing all the time.

'There's something behind this,' they said to each other. 'We should keep an eye on her and find out.'

They came quietly one night, looked through the keyhole, and were amazed to see a handsome young Prince, instead of a toad.

'Hallo! What a handsome Prince! ... If only we had known,' they said to each other.[6]

They heard the Prince saying these words to his wife, 'I must go on a journey tomorrow, and I'll be leaving my toadskin in the house. See that no harm comes to it, for I have to use it for another year and a day.'[7]

'That's good,' said the two sisters to each other.

Next morning, the Prince left, and his two sisters-in-law came to visit his wife.

'God! What beautiful things you have! You must be very happy with your toad!' they said to her.

'Yes, sisters, I'm truly happy with him.'

'Where's he gone?'

'On a journey.'

'If you like, little sister, I'll comb your hair for you – it's so beautiful.'

'I'd like that very much, good sister.'

She fell asleep whilst they were combing her hair with a golden comb,[8] and then her sisters stole her keys from her pocket, took the toad skin from the cupboard in which it was locked, and threw it in the fire.[9]

When she woke up,[10] the young woman was surprised to find herself alone. Her husband arrived a moment later, red with anger.

'Ah, unhappy woman!' he cried. 'You've done what I clearly told you not to; you've burnt my toad skin, to my and your misfortune. Now I must go, and you shall never see me again.'

The poor woman started crying, and said, 'I'll follow you wherever you go.'

'No, don't follow me; stay here.'

And he ran off, and she ran after him.

'Stay there, I tell you.'

'I won't stay, I'll follow you.'

And he kept on running; but run as he may, she kept on his heels. Then he threw a golden ball behind him. His wife picked it up, put it in her pocket, and went on running.[11]

'Go back home! Go back home!' he cried again.

'I'll never go back without you.'

He threw a second golden ball. She picked it up like the first, and put it in her pocket; then a third ball; but seeing she was still on his heels, he went into a rage and hit her straight in the face with his fist. Blood spurted and three drops fell on his shirt, leaving three stains.

Then the poor woman was left behind, and soon lost sight of the fugitive; but she cried out to him, 'Those three blood-stains will never wash out until I find you and make them go away myself.'[12]

Despite all, she continued her pursuit. She went into a great wood. Soon after, whilst following a footpath beneath the trees, she saw two enormous lions sitting on their behinds, one each side of the path. She was quite afraid.[13]

'Alas!' she said to herself. 'I think I'm going to lose my life here, for these two lions will surely eat me; but no matter, God keep me.'

And she went forwards. When she came close to the lions, she was quite surprised to see them lie down at her feet and lick her hands. She even stroked them over their heads and down their backs. Then she continued on her way.

Further on, she saw a hare sitting on its behind, by the side of the path, and when she was passing close by, the hare said to her,[14] 'Climb on my back, and I'll take you out of the woods.'

She sat on the hare's back, and he soon took her out of the woods.

'Now,' said the hare before leaving, 'you're close to the castle where the one you're seeking is to be found.'[15]

'Thanks, kind creature of the Good Lord,'[16] said the young woman.

She soon found herself in a great avenue of old oaks,[17] and not far away she saw some washer-women washing linen in a lake. She approached them and heard one of them saying, 'Ah! There must be a curse on this shirt; for two years I've tried every way I know to remove the three blood-stains from it, and although I've tried hard, I can't manage to do it.'

On hearing these words, the traveller went up to the woman who spoke thus, and said, 'Please let me have a go at that shirt, just for a moment; I think I'll be able to remove the three blood-stains.'

They gave her the shirt, she spat on the three stains, soaked them in water, rubbed them a little, and they soon disappeared.[18]

'A thousand thanks,' said the laundress. 'Our master's about to get married, and he'll be pleased to see the three stains have gone, for it's his best shirt.'

'Is there any chance of a job in your master's house?'

'The shepherdess left a few days ago and she hasn't been replaced yet; come with me and I'll recommend you.'

She was taken on as shepherdess. Every day she took her flock to a great wood which surrounded the castle, and she often saw her husband walking there with the young Princess who was going to be his wife. Her heart beat faster when she saw him; but she did not dare speak.

She still had her three golden balls, and often, to relieve her boredom, she played bowls with them. One day the young Princess noticed her golden balls, and said to her waiting-maid, 'Look! Look! What beautiful golden balls that girl has! Go and ask her to sell me one.'

The maid went up to the shepherdess and said, 'Those beautiful golden balls you have, shepherdess. Would you sell one to my mistress, the Princess?'

'I won't sell my balls; in my loneliness I've no other pastime.'

'Bah! You're unreasonable; look what a state your clothing is in. Sell one of your balls to my mistress and she'll pay you well; you'll be able to dress properly.'[19]

'I ask neither gold nor silver.'

'What do you want then?'

'To sleep with your master for a night!'[20]

'What! Wicked girl! How dare you speak like that?'

'I will not give up one of my golden balls for any other thing in the world.'[21]

The maid went back to her mistress.

'Well! What did the shepherdess say?'

'I daren't tell you what she said.'

'Tell me, at once.'

'She said, wicked girl, that she would only give up one of her balls to sleep for a night with your husband.'

'I see! But no matter, I must have one of her balls at any price; I'll put a drug in my husband's wine at supper time, and he'll know nothing. Go and tell her that I accept her terms, and bring me a golden ball.'

That night, on getting up from the table, the Lord was so sleepy that they had to put him straight to bed. Soon after, they let the shepherdess into his room. But though she tried hard, calling him by the tenderest names, embracing him, and shaking him vigorously, nothing could wake him up.

'Alas,' cried the poor woman in tears, 'have I lost after all my troubles; after so much suffering? And yet, I wed you when you were a toad and no one wanted you. And for two long years, in heat and cruel cold, wind, snow and rain, I've sought you everywhere without giving up; and now that I've found you, you sleep like a log! Ah, unhappy me!'[22]

And she sobbed and wept; but, alas, he did not hear her.

Next morning she went into the woods again, with her sheep, thoughtful and sad. The Princess came in the afternoon, as on the previous day, to walk with her maid. On seeing her coming, the shepherdess started playing with the two balls she had left. The Princess wanted to have a second ball, to make a pair, and she said to her maid, 'Go and buy me a second golden ball from the shepherdess.'

The maid obeyed, and, to cut the story short, the deal was made at the same price as the day before; to spend a second night with the master of the castle.

Once again the Princess put a drug in the master's wine, so that he had to go to bed straight after supper, and slept like a log. Some time later, the shepherdess was let into his room again, and once more she started to sigh and sob. A manservant who was passing the door by chance, heard a noise and stopped to listen. He was quite astonished by what he heard, and, next morning, he went up to his master and said, 'Master, things happen in this castle that you don't know about, but which you should know.'[23]

'Such as? . . . Tell me quickly.'

'A poor woman, seeming quite unhappy and upset, came to the castle a few days ago, and from feeling sorry for her, they took her on as a replacement for the shepherdess who had just left. One day, when the Princess was walking with her maid in the woods, she saw her playing bowls with golden balls. Straight away she wanted these balls, and sent her maid to buy them at any price from the shepherdess. The shepherdess asked not for gold nor for silver, but to spend one night in bed with you for each one of the balls. She's already given two balls, and spent two nights with you in your room, without your knowing anything about it. It's pitiful to hear her sighing and sobbing. I believe her mind may be deranged, for she says very strange things, such as that she was your wife when you were a toad, and that she's been walking for two whole years in search of you.'

'Can all this be true?'

'Yes, master, it's all true; and if you still know nothing about it, it's because the Princess put a drug in your wine at supper time, so that you had to be put to bed as soon as you got up from the table, and went into a deep sleep till morning.'

'Well! I'll have to watch out; you'll soon see some changes here.'

The poor shepherdess was disliked by the other castle servants, who knew she spent her nights in the master's bed, and they only gave her a piece of barley bread, like they gave to the dogs.[24]

Next morning, she went to the woods again with her sheep, and the Princess bought her third golden ball at the same price.[25]

When it was time for the evening meal, the master kept a careful watch. Whilst he was chatting with the person next to him, he saw the Princess pour a drug in his glass. He pretended not to notice, but instead of drinking the wine, he threw it under the table, when the Princess was not looking.

On leaving the table, he pretended to be sleepy and went to his room. The shepherdess went there also, shortly afterwards. This time he was not asleep; as soon as he saw her he threw himself into her arms, and they wept with joy and happiness at finding each other.[26]

'Now go back to your room, poor girl,' he said after some time, 'and tomorrow you'll see some changes here.'

Next day there was a great feast in the castle, for arranging the wedding-day. There were only Kings, Queens, Princes, Princesses and other distinguished persons. Towards the end of the meal, the future husband got up and said,

'Father-in-law, I need your advice on this matter: I have a pretty little box with a pretty little golden key; I lost the key and had another one made. But soon after, I found the old key, so now I have two. Which one do you think I should use?'[27]

'Always respect age,' replied the future father-in-law.

Then the Prince went into a nearby closet, and came straight back holding the shepherdess by the hand. She was dressed simply, but correctly, and, presenting her to the guests, he said, 'Well here's my first key, that's to say my first wife, whom I've found again; I've always loved her, and I'll never have anyone else.'

And they went back to their country where they lived happily together until the end of their days . . .[28]

And that's the story of the Toad Man. How do you like it?

The Vixen and The Oakmen

A fox had been hunted all day and the hounds were getting closer and do wha
she might she couldn't throw them off. 'Jump up and climb up me and ru
along the high, stone wall,' said the hawthorn tree.

'I don't think I could jump up anywhere now,' said she, 'but thank yo
kindly.'

'There's a water-gap in the stone wall,' said the hawthorn, 'and the othe
side is the forest. Squeeze through. The hedgehog does.'

'I'm not a hedgehog,' said the fox, 'but thank you kindly.' Then she hear
the hounds and squeezed herself inside and there she stuck and the hunt cam
by. They couldn't see her easily for she tucked in her brush and edged a bi
more under the thick, stone wall.

'The tip of your brush is sticking out,' said the tree. 'Push your nose out a
far as you like the other side of the wall. They'll have to go two miles roun
to find a gap to come round and see that.'

So she gave a wriggle and left most of her shoulder pelt on the stones bu
she got through, and even then she stopped to thank the hawthorn before sh
limped off.

Only one great hound heard her and came snuffling the small water-gap
Then he reached a great paw in and lifted his head to bay, but the hawthor
dropped a bunch of paigles [haws] down his throat and made him coug
instead. 'You give her a chance,' the tree told him. 'You're twice her size. G
round if you want to catch her up. She may be a vixen but she's got goo
manners. She doesn't cough and splutter all over my roots. Be off!' And th
hound went.

But the fox was very lame and it wasn't long before she heard men again
'I *must* rest,' she said and cowered in the brake ferns. But these men had axe
and whispered, even in the forest, and she heard what they said and when they
crept on their way she limped on hers, trying to hasten, for again she hear
hounds.

'O Holly Tree, block the way behind me, please! she said.

But the holly tree was a barren holly and wicked. 'I will if you come here,'
he told her, but she just looked at him.

'My poor little paws are too sore to walk on your leaves, Sir – you migh
hang me on your branches,' and she went well away from his clutch.

The hounds drew nearer again. Then she saw the great oak and crawled t
it.

'Please open and let me in. I bring news,' she whined. The Oakmen don' believe a fox's word, but they guard all forest beasts so they pulled her safe inside where she lay panting. At last she gasped, 'Your mistletoe bough – men with axes – going to cut it down – they said so – but they're scared. Am I in time to save it?'

'Did you come through all these dangers to tell us that?' said the Oakmen. She had.

'Then we'll forget Farmer Gregg's geese and ducks and hens,' they told her. 'We don't shelter thieves but we *can* shelter a true friend. The hunt has gone past and away, and now you must go too. Wipe your sore paws in our oaktree rainpool.' So she did and her coat grew again and her pads were healed.

'Keep away from the Barren Holly,' they said – she meant to – 'and never come here again.'

And she was off home to her den in the crags like a red flash and curled up and sound asleep in another minute.

When she woke Mr Fox had just brought home a fat goose. 'One of Farmer Gregg's, my love,' he said. 'He won't need it and you do. He's hanging high on the branches of a barren holly in the forest and another man with him. Eat the goose, love, and I'll just go back and bring a duck for supper.'

Gille Mairtin : Fox-God

At some time there was a King and a Queen and they had one son; but the Queen died, and the King married another wife.[1] The name of the son that he first Queen had was Iain Direach.[2] He was a handsome lad; he was a hunter, and there was no bird at which he would cast his arrow, that he would not fell; and he would kill the deer and the roes at a great distance from him; there was no day that he would go out with his bow and his quiver, that he would not bring venison home.

He was one day in the hunting hill hunting, and he got no venison[3] at all; but there came a blue falcon past him, and he let an arrow at her, but he did but drive a feather from her wing. He raised the feather and he put it into his hunting bag, and he took it home; and when he came home his muime said to him, 'Where is thy game today?' and he put his hand into the hunting bag, nd he took out the feather and he gave it to her. And his muime took the eather in her hand, and she said, 'I am setting it as crosses, and as spells, and s the decay of the year on thee; that thou be not without a pool in thy shoe, nd that thou be wet, cold, and soiled, until thou gettest for me the bird from which that feather came.'[4]

This is another mighty Tale from Gaelic-speaking Alban. The Tale is sometimes called Iain Direach, *after the human protagonist, but I prefer to credit the real hero, who is Gillie Mairtean, the Fox-Wildman. This particular telling is from Angus Campbell, a quarryman from Knockderry, Roseneath, and it was originally published in* West Highland Tales *by*

And he said to his muime, 'I am setting it as crosses and as spells, and
the decay of the year on thee; that thou be standing with the one foot on th
great house, and the other foot on the castle; and that thy face be to th
tempest whatever wind blows, until I return back.'[5]

And MacIain Direach went away as fast as he could to seek the bird fro
which the feather came, and his muime was standing with the one foot on th
castle, and the other on the great house, till he should come back; and h
front was to the face of the tempest, however long he might be withou
coming.

MacIain Direach was gone, travelling the waste to see if he could see th
falcon, but the falcon he could not see; and much less than that, he could n
get her; and he was going by himself through the waste, and it was comin
near to the night. The little fluttering birds were going from the bush top
from tuft to tuft, and to the briar roots, going to rest; and though they wer
he was not going there, till the night came blind and dark; and he went an
crouched at the root of a briar; and who came the way but *an Gille Mairtean*
the fox; and he said to him, 'Thou'rt down in the mouth a Mhic Iain Direach
thou camest on a bad night; I have myself but one wether's trotter and
sheep's cheek, but needs must do with it.'[7]

They kindled a fire, and they roasted flesh, and they ate the wether's trott
and the sheep's cheek; and in the morning Gille Mairtean said to the King
son, 'Oh son of Iain Direach, the falcon thou seekest is by the Great Giant
the Five Heads, and the Five Humps, and the Five Throttles,[8] and I will she
thee where his house is; and it is my advice to thee to go to be as his servan
and that thou be nimble and ready to do each thing that is asked of thee, an
each thing that is trusted thee; and be very good to his birds, and it well ma
be that he will trust thee with the falcon to feed; and when thou gettest th
falcon to feed be right good to her, till thou gettest a chance; at the time whe
the giant is not at home run away with her, but take care that so much as on
feather of her does not touch any one thing that is within the house, or if
touches, it will not go [well] with thee.'[9]

MacIain Direach said that he 'would take care of that'; and he went to th
giant's house; he arrived, he struck at the door.

The giant shouted, 'Who is there?'

'It is me,' said MacIain Direach, 'one coming to see if thou has hast nee
of a lad.'

'What work canst thou do?' said the giant.

'It is [this],' said MacIain Direach. ''I can feed birds and swine, and fee
and milk a cow, or goats or sheep.'

'It is the like of thee that I want,' said the giant.

The giant came out and he settled wages on MacIain Direach; and he wa
taking right good care of everything that the giant had, and he was very kin
to the hens and to the ducks; and the giant took notice how well he was doing
and he said that his table was so good since MacIain Direach had come, b
what it was before; that he had rather one hen of those which he got now
than two of those he used to get before. 'My lad is so good that I begin t
think I may trust him the falcon to feed'; and the giant gave the falcon t
MacIain Direach to feed, and he took exceeding care of the falcon; and whe
the giant saw how well MacIain Direach was taking care of the falcon, h

ıought that he might trust her to him when he was [away] from the house; ıd the giant gave him the falcon to keep, and he was taking exceeding care f the falcon.

The giant thought each thing was going right, and he went from the house ne day; and MacIain Direach thought that was the time to run away with ıe falcon, and he seized the falcon to go away with her; and when he opened ıe door and the falcon saw the light, she spread her wings to spring, and the oint of one of the feathers of one of her wings touched one of the posts of ıe door, and the door post let out a screech.[10] The giant came home running, ıd he caught MacIain Direach, and he took the falcon from him; and he said) him, 'I would not give thee my falcon, unless thou shouldst get for me the 7hite Glave of Light that the Big Women of Dhiurradh have[11]; and the giant :nt MacIain away.

MacIain Direach went out again and through the waste, and the Gille 1airtean met with him, and he said, 'Thou art down in the mouth MacIain ireach; thou didst not, and thou wilt not do, as I tell thee; bad is the night n which thou hast come; I have but one wether's trotter and one sheep's ıeek, but needs must do with that.'

They roused a fire, and they made ready the wether's trotter and the sheep's ıeek, and they took their meat and sleep; and on the next day the Gille 1airtean said, 'We will go to the side of the ocean.'

They went and they reached the side of the ocean, and the Gille Mairtean ıid, 'I will grow into a boat,[12] and go thou on board of her, and I will take ıee over to Dhiurradh; and go to the Seven Great Women of Dhurrah and sk service, that thou be a servant with them; and when they ask thee what ıou canst do, say to them that thou art good at brightening iron and steel, old and silver, and that thou canst make them bright, clear, and shiny; and ıke exceeding care that thou dost each thing right, till they trust thee the 7hite Glave of Light; and when thou gettest a chance run away with it, but ıke care that the sheath does not touch a thing on the inner side of the house, r it will make a screech, and the matter will not go well with thee.'

The Gille Mairtean grew into a boat, and MacIain Direach went on board f her, and he came on shore at Creagan nan deargan,[13] on the northern side f Dhiurradh, and MacIain Direach leaped on shore, and he went to take ervice with the Seven Big Women of Dhiurradh. He reached, and he struck t the door; the Seven Big Women came out, and they asked what he was eeking. He said he could brighten, or make clear, white and shiny, gold and ilver, or iron or steel. They said, 'We have need of thy like', and set wages on im. And he was right diligent for six weeks, and put everything in exceeding rder. And the Big Women noticed it; and they kept saying to each other, This is the best lad we have ever had; we may trust him the White Glave of ight.'

They gave him the White Glave of Light to keep in order; and he was aking exceeding care of the White Glave of Light, till one day that the Big Women were not at the house, he thought that was the time for him to run way with the White Glave of Light. He put it into the sheath, and he raised t on his shoulder,[14] but when he was going out at the door the point of the heath touched the lintel, and the lintel made a screech; and the Big Women an home, and took the sword from him; and they said to him, 'We would

not give thee our White Glave of Light, unless thou shouldst get for us th
Yellow [Bay] Filly of the King of Eirinn.'[15]

MacIain Direach went to the side of the ocean and the Gille Mairtean me
him, and he said to him, 'Thou'rt down in the mouth, MacIain Direach; tho
didst not, and thou wilt not do as I ask thee; I have tonight but one wether'
trotter and one sheep's cheek, but needs must do with it.'

They kindled a fire, and they roasted flesh, and they were satisfied. On th
next day the Gille Mairtean said to MacIain Direach, 'I will grow into
barque, and go thou on board of her, and I will go to Eirinn with thee; an
when we reach Eirinn go thou to the house of the King, and ask service to b
a stable lad with him; and when thou gettest that, be nimble and ready to d
each thing that is to be done, and keep the horses and the harness in right goo
order, till the King trusts the Yellow [Bay] Filly to thee; and when thou gettes
a chance run away with her; but take care when thou art taking her out tha
no bit of her touches anything that is on the inner side of the gate, except th
soles of her feet; or else thy matter will not prosper with thee.'

And then the Gille Mairtean put himself into the form of a barque
MacIain Direach went on board, and the barque sailed with him to Eirinn
When they reached the shore of Eirinn, MacIain Direach leaped on land, an
he went to the house of the King; and when he reached the gate, the gate
keeper asked where he was going. He said that he was going to see if the Kin
had need of a stable lad; and the gate-keeper let him past. He reached th
King's house; he struck at the door and the King came out and said, 'What ar
thou seeking here?'

Said he, 'With your leave, I came to see if you had need of a stable lad.

The King asked, 'What canst thou do?'

Said he, 'I can clean and feed the horses, and clean the silver work, and th
steel work, and make them shiny.'

The King settled wages on him and he went to the stable; and he put eac
thing in good order; he took good care of the horses, he fed them well, an
he kept them clean, and their skin was looking *sliom*, sleek; and the silve
work and the steel work shiny to look at; and the King never saw them so wel
in order before.[16] And he said, 'This is the best stable lad I have ever had, I ma
trust the Yellow [Bay] Filly to him.'

The King gave the Yellow [Bay] Filly to MacIain Direach to keep; an
MacIain Direach took very great care of the Yellow [Bay] Filly; and he kep
her clean, till her skin was so sleek and slippery, and she so swift, that sh
would leave the one wind and catch the other. The King never saw her so
good.

The King went one day to the hunting hill, and MacIain Direach though
that was the time to run away with the Yellow [Bay] Filly; and he set her in
what belonged to her, with a bridle and saddle; and when he took her out of
the stable, he was taking her through the gate, she gave a switch, *sguaise* with
her tail, and the point of her tail touched the post of the gate, and it let ou
a screech.[17]

The King came running, and he took the filly from MacIain Direach; an
he said to him, 'I would not give thee the Yellow [Bay] Filly, unless thou
shouldst get for me the daughter of the King of the Frainge.[18]

And MacIain Direach needs must go; and when he was within a little of the side of the sea the Gille Mairtean met him; and he said to him, 'Thou art down in the mouth, oh son of Iain Direach; thou didst not, and thou wilt not, do as I ask thee; we must now go to France, I will make myself a ship, and go thou on board, and I will not be long till I take thee to France.'

The Gille Mairtean put himself in the shape of a ship, and MacIain Direach went on board of her, and the Gille Mairtean sailed to France with him, and he ran himself on high up the face of a rock, on dry land; and he told MacIain Direach to go up to the King's house and to ask help, and to say that his skipper had been lost, and his ship thrown on shore.

MacIain Direach went to the King's House, and he struck at the door. One came out to see who was there. He told his tale and he was taken into the fort. The King asked him whence he was, and what he was doing here.

He told them the tale of misery: that a great storm had come on him, and the skipper he had was lost; and the ship he had thrown on dry land, and she was there, driven up on the face of a rock by the waves, and that he did not know how he should get her out.

The King and the Queen, and the family together, went to the shore to see the ship; and when they were looking at the ship, exceeding sweet music began on board; and the King of France's daughter went on board to see the musical instrument, together with MacIain Direach. When they were in one chamber, the music would be in another chamber; but at last they heard the music on the upper deck of the ship, and they went above on the upper deck of the ship, and [so] it was that the ship was out on the ocean, and out of sight of land.[19]

And the King of France's daughter said, 'Bad is the trick thou hast done to me. Where art thou for going with me?'

'I am,' said MacIain Direach, 'going with thee to Eirinn, to give thee as a wife to the King of Eirinn, so that I may get from him his Yellow [Bay] Filly, to give her to the Big Women of Dhirradh, that I may get from them their White Glave of Light, to give it to the Great Giant of the Five Heads, and Five Humps, and Five Throttles, that I may get from him his Blue Falcon, to take her home to my muime, that I may be free from my crosses, and from my spells, and from the bad diseases of the year.'[20]

And the King of France's daughter said, 'I had rather be as a wife to thyself.'[21]

And when they came to shore in Eirinn, the Gille Mairtean put himself in the shape of a fine woman, and he said to MacIain Direach, 'Leave thou the King of France's daughter here till we return, and I will go with thee to the King of Eirinn; I will give him enough of a wife.'

MacIain Direach went with the Gille Mairtean in the form of a fine maiden, with his hand in the oxter of MacIain Direach. When the King of Eirinn saw them coming he came to meet them; he took out the Yellow [Bay] Filly and a golden saddle on her back, and a silver bridle in her head.

MacIain Direach went with the filly where the King of France's daughter was. The King of Eirinn was right well pleased with the young wife he had got; but little did the King of Eirinn know that he had got Gille Mairtean. They had not long been gone to rest, when the Gille Mairtean sprung on the King, and he did not leave a morsel of flesh between the back of his neck and his haunch that he did not take off him.[22] And the Gille Mairtean left the

King of Eirinn a pitiful wounded cripple; and he went running where MacIain Direach was, and the King of France's daughter, and the Yellow [Bay] Filly.

Said the Gille Mairtean, 'I will go into the form of a ship, and go you on board of her, and I will take you to Diurradh; he grew into the form of a ship; and MacIain Direach put in the Yellow [Bay] Filly first, and he himself and the King of France's daughter went in after her; and the Gille Mairtean sailed with them to Diurradh, and they went on shore at Creagan nan deargan, at Cilla-mhoire, at the northern end of Diurradh; and when they went on shore, the Gille Mairtean said, 'Leave thou the Yellow [Bay] Filly here, and the King's daughter, till thou return; and I will go in the form of a filly, and I will go with thee to the Big Women of Diurradh, and I will give them enough of filly-ing.'

The Gille Mairtean went into the form of a filly. MacIain Direach put the golden saddle on his back, and the silver bridle in his head, and he went to the Seven Big Women of Diurradh with him. When the Seven Big Women saw him coming, they came to meet him with the White Glave of Light, and they gave it to him. MacIain Direach took the golden saddle off the back of the Gille Mairtean, and the silver bridle out of his head, and he left him with them: and he went away himself with the White Glave of Light, and he went where he left the King of France's daughter, and the Yellow [Bay] Filly which he got from the King of Eirinn; and the Big Women of Diurradh thought that it was the Yellow [Bay] Filly of the King of Eirinn that they had got, and they were in great haste to ride. They put a saddle on her back, and they bridled her head, and one of them went up on her back to ride her, another went up at the back of that one, and another at the back of that one, and there was always room for another one there, till one after one, the Seven Big Women went up on the back of the Gille Mairtean, thinking that they had got the Yellow [Bay] Filly.[23]

One of them gave a blow of a rod to the Gille Mairtean; and if she gave, he ran, and he raced backwards and forwards with them through the mountain moors; and at last he went bounding on high to the top of the *Monadh* Mountain of Duirradh, and he reached the top of the face of the great crag, that is there, and he moved his front to the crag, and he put his two fore feet to the front of the crag, and he threw his aftermost end on high, and he threw the Seven Big Women over the crag, and he went away laughing; and he reached where were MacIain Direach and the King of France's daughter, with the Yellow [Bay] Filly, and the White Glave of Light.[24]

Said the Gille Mairtean, 'I will put myself in the form of a boat, and go thyself, and the daughter of the King of France on board, and take with you the Yellow [Bay] Filly and the White Glave of Light, and I will take you to mainland.'

The Gille Mairtean put himself in the shape of a boat; MacIain Direach put the White Glave of Light and the Yellow [Bay] Filly on board, and he went himself and the King of France's daughter, in on board after them; and the Gille Mairtean went with them to the mainland. When they reached shore, the Gille Mairtean put himself into his own shape, and he said to MacIain Direach, 'Leave thou the King of France's daughter, the Yellow [Bay] Filly from the King of Eirinn, and the White Glave of Light there, and I will go into the shape of a White Glave of Light; and take thou me to the

the giant and give thou me to him for the falcon, and I will give him enough of swords.'

The Gille Mairtean put himself into the form of a sword, and MacIain Direach took him to the giant; and when the giant saw him coming he put the blue falcon into a *Muirlag*,[25] and he gave it to MacIain Direach, and he went away with it to where he had left the King of France's daughter, the Yellow [Bay] Filly and the White Glave of Light.

The giant went in with the Gille Mairtean in his hand, himself thinking that it was the White Glave of Light of the Big Women of Diurradh that he had, and he began at *Fionnsaireach*, fencing, and at *Sguiseal*, slashing with it; but at last the Gille Mairtean bent himself, and he swept the five heads off the giant,[26] and he went where MacIain Direach was, and he said to him, 'Son of John the Upright,[27] put the saddle of gold on the filly, and the silver bridle in her head, and go thyself riding her, and take the King of France's daughter at thy back, and the White Glave of Light with its back against thy nose; or else if thou be not so, when thy muime sees thee, she has a glance that is so deadly that she will bewitch thee, and thou wilt fall a faggot of firewood; but if the back of the sword is against thy nose, and its edge to her, when she tries to bewitch thee, she will fall down herself as a faggot of sticks.'[28]

MacIain Direach did as the Gille Mairtean asked him. When he came in sight of the house, and his muime looked at him with a deadly bewitching eye, she fell as a faggot of sticks, and MacIain Direach set fire to her, and then he was free from fear; and had got the best wife in Albainn; and the Yellow [Bay] Filly was so swift that she could leave the one wind and she would catch the other wind;[29] and the blue falcon would keep him in plenty of game, and the White Glave of Light would keep off each foe; and MacIain Direach was steadily, luckily off.

Said MacIain Direach to the Gille Mairtean, 'Thou art welcome, thou Lad of March, to go through my ground, and to take any beast thou dost desire thyself to take with thee; and I will give word to my servants that they do not let an arrow at thee, and that they do not kill thee, nor any of thy race, whatever one of the flock thou takest with thee.'[30]

Said the Gille Mairtean, 'Keep thou thy herds to thyself; there is many a one who has wethers and sheep as well as thou hast, and I will get plenty of flesh in another place without coming to put trouble on thee; and the Fox gave a blessing to the son of Upright John, and he went away; and the tale was spent.

The Tale of Tod

In the following totally brilliant bardic poem by the Green Knight (Stuart Akers) we find the Ancient Druidical wisdom alive and given fresh Awen. This mythological ballad gives us a near-perfect presentation of the teachings related to my rediscovered Keltic Shamanistic Calendar. Indeed, it was after a Kaer Eidyn Group meeting, when Start was travelling across a piece of moorland on his way back to the Scottish Borders, that the first main surge of inspiration came (some time after midnight out in the wilds). When I was given the poem to read the next week, I was immediately convinced that it had tapped into the wellsprings of the mighty ones. When Stuart later read The Tale of Tod to the assembled group, it was indeed a powerful event. That a student of the Druidical mysteries has been able to formulate a Tale containing complex well-woven symbolism should surely convince us that the ancient masters (who were the fountainheads of this very tradition) were able to do likewise. Thus, if academics and ill-educated pagans have not been able to comprehend the rich symbolism in Taliesin or Amhairgin's poem, it is because they have not spent enough time learning the proper Druidical keys, for, with the notes and Koelbren signs to guide you, The Tale of Tod is crystal-clear in its message. Only the profounder levels of meaning may yet elude the intelligent reader.

I am Tod
Right Reverend Bishop of the Wheel.
I stand in a high place
Vestments flapping
Mitre atop my head;
But my jaw is long and my teeth are sharp!

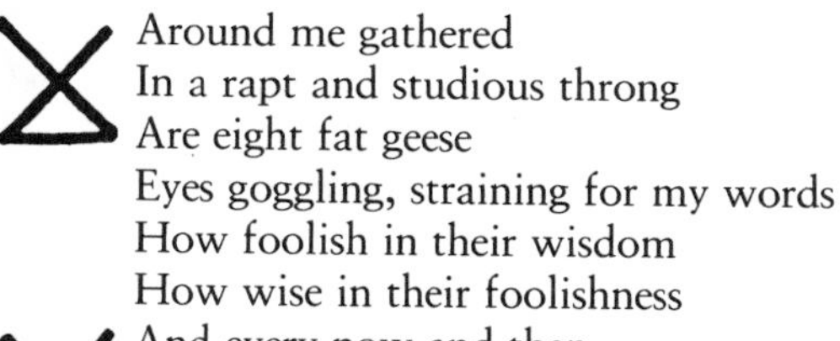

Around me gathered
In a rapt and studious throng
Are eight fat geese
Eyes goggling, straining for my words
How foolish in their wisdom
How wise in their foolishness
And every now and then
They cry, Ngeigh! Ngeigh! Ngeigh![1]

I raise my paw to command silence,
And speak to them
Of the hinge of two worlds;-
Of the horned King of the Wild Hunt,
Of the salmon in Black water and of
The *Erne*[2] pecking the shining back;
Of strangling ivy
Of the deep deep earth
Of the reeds soughing in Negt's cold wind,
Of the buried puddock[3]
Of the water ask[4]
Of the hunting *Kwn*[5]
And of the dark upcoming.

I am ceased and silence falls,
My eight geese are enspelled.
My eyes glitter and my jaws snap,
Some white feathers flutter in the breeze
And there be seven instead of eight
Crying, Ngeigh! Ngeigh! Ngeigh!

I raise my *Bachull* to command silence
And speak to them of the great hen
Pecking in the seed of truth;[6]
Of the unicorn and his horn of power
Of brave *Ruddock*,[7] of fruiting bramble
And of sweet-sounding *Awen*;
Of the cutting of round apple
Of the escape of great *Arty*[8]
And of the wild glimmer of red
Upon the eastern hills.

I am ceased and silence falls,
My seven geese are entranced.
I glitter through my eyes
And I snap my jaws
As like a nadder striking
And there be six instead of seven

Crying, Ngeigh! Ngegh! Ngeigh!

I shake a golden chain for silence,
And speak to them of the still pool
Wherein stands long-legged dawn[9]
The bright and yet the deceiver,
Of the lore of arse-foremost[10]
Of the fire-catching hazel,
Of swift timid bold *Keinach*[11]

Of the sharp tinder holly,
Of the Thunder God
And the riven holm[12]
Of the writhing wryneck
And the artful gowk,[13]

Of bright spangled truit starling
Jabbing in the earth.

I am ceased and silence falls,
My six geese are entrapped!
with a flash in my eyes
And a twist of my neck
My long jaws snap,
And there be five instead of six
Crying, Ngeigh! Ngeigh! Ngeigh!

I lift an arm for silence,
And speak to them of swift-turning
hawk;
Of the secret of the oaken door
And his guardian Druid wren.

I speak of hawthorn the lusty tree,
Of the leaning willow
By deep bright waters,
Of the living pulsating earth
Echoing in the boom of the water
bull[14]
O'er the endless fen;

Of fire-breathing *Drak*
Orange agin the Sun.

I am ceased and silence falls,
My five geese truly enamoured!
I smile most cunningly
I bite the flesh of wisdom
With a click of razor teeth
And there be four instead of five
Crying, Ngeigh! Ngeigh! Ngeigh!

I raise an eyebrow for silence,
And speak to them of high noonday
Of life! Life! Life! Life! Life!
I speak of the alder of *Bran*
The fire tree paddling in the stream;
Of the bright white transparency
Of bright white Nechtan[15]
Of the ash spear encompassed
With an hundred lightnings,
Nuin the ash raised up
Pure straight and tall;
Of the rattling snipe
Chasing his love course
through the azure sky,
Of bright white *Fin*[16]
And of *Nin*, most secret nettle.

I am ceased and silence falls,
My four geese truly enthralled!
I smile most benignly
And strike as the heather ask
A confused blur to mortal sight
And there be three instead of four
Crying, Ngeigh! Ngeigh! Ngeigh!

I wrinkle my nose for silence,
And speak to them of richness and
decline.
I speak of the bright Goddess
And her beloved rowan tree;
I speak of the red King's death[17]
The fall of the mighty lion!
O' dunnock shall Bend His Bow
And *Ruddock* shall fall pierced,[18]
Lugh the bright the powerful
Shall command the Sun go down,
The yew grove shall stand dark
Agin the dying day.

I am ceased and silence falls,
My three geese well ensnared.
I fasten them three
In my deadly stare
And lovingly lean downward
To pluck the first of the wise
Leaving two to cry,
Ngeigh! Ngeigh! Ngeigh!

I lick my lips for silence
And speak to them of the salt sea
Of *Tir-na-Og* and the western door.
I Speak of fear and exaltation
As the sun goes down
As Man in the Moon rides
A cloud-racked sky!
I speak of heather in deep purple
And soft honeysuckle,
Of raven purple and black
Tearing the dead flesh
And lifting his gutteral voice,
Of the hoary Kaledonian pine
Of *Peeswhaup* who will dance[19]
Before the dread door, crying
I know! I know! I know!
Will ye not enter
And taste of the mystery?

There comes utter silence
My two geese are as stone.
Will ye not enter?
Wisdom is death–life life–death;
Truth is now
And I snatch one
Leaving the other to cry,
Nay! Nay! Nay!
You shall not pluck me!
And so-saying,
He flies up into an elder tree.,
Nay! You shall never pluck me!
O' crafty subtle Tod!

Say you so? quoth I;
Why Ngeigh
I shall charm you in
From black water!
What is the dark mirror
Upon whom wisdom rests?
That is but the throat of Hell
The swallower and the disgorger![20]
Then in the twinkling of an eye
My vestments are off;
I stand resplendent in my fine pelt
naked beautiful and strong
In a freezing gale.
But the *Lynn* is an eddyless calm.

I raise my *Bachall*
Become a blackthorn bough
Sprouting life and blood.
Behold, I see the *Korbies*
Massing for Morrigan's feast,[21]
Behold, I hear the *Kwn* running the chase,

Behold, I feel wild Roebuck stamp his feet,
Peeswhaup is spinning and crying
A frenzied endless circle!

I gaze with love, skill and kunning
Upon wisdom in the pool of birth
My eyes send the power songs home
My jaws open in yawning gape
Wisdom flies in from dark waters
Casting off the feathered dress
And crying, Gwyddion! Gwyddion! Gwyddion![22]

I am Tod
Right Reverend Druid of the Wheel.
I stand in the house of beneath
My pelt russet and grey,
Nothing but a crane-skin bag
bulging at my flank.
I have tasted the knowledge,
I have stolen the lore,
I have eaten the flesh,
I have drunk the blood
At the crack of the worlds;
I walk the eternal wheel.

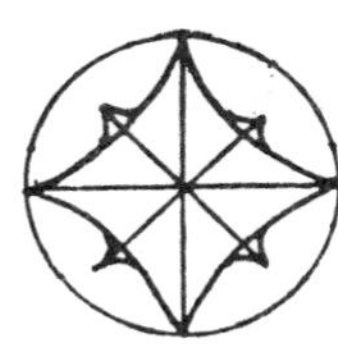

Poem Composed by
THE GREEN KNIGHT ©

Artwork of Tod in the Fiery Wheel
drawn by THE GREEN KNIGHT
(the Original is in Full Colour.)

Tam-y-Lynn

This wonderful ballad from the Borders of Alban is without doubt the most outstanding of the 'supernatural ballads' in the British tradition. It is full of esoteric significance, and in any of its dozen main versions the central storyline has been preserved complete. The rendition reproduced here is labelled 'A' in Childe's collection. Much of the richness and colour of the original language has been retained; footnotes have been provided for those who don't know certain words. My commentary and illumination of its Shamanism is given at the end.

O I forbid you, maidens a',
That wear gowd[1] on your hair,
To come or gae by Carterhaugh[2],
For young Tam Lin is there.

There's nane that gaes by Carterhaugh
But they leave him a wad,[3]
Either their rings, or green mantles,
Or else their maidenhead.

Janet has kilted her green kirtle
A little aboon her knee,[4]
And she has broded[5] her yellow hair
A little aboon her bree[6],
And she's awa to Carterhaugh,
As fast as she can hie.

When she came to Carterhaugh
Tam Lin was at the well,
And there she fand his steed standing,
But away was himsel.

She had na pu'd a double rose,
A rose but only twa,
Till up then started young Tam Lin,
Says, Lady, thou's pu nae mae.

Why pu's thou the rose, Janet,
And why breaks thou the wand[7]?
Or why comes thou to Carterhaugh
Withoutten my command?

'Carterhaugh, it is my ain,
My daddie gave it me;
I'll come and gang by Carterhaugh,
And ask nae leave at thee.'

Janet has kilted her green kirtle
A little aboon her knee,
And she has snooded her yellow hair
A little aboon her bree,
And she is to her father's ha,
As fast as she can hie.[8]

Four and twenty ladies fair
Were playing at the ba,
And out then cam the fair Janet,
Ance the flower amang them a'.

Four and twenty ladies fair
Were playing at the chess,
And out then cam the fair Janet,
As green as onie glass.

Out then spak an auld grey[9] knight,
Lay oer the castle wa,
And sayd, Alas, fair Janet, for thee
But we'll be blamed a'.

'Haud your tongue, ye auld fac'd knigh
Some ill death may ye die!
Father my bairn on whom I will,
I'll father nane on thee.'

Out then spak her father dear,
And he spak meek and mild;
'And ever alas, sweet Janet,' he says,
'I think thou gaes wi child.'

'If that I gae wi child, father,
Mysel maun[10] bear the blame;
There's neer a laird about your ha
Shall get the bairn's name.

'If my love were an earthly knight,
As he's an elfin grey,
I wad na gie my ain true-love
For nae lord that ye hae.

'The steed that my true-love rides on
Is lighter than the wind;
Wi siller he is shod before,
Wi burning gowd behind.'

Janet has kilted her green kirtle
A little aboon her knee,
And she has snooded her yellow hair
A little aboon her bree,
And she's awa to Carterhaugh,
As fast as she can hie.

When she cam to Carterhaugh,
Tam Lin was at the well,
And there she fand[11] his steed standing,
But away was himsel.

She had na pu'd a double rose,
A rose but only twa,
Till up then started young Tam Lin,
Says Lady, thou pu's nae mae.

Why pu's thou the rose, Janet,
Amang the groves sae green,
And a' to kill the bonie babe
That we gat us between?

'O tell me, tell me, Tam Lin,' she says,
'For's sake that died on tree,
If eer ye was in holy chapel,
Or christendom did see?'

'Roxbrugh he was my grandfather,
Took me with him to bide,
And ance it fell upon a day
That wae did me betide.

'And ance it fell upon a day,
A cauld day and a snell[12],
when we were frae the hunting come,
That frae my horse I fell;
The Queen o Fairies she caught me,
In yon green hill to dwell.

'And pleasant is the fairy land,
But, an eerie tale to tell,
Ay at the end of seven years
We pay a tiend to hell[13];
I am sae fair and fu o flesh,
I'm feard it be mysel.

'But the night is Halloween, lady,
The morn is Hallowday;
Then win me, win me, an ye will,
For weel I wat ye may.

'Just at the mirk and midnight hour
The fairy folk will ride,
And they that wad their true-love win,
At Miles Cross they maun bide.'

'But how shall I thee ken, Tam Lin,
Or how my true-love know,
Amang sae mony unco knights
The like I never saw?'

'O first let pass the black, lady,
And syne[14] let pass the brown,
But quickly run to the milk-white steed,
Pu ye his rider down.

Out then spak the Queen o Fairies,
Out of a bush o Broom:
'Them that has gotten young Tam Lin
Has gotten a stately groom.'

Out then spak the Queen o Fairies,
And an angry woman was she
'Shame betide her ill-far'd face,
And an ill death may she die,
For she's taen awa the boniest knight
In a' my companie.

'But had I kend, Tam Lin,' she says,
'What now this night I see,
I wad hae taen out thy twa grey een,
And put in twa een o tree.'

'For I'll ride on the milk-white steed,
And ay nearest the town;
Because I was an earthly knight
They gie me that renown.

'My right hand will be glovd, lady,
My left hand will be bare,
Cockt up shall my bonnet be,
And kaimd down shall my hair,
And thae's the takens I gie thee,
Nae doubt I will be there.

'They'll turn me in your arms, lady,
Into an esk[15] and adder;
But hold me fast, and fear me not,
I am your bairn's father.

'They'll turn me to a bear sae grim,
And then a lion bold;
But hold me fast, and fear me not,
As ye shall love your child.

'Again they'll turn me in your arms
To a red het gaud of airn;[16]
But hold me fast, and fear me not,
I'll do to you nae harm.

'And last they'll turn me in your arms
Into the burning gleed[17];
Then throw me into well water,
O throw me in wi speed.

'And then I'll be your ain true-love.
I'll turn a naked knight;
Then cover me wi your green mantle,
And cover me out o sight.'

Gloomy, gloomy was the night,
And eerie was the way,
As fair Jenny in her green mantle
To Miles Cross she did gae.

About the middle o the night
She heard the bridles ring;
This lady was as glad at that
As any earthly thing.

First she let the black pass by,
and syne she let the brown;
But quickly she ran to the milk-white steed,
And pu'd the rider down.

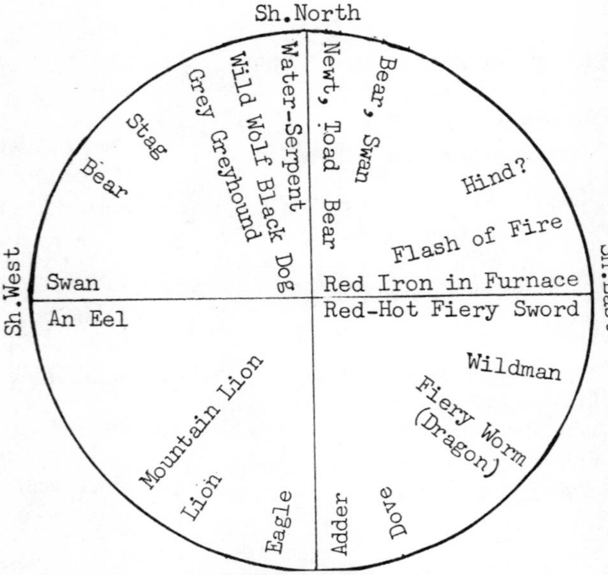

Sae weel she minded whae he did say,
And young Tam Lin did win;
Syne coverd him wi her green mantle,
As blythe's[18] a bird in spring.

Out then spak the Queen o Fairies,
Out of a bush o Broom:
'Them that has gotten young Tam Lin
Has gotten a stately groom.'

Out then spak the Queen o Fairies,
And an angry woman was she
'Shame betide her ill-far'd face,
And an ill death may she die,
For she's taen awa the boniest knight
In a' my companie.

'But had I kend, Tam Lin,' she says,
'What now this night I see,
I wad hae taen out thy twa grey een,
And put in twa een o tree.'

The complete story emerges if we piece together several of the parallel versions of this important ballad. How Tam-y-Lynn came to be enchanted and put under spells is revealed in version (I): 'There came a wind out of the North, A sharp wind and a snell, And a deep sleep came over me, And frae my horse I fell. The Queen of Fairies keppit me In yon green hill to dwell.' This 'green hill' is obviously a *Dun Sidhe*, a Faerie knoll; and the whole event was meant to have occurred next to a 'lady well' (Goddess fountain or *Lynn*); whether or not this was the well Tam-y-Lynn was later to guard we are not told (but I would presume so). That Tam-y-Lynn was not the knight's original name, but rather his title as 'the Guardian of the *Lynn* [Well]', needs to be emphasised. Also, the image of a well as a watery shaft surrounded by a stonework wall needs to be discarded, for the well may really have been like the sacred one I took my group to earlier this year, a large circular pond with an underwater central spring, the whole thing being sunk down into the ground, providing earthen banking, surrounded by trees (much more of a natural Shamanistic *Lynn* inhabited by frogs, and frequented as a drinking-place by other animals).

When maidens came to this *Lynn* for water or to bathe, they were expected to leave a token to the guardian (Tam-y-Lynn), especially if they had been presumptuous enough to have picked some of the blossoms from the Faerie rose/thorn bush. In Janet's case what she gave up was her maidenhead, as we hear in (I,10): 'He's taen her by the milk-white hand, Amang the leaves sae green, And what they did I cannot tell, The green leaves were inbetween.' Anyway, as Tam-y-Lynn and Janet appear to have fallen in love, this seems to have been quite fine. Tam-y-Lynn then relates his plan of escape, for he fears the Faerie tithe to the underworld (not 'Hell' as the Christian redactors have distorted it). Thus, on Samhain at a crossroads (anciently a geomantically 'betwixt and between' power-spot) Janet 'casts the magic circle round herself' and waits until: 'Betwixt the hours of twelve and one, A North wind tore the bent, And straight she heard Strange *Elritch* [elvish] sounds Upon that wind which went.' At the right moment she grabbed Tam-y-Lynn off his white steed and held onto him whilst the Faerie Queen tried to scare her into desisting by transforming her lover into various Faerie forms (taken from the Shamanistic Wheel). Other commentators have lacked the proper keys to indicate how all the forms mentioned in the various ballad versions represent *exact* Shamanistic Stations, not just vague notions; the above wheel that I've constructed proves this conclusively.

The Great MacVurich and the Faerie Mother-Beist

This Gaelic tale of a Shamanistic encounter was printed in Carmichael's Carmina Gadelica Vol. 5 in both Ghaidhlig and English. As it is given below I have improved some of the translation and a little of the style. If I had had more time I would have also tackled some of the inaccuracies in the translation of the verses into English.

Great MacVurich was out in the hill hunting for venison. He got a royal stag, and after gralloching the stag he slung the venison on his back. The man had to pass to the left of Loch Druidibig with the royal stag on his back.

In a cranny at the edge of the loch what should the man see but a tiny little creature. He lifted the poor little creature away with him in his breast and thus brought home the *Beist's* child. Hardly had he brought it home than the Mother-*Beist* came to the window and called out with a loud angry voice?, 'Out with my whelp, Great MacVurich!'

'For a bargain, *Beist*.'

'Out with my whelp, Great MacVurich, or the highest stone in thine ugly dwelling shall be the lowest stone in its foundation.'

'For a bargain,' said MacVurich.

'What is thy bargain, thou dirty rascal?' said the Beist.

'That thou build me a causeway across Loch Stadhlabhal on which my peats may be brought home and on which my cattle and sheep, my horses and goats, may pass back and fore without a white or red one among them.'

'Alas! alas!' said the *Beist*, 'though hard the task, it is better to fulfil it,' said she.

In the middle of the night the *Beist* came and called out at the window, 'That is ready, Great MacVurich; out with my bouncing boy.'

'No, except for a bargain,' said Great MacVurich.

'Let me hear thy terms, thou wicked man,' said the *Beist*.

'That thou bring home every single peat I have on the hill slope and make a stack of them on the hill at the end of the house.'

'Alas! alas! though the causeway was hard, harder still is it to bring the peats home and make them into a stack at the end of the house. But though the task is hard, it is better to fulfil it,' said she, setting out to the hill.

The *Beist* then came a third time and called out at the window, 'Great MacVurich, out with my bouncing pleasant boy, that is done.'

'Not yet, except for a bargain,' said Great MacVurich.

'Let me hear thy bargain, thou wicked man,' said the *Beist*.

'That thou build me a dwelling-house with nine couples in its roof, thatched with birds' feathers and no two feathers of the same hue.'

'Hard is the form of thy bargain, MacVurich,' said the *Beist*.

'Hard is the form of necessity, *Beist*,' said MacVurich.

The *Beist* laid the foundations of the house fairly neatly, and began on the mason-work; and Mary, Mary! 'tis herself that had the hand for it! There was but the one song coming from her mouth, she was ever crooning and murmuring thus:

'Clach air muin cloiche,
Clach air muin a dhà;
Càir mar sin na clacha
'S bidh am balla slàn.

'Stone on top of stone,
Stone on top of two;
Set the stones thus
And the wall will be complete.

'Clach air muin cloiche,
Clach ghlas r'h taobh;
Clach air muin cloiche,
Clach ghlas 'na h-aor.

'Stone on top of stone,
Grey stone by its side;
Stone on top of stone,
Grey stone to build it.

'Clach ri aghaidh cloiche,
Clach ri aghaidh dhà;
Clach ri aghaidh cloiche,
'S bidh am balla 'n aird.

'Stone in front of stone,
Stone in front of two;
Stone in front of stone;
And the wall will be up.

'Clach air muin cloiche,
Pinne chur san toll,
Leagan air gach leagan
Bho bhràigh gu bonn.

'Stone on top of stone,
A peg placed in the hole,
Layer upon layer
From the top to the base.

'Cabar ris a' chabar,
Sgrath air muin sgrath,
Reang air gach reang,
Criadh air criadh crath. [Gu cumail diar a mach

'Beam set to beam,
Divot upon divot,
Pole upon pole,
Clay on clay shake. [To keep out the drip

'It' air muin iteach
Bho 'n taobh a steach,
Sgrith sgrath sgolban
Bho 'n taobh a mach.

'Feather upon feathers
From the inside,
Gravel(?), divot, wooden wattle
From the outside.

'Sgrith sgrath sgolban
Gu ceann taigh a' chealgair,
Sgrios na nathrach obann [odhar
Air bogha a'bhalgair. [bhobag

'Gravel(?), divot, wooden wattle
To the roof of the deceiver's house,
The sudden destruction of the serpent [dun
On the scoundrel's vaulted roof.

'Gach fiodh sa choill ach fiodhagach, [itheagach
Gach fiodh sa choill ach fiodhagach,
Gach fiodh sa choill
Gu taigh na foill [Mhic Raing
Ach critheann chroinn is fiodhagach.' [eidheann, iubhar cam, draigheann dreang

'Every timber in the wood save the wild fig,
Every timber in the wood save the wild fig,
Every timber in the wood
To the house of treachery [Ranking
Save the aspen of the cross and the wild fig.' [ivy,
crooked yew, blackthorn

Thus she sang and sought until the house was finished. There was not Mother-bird in the beautiful blue sky that did not come with a feather to help with the thatching of the house, out of compassion for the Mother-*Beist*.

The *Beist* then came some time before cock-crow and she called out at the window and said, 'That is done, MacVurich; out with my whelp.'

'Here is thy whelp, thou great sly Bear-*Beist*, and let me not see thine eye or thy nose, thy paw or thy face, on this ground ever again.' And so saying MacVurich Mór of Stiligarry thrust the great *Beist's* offspring out at the window.

'Alas! alas!' said she, 'though the other conditions were hard, this is the worst predicament of all.' And she lifted the whelp on to her shoulders.

The *Beist* placed her little one on the ridge of her back, and singing the song that was in her head, she set foot:

'Is fada bhuam fhìn bonn Beinn Eadarra,
'S fada gun teagamh uam Bealach a' Mhorghain,

'Far from me is the base of Beinn Eadarra,
Far from me undoubtedly is Bealach a' Mhorghain,

Cul nam monaidhean, bràigh nam bealaichean,
Bonn nam bearraichean's Bealach a' Mhorghain.'

The back of the hills, the slope c the passes,
The base of the cliffs and Bealacl a' Mhorghain.'

Perhaps the first thing we need to do to put this Tale in context is to realiz that within the MacVurich (MacMurray) Clan there was a hereditary strea of Bards and Initiates practising Druidical Shamanism. This is nc speculation, but documentated historical fact. (That is not to say that the were not many ordinary peasant MacMurray clans-folk as well.) There we several of these MacVurich Initiates, and stories about their exploits are nc always clearly distinguished chronologically. More than one of the MacVu rich Initiates had dealings with the Faerie Wildfolk; one MacVurich wa reported to have gone daily up to the Faerie knoll with offerings of drops c milk and crumbs of bread for the rock spirits, the *Fridich nan Kreag*, (this kep him on good terms with these beings, who returned their magical blessings) as noted in chapter 6 page 143, another Chief of the MacVurichs, *Fear a Tom Dreis*, ('Man of the Bramble Knoll'), could Druidically produce winc from any quarter by moving the offerings made to the Wildfolk in the ston cups and basins. In this case MacVurich Mór blackmails the Faerie *Beist* int doing a prodigious amount of work. Indeed, the Edwardian and Victoria editors (good Presbyterians to a man) would have been fairer if they ha denomenated MacVurich as a bit of a 'monster', for he continually broke o changed his word; rather than the Faerie being (which I have preferred to leav in the Gaelic term *Beist*), for it kept its word at every turn. (Similar conduc can be noted in white man's broken 'treaties' with the native Red Indians.

Anyway, the Faerie *Beist* seems to have been a supernatural form of bea and may thus be similar to some of the bear-like creatures portrayed on Pictis symbol stones (from the same area and possibly the same period as the Tale) MacVurich Mór comes over as something of a bully as a ritual magician, fo the best Shamans prefer to be on better terms with their Otherworld allies That the Mother-*Beist* is being somewhat unfairly treated is supported by th fact that every mother-bird in the sky came and gave of its feathers out o compassion for the Mother-*Beist*.

Finally, the Victorian translators of the last two verses of poetry (and mor recent academics) have gone seriously wrong in their translation: having buil the house in the way described, I do not think the Faerie *Beist* was bein treacherous. In that it built the 'top of the dwelling' (*Kean Taigh*) in a certai way, and in leaving certain woods out of its construction, the redactor assumed the *Beist* was working a deception. I tend to think the very opposite I believe it may have been acting in kindness to construct a more pleasan dwelling (for most of the woods left out have Shamanistic West–North characteristics; whilst linking the roof to the arch of the sky, lightning and th serpent powers need not be bad for those who can work with Shamanisti South qualities).

Irrespective of the exact significances, in the end, when MacVurich obtain all his demands, he banishes the Bear-*Beist* and her whelp from their favourite hills and Glens. (Perhaps it is no karmic coincidence that latter highlanc history was to put all too similar a banishment on all too many Gaels.)

The Black Lad Of Loch Dring

The following short Gaelic Tales from the Western Highlands represent some of the clearest accounts of encounters with a Faerie Wildman. It is also important for Keltic spirituality that we note that even beings from Shamanistic North, 'Black Wildmen', etc., can be kind, gentle and benificent to those whom they feel deserve such treatment.

There was once a man of North Assynt whose name was Mac an Air.[1] It was said that this man was the father, and that a fairy-woman[2] was the mother of the Black Lad[3] [of Loch Dring[4]], but whether or no, the Black Lad has been seen on various occasions on the moors of the Highlands, particularly in the district of Loch Dring in Gairloch.

There was another man called Mulmoire MacRath[5] who dwelt at one time in Sannda of Gairloch, who [in the summer time] used to take his herds to the sheilings in the district of Loch Dring. He had a lassie for a servant whose name was Big Speedy-Foot[6] (*lit.* The Big Walker). One of this man's cattle went astray, and so his wife went in search of it. When Big Speedy-Foot grew weary of waiting for her mistress, and was beginning to think she was never coming back home, she also set forth. A certain little child, a daughter of Mulmoire's, beginning to wonder because neither her mother nor Big Speedy-Foot were returning, set forth after them; but the child had not gone far, when she got lost in the woods[7]. Then it was that the Black Lad, wearing a great headdress made of moss, which was bound about his head with a fillet of rushes[8], met her. He filled her arms full of flowers[9], and told her that her mother and Big Speedy-Foot had got home again and had brought the cow with them. He then set her safely on the road home.[10]

There used to be a big wild sort of man wandering about Gairloch called Murdoch the Minister, who lived on the peasantry. Murdoch was an exceedingly strong, wild man, who wore a suit of armour heavier than anyone else could wear.[11] On one occasion when roaming over the mountains, night overtook him when in the Loch Dring district, and he was obliged to seek rest in a deserted bothy. There was a certain great fierce bull, that used to attack people, and from which everyone used to flee; but Murdoch was so strong that he would wrestle with it until the animal of its own accord, ceased raging.[12] On the night in question the Black Lad met Murdoch, and there was a bitter fight between them[13], but it is very little that Murdoch would ever tell about it. He would sometimes remark that the Black Lad's eyes were as broad as plates. And people began to ask him 'Wert thou afraid, Murdoch?'

'There certainly was cause of fear,' Murdoch would answer, 'if there had been anyone to feel it.'[14]

The Laird of Sannda had Loch Dring for a summer grazing place or sheiling. He hapened to be passing over the mountains once, when night overtook him, and he was obliged to pass it in the Sheiling bothy. He was so thirsty that milk could not quench his thirst: he therefore asked one of his servants to go to the Well of Dringag for a drink of water; but not one of them would go for fear of the Black Lad. When they all refused, he was obliged to go himself; and according to the story I heard, he did not come back till

> daybreak. No one ever found out what sort of a fight took place between hir and the Black Lad: but in any case, the Black Lad was not see in the Loc Dring district for a long time afterwards. It was said that the Laird of Sannd wrung a promise from the Black Lad to leave the place; and that thereafter was in Assynt (his father's country) that the Black Lad was to be seen.[15]
>
> But long after the death of the Laird of Sannda, there was a cattle-herd i the Loch Dring district, called Big Deaf Hector, of whom it is related that h himself and his family had seen the Black Lad about the house, more tha once.[16]

It is worth reflecting upon *an Gille Dubh* (the Black Wildmans') attitudes to various humans; and different individuals' attitudes to the Black Lad.

Towards innocent young children (who bring no bad conditioning to the encounter) the Black Wildman will often show gentle kindness and humour, playing and sometimes even dancing with such youngsters. Towards a strong, upright and noble individual following the path of native Shamanism/ Druidism/Paganism/Esoteric Christianity, after an initial tussle of strength (to test worthiness), the Black Wildman is likely to act as a fierce but friendly guide and teacher of the mysteries. As for the frightened and misinformed members of the general public, the Black Lads are never likely to go anywhere near such folk, nor would the humans be likely to see such a being if passing by in a certain place. Towards powerful but unsympathetic individuals, the *Gille Dubh* is likely to agree to move out of the way and not trouble such an individual (but neither would he be available to help in magical tight-spots).

Of course, most ordinary folk would consider leaving such Otherworld beings well alone – fair enough. Even for those courageous enough to wish to attempt a contact with one of the Wildfolk, there are not many healthy 'wild' places left – and you have to be in the right place, at the right time, in the right state of personal-power. And to gain that personal-power may well require many years of careful training.

The Great Tuairisgeal Wildman and his Shamanistic Slaying

There was once a King of Erin, who was out of doors one day and had come to a certain hillock[1], when a rider met him there. 'Who art thou?' said the King.

'I,' said he, 'am the Young Tuairisgeal, the son of the Great Tuairisgeal[2].'

The [Young] Tuairisgeal asked the King to come and gamble with him on the morrow. On the morrow, accordingly, the King went to gamble with the Young Tuairisgeal. They played the game through, and the game went against the Tuairisgeal.[3]

'Take [the winnings of] thy gaming, King of Erin,' said the Young Tuairisgeal.

'The stake of my gaming is that I get the young woman whom thou hast there with thee.' He got the woman, and took her away with him.

'Now,' said she to the King, 'tomorrow thou wilt go again to engage in a gambling with the [Young] Tuairisgeal, and if thou win, demand from him as the stakes of thy gaming, the palfrey he has.'

On the morrow, the King went to meet the [Young] Tuairisgeal. They met each other at the hillock. 'Wilt come and play a game of chess[4] with me today?' said the Young Tuairisgeal.

'I will,' said the King.

They played the game through, and the game went against the [Young] Tuairisgeal. 'Take the stakes of thy gaming,' said the Young Tuairisgeal.

'The stakes of my gaming are that I get that palfrey of thine,' said the King. The Young Tuairisgeal gave the King of Erin the palfrey by the bridle (*lit.* the head).

Home went the King. 'Now,' said the woman, 'tomorrow thou wilt go again to gamble with the Young Tuairisgeal, but he will defeat thee, and he will lay binding spells upon thee that thou bring him word as to how his father, the Great Tuairisgeal, was put to death. And thou on thy part, shalt lay binding spells upon him that he shall lie stretched out on the hillock and propped up on his elbow until thou return.[5]

On the morrow, the King of Erin went to the hillock to hold a gaming with the Young Tuairisgeal. They met each other at the hillock.

'Wilt thou come [and play a game of chess with me today?' said the Young Tuairisgeal.]

'I will,' [said the King. They engaged in the game, but the Young Tuairisgeal won the game that day, and, for the King, that was indeed a cursed victory.]

'Take the stakes of thy gaming,' said the King of Erin.

'These are the stakes of my gaming – to lay thee under binding spells to

In the Scottish Gaelic tradition this Tale is known as 'the Chief Tale' or 'the Great Story', not only because it is a mighty good Tale, but also because it employs many of the key motifs in the Keltic spiritual tradition. Whilst being intellectually complex, the storyline also moves along at a cracking pace.

bring me word how my father, the Great Tuairisgeal, was put to death [and to bring his sword of light with thee, also[6]].'

'Then I lay thee under binding spells, that thou lie there stretched out on this hillock, and propped up on thine elbow, till I return.'

Home went the King of Erin. 'Now,' said the woman to him, 'thou must mount the palfrey's back, and visit the kingdom of Greece[7], and there thou wilt discover how the Great Tuairisgeal was put to death. There is not a living man in that kingdom who will not come to meet thee when they recognize the palfrey[8].'

On the morrow, the King mounted the palfrey, and departed. He travelled on till he came to the house of the Fair Knight[9]. The Fair Knight recognized the palfrey, and came forward to meet the King.

'What news hast thou? has thou tidings of my sister?' said the Fair Knight.

'I have,' said he, 'I have her at home in my house.'

'Thou must stay with me tonight,' said the Fair Knight. The Fair Knight laid hold of the palfrey, and ordered it into the stable, and took the King of Erin with him into the castle. He ordered food and drink to be set before him. This was done. The King ate and drank, and passed the night very pleasantly with the Fair Knight. Early in the morning, the King rose to depart. The Fair Knight also rose to see that he was well provided for. The King took food, and then they brought him the palfrey. 'Now,' said the Fair Knight, 'thou wilt be in the house of the White Knight tonight, and when he sees the palfrey, thou wilt be hailed as a chief, and welcome will await thee.' The King and the Fair Knight left farewell blessings with each other, and the King went off.

On and on he travelled, swiftly and cheerily, and never a stay did he make till he came to the house of the White Knight[11]. The White Knight met him, and laid hold of the palfrey. 'Hast thou tidings of my sister?' said the White Knight. 'That have I; I left her at home in my own house,' said the King of Erin. 'Thou shalt stay with me tonight,' said the White Knight. 'I will,' answered the King of Erin. [The White Knight ordered the palfrey into the stable, and took the King of Erin with him into the castle. He ordered food and drink to be set before him. This was done. The King ate and drank, and passed the night very pleasantly with the White Knight.] Early in the morning, [the King rose to go. The White Knight rose also to see that he was well provided for. The King took food, and then they brought him the palfrey. 'Now,' said the White Knight,] 'tonight thou wilt be in the house of the Black Knight, and he is the one who will tell thee what thou oughtest to do. When he sees the palfrey, thou wilt be hailed as a chief, and welcome will await thee.' The King and the White Knight left farewell blessings with each other, and the King mounted the palfrey, and was off.

On and on he travelled, swiftly and cheerily, never stopping nor taking ease till he came to the house of the Black Knight[12]. [The Black Knight recognized the palfrey, and came forward to meet the King.] 'Hast thou tidings of my sister?' [said the Black Knight.

'That have I; I left her at home in my own house,' said the King of Erin. 'Thou shalt stay with me tonight,' said the Black Knight. 'I will,' said the King of Erin. The Black Knight laid hold of the palfrey, and ordered her into the stable, and took the King of Erin with him into the castle. He ordered food and drink to be set before him. This was done. The King ate and drank, and passed the night very pleasantly with the Black Knight.] Early in the morning [the King rose to go. The Black Knight rose also to see that he was well provided for. The King took food, and then they brought him the palfrey.]

'Now,' said the Black Knight, 'there is a river[13] before thee or ever thou come to the kingdom of Greece. Thou art to take with thee nine bottles of wine, and nine wheaten loaves, and when thou arrivest at the river, thou shalt give the palfrey three loaves of bread and three bottles of wine, and thou shalt comb her hair the wrong way and then the right way, and if she will not then leap the river, thou must give her more [food and combing] until she does leap it.'[14] The King and the Black Knight then left farewell blessings with each other, and the King set forth.

On and on he travelled, swiftly and cheerily, never stopping nor taking ease until he came to the river. When he arrived there, he dismounted and gave the palfrey three bottles of wine and three wheaten loaves, and combed her hair the wrong way, and then the right way. When she had taken all that (wine, loaves, and the combing) he mounted her back, and made an attempt to leap the river, but all she did was to dip her head in it – nothing more. He dismounted, and gave her three more bottles of wine and three more wheaten loaves, and combed [her hair the wrong way and then the right way]. Again he mounted her back, and again he tried to leap the river, but all she did was to go up to her belly in it. Down he came again, and gave her three more bottles [of wine and three more wheaten loaves], and combed [her hair the wrong way and then the right way]. Then once more he mounted her back and tried again to leap the river, and this time she went over it.[15]

The Young King of Greece[16] saw the palfrey leaping the river, and set off to meet them.

[The palfrey saw him coming, and well she knew what he wanted.] 'Thou must hand me over, thou must give me to him in exchange for information as to how the Great Tuairisgeal was put to death,' said the palfrey to the King of Erin.

The King of Erin gave the palfrey to the King of Greece accordingly, and the King of Greece informed him where the man was who had put the Great Tuairisgeal to death.

He went into a house which the King of Greece had pointed out to him, and there [he found] an old man lying in a cradle[17]. The old man arose, and set forth with him. They never stopped till they came to a house situated in a certain glen. The old man opened the door, and they went in. He gave the King of Erin a golden chair, but seated himself in a silver one[18], and then did he begin to tell how the [Great] Tuairisgeal was [put] to death.

'A tale more painful than ear ever heard am I now going to tell thee. There was once a King of Greece who had three sons. His wife died, and he married another. The Young Queen was a bad step-mother[19]: and she turned the King's three children into three wolves[20].

'At that, the three fled to a mountain.

'She told [people] that there were three wild wolves killing the sheep belonging to her, and that these wolves must be killed.

'She sent blood-hounds and terriers off to the mountain. The blood-hounds followed the wolves, and killed two of them. The one who survived went to a rock, and got into the nest of a *Geere-veenach*[21], and stayed there for ten days. A ship went by, and passed close to the rock. The wolf gave a great howl of grief when he saw the ship. When the captain heard him, he sent two of the hands in a yawl[22] to fetch him. They saw the wolf putting out his tongue, and they brought the yawl close in and under the place where he was. When he saw the yawl coming close in under him, the wolf let himself fall down the rock, and into the yawl. They then took the yawl back to the ship. The *Geere-veenach* followed the vessel, but one of the hands snatched up a handspike in his fist, and kept her away. Then they fetched the wolf on board. They gave him some broth, but he would not touch that. Then they gave him the proper food (for dogs), and of that he ate some.[24]

'It was in another kingdom situated in Greece, that the vessel came to land. It was his [the wolf's] own father's brother who was King there. His father's brother, who was newly married, took the wolf from the master of the ship, and brought him to his own household.[25]

'His [the King's] wife was pregnant at the time, and in a short time she was delivered of a girl-child. There were three midwives waiting upon the Queen and upon the child. In came a Great Claw-like Hand[26] through the roof of the house, which seized the child, and took it away. The midwives did not know what to do, for it was they who had let the child go. They went, and killed a young cockerel, and rubbed the blood upon the wolf's teeth. They told his father's brother that the wolf had eaten the child, and that it ought to be burnt.

'But his father's brother's wife said that the wolf should be let alone until she should be pregnant again, and that when they would see what would happen. In time, she became pregnant again, and had a man-child.[27] The midwives were waiting upon her and upon the child. They never took any thought about what had happened before. In through the roof of the house came the Claw-like Hand and took the child away. The midwives killed a young cockerel as they had done before, and then clapping their hands (in grief), cried out that the crop-eared wolf had eaten the child. So now in any case, the wolf was to be put to death.

'But his [the wolf's] father's brother said that he would go to the smithy, and have an iron fastening made for him, and that they would forgive him on this occasion also. So his father's brother went to the smithy, and got the smith to make a strong iron leash, with which he fastened him. In course of time, the Queen was delivered again. The midwives were attending upon her and the child as usual. They never took a thought about what had happened before. In through the roof of the house came the Claw-like Hand and took the child away. But the wolf saw it. And breaking the iron leash, he leaped at the thing, and biting it through with his teeth, tore it off [from the shoulder][28]

'[He and the Claw-like Hand fell down on the floor, and before he could awake from his stunned condition, the Great Tuairisgeal, the giant who was outside, put in his other Claw-like Hand, and took away the child.[29] The wolf dragged the Claw-like Hand he had bitten off under the bed, and put it in a vessel.[30] The midwives killed a cockerel, beat their palms, and shouted that the wolf had eaten the child.]

'He was now to be burnt in any case. On the morrow, they began kindling a fire to burn him, and he was hiding under the cloak of his father's brother. [Then he fled to the hill.] When he perceived that the fire was now ready for him to be thrown on to it, he came back home, fetched the Claw-like Hand out of vessel and placed it before his father's brother.[31]

'"That shows that it was thou who wert faithful to me," said his father's brother. There was now no mention of burning him.

'His father's brother got a yawl the next day, and put out to sea. He saw an island, and went to it. Upon going ashore, he saw a castle in the island. He made for the castle, and went in. What should he see there, but the Great Tuairisgeal, asleep, and his own children along with him. He saw [the *or* a?] sword of light on a shelf[32]. He seized the sword of light, cut the Tuairisgeal's throat, and struck his head from off his neck. In the castle he found a magic wand[33]. He took his three children, the sword of light, the magic wand, and the head of the Great Tuairisgeal, and put them on board the yawl. Then he returned home.

'When he returned to land, the wolf met him. The King struck him with the magic wand, and he turned into a handsome and comely youth[34]. When he had become a handsome and comely youth, his father's brother said to him, 'Thou art the King of Greece.'

'On the morrow, he and his father's brother set forth, and arrived in the kingdom of Greece. They killed every man in Greece who raised a hand against them, and they burnt the stepmother. He [the late wolf] was crowned King over Greece that day.[35]

'Come! let us go over, and see if we can find the head of the Great Tuairisgeal ...'

They went over to a clump of rushes. Underneath the clump of rushes[36] there was a cauldron, and in the cauldron was the head of the Great Tuairisgeal. With a heave, the old man lugged it up out of the cauldorn, and handed it to the King of Erin, and with it he gave him the sword of light – 'Tell the Young Tuairisgeal,' said he, 'that it was I who slew the Great Tuairisgeal.'[37]

The King of Erin, taking the head and the sword with him, departed.[38] At the river of Greece, he met the palfrey. He mounted her back, and over the river she sprang. The same evening he was in the house of the Black Knight, and right hospitably was he treated there. He and the Black Knight spent the night gaily and merrily, with drinking and with music and with feasting. In the morning, the King arose and set out, and the next evening he was in the house of the White Knight, and was treated there no less hospitably. In the morning he rose and departed, and the third evening he was in the house of the Fair Knight. If he was treated hospitably by the other two Knights, he was certainly treated every whit as well in the house of the Fair Knight. They passed [the night gaily and merrily, with drinking, with music, and with feasting. In the morning the King arose.]

'Now,' said the Fair Knight, 'when thou comest to the end of thy journey thou wilt find that the Young Tuairisgeal has become a mere heap of bones on the hillock. Shout at him that thou hast come – shout again that thou hast come – shout the third time that thou has come. He will then raise himself up on his elbow on the hillside, and demand that the sword of his father be given to him. Do thou then hand him the sword, but when doing so, strike off his head; otherwise, it is thou who wilt get short shrift.' The King and the Fair Knight then left farewell blessings with each other.

The King came to the hill where the Young Tuairisgeal lay. Three times did he shout at him that he had come. At the third shout, the [Young] Tuairisgeal sat up on his elbow, and desired him to give him his father's sword. The King handed him the sword, but when in the act of doing so, struck off his head.[39]

Then he [the King] went home, but when he arrived, not a trace of his wife could he find.[40]

He went off in pursuit of his wife, and pressed on till he came to the house of the Blue-eyed Hawk of Slieve Brat. The Blue-eyed Hawk of Slieve Brat invited him to stay with him that night, and said that he thought the King a much better subject for hospitality than the Great Giant[41] who had had with him the King's prospective wife and lover. The King stayed that night in the house of the Blue-eyed Hawk of Slieve Brat.

In the morning when he was going, the Blue-eyed Hawk of Slieve Brat said to him, 'If any crisis come upon thee, remember me and I will be with thee.' He left a farewell blessing with the Hawk, and went off.

At night he came to the house of the Short-tailed Grey Hound of the Green Wood[42]. The Short-tailed Grey Hound of the Green Wood invited him in, and said that he thought the King a much better subject for hospitality than [the Great Giant who had had with him the King's prospective wife and lover. He stayed that night in the house of the Short-tailed Grey Hound of the Green Wood. In the morning, when he was departing, the Short-tailed Grey Hound of the Green Wood said to him, 'If any crisis come upon thee, remember me and I will be with thee].' He left a farewell blessing [with the Hound, and set forth].

At night time, he came to the house of the Otter of Rapid Stream[43]. [The Otter of Rapid Stream] invited him in, and said that he thought him a much better subject for hospitality than the Great Giant who had had with him the King's prospective wife and lover. He stayed that night in the house of the Otter of Rapid Stream. In the morning, when he was going, the Otter of Rapid Stream said to him, 'If any crisis come upon thee, remember me and I will be with thee.'] He left a farewell blessing [with the Otter, and departed].

That night he came to the house of the Giant, and there indoors he saw his own wife. She put him into a hiding place.

When the Giant came home, she said to him, 'If I only knew where thou keepest thy life [or soul] I would cover the place with branching tracery and pictures[44].'

The Giant named a place to her, and on the morrow, when he had left the house, she and the King of Erin decorated the place splendidly.

When the Giant came home, the ornamental work pleased him greatly. He said that that was not the place where his life was kept, but that it was in the stump of a tree; that there was a ram inside the stump; a wild duck inside the ram; an egg inside the duck; and that his life was in the egg.[45]

When the Giant had left the house on the morrow, he [the King of Erin] took an axe[46], and began to split that stump to pieces. Out of the stump leaped a ram, and the ram headed straight for the mountain.

'If I only had the Short-tailed Grey Hound of the Green Wood now, he would not be long in catching the ram.' He had scarcely said the word, when the Short-tailed Grey hound of the Green Wood came, bringing the ram with him in his mouth.[47]

They seized hold of the ram and split it open, and when they had done so, a wild duck leaped out of it. 'How useful would the Blue-eyed Hawk of Slieve Brat be now,' said he. Scarcely had he allowed the word to pass his lips when up came the Blue-eyed Hawk of Slieve Brat, bringing the wild duck[48] with him.

When they had split the duck open, they found an egg inside it, and when they broke the egg, a trout leaped out of it into the river. 'Good were now the Otter of Rapid Stream,' said he [the King of Erin]. He had scarcely said the word, when up came the Otter of Rapid Stream, bringing the trout[49] with him in his mouth. He seized the trout, and killed it, and the Giant fell dead at that very moment[50].

The King then took his wife with him, and came home to Erin. He sent word for his brothers to come, and she and he married. They had a merry and cheerful wedding, food and drink in plenty, inward contentment, music and dancing.[51]

The Queen of the Many-Coloured Bedchamber (The Rainbow-hued Bower)

Unlike the previous Tale, this one has been put into immaculate flowing gracious English, which more faithfully mirrors the dexterity of the original Gaelic. Perhaps the most astonishing thing about this Tale, however, is the graphic clarity with which it describes psychic happenings, some of which I know to be accurate to such experiences.

One day in the long ago, the sun shone down upon a green wood whose mightiest trees have since rotted at the bottom of the ocean, where the best masts find a grave. While the sunlight slept on the bosom of the foliage, a horseman galloped in the shade beneath. The great chief Fion, son of Cumhail, was looking for his knights, whom he had outstripped in the hunt.

He reined in his steed in a broad glade, and blew his bugle loud and clear. Beside the echoes repeated among the hillsides, there was no answering call. He rode on, pausing now and again to blow another and another bugle-blast, but always with the same result.

At length the wood grew more scattered, and presently he came out upon a stretch of plain where the grass was so green that it looked like emerald; and beyond it in the distance, at the end of the sloping plain, he could see the seashore, and the ocean rising like a wall of sapphire up to the farthest horizon.

Down by the shore he could see figures moving, and, thinking that his knights had found their way thither, he rode like the wind down the long, gentle slope towards them. As he drew nearer and nearer, he saw that there were twelve[1] of them, and they were playing at ball. By the mighty strokes they gave with the *coman*[2] he guessed that these were the twelve sons of Bawr Sculloge[3], for none but them could drive the ball so high and far. Tremendous were their strokes, and, when they ran after the ball, they outstripped the wind.

As Fion drew rein and dismounted, they stopped their play; and, drawing near, welcomed him loudly as the helper of the weak, and the protector of the green island against the white-faced stranger.

When he had returned their greeting, they invited him to join them in their game – if such an amusement was agreeable to him.

'Fion, son of Cumhail,' said one, 'here, take my *coman* and wipe away the vanity and conceit of all comers, for we are practising for a great contest.'

Fion took the *coman* and looked at it, holding it up between his finger and thumb.[4]

'I doubt if I could do much good with this plaything,' said Fion; 'it would break at first blow if I were to strike at all hard.'

'Never let that stand in the way,' returned the other. 'Wait!'

He then searched upon the ground among the blades of grass, and at length found a nettle, which he pulled up by the roots. Having breathed a charm over it, he passed it three times from one hand to the other, and lo, it was changed into a mighty *coman*[5], fit for the hand of Fion, son of Cumhail.

Then they were amazed at his terrific blows. The ball, struck by Fion, soared almost out of sight in the sky, and fell to earth far off. But, each time, the fleet-footed sons of Bawr Sculloge retrieved it.

At last Fion bared his arm to the shoulder, and, with a final blow, sent the ball out of sight. None saw it go; none saw it fall. They all stood and looked at each other.[6]

'My hand on it,' said the eldest son of Bawr, advancing to Fion. 'I live to admit that I never saw the game played till today.'

As they were speaking, a voice hailed them; and, turning seawards, they saw a small boat approaching. As soon as it touched the beach, a man sprang ashore, and hastened towards them.

'Hail! Fion, son of Cumhail!' he cried. 'You are known to me, though not I to you. My lady, the Queen of Sciana Breaca,[7] lays a knight's task upon you. Hasten forthwith, and have speech with her on her island.[8] The hand of Flat Ear the Witch is upon her, and her chiefs have advised her to summon you to her aid.'

'I know it,' replied Fion. 'The Salmon of Wisdom, which comes up from the sea, breeds knowledge in my brain[9]. I know what is passing in all the islands, but I fear that my efforts against witchcraft would be unavailing. Nevertheless, I will try. I will choose, from the twelve sons of Bawr Sculloge, three that I need[10], and together we will follow you to the island.'

'But, noble chief, you have no boat here, and mine will hold only one other beside myself.'

'Let not that trouble you,' replied Fion. 'I will provide a boat for us four, and we will follow you.'

With this he selected from the twelve sons the three that he needed. They were Chluas, Grunne, and Bechunach[11]. Then he plucked two twigs of a witch hazel that grew near by, and they all proceeded to the beach. There he held the two twigs out over the water, and, in a moment, the one became a boat and the other a mast with sail set.[12] He sprang in and the three followed, and presently they were speeding over the sea, setting their course by that of the stranger in his boat.

They sailed for many hours before they came to the island of the Queen of the Many-coloured Bedchamber[13]. There they passed between high rocks, and entered a quiet harbour, where they moored their boat to a stout pillar and set a seal[14] upon the fastening, forbidding any but themselves to loose it for the space of one year, for they knew not how long their quest would last. Then they went up into the palace of the Queen.

They were gladly welcomed and treated with the most generous hospitality. When they had eaten and drank, the Queen led them into a vast bedchamber decorated in the form and manner of the rainbow[15]. Over the ceiling were the seven colours in their natural order. Round the walls they ranged themselves in the same fashion, and even the carpet itself was formed of seven hues to correspond. If the rainbow itself had been caught and tied up in a room, the effect could not have been more remarkable. It was indeed a many-coloured bedchamber!

Taking Fion by the hand, the Queen led them all into a corner of the bedchamber, where she pointed to a little cot in which a child lay sleeping.

'I had three children,' she said as she stood at the head of the cot, while Fion and the others gathered round. 'When the eldest was a year old it was carried off by that wicked witch, Flat Ear. The next year, when the second one was twelve months old, it suffered the same fate. And now my youngest here, who is twelve months old today, has fallen sick, and I fear to lose him in the same manner. This very night the witch will surely come and snatch my child away unless you can prevent her.'

'Take comfort, fair Queen,' said Fion. 'We will do our best. If you will leave this chamber to us we will watch over your child and see that it comes to no harm. And, if it be possible to capture the witch, depend upon it we shall do so. Too long she has worked her wickedness upon these lands.'

The Queen thanked him and withdrew. Soon the sun was set, and, as the child slept on and the shadows gathered, Fion and the three brothers set their watch in the Many-coloured Bedchamber. Presently servants came in and set wine before them – honey-mead and Danish beer, and metheglin[16] and sweet cakes. And, while they regaled themselves, the servants brought chessmen and a board, and Grunne and Bechunach played chess[17] while Fion and Chluas watched by the bedside.

Hours passed while the two chess-players were absorbed in their game and the other two kept watch and ward. Then, towards midnight, while Fion was alert and wakeful, he saw Chluas sink his chin on his breast, overcome by an unnatural sleep. Thrice Chluas strove to rouse himself, but thrice he sank into a deeper sleep[18].

'Wake up, Chluas!' cried Grunne, as Bechunach was considering his next move. 'Wake up! We have a pledge to keep.'

Chluas roused himself. 'Yes, yes,' he said, 'we have a pledge to keep.' And then his chin sank gradually on his breast again, and he was once more a victim to the same unnatural sleep.

'Let him alone,' said Fion. 'I will watch.'

And the two brothers went on with their game of chess.

Suddenly a chill wind[19] swept through the bedchamber. The fire in the grate flickered, and the candles burned low: the child in the cot stirred and moaned.

'See that!' said Fion in a hoarse whisper, pointing to the fireplace.

They turned and looked. It was a long, lean, bony hand reaching down the chimney and groping in the direction of the cot. The fingers were spread out and crooked, all ready to clutch. Slowly the long arm lengthened and drew

near the cot. It was about to snatch the child, when Fion darted forward an
seized it in an iron grip.

There was a violent struggle, for Fion had the arm of the witch in h
powerful grasp. He held on so masterfully that the witch, in her frantic effor
to draw it away, fell down the chimney, rolled across the fire, struck Fion
terrific blow on the temple with her other hand, and then, falling on top c
his unconscious body, lay still, her shoulder torn and bleeding.[20]

Grunne and Bechunach quickly ran to Fion's aid, and, leaving the witch fo
dead, quickly withdrew his body and restored him to consciousness. Ther
when they turned to see to the witch, they found that both she and the chil
had vanished.

They sprang to their feet and roused Chluas roughly. But he sank to slee
again immediately.

'What shall we do?' they all asked of Fion.

'Follow!' said he, 'Follow where I lead. Grunne, pick up your bow an
arrows; Bechunach, knot your ladder of cords.[21] Follow me, both of you
Leave Chluas sleeping: he is not in his body; his Spirit goes with us, and w
cannot do without it[22].'

So Grunne gathered up his bow and arrows and Bechunach his rope, an
the three, leaving the body of Chluas like dead wood, went forth to seek th
witch.

They came to the seashore, loosed their boat, sped across the harbour an
out between the high rocks. Then, guided by the loosed spirit of the sleepin
Chluas[23], they sped forward on the ocean, driven by a freshening breeze. Al
the while the spirit-light, floating above the waves, led them on.

It was some two hours before dawn when they descried, in the distance, th
lighted tower of the witch, upon an island. A dull, red flame shot out from
it, and, as it turned for ever on itself, this flame lighted the sea around like
revolving wheel, clear and red against the surrounding blackness[24].

Nearer and nearer they approached it. Then Fion stood up in the boat an
chanted magic spells, raising his arms and sinking them again with finger
stretched and his palms downwards. Then with a loud cry he called for slee
to descend on the vile witch of the revolving tower.

Ere yet his cry had died away on the surrounding sea the red light ceased t
revolve. It was still, glaring dully. Then, as the boat touched the beach
beneath the tower, Fion commanded Bechunach to throw his knotted cor
and noose the topmost turret.

It was soon done. The noose caught, and held. And, in another moment
Bechunach, like a wild cat of the mountain[25], was climbing up. Fion an
Grunne followed, while the spirit of Chluas, who lay fast asleep in the Many-
coloured Bedchamber, guided and directed their every movement.

They gained a window of the tower and made their way in. Following th
gleam of the dull, red light, they went from room to room, and at last cam
to one where it shone clearly through the cracks of the door. They burst in
and stood aghast on the threshold at the sight that met their gaze.

There on the floor lay the witch, in a magic sleep, the blood flowing from
her shoulder, torn by Fion in the struggle. And there, around her, crying
bitterly, were the Queen's three children.

Fion stooped down and swept his arm round them, and took them asid and comforted them. Then he gathered the youngest to his breast, and, directing Grunne and Bechunach to see to the other two, he led the way to the window.

In a very short time they had all climbed down the rope ladder and were speeding away in the boat. But, as they left the island, the spell was released. The tower, with its wheel of red light, began again to revolve upon the waters, and they heard the witch's shriek of rage as she awoke to the pain of her wound, to find the children gone. It came again and again, that shriek of baffled hate and rage and pain. Then, as they looked back, they saw a dark form glide down the walls of the tower like a loathsome thing creeping head downwards[26]. It reached the foot and sped to the seashore. Then it seemed to loose a boat, and, in another moment, it was speeding in pursuit of them. Faster and faster over the waves it came.

'Quick!' cried Fion to Grunne. 'Draw your bowstring to your ear. You will not miss: the spirit of the sleeper will guide your shaft[27].'

Grunne fitted an arrow to his bowstring, and drew it to his ear. Then, as Fion shot forward his outstretched hands, casting a vivid light from his finger-tips[28] over the surface of the sea, the arrow sped with a twang and a whiz.

A terrible cry came back across the water. The witch, struck to the heart, threw up her arms, and, falling from her boat, sank in the sea.

Fion put down his hands, and then all was dark, save for a dull red light[29] which flickered and played above the spot where the witch had sunk; and they sped on.

Now they neared the harbour, and saw a multitude of people waiting, with torches waving. When they gained the foothold of the land, with the three children in their arms, the people raised a mighty cheer. The Queen heard it and hastened to meet them.

Great was her joy on receiving her three children at the hands of Fion. And she showered upon him every blessing, entertaining him and his comrades – the three sons of Bawr Sculloge – for a whole year. And every year thereafter – lest the deed be forgotten – on the anniversary of the day she sent a boat laden with gold and silver and precious stones, and shields and helmets and chess-tables and rich cloaks; and the sons of Bawr Sculloge invited Fion to join them in high festival on that day, for they said, 'Such deeds should never be forgotten.'

And, one morning in spring, Fion, son of Cumhail, went into the gardens and orchards about his palace and plucked many twigs from flowers and fruit trees, and with these he went down to the seashore. Holding them above the waves, he recited a spell, and immediately a boat was formed of the twigs – a trim little craft with sail set.[30]

He sprang in and steered his course for the isle of the Queen of the Many-coloured Bedchamber. And, as he sped over the waves, the boat began to bud; and green leaves appeared on the mast, and the spars and stays put out the growth of spring, till they shone like emerald in the sun.

When he came in sight of the island, the sides of the boat were covered with blossoms, the mast had put out a wealth of petals, and the sail and rigging were covered with flowering vines. Then, as he passed between the high rocks and entered the harbour, the watchers on shore saw a boat approaching, splendid with summer flowers, and on its mast were spreading branches

dropping down with luscious fruit[31]. Nearer and nearer it came, and when
touched the shore, Fion sprang out, and bade them gather the beautif
flowers and the ripe fruit and take them to their Queen.

And Queen Breaca valued this present more than any other he could ha
offered, because the manner of it was beautiful, and a Queen is a woman, an
a woman loves beautiful things above all else.

And Chluas, the sleeper – what reward had he? He claimed none, and no
knows what was his reward. Yet it is said that in the Land of Deep Sleep the
are rewards undreamt of by those who wake[32].

Fáinne Óir, Daughter of the King of Erin, and the Son of the King of Three Seas

Fáinne Óir[1], daughter of the King of Erin, was a small child when her moth
died. Her father married a second time, but if he did he made a castle for th
daughter in a place where no enemy could find or harm her.

In time after her marriage the second Queen had a daughter, ill-favoure
sore-headed; people called her Scaldhead. Well or ill this daughter wa
growing up, growing always, although she grew up without favour.

One day when the Queen was out walking she heard that the King had
child concealed from her, a daughter[2], Fáinne Óir, the most beautiful woma
in the world. She went home with her mind fixed and determined. In th
evening, as she sat at the table, she refused to taste food or drink.

'Are you ill?' asked the King. 'Or what trouble is on you?'

'I have no reason to feel well or be thankful,' said the Queen. 'We ar
married many years and you have never shown me your daughter, Fáinne Óir.

'What daughter have I?' asked the King.

'It is useless for you to deny,' said the Queen, 'and I'll never eat a bite a
one table with you till you bring me the daughter.'

At length and at last the King brought home Fáinne Óir, and they wer
passing the time pleasantly, the Queen and Fáinne Óir, keeping company par
of the day with each other.

The King's castle stood near the sea. In front of the castle was a beautifu
strand, white and smooth. Every morning Fáinne Óir went to the strand an
walked up and down lamenting her mother, who when alive used to wal
there and carry her own little daughter, fondling her, giving her fresh air
raising the child on her shoulder, showing her the world.

Now the King's daughter walked the strand every morning for a day an
a year lamenting her mother.

One day the son of Red Breast[3], the King of Three Seas – the Green Sea
the Red Sea, and the Black Sea – was sailing past on the water. He saw th
maiden and said, 'I must go ashore to see and know who that beautiful gir
is.'

He landed and went to Fáinne Óir.

'Good morning, fair maiden,' said the King's son. 'Tell me your name an
who are you.'

'My name is Fáinne Óir. I am a daughter of the King of Erin.'

'And I am the son of Red Breast, the King of Three Seas. In three days and three years I shall be here and take you home to my mother.'

Fáinne Óir was in love with the King's son already, and thought no man could equal the beautiful hero.

When the three days and three years were passed she put on a silk robe with gold tassels and a pair of red shoes of Spanish leather; her curled hair was dressed with diamonds; she was a beauty to look at.

'Where are you going?' asked her stepmother. 'I have never seen you dressed that way; you must tell me where you are going.'

'Three days and three years ago the son of the King of three Seas came to the strand outside, and I promised to meet him today.'

'Wait awhile, wait awhile,' said the stepmother. 'I will send your sister for company. I cannot let you go alone and not know what might happen to you.'[4]

The Queen dressed up her own daughter, Scaldhead, and as they were going she gave her a sleeping pin and spoke to her this way: 'When Fáinne Óir sits down on the strand tell her to let you look at her hair. She will do so. Thrust this pin in the hair.[5] Never mind her from that out. When the king's son finds her asleep he will wait, try to rouse her, and at last go away. Draw the pin then, and let her do what she likes.'

Fáinne Óir and her half-sister went to the strand and sat there, sat waiting near the water.

'Let me look at your hair,' said Scaldhead.

She did so. Scaldhead put the pin in, and at once Fáinne Óir was asleep. Soon the son of the King of Three Seas came, found the maiden asleep and could not rouse her.

'It's a pity for me,' said he, 'to come so far to you and now to be going without you.'

He drew out a pen, wrote three lines on the palm of her right hand, and departed. What he wrote on the hand was that he would come to the same place in a day and a year and to be on the strand there before him.

When the King's son had sailed out of sight, Scaldhead drew the pin and roused Fáinne Ór.

'Oh, why did you not wake me?' cried she to the sister.

'It failed me and the King's son to wake you,' said Scaldhead.

But Fáinne Óir knew well that the sister had done something to put her to sleep. They went home then together.

Fáinne Óir was taking good care of herself and growing up in great beauty, a wonder to look at, a delight to all people. When the day and a year were at an end she dressed again with great care.

'Where are you going now—' asked the stepmother.

Fáinne Óir told her.

'Stop,' said the stepmother. 'I will send your sister for company, to be sure that no danger comes to you.'

'I will not have her with me, I have no need of her company,' said Fáinne Óir. 'I will go alone this time.'

The Queen spoke to Fáinne Óir's waiting maid[6] in secret, and said, 'I will give you a fortune if you go with your mistress today to the strand. If she refuses to let you go never stop weeping and lamenting until she consents.

When she sits on the strand ask her to let you look at her hair. When she le
you look thrust this pin in it. Do nothing more, but wait till the hero, t
King's son, comes and goes. When he is out of sight pull the pin from her hai

The maid did all that the Queen said and went with Fáinne Óir.

'If I fall asleep,' said Fáinne Óir, 'and you see a ship coming, rouse me.

'I will, and why not?' said the maid.

The maid slipped the pin in her mistress's hair and Fáinne Óir fell aslee
Soon the son of the King of Three Seas came sailing in swiftly toward t
strand, and what did he find there but Fáinne Óir and she soundly sleepin
He tried to rouse her, tried once and a second time; no use for him. Then
tried a third and a fourth time; he could do nothing, and had to leave her

'Oh, 'tis too bad after my toil and long journey that I cannot wake you an
bring you away with me,' said the King's son. 'It is through enchantment th
you are sleeping whenever I come. Who is the cause of this? What can I d
I will wait still another year. I may bring you at that time.'

At parting he wrote on her palm, 'In a day and a year I shall come agai
Be not sleeping before me.'

The year passed, and on the morning of the day she arrayed herself
before.

'Where are you going this day?' asked the Queen.

''Tis no matter,' said Fáinne Óir. 'I have no reason to tell, and you hav
no call to know where I am going.'

'But you will need company wherever you are. Let the coachman go wit
you. He will bring word and tell us if anything happens to hurt you or if yo
go anywhere.'

Fáinne Óir consented.

Said the Queen to the coachman[7] in private, 'Find a chance to thrust thi
pin in her clothing.'

He found the chance, and she fell asleep. The coachman was walking bac
and forth till he saw a ship making towards land with great speed, and the so
of the King of Three Seas in it.

When the young hero found the maiden asleep he cried. 'Oh, bitterness
Thrice have I come and thrice are you sleeping before me; sleeping fron
enchantment and wicked enemies. But if I can do nothing more I will tak
three kisses before I go from you.'

He stooped down to kiss her. With the first kiss blood came from hi
nostril and fell on her robe in a round spot. At the second kiss he bled in th
same way, and the blood went through her clothes to her body. At the thir
kiss the blood fell on her breast and remained there.

'Farewell, farewell,' said he, 'whether we meet or meet not after this.' An
he went away heavy-hearted.

When Fáinne Óir woke she found the blood spots; she tried to remov
them, but could not, the blood remained fresh on her clothing and bosom. Sh
went home; her father was there at the castle before her.

'Good evening, my child', said the father. 'Have you heard news today o
seen anything strange?'

'I have not, but there is magic and evil around me, brought here by you
Queen. I am to go from you tomorrow, and never again shall I be in thi
castle.'

'If you are going, do not go until you visit your dead mother's chamber. No one has been there since she was taken from it, and none will go there again while I am here living.'

In the morning Fáinne Óir went to the chamber.

'Here is a gift,' said her father, 'that your mother left on her deathbed to give you, for she knew what trouble would come from your stepmother.'

He took from a box then a tablecloth[8].

'Take this,' said he, 'and whenever you are hungry or thirsty spread it out; you will have food and drink in abundance. Here, besides, is a token from your mother, a ring. Whether you are above ground or in the world under ground, look through it, and any place of lodging you seek you will see, or anything else that you want and are waiting for will come to you.'

Fáinne Óir left a blessing with her father, and went away walking and looking for the son of the King of Three Seas, expecting to find him here or there or in some place. She was travelling a long time without seeing hut, house, castle or building of any sort. At nightfall she came to a forest and said to herself. 'I am wearied with walking and must rest. If I sit on the ground, some wild beast may kill me; I will go up on a tree.' She climbed a tree and sat on a branch. 'Oh,' said she, 'but I have not looked through my ring. I will look through it now and see is there a house where I can find lodgings tonight, or must I stay here till morning.'

She looked and saw a fine castle near enough to her. 'I may find refuge there. I will try.' She slipped down from the tree, walked to the gate; and struck a blow on it. Soon a woman came out to her.

'What do you want, my good maiden?'

'Lodgings for this night. I walked far before I saw this castle.'

'Come in,' said the woman. 'But do you know the name of this castle?'

'I do not,' said the maiden.

'This is *Teach na Réalta* (House of the stars)[9]. You may stay here tonight.'

Next morning Fáinne Óir was for continuing her journey, but the woman stopped her and said. 'Stay with me, take service for a day and a year.'

'You would have a bad servant in me. I have never done work. I had many to serve me before I left home.'

'I ask no labour of you, but to be in my company a short time every day.'

Fáinne Óir stayed at the House of the Stars for a day and a year. All that time they spent two hours daily knitting a cap[10], and the cap was hardly made at the end of the year.

'As you are going now,' said the woman, 'take this cap, and if you see any one coming towards you put it on. You'll seem very pale and poor-looking, and will be unnoticed unless by the right man.[11] Here is an apple for you; if you are in dread, throw the apple over your shoulder and the greatest forest that ever was seen in the world will spring up in one moment behind you.'

Fáinne Óir left a blessing and went her way then. She travelled on many days. She had food and drink from the tablecloth. Once she was walking near a large river, and could see nothing beyond but a soft, swampy country.

'I may see something if I look through the ring,' said Fáinne Óir to herself. She saw the largest man she had ever laid eyes on, and the ugliest, and he coming up to her.

'Good evening, Fáinne Óir,' said he.

'What name is that for me?' said the maiden. The moment she saw the ma
through the ring she put on the cap, but too late.

'Oh, no use in denying or wearing a magic cap; you must come with me
You must be my bride.'

'Go your way. Never mind a poor orphan like me; leave me; leave me i
peace.'

'I will not let you go. I heard of you yesterday, and very glad am I to fin
you today.'

This man was terribly large, with legs so tremendously long that he crosse
at a step that broad river[12]. His name was Camchosa (Crooked Legs)[13]. H
took her up and away with him.

'Well,' said Fáinne Óir, 'I put you under bonds not to marry me for a da
and a year.'

He bore her to his castle and confined her in the highest chamber, but gav
her two hours every day to walk in the grounds of the castle. From grief sh
remained many days in the chamber, but at last she went out to move amon
people. While walking she saw a small house near the castle, and as she wa
passing a woman rose up in the doorway and looked at her. The woman wa
young, but in poor, worn garments.

'Indeed,' thought Fáinne Óir, 'I pity you greatly. You would be a beautifu
woman if you had clothing to suit you.' She said to herself then; 'The rin
gives me clothing in plenty, I will carry some to that woman, 'tis a pity to se
the like of her as she is.'

Fáinne Óir dressed the woman well on the following day, and she was a
fine a beauty as could be found here or there.

Fáinne Óir walked out on the third day, and when passing a second hous
an old man rose up in the doorway and looked at her. The old man wa
haggard and pale.

'Will you tell me, old man, why you are so poor and pale?' asked Fáinn
Óir.

'I am in hunger and suffering. All that I had was taken from me seven years
ago by Domhnall Donn[14] of the Eastern World. Only yesterday was I freed
from prison in this place. A day I get a bite to eat, and three days I get no bite.
It is from that the look comes that is on me.'

'Sit down and eat your fill now,' said Fáinne Óir taking out her tablecloth.

When he had eaten, the old man said, 'You have done so much forme that
I must do something for you. There is a woman living a whole year in this
place without hearing from her home or knowing how to get to it. She is a
sister of *Cleasaidher*[15], son of White Breast from the Western World, she was
taken awayby Donhnall Donn of the East, the father of Counchosa. Come
now to Cleasaidhe's sister.

When they went to the woman dressed by Fáinne Óir the old man said to
her, 'Write a letter to your brother and tell him that Fáinne Óir, daughter of
the King of Erin, is here, and that yourself is here with her.'

She wrote the letter, the old man took it, went to the river and threw in the
message.

'Go now, without stopping,' said he to the letter, 'till you find Cleasaidhe,
son of White Breast.'

In four days' time Cleasaidhe came out there on land before Camchosa's castle. He walked up to the front of it and struck the pole of combat.

'What do you want?' asked the messenger.

'Seven hundred champions for combat on each of the four sides of me.'

'I am living alone here,' said Camchosa, who came out at that moment, 'but I may be enough for you.'

The two closed in combat. Seven days and six nights they fought, when Cleasaidhe gave his enemy a truce. Cambhosa, bathed in his caldron of cure, took rest, then ate, slept, and drank, and was as fresh as the first day.

Early in the morning a dove[16] perched on a tree near Cleasaidhe and said to him. 'I'm not thankful to you; you are not so wise as you should be. Why give rest to that Camchosa? Never let him draw breath till you have him done. There is a round spot near his right arm. Touch that with your sword point and the strength will be gone from him. You will meet other trouble, though, when you have finished with Camchosa.'

Cleasaidhe had the knowledge now, and when the time came he touched Camchosa's spot with his sword point. Camchosa cried for mercy, begged for life.

'Leave the breath with me. I will be your servant here or in any place,' said he.

'I want nothing of you but to send out Fáinne Óir, daughter of the King of Erin.'

'That will be done,' said Camchosa.

Fáinne Óir was brought out, and very happy was she to part with Camchosa. Cleasaidhe went now to his ship, taking with him Fáinne Oir and his own sister. He raised his sails and went ploughing the deep sea. They were sailing on swiftly till the third day, when looking behind, Cleasaidhe saw many ships moving with great speed. When these ships were very near whom should he see on the foremost one but Dubhchosa[17], the magician, Camchosa's brother.

Fáinne Óir thought now for the first time of the apple she got from the Queen in the House of the Stars. She gave the apple quickly to Cleasaidhe.

'Throw this towards the ship,' said she.

He threw it, and that moment the tallest and thickest forest that ever was seen rose up through the ocean.

'Well,' said Dubhchosa, 'we have to turn home now till we bring men with sharp axes to hew down this forest. I'm greatly in dread it's too far they'll be gone from us when the forest is cut.'

They went home, and came back bringing men with sharp axes and cleared a way through the forest with much trouble and delay.

All this time Cleasaidhe was sailing on with great speed, and was within three days of the Western World when Dubhchosa was in sight a second time. Cleasaidhe increased his speed; still the magician gained on him so that when Cleasaidhe landed, Dubhchosa landed soon after and stood before him.

'Will you fight with swords or will you wrestle?' asked Dubhchosa.

'I have no choice,' replied Cleasaidhe. 'I'm as well used to the sword as to wrestling.' And they went at it with swords. They fought seven days and six nights on the strand of the Western World, till Dubhchosa asked for a truce and got it. The magician went to his ship then for rest and refreshment.

'By my word,' said Cleasaidhe, 'it is too bad for me to be waiting in this place without meat or drink.'

'No need of waiting,' said Fáinne Óir. 'I will give you food and drink in plenty.' With that she drew out her cloth and spread it. Food fit for a King or for a man's own mother was on it before them.

'By my word,' said Cleasaidhe, 'you are the best woman in the world. Not sorry am I for the toil and trouble if I can win you now or another time.'

Next morning the dove lighted on a tree near by and said to Cleasaidhe, 'Throw away your sword, take your enemy by the waist, and when you give him the first twist send him to his knees in the earth, at the second twist sink him to his waist, at the third to his shoulders. Tell him then to earn his life of you. He'll cry for mercy. You will answer that you have no mercy to grant and he none to get till he gives you the enchanted sword[18] and writes a letter with his blood, saying that you are the first hero in the world, and sends this letter to whatever place you tell him to send it.'

Cleasaidhe did all the dove said. The sword was delivered and the letter written.

'Where am I to strike this sword first?' asked he of Dubhchosa.

'Try it on the hardest block in the forest, and see what you'll cut with it.'

'By my word I can find no harder block than your own head, and for fear that you'd trouble me or another man after me, I'll take the head off you now.'

With that he swept the head off Dubhchosa with one blow of the sword. The head shot away through the air, and soon it was coming down with great speed. Cleasaidhe caught the head and struck the body in the breast and the heart with it.

'It was lucky for you that you did that,' said the head. 'If you had not I should be on my own body now, and the world would not part us or save you. If I am killed itself you will suffer severely; my father will meet you, and that very soon.'

Dubhchosa had barely stopped speaking when Domhnall Donn stood before Cleasaidhe. 'You have left my eldest son, Camchosa, without strength, you have killed my second son, Dubhchosa, but I'll have revenge and take your life now.'

'That is what you can never do,' answered Cleasaidhe.

'I have no time to argue. Will you use swords or will you wrestle?'

'It is all one to me,' replied Cleasaidhe.

They went at each other with swords then and fought for seven days and six nights, till Domhnall Donn asked for a truce. He got it, and went to his ship to rest.

'Oh, foolish man, you will ruin yourself,' said the dove to Cleasaidhe. 'Do what I tell you. Call for a truce tomorrow; write a letter then to the son of Black Breast[19] asking aid; throw the letter into the river; it will go to him; he will come quickly.'

Cleasaidhe did all the dove said, and on the morning following the letter the son of Black Breast was on the field.

'What brought you to this place?' said the son of Black Breast to Domhnall Donn. 'We have never troubled you in the Eastern World. Mind your life now, for there is no one here or there, in the East or West, underneath or above, who can conquer me.'

They closed in battle, and soon the son of Black Breast got the upper hand.

'Yield now,' said he.

'Leave my life with me, spare me,' begged Domhnall Donn.

'I will not kill you if you go home by the same way over which you came hither, without causing fog or enchantment; stop fighting for the rest of your life, and give me a letter in your own blood saying that I am the best hero in the world.'

Domhnall Donn wrote the letter, went to his ship, and sailed home by a straight course.

'Now,' said the son of Black Breast, 'we must stay here till midday tomorrow.' He wrote a letter to the son of Red Breast[20] and put it in the river. The son of the King of Three Seas received the letter in the underworld, and the following day drew up his ship in a harbour where no current could move it or storm come against it. He gave it the mooring of a day and a year, though perhaps it might not be three hours in the place. He went then to the son of Black Breast. 'Why did you send for me?' asked he.

'I sent for you because Fáinne Óir, daughter of the King of Erin, is here. There is blood on her breast and her dress; she will marry no man, she says, but the man who can take that stain from her. You saw her in Erin; Cleasaidhe saved her from Camchosa; I saved her from Camchosa's father. All three of us love her; we two have fought for her; who is to have her? We are here now, three cousins. You are seven years older than Cleasaidhe, son of White Breast –'

'I am,' said the son of Red Breast.

'Cleasaidhe is seven years older than I. Cleasaidhe has the seven years that he is younger than you to seek his fortune in, and I have the seven years that I am younger than Cleasaidhe in which to seek my fortune; we have no reason to fight for one woman. We will decide our fate this way: whichever of us will take the blood from the breast and dress of Fáinne Óir with a kiss will have her. I will give her the first kiss myself.'

He kissed her, but took no stain of blood.

Cleasaidhe, son of White Breast, kissed her and took no stain away.

The son of Red Breast, King of Three Seas, kissed her and that moment every trace of blood disappeared from her.

'You have the wife,' said the son of Black Breast, 'though it was not you who earned her; take her home to your mother now and keep her. It would be unseemly for three cousins to fight for one woman.'

He took her home, and the King's son said to Fáinne Óir. 'Rest here outside till I see is the castle prepared for you.'

He went inside.

'Have you the wife?' asked his mother.

'I have, the daughter of the King of Erin. I hope you will go out and bring her in and never trouble her in any way.'

The mother went out, embraced Fáinne Óir, and brought her into the castle. They sent then for all the great people and heroes of the world to come to the marriage, and no man of them knew whether the first day of the wedding or the last was the best. Oh, but they were full of delight, conversing, telling tales, singing, drinking wine with the odour of honey, no man drunk and no man dry.

The Son of the King of Erin and the Queen of Moving Wheel

There was a King in Erin long ago, and he had three sons.

On a day this King went out to walk with the Queen and look at the waves and the rocks on the strand. After they had walked for a time they saw a boat sailing in from the old sea (the distant sea)[1]. When the boat came to land they saw no one on board but a grey-haired old man[2], who came ashore and walked up to the King and the Queen.

'It is the wonder of the world to me,' said the old man to the King, 'that you never take thought of going out on the water to have amusement and pleasure for yourself.'

'How could I go on the water when I have neither ship nor boat?' asked the King.

'Walk into my boat with the Queen, and I will hold the cable while you sail and get as much sport as you like.'

The two entered the boat, and they were a good while inside sailing this way and that not far from land. At last the old man drew in the boat.

'Will you come out?' asked he of the King.

The King rose, and was coming out.

'It is a wonder to me,' said the old man, 'that you, a King, should be so thoughtless as to come out before the Queen. She might fall between the boat and the rock. You should let her go first, and keep your eye on her.'

The King stepped back and told the Queen to go first. The moment she stepped on the rock the grey-haired old man put his foot to the stem of the boat and gave a shove that sent it out nine leagues to sea.

The boat went tossing about in one direction and another till it came to Lonesome Island. The King left the boat then, anchored, and went his way walking till he came to a splendid castle[3] in the middle of the island. He entered the castle; there was no one inside but a woman, the most beautiful[4] that ever he had seen. That was the Queen of the Lonesome Island. She made ready a dinner, and both she and the King of Erin ate and drank at the one table.

Next morning she had breakfast ready before him. After breakfast they walked to the strand where the boat had been left, but neither ship nor boat was to be seen on sea or land. The King of Erin remained there with the Queen of Lonesome Island for a day and a year. The Queen at that time had a son three months old.[5]

'King of Erin,' said she, 'you may go home if you choose.'

The King made ready to start.

'Do not go,' said she, 'without marking this child in the way that you will know him surely if you meet him again[6].

'What mark am I to put on him?' asked the King.

'If you take off the small toe of his right foot it will do him no harm, and the mark will be certain.'

The King did that. The best ship ever seen was ready for him. He sailed away with fair wind and good wishes till he came to his own harbour with speed and in safety. While the King of Erin was on Lonesome Island word had gone out that he was lost. This word was going slowly from one place to another till it came to the White King.

Said the White King to himself, 'Now is my time to collect a fleet, sail to Erin, and take that land for my own use.'

He prepared a great fleet and went to Erin. At this time the son of the Queen of Lonesome Island was seven years old. His mother had been training him in all exercises and arts from one room of the castle to another[7], and great was his skill.

When the White King came with his fleet he sent a challenge to the King of Erin to fight for his crown or lie under tribute and pay the tribute without trouble.

The King of Erin sent back the answer that he would fight and die rather than lie under tribute to any man.

When his own three sons at home heard his trouble they hurried away to hide where no man could find them.

'Now,' said the Queen of Lonesome Island to her son, whose name was Wishing Gold[8]. 'It is very pleasant for us to be sitting here tonight, but with your father, the King of Erin, it is different. There is great trouble on him.'

'What trouble is on my father?' asked the boy.

'When I sent him wandering on the sea, so that he might come to this island, word went out of Erin through all lands in the world that he was lost. The White King heard this word at last, and now he has gone with a great fleet to take Erin for himself. Your father, unaided by anyone, will go out tomorrow to give battle to the fleet of the White King, and you must give him a day of assistance.'

'Has he not three sons older than I?' asked Wishing Gold.

'That matters not,' said the Queen. 'It was I that brought him to this trouble, and you must assist him.'

Wishing Gold made ready next morning, and, mounting a steed hurried off to Erin. When the King of Erin was going out, with his sword under his arm, to face the fleet, he saw a horseman rushing in on the water from the old sea[9], and he said to himself, 'I have time for delay. I will wait till I see where this horseman is going. There are men enough against me if the horseman is with me, and if it is going against me he is there are too many.'

When the horseman came to the fleet of the White King he closed with it and went through like a hawk through small birds, or a fox through hens, making one pile of men's heads, another of their bodies, and a third of their weapons. He killed all and spared none, till he came to the White King himself. Him he led, took under his arm, and threw down before his father and asked, 'Are we to kill this man or let him lie under tribute forever?

'I will not take his head without reason,' said the King of Erin. 'If he is willing to lie under tribute I will spare him. Oh, but I had not the luck to have the like of you for a son.' The boy drew the shoe from his right foot, showed that his little toe was missing, and told his story. The King of Erin knew his son then, and rejoiced.

The White King was glad to escape, and promised to pay tribute without trouble. Wishing Gold was for turning back on the spot to his mother, but his father would not let him go till he had spent two or three days in Erin.

Next day the King had a great hunt, and when they were starting, the Queen would not let Wishing Gold out of her sight.

'I like him so well,' said she, 'that I must have him with me while he stays in Erin.'

It was a delight to the King that the Queen was so fond of Wishing Gold, and he told him to stay with her that day.

When the King and his men had gone the Queen went to the old druid and said, 'I will have the head taken off you unless you tell me how to put an end to Wishing Gold.'[10]

'You are the worst woman I have ever seen,' said the druid. 'You wish to kill the boy who saved your husband and your kingdom.'

'I know well that unless I put him to death he will have the kingdom, and my own sons will be without it.'[11]

'Very well,' said the druid, 'I will tell you what to do. On the island where this boy was reared there are no banks; the place is flat and level. Take him now to the "Wonderful Banks"[12] beyond this castle, and he will say that in truth they are wonderful. You can say then that they are no wonder to you; that your own sons leap down from them and then spring back to the top again. When he hears this he will try to do it himself, and he will leap to the bottom.'

The Queen did as the druid advised. Wishing Gold leaped down, and when he was springing back and was near the highest point of the bank she was at the brink and pushed him; he lost balance, rolled down and out into the sea. He was dashed from one wave to another, till at last he was thrown in on an island. He rose and walked on to the middle of the island; there he found a house, and going in, saw a white trout[13] broiling on a spit before a fire. 'I will eat that trout,' said he to himself. Then he thought, 'It is not mine, and I will not touch it.' He went outside to look about, and saw hurrying towards him a terrible giant with five heads and five necks. The giant let such a laugh out of him that a man might have seen through his throat all that was in his body.

'You ugly beast,' said Wishing Gold. 'Why are you laughing like that?'

'I am glad to have your flesh to eat today; that's why I'm laughing,' said the giant.

'You haven't me yet,' said Wishing Gold.

The two then faced each other and began. Wishing Gold was better and far better than the giant, so he brought him to the ground, cut off the five heads, and sprang between them and the body.[14]

'If you had not done that,' said one of the heads, 'I should be now on my body, and neither you nor all the world could put me off again.'

'I have done a good work,' said Wishing Gold. Then he went to the house, saying to himself, 'I will eat the trout,' but he thought and said. 'By all that I have been taught, there never is one in a place but there may be more.' So he went out to look, and saw coming a far greater giant, with five heads and five necks.

As soon as the giant came near they closed in combat, but Wishing Gold was stronger and far stronger than the giant, and he brought him to the ground, drew his sword, cut off the five heads, and sprang between the heads and the body.

'Only that you did that,' said a tongue in one of the heads, 'I should be now on my body and all the world could not put me off.'

Wishing Gold went in thinking to eat the trout, and he ate it. As soon as he had eaten it he said to himself. 'There may be other giants in the place.' He went out and saw the third giant coming, and soon he was before him. They closed and fought in the way that they made hardness out of softness and softness out of hardness, and if people came from the lower to the upper world it was to look at the wonder of this battle that they came, but at last Wishing Gold was stronger and far stronger than the giant, so he put him to the ground, drew out his sword, cut the five heads off him, and sprang between the heads and the body.

'Only that you did that,' said one of the heads, 'I should be on my body now, and you, with all the world besides, would not put me off.'

'I've done a good deed,' said Wishing Gold. He went in then and sat down and said to himself, 'As these three were in one place their mother must be in it, too.' He rose and went out, and soon saw a dreadful old hag[15]' coming. He and she fell to fighting, and fought for three days and nights. Wishing Gold was doing no harm to the old hag, but the old hag was squeezing the heart out of him, until at last he was thinking, 'It is here my death is.'

That moment his mother's voice spoke behind him. 'Wishing Gold,' said she, 'think not that I am here to help you. If you were to lose your life ten times I would not help you, since you are so simple and keep not in mind what I've told you so often. It is a disgrace for a hero to fight three days and nights with an old woman. Often have I told you that all the world cannot do the old hag any harm while she has the long net[16] on her.'

By hearing his mother's words Wishing Gold grew strong, thrust the point of his sword in between the net and body of the hag and cut the net to the top of her head, when she had no greater strength than another, and he killed her. He went home with the mother then, and she was teaching him exercises and arts of all kinds[17].

The report had gone through the seven kingdoms[18] that Wishing Gold was lost. 'It is my time now,' said the White King. 'No need for me to be lying under tribute to the King of Erin. I will give him battle while he has no assistance.'

'I will go, too,' said the Spotted King. 'I will put the King of Erin under tribute to myself and make him release the White King.'

The two Kings made ready a great fleet and set out for Erin. When they reached land the Spotted King sent his message to the King of Erin: 'You are to release the White King and pay tribute to me without trouble, or fight for the kingdom.' The King of Erin sent back this answer: 'I will fight to my death before I will give up my own and go under tribute to any man.'

The battle was to be next day. The King of Erin's three sons[19] hid where no man could find them. Wishing Gold and his mother were sitting at home that evening.

'Very comfortable are we this night,' said the Queen of Lonesome Island, 'but it is not the same with your father in Erin; he has great trouble on him now.'

'What is the trouble that is on my father?' asked Wishing Gold.

When you were thrown down the Wonderful Banks by the Queen of Erin word went through the seven kingdoms that you were lost, and now the White King and the Spotted King have gone with a great fleet to conquer your father and lay him under tribute, you must give him a day of assistance tomorrow.'

'Sure, my father has three sons older than I.'

'It was I who began all this trouble,' said the Queen, 'when I sent your father wandering through the waters and brought him here, so you must help him.'

'You know how they treated me when I was in Erin before,' said Wishing Gold.

'I do,' said the mother, 'and I will put you in the way now to save yourself from the like again.[20] Here is a belt to tie around your body, and if man or woman wishes to harm you the belt will tighten and warn you.'

Wishing Gold mounted his steed and started for Erin.

Next morning the King of Erin was going out, with his sword under his arm, to face the enemy, when he saw a horseman riding in from the old sea.

'I may delay a while,' thought the King, 'if it is to help me that horseman is coming I have time enough, and if it is against me he is, I am too soon.'

When the horseman came he attacked the two armies, and went through them as a hawk through small birds or a fox through hens; he made a heap of their heads, a heap of their bodies, and a heap of their weapons, till he gave sore death to them all except the two Kings; these he took to his father, one under each of his arms, and asked, 'Am I to kill these men or put them under tribute?'

'Put double tribute on the White King and single on the Spotted King.'

The two kings promised to pay without trouble, and glad they were to escape, so they went away, each to his own place. Now Wishing Gold was for going home, but the father would not let him go without spending two or three days with himself.

Next day they had a great hunt, and Wishing Gold went to it, for the Queen dared not ask him to stay with her that turn. After all had gone she went to the old druid and said. 'I will put you to death unless you tell me how to kill Wishing Gold.'

'I will tell you how to do that,' said the druid. 'kill a cock, take the blood in a bottle to bed with you and say that you'll die very soon, take some blood in your mouth, then spit it out, send a horseman to the mountain with a message to the King saying that he'll not have a sight of you in life unless he comes quickly; and it is not one horseman or two that you will send, but one after another. When the King comes in haste and asks what trouble is on you, this is what you will say, "I cannot live unless you get a cure for me." "What cure must I get?" he will ask. Say to him, "There is nothing in the world to cure me but a bottle of water from the well at the castle of the Queen of the Moving Wheel in the Eastern world[21], and Wishing Gold can bring it." The King will say then, "That cure is what you'll never get."'

The Queen did as the druid advised and sent a horseman to the mountain to look for the King, and then a second, and then horseman after horseman. So the King hurried back and asked what was wrong with her.

'I am for death very soon,' said she.

'Is there anything to cure you?'

'Nothing can cure me but a bottle of water from the well of the Queen of the Moving Wheel in the Eastern world.'

'How can that be got?' asked the King.

'Wishing Gold could bring it if you would send him.'

'He will never go one step for it at my command,' said the King. 'You have three sons of your own, and I will not spare them if they like to go.'

The three made ready and were for starting.[22] Wishing Gold thought it a shame for him to stop behind, so the four went together. They travelled a very long time, till at length and at last they came to a house, and when they went in a fine woman met them. She caught Wishing Gold by the hand and gave him great welcome. She brought food and drink for the four, and an old man lying on a bed[23] called; 'Daughter, dear, who is this man, and you giving him such a welcome?'

'Wishing Gold, the son of your sister and of the King of Erin[24]. It is he that will give you the tidings, you have not heard the like of them for many a day.'

'Is it not bad, and too bad,' said the old man to Wishing Gold, 'that you are there and I here and I not able to go to you?'

'That is nothing,' said Wishing Gold. 'I will go to you.'

So Wishing gold drew his chair to the bed, and of all questions that the old man asked the first was: 'Where are you going, and what brought you this way?'

Wishing Gold told all from the first to the last.

'I have seen,' said the old man, 'many a King and King's son passing this house to look for that water, but never a man of them have I seen going home. It is better for you to go back.'

'I will never go back; I will lose my life or get the water.'

When the eldest son of the King of Erin heard of the great danger before him, the soul left him, and he fell dead[25].

'Well,' said Wishing Gold, 'if we were few enough before this, we are fewer now, but if we get the water we will bring you to life.'

Then they put the body in a box with green leaves to keep it fresh.[26] Next day the three travelled on till near night, when they saw a house in the distance. They hurried on. When they entered the house a fine woman caught Wishing Gold by the hand and gave him a warm welcome. She made ready a supper, and when they had eaten, an old man on a bed called out, 'How is it, daughter dear, that you have such welcome for this man?'

'It is not every one I would welcome in this way,' said she. 'This is the son of your sister and of the King of Erin; he will give news of the brother that you have not seen this long time.'

'It is bad that you are there and I here, and I without power to go to you,' said the old man to Wishing Gold.

'There is nothing wrong, except what is wrong with you, if you cannot come to me I can go to you,' said the King's son. He drew his chair to the bedside, and they began to talk.

'Where are you going?' asked the old man. 'I suppose it is not to see me that you are here.'

Wishing Gold told him everything.

'I have seen,' said the old man, 'Kings and Kings' sons enough to cover half the world going for that water, but never a man of them returning. If you take my advice you'll not go a step beyond this, but turn home in good season.'

'I will not turn home,' said Wishing Gold. 'I will go till I have the water or lose my life.'

When the second son of the King of Erin heard of the danger and of all who had lost their lives he dropped dead.

'I thought,' said Wishing Gold, 'that we were enough as three, but we are fewer now. If I get the water, however, I will bring him to life.' They found a box, packed the body in it with green leaves, and away they went next morning.

The two travelled all day till near night, when they came to a house, and were met by a beautiful woman, who welcomed Wishing Gold greatly. She brought supper, and then an old man lying in the corner cried out, 'Daughter dear, how is this that you have such welcome for a stranger?'

'Oh, this is the son of your sister and of the King of Erin,' cried the woman.

'Oh, nephew, it is bad enough that you are there, and I without power to go to you.'

'There is nothing wrong but what is wrong with you,' said Wishing Gold. 'I will go to you', and he drew his chair to the bed. The two began to talk.

'What brought you here?' asked the old man. 'I suppose it was not the wish to see me, though it would be no wonder if it was, and you my sister's son.'

'It was not,' said Wishing Gold. 'I am on my way to the kingdom of the Moving Wheel to get a bottle of water for the Queen of Erin.'

'I have seen many a King and King's son and champion going for that water, but not a man of them has ever come back. That is a terrible place. Between this and the castle of the Moving Wheel are three bridges on the Queen's land[27], guarded by three dogs of hers, and their mouths open so widely that you would think they could swallow the world. But as you have come this far, and as you are a son born for luck, you may get the water. The Queen sleeps only once in seven years, and then she sleeps for a day and a year[28]; when ready to sleep she raises her castle to the sky. When she is sleeping everything belonging to her, all her servants and guards are sleeping as well, though you would think they were awake, for all have their eyes open. If you cross the bridges, the greatest wall in the world is between them and the well, a wall with standing spears on top of it. But if you are such a champion as you seem, you may clear the wall. But near the four corners[29] of the wall are four cats[30], and the sight of these is enough to frighten any man. Each cat has a poison tail on her, and each has poison teeth, and eyes open and staring, as if to spring at you in an instant. If you pass the cats without trouble you will get the water. When you have lifted the water from the well you will see a tree in the middle of the garden, and on the tree three red apples, a large, a middle-sized, and a small one; pick the three apples and throw the largest one up to the sky, hit the castle and you will bring it a third of the way toward the earth[31], throw the middle-sized apple and bring it another third; catch the apple each time before it reaches the ground and put it in your pocket. Throw the small one and the castle will come to the earth. After that, unless you make a leap and catch the wheel at the corner, and keep it steady till the castle is settled, it will never stop moving[32]; then go to the kitchen door where there is a cart load of keys; strive to find the key of the hall door; you may not find the right key for a day and a year, and you may find it in a minute.'

When the third son of the King of Erin heard this he fell dead from terror.

'I see,' said Wishing Gold, 'I am worse off now, for I am alone.'

Next morning he washed his face and hands and started on; he travelled till he came to the first bridge. The terrible dog was there, with bared teeth and eyes staring, as if ready to spring.[33]

'A bird could not fly through the air and escape that dog,' thought Wishing Gold, 'but I will pass or lose my life.'

He went forward warily, crossed the bridge without trouble, for the dog was asleep; he passed the other two bridges in the same way, and cleared the wall at one bound, though it would be enough for a bird to fly over it, and sharp spears standing straight from the top. Wishing Gold was now in the garden; he walked up to the wall, watched the cats carefully, found them asleep, filled the three bottles with water, and set them aside. He went then to the middle of the garden, took the three apples from the tree, threw up the largest and struck the castle in the clouds; the castle came down one-third of the distance. He caught the apple, put it in his pocket, then threw the middle-sized one, and the castle came down the second third; threw the smallest apple and the castle came to the earth. Wishing Gold sprang at the wheel and kept it still till the castle was firm. He went next to the hall door, looked at the great pile of keys, and said to himslf, 'I might be here all my life before I could hit on the right key, but I have often heard my mother say that the key of the hall is the biggest of all.'

He picked out the biggest key and tried it, the door opened at the first turn[34]. In the door of every room he found the key in the lock from that out. He opened all the doors in the castle and came to the room where the Queen of the Moving Wheel was asleep. He wrote on a piece of paper that the son of the King of Erin had visited her while she was sleeping and left this paper in her bosom[35]. He came out then, locked all the doors behind him, threw the small apple at the castle, the castle rose in the air one-third of the distance; he threw the middle-sized apple, it rose another third; then the largest apple, and the castle went far into the clouds, where it had been before. He caught each apple as it came down and put them on the tree where he had found them, took the bottles, cleared the wall, crossed the three bridges and came to the third old man, his uncle, who was lying in bed, rubbed him with the water, and left him as young as a boy of fifteen; rubbed the youngest son of the King of Erin, and he came to life.

The two travelled on then till they came to the house of the second old man, rubbed him and he became as if fifteen years old; rubbed some on the second son of the King of Erin and he came to life.

The three travelled on till they came to the third old man, rubbed him with the water, made him young, rubbed the eldest son of the King of Erin; he came to life, and the four travelled on.

While they were walking, Wishing Gold in front, the three, who were a little behind, said among themselves, 'Wishing Gold will tell of all that has happened; it would be better to kill him and take the water ourselves.'

The belt of warning began to tighten that moment.

'I know,' said Wishing Gold to the three, 'what you would like, and I will tell you what I will do. I will give you the water; take it home. I will go my own road, to my mother, and never be seen again in Erin. If I give you the water and go it is not because I am in dread of you, for I could kill a hundre like you.[36]'

He gave them the water. They went home, and he went to Loneson Island. When they reached the castle the King was outside watching.

'Where is Wishing Gold?' asked he.

'It matters not where he is,' said they, 'When he saw what work was befor him he fell dead from fright. There was no good in him.'

'That is not true', said the father. 'Wishing Gold did the whole work an was killed. You stood back until all was over, and that is why you are here.

They would not confess. When the Queen of Erin heard that Wishing Gol wad dead, she had no need of the water. She sprang out of bed, as well as ever

Wishing Gold and his mother were exercising for a day and a year, an Wishing Gold was so active and skilful that in place of his mother driving hir through the rooms he was driving her, and she had as much as she could d to save herself. But one night, as they sat by the fire, she said. 'We are ver comfortable here, but there will be need of you in Erin tomorrow early.'

'I will never go to Erin! I have had my fill of that country.'

'No matter, you must go this time. When the Queen of the Moving Whee woke in her castle she saw before her a child three months old[37]. She spran out of bed. The line you wrote and left with her fell to the floor. She read i and is raging with anger. She has come now to your father's castle in Erin t destroy the kingdom or take the head off that son of the King of Erin wh entered the castle while she was asleep. She has challenged the King's eldes son to face her at midday tomorrow. She will know that he is not the man she will destroy him and his two brothers, and then your father and hi kingdom, unless you stand before her. I will tell you what to do. She is such a champion[38] that no one in the world is safe from her, but if you can b outside her tent in the morning before she rises, and have the first blow on th pole of combat which is there, and if you defend yourself from her first an second blow, I will save you from the third.'

Wishing Gold took his best weapons, and next morning early was in Erin outside the tent of the Queen of the Moving Wheel and had the first blow or the pole of compat. She made one spring out of bed and shouted:

'Who is this who has dared to strike a blow before my tent?'

'Your master,' said Wishing Gold.

'You will know who is master when I am before you,' replied she.

The Queen took her arms, came out, rose above him in the air, and came down. He defended himself from the crown of his head to the soles of his feet, and saved himself from her first blow.

'Good champion,' said she, 'this is what no one in the world could do before you. But if you saved yourself from the first you will not the second time.'

She rose above again, and as she came down he defended himself from the crown of his head to the soles of his feet, and saved himself the second time.

'Good champion,' said she, 'this is a thing which I thought no one in the world could do, but I will finish you now.'

'Wishing Gold!' cried the Queen of Lonesome Island, from behind, 'I would not spare the mother of my child, if the mother of my child would not spare me.'

'How can Wishing Gold be the father of my child?' asked the Queen of the Moving Wheel. 'It was prophesied from old that he was to be my husband, and it was for him that I was guarding myself[39]. It was written on the paper that fell from my bosom that the son of the King of Erin came to my castle.'

'Of course, Wishing Gold is the son of the King of Erin, because I sent the King of Erin wandering so that he might come to my island, where I was waiting for him, for there is no good blood in the world but what is in the King of Erin[40].'

When the Queen of the Moving Wheel heard all this, she caught Wishing Gold by the hand, kissed him, and had great welcome for him.

All went then to the castle of the King of Erin, and Wishing Gold and the Queen of the Moving Wheel were married[41]. Wishing Gold was giving presents to every one in the castle, and the Queen of Erin, who was anxious, cried 'Will you leave me without any gift?'

'I have not given your gift to any one yet,' said Wishing Gold.

He drew out a beautiful ring, the loveliest ever seen, and gave it to her.

She was delighted, and put it on her finger. The ring began to tighten.

'Wishing Gold,' said she,' I fear that your gift is not good.'

'My gift is a true one,' said he.

'Wishing Gold, take the ring from my finger.'

'The whole world could not take off the ring till you tell me the truth,' said Wishing Gold. 'The ring will have the finger off your hand and the head off your body unless you tell me who is the father of your eldest son.'

'Who is his father, but the King of Erin?'

'There is not a drop of the King's blood in his body.'

'Wishing Gold, take off the ring!' cried the Queen.

'The whole world could not take it off till you tell the truth, for 'tis a true gift.'

'Well,' said the Queen, 'the King and I had no children. I was in dread that the crown would be lost. The father of my eldest son is the King's pig-sticker[42].'

'So I believe,' said Wishing Gold. 'It is little good that is in him.'

'Take the ring off my finger,' cried the Queen.

'Not till you tell me who is the father of your second son.'

'The King's gardener[43].'

'I believe that, too,' said Wishing Gold. 'He was not much better than the eldest.'

'Take the ring off my finger,' cried the Queen.

'Not till you tell me who is the father of your youngest son.'

'The King's driver[44].'

'I see,' said Wishing Gold, 'whatever blood was in them was in the last.'

When the King of Erin heard all this he was raging, and said, 'I will have them all burned to ashes.'

'Do not burn them,' said Wishing Gold, 'leave them.'

The King of Erin married the Queen of Lonesome Island then, and went to live in her castle.[45] Wishing Gold and his Queen went to the kingdom of the Moving Wheel and lived there all their lives.

The Ankou
The Spirit of Death

In choosing to end this selection of Keltic Folk and Faerie Tales with a coupl about the Spirit of Death, I am not being negative in the slightest; indeed, deat can be a very positive teacher of the wisdom of life for those that can read hi 'signs'. One of the saddest actions of Orthodox Christianity towards the esoteri Gnostic Christianity was to suppress the teachings on reincarnation; and the par played by the Arkhangels Gabriel and Michael in the death process. Som Church fathers extended their folly by slandering the pre-Christian deities o death as 'evil', although this hardly suits Osiris, Keridwen or the Ankou. Thu the faithful sheep are offered mere 'carrion comfort' in some future 'resurrec tion', poor souls.

The Breton Ankou (Spirit of Death) has a Gaelic equivalent in Righ Geigea (King of the Dead); their prime Station is Shamanistic North (though they ar obviously at work throughout the year). Death plays a vital role in th harmonious cycle of life. New vegetation often springs from the decompositio of earlier plant-life; plants or animals have to die to produce food for our bodie as our rotting bodies may return nutriments to the earth, the worms and plant tree roots.

In Northern Europe, nature carries her highest load of death around mic winter; thus can be understood the midwinter rites to Righ Geigean (as those t Huorko, Kronos, Saturn and like Gods elsewhere). It is worth noting that Kin Geigean is the Black Wildman (Gogan) of Death. In Irish Lore Ri Geigea (Gigean/Guaigean), or his human actor, is described as a tall rough man, dresse hideously, smeared in soot, and carrying a scythe or sickle as a sign of office.

Likewise the ankou is depicted as a tall thin man, with long white hair an a face shaded by a large-brimmed felt hat; he carries a special scythe which ha its blade turned outwards so that, when he uses it, the Ankou drives it forwar rather than towards him. From the Breton tradition we read that:

> The Ankou's coach is similar to the ones they used in the old days fc transporting the dead.
>
> It is usually pulled by two horses harnessed in line. The one in front is thi emaciated, and scarcely able to stand on its feet. The one behind is fat, wit a shiny coat, and without a collar.
>
> The Ankou stands in the coach.
>
> He is escorted by two companions, both of whom walk. One of them leac the first horse by the bridle. The other has the job of opening field gates, an the doors of houses. He is also the one who piles the dead up in the coach; th dead whom the Ankou has harvested . . .
>
> When the Ankou sets out on his tour, they say his coach is filled wit pebbles so that it will go heavily, making more noise.

When he reaches a house where there is someone whom he must harvest, abruptly discharges his load, to make room for his new 'ballast'.

That is the cause of the sound of pebbles which is heard so often in homes here they are watching over a dying person, just at the time of the latter's st breath.

ittany it is also held that the last person to die in the year or the first to die e New Year becomes the Ankou; this is only saying that the one nearest the er Solstice is nearest to the Ankou. (This may well relate to the tithe to the rworld, mentioned in Tam-y-Lynn).

he preceding and following Breton Lore has been translated into English the collection of Anatole le Braz) by Derek Bryce.

Lucas
d by Marie-Yvonne Meringuy, Port-Blanc.)

ab Lucas worked at Rune-Riou. He went back every night to Kerdrenkenn here he lived with his wife Madelaine and five children, in the most iserable thatched cottage of that poor village. For Gab Lucas had only the n pennies that he earned by very hard work each day. This did not prevent m from having a happy nature and being a good worker[1]. The owners of une-Riou valued him. At the end of the week, they often invited him to end Saturday evening with them, drinking flip[2] and eating roast chestnuts. t the stroke of ten the farmer would give Gab his weekly wage and his wife ould always add some present for the household at Kerdrenkenn.

One Saturday night, she said to him,

'Gab, I've put a sack of potatoes aside for you. Give them to Madelaine on y behalf.'

Gab Lucas thanked her, threw the sack on his back, and set off home, after aving wished everyone good night.

It is a good three-quarters of a league from Rune-Riou to Kerdrenkenn. ab walked sprightly at first. The moon was shining, and the good flip he had unk warmed his stomach. He whistled a Breton air to keep himself mpany, happy that Madelaine would be pleased when she saw him return ith a good sack of potatoes. They would cook a large potful the next day; ey would add a slice of pork belly to it, and they would all enjoy themselves.

All went well for a quarter of a league.

But then the virtue of the flip wore off in the coolness of the night. Gab felt l the tiredness of the day's work come back to him. The sack of potatoes egan to weigh heavy on his shoulders. Soon, he no longer felt like whistling.

'If only a wagon would come by,' he thought 'But I'll have no such luck.'

Just then he reached the cross where the track from the farm at Nizilzi joins e road[3].

'Well,' said Gab, 'I can always sit on the steps of the cross for a moment, hilst I catch my breath.'

He set his load down, sat beside it, and lit his pipe.

The countryside was silent all around.

Suddenly, the dogs of Nizilzi began to howl pitifully.

'Why on earth are they making such a din?' wondered Gab.

Then he heard the sound of a cart coming along the road from Nizilzi. It badly greased axle went squeak, squeak[4].

'It looks,' said Gab to himself, 'as though my wish is about to come true They must be going for a load of sand. They'll take my sack right to my door.

He saw the horses come into view, and then the cart. They were terribl thin and emaciated, those horses. They were certainly not from Nizilzi because their horses were always so fat and shiny. As for the cart, its base wa made of a few loosely fitted planks; two rude hurdles served as sides. A grea gawk of a man, who was just as scraggy as his beasts, led this pitiful team. A large felt hat[5] shaded all his face. Gab could not recognize him. He greetec him all the same: 'Comrade, would you have room for this sack in your cart My back's aching. I'm only going as far as Kerdrenkenn.'

The carter did not reply.

'He must not have heard me,' said Gab to himself. 'That awful cart of his makes such a noise.'

The opportunity was too good to be missed. Gab hurredly put his pipe out stuffed it in his jacket pocket, grabbed the sack of potatoes, and ran after the cart, which was going fast enough. He ended by catching up with it, anc dropped his sack inside, letting out a sigh of relief.

But, how do you explain that? The sack went through the old planks anc landed on the ground.

'What sort of a cart is this?' said Gab to himself.

He picked up his sack, and once more put it in the cart, but this time further forward.

But the base of the cart had no solidity, for the sack and Gab went through it[6]. Both of them rolled on the ground.

The strange team continued on its way. Its mysterious leader had not even turned his head.

Gab let them move away from him. When they had disappeared, he took his own turn to go up to Kerdrenkenn, where he arrived half dead from fright.

'What's wrong?' asked Madelaine, seeing him so upset.

Gab told her his adventure.

'It's quite simple,' said his wife to him. 'You've met the coach of the dead.'

Gab almost had a fit. The next day, they heard the church bell ringing. The master of Nizilzi had died on the previous night, towards half-past ten[7].

The Coach of the Dead
(Told by Francoise, daughter of Jeanne Le Gac, 1890.)

It was a night in June, at the time when they leave the horses out all night.

A young man had taken his horses to the fields. He was whistling on his way back, for the night was clear and the moon was shining. He heard a coach coming towards him on the road; a coach whose badly greased axle went squeak, squeak.

He was sure it was the coach of death.

'At last I'll be able to see that coach with my own eyes,' he thought.

And he crossed the ditch and hid himself in a clump of hazels, so that he could see without being seen[1].

The coach came into view.

It was drawn by three white horses harnessed one behind the other. Two men accompanied it, both of them dressed in black and wearing wide-brimmed felt hats. One of them led the first horse by the bridle, the other was standing up in the front of the coach.

As the coach came opposite the hazel clump where the young man was hiding, its axle went 'crack'.[2]

'Stop,' said the man on the coach, to the one who was leading the horses.

The latter cried, 'Whoa!' and the team came to a halt.

'The axle pin's just broken,' said the Ankou. 'Go and cut what you need to make a new one from that hazel[3] clump over there.'

'I'm lost,' thought the young man, who right then regretted his indiscreet curiosity very much.

However, he was not punished there and then. The coachman cut off a branch, shaped it, inserted it into the axle, and then the horses continued on their way.

The young man was able to return home safe and sound, but, towards morning, he was taken with an unknown fever, and they buried him the next day.

NOTES TO THE STORIES

The Puddock Prince in the well

This is a typical Tale of a Prince 'under spells' (*fo gheasaibh*), who manages to become disenchanted when the Princess does what she is requested to do. I think it is of key importance that we note how the toad/frog being is associated with healing, in this case a healing draught from the magical well. This is vouchsafed not only from my own experience, but also from many things in the Folk tradition. For example, the healing herb 'mugroot/mugwort' is called in Irish Ghaidhlig *Buafannan Ban*, ('the white toad') or *Buafannan* ('the grey toad'); a cure for a sore eye was to get someone to lick the eye of a frog and then immediately lick the affected eye; the ashes of a burnt frog are said to stop haemorrhage; and frog spawn (called *Puddock Ruda/Rude/Rudd/Redd/Ride*, hence linked to Shamanistic Wheel) is a cure for erysipelas and other inflammatory diseases. A *Puddle-doo* (*Puddock dubh* – 'dark frog/toad') was often kept in the milk pail to promote the fertility of the cow's milk by making a connection through the *Bu-man* ('Wildman of the Cow-herds') to the earth spirit. (One description of the Keltic Earth Goddess (Luxuria) had her standing with a fox between her legs and a toad hanging from each breast; this has links with a folk remedy for the sore nipples of mothers who were suckling wains, for a frog or toad would be laid upon the tender spot to alleviate the problem.) The Prince, enchanted into toad/frog form, who continually wants to get a little closer to the Princess's bed, is paralleled in such Irish Folksongs as 'Cunnla'. The usual outcome of this sequence is sexual union; in this instance, however, the Faerie glamour is removed from him with an iron sword (*Glave*).

As a note on 'enchantment' into the form of another creature, one can perhaps distinguish 3 types of this process:

(1) Where a Druid or Initiate deliberately realigns his/her energy emanations to adopt a totem-form or whatever; such Shamans usually know how to readopt their normal human form.

(2) Where a trainee sorcerer or whoever 'accidentally' enters a Faerie domain, thereupon attracting an Otherworld form upon themself (which they may or may not be able to discard).

(3) Where a Faerie being deliberately enchants a form upon someone (as the Faerie Queen does to Tam-y-Lynn).

In general this 'enchantment' can either be shallow, i.e. a psychic 'appearance', or a more thorough transformation.

The Toad Man

First of all it would be worth noting how well respected a totem the toad/frog was in Ancient Gaul and Breizh (Brittany); this is demonstrated by three toads being the old heraldic emblem of Gaul. This Tale is replete with magic, some of which is only intimated at. (1) Yet again the enchanted 'toad' is found at a magical spring/well/fountain. (2) In this case the toad magically affixes itself to the father's face. I presume this is a Shamanistic extension of the quite considerable grip that toads sometimes possess (i.e., males in the breeding season), for this reason they may have been called Kraigean ('the well-pawed one'; also 'little stone'). (3) Although the Tale is somewhat Christianized, the Breton storytellers maintain quite a healthy disrespect for the Orthodoxy, demonstrated here by a wryly humorous perception on Church hypocrisy. (4) The toadskin is obviously a Shamanistic *Kokhul*, which he is being required to wear. (5) Opposite to my experience, but perhaps needed for this storyline. (6) Sexually jealous sisters. (7) From the sounds of his statement, it appears he was obliged to be in a toad form for one year and one day – perhaps on the orders of a Faerie being or a sorcerer. (8) and (10) The magic comb, like the earlier *Bar an Suan* ('pin of slumber'), may have had its points dipped in a sleeping poison, as well as being imbued with a magical charm. (9) With the destruction of his toadskin *Kokhul*/he could not complete his required term. (11) Perhaps a solar power object, but also the later means of reconciliation. (12) This common motif in Folktales shows that blood was considered especial to a single individual – something modern medicine abuses. (13) These non-ordinary lion-guardians denote a non-ordinary (i.e., magical) forest and hence the frontier to an Otherland. (14) A Faerie hare, what the Scandinavians would call a helpful troll-hare. (15) The Faerie hare obviously 'knows its stuff'. (16) Whilst appearing to conform to Christian convention, this phrase could also happily be used towards the Lord of the Animals – Kernunos. (17) An ancestral avenue to the castle. (18) As spittle bears a similar essence to blood, it is also sacred and was used for oaths/curses/healings. (19, 20, 21) The young heroine is not tempted

/ materialistic greed (unlike the 'Princess'), rather she wants to be with her ısband again, not just sexually, but also to re-establish their happy lationship. (22) This outlines her powers of endurance and commitment, a ust for anyone who wants to get very far on a 'Spiritual Path'. (23) Here we have he faithful servant', who, in some Tales, can symbolize the better qualities of e lower ego, the animal soul. (24) He is contrasted by the jealous, vindictive rvants, which can be those less than welcome aspects of our lower psyche. (25) he triple operation so common in Keltic and other traditions. (26) The nportant reunion. (27) The use of Keltic *Kunning* ('hound-wise') which blends ickery, symbolism and wisdom. (28) As well as the main storyline, this may so symbolize the reunification of various parts of the aspirant's psyche in the agical Otherworld which can then return to this world, all the happier for their ore permanent and stronger bonding.

The Vixen and the Oakmen

ı this truly amazing Tale from Brythonic Kumbria we are almost given an ısight into the relationship between trees, animals and their Faerie Wildfolk uardians. First of all it is the hawthorn tree (or *Huathe* Wildman) that helps this oor hounded vixen (thus the 'red-dog' is saved from the '*Luath* dogs, swift ounds). Next the infertile holly is encountered; even this unfriendly tree latterly as a place in the scheme of things. Finally the *Fynnoderee* Oak Wildmen save ıe trickster dog (fox = coyote) and, when they hear about the humans who were oing to desecrate the sacred mistletoe, they reward the fox family with their ick of meals. The tannin, etc., in the oak water would indeed heal (sore paws) nd revive (a flagging energy-body). The holly ends up as the gallows for the esecrators (echoing the Ancient Keltic way of disposing of criminals on Esus Axe God's) taran tree. Note hawthorn, oak and holly are all in Shamanistic ast sector in the Ogham Wheel.

Gille Mairtean

1) Quite often in traditional tales there is a 'wicked stepmother' who is omething of a black witch; part of the task in hand involves the hero/heroine rying to triumph over her. (2) This is normally weakly translated as 'Upright ohn', which omits a fair bit of more profound Lore, e.g. Iain/John is linked to stone of wisdom and power (see Clan Johnstone Lore), and Iain/Ewan/Ewan s linked to *Eon* (bird-totems); finally *Direach* is the name of a one-legged, one-yed and one-armed Wildman. These are some of the hero's channels to power. 3) The word translates as 'venison' but actually covers most game. (4) His tepmother (*Muime*) was a perceptive enough bad witch to feel and know that his particular feather came from a special power-bird. (5) In leaving her traddling the keep and the castle walls midst the ever-present winds of the Western Isles was a good magical counter-spelling by Iain. (6) An Gile Mairtean s a *kenning* for the Fox-Wildman/God who is most prominent in the Dark Quarter (Midnight, or Martinmas, November/December), as well as in the Red Quarter (dawn, or March as the crafty trickster). (7) In other fox Tales, such as he Slavic *The Lame Vixen/The Limping Fox*, it is a kind hero who shares his

meal with a starving fox; in this Tale the leader of the fox tribe returns th
kindness. (8) Five throttles = five necks – this fivefold giant with the Shamanist
South falcon may have some sort of connection with the five Ogham/Koelbre
signs of this quarter. (9) Like so many things in the magical Otherworld, and i
the dwellings of powerful Initiates/sorcerers, objects are imbued with awarene
such that they can, in a psychic way, cry out to their masters, as in (10). (11) Th
White Glave of Light means the steel sword polished up until it shines; it ma
also have connections with the sword of light that the Giant of the East wiel
at dawn to bring light over the sky. (12) In parallel Tales this is achieved b
magical sprigs of trees (Koelbren twigs). If the word *Diur-adh* (pronounced *Jur*
was originally linked to *Duir* of the oak station, then this would match th
sword's prime Shamanistic Station. (13) *Kreagan nan Deargan* means 'litt
Rocks of the bream fish'. (14) Large swords, claymores (*Glave-mor*), and th
like, were indeed heavy weapons. (15) Cream-coloured would have been a bett
translation than 'yellow', in the symbolical sense as well. (16) This is not poet
licence here, for prominent Keltic Kings and Chieftians did indeed use silver fo
the accoutrements of their favourite horses, hounds, etc.; and even gol
sometimes, for religious trappings. (17) Gateposts, door lintels, etc., were ofte
magically protected, either by 'invisible' spells or by magically charged run
Autiot carved glyphs. (18) Although this term might not have meant 'Franc
originally, even if it did it still could have been used symbolically here, i.e., fo
Shamanistic South-east (as Lochlann was employed for Shamanistic North
East). (19) Amongst the whole gamut of the Gille Mairtean (Tod Loweries'
shape-shifting abilities is the skill of producing Faerie music to lure the prize
lady aboard. (20) The esoteric (physical) connection between individuals (an
even some groups of people) and diseases is, not surprisingly, completely denie
by orthodox medicine. With such an attitude, much will continue to baff
science. (21) We start now to be given the real point behind this chain of events
MacIain was 'meant' to have this Princess as his bride. Probably the shrewd Gill
Mairtean had not even taken into account the failures needed to arrive at thi
union. (22) Here the Gillie Mairtean demonstrates that he is no sweet and gentl
angel by showing his teeth (as he does symbolically in *The Tale of Tod*). (23
This incident should remind you of the Gille Dakair and this magical nag (se
pages 181–184); also, a bay-coloured water-house (*Ech Uisge* in Sutherland
in the north of Alban) was reported to have in this way captured seven rider
– see *The Seven Herdsmen of Sollochie*. (24) It should be noted that Iai
Direach, thanks to the Gille Mairtean, has not only his true feminine partner
but is also acquiring power-objects as an Initiate can, thanks to his Wildfol
allies. (25) A *Muirlag* was an egg-shaped wickerwork basket with a hole in th
middle. The peasantry used them to transport hens, etc. Here a more noble bir
is carried in it. (26) As with much in the magical Otherworld, this does no
necessarily mean that the giant was totally dead, for, after such seeming-deaths
characters can reappear alive elsewhere. (27) See Note (2). (28) The edge of a
sword was and is used for magical protection; if you have the knowledge to carv
effective runes or Koelbren glyphs upon a magical weapon, then they return a
ill-wished spell back upon its sender. (29) This alludes to the different 'winds
in the Shamanistic Calendar (see Fig. 14 page 36). (30) That the red dog (fox
is called the 'Lad of March' is perfect for this Shamanistic Station. Thi
Shamanistic friendship once meant that no foxes were killed in the Western Isles

if only such a respect had been more widespread, we would not need the valiant hunt saboteurs of today.

The Tale of Tod

(1) *Ngeigh* is the primal Keltic word for the goose wisdom. (2) The *Erne* (sea eagle) feeding off the salmon of wisdom is a potent symbol of the Pictish mysteries. (3) The toad entombed in the winter mud/the spirit toad alive in the hardest rock. (4) Black water serpent/newt. (5) The hounds of Hell/Annwn and the black hound of North/East. (6) Keridwen as the 'black high-crested hen' giving birth to the Sun/Taliesin/Talorgan. (8) Great Bear God/King whose truth is in the apple. (9) Long-legged dawn: cranes/herons have their Shamanistic Station at dawn/East/fire. (10) Arse-foremost: Heyoka wisdom, reverse wisdom (e.g., Ku Roi and Myrddin). This branch of Initiation is still practised by North American Indian adepts. (11) *Keinach* is the Ancient Brythonic/Pictish Name for the hare. (12) Holm oak linked to the Thunder God Thor/Taran. (13) *Gowk* is the Ancient Brythonic/Pictish word for the cuckoo. (14) Water bull bittern. (15) *Nechtan* is the midsummer sky serpent (Pictish). (16) *Fin*: is the primal Keltic name for the bright white Horse God of Midsummer. (17) Red King's death: sacrifice of the Oak King/King William Rufus. (18) Dunnock ... Ruddock: the hedge sparrow symbolically kills the robin at this Station, that Robin may give his energy to the Dark Half. (19) *Peeswhaup* is the Pictish/Brythonic name for lapwing, the guardian Bird of the dark underworld. (20) Keltic underworld Initiation was sometimes symbolized by a 'monster' swallowing and then disgorging the human seekers. (21) The Feast of the Slain, the continual Feast of death (22) Gwyddion: The great Lord of the Cipher Speech linked to *Ngetal/Ngeigh* at the Winter Solstice.

Tam-y-Lyn

(1) Gold. (2) Carter Haugh, earlier Kerton Hall. The original is possibly Garten Hall, a Pictish and Brythonic phrase in the mysteries. (3) Token, pledge. (4) Lifted her green skirt a little above her knee: (5) Braided. (6) Brow. (7) Branch, in this case. (8) Go. (9) Grey-haired. (10) Will. (11) Found. (12) Sharply cold. (13) Hell was originally 'the underworld'. (14) Then. (15) *Ask* = a water serpent. (16) Red-hot sword-piece of iron. (17) Glowing embers. (18) Quickly, lively.

The Black Lad of Loch Dring

(1) 'Son of upon him'/'Son of the Plough.' (2) *Bean Sidh*. (3) *An Gille Dubh* (the Black Wildman). (4) A *Lochan*, also called *Tobar Dringaig* 'Well of the Slow ... water Crack'. (5) Mulmoire MacRath is properly 'Maol-Moire MacRath' = 'Great Tonsured One, Son of Good Fortune/the Wheel', i.e. a pagan priest or Druid. (6) 'wonderfully swift of foot' would have been better.

(7) *An Gille Dubh* is said to have treated the young girl 'with great kindness'. (8) The original Gaelic words also contain the image of an aura of light around the head. (9) A friendly gesture by one of these nature spirits. (10) In a parallel version he showed her all the way back to her house. (11) This wild 'minister' resembles one of the knights from the *Arthuriad.* (12) This 'great fierce bull' (*Tharbh Mór Fiadhaich*) may have been a wild auroch roaming the forest, or perhaps a supernatural bull. (13) These wrestling fights involve Shamanistic power, as did Ya'aqov's grappling with the wild angel in Genesis. (14) Charming Phraseology to say that he wasn't the man to be afraid, though the situation was indeed potentially frightening. (15) This Laird of Sannda, rather than try to get the Black Lad to work as his ally, preferred to ask the Wildman to move to another glen. (16) When the Laird died the Wildman was free to return to his natural haunts.

The Great Tuairsgeal Wildman and his Shamanistic Slaying

(1) A *Dun Sidhe*? (2) The Tuairisgeal is a ferocious type of Wildman best not to tangle with; the elements of his name seem to denote 'Sower of Confusion – Moon', a fierce Wildman of Shamanistic North. (3) and (4) The game of 'Chess' here talked about was *Fidchell*, a Shamanistic ritual board-game linked to trees, animals, etc. (5) This was one of the worst 'predicaments' to leave someone in; e.g., the Fianna/Arthurian Knights were roused onto their elbows by two, not three, blasts on the awakening horn. (6) The Sword (or Glave) of Light was one of the key weapons in Keltic mythology, occasionally appropriated by the Shamanistic North-east beings (as also happens in Scandinavian mythology) (7) Here 'Greece' indicates Shamanistic North-east, I think, its King being called Tuis in other Tales. (8) Horses are often vehicles of transport into the Otherworld. (9) Fair Knight from the Station of Shamanistic South-east, I believe. (10) That these knights are brothers to the Lady the King of Erin won from the Tuairisgeal is esoterically significant in terms of the linkages in the wheel. (11) With the White Knight we have obviously travelled round to Shamanistic south, and to the crack between the worlds. (12) Entering between the crack and down the central Column of existence we arrive at the Black Knight, Shamanistic North. (13) This river is a major barrier to crossing into an Otherworld dimension; it may equate with the river *Gjoll*/slide in Scandinavian mythology. (14 and 15) The purpose of the wine (spirit) might not have been more than to get the palfrey to feel high, for we should remember that the pig/pig-skin of Tuis, King of Greece, turned all streams of water which it walked through into wine for nine days. This relates to in and around *Muin*'s Oghan Station at Shamanistic North-east (equivalent to Dionysian revels). (16) It is appropriate to leave one's vehicle of travel with the King of this country (as Thor left his goats and chariot with Orvandel when he went off to fight some Frost Giants). (17) The old man was lying in a wooden bed (not a 'cradle'). (18) Thus we see in reality that he was a King of Old and also this Tale's Chief *Seanchaithe* (19) We encounter the bad witch of a stepmother again. (20) Although they were put into this shape, it is worth noting that the wolf-sons perform with

nobility and heroism in this creature of Shamanistic North. (21) Poor spelling of a *Gribhneach*, a gryffin. (22) A small boat like a curragh. (24) In a totem or *Nagual*-animal form the being adapts to what is natural for that creature. (25) This King seems to have psychically known who was within the wolf form, or at least to have felt a sympathetic bonding with it. (26) This rough hand belongs to the fierce Tuairisgeal. (27) The Queen also seems to have had a well-developed sense of awareness, over and above the normal. (28) The wolf-son here acts courageously and tears the arm off the Tuairisgeal (as Beowulf tore the arm off Grendel). (29) Made of strong stuff is this being. (30) The wolf shows wisdom as well as courage; whilst the midwives were a bunch of snivelling cowards. (31) The wolf thereby vindicates his honour, and in the process proves the widwives to have been spineless liars. (32) The sword is usually hanging from the wall. (33) The wand has power over Shamanistic transformation, etc. (34) Once the wand is applied, the Shamanistic North wolf form can be discharged. (35) i.e., Rules over his totemistic area. (36) It is significant that the head of the Great Tuairesgeal has been kept under a clump of rushes (Shamanistic North; sec. Shamanistic South) in a cauldron (mainly Shamanistic North). (37) Thus the old white-haired man turns out to be the hero who slew the Great *Tuairisgeal*. (38) He now retraces his route back into his own world. (39) In the parallel version of this Tale, the hero at least recounts the gist of the Tale to the debilitated Young *Tuairisgeal*, to give him an informed mind, before he puts him to death. (40) In the meantime another giant had made off with his wife! It thus turns out to be of vital importance that he makes friends with some 'helping creatures'; the first is the hawk or falcon *Lannair* (related to *Luis*) of Shamanistic South. (41) For 'Giant' we can translate *Gruagach* Wildman, much milder than the Tuairisgeal. (42) This *Kon* Hound of Shamanistic East is called *Mada Ruadh no Koille Krionaich* ('the Red/Great Hound of the Brushwood'). (43) The otter is Shamanistic West (– Shamanistic North) and is known as *Dobar-chu* ('Water-Hound') also as *Doran Donn an Uillt* ('Brown/Lord Otter of the Stream). (44) Evocative of Keltic knotwork and symbolical interweave. (45) The essence (soul) of the giant is within a series of layers within the Shamanistic Wheel. (46 and 47) In a parallel Tale, the axe (Shamanistic East) is applied to the trunk of an old holly tree (Shamanistic East) to release the ram (*Reithe*, Shamanistic East) which the hound (of Shamanistic East) chases. (48) The duck (*Lachu* Shamanistic South) is caught by the hawk (*Lannair* Shamanistic South). (49) The egg/trout (Shamanistic West) is caught by the otter (Shamanistic West). Some researchers believe it was the egg that was within the trout, not vice versa. (50) Anyway, when the final container is killed, the giant falls dead at Shamanistic North; thus the cycle is complete. (51) The hero's long struggles are over. He has mapped and found out the mechanics of the magical Otherworlds in the process.

Fig. M should make what happens at the end of this Tale crystal clear. Indeed, this may well be the first time this secret has ever been allowed into print from the storehouse of Keltic Initiatory wisdom.

For those who are interested in some sort of Qabalistic appraisal of the first half of the above Tale, see the Space Sphere (page 49). What seems to occur is a journey through the makrokosmic *Sephīrōth* in the East of the Space sphere round towards the South of the Space Sphere, then down from *Kether* (white) through *Da'ath*, *Tiphareth*, *Yesod* to *Malkuth* (black). From this point we cross

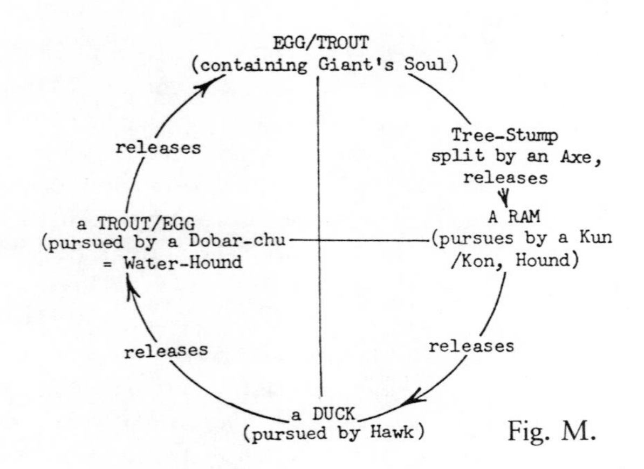

Fig. M.

over a magical river into an Otherworld. On Jacob's Ladder this would involve crossing over into another 'tree'; at a guess I would say *Malkuth* of *Yĕtzīrāh* down to an Otherworld dimension of *'Asayāh*.

The Queen of the Many-Coloured Bedchamber (The Rainbow-hued Bower)

In ancient times a hunt was one of the main methods that the higher powers could employ to shake a specific individual loose from his comrades, disorientating him, lead him to a strange locale, there to have a fateful encounter. Ball-games were initially a semi-sacred ritualistic activity, in which the ball represented the sun, in the main. These solar ball-games are recorded from all over the world, most noticeably in ancient South America and the Keltic lands.

(1) That there are twelve players in this Tale's game of *Hurley/Shinty* is no coincidence. (2) The *Koman* is normally a *Kromag* – that is, a playing stick with a bent end. (3) *Bawr Sculloge* seems to mean 'great resounding blow' (*sgaik* = prodigious skelp), which appears to fit the context of the Tale. (4) Great as these players are, Finn shows that he is tops in the game (as the *Lad Setanta* (Ku-Kulin did at Hurley). As a suitable-stick, Fion ('white') of mainly Shamanistic South receives a magically transformed stalk of nettle (*Nin*), due Shamanistic *South*. (5) Most fitting and no coincidence. With this suitable stick, Fion blasts the ball off into the sky; this is the cue for the Otherworld messenger to arrive and lay the knight's task upon Fion. (7) The lady is Queen of the Sword of Glinting Colours, which alludes to the rainbow scimitar that arches over the sky. (9) Fion (like Gwion) was imbued with secret knowledge when he was a lad. (10) Fion takes the triadic essence as his companions from the twelve. (11) The meaning of the names of the three he chooses seems to be as follows: *Chluas* = hearing of the inner ear; *Grunne* = accurate and exact; *Bechunah* = exact and precise. It is not surprising that the latter two end up being engrossed in playing chess at one part in this Tale. (12) In other Irish Tales, two *Krankar* (sprigs) of wych hazel are employed Shamanistically to construct a boat. (13) The Queen of the Many-

coloured Bedchamber is undoubtedly a Keltic Sky Goddess of the highest Shamanistic South. (14) The 'Seal' would be a magical one of a *Krankar*-Ogham nature. (15) A beautiful place of a mainly Shamanistic South character. (16) *Metheglin* is spiced mead/ale. (17) The two somewhat more intellectual of the brothers engage in *Fidchell* ('Shamanistic chess'). (18) Falling under an unnatural sleep was all to the good in the end. (19) 'Wind' presages a spirit, in this case from the North-east. (20) This incident has a parallel – *The Great Tuairisgeal* Tale. (21) Some of their other skills. (22 and 23) This shows that the Kelts had a clear psychic perception of out-of-the-body experiences. (24) That this revolving tower of the witch gave out a dull red light, two hours before dawn would seem to fit its Shamanistic Station of North-east–East. (25) This may be more than just poetic description; it may be Bechunach's totem animal, the lynx (Lug, mountain lion) of Shamanistic South. (26) This psychic description of what a fairly loathsome evil being looks like is accurate, as I can confirm. (27 and 28) The beam of light which shot out from Fion's fingers is a genuine psychic magical phenomenon, as I have seen it; and, for a magical strike, magical guidance is sometimes required. That Chluas ('hearing of the inner ear') should play a crucial part in killing flat *ear* the Witch is obviously not coincidental. (29) Some of the psychic residuum of a powerful being. (30) This is obviously employing knowledge of the *Krankar/Koelbren* sprigs under enchantment (as did Myrddin in the *Avellenau*). (31) The growth of spring has been transformed into that of high summer, which is indeed a suitable gift to Queen Breaca (who is similar to a Pictish Goddess of Summer that I have seen). (32) There are indeed untold treasures and sights of wonder in the psychic and Spiritual Otherworlds for those skilled enough to venture there.

Fánne Oir, Daughter of the King of Erin & the Son of the King of Three Seas

(1) *Fáinne Óir* means 'gold ring', 'golden ring', 'ring of gold'; hence she has solar associations (*Tiphareth*). (2) In other versions it is a concealed earlier son, see Tale No.1 in our series where the hero is 'Gold Apple' the exact male counterpart to 'Gold Ring' in this Tale. The wicked Queen represents the false side of earthly life. (3) The Son of Red Breast represents the spirit coming to awaken his counterpart. (4) Fáinne Óir is thwarted from following by the false Queen. (5) The false Queen of '*Asayāh* uses a *Bar an Suan* ('pin of slumber') the powerful 'forgetting' imposed by the false Goddess Planē according to gnostic teachings. Scaldhead (6 and 7) perhaps represents the distorted animal soul part of a human being, whilst the maid is perhaps the etheric body lead astray, and the coachman represents the passionate drives, the animal lusts. If so, these three stand in close similarity to the pig-sticker (equivalent to Scaldhead), the gardener (equivalent to the maid), and the driver (equivalent to coachman) found in Tale No.4 in our series. (8) The tablecloth operates like a lesser version of Gwyddnaw Garanhir's magic hamper and the Dagda's cauldron, etc. The cloth holds within it control over the generative laws; when it is unfolded, creation unfolds. We also discover the ring, which belonged to her mother, a Keltic Goddess. (9) *Teach na Réalta* centres on the Pole Star with the zodical belt around. We have clearly reached

Kether of *Yĕtzīrāh* on our Otherworld journey. (10) This cap, like fairy caps an the fish-skin caps of the Assyrian Gods, has the ability to give an enchanted fals appearance to its wearer. (11) Only one with Otherworld vision could se through this enchantment. (12) The primal River of Creation that pours throug at *Kether* of *Yĕtzīrāh*. (13) 'Crooked' is a fair enough translation, but *Cam* ha also serpentine and heavenly associations. (In another Tale we meet with *Donoch Kamcosa*.) (14) As the Lord and Judge of the Dead, Domhnall Donn i also Lord of Fate and Karma, thus the old man is in a karmic situation. To reac Domhnall's dwelling one usually has to sail Westwards from Eire till one reache *Tech n Duind iar n Érinn*' (Donn's house behind Ireland'). In this Tale 'th Eastern world' is being used for the 'Upper' Otherworld which still lies generall West–East of West if you like, rather than West of West, where his dwelling i to be found normally. (15) *Cleasaidhe* means 'One of Feats', i.e., 'One of Grea Deeds'. In another Tale we encounter a *Gruagach na g-Cleasan*, the *Gruagac* of the Feats, who is perhaps an equivalent of *Cleasaidhe*. (16) A spiritu messenger (some would say from the Goddess) to give sound counsel. (17 *Dubhchosa* means 'Black-legged One' (even as 'black' he is one of the goo forces, but of a harsher aspect). This apple gained from *Kether* of *Yĕtzīrāh* has th power in it to create a Magical forest anywhere in *Yĕtzīrāh*. An item from *Kether* always has the generative quality anywhere within its world tree. (18 This enchanted sword could be an quivalent of the sword of light or the swor stuck in a tree of other Tales; if so, it is to be found in the *Tiphareth* of *Braiā* region. These slayings are of course only symbolical, Initiatory overcoming (19) As Domhnall is often described as brown, dark, or black, it seems that hero is being called to match him in stature, namely the son of Black Breas There is no indication who Black Breast is, but I would suggest *Ri Doracha* ('th Dark King') or perhaps *Rig Rich is Garta* (the Coal-faced King) although th latter description is similar to some of Donn's eipthets. (20) Red Breast coul well be the spiritual Sun God (at *Tiphareth* of *Braiāh*). This river is the prim River of Creation and flows through all the worlds carrying certain messag with it. (21) The blood spots were created by his own broken heart, and thu return to him as his heart is healed in meeting Gold Ring (Fáinne Óir).

The Son of the King of Erin and the Queen of the Moving Wheel

(1) The Astral Sea, which pre-existed any physical earthly sea. To embark upo this sea is to go on a magical quest. (2) Grey-haired old man – note the *apparen* sex of this Inner World archetype; see who 'he' later becomes. (3) The castle i at the Centre of an island at *Kether* of *Yĕtzīrāh*, at the furthermost point in th Astral Sea. (4) Most beautiful, as were Banba, Fodhla, Eire, the Speir Ban, et (5) In other words they had made love when he first arrived. (6) Marking th Otherworld progeny to distinguish them later from other claimants. (7) She i behaving like Scathach, the Warrior Queen of 'Skye' or the Pictish Highland These area associations are really secondary to the Otherworld region in whic she has her Initiation/training centre. (8) Wishing Gold/Gold Fortune/Destin from Gold. As gold is solar, the destiny of the solar hero is connected wit

Tiphareth of *Braiāh* (Spiritual Sun Sphere) from *Kether* of *Yĕtzīrāh* (Turner of the Cycles). (9) His horse rides over/through the Astral Sea back to Earth/Erin, our plane of existence. (10) In Irish law the King and Queen were the only people superior to the Druids, and hence could command them in such a fashion. (11) The earthy Queen fears that the spiritual progeny will come to rule the earthly kingdom (as he rightly should, but the *Hylikoi* will always crave domination in this tooth-and-claw materialistic world). (12) 'Banks' here means 'cliffs'. (13) We are back in the magic Otherworld where the salmon trout of wisdom is at the centre of the feast. (14) When one has the opportunity to triumph, one must execute it cleanly, properly – else the opposition will grow strong from our mistake, such that we could not later conquer them. A definite law of magic workings. (15) The harsh, testing aspect of the Goddess. (16) The net symbolizes control over laws that govern and harness the energies of that plane. It would thus be holding together her magic powers and strength. Omphalos stones are often draped over with a net. Omphalos stones appear at the *Kethers* of *'Asayāh*, *Yĕtzīrāh* and *Braiāh* – the middle one of the three is also connected with *Tiphareth* of *Braiāh* and the beings who wield nets there – Thor, Mikhael, Merodach (Marduk) and to a lesser extent Herakles (Hercules). (17) Again we see the Scathach, Warrior Goddess capacity giving training as *Ku Khulain* was instructed. (18) Seven kingdoms, like the seven earths talked about in the ancient Qabalah. Seven *'Asayatic* power planes. (19) The three sons, the animal soul, the etheric, and the animal drives, the life forces; three aspects of the lower personality of each human being. (See notes 42, 43 and 44.) (20) These three aspects will not fight takeovers/possession. Note susceptibility of spiritualists and mediums. (21) The Eastern World – where the Sun rises. The moving wheel is at *Kether* of *Yĕtzīrāh*, at its centre is the Pole Star, and around this revolves the zodiacal belt. (22) The three aspects of the lower personality are often eager to start upon some new venture. Usually however they give up shortly thereafter, lacking the will power and ability to see it through. (23) Similar to wounded or invalid Kings in the Arthurian grail quest. (24) The old man on the bed is the brother of the Queen of Moving Wheel. (25) One by one the parts of the lower personality 'die' (give up on the quest). Indeed, even if they wished to proceed, they could go no further, for they would be entering regions/planes in which they could not function. (26) Note that the Irish knew the rudiments of body preservation; it probably has a deeper symbolic purpose (etherically) as well. (27) Many are the questers, but few manage to pass through this lofty region into the Spiritual world beyond. The three bridges are linked to the three paths that converge onto *Kether* (of *Yĕtzīrāh*) at this point. The three dogs are equivalent to the three-headed dog belonging to the King of the Underworld (Annwn) in other mythologies. (28) The change-over period between the cycles (the seven-period cycle), from Samhain to Samhain in the ritual year or W. Solstice to Solstice. (29) The four-square castle (equivalent to the Welsh *Kaer Pedryvan*). (30) The cats are the sharp-eyed Guardians. (31) Hovering in the Sky at *Kether* it is brought down through the three powers. (32) He is then instructed to halt the turning castle (Welsh equivalent is *Kaer Sidi*), which is similar to Arthurian turning castles and the world mill with its 'whirling eye of the millstone' in Scandinavian mythology (although they serve slightly different inner World purposes). (33) The terrible appearance of the dog is to scare off those unworthy of entry/Initiation. (34) One 'key' unlocks the next 'inner law'/'doorway'. The

Ladder of Learning. (35) He did more than write on a piece of paper, for he left her with child. (See note 37.) (36) The true Initiate is not particularly eager for worldly 'fame' or 'glory', but many of the worldly live for it. Also, he is willing to let those cloyed with worldly vanity enjoy false glory (for achievements not of their doing, for he knows full well that 'the truth will out' in time, and that he will be accorded appreciation commensurate with his true worth). (37) Wishing gold had obviously entered the castle and left her with child near the start of her year 'asleep'. (38) She is manifestly something of a Warrior Goddess in what follows, like other Irish Goddesses, and the Babylonian Ishtar. (39) The Spiritual Bride (beloved) holding herself in purity for her destined one. (40) Not a racial boast really; more properly it refers to the *Kether* of *Kether* of *'Asayāh*, the quintessence of quintessences as some might say. (41) Wishing gold and the Queen of the Moving Wheel are Spiritual equals and partners. (42) That which controls the life or death of the animal aspect: the animal Soul. (43) That which nurtures the vegetable aspect: the etheric body. (44) That which drives things on (if drover of animals). If a chariot driver, it is the factor which propels and controls the vehicle. Probably the former in a poor translation. In either case the animal (astral) drives of the lower nature/personality. (45) The King is raised up through *Yĕtzīrāh*.

The Ankou: The Spirit of Death

(1) The ebullient and positive nature of Gab Lucas may well have counted in his favour with the Ankou, such that no ill came of the encounter, unlike the situation with the young man in the next Tale. (2) *Flip* is a Breton cider drink laced with dark rum. (3) As in the 'Tam-y-Lynn' ballad, this magical encounter takes place at a crossroads. (4) The noise of the cart of the dead probably served a warning to keep well clear. (5) The large felt hat that shaded the face and one eye was also worn by Odin in his death aspect. (6) Thus the non-material, astral nature of this cart of the dead is made clear. (7) The correlation of such times and happenings are recorded from Folk traditions all over the world, and it is only the hardened skeptics who refuse to believe them; no matter, the Spirit of Death will claim them all the heavier.

The Ankou

(1) The motivation of this lad for seeing the death spirit was not impeccable, thus he suffers the consequences. (2) Not a coincidence, more a 'sign from the world', an omen. (3 and 4) It is perhaps worth nothing that 'towards morning', when he was stricken with fever (fire), is the Koelbren Station of the hazel.

CHAPTER 8

Relevance to Modern-Day

The Keltic Folktales recounted and discussed on the preceding pages and the Shamanistic Calendar that they are founded upon can provide enlightened guidance to several other branches of the esoteric sciences.

Nature-worship and paganism: It is to these subjects that this book has obvious, near-immediate, and also profound, dimensions of application. I trust that any reader who is pursuing a personally autonomous path in 'nature-worship' (i.e., reverencing the powers of nature without any previously worked-out hierarchy of dieties, working beneath 'the universal spirit') will have found much in this book delightfully stimulating, and conducive to enriching and deepening your understanding of your own path. (For some more practical suggestions, please consult certain of my other writings.)

Under the general banner of contemporary paganism go a variety of forms of Witchcraft, Wicca, Heathenism, Odinism and other native Paganisms. Some of the Scandinavian and Germanic Pagan groups following the Odinist tradition seem, to my eyes, best organized and well founded. This is partly due to the fact that their rituals can be built around a very ancient and dependable Nordic mythology, which has produced a near-continuous Pagan tradition from the Sagas to today; this has recently sparked off a reawakening of interest in the runic divination scripts. All further well-balanced growth in Odinism I welcome and respect, and offer this book as a good source of comparable and compatible Keltic Lore. Out of the wiccan groups that claim to be Anglo-Saxon in emphasis, I'm afraid I have perceived little genuine Anglo-Saxon Lore in their rites; at present they seem content with a very wishy-washy, watered-down version of Germanic paganism. Perhaps in the worst state of all, however, are those pseudo-Celtic wiccan groups; for the amount of Keltic language used by them is almost nil; Keltic art-symbolism is conspicuous by its absence (or its misapplication); the Keltic Gods and their mythological ascriptions are often hopelessly garbled; whilst extracts from Tuscan gypsy witchcraft, invocations to Graeco-Roman–Egyptian Goddesses (employing the relevant ritual gear), garbled Arabic spirit-invocations, indulgent sexuality, plus many other extraneous distractions, make a mockery of any alleged 'Celticness'. This hopeless pot-pourri of non-authentic Keltic withcraft is a disgrace to the British Wise Wyfes who once practised their many skills. What these so-called 'Celtic groups need to do is to throw out the trash, make a clean start, and then buckle down to relearn the proper Keltic pagan tradition (which needs none of those inappropriate irrelevances). To be positive as well as critical, the Keltic witch should be able to find enough ingredients within this book of mine to be able to construct more meaningful and authentic seasonal rituals in keeping with the Shamanistic Calendar, the eight Solar Festivals and the orbiting Lunar Esbats. With the right mythological ingredients employed, there may well be a greater possibility for magical success than there ever was with Gardnerian, etc., trash.

Jungian psychology: I think first of all that C. J. Jung deserves commendation for producing a form of psychology that comes nearest to the real esoteric sciences. He also merits credit for distinguishing the various psychological archetypes that operate in the creative depths of each human being. Jung also did very praiseworthy research into medieval alchemy, pointing out certain parallels with dream motifs and more general symbolism. Yet upon several major points Jung showed that he worked from *outside* the Initiatory mysteries, e.g., when he backed away from ascribing distinct reality and autonomy to the archetypes; or when he associated the Wildman with just the animal nature of man; or when he misinterpreted some dreams because he was still contaminated by the sick theories of Freud (the deviant psychology of whom should play no part in any noble religious or Spiritual path).

Personal totemism, dream analysis and alchemy: I feel that the content of the Shamanistic Calendar is of great help in finding out what totems apply to a particular person. Also, these Shamanistic ingredients are likely to occur in dreams in any part of Europe, for they are natural to the psychic ethos of this whole region; and on the Inner Planes all the archetypes of all the creature species are very much alive. I also feel that Keltic and European Shamanistic symbolism played *as* major a role in the formation of medieval alchemy as did Middle Eastern or Gnostic Christian source-streams (Compare Figs. N and O with the Shamanistic Calendar).

Esoteric astrology: I think that for too long the mainstream of astrology has been based primarily upon Middle Eastern teachings (all too imperfectly comprehended); for people using astrology in Europe and Keltia it makes sense to learn as much as we can about the Ancient Keltic and Scandinavian Star Lore. I also maintain that astrology is carrying large amounts of erroneous ascriptions and some material that is inapplicable to Keltic areas. Astrologers would gain some healthy new insights if they respectfully assimilated some of the Shamanistic Calendar Astro-lore.

Fig. N, from an alchemical manuscript, (Ripley Scrowle manuscript 1588) depicts the Winged Wyvern of the sky and summer locked in a cycle with the Web-winged Wyvern of the dark waters and winter; they turn thru the zodiac (depicted here anti-clockwise). Likewise in Fig. O from Bohme (which turns clockwise through calendar) note the Winged Sun and Y.H.V.H. at the Summer Solstice; and the cubic stone, Moon and walled city at Winter Solstice.

Fig. N.

Fig. O.

CHAPTER 9

Conclusions and Counselling on Choosing an Occult-Spiritual Path

From the lofty Mountain fastness
that shelters the Ambrosial City,
I can still hear Taliesin, the honey-tongued comforter, calling,
calling the wayward Spirits to return, saying –

'I am a peace-gained proficient
who addresses the Bards of the land;
it is mine to animate the courageous;
to persuade the unadvised;
to awaken the lame-tongued onlooker
I am a bold illuminator of the Righteous.'[1]

'I know the Art of Contemplation;
and it is pitiful that men will not come
to seek all the sciences of the world
which are treasured in my bosom,
for I know all that has been
and all that will be hereafter.'[2]

The above is an extract from my poem 'Proclamation from Caer Aidean', composed in June 1981, including (1) my translation of verses from Taliesin's 'Kadair Taliesin – The Chair of Taliesin' and (2) 'Hanes Taliesin – The Life-history of Taliesin'.

My most basic piece of advice as regards choosing a magical, religious or spiritual path is that it should be in harmony with the land upon which you are, for the most part, residing. It is a too little respected fact that each area of Planet Earth exudes an ethos and geomantic characteristics; thus if the spirituality you are practising is in harmony with this ethos and its associated beings, then things have a chance of working more beneficially; whereas if you are trying to impose a belief structure that is incompatible with the ethos of the land, then all you are likely to generate is friction.

Thus I do not necessarily think that Keltic religious mythology is either appropriate or of much use to people staying in, for example, Australia, South America, China or Africa. Indeed, I was amused to read that an English authoress had sent a batch of rituals (some of which were Keltic) to a magical group in Australia, to have the rituals 'tested out'; whatever 'great results' were then reported I would view with extreme suspicion and disbelief. For, from practical experience, Keltic Gods who, through their very names, are linked to the trees, creatures and land of Keltia, will only with extreme difficulty be evoked through Australian geomantic energies, plants and exotic creatures, which in many ways are the Shamanistic reverse/opposite of the Keltic. My general advice to magical folk staying in Australia is – with great respect seek to be taught the Aborigines' paths to wisdom; to those Westerners staying in Africa – all strength to the reflourishing of the native religions of the black man; to those in America and Canada – with great respect seek to learn the Red Indian medicine ways, for those were shaped by the holy soil of these lands (if Americans should still desire to try and follow their Keltic/Anglo-Saxon 'ancestry' then they should only do so with the greatest reverance for the essential sacredness of these Keltic 'roots'.

If in regard to these or similar cases you wish to employ worship of the Christ and Christian Gnostic principles, then it should be done as much as is possible in harmony with the ancient native tradition. For example the early Brythonic, Pictish and Culdee type of Christianity is more suitable to Keltia than any of the more Orthodox forms.

Finally I think it is a sign of an unbalanced religion if its members are too preoccupied with inter-human exchanges, to the neglect of all the other nature kingdoms. We incarnated to learn and experience from this rich world, to the fullness of our natural abilities. It should be a personal religious concern to interact healthily with many-faceted nature; and personally to help heal the ecological imbalance which faces us at present. That way we each stand to get most in return.

Whilst treading the Path may you have Love, Joy, Courage & Fortitude; and may you also cultivate Discerning Wisdom to Deepen Simple Faith.

Be ye therefore Wise as Serpents and harmless as Doves.

Bibliography

This is *not* a complete Bibliography of books I (or my close colleagues) have read that have a bearing on this Book, for many small but valuable items of Lore have been gleaned from widely scattered sources.

(For those that are interested, most of the Books, Monographs and Journals listed below by KALEDON NADDAIR can be obtained from: KELTIA PUBLICATIONS, 'KAER EIDYN', P.O. BOX 307, EDINBURGH, EH9 1XA, ALBAN (SCOTLAND).

(1) KELTIC MYTHOLOGY, FOLKLORE, FOLK AND FAERIE TALES

★ KALEDON NADDAIR – 'Esoteric Irish Folktales' (9 Booklets) Keltia Publ. Feb. 1984.

★ OTTA F. SWIRE – 'Skye, The Highlands, The Inner Hebrides, and their Legends' 3 books, Collins.

★ DERMOT O'BYRNE – 'Children of the Hills' Maunsel & Co. c1912.

★ JAMES STEPHENS – 'The Crock of Gold' Macmillan & Co., 1923.

★ JEREMIAH CURTIN – 'Irish Folk Tales' Talbot Press, Dublin, 1956.

★ JEREMIAH CURTIN – 'Myths and Folklore of Ireland' 1890.

★ JEREMIAH CURTIN – 'Hero-Tales of Ireland' 1894.

★ EDWARD DAVIES (Rev.) – 'The Mythology and Rites of the British Druids' 1809.

★ EDWARD DAVIES (Rev.) – 'Catholic Researches' 1803.

★ MILES DILLION – 'Early Irish Literature' The University of Chicago Press, 1948–72.

★ EUGINE O'CURRY – 'Lectures on the Manuscript Materials of the Ancient Irish'.

★ EUGINE O'CURRY – 'Manners and Customs of the Ancient Irish'.

★ S. H. O'GRADY – 'Silvia Gadelica' 1892.

★ T. F. O'RAHILLY – 'Early Irish History and Mythology' 1946.

★ T. C. LETHBRIDGE – 'Gogmagog – The Buried Gods' Book Club Associates, 1975.

★ MAIRE MACNELL – 'The Festival of Lughnasa'.

★ F. M. MACNEILL – 'The Silver Bough – Scottish Calendar Customs' William MacLellan, 1957.

★ JOHN RHYS – 'Lectures on Religion as illustrated by Celtic Heathendom' 1888.

★ ANNE ROSS – 'The Folklore of the Scottish Highlands' Batsford Ltd., 1976.

★ ANATOLE LE BRAZ – 'The Celtic Legend of the Beyond' Transl. by Derek Bryce, Llanerch, 1986.

★ F. M. LUZEL – 'Celtic Folk-Tales' (from Armorica) Transl. by Derek Bryce, Llanerch, 1986.

★ (Both 2 Books above from Llanerch Enterprises, Felinfach, Lampeter, Dyfed, Kymru.)

★ ELIZABETH MARY WRIGHT – 'Rustic Speech and Folk-Lore' Oxford University Press, 1913.

★ 'Folk-Lore' (from 1890 to date); 'Folk-Lore Journal' (1883–9); 'Folk-Lore Record' (1872–82) (from the Organs of the Folk-Lore Society).
★ J. F. CAMPBELL – 'Popular Tales of the West Highlands' Vol. 1–4.
★ JOHN DARRAH – 'The Real Camelot' (Paganism in the Arthurian Legends) Thames & Hudson, 1981.
★ T. D. SULLIVAN – 'The Voyages of the Sons of O'Corra' (in his book of Poems).
★ KUNO MEYER – 'The Colloquy between Fintan and the Achill' in Anecdota from Irish MSS.
★ J. R. R. TOLKIEN – 'Tree and Leaf' George Allen & Unwin Ltd., London, 1964–74.
★ J. JACOBS – 'Celtic Fairy Tales' 1892; 'More Celtic Fairy Tales' 1894.
★ P. W. JOYCE – 'Old Celtic Romances' Longmans Green & Co., 1920.
★ J. M. MACKINLAY – 'Folklore of Scottish Lochs and Springs' 1893.
★ AUGUSTA GREGORY (Lady) – 'Of Gods and Fighting Men' John Murray rep. 1978.
★ AUGUSTA GREGORY (Lady) – 'Cuchulain of Muirethemne' John Murray rep. 1978.
★ CHARLOTTE GUEST (Lady) – 'The Mabinogion' Alfred Nutt, 1904.
★ A. NUTT – 'The Voyage of Bran' 2 Vols. 1895.
★ ARCHIBALD CAMPBELL (Lord) – 'Waifs & Strays of Celtic Tradition' Vols. I–IV (Vol. II Donald McInnes (Ed), Vol. III J. MacDougall (Ed)).

(2) KELTIC RELIGION, FAERIE-FAITH AND GENERAL ESOTERICISM

★ KALEDON NADDAIR – 'From the Wildman to the Lord of the Forest' Keltia Publ. Oct. 1984.
★ KALEDON NADDAIR – 'Modern Keltic Druidism: An Assessment' Booklet, Keltia Publ. Dec. 1986.
★ KALEDON NADDAIR – 'The College of Druidism: A Guidebook' Keltia Publ. Feb. 1983–86.
★ KALEDON NADDAIR – 'Keltic Mythological Weapons, Magical-Objects and Sacred Treasures' Nov. 1987.
★ KALEDON NADDAIR – 'A Dictionary and Guidebook to The Faerie-Wildfolk' (in preparation).
★ BETTY KURTH – 'Die Deutschen Bildteppiche de Mittlelalters' Verlag Von Anton Schroll & Co. 1926.
★ JANET AND COLIN BORD – 'Bigfoot Casebook' Paul Elek, 1981.
★ BERNARD HEUVELMANS – 'On the track of Unknown Animals' Paladin, 1970.
★ EDWARD ANWYL – 'Celtic Religion' 1906.
★ EDWARD ANWYL – 'Celtic Heathenism in the British Isles' Camb. Med. Hist. Vol. ii, Ch. xvb, 1913.
★ EDWARD ANWYL – 'Ancient Celtic Deities' in Proceedings Gaelic Soc. of Inverness Vol. 26 p. 392.
★ LEWIS SPENCE – 'British Fairy Origins' Watts & Co. 1946.
★ EDWARD ANWYL – 'Ancient Celtic Goddesses' in The Celtic Review, Vol. iii, p. 26, 1906.

★ W. G. WOOD-MARTIN – 'Pagan Ireland' 1895.
★ W. G. WOOD-MARTIN – 'Traces of the Elder Faiths of Ireland' 2 Vols., 1902.
★ DUDLEY WRIGHT – 'Druidism: The Ancient Faith of Britain' London, 1879.
★ GUY RAGLAND PHILLIPS – 'Brigantia (A mysteriography)' Book Club Associates, London, 1976.
★ AFFLECK GRAY – 'The Big Grey Man of Ben MacDhui' Impulse Books, Aberdeen, 1970.
OWEN JONES (Ed.) – 'Myvyrian Archaeology' 3 Vols., 1801–7, rep. in 1870.
★ L. A. PATON – 'Studies in the Fairy Mythology or Arthurian Romance' Boston, 1903.
★ ISABEL HILL EDLER – 'Celt, Druid and Culdee' The Covenant Publ. Co. Ltd., 1938.
★ ROBERT KIRK – 'The Secret Commonwealth, of Elves, Fauns and Fairies' Eneas Mackay, 1933, orig. 1691.
★ KEITH CRITCHLOW – 'Time Stands Still' (Sacred Geometry etc) Gordon Fraser Publ., 1979.
★ A. D. HOPE – 'A Midsummer Eves Dream' Australian Nat. University Press, Canberra, 1970.
★ ALWYN REES AND BRINLEY REES – 'Celtic Heritage' Thames and Hudson, 1978.

3) KELTIC CIPHER-SCRIPTS AND LANGUAGE

a) *OGHAM & KRANKAR (Ghaidhlig Cipher)*

★ KALEDON NADDAIR – '*Ogham*, Koelbren and Runic' 2 Vols. Keltia Publications 1986.
★ DANIEL CORKERY – 'Hidden Ireland' Mercier Paperbacks, Dublin.
★ GEORGE CALDER – 'Auricept Na N-Éces – The Scholars Primer' (The Bardic Poetic Art) 1917.
★ CYRUS H. GORDON – 'Riddles in History' Arthur Barker Ltd., 1974.
★ E. W. B. NICHOLSON – 'Keltic Researches' London, 1904.

b) *OGHAMISED IRISH, SHELTA, etc.*

★ R. S. S. MACALISTER – 'The Secret Languages of Ireland' Cambridge University Press, 1937.

c) *KOELBREN (Kymraeg Cipher)*

★ KALEDON NADDAIR – 'Ogham, *Koelbren* and Runic' 2 Vols. Keltia Publ., 1986.
★ EDWARD WILLIAMS – 'Barddas' Llandovery Soc. for Preservation of Welsh Manuscripts.
★ ROBERT CRAIG MACLAGAN – 'Scottish Myths' (Notes on Scottish History And Tradition) Edin. 1882.
★ EDWARD DAVIES – 'Celtic Researches'
★ EDWARD DAVIES – 'The Mythology and Rites of the British Druids' 1809.

★ OWEN JONES – 'Myvyrian Archaeology' 3 Vols. 1801–1807.

(d) KELTIC LANGUAGE, HISTORY AND DECLINE

★ VICTOR EDWARD DURKACZ – 'The Decline of the Celtic Languages' John Donald Publ., 1983.
★ CATHAL O'LUAIN (Ed) – 'For a Celtic Future' Celtic League, 1983.
★ P. W. JOYCE – 'Irish Names of Places' 2 Vols., Longmans Green & Co., 1901.
★ D. B. GREGOR – 'Celtic – A Comparative Study' (on languages) Oleander Press, 1980.
★ 'Counting Out Rhymes' (Kymric basis in Scotland) Article in Transactions of Buchan Field Club. 9.
★ CORMAC – 'Cormac's Glossary' (compiled 9th–10th cent.) transl. by J. O'Donovan (Ed), 1868.
★ JOSHUA WHATNOUGH – 'The Dialects of Ancient Gaul' Harvard University Press.

(4) KELTIC HISTORY, ART-SYMBOLISM AND POETRY

★ KALEDON NADDAIR – 'Kruithnaeg (Pictish) and Keltic Art Symbolism' Book Feb. 1987.
★ KALEDON NADDAIR – 'Shamanistic Symbolism on Pictish Stones' Article in I.K. No.8 and TPS No.1.
★ KALEDON NADDAIR – 'Pictish Symbols and Indo-European Comparisons' Article in I.K. No.6.
★ KALEDON NADDAIR – 'Cup and Ring Marks, Rock Art and the Rock Spirits' Article in T.P.S. No.1.
★ KALEDON NADDAIR – 'Symbolism in Keltic Art' Article in INNER KELTIA No.3 (also Booklet).
★ KALEDON NADDAIR – 'The Search for Awen' (2nd Book of Poetry) Keltia Publ. Feb. 1985.
★ IAIN FRASER GRIGOR – 'Mightier than a Lord' (on Highland clearances) Acair Ltd., 1979.
★ RONALD W. B. MORRIS – 'The Prehistoric Rock Art of Galloway and The Isle of Man' Blandford, 1979.
★ FRANK G. A. KNIGHT – 'Archaeological Light on the Early Christianisation of Scotland' Clark, 1933.
★ AODH DE BLACAM – 'Gaelic Literature Surveyed' Talbot Press 1929–73.
★ VARIOUS – 'Traditional and Modern Gaelic Poetry from Ireland and Scotland' Poetry Australia No. 63 197.
★ MALCOLM CHAPMAN – 'The Gaelic Vision in Scottish Culture' Croom Helm Ltd., 1979.
★ ARCHIBALD B. SCOTT – 'The Pictish Nation, People and Church' Foulis, Edinburgh, 1918.
★ ELEANOR KNOTT – 'Irish Classical Poetry – Filicht na Sgol' (in English) Mercier, 1957–78.
★ DANIEL CORKERY – 'The Hidden Ireland' Gill and MacMillan, 1924–70, Mercier Publ. 1970–.

★ GEORGE BAIN – 'Celtic Art – The Methods of Construction' 1951–1977.
★ M. VAN HOEK – 'The Carved Rocks near Wooler' Oisterwijk, Holland, 1982.
★ ALEXANDER CARMICHAEL – 'Carmina Gadelica' 6 Vols., 1912.
★ SORLEY MACLEAN – 'Dean do Eimhir' – Poems to Eimhir' (in English) Northern House, 1979.

5) NATURE MYSTERIES, GEOMANCY, TOTEMISM AND SHAMANISM

★ CARLOS CASTANEDA – (1) 'The Teachings of Don Juan' (2) 'Separate Reality' (3) 'Journey to Ixtlan' (4) 'Tales of Power' (5) 'The Second Ring of Power' (6) 'The Eagle's Gift' (7) 'The Fire from Within' (1–6 on Penguin) (7 on Black Swan).
★ KALEDON NADDAIR – 'The Keltic Shamanistic Calendar' Book, Keltia Publications, Nov. 1987.
★ KALEDON NADDAIR – 'Some Secrets from The Shamanistic Calendar' Article in INNER KELTIA No. 8 and 9.
★ KALEDON NADDAIR – 'The Shaman and Ritual Drumming' Booklet, Keltia Publications, 1986.
★ KALEDON NADDAIR – 'The Pictish Shaman' Magazine No. 1, KRP 1985.
★ JOAN HALIFAX – 'Shaman – The Wounded Healer' Thames & Hudson.
★ LAME DEER AND R. ERDOES – 'Lame Deer' London, 1973.
★ FRANK HAMEL – 'Human Animals' Rider & Son, London, 1915.
★ OLOF ALEXANDERSSON – 'Living Water' (on the Work of Viktor Schauberger) Turnstone, 1982.
★ W. EDWARD MANN – 'Orgone, Reich and Eros' Simon & Schuster, New York, 1973.
★ T. C. LETHBRIDGE – 'E.S.P. (Beyond Time and Distance,' Sidgwick & Jackson, 1965 and 1974.
★ TOM GRAVES AND JANET HOULT – 'The Essential T. C. Lethbridge' Routledge & Kegan Paul, 1980.
★ LYNN ANDREWS – 'Medicine Woman' RKP.
★ LYNN ANDREWS – 'Flight of the Seventh Moon' RKP.
★ GEORGE HENDERSON – 'Survivals in Belief Among the Celts' Glasgow, 1911.
★ FULCANELLI – 'Le Mystere des Cathedrales' Transl. by Mary Sworder, London, 1971.
★ LYALL WATSON – 'Lightning Bird' Hodder & Stoughton, 1982.
★ LYALL WATSON – 'Heaven's Breath' Coronet Books, 1984–5.
★ LYALL WATSON – 'The Romeo Error' Coronet Books, 1974–76.
★ LYALL WATSON – 'Supernature' Coronet Books, 1973–4.
★ TOM GRAVES – 'Needles of Stone' Gothic Image, 1987.
★ ANDREE ROSENFELD – 'The Inorganic Raw Materials of Antiquity' Weidenfeld & Nicolson, London, 1965.
★ JANET AND COLIN BORD – 'Alien Animals' Book Club Associates, 1980.
★ CHARLES FORT – 'The Book of the Damned' Abacus, London, 1919–73.

★ CHARLES FORT – 'New Lands' Sphere Books Ltd., London, 1923–74.

★ M. CARON AND S. HUTIN – 'The Alchemists' Evergreen Books, London, 1961.

★ ALEXANDER ROBERT FORBES – 'Gaelic Names of Beasts (Mammalia), Birds, Fishes, Insects, Reptiles, etc.' (in Gaelic and English) Edinburgh, 1905.

★ WILLIAM R. CORLISS – 'Strange Life' (A Sourcebook on the Mysteries of Organic Nature) Vol. B.1. The Sourcebook Project, Maryland, 1976.

★ ALFRED WATKINS – 'The Old Straight Track' 1925–74, Abacus.

(6) TREE, PLANT AND HERB LORE

★ KALEDON NADDAIR – 'Keltic (and Indo-European) Tree Lore' Keltia Publ. Dec. 1987.

★ KALEDON NADDAIR, BELBUCCA AND EURIG AP GWILYM – 'Keltic Tree Lore,' 'Pagan-Woodcraft,' and 'Forestry and Ecology' Booklet, Keltia Publ. April, 1984.

★ ROBERT LAMB – 'World Without Trees' Magnum Books, 1979, 1980.

★ ROBERT FISHER – 'The English Names of our Commonest Wild Flowers' T. Buncle & Co., 1932.

★ GERALD WILKINSON – 'Trees in the Wild' Book Club Associates, 1976.

★ JOHN CAMERSON – 'The Gaelic Names of Plants' 1900.

★ DONALD ARMSTRONG – 'Plant Badges of the Clans' An Comunn Gaidhealach, 1970.

★ BARBARA FAIRWEATHER – 'The Highland Plant Lore' Glencoe and N. Lorn Folk Museum.

★ BRETT L. BOLTON – 'The Secret Powers of Plants' Abacus, 1974–5.

★ RICHARD FOLKARD – 'Plant Lore, Legends and Lyrics' 1884.

★ MRS M. GRIEVE – 'A Modern Herbal' Penguin Books, 1931–78.

★ J. FERGUSSON – 'Tree and Serpent Worship' 1873.

★ WALTON NICHOL – 'The Planters Kalendar' 1812.

★ PAUL FRIEDRICH – 'Proto-Indo-European Trees' (The Arboreal System of a Prehistoric People) 1970.

★ A. T. LUCAS – 'The Sacred Trees of Ireland.'

★ GORDON ROBINSON – 'Forestry as if Trees Mattered: A Bold Stand' Not Man Alone (Journal of US Friends of the Earth), August 1976, pp. 24ff.

(7) BIRD LORE

★ KALEDON NADDAIR – 'Keltic (and Indo-European) Bird Lore' Keltia Publ. Jan. 1987.

★ E. A. ARMSTRONG – 'The Life and Lore of the Bird in Nature, Art, Myth, and Literature.'

★ EDWARD A. ARMSTRONG – 'The Folklore of Birds' 1958.

★ FRANCESCA GREENOAK – 'All the Birds of the Air' Andre Deutsch, 1979.

(8) ANIMAL LORE

★ KALEDON NADDAIR – 'Keltic (and Indo-European) Animal Lore' Keltia Publ. May. 1987.

★ GILBERT WHITE (Rev.) – 'Natural History of Selbourne' Frederick Warne & Co.
★ W. H. HUDSON – 'The Book of a Naturalist' – Thomas Nelson & Sons, London.
★ WM. L. SIME (Rev.) – 'Nature Letters Book' McLagan & Cumming, Edinburgh.
★ ERNEST T. SETON – 'Mainly about Wolves' Methuen & Co., London, 1937.
★ ROY P. MACKAL – 'Searching for Hidden Animals' Cadogan, London, 1983.
★ DI. FRANCIS – 'Cat Country' David & Charles, London, 1983.
★ E. C. CAUTE – 'Ritual Animal Disguise' 1977.
★ BILL SCHUL – 'The Psychic Power of Animals' Coronet Books, London, 1978.
★ (9) INDO-EUROPEAN MYTHOLOGY, RELIGION AND ESOTERICISM

★ KALEDON NADDAIR – 'An Esoteric Interpretation of Teutonic Mythology' Q.R.P. 1980.
★ VIKTOR RYDBERG – 'Teutonic Mythology'
★ DONALD A. MacKENZIE – 'Teutonic Myth and Legend' Gresham.
★ HANS A. GUERBER – 'Myths of the Norsemen' Harrap.
★ PRUDENCE JONES – 'Sundial and Compass Rose' 8-fold Time Division in N. Europe. Fenris Wolf 1982.

(10) QABALAH

★ KALEDON NADDAIR – 'Qabalah: An Introduction' Booklet, March, 1987, Q.R.P.
★ Z'EV BEN SHIMON HALEVI – 'The Way of the Kabbalah' Rider & Co., 1976.
★ Z'EV BEN SHIMON HALEVI – 'A Kabbalistic Universe' Rider & Co., 1977.
★ Z'EV BEN SHIMON HALEVI – 'Kabbalah and Exodus' Rider & Co., 1980.
★ Z'EV BEN SHIMON HALEVI – 'Adam and the Kabbalistic Tree' Rider & Co., 1974.
★ Z'EV BEN SHIMON HALEVI – 'Kabbalah-Tradition of Hidden Knowledge' Th. & Hudson, 1979.
★ CARLO SUARES – 'The Sepher Yetsira' Shambhala/Stuart & Watkins, 1976.
★ CARLO SUARES – 'The Cipher of Genesis' Shambhala/Stuart & Watkins, 1970.
★ CARLO SUARES – 'The Song of Songs' Shambhala/Stuart & Watkins, 1972.
★ CARLO SUARES – 'The Resurrection of the Word' Shambhala/Stuart & Watkins, 1972.